A HISTORY OF THE FEDERAL RESERVE

ALLAN H. MELTZER

A HISTORY OF THE

Federal Reserve

VOLUME II, BOOK ONE, 1951–1969

THE UNIVERSITY OF CHICAGO PRESS • CHICAGO AND LONDON

Allan H. Meltzer is the
Allan H. Meltzer University
Professor of Political Economy
at Carnegie Mellon University
and Visiting Scholar at
the American Enterprise
Institute. He is the author
of many books, including
*A History of the Federal
Reserve: Volume I*, also
published by the University
of Chicago Press.

The University of Chicago Press, Chicago 60637
The University of Chicago Press, Ltd., London
© 2009 by The University of Chicago
All rights reserved. Published 2009
Printed in the United States of America

18 17 16 15 14 13 12 11 10 09   1 2 3 4 5

ISBN-13: 978-0-226-52001-8   (cloth)

ISBN-10: 0-226-52001-3   (cloth)

Library of Congress Cataloging-in-Publicatin Data

Meltzer, Allan H.
    A history of the Federal Reserve / Allan H. Meltzer
      p. cm.
    Includes bibliographical references and index.
    Contents: v. 1. 1913–1951—
      ISBN 0-226-51999-6 (v. 1 : alk. paper)
      1. Federal Reserve banks.   2. Board of Governors of
the Federal Reserve System (U.S.)   I. Title

HG2563.M383 2003
332.1'1'0973—dc21

2002072007

To Christopher C. DeMuth, Marilyn Meltzer, and Anna J. Schwartz

For their support and encouragement
over the many years this history was in process.

CONTENTS

The reference list and the index appear in volume II, book two.

PREFACE

The second, and last, volume of this history covers the years 1951 to 1986 in two parts. These include the time of the Federal Reserve's second major mistake, the Great Inflation, and the subsequent disinflation. The volume summarizes the record of monetary policy during the inflation and disinflation.

Early in the Fed's history, and even in its prehistory, few doubted the importance of separating the power to spend from the power to finance spending by expanding money. The gold standard rule and the balanced budget rule enforced the separation of government spending and monetary policy. By 1951, both rules had lost adherents, especially among academics and increasingly among policymakers and many congressmen.

The men who led the Federal Reserve during these years made many speeches about the evil of inflation. They made mistakes and gave in to political and market pressures for expansion. Many of their mistakes represented dominant academic thinking at the time. A minority view that opposed the policies was heard from some outsiders and some reserve bank presidents at meetings of the Federal Reserve, but most often it was dismissed or disregarded. The role of the reserve bank presidents fully justifies their continued presence on the open market committee. They often bring new or different perspectives that are not entirely welcome but valuable nonetheless.

The volume starts with the first major change in Federal Reserve policy following agreement with the Treasury to permit a more independent monetary policy. The volume ends following the second major change to a policy of disinflation. It would be comforting to see these changes as evidence that "truth will out." It must be added that both changes followed a shift in political support that facilitated the change. The change to an independent policy did not survive the 2007–9 crisis.

The Federal Reserve is said to be an independent central bank. The meaning of independence changed several times. In the years after World War II, Congress and several administrations recognized the political implications of unemployment and later of inflation. As a result, the Federal Reserve often found it difficult to follow an independent course. Mistaken beliefs and lack of courage sustained inflationary actions.

A subject that I do not raise in the text deserves mention. One of the outstanding achievements of the Federal Reserve in Washington and at the regional banks is the high level of integrity and purposefulness of the principals and the staffs. More than ninety years passed without major scandal. There are very few examples of leaked information. This fine record has been abused rarely. Although I find many reasons to criticize decisions, I praise the standards and integrity of the principals.

Volume 2 records some successes and achievements but many persistent errors. As in the earlier volume 1, I let the principals explain their reasoning. Much of the material uses the records of meetings of the Federal Open Market Committee. The Federal Reserve refers to these records as transcripts or memoranda of discussion. I refer to them as minutes. They find officials explaining their decisions many times but also showing an understanding of their mistakes and the reasons they continued.

It took six or seven years to complete this volume. To write a volume with such enormous detail I needed much help. It would have taken much longer without the support of the bright and energetic assistants who read and summarized the minutes and provided assistance in collecting data and searching archives. I thank the nine assistants who worked at different times on the volume for their often insightful contributions. Thanks to Matt Kurn, Mark de Groh, Richard Lowery, Randolph Stempski, Jessie Gabriel, Jonathan Lieber, Hillary Boller, Daniel Rosen, and Danielle Hale. I regard their efforts as indispensable. They were supported and assisted by the helpful library staff at the Board of Governors. Thanks are due especially to Susan Vincent and Kathy Tunis, who guided me and many assistants through the records, and thanks also to David Small, Debby Danker, and Normand Bernard of the Board's staff for their help and support.

To supplement the Board's records, I read the papers and records at the Federal Reserve Bank of New York. The reserve banks are not subject to the Freedom of Information Act. I am grateful to President William McDonough and to the archivist Rosemary Lazenby and her successor Joseph Komljenovich for making the records available and for their assistance and guidance through their extensive files. With the passage of time and the changed positions of Washington and New York, meetings of the New York directors became a less important source of information. The papers of the presidents and correspondence remained valuable.

Presidential libraries were a more important source of material after 1951. No one can read these volumes without seeing the influence of politics and politicians. Papers of presidents, presidential assistants, and other officials contain records of policy development and conflicts. I benefited from the able assistance of archivists and librarians at the Millar Center at the University of Virginia, the Missouri Historical Society for the papers of William McChesney Martin, Jr., the Kennedy Library in Boston, the Johnson Library in Austin, the Carter Library in Atlanta, the Ford Library at the University of Michigan in Ann Arbor, and the National Archive II for the Nixon papers and the Nixon Oval Office tape recordings.

To supplement the written records and documents, I interviewed several participants. All of the following graciously gave their time and interpretations. They were particularly helpful in describing the atmosphere in which decisions were made or rejected. I am grateful to each of the following: Steven Axilrod, Andrew Brimmer, Joseph Coyne, David Lindsey, Kenneth Guenther, Jerry L. Jordan, Sherman Maisel, William Miller, James Pierce, Charles Schultze, George Shultz, and Paul Volcker.

Sherman Maisel permitted me to use the diary that he kept during his years as governor. These were very helpful and, as instructed, they are now deposited at the Board of Governors.

On a visit to the research department in May 2003, I discussed the meaning of Federal Reserve independence with Governor Donald Kohn, Athanasios Orphanides, and Edward Ettin. Their comments helped me to understand how Board members and their staff regard this central concern of any monetary authority.

Along the way, I had the good fortune to have several readers who commented on drafts of the main chapters, in some cases on all of them. I am especially grateful to Marvin Goodfriend, David Lindsey, and Anna Schwartz, who read and commented helpfully and extensively on all of the historical chapters. Jerry Jordan, David Laidler, Athanasios Orphanides, and Robert Rasche made insightful comments on several chapters. Responsibility for accepting comments and for remaining errors or misunderstandings are, of course, mine.

Much of the archival material is in Washington. Without my long association with the American Enterprise Institute and its support for me and the many assistants named above, this work would not have been completed. I thank especially Chris DeMuth and David Gerson for their support. I benefited also from the support of the Tepper School at Carnegie Mellon University.

Several foundations provided support. I am especially grateful to my friend Richard M. Scaife for his many contributions and to the Sarah Scaife Foundation. The Earhart Foundation, the Lynde and Harry Bradley Foundation, and the Smith Richardson Foundation also gave helpful assistance. Thank you.

Alberta Ragan typed, proofread, and revised the manuscript several times. Her cheerful, capable, and willing assistance made completion much easier.

Finally, I owe much to my wife, Marilyn, whose support and encouragement were never in doubt and always present.

ONE

Introduction

Exact scientific reasoning will seldom bring us very far on the way to the conclusion for which we are seeking, yet it would be foolish to not avail ourselves of its aid, so far as it will reach:—just as foolish would be the opposite extreme of supposing that science alone can do all the work, and that nothing will remain to be done by practical instinct and trained common sense.
—Marshall, 1890, 779, quoted in Blinder, 1997, 18

The Federal Reserve that we find in these volumes is very different from the institution founded in 1913. Carter Glass, one of its founders, always insisted it was not a central bank. Its main business was the discounting of commercial paper and acceptances governed by the real bills doctrine and subject to the gold standard rule. The United States was an industrial economy, but agriculture retained a significant role and furnished about 40 percent of exports. Discounting facilitated the seasonal increase in loans that supported agricultural exports.

By the 1980s, when this volume ends, the United States had become a postindustrial economy, by far the largest economy in the world. The Federal Reserve was the world's most influential central bank. No one had denied it this title for at least fifty years. Much had changed. Discounting became a minor function. The gold standard was gone. Principal central banks issued fiat paper money and floated their exchange rates.

During its early years and for many years that followed, the Federal Reserve System's concerns included par collection of checks and System membership. Many small banks earned income by charging for check collection. The payee received less than the face amount of the check. Members were required to collect at par. Many small, mainly country, banks did not join the System to avoid par collection and to avoid costly reserve requirement ratios. Both problems ended by the 1980s when Congress made all banks adopt Federal Reserve reserve requirement ratios even if they declined membership.

The most significant change was increased responsibility for economic stabilization, a mission that officials first denied having. Two economic and political forces changed that belief. One was developments in economic theory beginning with the Keynesian revolution in the 1930s and later the monetarist counterrevolution in the 1960s and the Great Inflation of the 1970s.

The principal monetary and financial legacies of the Great Depression were a highly regulated financial system and the Employment Act of 1946, which evolved into a commitment by the government and the Federal Reserve to maintain economic conditions consistent with full employment. The Employment Act was not explicit about full employment and even less explicit about inflation. For much too long, the Federal Reserve and the administration considered a 4 percent unemployment rate to be the equilibrium rate. The Great Inflation changed that. By the late 1970s, the targeted equilibrium unemployment rate rose and Congress gave more attention to inflation control. The resolution was reinterpretation of the Employment Act as "a dual mandate" to guide policy operations at the end of the last century and beyond. The guide does not clearly specify how a tradeoff between the two objectives—low inflation and a low unemployment rate—should be made when required. But it is now more widely accepted that in the long run, employment and unemployment rates are independent of monetary actions, so that monetary policy is fully reflected in the inflation rate and the nominal exchange rate.

The founders of the Federal Reserve intended a passive but responsive institution with limited powers. Semi-independent regional branches set their own discount rates at which members could borrow. The borrowing initiative remained with the members. Creation of the Federal Reserve brought regional interest rates closer together. By the mid-1920s, the System became more active. Under the leadership of Benjamin Strong, it initiated action to induce banks to borrow or repay lending. From this modest start, open market operations became the Federal Reserve's principal and usually only means of changing interest rates and bank reserves. Discounting almost disappeared; advances became a very small activity used mainly for seasonal adjustment by agricultural lenders.[1] Following passage of the

1. The Federal Reserve can also change reserve requirement ratios to add or reduce available reserves. If it keeps the interest rate unchanged, the only effect of the change is to raise

Employment Act, the Federal Reserve at first recognized responsibility mainly for employment and to a lesser extent for inflation. The weight on inflation increased in 1979, a result of the Great Inflation.

Like most central banks, the Federal Reserve avoided taking risk onto its balance sheet. Until 2008 both by statute and by its own regulations, it limited the assets it acquired principally to Treasury securities, mainly short-term bills, and gold (or gold certificates after 1934) and foreign exchange. Originally the Federal Reserve tried to develop a market in bankers' acceptances, but it did not succeed. In 1977, it ceased open market operations in bankers' acceptances. Under pressure from Congress to assist housing finance, it purchased small volumes of agency securities in the 1970s.[2]

Small and Clouse (2004, 36) reviewed the legal and regulatory rules that apply to the Federal Reserve's asset portfolio.

> In usual circumstances, the Federal Reserve has considerable leeway to lend to depository institutions, but a highly constrained ability to lend to individuals, partnerships, and corporations (IPCs). The lending to depository institutions can be accomplished through advances (rather than discounts) secured by a wide variety of private-sector debt instruments. In discounts for depository institutions, the instruments discounted generally are limited to those issued for "real bills" purposes—that is agricultural, industrial, or commercial purposes. The Federal Reserve can make loans to IPCs, but except in unusual and exigent circumstances, the loans be secured by U.S. Treasury securities or by securities issued or guaranteed by a federal agency.[3]

The evolution that changed an association of semi-independent reserve banks into a powerful central bank reflects interaction between policy, events, and monetary theory. Volume 1 showed the importance of the gold standard and, even more, the real bills doctrine that had a powerful role in sustaining the Great Depression. This volume documents the role of Keynesian thinking in creating the Great Inflation and mainly monetarist thinking in bringing inflation back to low levels.

Intervention between monetary theory, policy, and events is one part of

---

or lower the multiplier applied to reserves and the transfer of bank reserves to or from the Federal Reserve.

2. In 2008, the Federal Reserve changed this policy. Abandoning all past precedents, it lent on relatively illiquid long-term debt. Within a few weeks more than half of its portfolio's consisted of longer-term debt. This represented a break with all previous central bank experiences in developed countries.

3. Small and Clouse (2004, 29) point out that it is clear that the "real bills" limitation in section 14 of the Federal Reserve Act applies to purchases of bills of exchange but unclear whether it applies to bankers' acceptances. The limitation does not apply to purchases of foreign instruments.

the story. Changing beliefs about the role of government is another. By the middle of the twentieth century, citizens (voters) in all the developed countries accepted that government had a responsibility to maintain economic prosperity. This raised a critical issue. Voters could punish an administration or Congress for actions of the Federal Reserve. Responsibility and authority remained separate.

The next sections discuss three main themes of this volume. First is the relation of monetary theory to monetary policy. Second is the meaning of central bank independence. Third is inflation, the dominant monetary event of the years 1965 to 1985.

The monetarist-Keynesian controversy had a large role in bringing about changes in policy. Federal Reserve officials never agreed upon a theoretical framework for monetary policy, but the controversy and research influenced them. In the 1980s, Chairman Volcker called his framework "practical monetarism." This was a major change from the approaches advocated by Chairmen Martin and Burns. Changing views about the meaning of central bank independence and its practical application contributed to the start, persistence and end of the Great Inflation.

THE KEYNESIAN ERA
In the early postwar years, policymakers assigned a major role in stabilization policy to fiscal actions. Monetary actions had a minor supporting role, mainly to support fiscal generated expansions or contractions by avoiding large changes in interest rates. Herbert Stein (1990, 50) listed the seven assumptions used in the early postwar versions of Keynesian economics. Stein described these assumptions as "the simple-minded Keynesianism that a generation of economists learned in school and which became the creed of modern intellectuals."

1. That the price level was constant, so that demand could be expanded without danger of inflation.

2. That the potential output of the economy, or the level of full employment, was given—that it would not be affected by the government's policy to maintain full employment.

3. That we knew how much output was the potential output of the economy and how much unemployment was full employment.

4. That the economy had a tendency to operate with output below its potential and unemployment above its full employment level.

5. That output and employment could be brought up to their desirable levels by fiscal actions of government to expand demand—specifically by spending enough or by running large deficits.

6. That we knew how much spending or how big deficits would be enough to achieve desired results.

7. That there was no other way to get to the desired levels of output and employment, the main implication of which was that monetary policy could not do it.

To economists in the twenty-first century, these assumptions and claims seem extreme, simplistic, even simpleminded. Three citations suggest how broadly it was held. First is the survey of monetary theory written for the American Economic Association's sponsored *Survey of Contemporary Economics* (Villard, 1948). Second is the 1959 report of the Radcliffe Committee in Britain, written after inflation had become a problem in Britain, the United States, and elsewhere (Committee on the Working of the Monetary System, 1959). Third is the American Economic Association's *Readings in Business Cycles* (Gordon and Klein, 1965). I cite these studies not because they were unusual but because they reflect the dominant or consensus views found in professional discussion, in popular textbooks such as Ackley (1961), and in econometric models of the period.[4]

Simple Keynesian ideas dominated the analysis in *Employment, Growth, and Price Levels* prepared by professional economists for Congress in 1959 (Joint Economic Committee 1959a). The report denied long-run monetary neutrality, gave no attention to expected inflation, and argued that the economy could not on its own achieve full employment and price stability without guideposts for wages and prices. Chairman William McChesney Martin, Jr., did not share this view, and the Federal Reserve's statement to Congress did not endorse it.

The Federal Reserve opposed securities auctions and helped to finance budget deficits, a main source of inflationary money growth after 1965. Treasury later began auctions. In time, the Federal Reserve ended "even keel" operations used to reduce interest rate changes during Treasury financings.

The early Keynesian model evolved. By the 1960s a Phillips curve relating some measure of inflation to output, the gap between actual and full employment, or unemployment became a standard feature. Prices no longer remained constant; aggregate demand could exceed full employment output, resulting in inflation.

What remained unchanged was the belief that money growth had at most the secondary role of financing deficits or fiscal changes to prevent interest rates from rising, or from rising "unduly." Policy coordination

---

4. This paragraph repeats Meltzer (1998, 9).

became an accepted policy program in the 1960s. In practice, coordination meant that monetary expansion financed government spending or tax reduction and also moderated the negative effects on employment of anti-inflation fiscal actions.

There is often not a close connection between academic research findings and recommendations and Federal Reserve actions. This was certainly true of the 1950s. Chairman Martin had little interest in economic theory or its application. His principal advisers, Winfield Riefler and Woodlief Thomas, revived a modified version of the 1920s policy operations that gave main attention to the short-term interest rate and credit market conditions. To mask its role in affecting interest rates, the Federal Reserve most often set a target for free reserves—member bank excess reserves net of borrowed reserves. Free reserves moved randomly around short-term interest rates.

Keynesian influence became much more visible in the 1960s. President Kennedy brought leading Keynesian economists into the administration. They continued the regular meetings, started in the Eisenhower administration, that brought the Federal Reserve chairman together with the president and his principal economic advisers. These meetings and other contacts sought to increase policy coordination and reduce Federal Reserve independence. And Presidents Kennedy and Johnson chose members of the Board of Governors who shared mainstream Keynesian views. As older staff retired, the Federal Reserve staff and advisers acquired younger economists trained in Keynesian analysis. By the late 1960s, the Keynesian approach dominated discussion.

Similar changes affected Congress. Avoiding recession became the priority. Hearings reflected the urgency felt by many to avoid an unemployment rate above 4 percent, considered full employment.

Chairman Martin at the Federal Reserve did not share these interpretations. He had a restricted view of both Federal Reserve independence and the power of monetary policy. To him, the Federal Reserve was independent within the government. This meant that Congress voted the budget. If they approved deficit finance, the Federal Reserve's obligation called for monetary expansion to keep interest rates from rising. Martin blamed the deficit for inflation. As he said many times, he did not understand money growth. Thus, he permitted inflation to rise despite his many speeches opposing the rise. Although he did not share the Keynesian analysis, he enabled their policies.

Federal Reserve policy relied on interest rate ceilings (regulation Q) to control credit expansion. Substitutes for bank credit developed to circumvent regulation. The euro-dollar market enabled banks to service their customers and money market mutual funds substituted for time deposits. Governor James L. Robertson especially recognized that the System should end reliance on rate ceilings, but the timing never seemed right. Opposition in Congress contributed to the lack of action. Also, the Federal Reserve did not distinguish between real and nominal rates, a problem after inflation rose. Brunner and Meltzer (1964) formalized the Federal Reserve's analysis.

THE MONETARIST CRITIQUE

Clark Warburton was an early critic of Keynesian analysis.[5] Warburton concluded from his empirical work that erratic changes in money growth were the main impulse producing recessions. Real factors had a secondary role. In the long run, money was neutral.

One of the earliest propositions of monetary economics, expressed in the quantity theory, claimed that the monetary authority determined the stock of money, but the public determined the price level at which the stock was held. In a modern economy with developed asset markets, an excess supply of money increases the demand for existing assets in addition to or in place of increases in commodity demand. Higher asset prices induce increased demand for investment.

Beginning in the mid-1950s, Milton Friedman and his students and collaborators produced theoretical and empirical analyses of the role of money. In *Studies in the Quantity Theory of Money* (1956), Friedman challenged the Keynesian view that money substituted only for bonds or, in practice, Treasury bills. In the most developed Keynesian models, wealth owners optimized their portfolio of bonds and real capital, then separately distributed short-term holdings between money and Treasury bills (Tobin, 1956 and elsewhere). Friedman treated money as part of an intertemporal portfolio; money holding substituted for bonds, real capital, and other stores of wealth as in classical analysis. The effect of changes in the stock of money were not limited to the interest rate on Treasury bills. Relative prices on domestic assets and the exchange rate or foreign position responded to the change in money.[6] In their *Monetary History*, Friedman and Schwartz (1963) showed that money growth had a major role in fluctuations, inflation and deflation.

5. Michael Bordo and Anna J. Schwartz (1979) review Warburton's work. This section is based on Brunner and Meltzer (1993, chapter 1).

6. This difference remains as demonstrated in discussions of a liquidity trap in the 1990s. Keynesian thinking emphasizes difficulties for monetary policy caused by a zero bound on nominal Treasury bill rates. A monetarist (non-Keynesian) responded that a central bank could buy other assets, longer-term securities, foreign exchange, or even equities. Brunner and Meltzer (1968).

Discussion and controversy went through several phases. Among the central issues were the properties of the demand for money, the distinction between real and nominal interest rates, real and nominal exchange rates, and between the short- and long-run Phillips curves.[7] By the late 1970s, economists reached a consensus on many of the disputed issues. In his presidential address to the American Economic Association, Franco Modigliani, a leading Keynesian economist, acknowledged that the monetarist position was correct on these issues (Modigliani, 1977). The principal remaining issue between monetarists and Keynesians that he did not concede was whether monetary policy should follow a rule or proceed according to the discretionary choice of officials. Issues no longer in dispute included the long-run neutrality of money, the effects of inflation on money wages, nominal interest rates, and exchange rates, and any permanent real effects of inflation. Four fundamental issues affecting monetary policy remained: the role of monetary rules, the definition of inflation, importance of relative prices in the transmission of monetary policy, and the internal dynamics of a market economy, particularly whether it is mainly self-adjusting.

Rules

Classical monetary policy was based on rules. The best-known rule was the gold standard, but other proposed rules included bimetallism, commodity standards, and real bills. The aim was to achieve price or exchange rate stability. Keynesian analysis shifted the emphasis from rules to discretionary actions by governments and central bankers. Monetary policy, at first, had the modest role of financing fiscal actions, as discussed above. Its responsibilities increased until it held a prominent role in stabilizing the economy. Discretionary actions intended to stabilize were based on judgments of current and possibly longer-term consequences of events and policy actions.

Early in the discussion of rules and discretion Friedman (1951) recognized the importance of information and uncertainty in choosing between a rule and discretionary actions. A well-intentioned policymaker may destabilize if he is misled by incomplete or incorrect information. Later work by Kydland and Prescott (1977) and a large literature that followed analyzed time inconsistency and the credibility of policy actions and announcements. Kydland and Prescott showed that the dynamic path that

---

7 Meltzer (1998) has a more complete discussion of the result of the controversy. Modigliani (1977) is a useful statement from a Keynesian perspective of the consensus reached at the end of the 1970s.

the economy follows depends on the choice of policy rules. A discretionary policy that made an optimal choice today was time inconsistent if it did not follow a rule restricting future actions. An individual or firm planning its future actions experienced increased uncertainty when faced by discretionary policy.

A major change in economic theory came with recognition of uncertainty and the role of information. This heightened attention to the role of expectations. Lucas (1972) developed earlier work on rational expectations.[8] Rational expectations raised a question about the meaning of discretion. In practice, many central banks responded by providing more and better information about current and future actions. Rational expectations implies that central banks depend on market responses and markets depend on central bank actions. Setting and achieving a target for inflation two or three years ahead is a recognized way of reducing uncertainty about future actions. Federal Reserve officials have not adopted a formal inflation target, but, for a time, they encouraged a belief that they try to hold inflation in the 1 to 2 percent range, and in 2007 they began to forecast inflation, output, and unemployment for three years ahead. In early 2008, however, they gave most weight to forecasts of possible recession and less weight to inflation.

These actions constitute a major change from the secrecy traditionally practiced by central banks. It recognized the developments in monetary theory about the role of information, the importance of anticipations, and the success achieved by foreign central banks that announced inflation targets. But United States governments have not adopted fixed rules and are unlikely to do so in the foreseeable future.

Central bankers continue to meet regularly to decide current actions. Prominent central bankers have explained why they do not commit to a fixed rule. The former chairman of the Federal Reserve, Alan Greenspan (2003), explained that a fixed rule could not take account of the many contingencies to which monetary officials might wish to respond. The contingencies are infinite and most are unforeseeable. Many of the contingencies arise from actual or potential financial failures. The monetary rules developed in the literature do not incorporate these contingencies. In the past, following Bagehot (1873 [1962]) the central bank or the government announced in advance that it would suspend the gold standard rule at such times and provide the increased reserves demanded. This became part of the monetary rule.

8. Brunner and Meltzer (1993) point out that rational expectations models usually assign considerable weight to information but zero weight to the cost of acquiring information.

Greenspan's successor, Ben Bernanke (2004), recognized that the central bank can do a great deal to reduce uncertainty about its future actions, but "specifying a complete policy rule is infeasible" (ibid., 8). He accepted Greenspan's reason for infeasibility. Mervyn King (2004), governor of the Bank of England, called for "constrained discretion." "Suitably designed, monetary institutions can help to reduce the inefficiencies resulting from the time-consistency problem" (promising one thing but later doing another) (ibid., 1). Otmar Issing, former chief economist and board member of the European Central Bank, expressed a similar position on many occasions (Issing, 2003, for example). He regarded as impossible in practice the idea of following a fixed rule.

The chapters that follow show that the Federal Reserve changed its objectives and its target many times. Often it did not have a precise target. Even after Congress required the Federal Reserve to announce an annual monetary target, it did not adopt procedures to achieve the target and allowed excess money growth to remain by following the practice called "base drift."

Table 1.1 from the 1980s shows the changing objectives pursued during 1985–88. The principal objective changed frequently, making it difficult for the public to plan. The Federal Open Market Committee (FOMC) did not announce the objectives at the time, and the statement of objectives was sufficiently vague that knowing the objectives would not help observers to anticipate policy actions. And because it chose four or five objectives, the public could only guess the relative importance of each or its influence on Federal Reserve actions.

By the 1990s, principal central banks followed King's "constrained discretion." Many used some version of Taylor's (1993) rule as a guide, but they deviated when they chose to do so. Several adopted inflation targets and gave more information about proposed actions and objectives. None followed a precise rule.

Definition of Inflation

Economists use two definitions of inflation, and laymen use some others. Monetarists define inflation as a *sustained* rate of change in some broad, general price index. The more common definition includes all price increases. Popular usage includes some relative price increases such as wage, asset price, or energy price increases; an example is "wage inflation."

Economic theory does not prescribe the choice of a stable price level over a stable sustained rate of price change. The former requires central bank policy to roll back or push up the price level following an event that

Table 1.1 Order in Which Policy Variables Appeared in the FOMC Directive

MEETING	FIRST	SECOND	THIRD	FOURTH	FIFTH
3/85 to 7/85	Monetary Aggregate	Strength of expansion	Inflation	Credit Market Conditions	Exchange Rates
8/85 to 4/86	Monetary Aggregate	Strength of Expansion	Exchange Rates	Inflation	Credit Market Conditions
5/86	Monetary Aggregate	Strength of Expansion	Financial Market Conditions	Exchange Rates	——
7/86 to 2/87	Monetary Aggregate	Strength of Expansion	Exchange Rates	Inflation	Credit Market Conditions
3/87	Exchange Rates	Monetary Aggregate	Strength of Expansion	Inflation	Credit Market Conditions
5/87	Inflation	Exchange Rates	Monetary Aggregate	Strength of Expansion	——
7/87	Inflation	Monetary Aggregate	Strength of Expansion	——	——
8/87 to 9/87	Inflation	Strength of Expansion	Exchange Rates	Monetary Aggregate	——
11/87	Financial Market Conditions	Strength of Expansion	Inflation	Exchange Rates	Monetary Aggregate
12/87 to 5/88	Financial Market Conditions	Strength of Expansion	Inflation	Exchange Rates	Monetary Aggregate
7/88	Monetary Aggregate	Strength of Expansion	Inflation	Financial Markets	Exchange Rates
8/88 to 11/88	Inflation	Strength of Expansion	Monetary Aggregate	Exchange Rates	Financial Markets

Source: *Economic Review*, Federal Reserve Bank of San Francisco, Spring 1989, p. 11.

raises or lowers it. If this is successfully carried out, the public can expect an unchanged price level over time. It incurs a cost because price adjustment is costly, particularly if the price level increased following a large increase in the price of oil or in an excise tax on a subset of goods.

The monetarist position lets the price level become a random walk. Energy price, excise tax increases, currency depreciation, or reductions in productivity raise the price level; opposite movements reduce the price level. These changes up and down often are spread through time. They appear as changes in the rate of price change, but they are not sustained.

Sustained money growth in excess of output growth induces a sustained increase in the rate of price change. Milton Friedman's often quoted statement that inflation is always a monetary phenomenon used the monetarist definition of inflation. It recognized implicitly that non-monetary price level changes are mainly relative price changes.

A central bank must choose whether to control the price level or the rate of price change. Each has different costs to society. Controlling the sustained rate of price change permits the price level to vary, probably as a random walk. Wealth owners have to accept price variability but can be more confident when planning lifetime asset allocation that inflation will be controlled. Controlling all changes in the rate of price change also incurs a cost. The monetary authority must force other prices to decline if oil (or other) prices rise and permit other prices to rise in the opposite case. Such changes induce allocative changes and temporary changes in output and employment. Experience under the classical gold standard suggests that these costs are not small.

In practice, some central banks ignore some transitory changes in the price level. The Federal Reserve targets the so-called core deflator for private consumption expenditures. This excludes changes in the prices of food and energy on grounds that these prices are volatile and that many of the changes are transitory. The public experiences the effects of food and energy prices and considers these changes as inflationary. In 2007 the Federal Reserve accepted responsibility for controlling these prices over the longer term.

The use of a core price index is an inexact way of separating transitory from persistent price level changes to get a better measure of sustained inflation. A superior alternative would use statistical estimation of the relative variance of the permanent and transitory components to estimate whether a given change is likely to persist. Muth (1960) suggested a procedure.

Persistent price changes—inflations—occur if sustained money growth rises in excess of sustained output growth. The inflation rate changes, therefore, if money growth rises relative to output growth or if normal output growth changes relative to money growth. The latter change occurred in the mid-1990s in the United States. It produced a fall in the sustained rate of inflation.

Implementing a monetarist policy to control inflation requires commitment to the low or zero inflation rule. Implementation of the policy requires judgment about the permanent rates of change of money and output. Many central banks now use an inflation target that they try to meet over two or more years.

The Role of Relative Prices

The simple Keynesian model of the 1940 and 1950s had a single interest rate representing the bond market or, in practice, the Treasury bill or federal funds rate. In the IS-LM model of that period, money was a substitute

for bonds; money growth had little direct impact on output or employment. The real balance effect was small. Usually the price level remained
fixed. Later a Phillips curve avoided fixed prices by making the rate of price
change depend on some measure of the output gap.[9]

Friedman's (1956) essay on the demand for money broadened the interpretation of interest rates to include relative prices of assets and output.
His analysis changed the explanations of the transmission of monetary impulses to include a wide range of substitutions between money and other
objects. In place of the Keynesian transmission from money to Treasury
bills found in textbooks and many versions of the Federal Reserve's econometric models, monetarists claimed that changes in the quantity of money
altered current and expected future prices on a wide variety of domestic
assets and the exchange rate.

In classical monetary theory, monetary policy changed the quantity of
real balances relative to the stocks of other assets and current consumption. Substitution occurred in many directions. An excess supply of real
balances induces changes in asset prices and spending; a deficient supply does the opposite. A change in the price of existing capital relative to
the price of current investment induces or discourages new production.
Changes in real balances relative to current consumption expenditure encourage or discourage spending.

There is no possibility of a liquidity trap—a condition in which monetary changes are impotent. If the nominal rate on short-term bills falls to
zero, this margin closes but other margins remain (Brunner and Meltzer,
1968). A central bank can always increase the quantity of real balances
by buying long-term debt, foreign exchange, real assets, or claims to real
assets until money holders find that they hold more real balances than
desired. To reduce money holdings people spend on consumption or non-
money assets, changing relative prices to restore portfolio balance.

In Federal Reserve history, deflation occurred several times. In some
periods, such as 1938, the nominal short-term interest reached zero or
slightly below. Each of these periods is highlighted in the text of the two volumes. Economic expansion followed monetary expansion. Other periods
of deflation, including the early 1920s, when the real interest rate reached
20 percent or more, do not show failure of monetary policy. The principal examples used by proponents of a liquidity trap are usually the early
1930s in the United States or the late 1990s in Japan. In both cases, mon-

---

9. Early discussions of the Phillips curve did not recognize that original data came from
a time when the gold standard anchored inflation and expectations.

etary policy was not expansive. Inept and inappropriate monetary policy in 1929–33 induced reductions in money growth, giving rise to anticipations of further deflation.[10]

The most comprehensive recent statement of modern macroeconomic theory, Woodford (2003), is an elegant, erudite development of the rational expectations model that currently dominates academic thinking. Like early Keynesian models, but for very different reasons, Woodford's analysis has a single interest rate that is set by monetary policy. All other interest rates reflect the current short-rate and rational expectations of the duration, magnitude, and influence of current policies and events. Prices and output are determined by aggregate demand and supply. Since the single interest rate is fixed by policy action, money has no independent role. All relative prices fully reflect current rational expectations of future events. Spending in this and other models depends on the long-term real interest rate. The central bank controls the short rate. A strong assumption about the expectations theory or the term structure of interest rates assumes away the problem of determining long rates.

Many central bank economists use this model. No central banker uses it. There are many reasons for this difference in approach. Three are most important.

First, rational expectations models give importance to information and anticipations of future events. Decision makers use all available information when allocating resources. This is an important advance. However, few models recognize the cost of acquiring information and differences in this cost in different markets. Further, the meaning or interpretation assigned to observations depends on the particular model or framework used. Federal Reserve policy discussions show that major differences in interpretation and anticipations were common. Members lacked a common framework of analysis, so they often differed about the expected policy consequences of current information.[11]

---

10. At a zero interest rate, as in Japan in the 1990s, central bank purchases of treasury bills provide no stimulus. The two assets are nearly perfect substitutes at a zero price. Later, expansion followed purchases of longer-term securities.

11. A well-known example from the 1990s was the conclusion drawn by Chairman Greenspan that productivity growth had increased. Other members of the open market committee expected an increase in inflation and wanted to raise the interest rate. Several years passed before all agreed about increased productivity growth. This is one of many examples with differences in interpretation of common information. Blinder (2004, 39, 43) discusses differences of interpretation and opinion on the FOMC during his term as a member. He concluded that committee decisions are less extreme, and less volatile (ibid., 48). Some work on committee decision making in monetary policy suggests relevant differences between the single policymaker assumed in economic models and committee decisions (Chappell, McGregor, and Vermilyea, 2005).

Second, abundant econometric evidence suggests strongly that prices of long-dated assets have separate roles in the transmission of monetary policy. Considerable research shows that expectations theory of the term structure of interest rates does not hold at times. The relation of long- to short-term rates changes. The same is true of other asset prices and especially exchange rates. One reason is the market's inability to estimate the term premium accurately. Different procedures give different estimates, often considerably different.

Woodford (2005, 886–87) recognizes that long-term rates contain information useful to the Federal Reserve in interpreting its policy, but he concludes that a central bank could not affect the economy by purchasing long-term bonds even when the short-term rate is zero. The experience of the Bank of Japan after 2002 and on several occasions in U.S. history supports the opposite conclusion; expanding base money and money by purchasing longer-term securities stimulated spending with a zero short-term interest rate. Blinder (2004, 77) concluded that "the implied interest rate forecasts (expectations) that can be deduced from the yield curve bear little resemblance to what future interest rates actually turn out to be. . . . Suffice it to say that the abject empirical failure of the expectations theory of the term structure of interest rates is a well-established fact."

The distinction between sustained rates of change and changes in the price level is important for the term structure. Devaluation or an oil price increase raises the reported price level. If the increased oil price is expected to remain, the effect on interest rates is mainly at the short end. An increase in inflation expected to be sustained raises rates along the entire term structure.

Third, to use the Woodford model, central bankers require reliable estimates of potential output and expected inflation. Research has shown that economists do not have such estimates and to date have not developed reliable estimates. This was a main reason for the large errors in predicting inflation in the 1970s, as Orphanides (2001) showed. And it is a main weakness of Phillips curve predictions of inflation and Woodford's model.

Role of Government

Monetarists and Keynesians held different visions of the role of the government and the private sector. Following Keynes (1936), Keynesians viewed the private sector of the economy as unstable, subject to waves of optimism or pessimism that produced economic booms and recessions. Government had to act as a stabilizer, at first by changing its expenditures and tax rates and later by adjusting interest rates.

Monetarists hold a contrary view. The internal dynamics of the private sector are stabilizing. Relative prices adjust to restore equilibrium. Declining tax collections and increased spending in recessions, built-in stabilizers, support recovery. Adjustment is not instantaneous, so government policy can nudge the economy toward equilibrium, but too often government policy worsens outcomes by doing too much or too little.

A standard monetarist complaint about the Federal Reserve from the 1950s to the 1970s was that it misinterpreted its own policy. When short-term interest rates declined, the Federal Reserve interpreted the decline as easier policy despite a decline in money growth. And it interpreted an increase in interest rates as evidence of more restrictive policy even if money growth increased. Failure to distinguish between real and nominal interest rates until the late 1970s was part of the problem, but not the whole problem. Until 1994, monetary policy was typically procyclical until late in the inflation or recession.[12]

The most damaging effect of the Keynesian belief in the role of government came after 1960. Administration economists argued that inflation would increase before the economy reached full employment output. Government had the role of limiting wage and price increases using guideposts and guidelines. This approach to pricing interfered in private decisions and, if successful, would have restricted prices and wages from reallocating resources efficiently. It concentrated attention on pricing in visible sub-sectors, especially those with strong unions. And it focused on price changes in those industries instead of general inflation.

Keynesian economists and policymakers repeated this claim but did not produce evidence to support it. After 1980, the Federal Reserve abandoned the claim and insisted instead that stable low inflation abetted economic expansion and high employment. After inflation declined, the United States experienced three long peacetime expansions punctuated by relatively mild recessions. Low, relatively stable inflation contributed to this outcome. Researchers differ on the degree.

Some monetarist analysis included a credit or financial market (Brunner and Meltzer, 1989, 1993, and 1968). This analysis recognized that money, government debt, and real capital are distinct assets held in portfolios. One function of financial markets is to allocate the stock of debt between banks and the public. This process is a factor in the determination of

---

12. Monetarists erred by insisting too strongly on direct control of money growth instead of an interest rate. Experience since 1994 shows that the Federal Reserve learned to adjust the interest rate counter-cyclically. The German Bundesbank and the European Central Bank use money growth as a "second pillar," that is, as an indicator of whether the interest rate is set appropriately.

asset prices and interest rates. Recent work by Goodfriend and McCallum (2007) returns to issues involving intermediation and financial markets.

Summary on Theory and Policy

The two-way relation between monetary theory and policy was never complete or precise. The Federal Reserve and other central banks became more professional as time passed and complexity increased. Economists with academic training and experience occupied leading roles at central banks. Much larger staffs and more policymakers came from academic backgrounds. No chairman of the Board of Governors came from a professional economics background before 1970. After 1970 all but one had that training and experience. Nevertheless, analytic errors and misjudgments had a large role in mistaken policy choices.

Cagan (1978a, 85–86) described the early postwar consensus on the role of money. "The quantity theory of money was not considered important, indeed was hardly worth mentioning, for questions of aggregate demand, unemployment, and even inflation . . . [I]f you traveled among the profession at large, mention of the quantity of money elicited puzzled glances of disbelief or sly smiles of condescension."

For very different reasons, the Federal Reserve ignored money growth until the mid-1970s, when Congress, over Arthur Burns's objections, required semiannual statements that included ranges for money growth consistent with administration economic policy. William McChesney Martin, Jr., chairman from 1951 to 1970, had no interest in economic theory and did not find it useful. Until very late in his chairmanship, he prevented his staff from making forecasts. He often said that he did not understand statistics on money growth. He opposed attempts to control inflation by controlling money growth. In 1969, he replied to Milton Friedman, saying: "I seriously doubt that we could ever attain complete control [of monetary aggregates], but I think it's quite true that we could come significantly closer to such control than we do now—if we wished to make that variable our exclusive target. But the wisdom of such an exclusive orientation for money policy is, of course, the basic question" (quoted in Friedman, 1982, 106).[13]

Except for control of money, monetarist arguments prevailed eventually. The Phillips curve tradeoff vanished in the long run, as Friedman (1968b) predicted. Policy distinguished real and nominal interest rates and exchange rates. Long-run neutrality of money again became standard

---

13. Friedman commented that Martin's response recognized that the Federal Reserve could control money growth, contrary to many earlier statements.

in economic theory. Strangely, models incorporating these ideas are now called neo-Keynesian (Ball and Mankiw, 1994).

Romer and Romer (1994, 56–57) concluded their study of postwar macroeconomic policy by finding that "monetary policy alone is a sufficiently powerful and flexible tool to end recessions." Contrary to the early Keynesian position, they found that "fiscal actions contributed only moderately to recoveries . . . [T]he historical record contradicts the view that fiscal policy is essential to ending recessions or ensuring strong recoveries." However, the authors found that frequently monetary policy was destabilizing, and procyclical instead of counter-cyclical. This was a main monetarist criticism from the 1960s on.

McCallum (1986) reviewed discussion of monetary and fiscal policy and critiqued criticisms of the Andersen and Jordan (1968) findings showing the relative and absolute importance of monetary policy for output. He concluded (McCallum, 1986, 23) that "an open-market increase in the money stock has a stimulative effect on aggregate demand." This conclusion would not be remarkable if it had not been denied by early Keynesians and challenged by critics of the Andersen-Jordan paper.

Modigliani's (1977) conclusion that the monetarist position was correct on main issues of theory and fact represents an end to the controversy. He did not accept a monetary rule, and neither has the economics profession. Central banks continue to target interest rates, but they give much greater weight to avoiding inflation and damping inflationary expectations.

Central Bank Independence

Interpretations of central bank independence have changed several times. The changes were not limited to the United States. At the end of World War II, the British Labor government nationalized the Bank of England and made it subservient to the Treasury, that is to the elected government. Fifty years later, a new Labor government made the Bank independent. The Bank and the government now agree on an inflation target. With few restrictions, the Bank is empowered to decide on its actions. After years of inflation and slow growth, the government accepted the importance of price stability for economic growth and the importance of independence for price stability.

The European Central Bank (ECB) requires governments to accept the independence of its member central banks. The ECB's legal mandate is price stability, interpreted to mean sustained low inflation.[14] Governments

---

14. Article 108 of the Maastricht treaty says: "Neither the ECB [European Central Bank] nor a national central bank . . . shall seek or take instructions from community institutions or

and ministers complain about the ECB's actions, but they have not changed its mandate. Change requires unanimous agreement.

The Federal Reserve Act gave the System independence that with few exceptions, as in wartime, administrations accepted until 1933. From 1933 to 1951, the Treasury Department dominated the Federal Reserve's decisions, at first by direct pressure and in World War II and thereafter by agreement.[15] Slowly after March 1951, the Federal Reserve regained some independence, but it remained responsible for assuring the success of Treasury debt sales. From 1961 to 1979, policy coordination, the emphasis given to avoiding recessions, and frequent Treasury debt sales restricted independence. The System gained increased independence for disinflation starting in 1979, and it retained its independence during the next quarter century. Testifying before a House subcommittee in 1989, Chairman Greenspan described independence as necessary to enable the central bank "to resist short-term inflationary biases that might be inherent in some aspects of the political process" (Greenspan, 1989, 2). Regrettably, the record does not show either a consistent avoidance of short-term pressures or avoidance of inflationary pressures from elected officials.[16] Cukierman (2006, 149) points out the difficulty of not knowing the value of potential output as a source of error, possibly large error, in achieving an inflation target while maintaining actual output close to potential output. Orphanides (2003a,b) demonstrated the relevance of this point.

Independence is never absolute.[17] There are two principal, formal restrictions in the United States. First, the Federal Reserve is the agent of Congress. The Constitution gives Congress authority to "coin money [and] regulate the value thereof"; in principle, Congress can withdraw the authority or restrict Federal Reserve actions. On occasion, it has discussed such restrictions and in the 1970s, Congress required the Federal Reserve to report on

---

bodies, from any government of a Member State or from any other body." This article restricts political influence in a way that U.S. law does not.

15. Marriner Eccles, chairman from 1934 to 1948, defined independence as "the opportunity to express its views in connection with the determination of policy" (Board Minutes, February 3, 1942, 8). See Meltzer (2003, 599, n. 27).

16. Former vice chairman Alan Blinder is a bit more explicit. "Central bank independence means two things: first, that the central bank has freedom to decide how to pursue its goals and, second, that its decisions are very hard for any other branch of government to reverse" Blinder (1998, 54). This leaves two critical issues open. First, does the central bank coordinate its policy with the administration so that it "independently" decides to finance the budget deficit? Second, how free is the central bank to choose its objectives? Does it have a broad mandate like the so-called dual mandate or does the administration choose the inflation target. The Federal Reserve is always concerned that Congress can restrict its independence.

17. Cukierman, Webb, and Neyapati (1992) discuss the problem of measuring independence in developed and developing countries.

its actions and plans. Second, the Treasury is responsible for international economic policy decisions. It can adopt a fixed exchange rate, requiring the Federal Reserve to intervene in the exchange market and to adjust interest rates and money growth consistent with the exchange rate target. On occasion, as in mid-1980s, the Treasury can agree on an exchange rate target, but the independent Federal Reserve sterilized most Treasury intervention. Table 1.1 above shows that it did not give priority to the exchange rate.

Informal restrictions on independence vary. Members of Congress and of the administration urge the Federal Reserve to adopt policies that they favor. One example repeated in 1968, in 1982, in 1991, and at other times is pressure to reduce interest rates when Congress approves a tax increase. In 1968 and 1982 the Federal Reserve responded to this pressure. In 1991, following the Bush tax increase, the FOMC reduced rates to spur the economy.

One manifestation of independence is budgetary authority. The government budget reports the System's spending as an appendix and records a transfer of 90 percent of Federal Reserve earnings as a fiscal receipt. In the Banking Act of 1933, Congress accepted that the Federal Reserve's receipts were "not to be construed as government funds or appropriated moneys." This freed them from congressional budget control (Hackley, 1983, 2). Members of Congress have introduced legislation making the system subject to the congressional appropriation process or cancelling its debt holdings, thereby removing its source of income. The legislation has never passed, mainly because a majority prefers to maintain independence. In 1978, Congress approved the Federal Banking Agency Audit Act, providing for audit of some of the Federal Reserve's transactions by the General Accounting Office. The act exempted transactions with foreign central banks and related to monetary policy actions (Hackley, 1983, 5). Since the Board lacks a source of earned income, the regional reserve banks pay an assessment to the Board.

Other aspects of independence are the non-renewable fourteen-year terms of Board members, the absence of Senate confirmation for presidents of Federal Reserve banks, commercial banks' ownership (but not control) of Reserve banks, the reluctance of Congress to approve legislation making the chairman's term coterminous with the president's, and service by Reserve bank presidents on the policymaking Federal Open Market Committee (FOMC). Other instances include the provision that Board members may be removed only for cause, and the removal of the Secretary of the Treasury and the Comptroller of the Currency from the Board in 1935. Congress has reconsidered each of these issues, some many times, but has not made a major change to reduce independence.

Hackley (1972, 195) concluded that the Federal Reserve Board of Governors and the FOMC are agencies of the executive branch. It is a "creation of Congress but so are other executive agencies." Hackley argues that the president appoints Board members and the Board, under congressional statutes, exercises governmental functions[18] (ibid., 195). I have not found evidence that members of the Congressional Banking Committee share this view. Federal Reserve governors are asked frequently if they are the agents of Congress; the expected answer is yes.

One informal but powerful restriction on Federal Reserve independence is its presence in Washington, the political capital. Board members, especially the chairman, are conscious of political developments and pressure to accede to them. Federal Reserve policy was an issue in the 1960 election and again in 1980. Arthur Burns as chairman was unusually partisan. He met with President Nixon regularly. Other chairmen and governors met at times with administration officials both at regular meetings and less formally. Pressure from Congress increased in the 2007–9 crisis.

Several administrations used appointments to influence Federal Reserve decisions. On the other hand, some presidents honor independence. President Gerald Ford was exceptionally careful not to influence Arthur Burns. However, the minutes or transcripts of FOMC meetings contain very few references to politics. Partisan action would threaten independence, so it has usually been avoided.[19] Wooley (1984, 109) concluded that "presidents generally get the policy they want from the Federal Reserve." Presidents Ford, Carter, and George H. W. Bush would not accept that conclusion. It remains true that Presidents Eisenhower, Ford, Reagan, and Clinton were less intrusive than Presidents Johnson and Nixon. The result was lower inflation when the Federal Reserve was less subject to and less responsive to administration pressures.

The monetary and political authorities have not agreed on a definition of independence. Often System officials speak about "independence within government," a convenient phrase that recognizes that independence is not absolute but leaves open where the limits of government authority lie. The limits change. President Reagan wanted lower inflation and did not criticize Federal Reserve policy. His administration did not agree on what they wanted the Federal Reserve to do, so Chairman Volcker ignored them. He did not talk to Treasury Undersecretary Sprinkel and did not get along

18. Hackley was the chief legal officer of the Board.

19. Wooley (1984, 129) summarizes political influence: "There is almost no persuasive evidence that the Federal Reserve is actively engaged in partisan manipulation." A finding that it engaged in political actions would probably end independence.

with Secretary Regan. The first Bush administration frequently criticized Federal Reserve policy publicly, and Chairman Greenspan publicly criticized as an attack on independence a letter written by a Treasury official to the FOMC members urging a reduction in interest rates. The Clinton administration did not discuss monetary policy publicly and avoided putting pressure on the System.

In practice, the Federal Reserve waited for political support before making major policy changes. Although members chafed under the 2.5 percent ceiling for long-term rates before 1951, they did not challenge the restriction until they had congressional support. In 1978 polling data showed a sharp increase in concern about inflation that persisted until spring 1982. More than 50 percent of those polled listed inflation and the high cost of living as the most important problem facing the country. In October 1978, 72 percent listed inflation and only 8 percent listed unemployment. The public wanted disinflation; the political process responded and the Federal Reserve changed its policy. By October 1982, when the disinflation policy ended, 61 percent listed unemployment as the most important problem. Only 18 percent still cited inflation.

President Nixon urged Arthur Burns to adopt more expansive policy prior to the 1972 election. Leading members of Congress agreed. The public expressed little concern about inflation. Only 20 percent listed inflation as their principal concern at election time.

Independence should be strengthened. Responsibility for policy outcomes should not be avoided in discussions of independence. An independent central bank can cause unemployment or inflation. The public generally blames the administration and Congress for these outcomes. They may lose office. Federal Reserve officials may be criticized, but they retain their positions. Following the two major errors of the twentieth century, the Great Depression and the Great Inflation, no Federal Reserve officials had to resign.

Responsibility and authority should be more closely aligned. At a Shadow Open Market Committee meeting in 1980, I proposed that the Federal Reserve Chairman and the Secretary of the Treasury should agree on the policy objective for the next two or three years. If the objective is not met, the president could ask for an explanation. He could then accept the explanation or ask for a resignation. Subsequently, several countries starting with New Zealand adopted variants of this proposal.

Inflation

The third major topic is inflation. Chapters 4 through 9 discuss four issues. Why did the Great Inflation start? Why did it take fifteen to twenty years to reduce inflation to low levels? Why did it end? Why did high inflation not return in the next twenty years?

Modern central banks no longer claim, as the Federal Reserve did in the 1920s and even in the 1950s, that they do not control the inflation rate. They may have meant the near-term or quarterly rate but, if so, they failed to make that explicit. Academic research and experience settled the issue about the long term. It left open the practical issue of how to measure inflation and how to choose a value for an inflation target.

Chairman Greenspan would not announce a numerical objective. He defined the absence of inflation as the point at which the public ignored inflation when making decisions.[20] President Poole of the St. Louis reserve bank favored a goal of "zero inflation properly measured" (Poole, 2005, 1). In practice, he proposed 1 percent inflation for an index that excludes "volatile food and energy prices" (ibid., 2).

Poole's definition recognized that in the short term, different indexes give different information. Over the longer term this is less of a problem. One reason is that one-time price changes and changes in relative prices distort inflation measures in the short term but are less troublesome over the longer term.

Central banks that announce inflation targets choose measures of the sustained rate of price change. The price level is allowed to change in response to the many largely random changes in productivity, excise taxes, exchange rates, or other relative price changes. In economic textbooks, these problems do not appear. They are very real to central bankers.

Otmar Issing (2003, 21) pointed to the information problem and the need for judgment. When analyzing expected inflation "no simple rules linking policy to one or two privileged indicators can substitute for an accurate examination of shocks and a careful analysis of their potential for transmission into prices over a sufficiently extended span of time ahead." This statement about short-term difficulty in interpreting data contrasts with his view about the longer term. "Money should grow at a rate that is consistent with trend growth in real output and the central bank's definition [sic] of price stability" (ibid., 21)

One example of the difficulties that the Federal Reserve had in deciding on the expected rate of inflation came in 2002–3, when the FOMC became concerned about deflation. An economy with very large budget and current account deficits and positive monetary growth was unlikely to experience

---

20. Pressed internally to give a quantitative measure, eventually he said 2 percent. The FOMC later adopted 1 to 2 percent but did not announce it, out of concern for congressional opposition to an inflation target.

deflation. And the deflations in 1920–21, in 1937–38, in 1960, and at other times show no evidence that deflation had significant negative, real effects. The 1929–33 experience differed because money growth declined faster than deflation, suggesting that deflation would continue. The expected deflation did not occur in 2002–3.

Orphanides (2001, 2003a,b) reported the errors in inflation forecasts during the 1970s. All the errors in the second half of the decade were underestimates of the inflation rate, strongly suggesting model errors. The Federal Reserve had difficulty forecasting the inflation rate at that time and later. In the 1980s, Paul Volcker disparaged staff forecasts and did not rely on them. Alan Greenspan (2007, 437) concluded that short-term forecasts are much less accurate than long-term.

As Issing insisted, setting an inflation target is easy. Achieving it in the short run is difficult because of the lack of accurate models of short-run behavior, the difficulty of distinguishing permanent from transitory changes in current data, measurement problems, especially the natural rate of output, and the often large data revisions. During the period discussed in the chapters that follow, unwillingness to persist in anti-inflation policies—often influenced by political concerns and pressures—had a large role.

REGULATION AND SUPERVISION

Financial problems and panics are recurring problems. Almost all countries have de facto or de jure deposit insurance programs. Often large deposits are uninsured but are protected against loss. The insurance limit in the United States started at $2500 in 1934 and is now $250,000. Adjusting for inflation, the new limit is at least seven times the initial limit.

Even in the absence of political pressures to avoid depositor losses, government-insured deposits require the government to regulate insured financial institutions. Absent regulation and supervision, some financial institutions would take large risks. This is particularly a problem if the institution's capital is impaired.

Financial regulation has two distinct functions. One is service as the lender of last resort—the lender willing to supply bank reserves when most other lenders will not. The other is portfolio regulation and supervision to limit risk taking, maintain prudent standards, and protect the payments system. This function now includes lending standards intended to protect low-income borrowers and to increase their access to consumer loans and mortgages.

In its ninety-year history, the Federal Reserve has never clearly defined its responsibility as lender of last resort or announced a strategy for responding to crises. It creates uncertainty by, at times, preventing failure of banks and other institutions and at other times permitting failure while protecting the payments system. Examples of bailouts include First Pennsylvania, Continental Illinois, and Long Term Capital Management. At other times, it permitted failures such as Drexel Burnham and several Texas banks. But during the Latin American debt problems of the 1980s, it protected the money center banks and did not require them to report their losses. Of course, the market value of the banks' shares fell as the market recognized the hidden losses.

Announcing a clear strategy tells financial institutions what to expect. It removes the uncertainty about whether there will be a bailout to prevent failures or whether the Federal Reserve will limit its action to preventing the spread of failures by providing liquid assets on demand against acceptable collateral. If the Federal Reserve makes the latter choice, prudent financial institutions hold collateral to prevent failure. This lessens the problem.

More than a century ago, Walter Bagehot urged the Bank of England to announce its strategy for responding to financial panics. He wanted the Bank to state publicly that it would lend freely at a penalty rate against adequate collateral. That strategy is as sound now as when he announced it.

The size of financial firms often appears as an excuse for bailouts. A policy of "too big to fail"—the policy followed in the United States—encourages giantism and risk taking by large institutions. These institutions should be allowed to fail like any other. Failure does not mean that the firm disappears. It should mean that management and stockholders lose. Unless insolvent, the firm is reorganized and continues under new management and owners.

Congress became dissatisfied with the way financial regulators acted. In 1991, Congress passed the Federal Deposit Insurance Corporation Improvement Act (FDICIA). FDICIA restricted bailouts by instructing regulators to close failing firms.

FDICIA is as close as the United States has come to announcing a strategy for responding to financial failures. Regulators, especially the Federal Reserve as lender of last resort, should make their strategy known and follow it.

Portfolio regulation and supervision went in two directions. After the 1970s, Congress eliminated many of the prohibitions adopted in the 1930s. Interest rate ceilings and restrictions of banking from other types of finance disappeared. Resolution of bank and thrift association failures required regulators to permit interstate branching and bank consolidation. But regulators received new powers over credit decisions especially affecting minorities and women.

Furlong and Kwan (2007) and Benston (2007) discuss several of the proposed changes in the United States. Congress approved several of the recommendations in modified form. It has not required banks to use subordinated debentures to shift risk from depositors or deposit insurance to investors (Calomiris, 2002). Agreeing on measures of financial risk proved difficult. Efforts to agree on international standards, the Basel accords, have proved unsatisfactory. A main reason is that the regulators failed to rely on incentives and diversification to enforce discipline. They chose regulation instead (ibid., 22–23). The accords encouraged banks to limit reserves by putting risky assets off their balance sheets. In 2007, these hidden risks became visible.

INTERNATIONAL

A central bank can direct its efforts at stability of either domestic or international prices. It cannot do both unless other central banks and governments agree on an exchange rate system. The Bretton Woods Agreement was such an agreement. The United States agreed to maintain the dollar at $35 per fine ounce of gold. Most countries agreed to maintain exchange rates fixed to the dollar or gold. Countries agreed to buy or sell dollars to maintain their fixed exchange rate. To correct a recognized weakness in the gold standard, countries could devalue or revalue to adjust to permanent changes in their equilibrium exchange rate. The agreement did not define permanent changes.

As the center of the system, the United States supplied dollars. The Bretton Woods period, 1945–1971, saw recovery in Europe and Japan. At first, most currencies remained inconvertible. By 1958 Western Europe agreed to convertibility on current account, and West Germany made the mark fully convertible. The United States began to experience balance of payments deficits. Payments for military assistance, defense, foreign aid, investment in Europe, and imports of consumer goods exceeded revenues.

The president and other officials repeatedly pledged their commitment to the $35 gold price. Whenever a problem arose during the Kennedy and Johnson administrations, they took administrative action—usually controls—to reduce the payments imbalances. Until 1968, the Treasury paid gold in exchange for dollars.

The Federal Reserve had a secondary role. Exchange rate and balance of payments remained a Treasury responsibility. The Banking Act of 1933 reduced the role taken by the New York Federal Reserve Bank in the 1920s. The Federal Reserve chose domestic policy, especially high employment, over international policy. To avoid painful increases in the unemployment rate, it did not persist in efforts at disinflation when unemployment rose. In 1971, President Nixon ended convertibility of the dollar into gold.

Attempts to restore a fixed exchange rate system after 1971 failed. By the mid-1970s, countries agreed to permit exchange rates to fluctuate. Principal European countries preferred fixed exchange rates, so they moved toward, and later adopted, a single currency.

Critics of floating exchange rates found many reasons to complain. Different effects of oil price increases, different rates of inflation, and changes in relative productivity growth produced large changes in exchange rates. Intervention to limit or prevent these changes added to the initial problems. Critics did not show that fixed exchange rates would be a better solution. Floating continued and remains.

A remarkable feature of policy under the Bretton Woods system was the inability or unwillingness to solve the basic problem—overvaluation of the dollar. Policymakers spent considerable effort developing a substitute for gold, the special drawing right (SDR). It had little importance. They did nothing to correct the more serious—and more obvious—problem, the overvalued dollar. Unilateral action by the United States forced attention to the so-called adjustment problem.

With some exceptions, the United States allows the dollar to float freely. The Federal Reserve sterilizes intervention. From 1985 to 1987, Treasury Secretary Baker first undertook to depreciate the exchange rate by agreement with other countries and then agreed to stabilize exchange rates. Like many political decisions, this one did not distinguish between real and nominal exchange rates. The agreement ended following the large worldwide decline in stock prices in October 1987.

RESEARCH

Improved research is one of the Federal Reserve's significant achievements. From the 1920s on, the System encouraged research on monetary theory, banking, and aggregate economics. At first, researchers concentrated on developing data series useful for judging the current position of the financial and economic system. Research expanded in the postwar years at the Board and the reserve banks. Research at Richmond and St. Louis was helpful in changing policy by pointing out deficiencies in accepted ideas and proposing alternatives. Minneapolis has been a leading developer and advocate of rational expectations models.

The Board's research staff took a leading role in developing large, econometric models of the economy. This effort focused staff attention on details of particular sectors. Policymakers have not found the forecasts from these models useful and have usually not followed them.

SUMMARY OF THE VOLUME

In the years 1951 to 1986 discussed in this volume, the world economy experienced a long period of sustained growth affecting more people in more countries than in any previous period. In the United States real per capita consumption more than doubled, more than an annual 2 percent compound average rate of increase. Although six recessions temporarily broke the economy's growth, by the end of the 1970s inflation had become the major economic problem. At its peak rate of increase, consumer prices rose 12.5 percent in 1980 or 12.2 percent excluding one-time changes in food and energy prices (Council of Economic Advisers, 1989, 373). For the period as a whole, consumer prices doubled and redoubled, more than a 4 percent average annual rate of increase.

Inflation was not at all uniform. It remained low until 1966, then rose with the financing of the Vietnam War and the Great Society. Inflation fell after 1984 and remained moderate in the late 1980s and beyond. Chart 1.1 shows these data. The Federal Reserve later chose to monitor the deflator for personal consumer expenditures excluding energy and food prices. In the short term this index differs from the consumer price index (CPI) mainly because weights on particular components differ in the two measures. Housing, medical care, and energy prices have been principal sources of short-term differences. Over a longer term, most broad-based

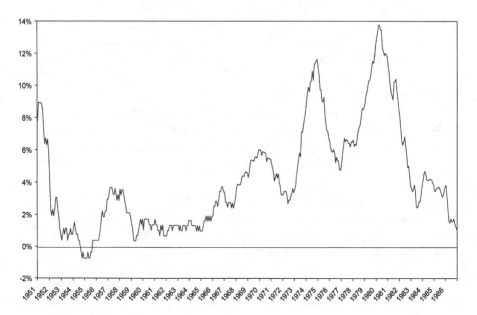

Chart 1.1. CPI inflation, 1951–86, measured year over year.

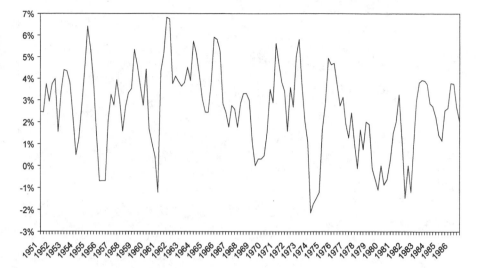

Chart 1.2. Productivity growth. Output per hour, business sector, 1951–86, measured year over year.

price indexes move together. Many short-term differences result from large relative price changes, not from sustained inflation.

Some economists attribute the Great Inflation to the end of price and wage controls or to the energy price increase. These changes affected the price level, temporarily raising the rate of price change. Persistent inflation shown in the chart, like all sustained inflation, resulted from excessive money growth.

Productivity growth is a noisy series (chart 1.2). It is not possible to know promptly whether changes are transitory or likely to persist. Economists have not agreed on the reasons for the decline in productivity growth in the 1970s despite substantial research effort.

Sustained changes in productivity growth are a main source of changes in expected output growth. Federal Reserve staff and many private sector economists use the difference between actual and expected output growth to forecast inflation. As Orphanides (2003a,b) showed, this was a main source of error in inflation forecasts in the 1970s. Meyer (2004) explained that it misled Federal Reserve economists who based inflation forecasts on the Phillips curve. Alan Greenspan did not rely on that model; his forecasts were more accurate in the 1990s.

Chart 1.3 shows that output growth is highly variable. Some research shows that the series is closely approximated as a random walk—that is, a series dominated in the short term by its random component. This is a main reason that quarterly forecasts using econometric models lack accuracy.

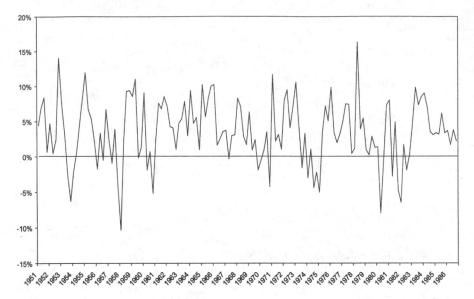

Chart 1.3. Real output growth, 1951–86.

Currency depreciation follows domestic inflation unless foreigners inflate even more. Until August 1971, the United States kept the nominal exchange rate fixed at $35 per ounce of gold. Most other countries fixed their exchange rates in relation to the dollar and gold. To maintain the $35 dollar gold price, the Federal Reserve would have had to choose exchange rate stability over the requirements of domestic policy. The standard interpretation of the Employment Act of 1946 at the time gave most importance to maintaining full employment. Until the late 1970s full employment was considered a 4 percent unemployment rate. When the signals from the foreign exchange market and the unemployment rate diverged, the Federal Reserve followed the unemployment rate.

The real exchange rate adjusts the nominal rate for differences in price levels at home and abroad. From 1951 through 1980 the real exchange rate declined persistently. In the early 1980s the United States ended high inflation. Chart 1.4 shows that from the mid-1970s on the real and nominal exchange rates moved together. Nominal exchange rate changes are the dominant short-term influence on real exchange rate changes.

Between 1951 and 1986, the annual average civilian unemployment rate varied between a low of 2.9 percent in 1956 and a peak of 9.7 percent in 1982. As Chart 1.5 shows, the unemployment rate rose quickly during

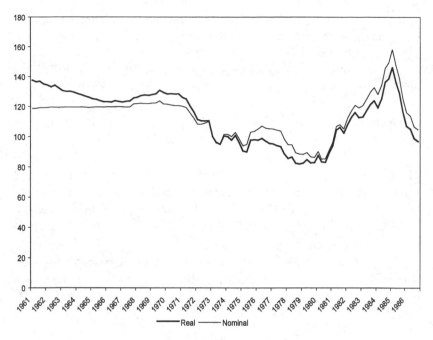

Chart 1.4. Trade-weighted exchange rates, 1961–86.

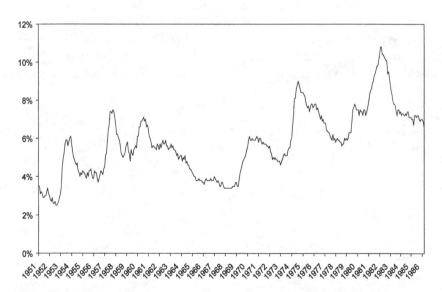

Chart 1.5. Civilian unemployment rate, January 1951–December 1986.

recessions as employers laid-off workers and reduced hiring. It declined slowly as the economy recovered. Local troughs in 1954, 1958, 1961, 1971, 1975, and 1982 show the effects of recession.

The Phillips curve posits a short-run negative relation between the unemployment rate and the inflation rate. The data suggest that the medium- or longer-term relation was positive in the 1970s and 1980s. On average the unemployment rate rose with inflation in the 1970s and both declined after 1982.

The chapters that follow use the real and nominal growth of the monetary base as indicators of the thrust of monetary policy. The uses of the monetary base consist of bank reserves and currency issued by the Federal Reserve. A common criticism points out that the uses of the base include mainly currency, much of it held abroad.

This criticism is mistaken. Sources of growth of the monetary base reflect mainly purchases of government securities by the Federal Reserve— injections of additional money or withdrawals. Currency held abroad is much more important for the level of the base and less important for interpreting the growth rate.

Chart 1.6 shows the growth rate of the monetary base. Inflation followed sustained increases. Charts in the following chapters show that recessions followed sustained declines in growth of the real base. The charts compare growth of the real base to the expected real rate of interest. Volume I showed that declining real base growth preceded every recession and that when signals from real base growth and real interest differed, the economy

Chart 1.6. Monetary base growth, January 1951–December 1986, measured year over year.

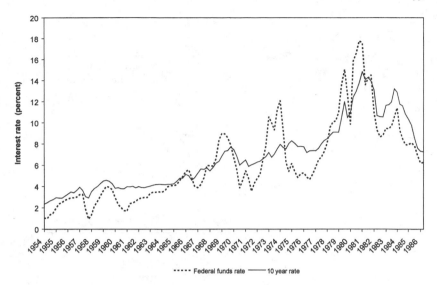

Chart 1.7. Long- and short-term interest rates, 1954:3 to 1986:4.

followed real base growth. The chapters that follow replace actual with expected inflation and reach the same conclusion

During the period discussed in these volumes, the Federal Reserve paid little or no attention to growth of the monetary base. Chart 1.7 shows long- and short-term interest rates for the period. The Federal Reserve used short-term rates as a target either directly or indirectly (free reserves, member bank borrowing, money market conditions) during most of the period. The period October 1979 to July or October 1982 is an exception.

Annual average short-term rates reflect mainly Federal Reserve actions. Rates on three-month Treasury bills varied from less than 1 percent in 1954 to more than 14 percent in 1982. Inflation expectations dominate long-term rates. Annual average of rates on ten-year constant-maturity Treasury bonds ranged from 2.4 percent (1954) to 13.9 percent (1982).

Interest rates typically rise during periods of economic expansion and decline in recessions. For most of the period, the Federal Reserve interpreted the rise or fall in interest rates, particularly short-term rates, as an indicator of its policy. When market rates declined, it interpreted the decline as an easier policy; when rates rose, it interpreted the rise as more restrictive. Usually, it slowed growth of the monetary base and money when rates fell and permitted faster growth when rates rose. Consequently, measures of money growth usually moved procyclically instead of counter-cyclically.

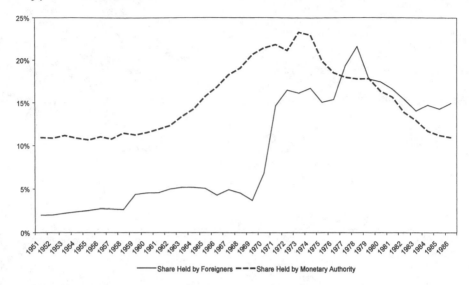

Chart 1.8. Percentage of total U.S. Treasury securities outstanding, by holder. 1951–86.

Chart 1.8 shows the substantial changes in ownership of the federal debt. As government deficits rose after 1964, the Federal Reserve "coordinated" its policy actions by financing a rising share—from 9 percent in the 1950s to almost 17 percent of a much larger debt in 1973–74. By 1985, the share taken by the Federal Reserve was again below 9 percent.

Foreigners financed a large share of large budget deficits in the 1970s and even larger deficits in the 1980s. The chart suggests a main reason. The jump in the foreign share in 1970–71 suggests that foreigners preferred to buy Treasury securities instead of permitting their exchange rates to appreciate against the dollar. The foreign share declined when the dollar appreciated in the early 1980s. It then began to rise again as the dollar fell relative to foreign currencies in the 1980s, especially in 1985 and 1986.

Growing foreign accumulation of Treasury debt eased pressure on the Federal Reserve to finance budget deficits and inflate. Interest rates, exchange rates, and inflation rates reflected the changing shares.

THE HISTORICAL CHAPTERS
Chapter 2 covers the years 1951–60, mainly the years of the Eisenhower administration. President Truman appointed William McChesney Martin, Jr., as chairman of the Board of Governors in 1951. Presidents Eisenhower, Kennedy, and Johnson reappointed him at the end of each four-year term. He retired in 1970.

Martin reorganized the Federal Reserve System. The System we now have is very different from the original. Martin eliminated the Executive Committee of the Federal Open Market Committee (FOMC), which made operating decisions about open market operations. To give greater role to the presidents of the regional banks and reduce New York's role, he increased the number of FOMC meetings from four to seventeen a year and worked to get the reserve bank presidents to take an active part. Also, he transferred the choice of manager of the open market account from the New York bank to the FOMC. Each of these steps increased the Board's role and reduced New York's. From its earliest days, Washington and New York struggled over control of the System. Martin settled the issue with Washington in charge. His moves gave the System greater cohesion but also made it more susceptible to political pressure.

In the 1930s and 1940s, the Federal Reserve's main concern was debt management. The March 1951 accord with the Treasury reduced that role. Gradually the System's main concern became support of the goals of the Employment Act, especially full employment. Inflation concerned Martin, and in the 1950s he worked to prevent it. In this he was greatly helped by the Eisenhower administration's support for budget balance except in recessions. Forceful Federal Reserve and administration action after the 1958 recession reduced the budget deficit, money growth, and inflation.

Martin also firmly supported the Bretton Woods system and accepted the importance of the fixed $35 gold price. The Federal Reserve had a supportive role, but Martin led the Federal Reserve into a cooperative arrangement to assist the Treasury by financing foreign exchange purchases and by arranging "swap agreements" with many foreign central banks.

Martin often described the Federal Reserve as "independent within government," a phrase that meant to him that the Federal Reserve would not fail to support Treasury financing operations. It could raise interest rates to prevent inflation caused by excess aggregate demand by private agents, but it would not force the government to finance budget deficits solely out of domestic and foreign saving.

To free itself from pressures to support the market for long-term debt, the Federal Reserve adopted the bills-only policy. It supported long-term markets only when there was a risk of failure of a Treasury issue. These interventions were infrequent. The policy had many critics in Congress and elsewhere who claimed that it contributed to higher long-term rates. After bills-only, the System made few purchases or loans on long-term debt until 2008.

Martin concluded that budget deficits caused inflation. He had little interest in economic theory, and he did not encourage or want economic theory used to guide monetary policy. His main concern was the money market. Instructions to the desk during these years were imprecise to give more influence to the manager.[21] Members of the FOMC used different measures to gauge the thrust of policy actions and did not attempt to reconcile them.

Chapters 3 and 4 cover the years of the Kennedy-Johnson administrations, the years up to 1965 in Chapter 3, 1965–69 in Chapter 4. Restrictive policies in 1959 ended inflation but caused a recession. The economy recovered in the early 1960s. Inflation remained low. The Kennedy administration promoted growth by instituting an investment tax credit, faster depreciation schedules, and the much-discussed 1964 tax reduction passed after Kennedy's assassination.

Problems continued. European currency convertibility strengthened the European currencies and increased a gold outflow from the United States. President Kennedy often expressed concern, and his administration introduced lending restrictions and promoted a policy of "twisting the yield curve" by lowering long-term rates to induce domestic expansion and raising short-term rates to attract foreign deposits and strengthen the dollar. The Federal Reserve abandoned bills-only and cooperated with the administration, but not enough to satisfy some of the administration's economists. The Johnson administration was less concerned about the gold outflow. Whenever the problem seemed acute, they introduced or strengthened controls on foreign lending.

In the 1962 report of the Council of Economic Advisers, the Kennedy administration claimed that inflation would start to rise before the economy reached full employment. They proposed guidelines for wage and price increases to suppress the rise in inflation. Reliance on guidelines or guideposts shifted attention away from Federal Reserve policy as a cause of inflation.

Kennedy administration economists wanted policy coordination. They especially wanted a voice and influence on Federal Reserve actions. Martin cooperated, believing he gained a voice in administration fiscal policy. He knowingly reduced Federal Reserve independence because he believed that the Federal Reserve could not control inflation if the administration ran large deficits. Eventually, he learned that coordination worked one way; the Federal Reserve adjusted its actions to the administration. When the Federal Reserve wanted the administration to increase tax rates to reduce the budget deficit, the Johnson administration and Congress were slow to act.

21. Transactions for the open market account are made in New York. The trading desk does the transactions.

When Congress finally approved a tax surcharge in 1968, the Federal Reserve lowered market rates to soften the expected effect on the economy. By the end of that year, Martin realized he had made a mistake. Inflation increased; the Great Inflation was under way.

The simple Keynesian model (Ackley, 1961) dominated thinking by the administration and the Federal Reserve staff. Although Martin did not share these beliefs or ideas, he did not offer an alternative. He distrusted most academic research, especially monetarist claims about money growth. Although he made many speeches opposing inflation, the inflation rate rose to 6 percent at the end of his term.

Chapter 4 discusses the emergence and growth of domestic inflation. Chapter 5 considers international aspects. Financing budget deficits at home produced inflation; financing them abroad put pressure on the dollar exchange rate. Controls produced temporary respites. By March 1968, the United States and foreign governments agreed to end sales of gold to non-government or central bank entities. This was the beginning of the end of the fixed exchange rate system.

Federal Reserve and administration officials repeated that there were three problems—liquidity (too many dollars to sustain dollar exchange rates), adjustment (the need to change exchange rate parities), and confidence (belief or anticipations that the Bretton Woods system would continue unchanged). The United States opposed any change in the dollar price of gold or devaluation of the dollar. Only Germany and the Netherlands appreciated their exchange rates by small amounts. Most others complained about inflation, called imported inflation, but preferred inflation to appreciation of their currency. Cooperation to maintain the system was lacking.

Creation and later issuance of the special drawing right (SDR) were the main international policy action to remedy problems of the Bretton Woods system. Ignoring the adjustment problem and misaligned exchange rates to concentrate on the liquidity problem is hard to understand or defend. The system had surplus liquidity. The main reason given for the attention to SDR creation was that in some distant future, if the United States stopped running payment deficits, a new source of liquidity would be needed. Gold production would not be sufficient.

SDRs never became an important means of settlement. In August 1971, the United States allowed the dollar to depreciate against gold and foreign currencies. After introduction of a surtax on imports and considerable wrangling, governments agreed to a new set of exchange rate parities. The agreement began to unravel in the winter of 1973. Thereafter, exchange rates floated, a few freely; most were managed by central banks.

President Nixon took office in January 1969. In 1970 he appointed Arthur Burns as chairman of the Board of Governors. The president promised to reduce inflation without a recession. A recession started in November 1969. The Federal Reserve soon gave up its efforts to reduce inflation and worked to reduce unemployment. Coming after a similar response to slowing economic growth and housing in 1966–67 and the tax surcharge in 1968, markets correctly interpreted these actions as evidence that the Federal Reserve gave more importance to avoiding a rise in unemployment than to preventing inflation. Anticipations of persistent inflation rose.

Burns was the most politically involved chairman since Marriner Eccles in the 1930s. He sacrificed Federal Reserve independence to the interests of the administration. He believed that labor unions and the welfare state made inflation difficult to control using monetary policy. FOMC supported his actions. Most of the members accepted that their first responsibility was to avoid an unemployment rate above 4 percent.

Congress challenged the Nixon administration to use price guidelines or controls to slow inflation. Arthur Burns was a leading advocate using a flawed argument that controlling prices would reduce inflation. Facing a reelection challenge for failing to use controls, the president reversed his often-stated opposition. Chapter 6 traces the decision to use controls and float the dollar in August 1971. It was a political success but a disaster for inflation control. Inflation reached new heights once controls ended. An increase in food and energy prices exaggerated the sustained consumer price index (CPI) inflation rate.

After President Nixon resigned, Gerald Ford encouraged the Federal Reserve to slow inflation. A recession interrupted the effort, but the reported inflation rate declined. Ford lost the 1976 election to James Earl Carter. The new administration chose to follow a more expansive policy. Chapter 7 traces policy developments at the end of the 1970s.

Carter administration economists renewed the use of guideposts and exhortation to prevent wage and price increases. These efforts failed again. Administration economists worked to get Germany and Japan to agree to coordinated expansion. Their idea was that exchange rates would remain bounded. Germany did not agree until the summer of 1978.

This policy failed also. By late 1978 inflation had increased. The dollar exchange rate fell. After a renewed attempt to use non-monetary means, the Federal Reserve raised interest rates. The dollar strengthened.

Another large increase in the price of oil pushed measured inflation to the peak shown in Chart 1.1 above in 1978–79. Public pressure, including polling data, encouraged President Carter to replace the Secretary of the

Treasury with G. William Miller, who had replaced Arthur Burns at the Federal Reserve. Paul A. Volcker became chairman of the Board of Governors.

Volcker was an anti-inflationist and a "practical monetarist." Within two months of becoming chairman, he convinced the FOMC that it had to control money growth and allow interest rates to move as much as required to slow inflation.

Volcker restored Federal Reserve independence and made a major change in its policy views. Instead of the belief that the economy required guidelines to reconcile low inflation and low unemployment, Volcker claimed that low inflation would encourage expansion and employment. The Federal Reserve's goal changed to reducing inflation.

Chapter 8 discusses policy actions from 1979 to 1982. With strong support from President Reagan and principal members of Congress, inflation fell to 4 percent by the end of 1982. The unemployment rate rose above 10 percent by fall 1982. A high unemployment rate, credit difficulties in the banking system caused by defaults on foreign loans, and congressional pressure brought a change in monetary policy in the summer and fall of 1982. The Federal Reserve returned to control of member bank borrowing and gave up efforts to control money growth. But it did not return to an inflationary policy.

The so-called experiment with monetary control is generally regarded as a failure. The experiment was never complete; the FOMC considered but did not adopt institutional changes that would have improved its ability to control money growth. Also, large changes in the public's asset allocation followed after Congress deregulated banking and financial markets. These changes made it difficult to interpret changes in monetary aggregates during the transition to a less regulated system.

Volcker distrusted forecasts and relied more on his judgment and interpretation than on economic models. His "practical monetarism" did not go much beyond a belief that money growth above output growth was a necessary condition for inflation. His courage and determination to lower inflation showed in his willingness to raise interest rates despite relatively high and rising unemployment.

Chapter 9 discusses actions taken from 1982 through 1986. Expectations of inflation as reflected in long-term interest rates and exchange rates (Charts 1.4 and 1.7 above) declined slowly. I date the end of the inflation in 1986, when the public seemed to accept that high inflation would not return soon.

Chairman Volcker and the FOMC did not follow any explicit economic theory. Volcker relied on his assessment of events and his guesses about the future. He gave most attention to member bank borrowing, and he denied that he used an interest rate target. The FOMC was more alert to inflation than in the 1960s and 1970s.

Chapter 10 concludes the volume. Federal Reserve policy remained much better than earlier until the mid-2000s. The economy experienced three long expansions followed by two relatively mild recessions. Variability of output and inflation declined; many called it "the great moderation."

I suggest some changes to improve monetary policy further. Although efforts to focus on longer-term objectives have been made, more needs to be done. The Federal Reserve needs to announce two strategies—one to guide its monetary policy operations, the other to guide its operations as lender of last resort. And it must insist on maintaining independence.

The history of an institution is a record of successes and failures. I have suggested principal reasons for the failures—the inability to agree on a broad framework for analyzing events, a failure to focus on medium- to long-term outcomes, and the difficulty or inability to resist political pressures much of the time. At the time of its creation, proponents and opponents recognized a principal issue: Would the Federal Reserve be controlled by bankers operating in their interest or by politicians operating in theirs? Over time, control shifted to the Board of Governors. Resistance to political influences often weakened. Insistence on independence from political pressures was not impossible but required more courage than was usually present.

TWO

A New Beginning, 1951–60

You certainly have the advantage over me of being closer to the market, but it may not be an unmixed advantage. The ticker may loom too large in your perspective and what from the point of view of the national economy are molehills may . . . appear to you as mighty mountains.

—Letter, Viner to Sproul, in Sproul papers, Correspondence, S–W 1940–1955, January 9, 1948

The March 1951 Accord with the Treasury opened a new era in Federal Reserve history. Once again, the Federal Reserve could claim to be independent, as its founders intended. It could raise interest rates without prior approval or consultation with the Treasury, at first only within the transitional limits set for the year by the Accord.[1]

The new arrangement reopened issues that had remained dormant. What did independence mean in practice? What goals should an independent central bank pursue? How could it reconcile independence with continued responsibility for the success of Treasury debt management operations? By what means could it efficiently achieve its goals? What guiding

1. Volume 1, chapter 7 discusses the details of the Treasury–Federal Reserve Accord of March 1951. The Accord ended a nine-year period during which the Federal Reserve consulted the Treasury before changing interest rates. In practice, the Treasury exercised a veto over interest rate changes. The Accord permitted the Federal Reserve to let the rate on long-term government bonds exceed 2.5 percent and let short-term rates rise to the discount rate. The Federal Reserve agreed to maintain orderly markets and shared responsibility for success of debt management operations with the Treasury. In practice this responsibility led the Federal Reserve to adopt an "even keel" policy of maintaining interest rates during periods of Treasury borrowing. This permitted money growth to increase especially when budget deficits rose in the late 1960s. The remaining provisions are in volume 1, 711–12.

principles should govern practice? How should it organize and operate to carry out its functions?

The Federal Reserve had not faced these issues since the 1920s. The Federal Reserve Act, as amended and amplified by other legislation, left much scope for interpretation. The old procedures developed under the gold exchange standard reflected very different organizational and economic arrangements. The Banking Act of 1935 shifted power from the federal reserve banks to the Board of Governors, eliminated the semi-autonomous nature of the reserve banks and moved control of open market operations from the reserve banks to an open market committee on which the Board had seven of twelve votes. It did little to clarify the system's mandate. The 1944 Bretton Woods Agreement established a fixed but adjustable exchange rate regime, although most currencies other than the dollar remained inconvertible until 1959. The United States' relatively large stock of gold was more than ample to satisfy any likely demand at the time, and, in truth, administration policy favored some redistribution of foreign exchange and gold holdings abroad. Of greatest importance subsequently, the Employment Act of 1946 committed the country to maximum employment and purchasing power but did not further define these terms. When passing the Employment Act, Congress did not explain how to reconcile its domestic employment goal with the Bretton Woods Agreement and with the political and military obligations the United States soon accepted as part of the cold war with the Soviet Union and its allies.

Domestic policy dominated international concerns during most of this period. The Federal Reserve recognized that international economic policy was principally a Treasury function, not their primary responsibility.

Under the Employment Act, Congress expected the Federal Reserve to do more than avoid another Great Depression. It expected the act to lower the average and variability of the unemployment rate, and for many years it gave much greater weight to unemployment than to inflation. The new emphasis on employment heightened congressional interest in what the Federal Reserve did, in how and why it made its decisions. Increased frequency of congressional hearings reflected this political interest. Later, rising pressure for policy coordination with the administration challenged the Federal Reserve to find ways of reconciling independence and coordination. It did not succeed.

Near the end of World War II, the Federal Reserve had engaged in domestic postwar planning, but it had not directly addressed or anticipated some of these issues. Its main concern was to avoid a return to the depressed high-unemployment economy of the 1930s. By 1951, with the Korean War under way, these concerns were no longer paramount. Its concern was resurgent wartime inflation. In the words of one of its principals: "Up to the time of the Korean crisis, the Federal Reserve was content to carry on a holding operation. It joined with the Treasury in opposing those who . . . counseled abrupt and vigorous use of credit policy to reduce the swollen money supply . . . In the face of the economic repercussions of the Korean crisis, however, such an approach was no longer practical" (Sproul, 1964, 234).

At first, the Federal Reserve made no effort to set objectives for employment and inflation or develop the means of achieving them. It began its independent operation about where it had left off in the 1920s. Minutes of meetings show that the System's principal concern was with current money market conditions, mainly control of the volume of member bank borrowing. By controlling borrowing, it expected to influence the banks' supply of credit and thus the pace of economic activity. If this were done properly, officials and staff expected the price level to fluctuate around some stable value, but they did not have a framework linking their actions to these objectives, and they made no effort to develop one.

Reversion to the practices of the 1920s is not entirely surprising. The new chairman of the Board of Governors, William McChesney Martin, Jr., was the son of a former Federal Reserve official. His father had served first as Chairman, later as governor and president of the St. Louis Federal reserve bank from 1914 to 1941. Martin reactivated the 1920s procedures with assistance from two staff members who served in the 1920s— Winfield Riefler and Woodlief Thomas. Riefler was assistant to the chairman and later Secretary of the Federal Open Market Committee. Thomas was research director and, after 1949, adviser to the Board.[2]

The structure of the modern Federal Reserve is, in large part, Martin's creation. In the 1950s especially, he restructured the open market committee and its operating procedures. Shortly after coming to the Federal Reserve, he chaired a committee that recommended changes in the relation of the Federal Open Market Committee (FOMC) to the manager of the System account, the type of securities purchased, and the frequency of FOMC meetings. By 1955, the FOMC had adopted a policy of purchasing only Treasury bills (except in crises), eliminated the Executive Committee, greatly increased the frequency of its meetings, expanded the scope of its deliberations to include not just open market operations but all the tools of monetary policy, and encouraged all FOMC members to contribute to the policy discussion.

2. Riefler joined the Board's staff in 1923. In 1933, he left the staff but returned in 1948 as assistant to the chairman and secretary of the open market committee. During 1941–42, he served as a director of the Philadelphia Reserve Bank. He retired at the end of 1959. Thomas left the staff from 1928 to 1934. He retired in 1966.

The 1950s were a period of experimentation and eclecticism. The System did not develop a broad policy framework to replace the analysis in the Tenth Annual Report of 1923. The Riefler-Burgess version of the real bills doctrine, inherited from the 1920s, soon faded away, leaving some traces behind. This notion emphasized the quality of credit as a way of controlling inflation. Real bills called for the discounting of productive credit to finance agricultural, commercial, and industrial concerns and for avoidance of speculative credit. The heightened role of open market operations and the reduced role of discounting could not be reconciled with the real bills doctrine. No single framework replaced real bills. Initially, the FOMC gave the manager qualitative guidance, characterized by imprecise directions such as "achieve slightly more ease (restraint)," "promote active ease," "respond to tone and feel," or "lean on the side of restraint." The main target was free reserves—excess reserves minus member bank borrowing—but members often did not agree on a specific range. Some members chafed at the imprecision of the FOMC directives and the autonomy left to the manager, but the directives remained imprecise.

The new arrangements were in some ways a replay of the early 1930s, when the Board expanded membership of the open market committee to reduce New York's influence. Martin's actions shifted influence away from Allan Sproul, president of the New York Reserve Bank until 1956. By eliminating the five-person Executive Committee, which Sproul dominated, he reduced Sproul's power; by restricting purchases to bills, he limited New York's discretion; by requiring all members of the FOMC to state their opinions and make choices, he diluted New York's influence. The long struggle between New York and Washington faded away. By the mid-1950s or thereabouts, Washington controlled the System.

In the 1920s, the Federal Reserve tried to control the level of member bank borrowing. It assumed that excess reserves remained constant. Recognition that excess reserves could change, as they did in the 1930s, shifted attention to free reserves, excess reserves minus borrowing. In the Federal Reserve's analysis, an increase in free reserves eased the money market; a reduction tightened the market. The new measure, like the old, carried the implication that increased member bank borrowing tightened the money market (and Federal Reserve policy) despite the increase in reserves and the monetary base that banks in the aggregate obtained by borrowing. This reasoning probably reflected the use of borrowing or free reserve targets as an imperfect substitute for an interest rate target. Since borrowing increased total reserves and the monetary base, other things being equal, increased money accompanied the increase in borrowing.

The free reserve framework failed to recognize that, at any level of free reserves or borrowing, policy could be lax or restrictive depending on what happened to the growth of money or credit. Although the minutes contain references to money growth, it remained in the background at FOMC meetings. Many members believed that, in the long run, excessive money growth caused inflation, but long-term considerations of this kind received less attention than short-term events reflecting both long-standing practices and Chairman Martin's lack of interest in statistics and in forecasts or projections of more distant concerns. Until the mid-1960s, the Federal Reserve operated under the Riefler rule; it did not make or discuss forecasts. Frequent meetings and the Riefler rule concentrated attention on current events.

Staff reports mention money growth frequently. The staff and some members compared average growth rates of money and output, and they recognized that monetary velocity had increased in the postwar years. At a 1958 meeting, the staff described System operations as influencing the economy mainly by changing the money stock but added that measures of reserves and money varied unpredictably (Memo, Thomas to FOMC, Board Records, February 25, 1959, 1). The staff confined its analysis to estimating the money growth rate, then using it to compute the appropriate level of required and free reserves. This procedure was subject to large errors, since the connection between money growth and free reserves was weak. There is no record of concerted efforts to improve the estimates. Their imprecision may have contributed to their neglect. The staff did not estimate demand for money or velocity equations. An exception is Garvy (1959), but his work was not mentioned in the minutes or used to project velocity.[3]

The Federal Reserve in the 1950s did not recognize or correct some of the principal errors that had misled it from 1928 to the early 1930s. It did not distinguish between real and nominal interest rates for many years. Use of a free reserve target gave monetary policy a procyclical bias. Lauchlin Currie (1968) had complained about the procyclicality of the operating procedures in the 1920s.[4] When output expanded and customer borrowing increased, banks borrowed from the Federal Reserve, and open market rates rose relative to the Federal Reserve's discount rate. The Federal Reserve interpreted higher nominal interest rates, increased borrowing, and reduced free reserves as evidence of restrictive policy. Often it allowed growth of the monetary base and money to increase, adding first

3. Garvy (1959, 55, 83) explained the trend in deposit velocity as a result of growing efficiency in the use of money. He expected the trend to continue.

4. Currie worked at the Board in the 1930s, but there is no mention of his monetary analysis in Board or FOMC records in the 1950s. Brunner and Meltzer (1964) emphasized procyclicality also; they showed that money growth was slower in downturns and recessions than in succeeding expansions.

to spending and later to inflation. When spending declined, the process worked in reverse.

The changed political climate that produced the 1946 Employment Act also produced lasting changes in the meaning of independence and the relation of the Federal Reserve to the administration and Congress. Treasury interference in the 1930s and 1940s mainly reflected the traditional interest of debt managers in financing at low nominal interest rates. In the postwar years, governments in all developed countries accepted responsibility for maintaining employment, smoothing fluctuations in economic activity, and preventing a return of the Great Depression. As understanding of the role of monetary policy in economic stabilization improved, political pressure on the Federal Reserve increased. Congressional hearings on monetary policy became more frequent, and Federal Reserve chairmen came under pressure to participate in policy discussions with the president, Treasury Secretary, and other senior officials. Chairman Martin accommodated requests for consultation but, at first, tried to limit his role to exchanging information about the economy and its prospects. He listened to administration and congressional concerns, offered reassurance, and defended his actions. To avoid calling public and congressional attention to meetings with administration officials, the meetings became regularly scheduled events in the late 1950s.

Heightened political interest in monetary policy induced the System to look for external supporters in Congress and among the public. Banks and financial institutions under regulatory control became a source of support, particularly after the 1956 Bank Holding Company Act increased the Board's power to approve or reject applications for new bank powers.

This chapter and the next two trace the increased importance of stabilization policy, growing recognition of the Federal Reserve's role, increased pressure on the Federal Reserve and its chairman, particularly in election years, and reduced independence. President Eisenhower and Treasury Secretary Humphrey became concerned about Federal Reserve policy in 1956 and wary of Martin's anti-inflation stance. Vice President Nixon blamed his defeat in the 1960 election on Federal Reserve policy, and both he and President Kennedy considered replacing Martin. The Kennedy and even more the Johnson administrations used policy coordination to restrict Federal Reserve independence.

The Federal Reserve did not, at first, link its operating procedures to the employment and price goals the Employment Act mandated. In the 1920s, it had denied any direct control over prices and output. It did not repeat these denials in the 1950s. But it made no effort to link its credit market framework to the broader and more remote goals it claimed to pursue. As in the past, it treated $500 million of borrowing (or equivalent free reserves) as "neutral," but it had limited understanding of how much output, employment, and the price level would change, or how inflation would change, if free reserves rose or fell by $100 million. And, it made no effort to find out for a decade or longer.

Under Martin, policy became more activist. The Federal Reserve responded to Treasury financing, output, unemployment, inflation, and later housing sales and other events. The founders' design of a largely passive institution that let gold flows and member bank borrowing determine the stock of bank credit disappeared. By the middle of the 1950s, the Federal Reserve intervened in the money market to smooth seasonal and longer-term changes and to manage the business cycle. Politicians gave most attention to unemployment and interest rates. The Federal Reserve responded by moving toward a labor standard. When the unemployment rate rose, reducing unemployment became the System's principal concern.

Within the free reserve framework, concerns about employment, Treasury financing, and other goals were not easy to reconcile with concerns about inflation. The annual inflation rate rose in steps from about 1 to 2 percent in 1953–54 to 3 to 4 percent in 1956–57, then declined toward zero at the end of the decade. Slow growth and recessions in 1953–54, 1957–58, and 1960–61 accompanied lower rates of inflation. Inflation, recession, and slower growth heightened interest in the economy's response to policy actions. Although problems of growth, inflation, and unemployment became more severe later, inflation rates in the mid-1950s were high compared to previous non-war years. The price level rose persistently for the first time in peacetime history. Economic performance at the end of the 1950s, especially relatively slow growth and a rising international payments imbalance were, in part, the price paid for inflation and, in part, for the disinflation that followed. Concerns that the Federal Reserve was responsible for slow growth became a political issue in the 1960 election.

One consequence of a positive inflation rate was that, on average, interest rates on long-term bonds and mortgages remained above short-term rates. The yield curve, relating short- to long-term rates, typically sloped upward, probably reflecting the belief that inflation would increase. Housing and mortgage credit increased. While it lasted, this was extremely favorable for thrift institutions that paid a short-term rate to depositors and earned the higher long-term mortgage rate.

The Federal Reserve Board's regulation Q set the maximum rate that commercial banks could pay on time and savings deposits. However, non-bank thrift institutions were not subject to regulation Q until later. They offered a rate slightly above the ceiling that banks could pay. As anticipated inflation increased, banks lost time and savings deposits to thrifts and others. In 1956, the Board raised the maximum ceiling rate by 0.5 percentage points to 3 percent. It was the first step in what became an effort to manage the deposit positions and lending of both the banking and thrift industries by controlling the level of the time deposit rate and the premium offered by the thrifts. The policy failed, eventually, like most efforts of its kind. Congress was slow to act and the Federal Reserve reluctant to press the issue. The end result of managing ceiling interest rates was the failure or disappearance of a large part of the thrift industry after short-term rates fell below mortgage rates when inflation slowed in the 1980s.

A second consequence of rising inflation was the beginning of concern about operating procedures and policy goals. The minutes of FOMC meetings show that from the middle 1950s on, some members of the FOMC questioned both the use of free reserves as a policy target and the ways in which the FOMC and the manager used free reserves to implement policy. Intermittent discussion began about policy objectives beyond the money market and the role of reserves or monetary aggregates as policy targets. The System moved from the relatively passive role of letting member bank borrowing and private decisions determine money growth and inflation to a more active policy of trying to manage the business cycle to achieve the goals of the Employment Act and respond to public and political pressures. It reassured itself that it could not be responsible for what happened because it did not have complete control; monetary policy, the minutes repeat, was only one influence on the economy.

This chapter uses the minutes of policy meetings and other materials to show how the System made policy decisions in the absence of a coherent framework. One reason for its absence and the often vague policy directives to the manager was the lack of agreement among officials on the most general principles of monetary analysis. Martin's beliefs were important also. He described himself as a market man; his concern was current market behavior. Economic analysis did not interest him because he did not find it useful. He not only did not have a model of the economy, he did not want one.[5]

Martin described his idea of independence as "independence within the government, not independence of the government." This was not just a phrase to satisfy congressional critics. It meant that the Federal Reserve

---

5. Romer and Romer (2002b) claim that the Federal Reserve had an appropriate or current model of inflation in the 1950s. They attribute successful policy to reliance on the model as a guide to policy. I find no evidence to support their claim. A more important factor was the Eisenhower administration's conservative fiscal policy during most of the decade. The Federal Reserve was not under pressure to finance budget deficits most of this decade.

had to assist the Treasury with debt finance. The 1951 Accord had not removed that responsibility; it had freed the Federal Reserve from its subsidiary role relative to the Treasury and made it co-equal. But Congress voted the budget and permitted deficits. The System adopted an "even keel" policy of supplying enough reserves to finance new or refunded Treasury issues at interest rates prevailing at or near the time of the Treasury's announcement of financing terms. Additions to reserves usually remained in the banking system and supported increased money and bank credit.

Deficits remained relatively small and were followed by surpluses in the 1950s. Consequently, the System's views on independence and even keel did not result in high, persistent money growth, so inflation remained low. The cumulative deficit for the 1960s was three times as large as that for the 1950s. Inflation rose, particularly after 1965, when persistent large budget deficits became the norm. Although Martin disliked inflation and opposed it verbally, his policies supported and increased it. This chapter traces the development of these beliefs about the System's responsibilities to the Treasury in the 1950s.

At the end of World War II, the United States was the main developed economy that had not suffered from destruction of its capital stock but had instead increased productive capital. It could fight a war in Korea, increase domestic consumption, export capital to rebuild foreign economies, and invest abroad without concern for its international reserves. At first the outflow of gold during the Korean War seemed an acceptable, even desirable, way to redistribute the world's monetary gold stock and strengthen countries' ability to move toward currency convertibility. Many believed that disproportionate U.S. gold holdings in the 1920s caused the breakdown of the gold standard in the 1930s. They did not want a repetition.

Attitudes began to change in the 1950s. Revival in Europe and Japan initially increased their imports from the United States, but later increased their exports of textiles, steel, automobiles, and other goods. Growing competition from foreign producers of particular goods created political issues that began to influence economic policy by the end of the decade.

The United States encouraged and at times exhorted the Europeans to end exchange controls on current account transactions and accept convertibility of their currencies into dollars. At the end of the decade, the principal trading nations adopted current account convertibility, and Germany agreed to make the mark convertible on both current and capital account.

Concern about membership in the Federal Reserve System continued. All national banks had to be members, but state chartered banks could choose. Many elected to remain outside the System. Membership was costly; it required a bank to hold required reserves without receiving any interest, to collect checks at par, thereby forgoing collection fees, and to submit to examinations that often were more demanding than examinations by state examiners. In June 1951, only 49 percent of commercial banks, with 93 percent of deposits, had joined the System. Nearly 13 percent of all banks did not collect at par. These percentages changed very little during the 1950s (Board of Governors, 1976, 27, 43, 61, 62).

To encourage membership, the Board changed required reserve ratios several times during the decade. Although the minutes generally do not explain the choice of this instrument, all of the changes were reductions. During the decade, the ratios declined at central reserve city, reserve city, and country banks from 24, 20, 14 to 18, 16.5, and 11. Membership did not change substantially, but influential members of Congress criticized these actions as a windfall for banks and a loss of interest payments returned to the Treasury. They pressed the Federal Reserve to stop reducing these ratios and rely on open market purchases to provide growth of money.

Some important changes in personnel occurred during the decade. Two prominent members of the FOMC left the System. Allan Sproul resigned in 1956 as President of the Federal Reserve Bank of New York after thirty-seven years of service in the System. A banker, Alfred Hayes, replaced him in New York. Marriner Eccles, former chairman of the Board, resigned in July 1951, after nearly seventeen years of service.[6] At the end of the decade, the influential Winfield Riefler retired from the staff. New Board members included Abbott L. Mills, Jr. (San Francisco), an Oregon banker, and James L. Robertson (Kansas City) in 1952. Robertson was a lawyer who had worked for the Federal Bureau of Investigation and spent many years at the Office of the Comptroller of the Currency. He brought needed expertise on banking

6. Other members of the Board in 1951 were: Edward L. Norton, Oliver S. Powell, James K. Vardaman, Jr., Rudolph M. Evans, and Menc S. Szymczak. Szymczak had served since 1933. Norton and Powell resigned in 1952 after serving about two years. Powell remained in the System until 1957 as President of the Minneapolis Federal Reserve Bank. Vardaman was a banker and a friend of President Truman who served as his naval aide before his appointment. He incurred the hostility of his colleagues for several reasons, including being too close to the White House and allegedly leaking information to the White House staff during the months leading up to the Accord. Martin's papers contain an unsigned memo written before Martin joined the Board with six pages of text and seventeen charts comparing Vardaman to other governors and detailing his faults. The memo said he was unreliable and undependable, and made "little effective contribution" to the Board's work. He lied about what he was doing, was absent nearly 40 percent of working days, and arrived late and left early when he was in attendance. He missed 33 percent of FOMC meetings and 30 percent of Board meetings. He publicly criticized other members of the Board including in press interviews. And he used Board property for personal activities (Martin papers, undated, probably 1950, untitled). Evans left in 1954, Vardaman in 1958 and Szymczak in 1961. A list of members is in an appendix to the second half of this volume.

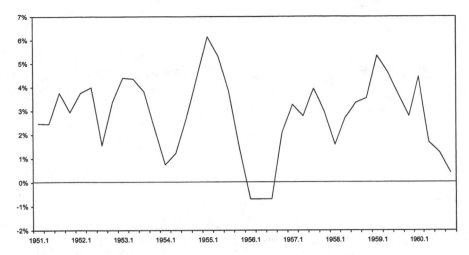

Chart 2.1. Output per hour, business sector, 1951–60. Measured year over year.

regulation and had strong views on monetary policy, on the use of repurchase agreements, and on the need to restrict the manager's autonomy.[7]

The 1950s was a decade of moderate growth with low but variable average inflation. Outcomes were among the best, on average, until the 1990s. Real GNP rose at a compound annual rate of 2.6 percent despite a relatively mild recession in 1953–54 and a deeper recession in 1957–58. Productivity and output per hour in the private sector rose at a 2.7 percent average annual rate. Chart 2.1 shows productivity growth and fluctuations. Productivity growth rose and fell cyclically but not uniformly. For example, productivity growth fell more in the relatively mild 1953–54 recession than in the more severe 1957–58 recession.

The percentage of the labor force unemployed (Chart 2.2) started the period at about 3 percent, averaged 4.5 percent for the decade, but rose above 7 percent in the 1958 recession (Council of Economic Advisers, 1971). Each cyclical rise in the unemployment rate started from a higher level than the previous rise. Many in Congress blamed the Federal Reserve for the rising average rate.

Inflation remained positive, at the time an unusual experience for the peacetime United States. As Chart 2.3 shows, inflation rose after 1953–55 and remained above its earlier range until the end of the decade. For

7. Martin recommended Mills and Robertson in a letter to President Truman (Martin papers, January 21, 1952).

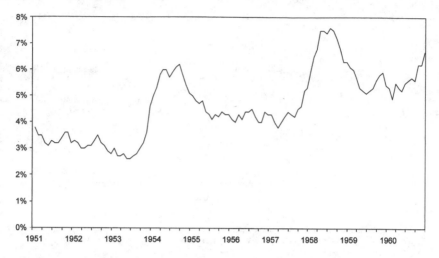

Chart 2.2. Civilian unemployment rate, January 1951-December 1960.

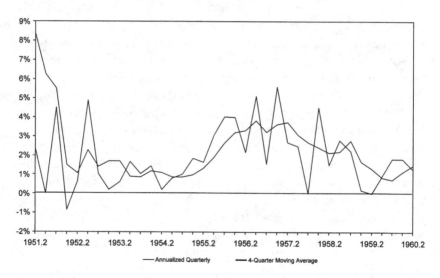

Chart 2.3. Change in GDP deflator, 1951:2–1960:2.

the period as a whole, inflation measured by the GNP deflator averaged 2.5 percent, with a peak rate above 5 percent in 1957. This experience was far superior to that of the next three decades.

Inflation contributed to a rise in real and nominal interest rates over the decade. The nominal rate on Treasury notes and bonds with three to five years of remaining life rose from about 1.5 percent in 1950 to approximately 4 percent at the end of the decade. At peak interest rates in 1959,

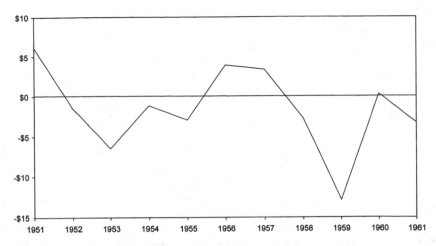

Chart 2.4. U.S. federal budgetary position (in billions).

the Treasury sold a 5 percent note, called the "magic 5s" because their coupon rate was above any yield the Treasury had offered since before the Federal Reserve started.

These and other data on interest rates, wages, and prices suggest that a change occurred during the decade. Inflation during World Wars I and II, and briefly during the Korean War, had not raised interest rates very much. Nor had the postwar years of pegged rates, despite the Federal Reserve's belief that it had become an "engine of inflation." A partial explanation is that the public did not expect inflation to persist, but it was also true that until the Accord they could sell their bonds at fixed rates to the Federal Reserve whenever they chose. In contrast, by 1959, long-term interest rates suggest that markets expected inflation to persist over time. Also, bondholders could no longer sell their bonds to the Federal Reserve without loss. Bond yields reflected the changed risk and expectation of inflation.

Contemporary observers pointed to budget deficits and (non-productive) expenditures for defense and foreign aid as a source of inflation. Despite President Eisenhower's many calls for fiscal prudence, and a budget surplus in three of the ten years, the government's fiscal position and policy were much different in the 1950s than in the 1920s. Secretary Andrew Mellon and Presidents Warren Harding and Calvin Coolidge ran large surpluses that they used to pay down debt and reduce tax rates; President Eisenhower had one tax cut that reduced high wartime rates by about 10 percent in 1954, but the public debt rose during his administration. Chart 2.4 shows that the Eisenhower administration achieved budget surpluses in 1956 and 1957 followed by a very large deficit by the standards of the time in 1959—2.5 percent of GDP. It made a major effort to restore budget

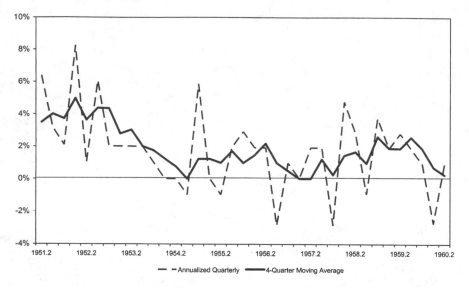

Chart 2.5. Base growth, 1951:2–1960:2.

balance in 1960. At one point, it called on the Federal Reserve to help by making an extra cash payment to the Treasury.

Judged by base money growth, monetary policy was highly variable around a relatively stable trend after 1952. In the first years after the Accord, System actions reduced average base growth to the 1 to 2 percent range, in which it remained for the rest of the decade. Chart 2.5 shows these data.

The System did not attempt to control or monitor the monetary base. The main source of the base is open market operations and changes in reserve requirement ratios. The Federal Reserve could sustain its choice of a short-term interest rate only by standing ready to buy or sell reserves (base money) as the market required. At different times, the same market interest rate might require large Federal Reserve sales or equally large purchases, hence falling or rising stocks of base money. Fixing a nominal interest rate can expand or contract money growth depending on the expected rate of inflation and expected real growth. The growth rates of the nominal and real monetary base relative to GDP show whether the Federal Reserve's choice of interest rates eased or restricted the growth of base money.[8]

8. Two common criticisms of the monetary base are: (1) the base consists mostly of currency, so it is demand determined because the System supplies currency on demand; and (2) as much as 60 percent of the monetary base is held abroad. First, on the sources side, the base consists mainly of the open market portfolio, and growth of the base reflects Federal Re-

Many contemporary observers blamed labor unions and businesses for inflation. The Economic Reports of the President in the later part of the decade exhort labor unions and corporations to moderate their demands in the public interest (Council of Economic Advisers, 1956, 1959). The Eisenhower administration did not offer numerical guidelines for wages and prices. That waited for its successors.

REDESIGNING THE FEDERAL RESERVE

For the first time since 1928, the Republicans, led by retired General Dwight Eisenhower, won control of the presidency and both houses of Congress in the 1952 election. Eisenhower had pledged to go to Korea to end the war if elected. A truce was declared on June 27, 1953. With the truce, growth of defense spending fell sharply from a 100 percent rate of increase in fiscal 1952 to a 13 percent rate for 1953. In fiscal 1954, defense spending fell more than 6 percent. Eisenhower's policy called for a balanced budget and reduced government spending. He firmly believed that government set the rules and promoted "conditions favorable to the exercise of individual initiative and effort" (Saulnier, 1991, 15). He immediately showed that deficit reduction and budget balance had priority over tax cuts by postponing the expiration of wartime excise taxes against opposition from many in his own party (Eisenhower, 1963, 202). He removed Korean War price controls soon after taking office and followed by closing the Reconstruction Finance Corporation, a relic of the Great Depression, retaining only small business lending in a new Small Business Administration.

The new administration appointed W. Randolph Burgess as Undersecretary of the Treasury. Burgess had spent many years as an officer of the New York Federal Reserve Bank. After leaving the New York bank to become vice chairman of National City Bank, he represented the second district on the Federal Advisory Council. He had spoken and testified against the policy of pegging interest rates.[9]

Martin believed that the new administration gave him an opportunity to separate monetary management from debt management. The Federal Re-

---

serve purchases. If the base rises rapidly because the demand for currency increases rapidly, that is a signal either that the economy is expanding rapidly at current interest rates, or that there is a run from bank deposits to currency. Second, foreign holdings are part of the stock of base money. Monetary policy should concentrate on base growth, not level. The former is not much affected by changes in growth of foreign holdings. See appendix.

9. As president of the American Bankers Association, Burgess actively opposed the Bretton Woods Agreement. He was willing to change his position if the Treasury agreed to changes. Harry Dexter White refused, but Congress included some of the changes (affidavit of E. M. Bernstein, in Sproul papers, Correspondence A–M 1936–1955, January 15, 1954). Burgess did nothing to change the IMF during his service at the Treasury.

serve did not peg bond prices after March 1951, but until November 1952 it supported refunding of Treasury certificates, usually by purchasing rights to the new issue. Almost a year of cooperation with the Treasury after the Accord had convinced him that the Federal Reserve would not free itself from support of Treasury issues if it continued to advise the Treasury on debt management. Martin appointed a three-person subcommittee of the FOMC, in April 1952, to recommend changes in operating procedures. He served as chairman. The other members were Abbott Mills, newly appointed to the Board, and Malcolm Bryan, president of the Atlanta Federal Reserve Bank.[10] The subcommittee completed its report in December 1952.[11]

The report was a main topic at the March 1953 FOMC meeting. After much discussion, the FOMC voted to change the wording of its directive to reflect its less active role in the long-term market. In place of "maintaining orderly conditions in the Government security market," the directive now read "correcting a disorderly situation" (FOMC Minutes, March 4, 1953, 22). The committee reaffirmed its commitment to rely on discounting to supply reserves, using Riefler-Burgess reasoning to explain how discount policy worked. Discounting "limits credit expansion, puts pressure on banks, and makes them more responsive to changes in the discount rate" (Annual Report, 1953, 87).[12] The subcommittee recommended that the Federal Reserve stop making specific proposals about the terms of

10. Abbott L. Mills, Jr., served on the Board of Governors from February 1952 to February 1965. Mills filled the vacancy left by Marriner Eccles's resignation. Mills was an active member with an independent view that he expressed forcefully at a time when most FOMC members did not. He favored expansive policies and dissented several times when the FOMC voted to tighten (Katz, 1992). Bryan was an economist who had taught at the University of Georgia before joining the System. He spent five years as vice chairman of a Georgia bank.

11. Robert H. Craft of Guaranty Trust served as technical consultant on leave from his bank. The complete report is printed in Joint Committee on the Economic Report (1954, 257–307), followed by comments by the New York Federal Reserve Bank. Martin wanted to commission the report in May 1951 but delayed a year to await the report of the Joint Economic Committee chaired by Congressman Wright Patman in 1952. Volume 1, page 715 discusses this report.

12. Riefler-Burgess reasoning refers to the work in the 1920s at the Board and the New York bank that provided the policy framework used in the 1920s and early 1930s. See volume 1, chapter 4. In the 1950s, Riefler continued to hold that banks did not borrow for profit and interest rate spreads did not affect the volume of borrowing. Karl Bopp at the Philadelphia bank took the opposite view. Rate spreads affected borrowing, according to Bopp. At New York, Sproul and one of the vice presidents, Harold V. Roelse, sided with Riefler (memo, Roelse to Sproul, Sproul papers, September 29, 1954). Robert Roosa took an intermediate position, arguing that the reason for changing discount (and other) rates was that "there's still room for profitability as an independent influence" (quoted in ibid., 1). Roelse's memo shows that the New York and Board staffs had resumed their quarrels from the 1920s. Roelse remarked that he rarely found much to agree with in Riefler's work.

Treasury issues. It concluded also that the account manager and the New York bank had too much discretion and that a few members dominated decisions.[13] The report obliquely accused Sproul of conflict of interest because he made operating decisions and participated in the policy discussion and the assessment of operations. It proposed to increase participation by the regional bank presidents and reduce New York's influence. In a letter to Sproul, Martin made two major criticisms of existing arrangements. First, members did not understand how the desk implemented FOMC decisions. The System would be embarrassed if Congress learned about this in a hearing. Second was the principal-agent problem that arose because the FOMC could not fire the manager (letter, Martin to Sproul, Martin papers, undated but likely July 1953). The entire discussion shows that Martin saw the problem as a lack of administrative control. He did not recognize that the FOMC could control the manager by giving precise instructions and assuring that the manager followed them.

One set of proposals made the manager an employee of the FOMC instead of the New York bank and gave the FOMC a separate budget and its own staff. Sproul opposed the change, arguing, in a five-page letter to Martin, that the recommendation confused policy and operations. The FOMC was a policymaking body; it was never intended to have operating responsibilities. He defended his own role vigorously, argued for continuing the manager's discretion, and defended the established practice of having the manager serve as a vice president of the New York bank (memo, Sproul to

13. The account manager operated the "desk" (trading desk) charged with execution of open market operations. At the time, the manager made the decisions about how much and when to provide or remove reserves. The subcommittee found other "anomalies in the structure and organization of the Federal Open Market Committee" (FOMC Minutes, revised, March 4, 1953, 27). It mentioned a separate budget, separate staff responsible only to the FOMC, and making the manager "directly responsible" to FOMC (ibid.). Sproul objected strongly, so these recommendations were put aside. The FOMC eventually took responsibility for appointing the manager, although he remained a New York bank vice president. The committee never implemented proposals about separate budget and staff. Sproul's response said that the problem was "to make an effective transit from policy to execution of policy" (Sproul papers, "Organization of Federal Open Market Committee," FOMC Correspondence, July–December 1953, February 18, 1953). He defended the manager's role and claimed that the proposed changes would not remove the gap between policy choice and execution. (No one suggested more explicit instructions to the manager.) Separately in a letter to Oliver Powell (Minneapolis), but sent to all FOMC members, Sproul charged the subcommittee with trying to appease congressional critics who wanted greater centralization of control in Washington. The Board wanted to strengthen its position and weaken New York, an old and continuing struggle (letter, Sproul to Powell, Sproul papers, FOMC Correspondence, July–December 1953, July 16, 1953). Martin responded, agreeing with many of the points Sproul made about the need for managerial discretion in executing FOMC directives. But he added that delegation could go too far. "The management of the Account, if it chooses, may make a lot of policy on its own" (letter, Martin to Sproul, Martin papers, undated but likely July 1953).

Martin, Sproul papers, February 18, 1953). Martin postponed discussion of the last issue to a later date so that the subcommittee could meet with Sproul (FOMC Minutes, March 4, 1953, 27). The FOMC discussed the proposed change in its relationship to the manager several times in the next few years. The manager remained a vice president of the New York bank, but he received his appointment as manager from the FOMC after 1955.

The subcommittee proposed a new form for the directive summarizing the FOMC's decisions. Martin's intention was to give more explicit directions to the Executive Committee. Once a year, the committee would reconsider general operating instructions, the first part of the directive. The second part would be a specific directive issued to the Executive Committee. The committee would then issue any instructions concerning direct purchases from the Treasury.[14] Instructions to the New York bank would follow. The last of these was not published as part of the Annual Report.

Martin's concern was not just operating control. He believed that the government securities market expected the Federal Reserve to limit losses on longer-term government bonds. As long as the manager intervened at various maturities, the market would expect the manager to do so. It would not develop its own arrangements for limiting risk to portfolio holders. A small decline in price would not call forth buyers willing to clear the market and conversely. Instead, the market would wait for Federal Reserve support. If the Federal Reserve did not support the price, Martin believed the market would expect the price to fall further; a fall in bond prices would therefore bring forth an excess supply and a further price decline. In the terminology used at the time, the market lacked depth, breadth, and resiliency.[15] Buyers and sellers did not support an existing price by taking advantage of small deviations from equilibrium to restore equilibrium.

One way to stop the manager from intervening, and to lessen Sproul's influence, was to make the manager report to the FOMC, where Martin

14. Authority to purchase limited quantities directly from the Treasury began as a temporary accommodation in the 1930s. In 1952, the Treasury requested Congress to make the authority permanent. The Board discussed the issue several times in 1952 and concurred in the Treasury request (Board Minutes, February 18, 1952, 5–6; November 4, 1952, 11–12).

15. Riefler coined these terms, which were widely used at the time. He said he chose depth, breadth, and resiliency because DBR were his son Donald's initials (Hetzel and Leach, 2001, 50). In a written response, Martin defined these terms as: "dealers willing to quote firm prices at which they will buy reasonably large quantities of securities, . . . [and] variations in quotations between successive transactions are minor." He also used "continuity" and "responsiveness" (Sproul papers, Flanders Hearing Folder 1, Roosa to Sproul, December 2, 1954). Robert Roosa at the New York bank criticized Martin for discussing the issue "in the rarefied atmosphere of theoretical discussion conducted in another world" (ibid., 3). This criticism of Martin is very wide of the mark.

could exercise control. With that option put aside, an alternative was to limit or eliminate operations in long-term securities.

Martin's subcommittee had concluded that the government securities market had not developed as a "self-reliant" market, even though the Treasury sold an issue in November 1952 without System support for the first time since the war began. One reason was that a "disconcerting degree of uncertainty existed . . . with respect to both the occasions which the Federal Open Market Committee might consider appropriate for intervention and to the sector in which such interventions might occur—an uncertainty that was detrimental to the development of depth, breadth, and resiliency of the market" (Annual Report, 1953, 89). It also increased the risk premium. The report recommended limiting policy actions to transactions in Treasury bills, a policy that became known as bills-only.

Bills-Only

By unanimous vote, the FOMC agreed on March 4, 1953, that: (1) operations for the System account would be confined to the short end of the market; (2) purchases and sales would be made only to meet the objectives of monetary and credit policy (not to support any pattern of yields and prices); and (3) during periods of Treasury financing, the System would not purchase maturing issues, when-issued securities, or issues with comparable maturity (FOMC Minutes, March 4, 1953, 40–42). Two years after the Accord, approval of the resolution ended the transition period.[16] The Federal Reserve increased its independence of Treasury.

The market soon tested the new policy. On the same mid-April day that Martin, in a speech, told the market that it would be free to set prices and yields in the long-term market, the Treasury announced that, to lengthen the maturity of outstanding debt, it would offer $1 billion of thirty-year bonds with a 3.25 percent coupon.[17] This was the first issue of long-term

16. The April 8 Executive Committee meeting approved unanimously a letter from Chairman Martin to President Sproul setting out the March 4 agreement. The letter limited operations to short-term securities (except in disorderly markets), and abandoned "rigid qualifications for dealers" (Executive Committee Minutes, April 8, 1953, 10).

17. The speech, called "The Transition to Free Markets," set out Martin's philosophy and beliefs about the role of monetary policy. It was, he said, "a mistake to claim too much for monetary policy . . . But it was equally misleading to conclude that this steady progress [since the Accord] would have been achieved without the aid of the monetary policies and actions that were initiated two years ago. . . .

"In a free market, rates can go down as well as up and thus perform their proper function of the price mechanism. . . .

"Under our government institutions and our economic system, the maximum benefits for all of us flow from utilizing private property, free, competitive enterprise, and the profit motive" (Martin speeches, April 13, 1953, 4).

bonds since the war. The yield was generous; at the time long-term Treasury bonds yielded slightly less than 3 percent. After an initial, positive response, market yields began to rise.[18]

At the May 6 Executive Committee meeting, the manager reported that "there was virtually no market for government securities at the present time" (Executive Committee Minutes, May 6, 1953, 2). Sproul wanted to intervene in the long-term market, but Martin wanted to maintain the bills-only policy (letter, Sproul to Martin, Sproul papers, December 4, 1953, 3). In the next three weeks, the System purchased $134 million and increased repurchase agreements. Banks reduced discounts by $513 million, more than offsetting the System's expansion. Long-term yields continued to rise.

Martin claimed that speculators subscribed to the bonds thinking that they would go to a premium. Instead, they went to a discount. As prices fell, speculators sold their bonds. Average yields on government bonds rose from 3 percent at the end of April to 3.19 percent in the week ending June 6. This was a large change at the time.

Later, he explained the importance of bills-only policy: "The market appeared constantly to expect action by the System which, by the standards of a free market, would be unpredictable and might seem capricious" (ibid., 7). He added: "[W]hen the Federal Reserve, with its huge portfolio and virtually unlimited resources, intervened in the market during Treasury refundings, many other investors tended to step to the sidelines and let the market form around the System's bids. This was a natural and highly rational investor reaction" (ibid., 9). As a consequence, the market was uncertain about the proper pricing of new issues. Martin then described characteristics of a properly functioning market, distinguishing transitory and persistent changes. "[F]luctuations resulting from temporary or technical developments are self-correcting without any official intervention. Of the movements that are not self-correcting, most reflect basic changes in the credit outlook which should be permitted to occur. Only very rarely is there likely to be a disorderly situation that would require Federal Reserve intervention for reasons other than credit policy" (ibid., 11). Disorderly and orderly proved difficult to define, as New York recognized at the time. The purpose of the change was to avoid giving the market reason to think that the Federal Reserve had resumed pegging interest rates (Sproul papers, Q and A for the Flanders hearings, answer to question 3).

18. The rise was not entirely unforeseen. Banks' loan demand rose following the end of selective credit controls in January 1952. To finance lending, banks sold $3.9 billion of government securities in the three months ending April 1953. Sproul told his directors in April that Treasury borrowing would increase in part because the Treasury would have to pay off maturing F and G bonds sold to big investors during World War II. However, two weeks later, he warned that economic expansion might be nearing its end (Sproul papers, FOMC meeting comments, April 2 and 16, 1953). In early May, he told the FOMC that increased Treasury borrowing might raise rates and "the market might become 'disorderly'" (ibid., May 7, 1953, 2). The policy of neutrality "has become a tight money policy—money can be tight even at rates of interest which 'look' low" (2). On the day the Treasury announced the issue, nine United States senators urged the Treasury to withdraw the issue as a "triple threat to the American economy" (quoted in Knipe, 1965, 87). This is an example of the heightened political interest in economic policy.

The manager continued to follow bills-only, purchasing (net) $848 million for the System account in the middle two weeks of June, a 3.5 percent increase in Federal Reserve holdings. In addition, the manager purchased long-term debt, including the 3.25 percent bonds, for the Treasury trust funds. By the end of the month, long-term yields were halfway back to the April level.

At the June 11 FOMC meeting, Sproul reopened discussion of bills-only, arguing that the market had not shown the promised resiliency. He accused proponents of bills-only policy of a "doctrinaire attitude on free markets" (Sproul papers, FOMC meetings, June 11, 1953, 3). Two Board members did not attend the meeting, and there was one vacancy on the Board following Oliver Powell's departure to become president of the Minneapolis reserve bank. The presidents, therefore, had a five-to-four majority at the meeting. They voted together to rescind the bills-only policy and permit the Executive Committee to decide what to purchase. The temporary market disturbance passed, and the two absent members returned. The FOMC again reversed itself and restored bills-only at its September meeting. This time the vote was nine to two with Sproul and Powell dissenting. The other presidents voted with the majority.

Sproul tried again to modify the decision at the December FOMC meeting. He proposed that the bills-only policy be adopted (or changed) at each meeting, and that the rule be rescinded unless explicitly approved. The majority argued that the rules could be changed at any time. By a nine-to-two vote, the committee rejected Sproul's motion. Only Joseph Erickson (Boston) joined Sproul.

Sproul did not give up. In March 1956, shortly before he retired, he prepared a twenty-three-page memo for the FOMC. He argued, as on previous occasions, that the bills-only policy had not increased, and would not increase, the depth, breadth, and resiliency of the long-term market. Dealer positions had fallen because risk had increased. Dealers had become brokers of long-term securities instead of market makers. In the same period, the floating supply of Treasury bills had declined, so the Treasury bill yield had become a less reliable indicator of money market conditions. For these reasons, he claimed operations in the short-term market did not affect the long-term market, as the committee had expected (memo, Sproul to Riefler, Board files, March 28, 1956).[19]

19. Martin hit back, rejecting Sproul's argument and his analysis. "I do not understand how any judgment about depth, breadth, and resiliency can be based on statistical comparisons of the volume of transactions in various sectors of the market when the market was pegged with the volume of transactions in those same sectors when the market was free" (Martin to FOMC, Board files, April 17, 1956, 1). Sproul responded, accusing Martin of an

Martin won the skirmish with Sproul over bills-only. He had the better argument: sporadic intervention in the long-term government securities market would lead market participants to anticipate support of particular issues during Treasury sales or market volatility. The Federal Reserve should intervene only for general monetary policy operations by supplying or withdrawing reserves. A "free market" would not develop if the Federal Reserve supported long-term bonds. Characteristically, Martin rejected the statistical tests that Sproul's staff and others developed to show that the long-term market had not developed greater depth, breadth, and resiliency. He did not deny that intervention in the long-term market would change long-term rates, an important issue for Sproul. He conceded that effects on long-term rates might be slower under bills-only. He wanted to prevent the market from depending on, and waiting for, System intervention. Sproul and his staff would not acknowledge the importance of this argument (memo, Gaines to Sproul, FOMC Correspondence, April 27, 1956).

Long-term rates move around an average (geometric mean) of expected future short-term rates. Interventions to change a long-term rate must also change other prices up and down the maturity structure. Later, research developed the expectations theory of the term structure, showing why interventions of the kind Sproul proposed were unlikely to succeed for long if at all.[20]

Sproul thought the FOMC was "foolish" to agree "for the record that we enter into open market operations solely to supply or absorb reserves" (letter, Sproul to Powell, Sproul papers, Correspondence 1952–55, September 17, 1954, 2). He believed that "this business of central banking requires a little more complicated approach than just 'putting in and taking out reserves' so as to maintain some figure or range of 'free reserves.' The cost of credit at short- and long-term is a central banking consideration as well as the supply of bank reserves" (ibid., 1). He believed also that "aid can properly and appropriately be extended to Treasury refunding operations by transactions in rights, when issued securities, and securities of comparable maturity; that it can be extended at times, more effectively in this way than by confining our operations to Treasury bills" (letter, Sproul to Martin, Sproul

---

all-or-nothing approach and reiterating his belief that the FOMC should use all available tools (Sproul to FOMC, Board files, May 3, 1956). Sproul left the FOMC a few weeks later. In 1961 purchases of all maturities resumed. Market activity slowed or ceased when the System purchased longer-term securities.

20. Modern work on the term structure did not begin until Meiselman (1962). By that time, bills-only had ended. Until the financial disturbances in 2008, the Federal Reserve held few long-term bonds. In 2008, more than half its portfolio was longer term.

papers, Correspondence 1952–55, December 4, 1953, 4). He doubted that "the market could develop into a broad, impersonal mechanism in which gradual and orderly changes in demand and supply conditions would be reflected in equally orderly changes in prices and yields, if only the System Account were out of the picture so that dealers might rationalize their expectations. The minority [New York] . . . viewed the market as one in which the major disturbing forces were the so-called 'natural forces' not the System Account. The principal uncertainty created by the Federal Reserve System stems from the possibility of shifts in its basic policy not from the areas of the market in which it might operate"[21] (Sproul papers, Q and A for Flanders hearings, questions 3, November 1954).

For Sproul's argument in favor of intervention to be correct, the desk would have to distinguish correctly between temporary and permanent changes in prices at different maturities. As the market learned to anticipate intervention, prices and yields would change, as Martin insisted. Sproul never tried to show that the manager would know how much to intervene and when to do so. He assumed that intervention would stabilize the market. Time and experience have not supported Sproul's views that the Federal Reserve could change the relative prices of securities of different durations other than temporarily or change security prices independently of changes in the stock of reserves or base money. Most central banks operate mainly or exclusively in the short-term market although they may buy and hold long-term securities. In the United States, Congress put pressure on the Federal Reserve at times to buy agency securities to encourage housing.

At the Board, Riefler put considerable weight on the role of forward-looking anticipations, long before they received much attention in academic work. He described government security dealers and market professionals as always trying "to ascertain the significance of all System policy actions" and adjusting their portfolios accordingly (Riefler, 1958a, 5). Markets, he said, do not try to counter System operations because of the size of the System's portfolio and because the System is a central bank, concerned about its policy objectives not its profitability.

Martin did not insist that policy could do no more than change the stock of reserves and let the market determine the relative prices of different

21. Even if one accepted that the principal source of market disturbance is Federal Reserve intervention, additional intervention or uncertainty about where the Federal Reserve would intervene would not smooth the market. New York refused to accept the Board's argument about dealer expectations and the suggestion that intervention would be a step toward pegging. To New York's chagrin, market newsletters emphasized this point (Gaines to Rouse, Sproul papers, bills-only, June–October 1954, June 9, 1954).

maturities. Theoretical arguments of this kind had little appeal for him. He would have dismissed the claim that he had adopted a "monetarist" position that the stock of reserves and base money were the key variables. He based his decision on the "practical" argument that, if the Federal Reserve intervened to support particular issues, it would soon be back pegging interest rates for the Treasury. He added, moreover, that there would never be a "free market" in Treasury securities if the market expected the Federal Reserve to limit price changes by intervening in the long-term market.[22]

The weak point in Martin's argument and the staff's support for bills-only was a failure to recognize that support for Treasury operations, whether by purchasing bills or bonds, increased the risk of inflation. Some of the staff, and possibly Martin at times, recognized the need to control money growth if they were to prevent inflation. They did not acknowledge that support of Treasury financings made monetary control more difficult. This became a problem in the 1960s.

Martin won the System's economic and policy dispute but lost the broader political skirmish.[23] Most academic economists who expressed their views on bills-only sided with Sproul. In journal articles and congres-

22. In a 1954 hearing, Martin responded to a written question by highlighting the uncertainty created by sporadic intervention borrowing in part from his speech on free markets. "The constant possibility of official action, which from the standpoint of investors and market intermediaries would often seem capricious, constituted a market risk which private investors could in no reasonable way anticipate and evaluate" (Joint Committee on the Economic Report, 1954, 24). Testifying to the Joint Economic Committee in 1959, Martin listed three ways that open market operations affect the economy. "(1) They change the volume of reserves. . . . (2) They affect the volume of securities . . . (3) They influence the expectations of professional traders and investors regarding market trends" (Martin, 1959, 19). The reference to expectations reflects Riefler's influence and gives an emphasis that did not appear in the academic literature for many years. Martin put the most weight on the change in reserves. This emphasis is also in other Federal Reserve publications at this time. Within the Federal Reserve, Sproul had been the leading opponent of pegged rates and neither wanted nor intended to go back to pegging. He seemed unable to accept that the long-term market would function efficiently without support. Martin, for his part, did not address the issue that bothered Sproul: if the Federal Reserve intervened in the short-term market, the market was not "free" but depended on the System's intervention. Martin's claim was that the Federal Reserve could not know the proper relationship between prices of different maturities (Joint Committee on the Economic Report, 1954, 235). Sproul did not respond directly to this argument. Martin also claimed that, unlike Sproul, he believed arbitrage occurred quickly (ibid., 230).

23. An example of press commentary is an editorial in the *Journal of Commerce,* a business newspaper. The December 14, 1954, editorial blamed bills-only for the declining share of long-term bonds in the Treasury market. The editorial made no mention of the Treasury's unwillingness to pay the higher interest rate on long-term bonds. The bills-only controversy illustrates the changed positions of New York and Washington. In the 1920s, Governor Benjamin Strong (New York) dominated policy actions and procedures. In the 1950s, New York could protest, but Washington decided.

sional hearings, they criticized bills-only as an unnecessary and costly restriction. Congressional opposition to bills-only gained strength as interest rates rose during the decade. The issue united Senator Douglas and Congressman Patman, who disagreed totally about pegged rates but agreed for different reasons that bills-only was wrong. In 1960, twenty-one senators urged the System to end bills-only and increase money growth to equal the rate of output growth (Board Minutes, March 15, 1960).[24] The Federal Reserve's efforts to defend the policy attracted few supporters.

Faced with intense, growing criticism of the bills-only policy, early in 1958 Chairman Martin appointed a special committee to review procedures after five years of experience. President Hayes initiated the review in a memo questioning whether the procedures and policies then in effect were optimal ways of achieving the System's objectives while aiding Treasury finance and improving the functioning of the dealer market for government securities. Although the Board's staff and the New York bank recognized some merit in each other's position, and they agreed on objectives, basic differences remained.

The broad issue between the Board and the bank concerned how Federal Reserve operations should change to recognize the existence of a large, outstanding stock of debt, often growing and frequently refunded. Both accepted an obligation to assist the Treasury to an extent consistent with the System's objectives. Growth of new, non-bank intermediaries was a second major change since the 1920s. Analysis at the time suggested that the existence of these intermediaries made a significant change in the transmission of monetary policy (see Gurley and Shaw, 1960).[25] Both staffs' responses accepted that markets would reflect the new conditions, but open market operations continued to work by changing the supply of reserves.

Much of the discussion restated earlier positions. The Board's staff claimed that there were no occasions since 1953 "when operations in securities other than bills would have made it easier to accomplish monetary policy objectives" (Memo, "Analysis of Issues to be Considered by Special Committee," Board Records, January 14, 1958, 3). The manager responded by citing some occasions when long- and short-term rates moved in op-

24. Martin responded on behalf of the Board, pointing out that bills-only was not a rigid rule. The System had intervened in November 1955 and July 1958 and on two other occasions had exchanged its holdings for other than bills (August 1959 and February 1960) (Board Minutes, April 14, 1960, letter, Martin to 21 senators).

25. Some secondary issues arose also. How could financing of the dealer market be improved? The manager wanted opportunity to swap securities with market participants, an issue that the FOMC had considered and rejected earlier.

posite directions, periods when he would have intervened in the long-term market.[26] This did not respond directly to the Board's statement, and it did not establish that the intervention would have been effective. In fact, aggressive reduction of short-term rates in a recession can increase expected future inflation, raising long-term rates.

The Board's staff and New York agreed that they could not produce evidence on the effectiveness of the policy by citing evidence from the long-term market. This required evidence on the counterfactual that no one could have. The Board's staff argued that every time the market seemed on the verge of becoming disorderly, it "fairly quickly made its own adjustments" ("Analysis of Issues," Board Records, January 14, 1958, 10). Support operations, they said, would have damaged the market's ability to adjust. The staff added several administrative complications that would have arisen if the System had operated, at times, in the long-term market (ibid., 11).

The Board's staff dismissed the suggestion that the FOMC should work to prevent, instead of correct, disorderly conditions. Prevention required forecasting and could quickly become an excuse for intervening more frequently, thereby increasing uncertainty for market participants. The staff then made the case for rules to reduce discretion: "Decision-making, moreover, is facilitated by having a set of recognized, well-conceived, generally workable ground rules and working principles as a basis for operations. . . . Perhaps more important is the desirability of public recognition of the principles, rules, and guides that govern monetary policies and operations"[27] (ibid., 26).

The staff response also contained a general statement of "working principles" that explained the staff's understanding of the way monetary policy affects the economy. The first principle is that "regardless of the instruments through which Federal Reserve credit is extended, the supply of bank reserves is affected" (ibid., 3). The report then discussed availability and the cost of credit as reflected in the correlation between free reserves and market interest rates, relative yields on securities, and the role of the government securities market. Missing is the earlier discussion of anticipations and the transmission of the monetary impulse via relative prices and real yields to the markets for output, investment, and consumer spending.

26. The manager presumed that the market was wrong and warranted correction. See his appendix to "The Ad Hoc Report—After Five Years" (Board Records, January 15, 1958). Differences in temporary and persistent changes in conditions would explain such movements.

27. This is a long, first step in the evolution toward greater transparency and what economists later called credibility and away from historic central bank secrecy. The staff, at this time, could see the advantages of a rule for intervention procedures but not for policy actions more generally.

Hayes's response remarked that "we are all very close to agreement as to the way in which the account should actually be administered" (Memo to Special Committee, Board Records, February 4, 1958, 1). He conceded, at last, that bills-only may have helped the market to make its own adjustments, and he agreed that "while Treasury financing operations unavoidably must be taken into account, any System efforts to facilitate them should be definitely subordinated to our primary objectives of monetary policy" (ibid., 1). Alas, like the Board and its staff, he did not explain how the subordination of Treasury financing to policy objectives could be reconciled with the System's reluctance to raise rates, steeply if necessary, to prevent Treasury financings from increasing money growth under even-keel policy.

Hayes accepted that most operations would be in the bill market. The main point of his memo was that the System should be more flexible. He again urged rewording the operating directives by introducing less restrictive language ("usually," "as a general rule") and permitting the desk to engage in securities swaps with the market.

The five-year review did not change the policy guidelines. Martin, the FOMC, and the staff continued the bills-only policy despite the continued opposition among prominent members of Congress and little support from academic research.

The Board's intellectual defense of bills-only did not claim that arbitrage was perfect or that long-term rates moved directly with short-term rates and only in response to such movements. To support the Board's position, Riefler (1958a, 1958b) relied on four main arguments; not all were present in each discussion.

First, the main direct effect of an open market purchase or sale came from the change in reserves, not from the change in the outstanding stock of securities. Hence, purchases or sales of long-term debt would not have much additional effect.[28]

Second, an indirect effect on expectations amplified the System's action. Market professionals "are not likely to operate against any trend in rates they think the System is trying to establish. . . . [W]hen System actions give rise to firm expectations among market professionals with respect to

---

28. As part of this argument, Riefler claimed that the multiplier of bank reserves was about 7, based on the reciprocal of the reserve requirement ratio (1958b, 1262, 1269). This calculation ignored leakages into currency. New York pointed out another error, "the continued effort to maintain the fiction that increases in reserve requirements . . . and the omission of any reference to the fact that, in every instance, the increase in reserve requirements led to increased sales of Government securities to the System" (Roelse to Sproul, Sproul papers, FOMC Correspondence, January–March 1952, February 5, 1952, 2).

interest rate trends, relatively small System operations may have important short-run effects on market quotations" (Riefler, 1958b, 1263).

Third, operations in the long-term market, even if frequent, "would indicate a feeling on the part of Federal Reserve authorities that existing prices and yields on long-term securities were out of line" (1958b, 1264). Since long-term bonds traded infrequently relative to bills, these actions would disrupt the market.[29] "Bill operations can also give rise to false or misleading expectations, but they are much less likely to do so" (ibid.).

Fourth, open market operations change the volume of securities that the market holds. Substitution and arbitrage spread this effect to securities along the entire maturity spectrum. Riefler put greater stress on substitution than on yield arbitrage. He dismissed theories that put buyers and sellers into "preferred habitat" maturities where they remained. He claimed a "high degree of actual substitutability . . . for many lenders" (Riefler, 1958a, 7).

The Board had the better analytic argument, but it did not win the point with Congress and academic critics. Many of the critics confused nominal and real rates of interest. Believing that the Federal Reserve could reduce long-term interest rates and refused to do so, the leading academic economists who prepared the *Report on Employment, Growth and Price Levels* for the Joint Economic Committee, chaired by Senator Paul Douglas, wrote:

> Just as the preaccord policy promoted artificially low interest rates, the policies pursued, particularly since 1953, have brought interest rates to levels higher than they should or need be. [T]he full potential of monetary policy to promote stability and economic growth has not been realized. (Joint Economic Committee, 1960b, 30)

Faced with this criticism and strong opposition in Congress,[30] the Board ended the bills-only policy in the fall of 1960 and in 1961 formally revoked the 1953 policy. The new administration wanted to keep short-term rates

---

29. Remembering the pegging period, Martin (1959, 20) wrote: "If an attempt were made to lower long-term interest rates by System purchases of bonds and to offset the effect on reserves by accompanying sales of short-term issues, market holdings of participants would shift by a corresponding amount from long-term securities to short ones. This process would continue until the System's portfolio consisted largely of long-term securities." This would not be true if the market expected rates to fall. Two years later, Martin endorsed the policy he rejected here. The written argument was likely the work of the staff.

30. In 1959, Congress refused the administration's request to remove the 4.25 percent ceiling rate on government bonds with more than five years' initial maturity until the Federal Reserve abandoned the bills-only policy. In 1960, the Joint Economic Committee made as its major recommendation for monetary policy that the Federal Reserve "abandon its discredited 'bills only' policy and acquire long-term bonds for the portfolio" (Joint Economic Committee, 1960a, 16).

up while lowering long-term rates. The Federal Reserve cooperated by occasionally buying long-term and selling short-term securities. Sproul was
elated (letter, Sproul to Hayes, Sproul papers, Correspondence, February–
March, 1961, March 14, 1961).

The bills-only policy may have contributed slightly to strengthening the
market for long-term Treasury securities, but the evidence is mixed. After
seven years, only a few government security dealers held positions in the
long-term market or made markets in those issues.[31]

In retrospect, much of the criticism of bills-only seems misdirected. If
there were gains for stabilization policy that the Federal Reserve could, but
would not, achieve, the Treasury could have changed its offerings to supply more (fewer) bills and fewer (more) long-term securities. Until 1959
debt management by the Treasury remained fully capable of maintaining
the composition of the debt that the Treasury wanted (or that was socially
optimal). For a brief period in 1959–60, the 4.25 percent ceiling restricted
what the Treasury could do.

Bills-only did not achieve the System's principal aim—to free itself
from responsibility for the success of debt management and support of
Treasury offerings. Treasury operations were a continuing concern. The
Federal Reserve held interest rates unchanged before, during, and after
Treasury sales. It intervened in the bill market frequently and delayed
policy changes to provide enough reserves so that banks could buy new or
replacement issues. It no longer counseled the Treasury on what it should
issue, but it estimated the reserves it would have to supply to make the
issues succeed.

For the System, the Treasury was not just another borrower. Some
members suggested that if many holders redeemed for cash (called attrition), the main effect would be that the Treasury would have to borrow
again. The Treasury and the Federal Reserve did not accept this view. Attrition was evidence of failure, a cause of embarrassment that both wanted
to avoid.

The Federal Reserve described its role as independent within the government, but independence within government included some support of
Treasury offerings.[32] Its policy, called "even keel," later severely restricted

31. In 1960 Congressman Wright Patman of the Joint Economic Committee commis-
sioned Gert von der Linde and me to study the dealer market. The conclusion in the text
is based on that study (see Joint Economic Committee, 1960). The Treasury supported or
did not criticize bills-only during the 1950s, but members of the FOMC began to tire of the
criticism and to urge greater flexibility (memo, Mangels [San Francisco] to FOMC and Bank
Presidents, Board Correspondence, February 24, 1960).

32. This was not new. In the 1930s, Treasury Secretary Henry Morgenthau held the Federal Reserve accountable for any change in market rates no matter how small. It took until

the number of days on which the Federal Reserve could change policy. All members did not always agree with this commitment, but a large majority did. Chapter 3 has a table showing "even keel" activity during 1966 to 1971.

Transforming the FOMC

The Banking Act of 1935 mandated four meetings of the FOMC in Washington each year. In the early 1950s these meetings set policy guidelines. The chairman and vice chairman of the FOMC met every two weeks with three other members of the Executive Committee to decide how much to buy or sell to achieve the full committee's objective and to instruct the manager.

In practice, New York dominated the Executive Committee. Sproul and the account manager, Robert Rouse, had much more information than the other members about the current and near-term position of the money market, prospective Treasury offerings, and other technical details. Consequently, New York could usually get its way. Although Martin and Sproul often agreed on policy, Martin wanted to increase Board control and the participation and influence of other FOMC members. He proposed to discuss termination of the Executive Committee at the June 1955 FOMC meeting and to include discussion of discount policy, changes in reserve requirement ratios, and margin requirements at FOMC meetings. The FOMC was the "heart of the System," and it should discuss all of these decisions, not leave some to the Executive Committee and others to the Board (Executive Committee Minutes, April 12, 1955, 5). New York's advantage weakened in later decades, so the regional banks became more important participants, but the Chairman dominated decisions.

In June, the time for a showdown with New York had come. In advance of the June 22 FOMC meeting, Riefler mailed a proposal to all the presidents that would abolish the Executive Committee and substitute full committee meetings every three weeks. The general counsel prepared a memo stating the required changes in by-laws, regulations, and procedures to adjust to the change. Martin repeated his earlier statement about increasing the FOMC's responsibility.[33] Sproul argued that the Executive Committee

---

the 1970s before the System recognized that its problems with the pricing of Treasury issues would be reduced if the Treasury auctioned its debt instead of fixing the price. Auctioning debt gradually freed the Federal Reserve from "even keel" operations. It became possible to slow inflation despite persistent, large budget deficits, although it did not have that effect for several years.

33. In 1953 Martin considered a legislative change to reduce the Board to five members (each with a ten-year term) and the FOMC to nine members, five from the Board and four from the reserve banks. New York would continue to hold a permanent seat. In testimony at

could meet quickly in an emergency and that the telephone was not a close substitute for "a face to face meeting at which ideas can be developed and debated, and the reaction of your associates to those ideas can be observed and taken into account" (FOMC Minutes, June 22, 1955, 7).

Several members pointed out that almost all members of the full committee had attended Executive Committee meetings that spring. New York was clearly on the losing side, just as it had been in 1930, when the Board urged an expansion of the committee to include all twelve banks instead of five. With little further discussion, the committee voted unanimously to abolish the Executive Committee and transfer its responsibilities to the full committee. The FOMC issued a press statement the following day, June 24, 1955. Slowly the regional bank presidents increased their role and appointed advisers to inform them about policy actions.

The vote settled an issue that was older than the Federal Reserve System: Where should control of monetary policy reside, in Washington, the political capital, or in the regional banks, particularly New York, where merchants and bankers had more influence? The Banking Act of 1935 had shifted power to Washington by giving the Board a majority on the FOMC, by putting the appointment of reserve bank presidents under Board control, and in other ways.[34]

To give a larger voice to the regional banks and the Board, while retaining influence over decisions, Martin instituted the "go around." FOMC members discussed conditions in the economy or in their districts, stated their concerns, and recommended policy action. Martin then summarized the views, described the consensus, and put his statement to a vote only if there was a change in the directive or substantial division. Members could dissent, but generally they supported Martin's consensus in the 1950s. Initially, this was a more substantial change in procedure than in practice, since many of the presidents did not have strong views. In time, new people with more training in economics or experience in financial markets became presidents of the reserve banks.

The change had two immediate effects. One was to lessen New York's

the 1952 Patman hearings, Martin had also proposed ending the prohibition against reappointment after a full term and limiting terms to six years. The Board staff prepared legislation. Martin discussed the proposal with Treasury Secretary Humphrey and Undersecretary Burgess and hoped that the new organization would be in place by March 1954 (letter with attachments, Martin to Burgess, Martin papers, April 8, 1953). Eccles had proposed a five-person board in 1935.

34. In the 1930s, Chairman Eccles tried to keep the presidents from voting at the FOMC and made New York alternate with Boston as a member of FOMC. The latter effort failed, and New York was made permanent vice chair in 1942. Gradually, New York recovered some of the influence lost in 1935–36.

dominance. Martin usually asked Sproul to speak first, after the staff briefing. Sproul always had prepared remarks and stated his position forcefully but was always courteous.[35] His descriptions of market conditions, current and prospective Treasury borrowing, and the economic outlook were carefully done and respected by the other members. Although the procedural changes reduced his discretion and independence, he remained influential. With the passage of time, the FOMC developed procedures for keeping regional presidents and their staffs informed about economic and market conditions and policy actions to a greater extent than under the older arrangements.

The second immediate effect was to shorten the policy horizon. A decision could always be postponed for three weeks to get more information or reduce uncertainty. Occasional efforts to focus on long-term inflation failed, displaced by near-term considerations, especially Treasury finance. Meeting every three weeks gave members an opportunity to delay decisions until they had more information.

Managing the Manager

Martin's 1952 ad hoc subcommittee also recommended that the account manager become an FOMC employee, instead of vice president of the New York bank. The open market account would remain in New York, but the manager would be responsible only to the FOMC and would have his own staff.

Sproul objected strongly when the FOMC discussed the issue in 1953, so the FOMC did not make a decision. After alerting Sproul by letter, Martin returned to the issue in February–March 1955. The Board's general counsel pointed out "the Committee is neither specifically authorized nor forbidden to employ its own staff" (memo, George B. Vest to Board of Governors, Board files, January 4, 1955, 2). However, counsel raised questions about whether the FOMC could use its earnings to pay a staff. He

35. Sproul's intensity of feeling and distrust of Martin's motives showed up in an exchange of letters about visitors from the Board to observe desk operations. Sproul accused Martin of sending "watchers" and argued that New York had "no other allegiance than to the Federal Open Market Committee, and no other purpose than to give effect to its policies" (Sproul to Martin, Sproul papers, FOMC Correspondence, January 4, 1952, 1). He then explained the reasons why a "watcher" would not work and should not be tried, ending with: "I would not want to have a 'watcher' in the house" (ibid., 3). Martin replied that he was "amused" by Sproul's comments, that he had not used the word "watcher," and that he did not intend to change the site of open market operations. Martin explained that he wanted more Board members and staff to understand how the market operated, and he included Treasury staff among the people who would gain from observing (Martin to Sproul, ibid., January 11, 1952). By June 1953, Sproul was "ready to accommodate such persons . . . [and] place them on our staff and payroll" (Sproul to Powell, Sproul papers, FOMC Correspondence, July 16, 1953, 3).

recommended that the Board get Congress to legislate, a step the Board usually was reluctant to take.[36]

Martin placed the issue on the agenda for the March 2, 1955, FOMC meeting. He reiterated the importance of having a manager who was responsible to the FOMC and not to the New York directors.[37] Further, "I want the whole Committee really to be responsible. I don't want operational responsibility limited to the New York Bank or to the manager of the account. That is the fundamental reason I make this proposal" (FOMC Minutes, March 2, 1955, 64). Martin then moved that the manager "be made more directly responsible to the Open Market Committee as a whole" (ibid.).

Sproul argued that the proposal did not raise an issue of principle. The manager was responsible to the FOMC. The FOMC reviewed the budget and accounts relating to the manager's work and, if it chose, could participate more fully in the budget process, the details of the manager's operations, and supervision of the account. He argued that all major issues could be resolved without making the manager an FOMC (or Board) employee. Further, Sproul objected that Martin's motion did not address operational issues. New York operated as fiscal agent of the Treasury and as agent for foreign central banks. He doubted that the manager's open market operations could be kept entirely separate from these operations of the New York bank. Also, someone had to supervise the manager's operation. Historically, New York had the responsibility. How would that change? Who would supervise? Finally, he questioned whether the System needed a new organization to make changes that would accomplish Martin's objectives or to remove any special advantage that New York's directors might have (ibid., 66–71).[38] Rather, the change would be taken as evidence that New York had lost the confidence of others in the System.

36. Martin sent Vest's letter to Sproul on February 14, 1955. Suggesting the state of relations, the letter addressed "Dear Mr. Sproul" and carried Martin's full name (letter, Martin to Sproul, Sproul papers, FOMC Correspondence, February 14, 1955). Martin also sent a letter to all the presidents outlining the proposed change. He planned a two-step procedure, first, a decision in principle to make the change followed by appointment of a subcommittee to recommend how the change should be made (ibid.).

37. "His selection is put up to us by the Board of Directors of the Federal Reserve Bank of New York as the man they have selected, one whom they believe to be satisfactory" (FOMC Minutes, March 2, 1955, 62).

38. "From the beginning of the Federal Open Market Committee they [New York directors] forswore any knowledge of open market operations which is not available to the directors of other Federal Reserve banks, and the by-laws of the Federal Open Market Committee would not permit them to have such knowledge" (FOMC Minutes, March 2, 1955, 71). One reason for the intensity of feeling was that the issue reopened a conflict that had been present from the start of the System but had remained below the surface after the 1930s. From earliest times, the Board regarded the reserve banks as representative of bankers, and some of the banks regarded the Board as overly political. Martin's claim that New York banks gained spe-

A heated discussion followed in which Martin maintained that the current arrangement was unacceptable, and Sproul urged that they vote on a specific proposal, not a vague sense of dissatisfaction. He insisted that the manager was responsible to the whole committee and objected strenuously when Board members claimed the contrary.

Sproul moved that a committee study the status of the manager and his responsibility to the FOMC. The FOMC defeated the motion by a seven-to-four vote with one president voting with the Board. The committee then approved Martin's motion to make the manager "more directly responsible to the open market committee" and appoint a subcommittee to bring back proposals to implement the new arrangement. This motion passed six-to-five with all presidents voting no (FOMC Minutes, March 2, 1955, 89–90). Subsequently, Martin appointed Canby Balderston, Watrous Irons (Dallas), Hugh Leach (Richmond), Martin, Robertson, and Sproul to propose a "structural and operating organization that will best implement the policies of the FOMC." The new committee contained three members who had voted in favor and three who had opposed.

Martin proposed that the FOMC choose the manager and set his compensation. The manager would be an employee of the FOMC and responsible to its members. Operations would remain in New York, but the New York bank would lose its special position (memo, "Status of the manager of the System Open Market Account," Board files, May 10, 1955). In October, Robertson went further. He endorsed Martin's proposal, but he also partly addressed a problem that Sproul emphasized and Martin neglected. The twelve members of the FOMC could not supervise the manager. They would often disagree about what the loose wording of the FOMC directives

---

cial advantage put New York on the defensive. Sproul cited the rules adopted by the New York bank that stated explicitly that "the board of directors under the by-laws and present practices of the Federal Open Market Committee cannot be informed adequately of the reasons for, or the possible extent and duration of, transactions in United States Government securities for account of the System Open Market Account" (letter, Sproul to Powell, Sproul papers, FOMC Correspondence, July 6, 1954). Sproul summarized New York's procedure: "They [directors] have been told what has been done—in effect what appears in our weekly statements" (ibid., 1). Affirmations of this kind did not change Martin's mind; he continued to press his argument. Possibly he remembered his father's experience in the 1920s, when directors voted on open market purchases and sales decisions for the individual reserve banks. The Banking Act of 1933 removed that decision and with it the need for directors to know (and take) a decision. See also Sproul's letter to Senator Paul Douglas (Sproul papers, FOMC Correspondence, March 11, 1954). Sproul wrote to object to Douglas's reference to "private bankers" making decisions at FOMC. Sproul's letter insisted that a reserve bank president was not the "representative of private bankers." He closed by saying: "I represent nothing but the public interest when I sit in meetings of the Federal Open Market Committee" (ibid., 2).

meant.[39] Robertson proposed giving supervisory responsibility to the secretary of the FOMC, Winfield Riefler at the time. If the secretary and the
manager disagreed, the FOMC would be asked to decide.

The special committee considered these and other proposals, but it
could not agree on any. The manager remained a vice president of the
New York bank.[40]

GUIDING PRINCIPLES

The Riefler-Burgess version of the real bills doctrine, which dominated
policy decisions in the 1920s and 1930s, faded in the 1950s. It did not
disappear entirely. Vestiges remained in concerns about speculative use of
credit for housing and the stock market. Aside from stock market margin
requirements, selective controls had expired. The Board used its authority
to change stock market margin requirements more frequently from 1951
to 1960 than in any other decade.

Several factors contributed to the reduced role of the real bills doctrine.
Government debt had grown in size. No one expected the government
to retire a large share of the debt by running budget surpluses, as in the
1920s. Banks had become accustomed to holding government securities
and, in a major departure from the principles embodied in the Federal
Reserve Act, using Treasury bills instead of acceptances (real bills) to adjust their portfolios. Open market operations in governments had become
the dominant means of changing bank reserves and the monetary base.
Although discounting remained an important source of reserves in the
1950s, most often Treasury bills, not acceptances or commercial paper,
served as collateral for discounts. Real bills declined in importance.

Changing Views about Discounts

The Riefler-Burgess framework minimized the role of the discount rate.
Banks borrowed only if necessary to meet reserve requirements. They did
not borrow to take advantage of differences between the discount rate and
lending or open market rates. The Federal Reserve ignored evidence con-

39. As long as the FOMC gave instructions such as "lean against the wind," "resolve
doubts on the side of ease" (restraint), and the like, the manager could exercise discretion,
and he did. The eventual resolution of the problem came in the 1970s, when the FOMC began
to give more precise instructions.

40. To increase scrutiny and monitoring of the manager's daily decisions by FOMC
members, Sproul responded to a suggestion by Governor Robertson and began a daily telephone call from the desk to the Board and to a reserve bank president currently voting on
the FOMC. Calls began on June 1, 1954, and have continued to the present (Sproul papers,
FOMC Correspondence, May 17, 1954).

tradicting this assumption until 1952, when banks borrowed relatively large amounts to take advantage of the spread in after-tax rates. Sproul summarized the then current position in a letter to Professor Elmer Wood.[41]

> Most often the discount rate and open market operations can be used together; the discount rate to symbolize the policy adopted, and open market operations to keep market rates and member bank borrowing in appropriate relation to the discount rate. At times of credit ease, this would mean sensitive money market rates below the discount rate and infrequent and minor borrowing in response to temporary needs of individual banks. At times of credit restraint, it would mean sensitive money market rates (except federal funds) at or maybe above the discount rate, with member banks having to borrow fairly frequently and in relatively large amounts so that, in the aggregate they would be in debt more or less continuously. (Sproul papers, Correspondence S–W, November 5, 1954, 2)[42]

The core concept remained. Sproul does not mention that advances against collateral had replaced borrowing on commercial paper. He retained the idea that restrictive policy drove banks to seek advances from the Federal Reserve. The Federal Reserve encouraged and might subsidize borrowing or advances by letting market rates rise above the discount rate. Conversely, when market rates declined in recession, the Federal Reserve penalized borrowing by making the discount rate a penalty rate.[43] Thus, discount policy contributed to procyclical growth of money and bank credit.

41. Wood wrote to Sproul supporting Sproul's opposition to the bills-only policy and urging the Federal Reserve to use the term structure of interest rates on government securities as the main policy guide. Sproul based his reply on a lengthy analysis by Robert Roosa, one of his staff (Sproul papers, FOMC Correspondence, October 26, 1954).

42. Sproul added a statement that makes sense only in the Riefler-Burgess tradition. "There are different kinds of reserve dollars and differences in the response of the banking system to their availability. We should take advantage of these differences" (Sproul papers, Correspondence S–W, November 5, 1954, 2). In Riefler-Burgess, the composition of reserves mattered. Banks used reserves supplied by open market operations to repay borrowing and expand. Reserves acquired by borrowing induced banks to contract, because they disliked indebtedness. In contrast, Madeline McWhinney (1952, 8) explained use of the discount window as a choice based on the cost and length of time for which the bank required additional reserves. Short-term demands could be satisfied by purchases of federal funds if they are "available in adequate volume at a satisfactory price."

43. Another oddity is the treatment of uncertainty. Both Roosa and Sproul said that, at times, the Federal Reserve should create uncertainty about future interest rates as a substitute for changes in rates. "[I]f for any reason . . . it proves impracticable or impolitic at times to exert influences that will lead to sizeable changes in the rates themselves, then by working on the uncertainty band instead the central bank may be able to maintain something like the desired degree of pressure upon the availability of credit" (Sproul papers, FOMC Memo, Roosa to Sproul, October 26, 1954, 11).

The System found it difficult to reconcile its belief about how discount policy worked with the volume of borrowing in 1952.[44] Sproul offered a different interpretation. Member banks remained reluctant to borrow because they "do not like to be in the position of having us able to tell them that they must reduce or eliminate their borrowing from us, which forces them to make other adjustments in their portfolios" (memo, Sproul to Trieber and Rouse, Sproul papers, FOMC Correspondence, September 26, 1952).

In 1954, the Federal Reserve modified its discount policy by changing the foreword to its regulation A, effective February 1955, governing a member bank's use of discounting. The revision stated the general principle that borrowing was a privilege and not a right of membership in the System. It was mainly a short-term loan to assist banks facing a sudden change in the demand for credit. It should not be used to profit from rate differentials or other opportunities. All members of the Federal Advisory Council opposed the change as a restriction on their right to discount (Board Minutes, September 21, 1954, 2–8). Defending the change in language, Governor Mills explained that a System study of the discount mechanism had shown that in 1952–53, "active use of the discount window . . . had provided additional reserves . . . in a super-abundant amount which had the effect of counteracting the restrictive open market policy" (ibid., 4). This contradicted Sproul's interpretation of borrowing and the interpretation of changes in free reserves, where an increase in borrowing indicated more restrictive policy. No one mentioned the inconsistency at the time, and no one mentioned that the Federal Reserve could raise the discount rate to restrict borrowing.

To mollify the bankers, the Board issued a statement that the "revised foreword is designed merely to restate and clarify certain guiding principles . . . [and] is not intended to further restrict or restrain access by member banks to the credit facilities of the Federal Reserve banks" (Annual Report, 1955, 83). This statement is, at best, misleading. In their discussion with the Federal Advisory Council, both bankers and Board members described the change as a response to the heavy use of the discount window in 1952–53.

44. Ralph Young, deputy research director at the time, summarized discount policy in 1952–53, a period with relatively large borrowing.

> It was definitely an experiment . . . in the pattern of System discount tradition. . . . The System followed the market rather than leading it and penalizing the use of reserve bank credit by means of the discount rate. It relied on the tradition against borrowing and the reluctance to stay in debt to restrain undue credit expansion. And the System was surprised that borrowing for profit went on and that monetary expansion during the period of build-up in member bank debt was so rapid. (FOMC Minutes, August 23, 1955, 15)

The Board reconsidered the role of discounting in its 1957 Annual Report, eliminating many of its long-standing beliefs. The System had changed discount rates eight times in 1955–57, seven increases and one reduction. The Board, at last, recognized that when one bank repaid its borrowing, another might be forced to borrow, so that aggregate reserves did not decline. And it recognized that increased borrowing offset open market sales and that the "attitude of member banks toward operating with borrowed resources varies from bank to bank" (Annual Report, 1957, 12). The System discouraged reliance on extended borrowing (ibid.). Many banks avoided borrowing because pressures to repay required portfolio adjustment. Discount rate increases reinforced banks' reluctance to borrow (ibid., 13).

The Board found no conflict between discounting and open market operations. Market and discount rates were interdependent. By raising the discount rate above the market rate, the System encouraged banks to adjust by selling securities instead of discounting. Short-term rates rose, reinforcing an open market policy of sales.

The Board did not reconcile this view of discounting with its use of free reserves as an indicator of ease and restraint. If additional discounting increased reserves, as the Board now recognized, a reduction in free reserves that increased total reserves was expansive, a point the Board did not recognize.

Other Changes

The Federal Reserve Act of 1913 incorporated the real bills doctrines and the gold standard as guiding principles. The use of Treasury bills as the principal asset used to adjust reserve positions could not be reconciled with the real bills view that inflation was the inevitable consequence of basing credit expansion on government securities (or other speculative assets).[45] In the 1950s, the System held a loose quantitative view. Inflation resulted from too much money growth and budget deficits.

Belief in the automaticity and benign properties of the gold standard faded also. As a member of the International Monetary Fund, the United States committed to maintain the price of gold at $35 an ounce. It committed also to the primarily domestic goals of the Employment Act. The latter dominated any concern about international effects of monetary policy in

45. By the late 1990s, the System had moved so far from its roots that many in the System expressed concern that budget surpluses and debt reduction would remove all outstanding Treasury bills. How could they conduct policy they asked, without government securities? The issue disappeared with the budget deficits in the early twenty-first century.

the 1950s.[46] The principal international concern was restoration of currency convertibility for current account transactions. With its large gold stock, unchallenged productivity, small share of exports or imports, and positive net exports, the international payments position seemed unimportant. By the end of the decade, however, concern about the capital outflow began to rise.[47]

Nothing in the 1950s compares to the Board's Tenth Annual Report or the Riefler (1930) and Burgess (1927) books. The staff's most complete statement of the role of monetary policy and the monetary transmission process is *The Federal Reserve System: Purposes and Functions*. The third edition (Board of Governors of the Federal Reserve System, 1954) summarizes staff views and understanding at the time.[48]

The staff's discussion of monetary policy was more complete than mainstream academic views of that time. In the Federal Reserve's best statements, monetary policy affects the economy mainly by changing investment in inventories and durable capital, but also by affecting mortgage lending and housing. These responses occur through four channels: borrowing and lending, changes in the money stock and cash balances, changes in expectations, and changes in capital values and wealth (Board of Governors 1954, 123–36).

Although the various elements were not combined in an explicit framework, the emphasis given to expectations, capital values, and relative prices (or capital values) suggests an underlying sophistication that anticipated much future research. Mixed with these elements were residues of earlier ideas, including banks' reluctance to borrow from the Federal Reserve. Growth of the money stock (usually currency and demand deposits) had a more prominent role than in the 1920s. At each FOMC meeting, the staff reported on growth of money and credit. Martin, Riefler, and others believed that to avoid inflation, money should grow at about the growth rate

46. Sproul wrote to Karl Bopp (Philadelphia): "We have been able largely to disregard our balance of payments in pursuing monetary policy" (letter, Sproul to Bopp, Sproul papers, FOMC Correspondence, May 16, 1955). Sproul then contrasted the United States with foreign central banks that daily "have to follow the foreign exchanges and the balance of payments" (ibid., 1).

47. In 1954, Chairman Martin testified against legislation to permit redemption of currency in gold, ending the embargo on private sales of gold. He acknowledged the safeguard that the proposal offered, "but there is no magic formula and no simple device." And "there is no danger, present or prospective, that this measure would avert." Other bills would have created a free gold market and restored bimetallism (Martin speeches, March 29, 1954).

48. Ralph Young supervised preparation. He replaced Emanuel Goldenweiser, who had supervised the two earlier editions.

of real output.[49] There was general recognition that the price level could change for many reasons, but excessive money growth was necessary for sustained inflation.

In response to a questionnaire sent as part of hearings chaired by Senator Ralph Flanders (Vermont), the New York bank wrote: "Although it is the general policy of the Federal Reserve System to promote a growth in the money supply in keeping with the long-term growth of the economy, it is unnecessary and impracticable for the System to attempt to enforce a change in the money supply month-by-month and year-by-year, either precisely parallel to the changes in overall economic activity, or at a rate of growth equal to the assumed or expected long-term growth of the economy" (Q & A Flanders, draft for question 4, Sproul papers, November 1954). The response explained why short- and long-term deviations occur with changes in velocity and economic activity and wartime budget finance. Wartime finance, the response said, produced a large increase in money that the economy absorbed as desired cash balances during the postwar economic expansion.

Again, in a letter to Senator Douglas, Sproul repeated that inflation had many causes, including excessive money growth. To guide central bankers, he proposed that "growth in the money supply should parallel the *long-term* growth in production activity. That calls for a policy of resisting too rapid expansion of bank credit and the money supply in boom periods . . . and resisting credit contraction in periods of recession" (letter, Sproul to Douglas, Sproul papers, Board of Governors Correspondence 1942–1956, August 31, 1953). Earlier, he had written, "Inflation can arise from a variety of causes even though the end result is too much money chasing too few goods" (letter, Sproul to Winthrop Aldrich, Sproul papers, Correspondence A–M, November 7, 1951)

---

49. One of the statements came in response to a question from Senator Joseph O'Mahoney (Wyoming).

> Senator O'Mahoney. What is the yardstick by which you measure the amount of money that ought to be created?
> Mr. Martin. Well, the yardstick—there is no firm yardstick, but we have looked on the normal growth of the country in terms of 2, 3, 4 percent, no fixed formula, and we have added to the money supply for that purpose. (Joint Economic Committee, 1956b, 127)

On another occasion, Martin described the proper rate of money growth: "Some people think the money supply ought to grow at the rate of 3 percent a year, while others may say 2 percent a year, while others may say 2 percent or 5 percent; I do not profess to know what the figure ought to be. . . . Growth in the money supply must be regulated according to the country's real needs" (Martin speeches, Pennsylvania Bankers 62nd Annual Convention, May 11, 1956, 10–11).

Emphasis on the role of sustained money growth as a cause of inflation appeared frequently in this period. This was a marked departure from the 1920s, when the System dismissed the roles of money and claimed to rely on the gold standard to control inflation, and the 1960s and 1970s, when money growth received little attention or was again dismissed as unimportant. The greater success at controlling inflation in the 1950s may reflect the presence at the Federal Reserve of Sproul, Riefler, and Thomas, all of whom gave prominence in their analysis to the long-term growth of money relative to output. All three left the Federal Reserve before major inflation started in the mid-1960s. Other voices, such as Malcolm Bryan (Atlanta), and Delos C. Johns, Darryl Francis, and Homer Jones (St. Louis), were unable to influence policy, in part because some of the Board's staff and others dismissed their views.[50]

There were two major shortcomings in the analysis of money. First was the failure to analyze the linkage between short-term changes in free reserves and longer-term changes in money and credit and between monetary aggregates and output and the price level. The Federal Reserve did not link its actions affecting interest rates and free reserves to demands for money and free reserves. Meigs (1962), Dewald (1963), and Brunner and Meltzer (1964) showed that free reserves were not closely related to the money stock (or other monetary and credit aggregates). The Federal Reserve in the 1950s carefully monitored, and reported, how much money, credit, and other variables changed. It made no effort to separate the effects of changes in supply and demand or to learn how these aggregates changed when free reserves changed. And it did not recognize or discuss the inconsistency between procyclical money growth resulting from using free reserves and short-term interest rates as indicators of policy stance and the counter-cyclical stance described in Sproul's letter to Douglas.[51]

The second major weakness was the continued failure to distinguish between real and nominal interest rates. In its handbook on changes in interest rates (Board of Governors, 1954), the staff offered useful discussion of changes in relative interest rates and asset returns, but there is not a word about adjusting market rates to remove the effect of inflation. Neither the staff nor the Board connected their discussion of inflationary anticipations

50. An early example is Sproul's comment to Roosa in 1959 about Malcolm Bryan (Atlanta). He described Bryan's views as "a legacy of a fundamentalist religious slant as bent and twisted by the University of Chicago, but it is also a consequence of his having had no experience in a money market" (letter, Sproul to Roosa, Sproul papers, Correspondence from Roosa, April 27, 1959).

51. Changing short-term interest rates frequently and counter-cyclically eliminated the inconsistency in the 1990s.

to changes in interest rates. High nominal rates were evidence of restrictive monetary policy. This error is one of the major reasons for the failure of monetary policy to control inflation in the 1960s and early 1970s.

Tradition or history is one reason for relying mainly on free reserves or borrowing as a policy target instead of an interest rate. No less important was concern that an interest rate target invited pressure from congressional populists, especially Congressman Wright Patman, to keep interest rates low. That explains the practice, common at the time, of denying that the Federal Reserve controlled any interest rate. "Traditionally, reserve banking operations are not directed toward establishing any particular level or pattern of interest rates" (ibid., 143).[52] A claim that the Federal Reserve controlled a short-term rate seemed certain to invite Patman and others to demand lower rates. Later, Volcker's decision to target reserves in 1979–82 avoided some criticism by attributing the rise in interest rates to market forces, not the Federal Reserve.

Another major difference between the 1920s or 1930s and the 1950s is in the choice of framework. In the earlier period, policymakers appealed to the real bills doctrine and the principles in the Tenth Annual Report to support their actions and to oppose intervention. In the 1950s, there was neither a common framework nor a common set of beliefs about monetary policy. The main common elements were the free reserve target and the loose commitment to full employment and price stability. The connection between the two was left to individual judgment, and there was considerable skepticism within FOMC about the accuracy of free reserves as a measure of ease and restraint.

The absence of agreement on a framework reinforced the very strong pressure to concentrate attention on recent events and near-term prospects, heightening the short-term focus and neglecting longer-term consequences. Although the Riefler rule prohibited forecasts, the staff occasionally looked ahead a few months. Martin had little confidence in economic (or other) theories of longer-term consequences. Martin's focus was on the money market. Although some FOMC members were aware that policy actions had effects that lasted longer than three weeks, these concerns did not affect the policy process or FOMC actions.[53]

52. The FOMC minutes contain many criticisms of free reserves. Even New York, which often favored relying on free reserves in the instructions to the manager, acknowledged the difficulty of specifying the level precisely. New York wanted to solve the problem by making the manager's discretionary authority explicit.

53. Martin often used a metaphor to describe how policy operated. "I think of it, that flow of money and credit, as I do a river or stream or a brook. . . . Our purpose in trying to see that this brook, this stream has a little bit of gurgle . . . that it doesn't overflow the banks and flood the fields" (Martin testimony, v. 1, Board Records, January 12, 1956, 7–8). He used the

The System did not dismiss longer-term concerns entirely. For example, in 1959 Delos Johns (St. Louis) urged that the System use the money stock as the principal guide to policy operations. Woodlief Thomas responded: "The money supply is the principal *quantitative* end of Federal Reserve policy, because System operations exercise their influence primarily through the money supply, although there are broader and more complex ultimate objectives" (Thomas to FOMC members, Board Records February 25, 1959, 1; emphasis in the original).[54]

Others faulted the System for its lack of quantitative targets but did not want to use money or money growth as part of the manager's instruction. Balderston shared Bryan's concern about control of the manager's actions, but he usually favored free reserves as a target (memo, Balderston to FOMC, FOMC Minutes, April 3, 1957).[55] Still others favored total reserves as a more accurate quantitative target. But some opposed precise quantitative targets, preferring to give the manager discretion and permit him to exercise judgment. The New York bank was in the latter group. Though it claimed to favor more precise instructions, it would point out the pitfalls of being overly precise. Hayes's response to Balderston developed this reasoning (memo, Hayes to FOMC, FOMC Minutes, April 15, 1957).

Independence and Political Influence

The Federal Reserve had always been aware that Congress could change its status, but political influences inserted themselves in the 1950s to a much greater degree than in the 1920s. Congressional approval of the Employment Act made a major difference. The Federal Reserve had for-

---

same metaphor when I interviewed him in 1963 as a temporary staff member of the House Banking Committee. Throughout his term, the minutes show no evidence of his interest in a more precise framework.

54. The memo then discusses the importance of the money supply for System operations and the difficulty of interpreting short-term changes. He observed correctly that "[i]t is not possible, or even desirable, to relate day-to-day or even week-to-week operations precisely to the money supply" (Thomas to FOMC members, Board Records, February 25, 1959, 2). However, money supply affected short-term projections of reserve needs by the Board's staff. Deviations of money from its projected path gave the FOMC reason to change the path. But Thomas did not provide a means of making the change effective by linking it to the current target.

55. Balderston's memo recognizes several weaknesses. First, correlation between free reserves and Treasury bill rates was low for short periods and even for a month or a quarter. Second, large borrowing may supply reserves and change the interpretation of a decline in free reserves. Third, he cited other changes in borrowing that affect interpretation of a given level of free reserves. Fourth, he recognized that the interpretation of a given supply of free reserves would vary with the strength of demand for free reserves (Balderston to FOMC, FOMC Minutes, April 3, 1957). Comments about the relation of free reserves to interest rates suggest that the System paid attention to interest rates but would not say so publicly.

merly denied that it could control output and the price level. Now it shared responsibility with other agencies for economic welfare. Martin often described this mix as independence within the government.[56]

New responsibilities changed the meaning of Federal Reserve independence in practice. In its early days, President Wilson started a tradition of not interfering in Federal Reserve decisions. Although Treasury Secretaries were members of the Board, *ex officio*, until 1936 they usually did not attend Board meetings. The Roosevelt administration ended this tradition of independence. Before the war, and even more during the war, Secretary Morgenthau wanted low nominal interest rates. In the 1930s, he either used, or threatened to use, the Treasury's trust accounts and the Exchange Stabilization Fund (ESF) to buy securities and lower interest rates if the Federal Reserve did not support his policy or accept his judgment. This threat may have been empty. The resources of the ESF were limited. The Federal Reserve, however, avoided conflict, sacrificing independence. During the war, the Federal Reserve agreed to maintain a pattern of interest rates after April 1942. In effect, the Treasury could veto interest rate changes.

The large outstanding debt after World War II, its short maturity, and the need to refund or borrow frequently made Treasury Secretaries and Budget Directors very conscious of interest rate changes. Although the Federal Reserve had been freed of Treasury control in 1951, its supporters in Congress favored some type of coordination with the administration. Independence did not mean to them that the Federal Reserve would ignore debt management (Subcommittee on Monetary, Credit, and Fiscal Policies, 1950, 4).

Chairman Martin worked hard to avoid involvement in decisions about the choice of debt instruments, and he succeeded in reestablishing and strengthening greater separation of monetary and debt management policies. The meaning he assigned to independence, however, did not go so far as to make the Treasury pay whatever interest rate the market might demand. From the very beginning of his tenure, Martin saw the Federal Reserve and the Treasury "as partners in promoting the welfare of the government securities market" (Senate Committee on Banking and Currency, 1951, 5).

Martin explained what he meant by "independent within the government." The Federal Reserve had to recognize that

56. The view was general within the System. "The Federal Reserve does not have, never has had, and never has claimed to have an independence in monetary affairs which divorces it from the general economic policies of the Government" (Sproul, 1964, 236). However, Sproul said "an independent Federal Reserve System is one that is protected from narrow partisan influence" (Joint Economic Committee, 1952, 508).

Congress appropriates the money; they levy the taxes; they determine whether or not there should be deficit financing. The Treasury then is charged with the responsibility of raising whatever funds the Government needs to meet its requirements. . . . I do not believe it is consistent to have an agent so independent that it can undertake, if it chooses, to defeat the financing of a large deficit, which is a policy of the Congress. (Subcommittee on Monetary, Credit, and Fiscal Policies, 1950, 231)

Martin also said repeatedly that the Federal Reserve could not refuse to finance a deficit that Congress approved. He told a news magazine, "[W]e have no obligation to finance the Treasury at just any rate, arbitrarily chosen. But we do have an obligation to see that the expenditures which are authorized by the Congress are met" (quoted in Kettl 1986, 84). He never went beyond ambiguous statements of this kind. He made it clear that to him independence did not permit the Federal Reserve to prevent inflation if the administration and Congress ran large budget deficits. His was a very narrow definition of independence. He could not prevent inflation if the deficit remained large, so he could not meet the primary responsibility of an independent central bank—to maintain money's purchasing power.

Even keel policy was one way of contributing to Treasury finance. Governor Balderston defined an even keel as "no greater ease or tightness at the end of the financing period than at the beginning, with the supplying of only such additional reserves during the period as will take care of the additional drain on reserves caused by the financing itself. Theoretically the amount of such reserves required would be 18 per cent of the amount of each financing taken by the banks" (FOMC Minutes, August 18, 1959, 37). Under this policy, reserves increased during a Treasury offering to keep interest rates from rising in that period, and the reserves remained in the market after the financing ended, unless the System explicitly changed policy.[57]

The role that Martin accepted as part of the Federal Reserve's responsibility went beyond even keel. Congress decided expenditures and tax rates. If the Treasury had to borrow to finance a deficit, he believed the Federal Reserve had to assist, mindful of the inflationary consequences

---

57. Bremner (2004, 79) quotes Martin as saying in 1953, "The System no longer needs to inject periodically into credit markets large amounts of reserve funds which are difficult to withdraw before they have resulted in undesirable credit development." This misinterprets even keel. Knipe (1965, 27) noted that "even keel" did not have a single definition. He listed four: "(1) an unchanged level of free reserves, (2) a changed level of free reserves but changed in such a way that the Board thinks the market effect is unchanged, (3) an unchanged level of some interest rate, or bond yield, or group of interest rates and bond yields, or (4) steady progress in a policy direction already determined." As Knipe noted, ambiguity applied as well to terms such as neutrality. In practice the manager made the final decision, and the FOMC and Treasury would not complain unless the Treasury issue failed.

of too much assistance. His initial thought was: "The Federal Reserve must do everything in its power to see that the Treasury is successfully financed, but neither the Treasury nor the Federal Reserve should succumb to the temptation to ignore the judgments of the market through our price mechanism in arriving at financial decisions" (Martin speeches, Speech to the 18th Annual Convention of the Independent Bankers Association, May 19, 1952, 3).

What if the Congress continued to run persistent deficits? Martin believed that there were limits beyond which the Federal Reserve could not insist upon its independence. Independence within government meant to him that the Federal Reserve would help the Treasury sell its securities. He explained this responsibility in a 1956 speech:

> The Federal Reserve's task of managing the money supply must be conducted with recognition of the Treasury's requirements, for two reasons: One, the Federal Reserve has a duty to prevent financial panics, and a panic surely would follow if the Government, which represents the people as a whole, could not pay its bills; second, it would be the height of absurdity if the Federal Reserve were to say in effect that it didn't think Congress was acting properly in authorizing expenditures, and therefore it wouldn't help enable the Treasury to finance them. (Martin speeches, Speech to Pennsylvania Bankers, May 11, 1956, 10)

Martin recognized that the Treasury had a responsibility also. It should conduct its operations in ways that did not jeopardize economic and currency stability. What if it did not? "Nobody has given the Federal Reserve the authority to tell the Congress what appropriations it should make, and the Treasury financing must always be a major consideration of our policy. But that does not mean that either the Treasury or the Federal Reserve can ignore the market and dictate what the rate should be" (Martin speeches, January 12, 1956, 19).

"Independence within the government" was not just a nice phrase. Repeatedly, Martin emphasized that the Federal Reserve's obligation to help the Treasury differed from its responsibility toward the private sector. By implication the Federal Reserve was the residual buyer of government debt, whether new offerings or refinancings. The Federal Reserve was not obligated to avoid interest rate increases that it regarded as appropriate or to prevent the failure of private offers. It could raise interest rates even when the market held new private issues awaiting placement.[58]

58. The Federal Reserve was less independent than the German Bundesbank. Even a strong chancellor like Konrad Adenauer learned that he lost public support when he criticized

Beyond citing the role of Congress in voting the budget, Martin never ex-plained why the Federal Reserve had to limit interest rate increases during Treasury financings. Failure of a Treasury issue (as sometimes happened) was an embarrassment, not a calamity. The Treasury would have to return to the market with a more attractive offer. Even if the Federal Reserve would supply reserves to prevent failure, interest rates could be raised as required for stability once the market absorbed the issue. Further, the Federal Re-serve and the Treasury could substantially reduce the risk of "failures" by auctioning Treasury notes and bonds. Both resisted this solution until the early 1970s perhaps out of concern for a failed attempt in the 1930s.

This interpretation of independence suggests one reason why the Fed-eral Reserve under Martin permitted inflation to increase in the 1960s. And it explains an important difference between Federal Reserve policies in the 1950s and 1960s. Martin was very concerned about inflation and was willing to tolerate three recessions in the 1950s to avoid or reduce inflation. Several times, he raised interest rates enough to slow or stop a private investment boom. In contrast, he was slow to respond to inflation in 1957 and after 1965. Despite his concerns and frequent warnings, ex-pressed publicly and privately, consumer prices rose 6 percent in his last twelve months at the Federal Reserve.

This interpretation may explain, also, why the Federal Reserve com-plained frequently about deficit finance. In the view of its principals, deficit finance required higher interest rates, an unpopular action always subject to criticism in Congress. Deficit finance also raised the issue of Federal Reserve independence and, on its interpretation, could make control of inflation impossible within the range of interest rates it considered politi-cally feasible.

Later, the Federal Reserve and other central bankers learned about the distinction between real and nominal rates. They could not prevent mar-ket interest rates from rising by limiting increases in short-term rates. At most, they could delay increases in real rates and only as long as markets did not anticipate that inflation would rise higher.

The government's commitment to maintain maximum employment and purchasing power in the Employment Act created pressures of a different kind for policy. Vivid memories of the Great Depression, and alleged Republican responsibility for it, made the Eisenhower adminis-tration, including the president, sensitive to rising unemployment and

the bank for raising interest rates in 1956. See Neumann (1999, 290–91). The occasion, how-ever, was an increase in private demand. But the Bundesbank used the incident to establish its independence and could defend itself against political pressure thereafter.

falling output. In the 1952 presidential campaign, Eisenhower pledged to use the power of the federal government to prevent another depression (Eisenhower, 1963, 304). During the 1953–54 recession, he "talked to the secretary of the Treasury in order to develop real pressure on the Federal Reserve Board for loosening credit still further . . . Secretary Humphrey promised to put the utmost pressure on Chairman Martin of the Federal Reserve Board in order to get a greater money supply throughout the country" (Ferrell, 1981, 278).

The main channel of communications became weekly meetings of the Federal Reserve Chairman and the Treasury Secretary. Later, meetings with the Council of Economic Advisers provided another channel for exchange of views. After 1956, President Eisenhower began periodic meetings with Martin, Secretary Robert Anderson (who replaced Humphrey in 1957), and CEA Chairman Raymond Saulnier, who replaced Burns. After the 1960 election, the Budget Director joined the group. In the Kennedy administration, the group became known as the Quadriad. Martin was careful to remain nonpartisan in these meetings and to avoid making commitments about future monetary policy, but he did not always succeed in the 1960s. Even if he avoided commitments, efforts to coordinate policy further limited independence.[59] This challenge became intense in the 1960s, when Martin tried to coordinate actions with President Johnson and some of his staff. Coordination began as an exchange of information, but it evolved into a restriction on Federal Reserve independence.

Appointments are another method by which the administration could influence the Federal Reserve's decisions. In the early years, many appointees stayed a full term or longer. Salaries declined in real terms, particularly after inflation in World War II and in the 1970s. Opportunities in banking and finance increased. A president might appoint a majority of the Board, but members did not always vote along partisan lines. Loyal appointees could report on the Board's attitudes, as James K. Vardaman did during the System's difficulties in the pre-Accord period, or listen carefully to the administration's position. Two of President Truman's appointees, Mills and Robertson, dissented frequently (Havrilesky and Gildea, 1990, Table 1).

---

59. Sproul opposed formal coordination and regarded the Council of Economic Advisers as "a discredited body in terms of objectivity" (Sproul papers, FOMC meeting comments, July 7, 1952). The reference may be to the Truman council headed at the time by Leon Keyserling, a New Deal economist with strong statist views. New York was very critical of the reports prepared by the Council in part because the Council opposed raising interest rates and favored selective credit controls (memo, Roelse to Sproul, Sproul papers, FOMC Correspondence, January 28, 1952).

The Martin Federal Reserve

By the mid-1950s, Martin had reorganized the Federal Reserve. The Board was more fully in control of the FOMC than at any previous time. Martin had obtained centralization of authority at the Board with the agreement of most reserve banks, and he did so in a way that did not disrupt operations and decisions.

The FOMC became the center for policy decisions. The traditional separation of powers between the Board and the FOMC did not disappear formally. Banks still sent requests for discount rate changes to the Board for decision. The Board decided in advance that it would approve discount rate changes requested by the reserve banks. But the main decision was frequently a collective decision made at the FOMC meeting and ratified by the reserve bank directors for transmission to the Board.

Open market operations remained the main policy instrument most of the time. Martin exerted his influence on these decisions using the "go around" in which members expressed their opinions, and he stated the "consensus." Members rarely challenged the consensus, and Martin was never defeated once the new procedures were in place. Occasionally, he spoke first to structure the discussion. Often he was willing to wait weeks, even months, until a consensus formed. His difficulties in gaining a consensus increased greatly in the 1960s, after Presidents Kennedy and Johnson had appointed a majority of the Board members.

Martin saw himself and the Federal Reserve as the main, perhaps only, force against inflation. He did not want to become what he called a crusader, but he often described the Federal Reserve's role as alone in a struggle against powerful forces, using metaphors about "leaning against the wind" or "taking away the punchbowl." And he often told his colleagues, as in 1957, that "the System was the only instrument of Government that was fighting inflation" (FOMC Minutes, December 17, 1957, 40). When the Democrats made his policies an issue in the 1960 political campaign, he drafted a letter describing his principal objectives: "(1) that a genuine effort be made, by those in authority, to preserve the purchasing power of the dollar that is so vital to our economy and the preservation of our society; and (2) that the Federal Reserve be allowed the freedom from political interference necessary for it to contribute its part to that effort" (draft letter, Martin papers, December 20, 1960).[60]

60. The letter is not addressed and has no salutation or close. The drafting has several corrections and insertions suggesting that Martin typed it personally. The last paragraph contains: "It is these things that matter—not what happens to me" (draft letter, Martin papers, December 20, 1960). This suggests that Martin may have considered resigning or perhaps

Martin offered to resign when Eisenhower became president. He told the president that he was a Democrat. After taking time to consider the decision, Eisenhower asked him to remain. He did not offer to resign after the 1956, 1960, 1964, and 1968 elections, but he considered resigning at other times. In 1960 he explained that Kennedy made monetary policy an issue in the election. The Democrats had argued that monetary policy had been too tight. Therefore, he had an obligation to remain until the end of his term (memo, Tobin to Heller, Gordon, and Solow, Heller papers, May 30, 1961).[61]

The analytic level under Martin in the 1950s did not venture much beyond metaphors and ambiguity.[62] Although the System accepted a role in maintaining full employment and price stability, I have not found any discussion in the 1950s of what these terms meant in practice. Many FOMC members recognized that to control inflation, money growth should equal the average growth of output over several years, but the connection between System policy and money growth remained as imprecise as other relations.

In June 1956, Allan Sproul resigned as president of the New York Federal reserve bank. A New York banker responsible for international lending, Alfred Hayes, replaced him. With Sproul's departure, Martin lost his most skilled and knowledgeable colleague and adversary. In his usual cautious way, with courtesy to others, Martin could direct Federal Reserve actions without facing significant challenge until the 1960s brought a new group of Board members with less concern about inflation, or perhaps greater confidence in their ability to limit it "later."

---

expected President Kennedy to ask for his resignation, since one of Kennedy's advisers, James Tobin, had proposed publicly that Martin be replaced. The letter suggests that Martin understood the importance of independence.

61. Martin had "a fine private job offered to him at that time" (Heller papers, May 30, 1961). Monetary and economic policy were issues in the 1968 election, so Martin did not offer to resign when President Nixon took office.

62. Romer and Romer (2002b) correctly point out that the Federal Reserve generally followed a non-inflationary policy in the 1950s. However, they credit the Federal Reserve with a more coherent analysis than the record suggests. The Federal Reserve responded to rising prices especially if brought about by strong private sector demand, and they relied on some vague relation of money growth to growth of real output as an indicator of inflationary pressure, but their analysis did not go beyond this general level. Often Martin rejected a role for money growth. One apparent reason for the generally successful anti-inflation policy appears in the Romers' figure 3. Most of the time free reserves and short-term interest rates were correlated negatively. The main exception was 1955–57, when inflation rose. Also, standards have changed. Price increases of two or three percentage points were considered serious in the 1950s, especially by Martin. I believe the difference in the size and persistence of budget deficits in the Johnson years compared to the Eisenhower and Kennedy years offers a better explanation of the difference in outcome.

DOMESTIC POLICY ACTIONS, 1951-53

In the months between the start of the Korean War and the Accord, Congress enacted legislation authorizing the Federal Reserve to control the use of credit. The Board reinstituted regulation W, for consumer durables, and regulation X, for real estate credit. It was one thing to allocate such credit during World War II, when production controls limited the amount of durables or housing produced. It was quite another to control credit in a competitive market with firms producing and consumers demanding durables. Regulation induced innovations to circumvent them. The Board's staff summarized the lesson learned:

> [I]ndustry lawyers proved to be highly adept at developing arrangements that effectively circumvented the letter of Reg. W. Fed regulators found themselves lagging far behind industry lawyers, first in ferreting out the loopholes, and then in devising measures to close them. Similar enforcement problems developed in the administration of regulation X.
>
> This generally negative experience with mandating credit allocation problems strongly influenced Fed attitudes. Each time Congress has subsequently proposed new programs for direct credit regulation, Fed officials have taken a negative view of their feasibility. (Stockwell, 1989, 19)[63]

Remembering World War II, President Truman proposed and Congress approved price and wage controls. They remained in effect until 1953, when President Eisenhower ended them.

On March 9, 1951, the Board instituted a Voluntary Credit Restraint Program. Its purpose was to restrain "inflationary tendencies" while financing "the defense program and the essential needs of agriculture, industry, and commerce" (Annual Report, 1951, 85). The underlying notion that loans for speculating, carrying securities, or financing real estate contributed to inflation shows the continuing influence of the real bills doctrine.

Most members of the Board and the bankers on the Federal Advisory Council favored direct controls, at least initially. Governor James Vardaman thought production controls would be more effective, but he voted

---

63. Martin held a very different view when he came to the Board. He told the members of the House Banking and Currency Committee that "selective measures of credit restraint are an effective and necessary supplement to general credit measures" (Martin testimony, House Banking and Currency Committee, May 10, 1951, 3). His 1956 testimony records his change of opinion. After listing some benefits, he opposed use of selective credit controls except in "recognized emergencies." Controls, he said, interfere with resource allocation and are difficult to administer and enforce without public acceptance and support (Testimony, Joint Committee on the Economic Report, Board Records, February 7, 1956). Martin did not use real bills arguments in his testimony. He described selective controls as a supplement to general controls, not a substitute.

for the credit control program. Little more than a year later, the Board suspended the voluntary program, on the recommendation of its advisory committee. A few weeks later, it suspended controls on consumer credit (Board Minutes, May 2, 1952). Formal authorization for consumer credit controls expired on June 30, 1952. Real estate credit controls continued until September 16, 1952, when housing starts remained below 1.2 million for the third month.[64]

Nevertheless, the Board removed controls reluctantly. Sproul later wrote that "the regulation of consumer credit was first weakened, and eventually abandoned, by Congressional action, contrary to the recommendations of the Federal Reserve System" (letter to Sumner Slichter, Sproul papers, September 29, 1952).[65] General price controls remained in effect.

At about the same time, the Board considered, but did not adopt, a reduction in margin requirements for purchasing and carrying securities. The governors agreed that the volume of stock market credit, about $1.3 billion, was not excessive. Those who opposed the reduction argued that the Treasury would have to borrow and that private borrowing had increased.[66] (Board Minutes, June 11, 1952, 12–14; July 31, 1952, 7) Margin requirements remained at 75 percent until February 21, 1953, when the Board reduced the percentage to 50 percent.

Monetary Actions, 1951–53

In retrospect, the first two years after the Accord were a period of economic expansion with low inflation or stable prices. Once the boom in consumer and government military spending slowed, real GNP growth fell from 5 to 6 percent in the middle quarters of 1951 to a 2 to 3 percent annual rate for most of 1952. Consumer prices, subject to price controls until 1953, rose at an annual rate of 1 to 2 percent. The Federal Reserve avoided the postwar deflation, a feature of postwar experience after World War I and, earlier, in Britain after the Napoleonic Wars.

Deficit finance had a modest influence on monetary policy. The government budget had a $6 billion surplus in fiscal 1951 and a modest deficit

64. Amendments to the Defense Production Act in 1952 authorized the Board to remove the controls, with the concurrence of the Housing and Home Finance Administrator, after three months of relatively slow housing starts. The Board had opposed the language of the Defense Production Act authorizing control of real estate credit as unclear. "Our experience . . . has been such as to show that many questions arise" (Board Minutes, March 23, 1951, 11).

65. The letter was a very critical response to articles by Sumner Slichter in popular magazines criticizing the Federal Reserve for not being more aggressive about controlling credit. Slichter was a well-known Harvard professor of labor economics.

66. Governor Vardaman favored the reduction, arguing that the decision should be based only on stock market credit, but he voted with the majority.

in fiscal 1952, despite the war and continued foreign assistance under the Marshall Plan. For the first time, war finance was not inflationary. The Accord created some uncertainty about future interest rates but reduced uncertainty about future inflation. The stock market responded by falling after the Accord, then resumed its rise. Total returns to common stocks (dividends plus capital gains) reached 22 percent in 1951 and 16 percent in 1952.

The Accord provided for a gradual change, not a sudden wrench in policy. Observers at the time saw the agreement as a modest step that settled a conflict over long-term interest rates (Morris, 1951, 1). The text of the agreement encouraged that interpretation. It first announced a new twenty-nine-year, non-marketable bond with a 2.75 percent coupon issued to replace 2.5 percent marketable bonds that the Federal Reserve had been buying to prevent the bonds from going below par. The next paragraphs referred cautiously to the Federal Reserve's increased role. If private holders tried to sell long-term securities, only "a limited volume of open market purchases would be made after the exchange offering was announced" (Annual Report, 1951, 100). The Federal Reserve pledged to maintain orderly markets at scaled-down prices. It pledged to "immediately reduce or discontinue purchases of short-term securities and permit the short-term market to adjust to a position at which banks would depend upon borrowing at the Federal Reserve to make needed adjustment in their reserves" (ibid., 100).

The immediate outcome differed considerably from the promise. The FOMC held more bills and long-term bonds after the Accord than before. The rate of purchase increased. Member bank borrowing remained within a narrow range until mid-1952. Table 2.1 shows average bill and long-term Treasury bond holdings at the Federal Reserve before and after the Accord.

As part of the Accord, the Federal Reserve agreed to keep the discount rate at 1.5 percent until year-end 1951. Discount rates remained unchanged until early 1953. Member bank reserve requirements remained unchanged also between January 1951 and July 1953.[67]

The Accord is described frequently as freeing the Federal Reserve to pursue an independent policy. This is a partial truth. The Accord eliminated the Federal Reserve's commitment to maintain the 2.5 percent long-term rate and any particular pattern of yields. The Federal Reserve could change interest rates, and especially it could raise them. But it retained re-

---

67. In May 1951, the Board considered asking Congress for the authority to set reserve requirements against loans at all insured banks. The Board could not agree on a workable formula, so it did not make the request (Board Minutes, May 22–23, 1951).

Table 2.1 Federal Reserve Holdings of Bills and Bonds ($ millions)

		BILLS, 90 DAYS OR LESS	BONDS, 10 YEARS OR MORE
	1950		
	November	1833	3139
	December	3631	3488
	1951		
	January	1709	2630
	February	1527	2828
Accord			
	March	1727	3483
	April	3092	3859
	May	4525	3983
	June	2128	4111

End-of-month values. After June 1951, the Federal Reserve began to reduce its holdings of long-term bonds.
Source: Board of Governors (1976, 488).

sponsibility for preventing Treasury offerings from failing, and it agreed to supply reserves to permit Treasury notes and bonds to be sold at the price the Treasury offered. Martin called this independence within the government. Martin's achievement was to establish the structure and procedures that gave the Federal Reserve its independence within the constraints set by the budget, congressional pressure, administration exhortation, and the requirements of the Employment Act. By the 1960s, the prevailing political interpretation of the Employment Act constrained monetary policy to achieve a 4 percent unemployment rate.

In the two years following the Accord, the Federal Reserve eased its way gradually into monetary control. It had to relearn control techniques in an environment with a large, outstanding government debt. It had to become convinced that changes in interest rates, credit, and money influenced the pace of economic activity and inflation. It had to acquire some sense of the quantitative effects of its actions and the markets' reactions. And it worried about the political response to higher interest rates and policy actions taken independently of the Treasury and the administration.[68] It was slow and hesitant at first, but it gained confidence.

68. These concerns were real. The New York bank's staff reported that a note to the 1952 Economic Report of the President, written by Vice Chairman John D. Clark, expressed "violent opposition to the actions taken by the System which have resulted in higher interest rates" (memo, Roelse to Sproul, Sproul papers, FOMC Correspondence, January 28, 1952, 1). The report itself supported the System's actions as a contribution "to the relative stability of the last nine months" (ibid., 1). In Congress, the Patman committee issued its report early in 1952. Sproul's discussion described the report as "pretty reasonable" (Sproul papers, FOMC meeting comments, July 7, 1952, 1). Sproul expressed concern, however, about proposed

Table 2.2   Interest Rates after the Accord (percent)

WEEK ENDING	NEW ISSUES 90-DAY BILLS	3–5 YEAR TREASURY	LONG-TERM TREASURY
1951			
March 3	1.39	1.69	2.40
March 30	1.53	2.05	2.51
June 30	1.53	2.02	2.66
Dec. 29	1.86	2.24	2.74
1952			
June 28	1.68	2.09	2.62
Dec. 27	2.23	2.36	2.79
1953			
June 27	1.95	2.81	3.09

Source: Board of Governors (1976).

Discounting and open market purchases and sales were the Federal Reserve's principal means of affecting the money market. Almost a month passed before the Federal Reserve allowed interest rates on long-term bonds to rise from 2.40 percent, in the week of the Accord, to 2.5 percent. In the first month of the Accord, the System bought nearly $400 million of long-term bonds to avoid a sharp price break. By June 30, the average rate on long-term bonds reached 2.66 percent. Table 2.2 shows the rise in interest rates from the Accord to June 1953.

Interest rates rose at all maturities. By the standards of later years, the rise seems moderate. By the standards of the times, it was less so. Interest rates had not changed as much in any six-month or two-year period for decades, nor had they reached the 3 percent level since the early 1930s.[69]

The Federal Reserve used member bank borrowing (discounts and advances) and free reserves as policy indicators. During 1951, member bank

consultation with the president and the administration if "set up by Executive Order and under [the] chairmanship of Chairman of the Council of Economic Advisers, a discredited body in terms of objectivity" (ibid., 2). Sproul also expressed concern about the recommendation that labor members be appointed to the Board of Governors and the banks' boards of directors.

69. Initially, rates changed slowly, as noted in the text. At the April 5 FOMC meeting, the account manager talked about pegging the long-term bond at $99 by purchasing as much as $50 million (FOMC Minutes, April 5, 1951, 4). The Executive Committee did not agree on whether rates should rise slowly or quickly. Ray Gidney, president of the Cleveland bank, recalled that in 1920 bonds had fallen rapidly to $82 once the Federal Reserve removed the peg. John H. Williams, from the New York bank, favored rapid decline. Chairman Martin acknowledged that the $99 floor acted as a new peg. That had to be avoided, but the System "must be in there aggressively helping [buying] to make the market" (ibid., 7). The decision gave the account manager instructions to "maintain an orderly market" after the Treasury completed its refunding.

borrowing generally remained below excess reserves. The Federal Reserve interpreted positive free reserves, between $100 and $500 million, as evidence of relative ease.

The first signs of a major change in procedures came in mid-1952. As the Federal Reserve proposed in the Accord, and repeated at FOMC meetings, it returned to the classical approach of relying on member bank borrowing to adjust reserve positions and the money market.[70] From mid-1952 to May 1953, member banks borrowed more heavily than at any time since the early 1920s. Weekly borrowing remained above $1 billion for most of the year, with a peak of $1.8 billion in mid-December 1952 to provide the seasonal increase. Free reserves remained negative.

At 1.5 percent, discount rates remained about 0.8 percentage points below the rate on prime commercial paper. Borrowing had become profitable for the first time since the 1920s. The Riefler-Burgess framework claimed that banks borrowed for need and not for profit, so the Federal Reserve, at first, regarded the borrowing as evidence of robust demand and tight money.[71] After months of heavy borrowing, it began to restrict borrowing by raising rates and later discouraged banks from using the discount window to adjust their position. In January 1953, discount rates increased to 2 percent at all reserve banks.[72] Borrowing declined but remained above $600 million until open market rates began to fall in the summer of 1953.

Annualized growth of the monetary base offers a different interpretation of policy thrust. Base growth rose from 2 to 3 percent in 1951 to 3 to 5 percent in 1952. As on many other occasions, nominal interest rates and

70. Members of FOMC, including Chairman Martin, often criticized the organization of the market in which the Federal Reserve conducted open market operations (FOMC Minutes, May 7, 1951, 1–2). The FOMC did its transactions with "recognized" dealers. The New York bank favored this arrangement because the recognized dealers provided them with information about the market and about the individual dealer's positions and transactions. The manager talked to two or three dealers about the market each morning before the market opening. Chairman Martin's concern was that the manager gave information to the dealers. Allan Sproul urged the New York staff to study the dealer market and propose changes. At the May 17 FOMC meeting, Martin chose to chair the study and keep control of the study at the Board, another of his efforts to shift control and decisions away from New York.

71. "The discount mechanism, while supplying reserve funds temporarily, tends to discourage expansion of bank credit. While banks are in debt, they are under pressure to repay and hence are likely to be conservative in expanding their own loans" (Annual Report, 1952, 5). Knipe (1965, 85) mistakenly describes the increase in borrowing as evidence of tighter policy following publication of the Patman committee report. Borrowing increased from $365 million in April to more than $1 billion in July. Annual growth of the monetary base rose from 3.67 to 4.52 percent in the same period.

72. The Board also controlled the ceiling rate on V-loans to defense contractors. Once the discount rate increased, the American Bankers Association asked for an increase in the ceiling rate on V-loans. The Board declined (Board Minutes, January 28, February 6, April 27, May 12, May 19 and 20, 1953).

free reserves suggested that policy had tightened; growth of the monetary base suggested policy had eased.

The Accord did not cause an abrupt change in policy discussion. The FOMC continued, at first, to focus on debt management and long-term interest rates. It continued to offer advice to the Treasury. Relations improved; the Treasury more readily accepted the committee's suggestions about the pricing and maturity of its issues. Independence did not prevent Board members from participating in Treasury meetings (Board Minutes, February 19, 1952, 13–14).

The Treasury's offer in April 1951 of a 2.75 percent non-marketable bond, callable in 1975, enabled the Treasury to exchange $13.5 billion of the 2.5 percent bonds callable in 1967. The Open Market Account took $5.6 billion (41 percent).[73] Thereafter, the Federal Reserve allowed the interest rate to adjust upward. By late June, the longest Treasury security sold at a discount from par value of $3.25 per $100 (FOMC Minutes, June 27, 1951).

The System and the Treasury tried to balance several different objectives. The average maturity of government debt had declined during the pegging period. Both believed that extending average maturity required long-term interest rates to rise more than either wanted to accept at the time. Also, the System wanted to let the market determine short-term rates. It had agreed to keep the discount rate unchanged during the transition, and it believed that raising short-term rates would raise long-term rates as holders of long-term debt shifted into short-term securities.[74]

At the May meeting, Woodlief Thomas started the first discussion of objectives in many years by remarking that "inflationary pressures arose from the creation of additional money through credit expansion and through increased turnover of money" (FOMC Minutes, May 17, 1951, 3). Marriner Eccles observed that, with the government budget balanced, the Federal Reserve could prevent inflation if it limited growth of bank reserves (ibid.,

---

73. During the exchange offer in April 1951, the account manager, Robert Rouse, told the Executive Committee that he had purchased the 2.5 percent bonds and anticipated purchasing more to hold the price to $99 during the exchange offer (FOMC Minutes, April 5, 1951, 2). At this time, and for many subsequent years, the FOMC maintained a "stable" bond market, holding rates within a narrow range for two weeks before a Treasury offering and during the offering (ibid., 5). Later this policy was called "neutrality" and, still later, "even keel," discussed earlier.

74. Discussion of Treasury financing often became animated. At the September 25, 1951, meeting of the Executive Committee, Allan Sproul proposed four options to present to the Treasury. Chairman Martin argued against one option and voted against the proposal. The majority voted with Sproul, and Martin duly forwarded the recommendation to the Treasury (Executive Committee Minutes, April 25, 1951, 8–9). There is nothing in the record to suggest that this experience affected his subsequent decision to abolish the Executive Committee.

4). Chairman Martin had little interest in discussions of this kind. He turned the discussion to current operations.

Frequent Treasury refundings interfered with Federal Reserve operations in this as in many subsequent periods. In early June 1951, for example, member bank borrowing increased to $538 million and excess reserves fell. "[T]he money market for the first time in years became tight for an extended period and interest rates moved upward" (Sproul papers, Board of Directors, memo, June 7, 1951, 1). The System "then faced an obligation both in terms of orderly markets and our accord with the Treasury to do whatever we could to assure the success of the financing. The success would be measured in the light of market acceptance of the offering and the climate thus created for future refundings and . . . the so-called attrition" (ibid., 1).

Raising rates encouraged attrition by imposing losses on those who accepted the Treasury offer. To avoid losses the Treasury offered a premium over current rates, but the premium on new issues lowered the prices of outstanding debt. The System's commitment to support the market during refundings required them to buy, at times heavily. Sproul told the New York directors that the Treasury worked with them "in terms of an integrated debt management-credit control program" (ibid., 2). In fact, monetary policy often yielded to debt management as it had before the Accord.

Traditionally, the FOMC decided how to provide the autumn seasonal increase in August or September. In 1951, the FOMC believed that economic expansion would continue, although it expected housing starts to fall. Uncertainty about the amount of defense spending clouded the outlook. Woodlief Thomas added that "the money supply might show a further expansion of as much as $7 billion," nearly 6 percent (Executive Committee Minutes, August 8, 1951, 4–5). This was possibly the first reference to money supply at an FOMC briefing.

The discussion that followed reached a consensus that the System should follow a "neutral" policy. The term neutral policy or neutrality occurs frequently, at the time, without definition. The context suggests that policy is neutral if changes in open market rates do not affect the rate on outstanding Treasury issues. Later, the New York bank's staff defined neutrality as "a policy dedicated to maintaining the volume of bank reserves . . . on an approximately stable level" (Central Subject Files, May 8, 1952, Box 1433). For the rest of the decade and beyond, the conflict continued between the System's wish to remain "neutral" during Treasury refundings and financings and its desire to pursue its goal of low inflation.

Although inflation remained low, the FOMC remained concerned that continued spending by the private sector, wartime deficits, continued Treasury borrowing, and frequent refundings made inflation inevitable.[75] To reduce uncertainty about timing, the Treasury began to put refundings on a regular schedule. Some members of FOMC wanted the Treasury to extend maturity by offering more long-term debt at higher interest rates.

Chairman Martin held a fiscal theory of inflation at the time. He expressed concern that open market operations could not prevent inflation under the anticipated defense spending and projected budget deficit (FOMC Minutes, October 4, 1951, 8). Since he believed that the Federal Reserve had to assist the Treasury in financing the spending that Congress approved, fiscal deficits meant either higher interest rates or additional money creation, usually both. Others added that the administration was unlikely to ask for additional tax increases. Several FOMC members favored higher interest rates to prevent inflation. President Bryan (Atlanta) urged more attention to this longer-term problem and less emphasis on short-term financing. Martin ended the discussion by sidestepping the issue of higher rates and emphasizing the need to attract more money into government securities other than by rate increases (ibid., 10).

The FOMC voted to appoint a committee to study long-term debt management and to recommend policy to the Treasury. In November, it abandoned the pegs it still used, while maintaining a commitment to orderly markets.[76] For the first time since 1942, a Treasury financing had no support. Soon after, President Sproul suggested that the New York directors consider increasing the discount rate (Sproul papers, Board of Directors, December 20, 1951, 1).[77]

Economic activity remained expansive early in 1952, and System discussion anticipated continued high-level activity.[78] The New York bank operated under a directive calling for a neutral policy "under which market forces of supply and demand are permitted to have their effect with a minimum of System intervention except to the extent necessary to promote

75. At about this time, the Board's staff estimated that government spending would rise from $58 to $84 billion in the next two fiscal years, an increase of nearly 50 percent. The actual increase was about 15 percent.

76. It voted "to carry on operations in both short-term and long-term Treasury securities for the purpose of maintaining an orderly market and that the points previously fixed below which long- and short-term issues would not be allowed to decline had been abandoned" (Executive Committee Minutes, November 14, 1951, 2).

77. Earlier, the Federal Advisory Council favored providing additional reserves by reducing reserve requirement ratios (Board Minutes, September 18, 1951, 3). The council frequently pointed to the conflict between policies to restrain credit expansion and government spending and lending programs to assist veterans, farmers, and others to buy houses and farms.

78. At the March 1, 1952, meeting Winfield Riefler, assistant to the chairman, became Secretary of the FOMC.

orderly market conditions" (Executive Committee Minutes, April 4, 1952, 9). The staff interpreted the directive to mean that normally the System would stay out of the market. After some discussion, the Executive Committee agreed to a "somewhat freer interpretation" (ibid., 12). That decision gave the manager more discretion, a result that Martin and some other members would later regret.

At mid-year 1952, the staff said that the economy would maintain "the current balance of high economic activity and low inflation" (FOMC Minutes, June 19, 1952, 7). Concerns remained about Treasury deficits to finance Korean War expenditures. Restraint depended on greater reliance on monetary policy (ibid., 7). The staff suggested a discount rate increase.[79]

The pleasant economic prospects forecast in the spring hid some problems. Governor Rudolph Evans pointed out that the System's objectives included: (1) extending the maturity of the debt by having the Treasury issue more long-term bonds; (2) reducing banks' holdings of governments; and (3) reducing bank loans to slow inflation. The Treasury was reluctant to raise the interest rate.[80] Evans believed that the combined effect of deficits financed with short-term debt and bank credit expansion would bring inflation.

Evans's concerns gained support the following month, when the staff raised its projection for the rest of the year and warned about increasing price pressures (Executive Committee Minutes, July 22, 1952, 3–4). A strike in the steel industry temporarily reduced these pressures, so the FOMC changed its policy stance from neutral. It agreed to "provide some controlled relief [to the market] through open market operations while forcing member banks to increase their borrowing" (ibid., 5). The new policy was, in fact, a modest step toward restriction.

With member bank borrowing above $1 billion, the Executive Committee regarded the market as tight when it met a month later. Staff at New York and Washington suggested that economic growth, Treasury borrowing, and seasonal expansion required $1 to $2 billion of additional reserves. Sproul favored letting member bank borrowing rise above $2 billion. Martin was uncertain. He was inclined to supply more reserves through open market purchases. The decision soon shifted in Martin's direction. The Treasury, on the advice of the Federal Reserve, had issued a

79. The FOMC voted to permit each reserve bank to purchase prime bankers' acceptances at rates set by the FOMC. The first move to coordinate market operations in the 1920s was made to centralize purchases of acceptances (letter, Riefler to Sproul, Sproul papers, June 27, 1952). See volume 1, chapter 4.
80. Attempts to sell long-term bonds without raising rates failed. In June the Federal Reserve purchased $300 million in the market to support a Treasury issue.

fourteen-month 2.125 percent certificate. The issue was not attractive, despite its higher rate, because market rates increased between the decision and the announcement. The Executive Committee felt obligated to support the issue but was uncomfortable with the need to do so.

The FOMC remained unhappy with the choices it had to make between debt management and monetary policy. The Accord had allowed interest rates to rise, but Treasury debt operations continued to influence Federal Reserve actions. Chairman Martin expressed concern that the FOMC strengthened this obligation by continuing to make specific recommendations to the Treasury in a letter signed by the Chairman. The post-Accord arrangement produced harmonious relations with the Treasury, but it took the FOMC back toward fixing rates to assist the Treasury.[81] Despite its concerns, the FOMC did not change its "neutral" policy during the October financing. A change would have required higher interest rates, a step that the committee did not want to take. It continued to support the new certificate issue until October 8, when it voted to restrict operations to the short-term market.

New York, as usual, found an argument for leaving more discretion to the manager and the New York bank. Sproul cited technical problems in carrying out specific instructions. The staff had difficulty foreseeing economic developments, the final guide to credit policy. Also swings in factors affecting reserves showed the administrative difficulties of fixing a pattern or program by committee action (Sproul papers, President's Conference, September 24, 1952, 3). These difficulties may explain some of the short-term variability in data for the period, but they point up the short-term focus. Sproul also complained that the instructions changed frequently. "One time the guide . . . might be interest rates and at another member bank borrowing" (Sproul papers, draft, August 13, 1952). Martin and the Board wanted more control, not less. They did not yet know how to instruct the manager in a way that would maintain control while permitting the manager to respond to daily or hourly changes in the money market.

The expansion of output, credit, and member bank borrowing continued through the fall. In a statement to the Joint Committee on the Economic Report (1954, 7) Martin later described the expansion as a "bubble on top of a boom." The Executive Committee noted that borrowing often exceeded $1.5 billion, but it took no action. Sproul proposed a discount rate increase

81. The Treasury was unhappy also. During the August refunding it had to pay cash (attrition) for 17 percent of the expiring bonds. The Federal Reserve bought an additional 7 percent ($430 million). In the October refunding, attrition was 8 percent, System purchases 17 percent.

at the November meeting. Reversing years of System discussion, he recognized that banks borrow for profit. He told the Executive Committee:

> Borrowing from the Federal Reserve as a deterrent to bank credit expansion is losing its force because of (a) the profit spread, (b) the excess profits tax,[82] (c) the idea that banks are finding it difficult to sell Government securities. (Executive Committee Minutes, November 25, 1952, 8)

Chairman Martin agreed.

Bank credit and member bank borrowing continued to rise. The staff estimate of credit expansion was 50 percent above the anticipated seasonal demand (FOMC Minutes, December 8, 1952, 4). In January, the Philadelphia and Cleveland banks voted to raise their discount rates to 2 percent. Concerned that a boom had started, Chairman Martin took up the requests at the January 9, 1953, Board meeting.

Winfield Riefler spoke first, supporting an increase. He believed a boom had started after the election of a Republican administration and a Congress committed to reducing tax rates. Capital expansion took too many resources relative to consumer durables. Rapid growth of credit sustained the expansion (Board Minutes, January 9, 1953, 4 and 9). Woodlief Thomas favored a small increase also. "[M]ember banks might get in the habit of borrowing and the act of borrowing might not be adequately restrictive" (ibid., 5).

The governors were divided between an increase of 0.25 and 0.5 percentage points. Martin said "it would have been better if the rate had been raised some time ago" (ibid., 11). He favored a 0.25 increase. "[A]n increase to 2.25 percent might be likely to create a turmoil in the market" (13).

The lengthy discussion at this meeting shows prevailing opinion on the role of monetary policy. Elements of the Riefler-Burgess framework carried over from the 1920s.[83] The Board and the staff had not yet developed Keynesian views, with the possible exception of Governor Menc Szymczak, who emphasized the dominant role of fiscal and debt management policies. Monetary policy could support fiscal policy by "supplying the money and credit required by a high level economy" (13).

The Board delayed the decision for a week so that New York could be

---

82. The tax reduced the after-tax cost to profitable banks and the customers who borrowed from them. The discount rate was almost 0.5 percentage points below the rate on three-month bills at the time.

83. There is even a brief discussion of whether the market anticipated the increase to 2 percent, so that it was fully discounted. The following week, the Federal Advisory Council discussed a discount rate increase. It told the Board that it opposed an increase (Board Minutes, February 17, 1953, 13–16).

among the first to announce. Effective January 16, the Board approved an increase of 0.25 (to 2 percent) at eight of the twelve reserve banks. The others followed within a week. Sproul's presentation to his New York board could have been written in the 1920s. "We forced the banks to borrow every bit of the increased reserves they needed to support credit expansion. . . . It is time to bring the discount rate into line with open market policy" (Sproul papers, Board of Directors, January 15, 1953, 2–3). The only new element is explicit recognition of the market's anticipation. The market has "already adjusted to an increase" (ibid., 3).

The rise in the discount rate changed the profitability of borrowing relative to holding government securities. In the three months January to March, commercial banks reduced borrowing by $1.2 billion and sold $3.9 billion of government securities.

Political Fallout

Raising interest rates is rarely popular. This time was not an exception. Sproul warned his directors not to overplay the idea of more flexibility in the use of the discount rate or a return to orthodox central banking. "[T]here are still limitations on our freedom with respect to the discount rate" (Sproul papers, FOMC meeting comments, January 8, 1953, 4).

Senator Paul Douglas had taken the lead in Congress to free the Federal Reserve from subservience to the Treasury.[84] Falling money growth (M_1) in the first half of 1953 followed by rising Treasury yields and problems in the bond market in June gained his attention. At the time, the annual rate of increase in consumer prices was between zero and 1 percent; this measure of inflation had declined from the 2 to 3 percent range of 1952. Douglas wrote to Eccles, who supported his view, criticizing Federal Reserve policy for shifting to deflation after the Eisenhower administration took office. Eccles and Douglas argued that the Federal Reserve had ignored the falling money supply.

Sproul responded to Douglas. He denied that policy was deflationary. Short-term changes in the money supply were not very informative. He doubted that a policy of keeping growth of the money supply "directly proportional to changes in production and employment . . . on a year-to-year basis is likely to be most conducive to the maintenance of stability in the economy at high levels. . . . [A] better theory for the guidance of central bankers . . . is that growth in the money supply should parallel the long-

---

84. Douglas, a former distinguished economics professor at the University of Chicago, enjoyed the status of an expert who was looked to by many of his colleagues in Congress. For Douglas's role in ending Treasury dominance, see volume 1, chapter 7.

term growth in productive activity" (letter, Sproul to Douglas, Sproul papers, Board of Governors Correspondence 1953–54, August 31, 1953, 4–5). Unlike Martin, Sproul believed that the maintained growth of money was a leading indicator of inflation.

Douglas was not the only critic. The rise in yields and the discount on government bonds aroused fears of recession or depression and considerable criticism of the Federal Reserve and its new policy. On May 11, twenty senators and representatives introduced a resolution requiring the Federal Reserve to support government securities at par.

The Eisenhower administration had no interest in restoring an interest rate ceiling. At the Treasury, Undersecretary W. Randolph Burgess, a former Federal reserve bank officer, had criticized the pegging policy when it was in effect. Arthur Burns at the Council of Economic Advisers, despite his reputation as an advocate of free markets, favored the use of credit controls "when economic activity is high and rising and prices seem to be moving upward" (Senate Committee on Banking and Currency, 1953, 2).[85] This support for supplementary policies was a preview of his advocacy of price and wage guidelines and support of price controls in the 1970s.

The Federal Reserve may have been misled by the decline in member bank borrowing and steady increase in free reserves from $-692 million in May to $-495 million on June 17. To dampen criticism from Congress, the Treasury, and elsewhere and respond to declines in agricultural prices and concerns about recession, the Board discussed a reduction in reserve requirement ratios at its June 16 meeting.[86] The following week, it esti-

85. The Truman Council of Economic Advisers had squabbled in its meetings with the president and lost support in Congress and the administration. Congress appropriated funds only to the end of March 1953 and left to President Eisenhower to decide what to do. Technically, Burns served from March to July as Economic Adviser on a special three-month appropriation. He proposed to reorganize the council, make only the chairman responsible for briefing the president, eliminate the vice chairman, and appoint an advisory board on economic growth to bring the Council into formal relation with other economic agencies (Hargrove and Morley, 1984, 96–97). Burns warned Eisenhower about a recession in September 1953, a correct forecast that strengthened his relation to the president.

86. The discussion began in April when "Governor Evans said he would look with some favor on a reduction in reserve requirements in the event of a downturn, particularly in view of recurrent complaints from country member banks regarding the inequitable position in which they were placed with respect to their non-member competitors" (Board Minutes, April 22, 1953, 3). Treasury Undersecretary Burgess urged Martin to reduce reserve requirement ratios. Martin urged the Treasury to offer an interest rate "substantially over the market" (FOMC Minutes, June 6, 1953, 6). Industrial production rose 10 percent in March and 5 percent in April (at annual rates). The concern about recession was probably related to the anticipated Korean armistice and the belief that recessions follow after wartime spending ends. The armistice came on June 27, and a recession followed. The New York Clearing House Association and others also expressed concern about a recession.

mated that the Treasury would borrow about $6 billion of new funds. It de-cided to supply part of the increase by reducing reserve requirement ratios for net demand deposits by two percentage points for central reserve city banks and one percentage point for all other members.[87] The new ratios became effective at different dates between June 24 and August 1. The vote was four to 1, with Governor Robertson voting no because he thought the reductions should be smaller.[88]

Robertson's dissenting statement recognized that most of the reserves released by the change would be withdrawn through open market opera-tions at unchanged interest rates. Staff estimates of Treasury borrowing and free reserve demand concluded that $1.5 billion of additional reserves would be needed to keep free reserves between $500 and $600 million for the rest of the year, but Robertson expected that only about $200 million of the reserves released would remain in the market. He preferred a smaller reduction followed by another reduction later in the year.

Robertson was right. With short-term interest rates unchanged, the de-mand for reserves declined approximately by the amount released. The measures that the FOMC used to judge its operations suggest little change in reserve availability or market ease. New issue yields on Treasury bills declined by 0.06 percentage points, but free reserves declined slightly. In the next three months, total bank reserves fell by $700 million, offsetting part of the change in required reserves. Thus, a principal result of lower reserve requirements was to reduce the cost of System membership.

The monetary base, adjusted for the change in reserve requirements, fell precipitately in the second half of the year. Chart 2.6 shows annual growth of the real value of the monetary base and the real interest rate in 1953–54. Data on anticipated inflation are not available for this period, so the real interest rate is an expost rate obtained by subtracting the most recent annual rate of price change from the long-term Treasury rate. Real interest rates fell one percentage point early in the recession, then rose to about 2.5 percent as the recession ended. The sharp deceleration of money, the change in the real interest rate and the rapid reduction in defense

87. Alternative proposals were: (1) to increase open market purchases substantially and increase the discount rate to show that policy was not inflationary; and (2) to make a modest increase in open market purchases. Those favoring the reduction in reserve requirement ratios wanted a strong gesture to show that the System did not want deflation.

88. There were two vacancies on the Board. In August, President Eisenhower appointed C. Canby Balderston and Paul E. Miller. Miller died within two months of his appointment. In March 1955, Balderston became vice chairman. Balderston was a Board member from August 1954 to February 1966. Before coming to the Board, he had served as dean of the Wharton School at the University of Pennsylvania and also as deputy chairman of the Phila-delphia reserve bank.

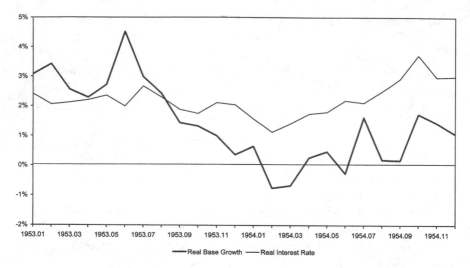

Chart 2.6. Real base growth versus real long-term interest rate, January 1953–December 1954 . Real base growth measured year over year; long-term interest rate measured as yield on Treasury securities with maturity greater than ten years.

spending following the armistice helped to bring on or sustain the 1953–54 recession.[89] As on several other occasions, real base growth is a better indicator of recession and recovery than the real interest rate. Real base growth started to fall in March, and fell more decisively in June 1953. The National Bureau marks July as the peak in the economy. Real base growth began to rise in March 1954; the trough in the economy came two months later.[90]

THE 1953–54 RECESSION

The June 1953 reduction in reserve requirement ratios came just as the economy slowed. The National Bureau of Economic Research (NBER) described the downturn as a "sharp recession."[91] It lasted ten months, ending

89. In the year ending second quarter 1954, government purchases declined 20 percent. At their peak, government purchases were 16 percent of GNP, but their decline in the year was 119 percent of the decline in GNP. The total fiscal impulse for calendar 1954 was smaller because excise tax reduction took effect in January 1954. A major income tax reduction became effective after the recession ended. Saulnier (1991, 65) says that military contract awards done in the United States at the peak in first quarter reached nearly $11 billion. By fourth quarter 1953, such awards had fallen to $1.6 billion. GNP was about $350 billion.

90. The expost real long-term interest rate rose about 0.5 percentage points between March and July 1953. During the early months of the recession, the rate declined slowly to 0.96 percent in February 1954. By June 1954, it was back to 2 percent. Romer and Romer (1994, 18) computed the real value of the federal funds rate in recessions and recoveries. Their measure increased procyclically for the first three quarters following the peak; the recession lasted ten months.

91. The NBER defines a sharp recession as a recession of intermediate severity, less se-

in May 1954. Real GNP fell 3.2 percent and industrial production 9.4 percent. Unemployment increased to a peak rate of 6.1 percent (Zarnowitz and Moore, 1986, Table 7).

This was the first recession under a Republican president since 1929. It worried an administration sensitive to criticism about its economic management and its emphasis on fiscal prudence, budget cutting, and size of government. Its critics claimed that it lacked concern about rising unemployment.[92] When CEA Chairman Burns told the cabinet in September 1953 that a recession had started, Eisenhower "recalled the Republican party's commitment to use the full resources of the federal government to prevent another 1929" (Eisenhower, 1963, 304).

The advent of recession was not a complete surprise. In May, the Federal Advisory Council told the Board that a nine-to-three majority believed "that the probability is for a moderate downturn in business in the next months" (Board Minutes, May 19, 1953, 2). The Council expressed particular concern about excessive automobile inventories and production. Chairman Martin responded that "in his judgment the probable trend of business would be downward" (ibid., 6). He still held to the old notion that recessions had a desirable, purgative effect.[93] Nevertheless, both the Republicans and the Federal Reserve now accepted federal responsibility for counter-cyclical policy. The new view responded to the public consensus that business cycles were a legitimate problem for government policy, not the unavoidable working of fate. This view had influenced Congress as reflected in the Employment Act of 1946, the 1952 Patman hearings, the 1954 Flanders hearings, and at the end of the decade the extensive *Report*

---

vere than a major depression, more severe than a mild recession. The scale is relative, based on the expost characterization of recessions (Zarnowitz and Moore, 1986).

92. In his presidential campaign and as president Eisenhower emphasized that he believed government had to take an active role against unemployment and recession. He would not raise taxes to balance the budget, as Hoover had done in 1932. The administration developed a stand-by public works program, in the event of a deeper recession, but it never implemented the program (Eisenhower, 1963, 307). The government reduced tax rates in 1954, fulfilling the campaign promise to lower wartime tax rates (Stein, 1990, 301, 305). A $7.4 billion tax act passed on August 16, 1954, after the recession ended, and $5 billion of Korean War excise taxes expired in January 1954 (Eisenhower, 1963, 297, 303). The top bracket rate remained at 85.7 percent at $1 million under the new law, and the lowest bracket had a 4 percent rate at $3000.

93. In Martin's opinion, "an adjustment was desirable for the economy which had been at too high a level for too long" (Board Minutes, May 19, 1953, 6). He hoped the adjustment would occur serially, not all at once. The purgative effect would lower prices. Most of the Federal Advisory Council agreed (ibid., 7). They agreed also that monetary policy was too tight, citing rising interest rates, the banks' demand for discounts, and the decline in bond prices below par that, they claimed, made banks reluctant to sell bonds. Martin later described his policy in this recession as "leaning against the wind."

on Employment, Growth and Price Levels prepared for the Joint Economic Committee (1960b). These congressional and public pressures encouraged the Federal Reserve to respond more actively to rising unemployment than in the 1920s and 1930s. Inevitably, issues about employment and business conditions became intertwined with the dispute over the bills-only procedures.

The 1953–54 recession was the Federal Reserve's first major trial after it regained independence. Its performance was mixed. It recognized the slowdown promptly and voted to provide additional ease. In June, a month before the start of the recession, the FOMC decided on a policy of "aggressive supplying of reserves to the market" rather than "exercising restraint upon inflationary developments" as agreed at the March meeting (FOMC minutes, June 11, 1953, 93).[94] The committee listed doubts about strength in the economy, concerns about a policy "more restrictive than was desirable" (ibid., 93), and the Korean armistice.

The bond market gave an additional reason for deciding to ease policy. Prices of the Treasury's new 3.25 percent thirty-year bonds dropped below par.[95] Martin had warned the market in April that the Federal Reserve had adopted a bills-only policy and would not support the long-term bond market except in disorderly periods. This left the market uncertain about how far bond prices would be allowed to fall. Selling increased. The Treasury had not made such a pledge, so it supported the new issue bond market, and the FOMC bought bills. In July, long-term Treasury yields began to fall in response to the Treasury's support operation, Federal Reserve easing, and the start of the recession. By year-end long-term Treasury rates had fallen to the level at the start of the year.

Martin criticized the desk for "(1) failing to purchase Treasury bills more aggressively prior to June 1 and June 2 and (2) failing to notify the Executive Committee that a disorderly market existed on June 1" (memo, Robert Link to Tilford Gaines, Sproul papers, FOMC Correspondence,

94. In Brunner and Meltzer (1964), we used the Board's Annual Report for 1953 to 1964 to register FOMC decisions on a scale from +1 (active ease) to −1 (active restraint) based on statements in the directive. We scaled this meeting +1 and the next meeting, in September 1953, + 1/2. As in the text here, we compared the scale value to the change in free reserves, the indicator used by most of the Board and FOMC members. Boschen and Mills (1995) use a scale from −2 (strongly reducing inflation) to +2 (strongly promoting growth). They record an end to mild anti-inflation actions in June, a mild shift to expansion in October followed by a strong expansionary policy starting in December. Romer and Romer (1994) date the start of monetary expansion in July and record the shift to "active ease" in September 1953. Their scaling neglects the FOMC's strong statement in June.

95. Eisenhower's first State of the Union Message proposed lengthening the average maturity of the debt. This policy had wide support in the financial markets (Saulnier, 1991, 50).

November 7, 1955, 2). The New York bank attributed the market break to rising interest rates, including an increase in the prime loan rate at the end of April, heavy demands for capital, and government borrowing. It used free reserves to establish that the desk had eased the money market, allowing member bank borrowing to decline by $600 million in May and early June without offset. But new issue Treasury bill rates increased nearly forty basis points, so the free reserve data probably misled the manager on this as on other occasions. The manager's instructions at the time were that "reserves should be supplied in sufficient volume to prevent further tightening but not in such volume as to ease the degree of credit constraint" (memo, Gaines to Roosa, Sproul papers, FOMC Correspondence, November 9, 1955, 3). Martin explicitly rejected any specific measure of ease or restraint.

The manager had discretion. He purchased more than $300 million of bills, a relatively large volume, in the four weeks ending June 3, and the Treasury supported its new issue by purchasing $3.5 million for its trust accounts in early June. Nevertheless, bond prices fell by as much as 1.25 points at the end of May and an additional half point in early June. The report of the ad hoc subcommittee appointed by the FOMC in 1955 said that a disorderly market occurred "when selling feeds on itself so rapidly and so menacingly that it discourages both short coverings and the placement of offsetting new orders by investors who would ordinarily seek to profit from purchases made in weak markets" (ibid., 7). The manager and Chairman Martin disagreed about whether this condition had been met on June 1. The manager's main defense was that his bill purchases, the Treasury's bond purchases, and the (false) rumor that the Federal Reserve had purchased bonds stopped the price decline.

From a cyclical standpoint, the injection of reserves to assist the market was fortuitous, since it provided additional reserves just as the economy reached a peak. The reduction in reserve requirement ratios became effective early in July. The interest rate on Treasury bills declined. By year-end, monthly average free reserves had more than doubled since June, and bill rates were at 1.63 percent, near the lowest level in two years. By these standards, monetary policy had eased, but these signals were misleading, influenced more by the decline in borrowing and spending than by Federal Reserve actions. In contrast, annual growth of the nominal monetary base declined from a peak of 5.3 percent in June 1953 to 1 percent at year-end. With a positive, but relatively low, rate of increase in consumer prices, growth of the real value of the base was below nominal base growth (Chart 2.6 above). The base data suggest that prevailing interest rates remained above the level at which the public chose to increase transaction balances.

In September, the FOMC adopted a policy of "active ease" to avoid de-flationary tendencies. Inflation fell. Growth of industrial production remained strong through the summer, rising at annual rates of 17 percent and 10 percent in July and August, as the FOMC noted at its September meeting. The FOMC minutes reported slowing economic activity in retail sales, construction, personal income, government spending, and inventory accumulation. These declines more than offset growth of industrial production. Farm incomes fell, and real GNP declined in the third quarter.

In December, the FOMC described the decline in the economy as moderate but unmistakable. The directive to the manager called for "promoting growth and stability in the economy by *actively* maintaining a condition of ease in the money market" (FOMC Minutes, December 15, 1953, 5). In response, free reserves rose. The increase came from two main sources, a relatively small seasonal increase in the System's open market portfolio and a $500 million decline in Treasury cash in the first half of November.[96] The latter reflected an unusual event, Congress's failure to increase the ceiling on Federal government debt. To pay its obligations, the Treasury used the profit remaining from the 1934 devaluation that had been left in the general fund in gold, part of Treasury cash. This action increased Treasury deposits at the Federal Reserve, but the money was spent, increasing bank reserves and the monetary base.

Real GNP in 1954 was slightly below the average for 1953, but the economy recovered slowly after the second quarter.[97] In August, the administration and Congress agreed on a 10 percent reduction in income tax rates, retroactive to January. With the war over, Federal purchases of goods and services, adjusted for price changes, worked in the opposite direction, declining 18 percent from peak to trough of the recession. The Federal Reserve continued the policy of "active ease."

Interest rates on new issues of Treasury bills remained 1 percent or below until mid-December 1954.[98] Free reserves remained in the range $500

96. Treasury cash includes the Treasury's holdings of gold, silver dollars, Federal Reserve notes, and other minor items. A decline in Treasury cash increases bank reserves and the monetary base.

97. The National Bureau dates the end of the recession in May 1954. Real GNP increased beginning in the second quarter, but industrial production did not begin a sustained rise until October. FOMC described the recovery in summer as sluggish, with "unusual stability" (Executive Committee Minutes, July 20, 1954, 3).

98. In a reprise of the 1930s, the bankers on the Federal Advisory Council complained in May that rates were too low (Board Minutes, May 18, 1954, 9). They were not alone. The Life Insurance Association complained also (letter, Carroll Shanks to Martin, Sproul papers, FOMC meetings, March 1, 1954.) Later, New York explained that short-term rates were lower than intended. It blamed bills-only policy (Sproul papers, Q and A for Flanders hearings, question 3, 1954, 11.). At the time, however, the main argument was uncertainty about estimates of

to $600 million that the Federal Reserve regarded as evidence of an "easy" money market. With the discount rate above the Treasury bill rate, banks reduced discounts, increasing free reserves. In the System's analysis, the reduction in discounts was evidence of an easier policy. The monetary base rose modestly (see Chart 2.6 above).

The Board reduced discount rates to 1.75 percent in February and 1.5 percent in April 1954.[99] At the same time, the FOMC reduced buying rates for acceptances. Unlike the 1920s, when the System had tried to foster an acceptance market by holding the acceptance rate below the discount rate, it now held its buying rate at the discount rate.

Periodically the Board considered changes in the system of reserve requirement ratios. The main problem was that the high reserve requirement ratios raised the cost of membership.[100] Martin appointed a committee to revisit the issue but, as on many earlier occasions, it could not reach agreement on the type of change to recommend (Board Minutes, November 27, 1953, 3). There was general agreement that reserve requirements should be uniform but no agreement on the level or how to phase in the change. The issue did not go away. A letter from the New York Clearinghouse requesting the Board to change New York's classification from central reserve to reserve city led to discussion of the pros and cons of a general reduction in these ratios (Board Minutes, April 23, 1954, 5–6). The Board asked the Federal Advisory Council for its view. It favored a reduction, timed to pro-

---

reserve positions and the need for "a substantial cushion on the downside against forecasting errors" (memo, Sproul to Roelse, Sproul papers, FOMC comments, May 13, 1954.). Earlier, the Federal Advisory Council opposed an increase in regulation Q rates paid on time deposits, a mistake they would later regret. The issue arose because the New York State Banking Board removed ceiling rates for mutual savings banks. The Council said that higher rates would encourage "unsound" practices (Board Minutes, November 17, 1953, 9–10).

99. An unusual incident speaks to tensions within the Board. After each Board meeting, members initialed the minutes. Governor Vardaman refused to initial the minutes for March 19, 1954, because he was angry about what had happened and did not think the minutes reflected the specific event accurately. The minutes report that Vardaman came to the 10 a.m. meeting for one hour, announced that he would have to leave to attend another meeting, and asked that the agenda be changed to permit him to suggest amendments to a letter the Board intended to send to a member of Congress. The Board refused, and Vardaman left without making his comments. Instead of signing the minutes, Vardaman wrote on the cover sheet: "As long as I have been on the Board, there has never been an occasion when a member has been denied the opportunity to voice his views on a proposal" (Board Minutes, March 19, 1954, initials page). He accused the Board of not stating the facts accurately, probably a reference to the absence of a statement saying that he had been prevented from offering amendments. Chairman Martin wrote alongside: "The minutes state the facts properly."

100. The number of state member banks declined from 1901 in 1951 to 1871 in 1954. Only 21 percent of state banks (with 65 percent of deposits) were members in 1954. Including national banks, Federal Reserve members represented 48 percent of all banks and 85 percent of deposits (Annual Report, 1954, 44).

vide additional reserves to permit banks to buy the Treasury's new issues (Board Minutes, May 18, 1954, 9–10).[101]

Until December 1954, seven months after the recession ended, the System continued the policy of "actively maintaining a condition of ease in the money market" (active ease) agreed upon at the December 15, 1953, meeting. The FOMC carefully followed conditions in the economy; it was aware at its June 23, 1954, meeting that the decline in production and consumption had moderated and, in September, that the economy had "moved sideways" during the summer. The Federal Advisory Council reported as early as May, the month of the NBER trough, that "the decline is leveling out. . . . [T]here is much more optimism" (Board Minutes, May 18, 1954, 5). At its September meeting with the Board, the Council noted that the recession had ended, but it did not expect "any significant upsurge or decline . . . in the next three months or in the first quarter of next year" (Board Minutes, September 21, 1954, 8).[102] This judgment proved wrong.

In October, the recovery strengthened. By November, Chairman Martin expressed concern about a speculative boom. "[T]here were indications of an exuberance of spirit among intelligent businessmen with respect to 1955 business prospects that seemed to him to be dangerous" (Executive Committee Minutes, November 9, 1954, 10–11). Most other members did not share his concern. They were wrong. In the next six months, industrial production rose at a 21 percent annual rate, and the unemployment rate fell from 6 to 4.7 percent. With real GNP rising at a 5 percent annual rate, Chairman Martin proposed to "re-examine the active part of the phrase 'active ease'" (FOMC Minutes, December 7, 1954, 5). Sproul agreed, but Vice Chairman Balderston opposed any announcement of a change on grounds that the announcement would mislead the public. Martin dissented strongly; he did not want the words "active ease" to remain in the directive. His concern was inflation. "[H]e did not believe that inflation provided jobs for people on a sustained basis although it might temporarily promote jobs" (ibid., 22). The committee agreed to remove the word

101. The Council estimated the Treasury would soon borrow $10 to $11 billion on new issues.

102. The Council praised the System's response to the recession but criticized the low interest rate policy that brought short-term rates on commercial paper and acceptances back to the levels of the 1948 recession. In February, the Council urged that "it would be proper policy to sell bills to an amount approximately offsetting the decline in loans" (Board Minutes, February 16, 1954, 8). This statement amplified the Council's concern about "undesirably cheap money" (ibid.) that lowered bank earnings. The Council divided on whether the February reduction in the discount rate was desirable. Earlier the FOMC had increased the rate on repurchase agreements to 2 percent.

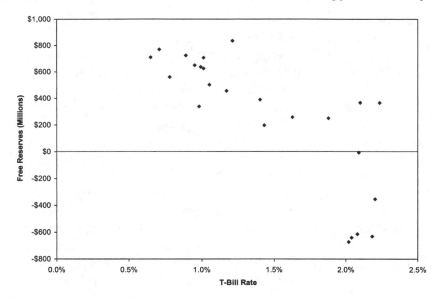

Chart 2.7. Free reserves versus ninety-day T-Bill rate (auction), January 1953–December 1954.

"active." Some members wanted to remove the word "ease" also, but the majority opposed.

A few weeks later, the Executive Committee heard that "a vigorous economic recovery was now visible and tangible." The members voted to keep free reserves in the $300 to $500 million range.

Chart 2.7 shows levels of free reserves and a short-term interest rate during the recession and surrounding months. The two variables are negatively related. Although there is considerable variation, low levels of the Treasury bill rate generally accompany large positive values of free reserves. Both measures offered the same general interpretation of the policy stance. For example, during "active ease" in the fall of 1954, the Treasury bill rate and free reserves remained about 1 percent or less and $650 to $700 million respectively. A shift from "active ease" to "ease" in December 1954 raised the bill rate by 0.25 percentage points and reduced free reserves by about $250 million. In contrast, during the same period, growth of the monetary base remained between 0.5 percent and −0.5 percent.

In a significant departure from its earlier experience, the Federal Reserve responded to measures of economic activity when choosing policy, and it took a more active role. Guided by the real bills framework in the 1920s and early 1930s, the System had generally let banks take the initiative for expansion by increasing the volume of discounts. The System had a more limited role. Its open market purchases encouraged banks to repay borrowing during a contraction, but monetary expansion usually had to wait for economic recovery to increase member bank borrowing.[103]

In contrast, the minutes for the 1953–54 recession do not show any FOMC member urging the System to wait for borrowing to increase. No one opposed open market purchases or described them as a source of speculative credit. These older ideas did not disappear completely, but they no longer dominated policy decisions or justified inaction. Everyone in authority accepted that the System's responsibilities included intervention to moderate fluctuations in economic activity even if they believed that recessions had a beneficial effect.

Policy operations remained procyclical, however. Money growth was higher in the expansion than in the recession. As before, the principal reason was that the Federal Reserve interpreted the decline in member bank borrowing and rise in free reserves as evidence of ease. Although it had not yet adopted an explicit, numerical free reserve target in its directive, by 1954 it often instructed the account manager to keep the level of free reserves within a specified range.

Federal Funds[104]

Growth of the public debt, particularly short-term debt, provided a market in which the Federal Reserve could conduct open market operations on a regular basis. It used this market to smooth fluctuations caused by changes in Treasury balances, float, seasonal demands for currency, and random events and also to change free reserves. Growth of the federal funds market, in which banks and corporations bought and sold claims to balances at the reserve banks became the lowest-cost way for banks to adjust reserve positions to meet requirements.[105] Reserve balances linked the two markets. The federal funds market started in the 1920s, disappeared with low nominal interest rates from the 1930s to the middle 1950s, then returned and became the principal market for reserve adjustment.

103. Governor Strong (New York) received considerable criticism for open market purchases in 1924 and 1927. Many blamed his 1927 actions for the stock market boom and subsequent economic collapse. The point of the criticism was that the purchases financed speculative credit, not real bills. See volume 1, chapters 4 and 5.

104. The Board's staff explored many different ways to analyze the economy. One of these was "flow of funds," a vast accounting system that sought to mimic national income accounts by recording changes in balance sheet positions. See Board of Governors (1955). This substantial effort produced a comprehensive system of accounts, but it failed to provide a useful framework for monetary analysis.

105. A buyer of federal funds received an immediately available deposit at a reserve bank. It paid by issuing a check payable at the clearinghouse on the following day. The buyer obtained funds immediately and paid the interest rate for one day (or longer). Free reserves are the difference between excess reserves and member bank borrowing.

One consequence of the increased use of federal funds was that the call loan market did not resume its former role. The call money post at the stock exchange closed for lack of business. Loans to brokers and dealers continued, but they no longer had a major role in banks' adjustment of reserve positions. The federal funds rate, not the call money rate, took over the role of adjusting the excess demand and supply for reserve balances.

The increased importance of the Treasury bill market gradually changed beliefs about the effects of a large government debt. In the 1940s, many economists and Federal Reserve officials expressed concern that a large outstanding debt hampered the use of monetary policy. The concern was that increases in interest rates caused bond prices to fall, imposing wealth losses. Small changes in interest rates would have little effect and large changes would be disruptive.

By the mid-1950s, these concerns no longer seemed relevant. Most people on both sides of the discussion of bills-only policy believed that interest rate changes were desirable and necessary. The Federal Reserve accepted the changed interpretation in a 1952 pamphlet. It now said that a large debt "induced much greater sensitivity to small changes in interest rates, and especially to changes in the direction of rates" (Roelse, 1952, 7). The essay concluded that it was unlikely that policy operations would require interest rate fluctuations similar to the relatively large fluctuations in call money rates in the 1920s (ibid.).[106]

The Board also changed the rules for issuing currency. Instead of returning all notes to the issuing reserve bank, banks could reissue currency of other banks.

RECOVERY AND EXPANSION, 1955–57

Recovery from recession and the subsequent expansion lasted thirteen quarters. Real GNP rose at an average 3.4 percent annual rate and industrial production at a 6 percent average rate. These averages hide the character of the recovery and expansion. Year-over-year growth of indus-

---

106. The new interpretation reflected the thinking of Robert Roosa at the New York bank. Roosa (1951) challenged the orthodox view at the time, claiming that since banks held a large volume of government securities, the central bank was "capable of reaching any segment of the rate structure" (ibid., 271). This accorded with New York's position that operations should be conducted at all maturities. Roosa highlighted "availability." By reducing availability and raising interest rates, he claimed the Federal Reserve made lenders less willing to lend. Availability, or its absence, dominated the rate change; and Roosa's emphasis is on the desire of lenders to lend, not on the willingness of borrowers to borrow or the cost of capital relative to the return on investment. Rising interest rates affected investors by creating uncertainty, thereby inducing investors to shift into short-term securities. Roosa's conjectures remained incomplete and, as noted by Robertson (1956, 70), required borrowers and lenders to draw opposite inferences from a change in interest rates.

trial production remained between 10 and 14 percent through most of 1955, declined sharply in 1956, owing partly to strikes, before returning to annual growth of 2 to 4 percent until the start of the 1957–58 recession. Output per hour, Chart 2.1 above, shows a similar pattern.

Year-to-year changes in the consumer price index remained modestly negative from September 1954 through August 1955. As noted years later, CPI changes overstate the rate of inflation, so the deflation in this period may be somewhat greater than reported figures show. The economy continued its recovery and, as in several earlier periods of modest deflation, output rose. There is no evidence of the monetary impotence that many economists suggest comes with deflation. Monetary actions remained effective despite the alleged zero bound on nominal interest rates often cited as a source of problems in economic models with a single interest rate.

Deflation did not last. While it lasted, it had no effect on Federal Reserve policy, and the Federal Reserve paid no attention. By late 1956, annual CPI inflation reached 2.5 percent on its way to 3.5 percent in the spring and summer of 1957.[107]

The FOMC continued to rely mainly on free reserves both to guide policy and implement it. Explicit targets for free reserves supplemented general guidelines such as "slightly more ease" or "active restraint" used earlier in the 1950s. Not all of the members used free reserves as their target, but that did not prevent them from criticizing the manager's frequent failures to hit the target.

Some FOMC members characterized "ease" and "restraint" more explicitly. Sproul offered the most complete statement using multiple measures including the relation of the discount rate to "sensitive" market rates, the extent to which banks obtained reserves by borrowing or open market operations, and the absolute level of market rates.[108] His characterization moved away from the 1920s Riefler-Burgess framework. The discount rate had a more important role and functioned, at times, as a penalty rate. No-

107. The implicit price deflator shows a very different pattern (Chart 2.3 above). There is no deflation. The lowest reported rate is 0.2 percent in third quarter 1954. The average rate of increase in 1955–57 is 3.4 percent, and there is no trend in the quarterly rates of increase (U.S. Department of Commerce, 1989).

108. Sproul had four categories: active ease, ease, neutrality, and restraint. He defined "active ease" as: ample excess reserves to meet borrowing needs; market rates low and falling absolutely and relative to the discount rate; banks borrow little from reserve banks and obtain reserves from open market operations (FOMC, January 11, 1955, 10–12). Sproul's commendable attempt to define terms failed to distinguish real and nominal changes. He rejected use of free reserves, citing distribution of reserves as one reason, then added: "We may find that . . . we can and should get rid of the idea of free reserves, and of free reserves themselves, but I still want to move gradually" (Sproul papers, FOMC Comments, January 11, 1955, 8). The distribution of reserves refers to the proportion of excess reserves at country banks.

table also was Sproul's emphasis on interest rates in addition to borrowing and the reduced role of free reserves as an indicator of ease or restraint.

Knipe (1965, 11), who worked for Chairman Martin at this time, characterized policy discussions and directives to the manager as shifting "from one expression of interest to another, often with no clear relationship to the policy actually in force." He added: "While nearly all the directives and most of the other material in the records of the Federal Open Market Committee may read as though the purpose was to conceal, rather than to reveal, a change from one particular ambiguity to another did occasionally correlate with policy changes" (ibid.). Like Maisel a decade later, Knipe deplored the absence of "an account of how policy was made" (ibid.).[109]

Policy actions in the 1954–57 period had a classical central banking flavor. The discount rate increased from 1.5 percent to 3.5 percent in seven steps. During the same period, the rate on prime commercial paper rose from 1.3 percent to 4 percent, 0.7 percentage points more than the discount rate (Board of Governors, 1976, 681–82). The rise in the discount was less than the increase in the annual rate of consumer price inflation, so expost real discount rates declined. The Federal Reserve's action was less restrictive than they, and others, believed at the time.

Levels of free reserves show little relation to reported inflation. Such relation as occurred was perverse; deflation came in 1955 when free reserves were positive, and inflation rose most rapidly in 1957 when free reserves remained about −$500 million. The FOMC believed that it had tightened policy during this period. Annual growth of the monetary base, however, remained between 0.5 and 1.5 percent in the two years ending August 1957, a mildly deflationary policy that showed no sign of change. (See Chart 2.5 above.)

Neither base growth nor free reserves adequately explain the shift from rapid to moderate expansion. Chart 2.8 shows that the modest changes in the federal funds rate in 1957–58 are much smaller than the increase in inflation, a pattern that returned during the Great Inflation. The inflation adjusted (real) federal funds rate reached a peak in 1955–56 and turned negative in 1957, an unplanned and unwelcome easing of monetary policy brought about in considerable part by rising inflation in 1956–57.

As in the 1930s, Federal Reserve officials did not distinguish between nominal and real interest rates. Unlike the early 1930s, however, the inflation rate was positive after 1955, so the real interest rate (and real free

---

109. In their report for the Banking Committee, Brunner and Meltzer (1964) noted the inchoate nature of Federal Reserve directives and policy statements at the time and proposed an explicit framework.

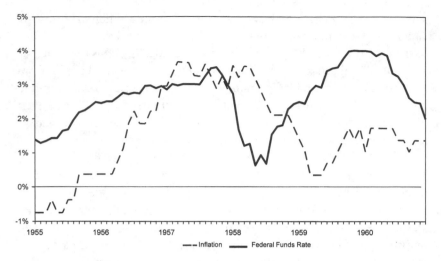

Chart 2.8. Federal funds rate versus inflation, 1955–60. Inflation measured as year-over-year CPI.

reserves) was lower than the nominal rates the FOMC watched. Its efforts to tighten policy failed in part because its failure to make this distinction prevented it from tightening enough.

Budget position does not explain inflation either. Under the Eisenhower administration's policy of fiscal restraint, surpluses in 1956 and 1957 replaced a modest deficit in 1955. This may explain why contemporary observers blamed inflation on wage increases and talked about cost-push inflation brought about by union power.[110]

With money growth modest and GNP rising more rapidly, monetary velocity—the ratio of GNP to the money stock—rose at an annual rate of 5 percent during the 1954–57 expansion.[111] The Federal Reserve hinted that the increase in velocity reflected the combined effects of rising economic activity and inflationary expectations.[112] The same forces worked

110. Growing union power would be required, but neither union power nor growing union power could explain why inflation was negative in much of 1955 and declined in 1958 and 1959.

111. Friedman and Schwartz (1963, 615) note the more rapid growth of a broader monetary aggregate (M_2). As in the late 1920s, slow growth of the monetary base in a period of rising demand for credit and money led banks to induce customers to increase time deposits, thereby reducing average reserve requirement ratios. Banks could peg interest on time deposits.

112. "A rising velocity of circulation of money . . . is typical of periods of increasing economic activity. . . . An increase in velocity is also likely to occur in inflationary periods when expectations of rising prices provide an additional incentive to minimize the holding of cash balances" (Annual Report, 1956, 10–11). In the light of this statement, it is puzzling that the

on interest rates also. Both short- and long-term rates rose during the expansion as the world economy expanded, domestic investment increased rapidly and, after the middle of 1956, consumer prices began a sustained rise that brought them from the mild deflation of 1954–55 to a 3.5 percent annual rate of increase in 1957. This was a high rate of peacetime inflation by the standards of the time.

The rise in velocity slowed after inflation declined, then remained low, from 1958 to 1961. The continued, but slower, rise in velocity reflected several forces at work during the period, including technological improvements in banking and finance that reduced desired cash balances and growing optimism about prospects for growth in the United States and other market economies. Optimism about future growth increased the demand for capital and claims to capital.

Anticipated inflation or the end of deflation seems too small to account for the growth of actual (real) balances in this period. The one available measure of anticipated inflation for the period is a survey of market opinion known as the Livingston Survey. The survey data in Charts 2.9 and 2.10 show a rise from anticipated deflation to anticipated price stability in 1955 followed by continued price stability. Although the Livingston Survey has been found to be biased downward, the bias would have to be large to accommodate much anticipated inflation at this time.

Federal Reserve Actions 1955

The System started 1955 by raising margin requirements on stock purchases and short sales from 50 percent to 60 percent. The Board acted in executive session, so no record of the reasoning exists. The Board's announcement said the increase "was designed to prevent the recovery from being hampered by excessive speculative activity" (Annual Report, 1955, 82).[113] The reference suggests concern that credit was used for speculative purposes instead of "real" activity. Sproul subsequently commended the Board for "warning concerning the use of credit in the stock market . . .

Board did not take the next step of recognizing that expected inflation would raise nominal interest rates also.

113. Stock price increases slowed modestly following the change. On April 22, the Board again increased margin requirements by ten percentage points to 70 percent. Again the decision was made in executive session. The Annual Report (1955, 84) explains the Board's intent to "prevent excessive use of credit" from adding to speculative pressures. The Board discussed an additional increase, to 80 percent, on September 21, but decided against it. This time the discussion is on the record. The main concern is the use of credit for speculation, but the rate of increase in credit and stock prices had fallen, so the only decision was to request data on margin balances (Board Minutes, September 21, 1955, 10–11).

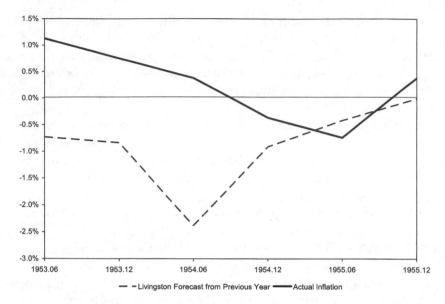

Chart 2.9. Livingston Survey of anticipated inflation versus actual inflation, June 1953–December 1955.

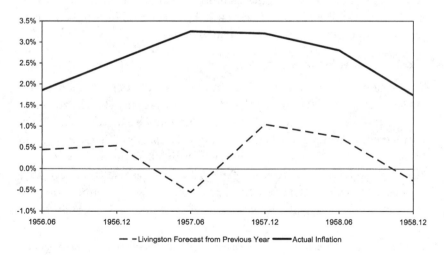

Chart 2.10. Livingston Survey of anticipated inflation versus actual inflation, June 1956–December 1958.

[and for] proper use of a selective control" (Sproul papers, FOMC comments, January 11, 1955, 1).

The Board reacted to the rise in equity prices. In the latter half of 1954, the Standard & Poor's (S&P) index of stock prices maintained a 30 to 35 percent average rate of increase for more than six months. In August

1954, the S&P index passed the nominal 1929 peak. Despite the impressive rise, the price level (deflator) had increased more than 75 percent in the same period, so the real value of the index remained far below its 1929 level.

The Federal Reserve was very alert to inflation in this period. On January 5, Chairman Martin asked Riefler to poll the members of the Executive Committee to learn whether current policy "should be tighter than had been decided" a week earlier at the December 28 meeting. All members agreed that policy should be tighter (Riefler to files, Correspondence, Board files, January 5, 1955). The following week, Martin held a special FOMC meeting to discuss the strong recovery and "the possibility that inflationary seeds may be germinating" (FOMC Minutes, January 11, 1955, 7). His conversations with businessmen showed extreme optimism in the business community.[114] Also, the level of free reserves remained between $400 and $700 million, a level that he thought was too high.

Sproul saw no reason for tightening. He acknowledged that the recovery had strengthened and would continue, but the "revival reflects more a cessation of deflationary influences than the emergence of new and continuing expansionary forces" (Sproul papers, FOMC comment, January 11, 1955, 6). Sproul expressed skepticism about incipient inflation. Although he opposed a shift to more restrictive policy, he was willing to accept Martin's proposal to change the directive modestly, from "promoting growth" to "fostering growth" (FOMC Minutes, January 11, 1955, 14).[115] The other members differed widely on whether and how they should change the directive. Balderston favored a reduction in the discount rate; H. G. Leedy (Kansas City) proposed restraint. After much discussion, the members voted to change the directive as Martin had suggested. The directive to the manager called for "fostering growth and stability in the economy by maintaining conditions in the money market that would encourage recovery and avoid the development of unsustainable expansion" (ibid., 24). That left the decision to the manager.

President Bryan (Atlanta) abstained on the vote. In a lengthy statement, he complained that he was prepared "to discuss appropriate policy

114. The Federal Advisory Council told the Board that the Council was unanimous in predicting good business in the months ahead. He said that it was the first time in his nineteen years on the Council that there had been such agreement (Board of Governors, February 15, 1955, 2). The Council had doubts and concerns about the second half of the year.
115. Sproul's statement included the definitions of "ease" and "restraint" discussed above. Martin replied that everyone should read Sproul's definitions. "One of the biggest problems of the Committee was understanding the terms that were used in describing credit policy and in translating those terms into instructions or directives" (FOMC Minutes, January 11, 1955, 14). But he did not instruct the staff to develop more precise definitions.

in terms of reserves and money rates" (ibid., 24). They had instead spent their time discussing "textual changes in the directive . . . [He was not prepared] to appraise the significance of the textual changes actually adopted, or the magnitude of the policy changes contemplated by the changes of language" (ibid., 25). He urged them to adopt quantitative measures, as Sproul had attempted to do, to "better discharge our responsibilities, within acceptable canons of delegation as between principal and agent" (ibid., 26)

Bryan's criticism was the first of many attempts by FOMC members to get better control of operations by making committee recommendations more precise. These efforts eventually succeeded when the FOMC adopted a numerical target for the nominal federal funds rate. That came many years later, after Martin had retired.

Although the Federal Reserve made many changes to avoid supporting, or appearing to support, the Treasury market, it gradually adopted a firm policy of avoiding changes in free reserves and interest rates for the two weeks surrounding Treasury debt operations. By 1955, this procedure, known as "even keel," had become standard practice. The practice was so well understood that the committee could vote for "even keel," without defining it, as it did on January 25, 1955, and many other occasions.

Economic growth remained robust through the spring and summer. Between January and August, the FOMC made only one change in the operative clause of the directive to the manager.[116] In the same period, free reserves declined from $400 million to $90 million, and the federal funds rate rose from 1.37 percent to 1.68 percent. No one questioned these changes or asked how the manager could interpret the directive as requiring changes in money market conditions.

A possible explanation for the change is that the System raised the discount rate by 0.25 to 1.75 percent effective April 14 and 15 at eight reserve banks. By May 2, discount rates were again uniform. Under an "easy" policy, as described by Sproul, "sensitive money market rates move up toward the discount rate" (FOMC Minutes, January 11, 1955, 11). Since the

---

116. The May 10, 1955, meeting discussed Sproul's motion to change the directive to reflect the end of the recovery phase. He proposed to substitute "avoid the development of unsustainable expansion" for "fostering growth and recovery." Sproul made clear that he envisaged no change in policy. "[W]e should hold steady for the next month or six weeks" (FOMC Minutes, May 10, 1955, 7). A steady policy, he said, would keep free reserves about zero and "interest rates in line with the present discount rate" (ibid.). The committee discussed whether the directive should "foster growth" or "foster stability." After much discussion of "fostering growth," "orderly growth," "stable growth," and "stability" (ibid., 9), the committee voted unanimously for Sproul's proposed change.

discount rate increased, apparently money market rates could rise without a change in the directive.[117] A problem with this explanation is that market rates rose before the discount rate.

The Kansas City reserve bank was the first to request a higher discount rate. It based its request on the desire "to place the [discount] rate in closer relationship with short-term market rates that had moved upward in response to strong demands for credit" (Board Minutes, April 13, 1955, 2). It seems clear that the account manager did not prevent the change in market rates on this occasion, as on many others in the 1950s and 1960s. At the time the FOMC relied on qualitative targets, or wide ranges for free reserves. Members could criticize after the fact, but they often disagreed on whether or not the manager followed the directive or acted independently.[118]

Sproul missed the directors' meeting on April 14, when New York voted for the increase. He believed the increase was too early but "the timing of the change was forced by the Treasury's needs" (Sproul papers, FOMC comments, Board of Directors, April 21, 1955, 1). He recognized that, by its choice of procedures, the Federal Reserve remained responsible for debt management. He found this "disturbing. Despite our break for freedom, monetary policy has to recognize the continuing need for coordination with Treasury financing" (ibid., 2).[119]

In the early 1950s the Federal Reserve renewed its traditional interest in encouraging the acceptance market, perhaps out of habit, perhaps as a remnant of the real bills doctrine. Perhaps also relevant, Sproul wanted

117. The Bank of England raised its discount rate twice in the winter of 1955. Sproul noted the change in March, but argued against responding. The domestic situation did not require a change, and "it might be helpful to have as wide a spread as possible in short rates" (correspondence, Sproul to Sherman, Board records, March 8, 1955, 2). Although control of international policy had shifted to the Treasury, New York, as in the 1920s, wanted to help maintain the fixed exchange rate system and restore convertibility without causing inflation at home. Support for the UK policy was a secondary reason for opposing an increase in discount rates in March. "Finally, there is the question of international money market relationships to which we are again paying some attention. . . . [T]emporary relief to the British position . . . would be in our long run interest" (Sproul papers, FOMC Comments, March 2, 1955, 2–3).

118. The claim that the manager frequently moved in advance of FOMC decisions is made and supported in Brunner and Meltzer (1964).

119. On the same day, the Board approved a letter to the federal reserve bank of Chicago asking about personnel policies. The letter noted that the bank "has no negroes presently employed and apparently has been following a policy which operated to preclude the employment of negro applicants" (Board Minutes, April 22, 1955, 12). The letter instructed the directors that if such policy exists "it is neither defensible nor in line with sound personnel policies" (ibid.). The letter was sent a decade before the non-discrimination legislation of the 1960s.

to increase the manager's options by relaxing the bills-only policy.[120] Governor Robertson asked whether the account manager could purchase bankers' acceptances. Sproul replied that, under bills-only, he could not.[121] Sproul urged a change in the rule (Executive Committee Minutes, February 8, 1955, 2–6). Martin agreed to reopen the subject at the next FOMC meeting.

The Board's staff considered several options before the meeting, including purchases of acceptances for the System account by individual reserve banks at posted prices and at market prices. The manager, Rouse, favored use of market rates. The discount rate would serve as an upper limit. He wanted authorization to use bankers' acceptances in repurchase agreements (memo, Riefler to George B. Vest, Board files, February 25, 1955).

The FOMC agreed to acquire bankers' acceptances as part of the System account, permit individual reserve banks to make repurchase agreements with non-bank dealers using acceptances, and eliminate the posted buying rate. Governor Robertson opposed the motion. He preferred to continue posting an acceptance rate and purchasing all offers to sell at that rate. He favored this traditional method as a way of encouraging the acceptance market by maintaining a rate advantage over commercial loans (FOMC Minutes, March 2, 1955, 48–49; March 29, 1955, 15–17). Robertson and Mills wanted to restrict the manager's options to increase committee control and the manager's accountability. Sproul and Martin agreed to limit purchases to $25 million.[122] The weekly average of System holdings did not remain above $25 million until December 1956.

120. In March 1954, the FOMC instructed the manager to buy up to $30 million of acceptances. At the January 11, 1955, Executive Committee meeting, the FOMC abolished the minimum-buying rate for acceptances and substituted the market rate. Governor Robertson opposed this on the grounds that the market "was growing and broadening without help from the committee" (Executive Committee Minutes, January 11, 1955, 4–5). Governor Mills, harking back to the 1913 act, wanted to "further the use of a form of financing that will strengthen and enlarge the United States as an international money market" (memo, Bankers' Acceptances, Board files, October 11, 1955). He opposed direct purchases by the reserve banks, believing that this would change the relative yield and reduce the market's scope.

121. Sproul had argued for operations in short-term securities other than bills on June 23, 1953. Martin opposed on grounds that "it was a step backward from the free market concept." Mills and Szymczak opposed also on grounds that it would lead back to pegging (memo, Riefler to Sherman, Board files, February 9, 1955, 1). Riefler noted that the issue had not been discussed since that meeting.

122. Robertson also objected to excessive use of repurchase agreements to supply reserves temporarily. He questioned the legality of repurchase agreements, because they were loans even if not classified as such. But he did not oppose them on that ground. He proposed to limit repurchase agreements to providing loans to non-bank dealers in government securities at a rate equal to the banks' discount rate. Sproul opposed vigorously. He argued that bank borrowing was a privilege of membership and that the analogy comparing bank and non-bank dealers was false. Although his definition of restraint contemplated the discount

Martin was not given to hyperbole or exaggeration. In a rare statement of satisfaction, he described the early months of 1955 as "the most prosperous period the country had ever been in" (FOMC Minutes, June 22, 1955, 43). He warned against excessive optimism about what monetary policy could do.

Concerns about excessive expansion increased by early August. The staff briefing for the August 2 FOMC meeting described the economic situation as positive, but the expected seasonal deceleration of activity had not occurred. Several industries operated at or near capacity. Auto purchases were at record rates, 40 percent above the previous year. Unemployment fell below 4 percent of the labor force, the lowest rate in almost two years. Weekly yields on new bill issues, after remaining in a narrow range during May and June, rose almost 0.5 percentage points from July to early August. Bill rates were now above the discount rate.

Since the start of the year, rates on three- to five-year Treasuries had increased from 2 to 2.75 percent; long-term governments rose above 3 percent in early August, and mortgage rates had increased, a change the System believed would slow home construction. Farm and food prices continued to decline, but prices of industrial materials continued to rise. Productivity growth slowed.

Discount Policy

Chairman Martin usually waited to speak about monetary and credit policy until he could interpret the views he had heard. In August 1955, he spoke first, urging the whole committee to discuss discount policy and reviewing the actions of the past two weeks. The market was full of rumors of an impending discount rate increase. He had discussed the issue with Treasury Secretaries Humphrey and Burgess, with Chairman Burns (CEA), and with his Board.[123] He expressed concern that "all the danger signals

rate above market rates, he now argued that a penalty rate would eliminate borrowing and repurchase agreements. Robertson and Mills, especially the former, continued to annoy Sproul by opposing any increase in New York's authority and by insisting on a strict bills-only policy. When put to a vote, however, Robertson's proposals to restrict use of repurchase agreements drew no other support (FOMC Minutes, July 12, 1955, 11–12). Robertson's opposition to repurchase agreements reopened an issue from the 1920s. Adolph Miller, a member of the Board from 1914 to 1936, had wanted to eliminate all repurchase agreements. In October, Mills and Robertson objected vigorously when the manager asked to lift the ceiling to $50 million. The arguments were the same on both sides. By December 1959, weekly averages reached $70 million seasonally. Generally, the account had $20 to $40 million in 1959 and 1960.

123. Martin asked Humphrey, Burgess, and Burns whether they favored two 0.25 increases or a 0.5 percentage point increase. They chose 0.5 all at once but, within a few days, reversed their recommendation out of concern for the purchasers of the Treasury's recent issue of 3 percent bonds. The Board also favored an increase of 0.5 to 2.25 percent (FOMC

[for inflation] . . . are now flashing red" (FOMC Minutes, August 2, 1955, 13).[124] He favored a 0.5 increase in discount rates to 2.25 percent, but he noted that Winfield Riefler believed it would be disruptive. He also wanted to change the directive to "restraining inflationary developments in the interest of sustainable economic growth" (ibid., 14). His aggressive stance contrasts with his less forceful actions in the late 1960s.

Sproul agreed with Martin about the risk of inflation, but he was less certain that the risk was imminent. He questioned whether the economy had reached its capacity. He favored a 0.25 percentage point increase in the discount rate and an open market policy that would force member banks to increase borrowing and raise interest rates. A 0.5 increase gave "expression to a judgment about a future economic situation which we do not yet have to make." Once again, it placed too much of the burden on credit policy: "Credit policy can't do the whole job, and shouldn't try to do it" (ibid., 21–22). Sproul, like Riefler, warned of the possible credit market reaction to a 0.5 percentage point increase.

As usual, the outlook was uncertain, so the members did not agree about what to do. Bryan (Atlanta) reminded the members that the U.S. had experienced inflation only in wartime or postwar periods. Money supply had increased modestly. Free reserves had become negative. Twelve-month CPI inflation was between 0 and -1 percent. In the weeks before the meeting, interest rates had increased. He favored no increase in the discount rate and a rise in short-term market rates (ibid., 31–32). This would allow discounting to act as "a safety valve" if they had misjudged the current situation.

Other members expressed a wide range of opinions. Balderston had earlier favored a 2.25 percent discount rate (0.5). He reaffirmed his position. At the opposite pole as usual, Mills favored adding reserves to offset the reserves withdrawn by repurchase agreements. Despite these differences, the committee voted unanimously to adopt Martin's proposal to change the directive to emphasize "restraining inflationary developments."

As agreed at the FOMC meeting, Martin, Balderston, and Sproul met with Treasury representatives and Chairman Burns to report on the discussion at the meeting. Administration officials were divided also. Secre-

---

Minutes, August 2, 1955, 11). Eight of the ten reserve bank presidents at the meeting favored the smaller increase. Three banks had submitted increases. A 0.5 percentage point increase would be the largest since 1937.

124. Martin was both pessimistic and prophetic about the political response to inflation. "[O]nce such action [inflation] has occurred, neither monetary policy nor anything else could effectively restore the purchasing power of the dollar without creating such distress as to preclude its usefulness" (FOMC Minutes, August 2, 1955, 13).

tary Humphrey now favored the smaller increase, but could accept the 0.5 increase, if the System agreed to prevent a disorderly market. Chairman Burns expressed concern that a 2 percent rate was not high enough. He favored 2.25 percent (Board Minutes, August 2, 1955, 2–3).[125]

After much discussion about the public relations and market problems of announcing different rates for different banks, the Board voted unanimously to approve action by Cleveland's directors to raise the discount rate to 2.25 percent and to approve 2 percent rates requested by Chicago, Boston, and Atlanta.[126] It was late in the day, so the increases were made effective August 4. At the next weekly Treasury bill auction, rates increased by 0.45 percentage points from the preceding week, suggesting that the market had not anticipated the change.

Within a few days, all remaining reserve banks adopted the 2 percent discount rate. Several governors expressed concern that Cleveland might lower its rate to match other banks. They preferred that all banks move to the higher rate. There was a sense of impending crisis. Governor Vardaman said that if the reserve banks delayed raising their rate to 2.25 percent, "he would be willing to exercise the Board's prerogative and fix that rate" (Board Minutes, August 18, 1955, 7).[127] Merchants had started to build large inventories for Christmas. It would be "unfair" to delay further restraint. Balderston supported him. He wanted a penalty discount rate imposed on the reserve banks if they did not approve the increase. He suggested that 2.5 percent might be more appropriate, if the Board imposed a rate. This would have meant a 0.75 increase, a very large increase imposed in a highly unusual way at a time of modest deflation or price stability.

At the August 23 FOMC meeting, Martin raised two issues: whether the discount rate should be a penalty rate, and whether it should lead or follow market rates. Riefler reviewed the history of discount policy. Traditionally, the committee used open market operations to remove reserves and increase market rates before increasing the discount rate. The failure

125. Burns later described the incident. "In 1955, I was pushing Bill [Martin] hard, along with Sproul, to pursue a tougher monetary policy because the economy was heating up, and the Federal Reserve was not moving fast enough in my judgment. That was also the thinking of Sproul" (Hargrove and Morley, 1984, 104). Note that at the meeting, Sproul opposed the larger increase, whereas Martin favored it. Burns's memory may have been faulty. As the text suggests, Martin was more concerned than Sproul about incipient inflation.

126. At the same meeting, the Board agreed to appoint Alexander Sachs, Jacob Viner, and Edward Shaw as consultants to explore an "appropriate research approach to longer-term financial problems" (Board Minutes, August 2, 1955, 7). This action recognized the overemphasis on current and near-term events and relative neglect of longer-term implications of monetary actions, a problem that continued.

127. The Board had ordered reserve banks to change their rates only twice before, in 1919 and in 1927.

to adopt a "penalty rate has created a problem for us of administering the discount facility in such a way as to prevent member bank abuse of the discount privilege by over-borrowing" (FOMC Minutes, August 23, 1955, 10).[128] He favored increasing the discount rate until it served as a penalty rate. Riefler reported on his analysis, showing that it takes "a very large volume of negative free reserves to put the market bill rate above the discount rate . . . The normal position is for the bill rate to be below the discount rate" (ibid., 12). The force driving that result was that banks sell bills when the discount rate is above the bill rate and discount when the rates reverse relative position. Goodfriend (1991) offered a more formal analysis of this issue.

Young urged the committee to experiment with control procedures. With a penalty discount rate, "the System can then broadly govern the volume of reserves needed for growth through open market operations while at the same time restraining an undue credit expansion financed primarily on borrowed reserves" (FOMC Minutes, August 23, 1955, 15).[129]

Martin concurred in the staff proposal, but several members of the committee remained skeptical or opposed. The committee resisted Martin's effort to decide whether the discount rate should lead market rates higher. It did not make a decision.

Following the meeting, effective August 26, Atlanta joined Cleveland at 2.25 percent. Other banks soon followed. By mid-September, all banks had adopted that rate. Bill rates rose to 2.1 percent in mid-September (from 1.7 in late July); the discount rate was a penalty rate. Borrowing declined briefly, then rose to the highest level since 1953, a monthly average of $800 million for September.

Sproul missed the August 23 meeting, so he reopened the discussion

128. Here Riefler accepts that banks borrow for profit, contrary to the assumption in Riefler (1930). He recognized that this change conflicted with the interpretation of negative free reserves, large borrowing, as necessarily restrictive. Ralph Young, the research director, followed Riefler. The staff now favored a penalty rate during periods of economic and credit expansion. The main change from the 1920s affecting borrowing and the role of the discount rate, Young said, was that there was now a single, dominant instrument in the money market—Treasury bills. In the 1920s, there were many different instruments, so it was not clear where to set the penalty rate. This is very similar to some reasoning used to give up the penalty rate after the 1920–21 recession. One of the reasons at that time was that the U.S. market was unlike the London market, where bankers' acceptances were the main instrument for banks adjusting reserve positions. See volume 1, chapter 4. As Sproul noted at the next meeting, it was not the only reason.

129. Young argued also that excessive credit expansion cannot later be contracted by counter-measures, at least not without serious deflationary dangers of "chain-reaction potential." He favored strong action to prevent "the bubble on top of the boom" (FOMC Minutes, August 23, 1955, 15).

of discount policy three weeks later. He forcefully opposed Riefler and Young's arguments for a penalty rate, partly because he disliked rules as guides to policy, but he disagreed also with their substantive claims.[130] The penalty rate tradition in central banking was a British, not a U.S., tradition. The System had abandoned a penalty rate as inapplicable to the U.S. not only because there was no single dominant asset used for reserve adjustment, as in Britain, but also because there were many small banks. Discounting helped small banks to adjust to temporary changes in reserves. Further, Sproul denied that Treasury bills had become the dominant means of adjustment. "I doubt if we are much closer than we were to having a single short-term market rate against which a penalty discount rate could be uniformly set" (FOMC Minutes, September 14, 1955, 22). This ignored the growing importance of the federal funds market.

Sproul accepted that the discount rate had remained above the bill rate most of the time in the past two years. He opposed "a timeless or rigid formula to achieve this result" (ibid., 23). And he questioned whether the System would follow a rule that required "shoving the discount rate up, during periods of credit restraint, with real risk of creating disorderly conditions in the capital markets."[131] Appealing to the other presidents, he argued that the rule would "reduce the role of the directors of the individual banks in setting discount rates" (24). It would, in short, further reduce regional bank autonomy.

Karl Bopp of the Philadelphia bank, later its president, had the more persuasive argument. He showed that the Riefler-Young formula required another increase in the discount rate. Only Governor Robertson favored the increase and only after the Treasury completed its October financing.

Uncertainty following President Eisenhower's heart attack in September put a temporary hold on policy changes. A telephone conference on September 26 decided to maintain an unchanged policy, despite a sharp decline in stock prices that day, but to show concern for the market's anxiety by showing a temporary increase in reserves for the statement week. On October 4 Robertson read a memo to the FOMC criticizing policy as "wholly inadequate" and "too slow to act" (memo, Re: Open Market Operations, Board files, October 5, 1955, 1). Sproul responded by recommend-

---

130. Sproul and others at the New York bank did not think highly of Riefler. Sproul's statement on discount policy starts by criticizing Riefler and Young harshly for not making their papers available in advance of the meeting (FOMC Minutes, September 14, 1955, 21).

131. This statement suggests that banks would adjust by selling Treasury bills or other securities instead of discounting, thereby forcing higher rates. This is as close as Sproul came to hinting at the negative political response to discount rate increases in 1920, a principal reason for abandoning the penalty rate at the time.

ing a modest reduction in free reserves to −$300 million and moving the short-term rate close to the discount rate. He believed that "the effectiveness of credit restraint is greatly influenced by opinions about the future and because opinions about the future may be undergoing some revision, I [favor] . . . a policy of maintained but not intensified pressure" (FOMC Minutes, October 4, 1955, 24).

Robertson again raised the issue of the discount rate at Board meetings on November 3, 9, and 16. The market did not anticipate an increase, so they would have the benefit of surprise (Board Minutes, November 3, 1955, 10–11). He considered surprising the market an advantage, and "[h]e considered an increase in the rate almost a necessity . . . [S]uch a move at this time would have a real impact" (Board Minutes, November 9, 11). Although new issue Treasury bill yields were above the discount rate, Chairman Martin hesitated. He saw merit in Robertson's argument, but he remained uncertain.

None of the reserve banks had requested an increase. Robertson favored acting without a request. After discussion, the Board agreed to send telegrams to each reserve bank, urging them to discuss an increase at their next meeting.[132]

Although several reserve banks held directors' meetings, none increased the discount rate that week. Discussion resumed at the FOMC meeting the following week.[133] Most of the presidents favored an increase, but Irons (St. Louis) was reluctant, and Sproul favored the increase but opposed a tighter policy. Martin shared his view. He favored an increase in the discount rate but "that did not mean that the supply of money also should be decreased" (FOMC Minutes, November 16, 1955, 23).[134]

132. The telegram was careful not to trample on the directors' prerogative, but it was disingenuous. "This move is not in any sense a suggestion that your directors act to increase the rate" (Board Minutes, November 9, 1955, 13–14).

133. The previous day, November 15, the Federal Advisory Council forecast continued growth in the first half of 1956 at a slower pace. The economy was near capacity. "There is a uniformly optimistic outlook" except for farmers (Board Minutes, November 15, 1955, 2). The Council opposed an increase in the discount rate and favored an unchanged policy stance (ibid., 20).

134. On November 3, Woodlief Thomas circulated a memo containing a chart showing the relation of the discount rate to free reserves and Treasury bill rates. "When borrowings exceed excess reserves, . . . the discount rate seems to set an upper limit on the rise in the bill rate regardless of the volume of net borrowed reserves. This indicates that when the bill rate is close to or above the discount rate, banks prefer to borrow rather than sell bills. . . . Thus at such time . . . the discount rate is probably the significant element of restraint" (memo, Thomas to FOMC, Board files, November 3, 1955). Sproul accepted the first conclusion but doubted that the discount rate was the appropriate measure of restraint. This follows "only if restraint is defined wholly in terms of the bill rate" (Sproul papers, FOMC comments, November 16, 1955). The exchange shows that members did not agree on measures of ease

The Board did not force the banks to increase, but it took the unusual step of voting in advance to approve a discount rate increase of 0.25 to 2.5 percent for any bank that made the request. By November 22, all reserve banks were at 2.5 percent.

Treasury Problems

Soon after the new discount rates took effect, the Treasury announced a refunding offer of $12 billion of 2.625 percent one-year certificates. The initial response showed the offer was properly priced. The "when issued" securities soon fell below par on the expectation that a large number of holders would redeem for cash. The Treasury formally requested the Federal Reserve to support the issue by buying the "when issued" certificates. Doing so would violate the bills-only policy, at least temporarily. But any temporary deviation would raise a question about future actions.

Sproul favored the purchases and suggested putting reserves into the market on the settlement date, extending the length of repurchase agreements to carry them over the New Year holiday, and purchasing "when issued" certificates as needed. Martin was reluctant, but he was willing to make an exception and let it be known that they would not return to the support policy.

Mills opposed on grounds that there was no emergency. If they did not intervene, the Treasury would have to pay cash and, probably, sell additional bills to raise cash. He was willing to extend the length of repurchase agreements to aid the market without violating bills-only policy. Robertson and Vardaman joined Mills in opposition. By a vote of nine to three, with all member presidents joining the majority, the FOMC voted to purchase $400 million of "when issued" certificates. This was the first departure from bills-only. On settlement day, December 8, the manager informed the committee that free reserves had fallen from –$300 to –$500 and interest rates had increased. The System supplied additional reserves by purchasing bills and offering repurchase agreements, but it used less than half of the $400 million to purchase "when issued" certificates.

Looking back a few weeks later, Martin said that the System would have been open to the charge of being "doctrinaire" if it had not responded to a direct request from the Treasury. He remained convinced that the principles reflected in the bills-only policy were correct. "Nevertheless, every time we give way on those principles we encourage the market to think that the System has been 'panicked' into taking a position to bail the Treasury

---

and restraint or on the effect of a higher discount rate. They never discussed how monetary policy affected the economy.

out" (FOMC Minutes, December 13, 1955, 25).[135] Sproul argued that the longer the committee went without making an exception, the more concern in the market when it made an exception. "This would mislead the market" (Sproul papers, FOMC Correspondence, December 13, 1955, 1).

The discussion continued. In January, Robertson wrote a memo criticizing the decision to assist the Treasury by purchasing "when issued" securities. The purchases abandoned the March 1953 policy agreement. It was a long step back toward support of the Treasury market, and it reduced independence.

Sproul's response did not hide his irritation. He accused Robertson of reverting "to the pronouncements of the 1952 Ad Hoc Subcommittee report," oversimplifying recent experience, and treating the 1953 policy as if "the commandment [bills only] had been chiseled in stone and could only be sandblasted out" (memo, Sproul to Sherman, Sproul papers, January 24, 1956, 2). Sproul pointed out that the FOMC regularly assisted Treasury debt management through its even keel policy and by lending directly to the Treasury. Even keel at times had required the FOMC to accept a "temporary halt in a policy of tightening credit which we intended to pursue" (ibid., 3). The System put additional reserves into the market, if needed, to assist the Treasury with its financing, but it left to the Treasury the decision about how to support its new issue.

Robertson wanted to notify the Treasury that it should not expect support in the future and that the departure from policy was a temporary change. Sproul replied that the Treasury understood that, and Martin agreed that they did not need a statement to the Treasury.

Total System purchases of certificates for the week reached $167 million. The committee discussed an announcement to call attention to the departure from policy and to indicate that it was exceptional. It decided not to issue the statement.

The decision to assist the Treasury financing irritated Senator Douglas. Douglas favored coordination of Treasury and Federal Reserve policy but expected each agency to operate independently. Although he opposed bills-only, he also opposed setting the policy aside temporarily to support a Treasury refinancing. This violated Federal Reserve independence that he had

135. Bremner (2004, 92) reports that Martin agonized about intervention and support all night. Governor Robertson offered a lengthy statement that pointed to mistakes by the Treasury. The Treasury had issued securities at year-end, when there was a heavy demand for cash. The solution should be to either avoid Treasury sales at such times or supplement the sales by additional sales of Treasury bills to pay for the attrition (shortfall). He preferred to have the Treasury borrow from the Federal Reserve for a few days, until they raised cash, instead of asking the Federal Reserve to support their issue (FOMC Minutes, December 13, 1955, 27–28).

worked hard to achieve in the 1949 hearings and in 1951. If the Treasury mispriced an issue, they should accept their failure and not depend on the reserve system to rescue them.

Martin defended the decision, citing the limits that he always placed on Federal Reserve independence and the need to assist in Treasury finance. At the Senate Banking Committee hearing on Martin's reappointment as governor and Chairman, Douglas was critical also of the 1955 decision to raise the discount rate four times instead of increasing reserve requirement ratios. The latter had the effect of transferring additional earnings to the Federal Reserve and later to the Treasury. Martin explained that "our policies are not directed to rewarding or punishing banks" (memo, Reserve Board Policy, Board files, January 20, 1956, 1). Douglas remained dissatisfied and abstained on the vote to reconfirm Martin.[136]

Responding to Inflation and Variable Growth

At the end of 1955, the FOMC looked back on a year of high and rising economic activity with a general feeling of confidence. Most of the members expressed concern about the easier market conditions following support of the Treasury offering, although there is no evidence in free reserves or short-term interest rates of more than a small change.

A 19 percent increase in real expenditure for plant and equipment was the major source of the 1955 boom. By early 1956, the boom began to slow. Growth in 1956 was highly variable, weak in the first and third quarters, stronger in the other two quarters. Unemployment was much less variable, remaining between 3.9 and 4.3 percent throughout. The Federal Reserve changed its direction several times, first recognizing the slowdown early in the year, then the renewed acceleration of investment and output and, still later, renewed deceleration followed by acceleration at year-end. A steel strike during the third quarter temporarily restrained industrial produc-

---

136. The vote was twelve to zero to confirm. At a later hearing, Martin discussed relations with the administration. The issue was the contentious 1956 increase in the discount rate, but it suggests the extent of coordination and independence at the time.

> In February of that year [1956], Governor Balderston and I had a meeting with Secretary Humphrey and there was a disagreement as to the nature that the economy was developing. We were so convinced; we discussed it with various people, and in a series of meetings from about the middle of February until the last week in March the position of the Federal Reserve . . . was . . . to go up in the discount rates. . . . [T]here was no "meeting of the minds. . . . [W]e acted." (Senate Committee on Finance, 1957, 1362)

At the hearing, Douglas asked Martin for the names of the FOMC members who voted to support the Treasury issue. Martin agreed to supply the names if the FOMC members agreed. Later, he forwarded the names to the Senate committee.

tion and output and contributed to inventory building followed by destocking. In November, the directive recognized "international conditions" for the first time in the postwar years.

Inflation reappeared. The annual rate of consumer price increase rose from 0.25 percent at the start of the year to 3 percent at the end. The disparity between the rise in the consumer prices index and GNP deflator narrowed. Both showed evidence of inflation. One common interpretation attributed the rise to wage pressures that raised production costs. Sproul considered two possible outcomes. Higher prices "might encounter consumer resistance which would have a dampening effect on production and employment, or . . . it might generate an inflationary spiral (Sproul papers, FOMC comments, March 27, 1956, 1).[137]

For the first time, Sproul recognized publicly that the Employment Act created conflict over what the Federal Reserve should do. "Should it expand to try to head off a decline in production and employment[?] The second and more difficult case would raise questions as to whether the central banking system should make credit so dear and difficult to obtain as to cause a decline in production and employment as the lesser of two evils. We haven't yet had to run head-on into the philosophy of the Employment Act of 1946 to that extent and it wouldn't be easy, so maybe we had better hope that some degree of economic responsibility on the part of management and labor will avoid presenting us the problem in serious form" (ibid., 1–2).

Others did not comment and may not have shared Sproul's view. Martin and others argued that the System had to finance part of the Treasury deficit but could control inflation resulting from private actions. Sproul's statements suggest some doubt about the System's willingness to create unemployment to stop price increases.

The Federal Reserve's response to changing conditions left no imprint on member bank borrowing or growth of the monetary base. Monthly average borrowing remained in the $700 to $800 million range, and annual growth of the monetary base fluctuated around 1 percent. The monthly average for the federal funds rate rose steadily from January through September, then remained just below 3 percent. With inflation rising, expost real interest rates declined during the year. If we accept the Livingston Survey, Chart 2.10 above, forecasters did not anticipate inflation. Even a

---

137. Sproul does not explain why prices would continue to rise. He may have believed that workers would try to restore real wages, but this point was never made. Arthur Burns at the Council urged the Federal Reserve to ease, despite the inflation. On this and other occasions during his years at the Council, he did not hesitate to pressure Martin and the Federal Reserve. Later, as Martin's successor, he objected vigorously to "interference" by the administration.

reported 3 percent inflation rate did not raise anticipations above 1 percent.[138] These data suggest, therefore, that the rise in inflation was largely unanticipated.

Rising nominal short- and long-term interest rates and rising inflation reduced desired money balances per unit of output and raised monetary velocity. Expost, the rise in monetary velocity explains by far the largest part of the 5.5 percent reported increase in nominal GNP for 1956.

Slow growth at the start of 1956, a presidential election year, alarmed the president and some of his advisers. Arthur Burns at the Council of Economic Advisers wanted an easier policy at the first sign of slower growth in January. Others in the administration joined in the public criticism of the Federal Reserve, and Congressman Patman held hearings on the conflict (Kettl, 1986, 89). Later, Burns admitted that Martin had been right (Hargrove and Morley, 1984, 104).[139] Eisenhower remained in the background but encouraged the effort. When the conflict became public, he supported the Federal Reserve's independence, and the conflict ended.[140]

The administration's concerns about Martin and the Federal Reserve did not prevent renomination and reappointment, effective February 1956, to a full fourteen-year term as a governor and a new four-year term as chairman. Martin's principal critics at Senate hearings on his reappointment expressed two main concerns: the Federal Reserve would be too independent and would forget that it was a creature of Congress; and the

138. Chart 2.10 compares actual inflation to the anticipations in the annual survey taken one year before. The Livingston survey taken in 1957 did not show much response to the 1956 data. Croushore (1997) surveyed the literature on bias and rationality of the Livingston Survey. He concluded that both bias and rationality of forecasters' anticipations were not easily supported or rejected for the entire data set. Forecasts for the 1950s, however, appear systematically biased downward by about one percentage point (ibid., 6).

139. Burns claimed that his relations with Martin remained cordial. "[I]t's hard to have a clash with Bill Martin" (Hargrove and Morley, 1984, 104). His relation with Secretary Humphrey was less pleasant. There were many clashes based both on personality and substance.

140. The Joint Economic Committee (1956a) held hearings on the discount rate change at which Secretary Humphrey and Chairman Burns testified against the increase. At Eisenhower's urging, Humphrey told Martin before the meeting that he should resign instead of opposing the president. Martin replied that he would resign if his leadership were to be opposed by the administration and informed the Board about his possible resignation. Humphrey and Burns continued to press the president to criticize Martin, but Eisenhower, after talking to Martin and receiving a promise to ease credit if the economy slowed, decided against. He said later that "overruling of the financial experts with a purely political judgment" was not in order (quoted in Saulnier, 1991, 87). Eisenhower subsequently responded to questions from the press on April 25 and May 4. On both occasions, he expressed confidence in the Federal Reserve and added, "I personally believe that if money gets . . . too tight, they will move in the other direction" (FOMC Minutes, May 9, 1956, 24–25). The minutes of this meeting include excerpts from Eisenhower's press conferences. Some business leaders criticized the increase also (Bach, 1971, 260).

bills-only policy kept long-term interest rates too high, thereby reducing investment.[141]

Martin's desire to build a consensus slowed the System's response to economic weakness. The FOMC first noted public comments about an economic downturn at its January 10 meeting. Young dismissed the comments as overly pessimistic and without empirical support. Others were less certain. Delos Johns (St. Louis) favored less restraint because growth had slowed. Joseph Erickson (Boston) and Oliver Powell (Minneapolis) reported slower growth also (FOMC Minutes, January 10, 1956, 2, 10, 16, 21). These were minority views. The FOMC took no action.

Policy change received more support two weeks later. The FOMC recognized uncertainties in agriculture, housing, and automobile markets. Perhaps in response to administration criticisms, Martin disagreed with the consensus at the meeting (FOMC Minutes, January 24, 1956, 7–8). He favored some easing to a level of free reserves close to zero, an increase of $250 million. The committee agreed to return to the directive in effect in June 1955.[142] It continued the instruction to restrain inflation but added that the manager should also take "into account any deflationary tendencies in the economy" (FOMC Minutes, January 24, 1956, 21). Free reserves remained unchanged in February.[143]

141. Senator Paul Douglas did not vote for Martin's reconfirmation. Douglas opposed the bills-only policy and criticized Martin for unwillingness to respond to congressional criticisms of the policy. Douglas repeated Martin's own words back to him: "I have had typed out this little sentence which is a quotation from you. 'The Federal Reserve Board is an agency of the Congress'" (U.S. Senate, Committee on Banking and Currency, 1956, 5). Several senators criticized the departure from bills-only in 1955. At the same hearing, Senator Fulbright said, "I do not believe there is any real independence" (ibid., 67). Martin defended the System but repeated that his view of independence within the government meant that "it is our endeavor to see that the Treasury is successfully financed. . . . neither the Treasury nor the Federal Reserve benefit by having the Treasury fail" (ibid., 22).

142. Martin made the following statement suggesting dissatisfaction with free reserves as a policy target but not offering a substitute: "We may say that we should maintain the pressure we now have in the market but I do not believe we or the public knows what the degree of pressure is that we are maintaining" (FOMC Minutes, January 24, 1956, 17). Martin went on to argue that the manager should have more flexibility—"putting our foot on the brake pedal but not pressing on the brakes" (ibid., 17). He was reluctant generally to cede authority to the manager but unable, or unwilling, to go beyond picturesque imagery to issue precise instructions. Martin then referred to the November election and the pressure to ease policy. "[W]e ought to make it plain that we are not being influenced by political considerations . . . But that is just digging the System's grave so far as effective policy is concerned" (ibid., 18). The reference is unclear but probably refers to criticisms of bills-only. Martin stated that he referred to the ability to carry out policy, not a political threat to formal independence.

143. In February, Martin testified on the renewal of authority to purchase limited amounts of securities directly from the Treasury. He presented a table showing the amounts outstanding since March 1942, when the authority began. The maximum amount outstanding was $1.3 billion in March 1943. Usually the amounts were much smaller, and there are several

Martin stated the consensus at the February 15 meeting as requiring no change in the directive but the trend should be toward ease, rather than restraint. Robertson, who favored restraint, challenged the interpretation, one of the few times this happened in Martin's tenure as chairman. The committee voted to keep the directive unchanged but did not discuss Robertson's objection or Martin's response. This left the decision to the manager or to the New York bank. Most weekly average market interest rates remained unchanged until April.[144]

The Federal Advisory Council did not share the concern about growth. Members told the Board that they expected the high level of activity to continue, and they warned that prices might rise. Higher minimum wages enacted by Congress would raise wages across the entire wage structure (Board Minutes, February 21, 1956, 13).[145] Adding to concern, the Board's staff reported that growth of industrial production and gross national product had stagnated and the prices of industrial materials had increased "substantially" in the past year (FOMC Minutes, March 6, 1956, 27). Conditions in the economy seemed mixed. The staff favored an increase in discount rates and fewer open market purchases. The Treasury had an offering, so the FOMC did not approve a change in policy until the March 27 meeting.[146]

---

years in which no borrowing occurred (Martin testimony, Board Records, v. 1, Statement, February 29, 1956).

144. The committee agreed to permit the International Monetary Fund to invest $200 million in U.S. Treasury bills, to treat the purchases in the same way that it treated purchases by foreign governments, and to prevent such purchases or sales from affecting policy objectives.

145. In November, Governor Robertson proposed that the Board ask Congress to amend the Federal Reserve Act to permit member banks to count vault cash as part of required reserves (Board Minutes, November 1, 1955, 10). The Board asked the Federal Advisory Council to comment on the change. The change was in their interest, so they voted eleven to one to make it. When adopted the proposal would reverse the 1917 decision by amending Section 19 of the Federal Reserve Act. The Board's proposal sought to use a defense emergency as the reason for the change. The reserve bank presidents favored the change, but they did not want to limit the change to a defense emergency (Board Minutes, January 25, 1956, 2–4). The Board agreed to submit a request for legislation. The change did not become effective until 1959–1960, when the Board, in steps, allowed vault cash to be counted as part of reserves. The Board could not anticipate the importance of the change; it occurred before automated teller machines (ATMs) became available. By the 1980s, many banks could satisfy their required reserve holdings with the vault cash in their ATMs. In effect, the required reserve ratio was no longer a binding constraint.

146. The committee voted to allow the New York bank to continue operations in the bankers' acceptance market. Robertson objected strenuously on the grounds that intervention interfered with the development of a free market. No one seconded his motion to terminate operations. A memo that the manager prepared for the meeting partly supported Robertson's position. The memo noted that System activity in the acceptance market had negligible effects on trade finance. Operations had helped dealers hold acceptances, especially when the market

The tone three weeks later was very different. The staff report to the FOMC highlighted renewed growth of consumption and investment spending, business' demands for credit, and concerns about rising prices. The staff again suggested an increase in the discount rate to slow borrowing. Sproul agreed that growth had resumed, but he was cautious about responding too vigorously to the prospect of inflation. He opposed a discount rate increase. The members divided; six favored an increase, ten favored delay or opposed change. The committee voted to change the directive, by removing the clause about deflation inserted in January. The instruction once again called for "restraining inflationary developments in the interest of sustainable economic growth" (FOMC Minutes, March 27, 1956, 36). And once again, there was no connection between the changes in words and actions. New issue rates on Treasury bills fell following the meeting.

One reason for delaying action was an unwillingness to raise rates until there was evidence of inflation. The members did not have a theory of inflation against which they might appraise developments, and they did not distinguish transitory and persistent change. Most of the comments about inflation referred to reported changes in particular prices, not a persistent rise in the general price level. The more potent reason was a political concern, the extent to which interest rates would have to rise, a concern that remained an obstacle to inflation control in the 1960s and 1970s. Sproul warned independence was not well supported, that "the Committee would be fooling itself if it thought it could prevent this wage-cost spiral short of adopting a very severe monetary policy. Whether the System would have the assent of the Government and of the public to such a course seemed to Mr. Sproul to be a real question" (ibid., 33). Vardaman shared this view. Stopping the wage-cost spiral "could easily result in the destruction of the System" (idem.).[147] Bryan (Atlanta) pointed out that delay would require still higher interest rates, but his remark drew no support from Martin or Sproul.

A week later, Bryan notified the Board that Atlanta's directors had voted to increase its discount rate by 0.25 percentage points to 2.75 percent.

---

was under "strain," but rates had not become more flexible. Dealers pressed for purchases when market rates started to rise (memo, Rouse to FOMC, Board files, March 2, 1956, 1–7). The March 6 meeting also reappointed the manager. Martin voted for the appointment but noted that he objected to the procedure under which the New York directors chose the manager and promised to have a committee meeting to recommend new procedures. This issue had been left unresolved since the 1952 ad hoc committee report.

147. The same concern arose in the 1920s and in the early postwar years. After the System raised the discount rate to 7 percent in 1921, it was reluctant in later years to consider raising rates to 6 percent or more. In the early postwar, concern about the effects on debt values delayed action. See volume 1, chapters 4 and 7.

Philadelphia joined Atlanta. Martin was under considerable pressure from administration officials to avoid higher interest rates. The staff, however, pointed to a 5 percent increase in demand for credit in February and increases in interest rates on long-term bonds. They attributed the higher bond yields to a "turn around in the thinking of market participants who previously had anticipated some relaxation of Federal Reserve policy" (Board Minutes, April 6, 1956, 14). With higher yields, banks preferred to borrow at the discount window instead of selling bills from their portfolios.

Governors Mills, Robertson, Charles N. Shephardson, and Szymczak favored the rate increase. Martin, Balderston, and Vardaman were not at the meeting, but Martin phoned to ask for a delay until the following week, when all Board members would be present and other banks could reach a decision. The Board had notified all other banks about the request for an increase following Atlanta's decision.

Effective April 13, the Board approved increases to 3 percent at Minneapolis and San Francisco and 2.75 percent at nine reserve banks. Chicago followed a week later. The Board authorized a 3 percent rate at any bank that chose to adopt it. The System had shown its independence by winning its first confrontation with an administration in an election year.

The consequences were much less than the administration feared. Between February and April, the federal funds rate rose 0.12 percentage points, and member bank borrowing increased $200 million. Weekly data showed increases of 0.35 to 0.5 points on Treasury bills and notes by the end of April with the largest increases at the shorter term. Though relatively small, the increases in Treasury bill rates brought these rates to their highest level since 1933. Annual growth of the monetary base remained in the neighborhood of 1 percent. Stock prices continued to rise until May.[148] The administration later recognized that the increase was appropriate. They did not protest the next increase in August (Saulnier, 1991, 92).

On April 27, Sproul resigned as president of the New York bank, effective June 30.[149] He attended his last open market meeting on May 9 and used the occasion to propose six studies of operational and procedural

148. At the April 17 meeting, Ralph Leach (Richmond) remarked that commercial banks in his district held few Treasury bills. He then illustrated how rare borrowing on commercial paper had become. Bankers had inquired about discounting eligible commercial paper, and one bank planned to borrow in that way in the next week (FOMC Minutes, April 17, 1956, 15).

149. Martin praised Sproul for his contributions to the System and invited him to return for the next meeting and to participate as long as he remained in the System (FOMC Minutes, May 9, 1956, 23, 38).

changes. Controversy arose over only one, "swaps," to permit the manager to exchange one type of bill for another when the maturity distribution of the bill portfolio was unbalanced. Other suggestions called for studies of operating procedures, the relation of monetary policy to debt management (jointly with the Treasury), the financing of government securities dealers, and operation of the federal funds market.[150] He did not include a study of the effect of monetary policy on economic activity.

Two weeks later, the economy again appeared less buoyant. The Federal Advisory Council (FAC) gave a mixed review. Only two members thought the economy would expand. Four expected a decline, and six expected the level to remain the same (Board Minutes, May 22, 1956, 4). Members from manufacturing regions were the most pessimistic. Industrial production fell in May and June. The FAC members favored keeping policy unchanged, unless business deteriorated. The staff report at the FOMC meeting the following day gave a similar mixed report on the economy. Consumer spending had slowed, but plans for investment remained robust.

Chairman Martin did not follow his usual custom of speaking last and forming a consensus. He spoke first, indicating that he wanted to change the directive by restoring the phrase "while taking into account any deflationary tendencies" that the committee had removed in March. The members agreed. Balderston proposed purchases of $400 to $500 million to increase free reserves to −$250 million. Martin went further. He preferred to raise free reserves toward zero over the next few months, but he described the change as a "shift in emphasis and not a change in policy" (FOMC Minutes, May 23, 1956, 29). Some members questioned both his recommendation and his characterization that this was not a change in policy. Following the meeting, borrowing declined and free reserves increased from monthly averages of $971 and −$504 in May to $769 and −$195 in June. The monthly average federal funds rate, however, remained about the same.

Once again, the intense focus on current reports, mistaking temporary for permanent change, misled the FOMC. Optimism soon returned. By late June, projections for output had become more positive, and pro-

150. The Board published the federal funds market study in Board of Governors (1959). Riefler had reported earlier on experience with short-term debt since the Accord. His study traced many of the differences between the markets for bills and certificates to differences in the way the Treasury marketed the two types of security. The Treasury had experienced attrition when marketing certificates and short-term notes but not when marketing bills. The study correctly attributed the difference to the use of auctions for Treasury bills versus fixed price offerings for certificates. Errors in pricing led to attrition or excess demand. The study also mentioned the greater frequency of bill offerings and other technical details (memo, Riefler to FOMC, Board files, April 10, 1956).

jected inflation remained low.[151] In July, the staff described the economy as "showing broad strength," despite the start of a steel strike. Actual inflation exceeded the Board's projections; consumer prices in May had the largest one-month increase in two years; average hourly earnings rose 6 percent from the year before.

William Trieber (New York), temporarily replacing Sproul, wanted to lower free reserves to −$400 million. Others expressed uncertainty about whether to ease or restrain the growth of credit. H. N. Mangels (San Francisco) and Powell (Minneapolis) discussed lowering their discount rates from 3 to 2.75 percent to align with the other banks, but Martin opposed any change while the Treasury was selling bonds.[152]

Alfred Hayes became president of the New York bank on August 1 and vice chairman of the FOMC on August 7 for the remainder of Allan Sproul's term. He remained until August 1975. His first FOMC meeting coincided with the British-French-Israeli invasion of Egypt to protect the Suez Canal from nationalization by the Egyptian government. Commodity prices began to rise with the outbreak of hostilities.

The slowdown in the economy had ended by the time of the August 1956 meeting. The staff reported that the economy showed renewed strength. The steel strike settlement raised wages, followed by higher steel prices. Hayes feared that "this was likely to start a chain reaction in other industries," a reference to prevalent concerns about inflation caused by rising costs, especially labor costs, pushing up prices, called cost-push inflation (FOMC Minutes, August 7, 1956, 10).

Hayes called for more restraint and lower free reserves, but he opposed an increase in the discount rate at that time. Most members agreed to defer a change in the discount rate until the Treasury completed its financing. As in the early postwar years, several expressed concern that monetary policy alone could not prevent inflation.[153] Only Robertson forcefully urged

151. The manager indicated at this meeting that he now watched the federal funds rate, not the Treasury bill rate. The bill rate could move for reasons unrelated to policy, for example, the sale of bills at quarterly corporate tax dates.

152. Abbott Mills commented on the excessive concern for free reserves and borrowing and the neglect of changes in the economy. "[T]he Committee's decisions are built so largely around market considerations that it is in danger of losing sight of its responsibilities for making credit adequately available" (FOMC Minutes, July 17, 1956, 33). On July 27, the executive committee of the Minneapolis bank voted to lower the discount rate to 2.75 percent. Country banks resented the 3 percent rate at a time when crops had to be marketed. The Board deferred action, citing Martin's concern about the national implications of a rate change during a period of Treasury financing.

153. The staff reported the annual increase in consumer prices reached 1.5 percent in June and that the rate of increase had continued in July. (In the year to May, annual rates of inflation had increased from −0.5 to 1 percent. May, June, and July show large monthly

a restrictive policy. The FOMC "should not credit monetary policy for keeping an even keel when things go well and deny responsibility when inflationary pressures seem to get the upper hand" (FOMC Minutes, August 7,
1956, 15). His statement received no support. At the opposite pole, Mills
argued that money was tight. Further tightening would reduce investor
confidence, "unsettled by the international tensions resulting from the
Suez Canal crisis" (ibid., 16).

Martin summarized the discussion in a lengthy statement, highlighting
the wage-cost spiral. "We are bordering on a state of over-employment . . .
[T]he steel strike had been a disaster" (ibid., 32). His recommendation
was to stay on an even keel until buyers completed payment for Treasury
securities while resolving "doubts on the side of tightness" (34). The only
decision was unanimous, to remove the clause reinserted in May that took
account of deflationary forces.[154]

The FOMC met again two weeks later. Member bank borrowing had
nearly doubled, and interest rates had increased at all maturities in response to market demand and the expected increase in the discount rate.
Rates on three- to five-year governments reached 3.5 percent, the highest
level since 1930. Banks raised their prime lending rates before the meeting. The reported increase in consumer prices, 0.7 percent for the month,
raised the annual rate of inflation to 2 percent, the highest rate since 1952.
A 7 percent increase in steel prices, following the strikes, convinced the
members that inflation would continue. Most members ignored the distinction between relative and general price changes.

The rapid rise in interest rates on short- and long-term maturities in
August 1956 contrasts with the much smaller response of interest rates
to much higher reported rates of inflation after World War II. One difference was that the Federal Reserve pegged rates in the earlier period, but
this explains only part of the difference. Holders did not sell most of their
bonds despite the reported inflation. In 1956–57, holders promptly sold
bonds, raising yields in response to inflation. One plausible explanation of

increases.) The proximate arithmetic cause was not higher wages. Agricultural prices had
lagged earlier in the decade. The report showed that they had increased 10 percent since the
previous December.

154. The FOMC again discussed several memos on whether the manager should engage
in "swaps" to balance the maturity distribution of the bill portfolio. Sproul's memo before his
retirement restated the reasons for engaging in swaps. Robertson responded, restating his
argument that the benefits were small and could be achieved in other ways. Trieber presented
New York's case at the meeting. Martin opposed, generally, but would permit limited authorization. The only decision was to solicit dealer opinion and revisit the issue. A month later,
the committee discussed the issue at length again, repeating most of the earlier arguments.
Finally, on September 25, the FOMC decided against portfolio swaps.

the difference is that the public expected inflation to persist after 1956, but not after 1947. The Livingston Survey (Chart 2.10 above), however, shows a rise to only 1 percent in the inflation rate predicted for 1957.

This time the administration did not object to the rate increase, despite the election (Saulnier, 1991, 92). The rise in inflation convinced Martin's critics that he had been right. Long-term interest rates did not peak until shortly after the peak in inflation in the fall of 1957, additional evidence of the market's new-found concern that inflation would not only rise and fall but would persist.

The FOMC responded to inflation by suggesting a 3 percent discount rate at the ten banks still at 2.75 percent, a move that followed the market.[155] Several members suggested an increase of 0.5. Only Governor Mills expressed concern that policy was too restrictive. He warned about a "destructively restrictive credit policy" that could cause "waves of unemployment with consequences both to the Federal Reserve System and the economy" (FOMC Minutes, August 21, 1956, 21). Borrowing declined slightly after the increase in the discount rate, raising free reserves, but the federal funds rate rose to nearly 3 percent, a percentage point above the year's earlier level.

Chairman Martin complimented the members on avoiding targets for free reserves. Although he expressed concern about inflation, the consensus, he said, was to avoid any change in open market policy. The FOMC was reluctant to tighten further until after the election. Martin urged the committee on September 11 to neither ignore nor be influenced by the election, but Robertson said he would argue for a tighter policy if it were not for the coming election (FOMC Minutes, October 16, 18).

The larger problem was lack of agreement about what should be done.[156]

155. The Board made the change on Friday despite a Treasury bill auction the following Monday. Martin noted that the market anticipated the change, so it would not surprise the market. Bill rates rose fifty-eight basis points from the previous weekly auction.

156. The members did not agree about what should be done or why. One group, concerned about the seasonal demand for reserves, proposed to reduce reserve requirements on time deposits by one percentage point to supply $400 million of reserves. Bryan (Atlanta) pushed his proposal to improve the competitive position of country banks relative to thrift associations and to help finance crop inventories. Only three others joined Bryan. Hayes wanted to tighten (after the next Treasury financing) by selling bills and forcing banks to borrow reserves. To assist their borrowing, he proposed easing regulation A governing use of the discount window. During the Treasury financing, the System should provide "whatever reserves should be needed to permit the banks to do their part in a successful program" (FOMC Minutes, September 25, 1956, 10). Leedy (Kansas City) proposed reducing reserve requirement ratios in New York and Chicago to assist the Treasury. Mills favored a somewhat easier policy. Robertson wanted to tighten. Governor Shephardson expressed concern about the stability of the dollar. He favored a penalty rate to discourage continuous borrowing by a few banks.

The staff report for the September 25 meeting tried to reduce concerns about persistent inflation. Ralph Young noted that growth of the money stock (M_1) was below the growth of real GNP for the year. For the previous five years, the two growth rates were about equal.[157] The System had followed a counter-cyclical policy by keeping money growth below the growth of real output, raising interest rates, in the face of increased demand for goods and credit. There is no sign in the members' comments that they recognized the implications of his statement or accepted it as a policy guide. In later testimony, Martin disagreed, describing policy in retrospect as slightly too easy in 1955–56 (Joint Economic Committee, 1957, 606).

The Federal Advisory Council told the Board on September 18 that business continued at a high level in all districts. Housing starts were below the previous year, so the administration eased mortgage credit in September to encourage housing purchases before the election.[158]

The System made no other changes in policy before the election. The federal funds rate remained near the discount rate at about 3 percent, but long-term rates continued to rise. In October, the Treasury experimented with auctioning longer-term Treasury bills instead of taking bids at a fixed price. The auction was successful for the Treasury, and it reduced pressure on the Federal Reserve to support a fixed price, but it did not become standard practice.

Three issues that would reoccur many times arose as the year ended. First, the Treasury bill rate rose above the discount rate. Second, the fixed exchange rate for the British pound came under pressure.[159] Third, rates on

157. "The slower growth of the money supply this year is to be attributed in part to Federal Reserve policy. That policy since 1951 has been geared to counter-cyclical objectives in the short-run and orderly growth at sustained high levels of activity without inflation over the longer-run" (FOMC Minutes, September 25, 1956, 4).

158. Martin asked the bankers on the FAC three questions that indicated his concerns at the time: (1) does tax deductibility of interest payments reduce the deterrent effect on borrowing? (2) have demands for long-term financing of investment increased relative to demands for short-term financing and, if so, are bank portfolios less liquid? (3) are large and preferred creditors satisfied while legitimate demands of smaller business are not? FAC members replied that real estate credit and loans to carry securities were most sensitive to the interest rate, but that much borrowing was not. Council members dismissed the second question and said there was no evidence of relatively greater restriction on loans to small business (Board Minutes, Sept. 18, 1956, 11–16).

159. Britain's currency problems in late 1956 followed the invasion of Egypt (with France and Israel) after President Gamal Nasser of Egypt nationalized the Suez Canal. The canal had been owned by British and French investors. Despite continued exchange controls in Britain, reported gold holdings fell to a low of $1.77 billion in December 1956, a loss of about $250 million from the previous year. Britain also sold about 30 percent of its holdings of U.S. Treasury securities (Board of Governors, 1976, 916, 968–69). The U.S. Treasury sold a special issue of $1 billion of Treasury bills to assist the British by absorbing the capital inflow.

federal funds, Treasury bills, and all longer-term instruments rose above the fixed ceilings on time and saving deposit rates administered by the Federal Reserve under the Board's regulation Q.

At the FOMC meeting on October 16, New York asked for guidance about the rise in Treasury bill rates above the 3 percent discount rate. The market anticipated an increase in the discount rate.[160] By December, new issue bill rates were nearly 0.25 percentage points above the discount rate. The FOMC's only monetary policy decision was to add the words "while recognizing additional pressures in the money, credit, and capital markets arising from seasonal factors and international conditions" to their continuing directive calling for "restraining inflationary developments in the interest of sustainable economic growth" (FOMC Minutes, December 10, 1956, 29). Only Governor Mills favored reducing interest rates below the discount rate by open market purchases. None favored an increase in the discount rate, although Mangels (San Francisco) thought his directors might soon vote an increase.[161]

Regulation Q. The Banking Act of 1933 empowered the Board to set maximum interest rates on time and savings deposits. A common belief at the time was that competition for time and savings deposits had contributed to stock exchange speculation by financing speculators. Banks, it was said, would not reduce deposit rates, so they took more risk instead. The Board initially set the rates at 3 percent. On January 1, 1936, it lowered ceiling rates to 2.5 percent, where they remained. By late 1955, open market rates on new issues of Treasury bills temporarily reached the regulation Q ceiling. A year later, open market rates were well above posted ceiling rates.[162]

The Board held discussions of ceiling rate violations throughout 1955. As usual when prices (rates) are controlled, there were ways around the

---

The Federal Reserve purchased between $60 and $70 million to support the offer. The pound weakened against the dollar, but Britain did not devalue.

160. The concern at the time was that the volume of float would rise. If the manager offset float by selling Treasury bills, bill rates might rise further above the discount rate. Martin used the occasion to define "feel of the market." If float reduced borrowing and increased free reserves while the System account maintained the same degree of tightness that the committee had been trying to have, he would not be bothered by the increase in bill yields (FOMC Minutes, October 16, 1956, 34). The statement left discretion to the manager, as Martin recognized, and avoided stating how to judge the degree of tightness. It relied on a judgment about persistence of higher bill yields.

161. When the manager first asked permission to buy and sell acceptances, Robertson suggested the manager would soon ask to enlarge operations. In December, the FOMC increased the account to $50 million over objections by Robertson and Carl Allen (Chicago). The principal objection was that purchases supported a price.

162. The ceiling rates were maximum rates. Non-member banks could not pay more than the maximum rate set by state agencies for their state (Board of Governors, 1976, 638).

ceiling. Banks offered an array of services—free safety deposit boxes, advisory services, use of foreign exchange facilities, etc.—and reduced rates on loans to circumvent the ceiling (Board Minutes, April 19, 1955, 12). Cases of this kind had occurred in the past, but their frequency increased as interest rates rose. The Board had considered, but not adopted, a general statement about what constituted payment of interest in violation of the ceiling, knowing that an explicit statement opened opportunities to circumvent it. The Board's only general policy was not to have one by leaving most cases to the examiners to decide on a case-by-case basis.

The Federal Advisory Council also could not state a general policy specifying what constituted indirect payment of interest. They favored self-policing by individual banks, and they agreed with the Board that the main violation of the law was the absorption of exchange charges by large banks to obtain correspondent balances of non-member banks that charged customers for collecting checks.[163] The reserve banks disagreed with the FAC; they did not want to announce "self-policing." The Board continued its policy of relying on examiners.

The next challenge to the existing ceiling came in December 1955, when a New York bank asked permission to compound interest payments monthly instead of quarterly. Several governors supported Governor Robertson's proposal to increase the ceiling rate to 3 percent as an alternative. The reserve banks, representing many of their members, opposed any increase. The Board agreed to permit monthly compounding but left the maximum rate unchanged. The new rule applied to time deposits but not passbook savings.

Ceiling rates became a frequent topic for discussion at Board meetings in 1956. The record suggests the number of unforeseen problems that arise when price controls become effective.[164]

Most of the governors favored higher rates to recognize changes in

163. The Board's practice was more restrictive than the FDIC's. The Board asked the FDIC to adopt a common standard, but the FDIC declined (Board Minutes, March 25, 1955, 9–10). Some member banks complained about the advantage to state non-member banks that were members of FDIC.

164. The State of North Carolina did not permit its treasurer to deposit state funds in banks that paid less than the yield on Treasury bills. The legislature was not scheduled to meet, and the banks were under pressure to hold the deposits and reserves so that they could lend to farmers for spring planting (Board Minutes, April 30, May 9). If regulation Q ceilings changed, Treasury saving bonds would be at a disadvantage. Congress would have to increase the rate to avoid runoff. Changes would alter the competitive position of non-member banks and thrift associations unless other regulations changed at the same time. Raising rates on short-term time deposits would attract spillover from demand deposits and thus expand credit by lowering average reserve requirement ratios (Board Minutes, June 27, 1956, 5). Ceiling rates also caused New York banks to lose deposits to foreign banks.

the market and to maintain competition. Several of the staff opposed any change. Riefler made the most forceful statement, arguing that banks would use time deposits to expand their non-commercial banking activities. He opposed "mixed banking . . . a mixture of long- and short-term banking in one institution" (Board Minutes, August 24, 1956, 13). Furthermore, higher rates allowed banks to issue "a due bill on the government" (deposit insurance) to expand their long-term, high-yield investments (ibid., 14). Governor Szymczak agreed with Riefler, while Governors Vardaman and Shephardson argued that Riefler's argument would permit less regulated competitors to take over banking functions. Governor Robertson said that if the statutes could be rewritten, he favored elimination of interest rate regulation.

Chairman Martin postponed further discussion until after a meeting of the FAC. At first, he had been persuaded by Riefler's argument, but he was now uncertain. The Comptroller and the FDIC opposed any increase. The Treasury had not taken a position, but it considered asking Congress to increase interest rates on savings bonds.

The Federal Advisory Council unanimously favored higher ceiling rates on deposits with no more than six months maturity. These rates would rise from 1 to 1.5 percent under ninety days and from 2 to 2.5 percent from ninety days to six months. New York banks had lost time deposits to foreign banks because of the low ceiling rates. The higher rates also attracted deposits of state and municipal governments (Board Minutes, September 18, 1956, 26–33). A week later, the reserve bank presidents agreed with the proposed change also.

Chairman Martin discussed the proposed change in ceiling rates with Secretary Humphrey, and the Board notified the FDIC of the proposed change. Finally, on December 3, effective January 1, the Board rejected the FAC proposal and voted to increase to 3 percent the ceiling rates on all savings deposits and on time deposits with six months or more to maturity. It voted to increase to 2.5 percent the rates on time deposits with more than ninety days and less than six months maturity. Rates for shorter-term time deposits remained at 1 percent. The FDIC changed its rates also.

Governor Robertson voted against the change, although he had been one of the first to endorse higher rates when discussion began early in the year. He believed that higher interest rates would raise bank costs, making it more difficult to raise capital, and encourage banks to take risky positions. Higher rates would not increase the amount saved; it would redistribute the stock of savings deposits among institutions (Board Minutes, November 30, 1956, 10–11). These were the arguments made earlier by Governor Mills, who now voted for the change.

The rise in market rates was the critical factor bringing the Board to a decision. Rates had increased to 3.5 percent on long-term Treasury bonds and to 3 percent for the shortest maturities. Martin believed savers should share in the higher rates, and Szymczak, who had initially opposed any change, gave that as a reason for changing his mind (Board Minutes, December 3, 1956, 18). As part of the change in rates, the Board permitted banks to compound at less than quarterly intervals provided the compound rates did not exceed the new ceilings.

Several months later, the Board asked the Federal Advisory Council about the response to the change in ceiling rates. It learned that (1) banks that raised their rate to 3 percent "experienced a material increase in savings deposits"; (2) the increase in savings deposits was mainly a reallocation of assets, not a change in the saving rate; and (3) some banks responded by seeking higher rates on their earning assets (Board Minutes, May 14, 1957, 16–20). FAC President Robert V. Fleming added that there had not been a large shift from demand to time deposits.

End of the Expansion

Members of the Federal Advisory Council looked ahead optimistically at their November 1956 meeting. Most told the Board that business would continue to be good in the first half of 1957. They warned, however, of lower profit margins, inventory accumulation, and the drought affecting much of the country (Board Minutes, November 20, 1956, 2). The FAC remained optimistic at its February 1957 meeting, but it repeated its concern about profits and added concern about investments. "[N]arrowing of the profit margin tends to make business investment less attractive" (Board Minutes, February 19, 1957, 2). FAC members reported some evidence of excess plant capacity after the long investment boom (ibid., 18).

In the first part of 1957, the economy continued the variable pattern of 1956, growing moderately in the first and third quarters, declining slightly in the second quarter. Industrial production rose in only four of the first eight months, followed by recession after August. The civilian unemployment rate remained near 4 percent.

The new element was persistent inflation. The GNP deflator and consumer prices both rose at a 3.75 percent average rate before the recession. The government budget remained in surplus, and money growth remained below the growth of real GNP. Monetary velocity continued to rise with interest rates, inflation, and new ways of economizing on cash holdings, including the spread of deposit banking. The public reduced its very large wartime accumulation of cash balances relative to income.

By January, the S&P index of stock prices was 6 percent below its peak in July 1956. The index fell in three of the next eight months, reflecting the variability of output and economic activity, higher inflation, and interest rates. The Board discussed a reduction in stock market margin requirements in January, but decided against a change.[165] In April, the New York Stock Exchange asked the Board to reduce margin requirements because volume had fallen. The Board's staff reported that "margin changes appeared to have had an immediate and perceptible impact on the level of stock market credit but no consistent or sustained effects on stock prices or trading volume" (Board Minutes, April 23, 1957, 8). The Board decided that inflationary psychology and ample buying power in margin accounts suggested that requirements should remain unchanged. Margin requirements remained at 70 percent until January 1958.

Judged by member bank borrowing and free reserves, monetary policy became more restrictive. Judged by the federal funds rate or growth of the monetary base, policy remained unchanged. Judged by growth of the real monetary base, monetary policy remained restrictive until after the recession began. Judged by the Board after the fact, circumstances called for more restrictive policy. It tightened policy by raising the discount rate and reducing holdings of government securities, so that banks were forced to borrow more at a higher discount rate while adjusting to the new conditions (Annual Report, 1957, 7, 32).

At the start of 1957, the staff described credit market developments as "ominous in their implications" (FOMC Minutes, January 8, 1957, 5). Borrowing at the turn of the year had increased rapidly. At a time when System policy called for tightness, borrowed reserves began to decline. The reason was that the manager acted in anticipation of large credit demands by purchasing $1.3 billion in December in the belief that "because of reduced liquidity positions, banks might be reluctant to supply these rather large credit needs" (ibid., 6). The manager relied on the "feel of the market." The decline in borrowing and the credit expansion showed that he had misjudged the credit situation.[166]

The manager, who was the target of the criticism, dismissed it citing the

165. The reasoning was convoluted. The staff memo reported that conditions had changed since the last increase in April 1955. The present level of margin requirements could not be justified on grounds used to support the last increase. However, the economic outlook remained positive, so a reduction could be misinterpreted as an easier policy stance (Board Minutes, January 18, 1957, 24–25).

166. "These developments illustrate the difficulty of relying upon the feel of the market and the level of interest rates as criteria for System operations . . . To attempt to relieve . . . tightness means facilitating the expansion" (FOMC Minutes, January 8, 1957, 7–8). The staff report did not propose an alternative measure to replace free reserves or borrowing, but the quoted comment shows the changed interpretation of borrowing and free reserves.

difficulties of operating at the end of the year. The figures for borrowing and free reserves did not give the right impression. Interest rates had increased. The manager thought "it would be possible to recapture the spirit although not the amount of net borrowed reserves that existed early in December" (ibid., 37). The "feel of the market" was the best guide, he said.

Governors Shephardson and Robertson wanted to increase the discount rate and reduce free reserves to counteract inflationary tendencies, but Hayes did not want a higher discount rate. Agreement was hard to reach, since there was no agreement on what constituted ease or tightness and how these terms related to what was happening in the economy. The consensus was to reduce free reserves and change the directive to remove the reference to seasonal factors.

Events continued to surprise the committee and the manager. Demand for credit declined, and market interest rates fell during the winter. Shephardson and Robertson continued to press for a more restrictive policy to reduce inflation. Robertson, looking back, criticized policy in 1956 for responding too quickly to temporary periods of slowing demand. In a prophetic statement he warned that the committee had to distinguish between permanent and temporary changes. The System "cannot effectively curb inflationary developments if we adopt a policy of easing every time there is a temporary lull in an expansion" (FOMC Minutes, February 18, 1957, 23). Most others worried more about the need to prevent attrition in Treasury refundings and short-term changes in the economy. Data showed a decline in industrial production and slower increases in commodity prices. Chairman Martin read the consensus as favoring the status quo.[167]

The budget added to the FOMC's concerns. After two years of budget surpluses, the administration's 1958 budget asked for a 10 percent increase in spending. Secretary Humphrey, in an unusual move, criticized the budget, especially increased spending, and asked Congress to reduce his administration's requested spending to avoid "a depression that will curl your

167. The lack of clarity in the instructions to the manager continued to create difficulties in deciding whether he had followed the FOMC's instructions. Free reserves fell in January, but the staff described policy as easier. The staff (Thomas) argued that "the ease referred to in January . . . was not because the System was not carrying out a restrictive policy but resulted entirely because credit was being liquidated very rapidly" (FOMC Minutes, February 18, 1957, 38–39). Martin added: "There was no point in trying to pursue a more restrictive policy if the objectives were being carried out" (ibid., 39). These statements shift the measure of ease and tightness from free reserves to credit growth. Free reserves "eased" because borrowing declined with the decline in bank lending. The statements recognize the problem with use of free reserves, but the FOMC resisted choosing another measure of ease and restraint. The main reasons were lack of agreement on an alternative and a reluctance to target an interest rate.

hair" (Saulnier, 1991, 103).[168] Apparently he thought an enlarged budget causes depression. Eisenhower agreed despite the obvious criticism of his administration's budget. The System's concern was that the budget provided additional stimulus to an economy faced with excess demand and inflation.[169] To the Federal Reserve, an expanding budget caused inflation. Its policy of financing deficits by issuing money reinforced this conclusion.

At Hayes's suggestion the FOMC changed the directive at the March 5 meeting to reflect its concern about the outlook. It added the words "recognizing uncertainties in the business outlook, the financial markets, and the international situation" to its concern about inflation (FOMC Minutes, March 5, 1957, 20, 42). The FOMC reappointed Robert Rouse as manager of the open market account without complaint from Martin.

Governor Mills asked whether the very slow growth of the money stock was consistent with economic growth. The System's purported policy of keeping long-term growth of money equal to the growth of output did not contemplate a "static money supply." Woodlief Thomas dismissed this concern, saying, "[I]t was necessary to look beyond the measure of the volume of credit to the flow of funds" (ibid., 17). He did not offer a specific measure. Chairman Martin added that "the only way in which we could have growth without inflation . . . was by reducing spending and increasing saving" (ibid., 18).

A forthcoming Treasury offering was a main concern. As usual, Mills favored supplying enough reserves to support the offer (ibid., 28). Robertson warned against "the kind of situation which had occurred time and time again of easing up the market just before a Treasury financing and then of tightening immediately afterward" (ibid., 29). Balderston, Irons (Dallas), Allen (Chicago), Fulton (Cleveland), and Bryan (Atlanta) sided with Robertson. Most of these members favored letting banks borrow to

---

168. To restrict expansion, the administration increased the interest rate on FHA (housing) loans by 0.5 to 5 percent and ended accelerated depreciation schedules to reduce demand for investment. This was a perverse procyclical move. The proposed 1958 budget predicted a surplus of $1.8 billion.

169. At about this time, the Treasury asked the Federal Reserve to exchange some maturing securities for longer-term securities to help extend the maturity of the debt. The Treasury claimed that market participants would be encouraged to take longer-term bonds at refundings if the Federal Reserve was willing to take them also. This violated bills-only policy. The Federal Reserve staff (Riefler) proposed instead to exchange a large part of the System portfolio for a non-marketable perpetuity that paid interest at a 1 percent rate. The new bond would be convertible into Treasury bills if in the future the Federal Reserve needed bills to reduce the monetary base. The main purposes of the proposed exchange were to reduce the Treasury's interest cost by $400 million and the System's large revenues. Since the Federal Reserve paid most of its excess revenue to the Treasury, any effect would be small. The System did not adopt either proposal.

obtain reserves instead of using open market purchases. This reflected the persistent belief that policy tightened if banks borrowed. Chairman Martin concluded that the majority opposed "too much encouragement to the Treasury financing" (40).

Robertson thought he had finally gained support for his opposition to the policy of assisting the Treasury. He soon found that he was mistaken. The account manager purchased securities and allowed borrowing to decline. At the next FOMC meeting, Robertson was angry. He made a lengthy statement "as dispassionately as possible," accusing the manager of allowing bill rates to decline just before the Treasury offering, contrary to the consensus and to the even keel policy (FOMC Minutes, March 27, 1957, 4–5). Rouse replied, defending his actions and asserting that "there were pressures in the market that were not apparent from the figures presented. . . . Some members of the Committee might not realize the serious situation that the Treasury faced" (ibid., 5–6). Hayes defended the manager. Rouse added that he had kept the market too tight.[170]

Robertson then drew the correct conclusion. The problem lay in the statement, not the interpretation. The error was the "inadequacy of the steps the Committee had taken to specify what it wanted" (ibid., 8). He regarded the manager's actions as inconsistent with the committee's decision, but he recognized that other interpretations could be made. Allen (Chicago) agreed with Robertson, but Martin defended the manager. As long as Martin and several others on the FOMC opposed giving more explicit instructions, the manager had considerable autonomy. Neither the minutes nor the background papers make clear the extent to which Martin or Sproul influenced his decisions outside of the meetings.

Ralph Young used his regular briefing to explain why expectations of inflation had become established.[171] He described the appeal to businesses of negative real interest rates, perhaps the first time that idea appeared in a Federal Reserve statement and certainly the first time anyone at the Federal Reserve developed the idea at an FOMC meeting. Households and firms that borrowed to finance purchases of durables or invest in plants and equipment had paid little to borrow. "Little wonder, with prices con-

---

170. The weekly average federal funds rate remained 3 percent throughout, but the Treasury bill rate declined. Hayes explained the decline as resulting from an unanticipated increase in the demand for bills (FOMC Minutes, March 27, 1957, 8).

171. "Creeping inflation was no longer a theory, it was a fact being realized. Moreover, the process was predicted to continue, with more and more confidence, for the longer-run" (FOMC Minutes, March 27, 1957, 14). Young then cited three reasons. Monetary policy had validated the postwar increase in prices and the Korean price increases. It had moved aggressively to stop the recession of 1953–54. Young gave a numerical example showing how an (unanticipated) inflation reduced the real value of a corporation's debt.

tinuing to advance and expectations of a longer-run uptrend increasingly widespread, that business demands for short- and long-term credit multiplied" (ibid., 14).

Young then challenged the committee to choose between price stability and rapid response to cyclical and temporary fluctuations.[172] A similar idea later became prominent as the Phillips curve tradeoff between inflation and output or employment. Erickson (Boston) complimented Young on his statement. Shephardson, Balderston, and Robertson wanted the committee to give more attention to long-term goals, but they did not suggest procedural changes. Most of the members confined their comments to conditions in their districts. Policy remained unchanged with an admonition to err on the side of restraint.

Pressure from the Eisenhower administration to ease policy increased. Raymond Saulnier, the new chairman of the Council of Economic Advisers, told Martin that policy was too tight (Bremner 2004, 107). Humphrey and Burgess expressed concern about problems the Treasury faced in marketing its debt. Martin called a telephone meeting of the FOMC to discuss a warning from Undersecretary Burgess that the Treasury's current issue would fail. Dealers expected 25 percent attrition (FOMC Minutes, telephone meeting April 24, 1957, 1, 4). Rouse reported that many dealers shared Burgess's view. They believed policy was too tight.

In the most recent week, member bank borrowing reached $1.2 billion and free reserves fell to −$700 million, about $100 million lower than planned. Interest rates on Treasury securities rose modestly during the month. An increase in float increased reserves, but usually the Federal Reserve offset the change.[173] Remembering Morgenthau's policies in the 1930s, the Treasury threatened to shift its balances from reserve banks to commercial banks to increase bank reserves.

Allen (Chicago) said the Treasury wanted a bailout by the Federal Reserve[174] (FOMC Minutes, April 24, 1957, 7). Hayes wanted the instructions changed to give the manager discretion to make repurchase agreements. The committee voted to maintain restraint but assist the Treasury by giving the manager leeway to prevent further tightening.

---

172. In a clear warning of the risk that would become reality, Young said: "The Committee needs to consider carefully at this time whether it should not regard the objective of a stable value of the dollar as overriding the objective of adjusting flexibly and promptly to short-run cyclical changes in activity. It needs to weigh the risk that monetary policy may lose strategic opportunity to make its discipline effective" (FOMC Minutes, March 26, 1957, 15–16).

173. Some of the problems were transitory, for example a rise in float because of a Railway Express strike.

174. Carl E. Allen, Jr., was the fourth president of the Chicago bank. He served from October 1, 1956, to December 31, 1961. He was a strong proponent of price stability.

Hayes missed the committee's next meeting. His alternate, William Trieber, discussed New York's view of the relation of the Federal Reserve to the Treasury and the government. New York's view was similar to Martin's and, like Martin's, restricted the meaning of independence. Congress set the budget and government spending. The Federal Reserve could discourage or postpone private spending, but "such a purpose is inapplicable to Government borrowing. The Government must be financed." The Treasury determined how the Government was financed by setting the terms of its issues. The Federal Reserve had to coordinate its actions with the Treasury while maintaining responsibility for credit policy. If the Treasury priced its securities "in line with market rates . . . the System has responsibility to avoid action that may jeopardize the financing" (FOMC Minutes, May 7, 1957, 11–12).

Turning to recent problems, Trieber expressed most concern about the Treasury's use of its cash balance to increase bank reserves.[175] The Federal Reserve, for its part, must consider the Treasury's problems. If it failed to do so, it could lose its independence.

Robertson argued that the Treasury's use of its cash balances was "an obvious and unjustifiable attempt to interfere with Federal Reserve credit policy" (ibid., 22). The "Treasury should be obliged to compete with other borrowers for available funds and the System should avoid as much as possible making things easier for the Treasury with the result of creating a situation inconsistent with the System's broad objectives" (ibid., 21–22).

Mills sided with Trieber. He believed that some members failed to distinguish "what was theoretically possible . . . with what was practically attainable" (ibid., 22). He thought the manager should have latitude to gauge the feel of the market and to balance the need to prevent over-expansion of credit against the Treasury's requirements.

Chairman Martin tried to find middle ground between the conflicting views. "If the Committee ignored theory completely, it would be in trouble, and if it ignored practice, it also would be in trouble." He agreed with Governor Vardaman on the value of studying communications problems with the Treasury, but the timing was not right. Once again the Federal Reserve looked directly at the conflict between implementing its policy and

175. "When, however, the Treasury manages its accounts for the specific purpose of increasing, or otherwise influencing, bank reserves, it is engaging directly in the act of credit management for which the Federal Reserve has primary responsibility. That we do not want" (FOMC Minutes, May 7, 1957, 12). This was reminiscent of several clashes between Chairman Eccles and Treasury Secretary Morgenthau in the 1930s. Then as in 1957, the Federal Reserve did not want the Treasury to take over its function. The Treasury wanted to reduce its borrowing cost. Trieber did not mention that open market sales could reverse the Treasury's action.

maintaining an even keel to help the Treasury, then looked away. On this critical issue, Martin failed to exercise leadership or consider what might be done. Like others who argued for taking practical considerations into account, he had no suggestions about how or when to remove the reserves added during these periods of Treasury support.

Inflation continued to increase. The twelve-month average inflation rate reached 3.75 percent in April, the highest rate since the early months of the Korean War, before the Accord. Anticipations of continued inflation also increased and spread, as Young had warned. The Board was aware of the changed anticipations. The Federal Advisory Council told the Board that "the business community views with concern the rising price level and the increase in the cost of living. . . . [T]here is a tendency to consider only the immediate future and to grant wage increases, especially if they can be absorbed largely or entirely by higher prices" (Board Minutes, May 14, 1957, 10).

As anticipations of inflation became firm, wages, prices, and interest rates increased. The System now faced the problem that would remain. People complained about inflation, but they complained also about higher interest rates and tight money. William Mitchell, a member of the FAC, reported that businessmen would understand the reason for tight money, if it was explained. He urged the Board to undertake an educational campaign, but Martin demurred on the grounds that the System "might be accused of being in the political area" (ibid., 12).[176]

All but one member of the FAC believed business conditions would remain favorable or become stronger. The Board's staff shared this view. Several FOMC members suggested increasing discount rates at the May 28 meeting, and Martin agreed that they should have increased the discount rate earlier. He was "alarmed about the picture; and 'alarmed' was the correct word to use" (FOMC Minutes, May 28, 1957, 33). He remained hesitant, however, because any actions would "compound the system's and the Treasury's difficulties" (ibid., 34). The System had to support a seasonal increase in demand for credit. The Treasury had to refund debt and maintain ownership of $55 billion in savings bonds. If rates rose, or were expected to increase, there might be a run from savings bonds.

176. Martin recognized that as anticipations of inflation firmed, it became more costly to reduce inflation. At a meeting with the FAC, "Chairman Martin inquired whether the public was growing increasingly cynical about the possibility of resisting inflation, and to this question Messrs. [William R.] Mitchell, [Robert V.] Fleming, [Homer J.] Livingston, and others indicated that such a tendency was developing. Chairman Martin went on to say that this compounded the difficulties confronting those who would resist inflation" (Board Minutes, May 14, 1957, 12). FAC President Fleming explained that with full employment and strong demand, businessmen became reluctant to resist demands for higher wages if it meant a strike.

He favored increasing the discount rate, but not right away. He thought the situation was "at a most critical juncture in the battle against inflation" (ibid., 36). On one side was a continued rise in velocity and a flight from the dollar, on the other a run on the Treasury. It was best, he concluded, to maintain current policy. Hayes responded to Martin's statement by saying that he did not see the need for a higher discount rate. "He had not reached a conclusion that the inflationary forces were very definitely and strongly in the ascendancy" (ibid., 38). With its two leaders opposed and the others divided, the committee did not act.[177]

Discussion of the discount rate, inflation, and Treasury financing continued without resolution. Johns (St. Louis) believed "the System must assist the Treasury in its coming financing. I think this should be done without pique . . . not as a bailing out of the Treasury, but as a move in the public interest" (FOMC Minutes, June 18, 1957, 15). Raising the discount rate would flaunt their independence because the case was not strong. Mills, Vardaman, and Hayes agreed. The System must satisfy the government's demand for funds in the public interest. Pressure to aid the Treasury came from Congress also. On May 31, Congressman Wright Patman sent a threatening telegram to Martin asking him to "carefully weigh the consequences—both for the Treasury and the Federal Reserve of the continued refusal of the Open Market Committee to facilitate Treasury borrowings. . . . The time has come for the Open Market Committee to make a decision. Will the Federal Reserve be restored to its intended function of providing the economy with the money and credit necessary to carry on commerce and trade, and of aiding the Treasury in its borrowings . . . or shall the System insist on standing aloof . . . " (telegram, Patman to Martin, Board files, May 31, 1957). Patman then urged the Federal Reserve to buy bonds until they reached par from the 12 percent discount at which some sold. This would mean a return to the pegging policy of 1942–51. The Federal Reserve's position continued to be that independence did not remove its obligation to prevent failure of a properly priced Treasury offering. "While Federal Reserve policy may at times seek to discourage or postpone private borrowing . . . such purpose is inapplicable to government borrowing. The

177. Although the circumstances were very different, the timing recalls the long delay in 1929 before deciding to increase the discount rate. In both periods, the System finally increased the discount rate in August, just as the economy reached a peak. This time, however, the two sides had reversed positions. New York was reluctant to move, while members of the Board—Robertson, Shephardson, and Balderston—were most eager. Growth was much stronger in 1929, and inflation was much higher in 1957. Stock prices began to increase, a move that the staff (Thomas) interpreted as evidence that the public expected inflation to continue (FOMC Minutes, June 18, 1957, 10). Thomas's statement does not explain why he believed inflation should increase stock prices.

government must be financed" (letter, Trieber to Vardaman, Board files, May 7, 1957). This repeated the System's justification for even keel policy and for its occasional efforts to help the Treasury sell its bonds.

A few members remained opposed. Bryan argued that the System risked "frittering away . . . the integrity of the American dollar" (ibid., 17). Fulton (Cleveland), Robertson, and Shephardson agreed with Bryan. Allen (Chicago) wanted the banks to raise their prime rates before the System increased its rates. With no consensus on what to do, the FOMC did nothing.[178]

The discount rate remained below the bill rate, and inflation remained at 3 to 3.5 percent, but several FOMC members continued to oppose tighter policy, including a discount rate increase.[179] A split developed in the FOMC. One group, led by Hayes, argued that raising the discount rate would raise market rates but leave the Treasury no better able to compete for funds (FOMC Minutes, July 9, 1957, 13). Those favoring a higher discount rate split also. Some wanted an immediate increase; others preferred to wait until after the Treasury completed its forthcoming financing.

Waiting for the Treasury meant a month's delay.[180] The July 30 meeting came just after the Treasury had completed its financing. The bill rate jumped to 3.36 from 3.17 percent a week earlier (FOMC Minutes, July 30, 1957, 3). Rouse reported that the market anticipated increases in the discount rate and the prime rate when the Treasury offering was in the market, but neither he nor others recognized that the anticipation weakened the case for an even keel policy.

Inflation continued. The staff reported wage increases of 1 percent a

178. Woodlief Thomas reminded the FOMC that money growth remained low, about 1 percent for the past two years. Velocity continued to rise, a result, he said, of the liquidity built up in the war and early postwar. The increase in monetary velocity financed the rise in prices and wages. Velocity had increased 7 percent in 1956 and 5 percent in the most recent twelve months (FOMC Minutes, June 18, 1957, 9). For the entire expansion, 1954:2–1957:3, velocity increased 14.5 percent or an average of 4.5 percent a year. At the New York bank, Garvy (1959) studied the postwar rise in velocity and concluded, as Thomas had, that much of it was due to the excess money balances accumulated in the war and early postwar. Friedman and Schwartz (1963, chapter 12) accept this explanation also. On that interpretation, the adjustment was a change in level that would end without additional System action.

179. The 3 to 3.5 percent is the annual rate of CPI increase. The FOMC minutes report a much higher number, 8.5 percent (4.25 percent a year) for the period since mid-1955 for all commodities other than food (FOMC Minutes, July 9, 1957, 7).

180. Robert B. Anderson and Julian Baird replaced George Humphrey and W. Randolph Burgess as Treasury Secretary and Undersecretary. Baird was a Minneapolis banker. Anderson came from Texas, had served as Secretary of the Navy, then as Deputy Defense Secretary in the Eisenhower administration. Earlier he had been vice chairman of the Board of the Dallas Reserve bank. Martin announced that the Board had appointed the members of a committee to study the underwriting of Treasury issues.

month in May and June and a 5.5 percent annual increase in GNP reflecting "rising prices and inventory accumulation in anticipation of further rises" (ibid., 6). Martin agreed with Mills that the System had to increase restraint before the next Treasury financing. Hayes disagreed. He thought the economy continued at a high level but growth showed evidence of slowing.

Finally, on August 8, as the economy reached a peak, the Board approved requests from four banks to raise their discount rates to 3.5 percent, the highest nominal rate since February–March 1933. Governor Vardaman opposed the increase but voted for it to make the vote unanimous (Board Minutes, August 8, 1957, 5). Within the month, all other banks followed. New York and Cleveland came last, two weeks later.[181]

The August 8 decision came two days after major banks raised their prime lending rates. This removed one of the obstacles, reluctance by some governors to lead the market up. A problem with their argument is that rates on a wide variety of instruments had increased much earlier; Treasury bill rates had been above the discount rate since May. Following the announcement, open market rates rose higher. Federal funds reached 3.5 percent by the end of August; in September, Treasury bill rates were again above the discount rate. Banks continued to borrow $900 million to $1 billion of reserves. With reported inflation at 3 to 3.5 percent, the real value of the discount rate remained near zero. Misled by the nominal rate, the Federal Reserve thought it had acted decisively.

At his reconfirmation hearing in 1956, Martin had described the Federal Reserve's objective as "leaning against the wind." Whatever he may have intended, the System was slow to act against rising inflation. The variable growth of output explains part of the delay. Neglect of the difference between real and nominal rates, concern for Treasury refinancing problems, and reluctance to raise rates to levels not experienced in twenty-five years played a role also. The problem of agreeing on effective action returned many times in the next twenty years.

Martin's style also played a role. He worked by consensus, rarely leading the FOMC by speaking first. He could shade the interpretation, when the committee was close to a consensus, but his procedure did not lead to a decision when the committee divided. In 1957, Hayes and others did not share his views or accept his warnings about the dangers of inflation. There was no consensus and no action.

---

181. Trieber (New York) explained that the New York directors believed the outlook was "less buoyant." The policy of restraint seemed "to be achieving its objectives" (FOMC Minutes, August 20, 1957, 11).

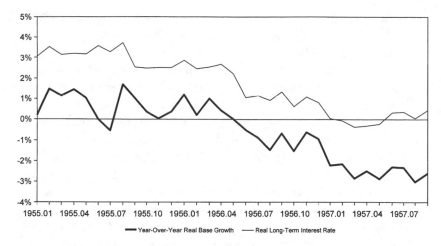

Chart 2.11. Real base growth versus real long-term interest rate, January 1955–September 1957. Real base growth measured year over year; long-term interest rate measured as yield on ten-year Treasury bonds.

Short-term interest rates remained about equal to the inflation rate, but long-term rates rose in the spring and summer partly reflecting the expectation that inflation would continue. The combination of strong domestic and foreign demand for goods, slow growth of the monetary base, rising domestic costs of production, and a 10 percent (about $1) increase in the price of crude oil slowed the economy. Chart 2.11 shows that growth of the real monetary base remained negative for more than a year before the end of the expansion and declined at a rising rate early in 1957. Expost real interest rates fell during 1956 and remained near zero early in 1957; rates rose modestly after the first quarter but remained below 1 percent. Once again, the shrinking value of the real base more than offset the stimulus from falling real interest rates early in the year. Later, the rising real rate modestly reinforced the effect of negative real base growth, slowing the economy and contributing to recession. These measures suggest that monetary policy was again procyclical.

THE 1957–58 RECESSION

The National Bureau chose August as the peak of the expansion. As in 1929, the discount rate increase came too late. Unlike in 1929, however, the recession was brief, lasting only eight months. It was not mild. The National Bureau ranks the severity of the 1957–58 recession in the middle of fourteen recessions from 1920 to 1982 (Zarnowitz and Moore, 1986, Table 7). Industrial production and real GNP fell 13.5 and 3.3 percentage points respectively. The unemployment rate reached 7.5 percent (after the cyclical trough) and, for the first time in a postwar cycle, remained above 7 percent for six months.

The Eisenhower administration relied heavily on the Federal Reserve and the built-in fiscal stabilizers as the economy slowed, but it substantially increased aid to agriculture, extended unemployment compensation benefits, and accelerated defense spending, reversing reductions made the previous year. Total outlays increased more than $15 billion, 20 percent of 1957 outlays. The result was a $3.3 billion budget deficit in 1958 and $12.1 billion in 1959 (Office of Management and Budget, 1990). The 1959 deficit was 2.5 percent of GNP, about the same as in 1953 (ibid., 17). By the standards of the time, these were large peacetime deficits.

The administration considered, but did not implement, a tax cut. President Eisenhower and Treasury Secretary Anderson expressed concern about the effect of budget deficits on future inflation and their desire for "fiscal responsibility." They did the unusual—expressing concern for the long-term consequences of actions. They would propose tax reduction only if the recession appeared likely to deepen (Ewald, 1981, 288–89).[182] President Eisenhower believed that the system would resume growing without additional stimulus (Saulnier, 1991, 10). The president neutralized political pressure for reduction in individual tax rates by asking Congress to act first on extension for one year of excise and corporate tax cuts approved earlier. By the time Congress acted, recovery was under way (Saulnier, 1991, 114). The Democratic leadership in Congress agreed to act together with the administration or not at all (Stein, 1990, 342–44).[183]

By spring 1957, R. J. Saulnier, at the Council of Economic Advisers, recognized that the economy had slowed. He urged the Federal Reserve to ease policy, but Martin and others were more concerned about current inflation than about possible future recession (Hargrove and Morley, 1984,

182. Vice President Nixon and Arthur Burns urged tax reduction but they were not successful (Stein 1990, 330, 342).

183. In the January 1958 Economic Report of the President, the Council recognized slow money growth in 1957 but did not assign responsibility for the recession (or use the word) (Council of Economic Advisers, 1958, 6). The president's message blamed the inflation on business and labor and suggested that wage increases above productivity growth slowed the economy (ibid., v). The administration's legislative program did not mention a tax cut or fiscal stimulus to moderate the recession. Emphasis was on achieving a budget surplus as the economy recovered (ibid., 55–57). A year later, the report highlighted monetary ease, extension of unemployment benefits, expanded government credit for housing, and other fiscal adjustments but also the resiliency of the private sector in a free economy (Council of Economic Advisers, 1959, 30–42). This list was opposite to the popular Keynesian view in its emphasis on the resiliency of the private sector.

124–25).[184] Eisenhower shared their concern.[185] Further, Saulnier had a National Bureau perspective about fluctuations and recessions; they were partly a consequence of the previous boom, a natural result of excessive expansion. Contraction, in turn, would be followed by renewed expansion. But he believed, also, that monetary policy had been too restrictive.[186]

The Federal Reserve responded slowly to the recession. The twelve-month rate of increase in the CPI remained between 3 and 3.5 percent through the recession, although the rate of increase in the GNP deflator slowed. But the slow response to recession also reflected a delay in recognizing that a recession had started. Until mid-November, 2.5 months after the peak, the FOMC directive continued to call for "restraining inflationary developments in the interest of sustainable economic growth." Although there was some recognition in September that the economy had slowed, and the FOMC made a small step toward easier policy at the October 22 meeting, it delayed major action until November, three months after the peak (Brunner and Meltzer, 1964, 67).[187]

At the September 10 meeting, both the staff and the members commented on growing pessimism about the outlook, but Hayes argued that it would be confusing to the market to ease policy so soon after raising the discount rate. Market rates had reached the 1929 level, and short-term

184. Saulnier described his difference with the Federal Reserve as "not a strong difference" (Hargrove and Morley, 1984, 27). Looking back, Saulnier did not regret that he had not urged a more expansive policy (ibid., 26). Opportunities for exchange of views increased in this period. In October 1957, the administration took a major step toward policy coordination and away from Federal Reserve independence. At Secretary Anderson's suggestion, Saulnier, Anderson, Martin, and Gabriel Hauge (White House staff) began to meet with the president. This was a forerunner of the Quadriad meetings in the Kennedy administration. The press release recognized the innovation—the first official body to bring the chairman of the Board of Governors to a periodic meeting with the president and his advisers.

185. "We want to do everything that is feasible and practical to stimulate recovery, and at the same time keep our own financial house in order" (Ferrell, 1981, 353). Saulnier gave a more detailed account. The administration wanted to renew some excise tax reductions in March 1958. They did not want to mix these renewals with a tax cut, so they delayed a reduction in personal income tax rates until after the excise tax bill passed. By that time, the recovery had started. Also, Saulnier claimed that he did not expect the decline to continue or cumulate (Hargrove and Morley, 1984, 151–52).

186. "I think monetary policy helped bring it on. But, you know, when you go through a great capital goods boom, you are going to pay for it. It's an unsustainable rate of increase" (ibid., 151). Statements of this kind suggest an inevitability about recession, a repeat in milder form of language about the Great Depression as "an inevitable consequence" of the previous boom. Later, Saulnier (1991, 99–100) changed his mind and blamed the Federal Reserve for the recession.

187. Romer and Romer (1994, 26) agree that November is the first month with a change in policy, but they describe the Federal Reserve as acting promptly. Boschen and Mills (1995, 43) date the policy change in November as well.

rates were above long-term rates.[188] The consensus kept the directive and policy unchanged. Martin commented that they were making progress against inflation.

The Federal Advisory Council reinforced the FOMC's sentiment. In mid-September, they told the Board that "business will continue strong for the balance of the current year" (Board Minutes, September 17, 1957, 2). The Council also reported a widespread belief that inflation was inevitable. It claimed that companies had increased plant and equipment spending to avoid higher prices (ibid., 13). The Council favored a continuation of the policy of monetary restraint (17).

Three weeks later, Ralph Young's staff report recognized that the economy had slowed and inflationary pressures had lessened. GNP data for the third quarter showed real GNP unchanged and inflation at a 4 percent annual rate. On average real GNP had not increased for three quarters. Industrial production remained at the June level, but consumer spending was strong.[189] Sixteen members favored no change in policy. Two urged greater restraint. Chairman Martin expressed surprise at the near unanimity and did not question it.

Between the meetings on October 1 and 22, the Soviet Union sent the first rocket and manned capsule into outer space. Anticipations of increased defense and space spending raised interest rates and reduced stock prices. The S&P index fell about 7 percent between early and late October. Although industrial production declined slightly, and concerns about inflation abated, the only action the FOMC took was to "resolve doubts on the side of ease."[190] The federal funds rate remained at 3.5 percent until after the November meeting, but free reserves increased.

At last, the staff recognized that "expansive forces had eased, and contractive forces had become more prominent" (FOMC Minutes, November 12, 1957, 5). Hayes added, "At least a mild downturn in business activity is

188. Governor Robertson complained that the manager had allowed free reserves to increase. He accused the manager of not following the committee's instructions. The manager agreed that free reserves had increased, but he claimed it was unintentional (FOMC Minutes, September 10, 1957, 16–17). In fact borrowing had declined following the increase in the discount rate and the start of the recession.

189. Later data show a 2.4 percent increase in real GNP in the third quarter and an average rate of increase of 1.7 percent for the year (U.S. Department of Commerce, October, 1988). A large decline (6.1 percent annual rate) came in the fourth quarter.

190. Using a scale from +1 to −1, Brunner and Meltzer (1964) mark a small (1/8) policy change based on the FOMC's statement. Hayes commented that the New York directors thought that the System was slow to act. They wanted a "somewhat less restrictive policy" (FOMC Minutes, October 22, 1957, 13). Hayes suggested that the FOMC begin to ponder discount rate reductions, open market purchases, and lower reserve requirement ratios for central reserve cities.

under way, and there is widespread belief that it will probably continue well into 1958."[191]

The committee voted nine to one to change the directive to "fostering sustainable growth . . . without inflation, by moderating the pressure on bank reserves" (FOMC Minutes, November 12, 1957, 53). Martin and several others favored a 0.5 percentage point reduction in the discount rate to 3 percent within a few weeks and free reserves of –$100 to –$250 million.[192] Governor Robertson cast the dissenting vote. He called attention to "inflationary potentials" and the need for continued restraint (ibid., 54).

The reserve banks did not wait weeks to vote reductions in their discount rates. The day after the FOMC meeting Undersecretary Baird met with the Board to express concern that the Board's upcoming action would not be known in the market when the Treasury announced its securities offering that afternoon. He wanted the Board to announce the easier policy so that he could get a lower rate on his sale (Board Minutes, November 13, 1957, 1–2). The Board would not make an announcement, but it agreed to announce the discount rate changes, if the reserve banks voted for them. The Treasury agreed to delay its offering. The following day, Richmond, Atlanta, and St. Louis voted to lower their discount rates to 3 percent. New York voted for 3.25 percent, but the Board would not approve. New York reconsidered and voted "reluctantly" for a 3 percent rate (Board Minutes, November 14, 1957, 8). By December 2, a uniform 3 percent rate prevailed. Rates at the weekly Treasury auction declined very little.

Governor Robertson voted against the reductions.[193] He did not see the need for a lower rate. The "dangers of continuing inflation are as great today as the dangers of deflation" (ibid., 8). He also disliked the assistance given to the Treasury by reducing the rate just before the Treasury offering. Although he acknowledged that "fiscal and monetary operations must be appropriately coordinated, the facilitation of Treasury financing operations should never be the sole motive" (ibid., 9).

191. At about this time, the Federal Advisory Council reversed its earlier position, recognizing that a moderate decline had begun. They anticipated that the decline would continue for the rest of the year and the first half of 1958. They blamed "international events," probably a reference to the increase in oil prices and the Soviet Union's achievement in space. Several members criticized the discount rate reduction made the previous week. They wanted more reserves. Although they did not say so, lower interest rates and increased reserves had opposite initial effects on bank earnings (Board Minutes, November 19, 1957).

192. The staff reported an unemployment rate of 4.6 percent, a 0.4 percentage point increase, and rapidly rising claims for unemployment compensation. Consumer prices continued to rise at a 4.2 percent annualized rate in November. The twelve-month rate of inflation had fallen to 3.2 percent from a peak of 3.7 percent in March and April 1957.

193. In an unusual gesture, Robertson dissented again, when the FOMC renewed the directive without change at the December 3 meeting.

The last comment drew a response from Martin. He defended the action as preemptive against a "deteriorating trend" in the economy. The System acted to "play fair and open with the investing public" (ibid., 9–10). Clearly, the Treasury, not the public, would benefit directly. The action was a direct attempt to lower interest cost and, therefore, inconsistent with the usual even keel policy and the principles of the Accord. Chart 2.8 (above) shows the decline in the federal funds rate that began at this time. Growth of the monetary base increased in December.

The next move came in mid-December. For the first time, Ralph Young described the decline as a recession, and Woodlief Thomas warned that reserves should be increased. Chairman Martin did not wait to speak last. Following the gloomy staff reports, he proposed a change in the directive. This was the last meeting of the year, so the change would appear in the Board's Annual Report for 1957 (FOMC Minutes, December 17, 1957, 12). Hayes agreed and proposed mentioning recession in the action clause so the System would appear alert when the report appeared in the winter.

The statement called for "cushioning adjustments and mitigating recessionary tendencies" (ibid., 44). Although the members had expressed different opinions, no one dissented. Martin then agreed with the slim majority that favored zero free reserves, a less restrictive position than many wanted. Only Watrous Irons (Dallas) expressed reservations.[194]

During the winter, the recession worsened considerably. In November, December, and January, industrial production fell at about a 25 percent annual rate. Unemployment rose to 5.8 percent, more than two percentage points above its trough and the highest rate in nine years. Monthly consumer price inflation rates fluctuated, but the annual rate remained between 3 and 3.5 percent. The System faced a simultaneous rise in prices and unemployment, later called "stagflation."

The FOMC took no action at the January 7 meeting. Opinion was divided. The staff and some members said the recession had worsened, but they expressed concern about inflation also. Others opposed any policy change. Lacking a consensus, Martin proposed to err on the side of ease but keep the directive unchanged.

Free reserves increased as banks repaid their indebtedness. At first, short-term market rates remained in a narrow range unrelated to the level

194. Since this was the last meeting of 1957, the chairman looked back and forward. Despite the recession, he described himself as more optimistic than a year earlier. The main reason he gave was that a year earlier, the Federal Reserve had stood alone against inflation. It had been in danger of becoming too narrowly focused on that one goal, becoming "a crusader against inflation and . . . [unable] to reverse its posture in time" (FOMC Minutes, December 17, 1957, 40–41). The reason for optimism was that the System had responded flexibly.

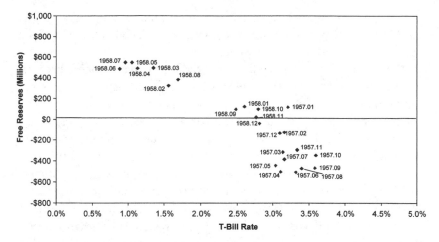

Chart 2.12. Free reserves versus ninety-day T-bill rate (auction), January 1957–December 1958.

of free reserves. As Chart 2.12 shows, this changed in the winter of 1958. Interest rates fell as free reserves rose. Expost real, short-term rates became negative.

A main reason for the change was an increase in growth of the (seasonally adjusted) monetary base in February and a reduction in discount rates. The latter started as a decision by the Philadelphia directors, on January 16, to reduce their rate to 2.75 percent.[195] The Board's staff favored the reduction. They expected the economy to continue declining. The Treasury would soon be in the market, but there was time to make the change. With the bill rate almost 0.5 percentage points below the discount rate, the market anticipated the move. Governor Szymczak wanted to wait until after the Treasury financing; Governor Mills wanted to act. The Board postponed its decision but agreed to notify all other banks of Philadelphia's request.

Four days later it approved the reduction on a four-to-two vote with Szymczak and Robertson opposed. Treasury bill rates declined by 0.5 percentage points (to 2.59) at the next weekly auction. Szymczak opposed because the Treasury would soon offer securities for sale. The Board had accommodated the Treasury in December. Another reduction timed before a Treasury offer risked "giving the impression that that is a pattern to be followed" (Board Minutes, January 21, 1958, 11). Robertson's reasoning differed. In a prescient warning about the problems of the 1970s, he pointed to the risk of continuing inflation. "Up to this time there has been no general downward readjustment of . . . prices, and if we move too rap-

195. Boston, New York, and Minneapolis had voted for no change.

idly to ease the downturn, we will be in a position of placing a floor under existing high prices and our country's history will be one of moving from one high price level to another" (ibid., 12).

Within a few weeks all banks except San Francisco reduced their discount rates to 2.75 percent. Earlier in January, the Board reduced stock market margin requirements from 70 to 50 percent. The vote was unanimous. These actions, signaling the Board's intention to respond to the recession by reducing interest rates and encouraging higher asset prices, produced the first monthly increase in the S&P index in six months.

The FOMC minutes continued to report deepening recession, mainly in the capital goods sector. As the decline deepened, attitudes within the System began to change. Hayes now told the FOMC it should "give major attention to the unfavorable realities of the present rather than the possible resumption of an inflationary threat in the future" (FOMC Minutes, January 28, 1958, 9). Later in the meeting, Hayes added that the New York directors believed that "the System had not done enough in the way of open market operations or otherwise" (ibid., 42).[196]

Erickson (Boston), Williams (Philadelphia), Bryan (Atlanta), Johns (St. Louis), and Fulton (Cleveland) supported Hayes. There was strong opposition from Robertson and Shephardson at the Board, and Irons (Dallas). Allen (Chicago), Deming (Minneapolis), and Mangels (San Francisco) made a spirited defense of inaction. Allen said he opposed the recent reduction in discount rates and urged the committee to give more weight to price stability.[197]

Hayes criticized use of free reserves as a target. If retained, the level should be raised but, in a statement showing that he chose the arguments that made his case, he cautioned that "we might find ourselves successfully maintaining this target while total reserves and the total money supply were still shrinking. Therefore, I would urge emphatically, as suggested by Malcolm Bryan at the last meeting, we try to devise a new type of guide for open market policy under present conditions that will focus attention on the

196. Martin's response seems uncharacteristically sharp, reflecting his sensitivity. "We should never get into the record that the directors of a reserve bank were recommending a change in reserve requirements since many directors are also bankers. . . . [T]his had come up on the Hill a number of times. . . . He was defending all of the Committee members and the presidents against the charge of being dominated by the bankers" (FOMC Minutes, January 28, 1958, 43).

197. Allen correctly saw that the market would recognize that unemployment was the primary concern. "I do not feel that the Committee's actions of the past several months have made the contribution which they might have made in that direction. . . . [We would have] a better chance of winning out against inflation if our easing policy were not proceeding so rapidly today" (FOMC Minutes, January 28, 1958, 20).

total reserve and the money supply rather than the amount of free reserves" (ibid., 11). Martin took no part in this discussion. The Treasury would soon come to market. The System followed an even keel until the next meeting.

Staff reports remained bleak. There was no sign of an upturn, but there was also no consensus within the FOMC. The division that emerged in January remained in February. Hayes opposed reducing the discount rate. Robertson argued that the System had done as much as credit easing could do, pointing to the decline in nominal short-term interest rates as evidence. He urged the members to "give our previous actions a little time to take effect." Using words reminiscent of the 1920s, he worried that excessive ease ("overease") "would so contribute to misguided financial decisions that it would enhance the likelihood of the economy having to go through a protracted period of severe liquidation and structural realignment before it recovers" (FOMC Minutes, February 11, 1958, 18).

Martin summarized the consensus as relatively optimistic. He opposed another reduction in discount rates because it would suggest that the System was in a panic. He favored continuing the even keel policy, leaning toward ease. Despite expressed differences no one dissented.[198] Congress was likely to hold hearings to highlight differences.

Neither Congress nor the Federal Advisory Council was optimistic about recovery. During the winter the Board received letters, and undoubtedly verbal suggestions, from members of Congress urging more aggressive action.[199] The FAC favored moderately easier credit, including a reduction in reserve requirement ratios. Most members argued that lower interest rates should be reinforced by increased availability of reserves. The proper action would be open market purchases; it recognized that lower reserve requirement ratios, with interest rates unchanged, would increase bank earnings but not bank reserves.[200]

198. The FOMC discussed the preliminary report of a System committee that studied float. One recommendation called for less attention to float—offset only "unusual fluctuations," leaving the market to adjust to others. The manager, Rouse, was hesitant. Another recommendation called for a longer period of deferred availability credit, basically an interest-free loan to the banks during the check collection process. The only decision asked the manager to provide daily data for further study. The discussion did not join the issue between those who wanted to focus on the main goals of policy and those who believed the System should concern itself with daily or hourly fluctuations in the money market.

199. One letter from Congressman Wilbur Mills, chairman of the Ways and Means committee, reflected the agreement with the administration to work together on tax reduction. Mills reminded Martin that he had asked that the "monetary authorities should be given an opportunity to cope with recessionary trends before tax reduction was undertaken" (Board Minutes, January 20, 1958, 2, letter, Mills to Martin). Mills reported also that bankers believed that "Federal Reserve actions had not been sufficiently vigorous" (ibid., 2).

200. The FAC preferred monetary to fiscal measures. "A substantial reduction in taxes

The FOMC meeting on March 4 changed the directive without changing policy action. Hayes proposed that the directive read "combating economic recession," but Martin preferred the milder "contributing further
by monetary ease to a resumption of stable growth." Most of the discussion
at the meeting suggested that the recession continued and deepened. The
general sentiment was to maintain free reserves but lower the discount
rate. Johns (St. Louis) proposed a 0.75 percent reduction, but Karl Bopp
(new president at Philadelphia) reminded the members that 1929 was the
only time the committee had reduced that much. Martin left the decision
about discount rates to the reserve banks.[201]

Two days later, the Board approved reductions of 0.5 percentage points
(to 2.25 percent) at New York, Philadelphia, and Chicago. All remaining
banks soon followed. Treasury bill rates declined 0.23 percentage points
at the next auction. By the end of March, the federal funds rate was about
1 percent, the lowest rate in four years. Again, there is no evidence that
monetary actions had become futile. Rates on long-term Treasury bonds
changed very little.[202] Borrowing fell to about $100 million and free re-
serves rose to $500 million. The System believed its policy was extremely
easy. It had moved in response to the recession despite continued inflation
of 3 percent or more.

---

and a sharp acceleration in the rate and magnitude of government expenditures might curtail and soon reverse the continued downtrend in business which the Council anticipates.
However, the ultimate cost to the economy of such extreme measures might be significantly
greater than the short-run advantages" (Board Minutes, February 18, 1958, 2).

201. The March meeting changed the composition of the FOMC and renewed all the
directives and operating policies. Martin again objected to the arrangement under which
New York chose the manager and New York objected to the bills-only policy. Hayes proposed
to introduce "as a general rule" to weaken the commitment to bills-only, but Martin did not
agree. Hayes's was the only dissent. The FOMC also agreed, over Mills's objection, to extend
the manager's authority to include purchases of acceptances from foreign banks. Also, Congress had increased the ceiling on public debt from $275 to $280 billion, so the committee
withdrew temporary authority to sell debt to the Treasury in exchange for gold certificates.
The staff raised a question about what should be included in the Record of Policy Actions
published as part of the Board's Annual Report. A problem arose because the FOMC regularly
discussed discount rate changes, a decision left by law to the reserve banks. One suggestion
would have omitted all references to discount rate changes. The Committee rejected that
suggestion and decided to make clear that "this was discussed in an objective fashion as
something within the responsibility of the directors of the Federal Reserve banks" (FOMC
Minutes, March 25, 1958, 5). A second problem was that "the record for the first six months
of 1957 . . . did not seem to justify the policy of restraint actually adopted" (ibid., 5). This is
as close as the FOMC came to recognizing that it had made a mistake. It did not compound
the mistake by adjusting the record.

202. Hayes commented on the widening spread. He blamed it on "the congestion in the
capital markets" (Notes for March 4, 1958, FOMC meeting, Board Records, March 17, 1958,
3). He did not mention that long-term rates probably reflected unchanged anticipations of
inflation over the longer-term as President Allen suggested earlier.

The following day the Board reduced reserve requirement ratios by 0.5 percentage points from 20, 18, and 12 percent for demand deposits at the three classes of banks, effective February 27 in central reserve and reserve city banks and on March 1 for country banks. Governor Mills opposed the action, but he voted for it to keep unanimity.

The Board's action came after renewed consideration of the structure of reserve requirements. Martin had encouraged the American Bankers Association (ABA) to study the issue and suggest revisions, including uniform reserve requirement ratios and a target date for phasing in the new arrangements. The Board was not willing to go to uniform requirements; although it seemed unaware of the hostile political response to any reduction in reserve requirement ratios, it believed that political considerations made it necessary to have different requirements for small and large banks (Board Minutes, February 21, 1958, 5–6).[203] After discussion with members of the ABA committee, the Board added a provision making maximum reserve requirement ratios for central reserve city banks 20 percent, the same as for reserve city banks. The Board then approved the proposed regulation by a vote of five to two. Robertson and Vardaman objected to the provision lowering requirements for central reserve city banks; the ABA subsequently endorsed the proposal (Board Minutes, March 18, 13–15, April 2, 1958, 6–7).

The Board next considered a further reduction in reserve requirement ratios. The Treasury would soon offer from $3 to $5 billion of securities. Since the Board did not announce its open market operations, Martin preferred to add reserves by reducing requirement ratios so that the market would know about the change before the Treasury offer. By unanimous vote the Board reduced reserve requirement ratios by 0.5 percentage

---

203. The Board's staff began by reviewing the proposal for reserve requirements based on deposit turnover developed in the early 1930s. The Board again rejected that plan as difficult to administer and complex. Robertson proposed counting vault cash as reserves and graduating requirements according to bank size without accepting the uniformity or the time schedule proposed by the ABA (Board Minutes, February 3, 1958, 5–6). Balderston favored different requirements for time and saving deposits, but others noted that separation would be difficult to enforce. Robertson's proposal drew considerable support, but the Board broadened it to include several different categories of banks by size and location. The Board wanted discretion to vary requirements for particular types of banks; small banks in reserve cities or large banks classed as country banks are examples. Martin noted that the Board's proposed legislation would permit uniform reserve requirements, as proposed by the ABA. Others objected that the proposal would stimulate many requests for exemption and reclassification. All parties agreed that the prevailing classification was inequitable, penalizing especially small banks in reserve or central reserve cities. The ABA would not join in supporting the Board's proposed legislation. They insisted on uniform requirements of up to 14 percent for all banks (Board Minutes, March 6, 1958, Appendix item 1).

points, effective March 20 for central reserve and reserve city banks and April 1 for country banks. Requirements were now 19, 17, and 11. The ratio for time deposits remained 5 percent. The Board did not mention pressure from the ABA as a reason for choosing to lower reserve requirement ratios. It continued to act as if lower ratios with unchanged interest rates permanently increased available reserves.

Through April and early May, several FOMC members favored additional ease. In May, even Robertson urged free reserves of $800 million, $300 million above the April average (FOMC Minutes, May 6, 1958). The federal funds rate fell below 1 percent in May, reaching 0.2 percent at the end of the month. Martin remained cautious and concerned about public relations. His summaries of the consensus were less expansive than statements by a majority of the members.[204] He preferred to reduce reserve requirement ratios.

On April 16, the Board's Executive Committee discussed a further reduction in reserve requirement ratios. Hayes called to say that he would propose a 0.5 percentage point reduction in the discount rate to 1.75 percent at the directors meeting that day and would like to announce the change at 4 p.m., after the close of trading.[205] Mills questioned why the System now relied on changes in reserve requirement ratios and the discount rate instead of open market purchases. He did not point out that a reduction in the discount rate to 1.75 percent would leave the discount rate one percentage point above the federal funds rate, so banks would continue to use the funds market and avoid discounting.

Martin responded that if Congress approved the Board's proposal and allowed vault cash to be counted as reserves, the proposed reserve requirement ratios would narrow differences in reserve requirement ratios for the three classes of banks. He believed that the proposed actions on reserve requirements and the discount rate would "remove the need for further System actions for some time to come." He made clear, however, that the proposed adjustment toward lower required reserve ratios was not taken to ease the market. It could be made, he said, "without interfering with over-all monetary policy" (Board Minutes, April 17, 1958, 8).

The gold outflow was one of his concerns. Like his predecessors in

204. At the May meeting, he opposed changing the directive to say "continuing to combat the recession" because it "might imply that the Committee had been unaware of the recession earlier in the year" (FOMC Minutes, May 6, 1958).

205. The staff briefing noted early signs of an end to recession. Required reserves had increased and currency had not shown the expected post-Easter decline (Board Minutes, April 17, 1958, 3). Thomas estimated that the proposed reduction would release $450 million of reserves (see text).

1936, he noted that if the gold outflow reversed, the Board could raise reserve requirement ratios. "The Board should look for opportunities to make reductions when consistent with credit policy" (ibid., 9). After further discussion, the Board approved unanimously an immediate 0.5 percentage point reduction for central reserve city banks and a further 0.5 reduction for central reserve and reserve city banks a week later. The Board left the country bank ratio unchanged. When the change became effective the requirement ratios were 18, 16½, and 11.

Although the Board did not have a formal request for a lower discount rate, it approved reductions to 2 percent or 1.75 percent, effective the next day for any reserve bank that acted that day. New York, Philadelphia, Chicago, St. Louis, and Minneapolis lowered their rates to 1.75 percent. All other banks followed. San Francisco and Dallas waited until May 1 and 9. Treasury bill rates continued to fall, as banks purchased bills following the reduction in reserve requirement ratios, but long-term rates began to rise in the first week of May.

Annual growth of the monetary base remained at 2 percent throughout the spring. Though lower than potential growth of the economy, base growth was at the highest rate in almost four years. Real base growth remained negative until August. Expost long-term real interest rates remained near zero through April, the last month of the recession according to National Bureau dating. Thereafter expost real interest rates rose. As often before, the rise in real rates contributed to the Federal Reserve's misinterpretation of its actions. It interpreted the decline in nominal rates as an indication that policy had eased. This ignored both the effect on rates of the change in anticipated inflation and the change in economic activity. Chart 2.13 shows the acceleration of the real base in February 1958, a few months before the start of the recovery. Again, faster base growth offset the restrictive effect of rising real interest rates.

The Federal Reserve had faced inflation and rising unemployment. At first, it moved slowly to stimulate spending out of concern for inflation. As unemployment and the output gap rose, it shifted to more expansive policy actions. This set a pattern to which it returned in the late 1960s. As Governor Robertson warned, once the public learned that rising unemployment (or the output gap) had highest priority, it expected inflation to persist. Thus, stagflation (persistent inflation and unemployment) became a problem in later years.

The System was slow to recognize the start of recession and slow to recognize its end. It was not alone. Congress approved supplementary unemployment compensation on June 4, after the recession had ended, and repealed transportation taxes on August 1. The Federal Advisory Council

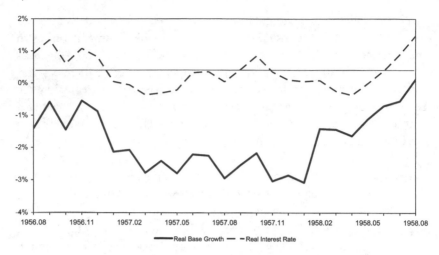

Chart 2.13. Real base growth versus real interest rate, August 1956–August 1958. Twelve-month moving average growth rates.

told the Board in late May that "although the rate of decline in business activity may have lessened, the economy continues a moderately downward trend" (Board Minutes, May 20, 1958, 1). The Council favored maintaining the degree of ease and did not want further reductions in the discount rate. Industrial production rose at a 12 percent annual rate that month.

THE SHORT EXPANSION, 1958–60

The Federal Reserve had decisively increased free reserves and lowered interest rates during the recession, and the administration permitted a large peacetime budget deficit.[206] Concern about inflation rose with the recovery and the budget deficit at both the Federal Reserve and the administration. The Federal Reserve responded without hesitation to inflation concerns. The administration did not do much about the 1959 deficit, but it was determined to bring the deficit down in 1960. It succeeded; 1960 had a small surplus brought about by an $11 billion increase in receipts and a $2 billion reduction in spending.

The Federal Reserve tightened policy soon after recovery seemed assured. Table 2.3 uses annual dollar change in the gross public debt to suggest the magnitude of the budget deficit and the sharp turn from fiscal re-

206. In a letter to a banker, Hayes remarked: "Undoubtedly, the size of the prospective deficit . . . was a shock to the market and accentuated fears of further inflation that had already been aroused by discouragement over the lack of progress in bringing the wage-price spiral under control" (letter, Hayes to Hillestad, Sproul papers, Correspondence, December 4, 1958.).

Table 2.3   Fiscal and Monetary Action, 1957–60

	AUGUST 1957	APRIL 1958	DECEMBER 1958	DECEMBER 1959	MAY 1960
Annual growth of the monetary base, nominal (%)	0.85	1.55	2.31	0.91	0.25
Annual growth of the monetary base, real* (%)	−2.63	−1.98	0.56	−0.58	−1.69
Federal funds rate (%)	3.24	1.26	2.42	3.99	3.92
Real federal funds rate* (%)	−0.24	−2.27	0.67	2.50	1.98
Free reserves	−471	492	−41	−459	198
Annual change in gross public debt (billion $)	−1.0	1.0	8.0	6.5	2.2

*Real values obtained by subtracting twelve-month rate of change of consumer prices.
Source: Debt from Board of Governors (1976, 870–71).

straint to ease and back to restraint. Several real and nominal magnitudes measure the size of monetary expansion or contraction.

The Federal Reserve's principal measures of ease, free reserves and the federal funds rate, recovered quickly and decisively. By December 1959, both were back at the levels reached at the August 1957 peak. Growth of the nominal monetary base, after expanding rapidly, fell back to its August 1957 rate also. The real federal funds rate suggests a much tighter policy than at the earlier peak. As the deficit declined, fiscal thrust also turned contractive. By April 1960, the deficit fell to $2 billion and, in the first quarter of 1960, the budget had a $7 billion surplus at annual rates.

The Federal Reserve and the administration managed to achieve their principal objective, preventing the stimulative policy during the recession from generating persistent inflation. In 1959 and 1960, the annual increase in the consumer price index remained between 0 and 2 percent. Arthur Burns recognized later that the reversal from highly expansive to contractive policies was too abrupt and too large a change (Burns and Samuelson, 1967). He attributed the decisions to "excessive concern over inflation" (ibid., 6) resulting from the recent experience in 1956–57, but he recognized that the reductions in government spending in aggregate "came to a much larger total than our fiscal authorities had either planned or advocated" (ibid., 7). He ignored the likely effect on anticipations. By promptly removing the stimulus, policy reversed the growing belief that inflation would continue. Inflation and anticipations of inflation remained low for several years.

The early recovery was robust, 9.8 percent growth of real GNP in the second half of 1958, and more than 6 percent in the first half of 1959. In August the unemployment rate began to fall. By January 1959, it reached 6 percent, 1.5 percentage points below its peak. Industrial production started to rise in May 1958. By January, it had reached its previous peak. In the first year of recovery, production increased 20 percent.

Inflation remained a short-term problem. The twelve-month rate of change of consumer prices did not fall below 3 percent until June 1958, after the recession ended. The CPI inflation rate fell toward 1 percent or less in 1959, but the deflator continued to rise. The administration's concern for fiscal responsibility gave priority to reducing the size of the deficit and growth of government spending (Council of Economic Advisers, 1959, 48–52).[207] The president asked, also, to make price stability an explicit goal of economic policy (ibid., 52).

Federal Reserve policy actions remained restrictive, as Table 2.3 (above) suggests. Annual growth rates of the monetary base rose above 2 percent in only one month of the twenty-four-month expansion. In the two years of expansion, the cumulative increase in the base was 1.7 percent. Interest rates rose under the influence of robust growth, moderate inflation, and restricted monetary growth. Treasury bill rates increased 1.7 percentage points (to 2.6 percent) in the first six months of recovery, and ten-year rates rose almost a full percentage point.

Together, fiscal and monetary actions set the stage for a brief but rapid decline in the unemployment rate to a level well above previous periods of recovery and expansion (see Chart 2.2 above). Recovery then slowed and ended. Tight policies made it the shortest postwar recovery to that time.

Federal Reserve Actions

Once again, the Federal Reserve promptly recognized the turning point but was slow to act. At the first FOMC meeting after the trough, May 27, 1958, the staff reported that the recession was near its end. Woodlief Thomas warned of inflationary tendencies in the recovery. New York was less certain. Hayes saw no sign that the recession was over (FOMC Minutes, May 27, 1958, 9). He favored another reduction in reserve requirement ratios, even during the forthcoming Treasury financing. Six FOMC members agreed, although most preferred to wait until the Treasury completed the financing. Martin favored an even keel, and the FOMC agreed unanimously to do nothing. Free reserves remained about $500 million, and the federal funds rate reached a low of 0.2 percent for the week ending May 28. Long-term Treasury yields remained above 3.1 percent, a wide spread over the funds rate, probably reflecting some anticipation that inflation would follow the aggressive fiscal stimulus.

---

207. The report asked for a line item veto, a request that would recur with greater emphasis in future years (Council of Economic Advisers, 1959, 51).

Hayes held to his interpretation: "there is certainly no evidence yet point-ing to any substantial recovery in 1958" (FOMC Minutes, June 17, 1958, 10). He saw the inflation outlook as "more encouraging than at any time in the last few years" (ibid., 11). In an unusual move, he challenged Martin's statement of the consensus calling for no change in policy. He thought a majority favored a reduction in reserve requirement ratios, to meet the holiday demand for currency, but Martin believed the money market was too easy. The committee voted unanimously to make no changes.[208]

In May, the Treasury offered to refinance $9.5 billion of maturing secu-rities by issuing either a 2.625 percent seven-year bond or a 1.25 percent one-year certificate. With the end of recession still uncertain, holders ex-changed $7.5 billion for the new seven-year bond. "This was a surprise to the market and suggested that a sizeable amount of the newly acquired securities were speculatively held" (*Federal Reserve Bulletin,* August 1959, 5). The market soon received information that caused bond yields to rise. Estimates of the government deficit for fiscal 1959 suggested that it would be the largest since World War II.[209] Much of the Treasury's demand for new financing would come in the fall, when the Treasury would also have large demands for refinancing. By mid-June, "observers took into account that economic recovery might already have begun," ending the period of credit ease (ibid., 5). Holders began to sell the new seven-year bond and other long-term bonds. The Treasury intervened in the long-term market in June and July, purchasing almost $600 million for its accounts, but the System limited its purchases to bills.[210]

By early July, Ralph Young's staff report concluded that the recession had

208. At the June 25 Board meeting, the reasoning became clearer. There were problems in the bond market (see text) following a Treasury issue. Government securities dealers had large positions, evidently speculating on a continued decline in long-term rates. The System had supplied about $600 million in open market purchases in the previous two weeks (Board Minutes, June 25, 1958, 7). Martin was cautious, citing labor negotiations. Mills, Robertson, Vardaman, Shephardson, and Balderston agreed that the System should act only, if at all, in the open market. Szymczak wanted to use the opportunity to reduce reserve requirement ratios and believed that there was a "need for reserves" to allay uncertainty (ibid., 10).

209. The unified budget deficit reached $12.8 billion, a record peacetime nominal vol-ume of borrowing to that time. The following year, the budget had a small surplus. Saulnier (1991, 124) responded to critics of the large fiscal tightening by noting that part of 1959 spending was a payment to the International Monetary Fund that had no economic impact on the U.S. economy. Nevertheless, the spending had to be financed.

210. An exceptionally large number of speculators bought the new bond issue anticipat-ing further reduction in interest rates by the Federal Reserve. Many of the purchasers bought on margin, with as little as 5 percent equity. Bremner (2004, 108) reports that one small banker purchased and resold $500 million in this way. Total loans secured by Treasuries reached $6.1 billion compared to a $7.4 billion issue, evidence that the bonds were not held in permanent portfolios.

ended. Several presidents agreed, and proposed either a prompt or near-term increase in the discount rate. Hayes remained skeptical about the recovery and concerned about Treasury issues. He favored giving less attention to free reserves and more to money supply growth, which remained slow. Mills and Szymczak shared his concern about the Treasury market.

Thomas's staff report warned that the Treasury bond market was weak, despite the large increase in reserves. Speculators had closed out their positions, and time deposits had increased substantially because their return was favorable. The banks had expanded credit, and additional expansion seemed likely. Then he added a statement that could have been written by a 1920s real bills advocate. "The experience of June is an example of the pitfalls that may be encountered in following a path of forcing down interest rates and stimulating credit commitments regardless of current needs . . . Is economic recovery aided by such false and temporary movements?" (FOMC Minutes, July 8, 1958, 13).

Although the recovery was only two months old, Martin favored an increase of 0.5 percentage points in the discount rate after the even keel policy ended, but he asked the presidents not to initiate a discount rate change before the next meeting. In the interim, he favored operating "within the color, feel, and tone of the market" (ibid., 46). He found it difficult to know what to do. The week after June 19 "was one of the worst that he had spent since coming into the System, with many people who were stirred up about rumors of a change in System policy calling him with various kinds of stories" (ibid., 42). "The System ought to do something that would be really clear-cut" (ibid., 43). But it should "not do anything to create more difficulty for the Treasury than necessary" (ibid., 44).[211]

With so much hesitation in the leadership, the only decision taken instructed the manager to keep free reserves at about $500 million. Irons (Dallas) suggested eliminating the free reserve target, substituting a measure of reserve availability. Hayes agreed in principle, but he favored retention because the public was accustomed to watching free reserves.

Once again, the System recognized that it did not have firm control of interest rates, but it was unwilling to move decisively to increase control. The next move came from the market. On July 15, the FOMC held a telephone meeting to discuss the proper response to a political crisis in the Middle East that involved sending 3,500 Marines to Lebanon. Bond prices

---

211. The Board also heard by telegram from Congressman Patman, who asked what the Federal Reserve would do "to check the jungle-like activities being carried on by gamblers and speculators." He urged them to abandon the bills-only policy (Board Minutes, July 16, 1958, 1). Patman sent another telegram on July 21 commending the FOMC for supporting long-term bonds.

fell sharply on the news, but selling remained orderly. The System did not act for three days. On July 18, Rouse told a telephone meeting that the market was falling and "the Treasury could not, in its opinion, deal with it" (FOMC Minutes, telephone meeting, July 18, 1958, 2).[212] Rouse regarded the situation as an international emergency but, since some buying continued as the market declined, he did not call the market disorderly. He asked for authority to purchase up to $50 million of long-term securities that day, "with the expectation of using less than $25 million" (ibid., 4). The committee voted the authority, with Robertson and Mills dissenting, because the markets were not disorderly. Martin, too, expressed reluctance to violate bills-only, but he voted to approve purchases.[213] On Friday July 18, the account bought $27 million, a small fraction of the Treasury's prior intervention (Board of Governors, 1976, Table 9.5, 490). Subsequently, it purchased $1.1 billion of the new issue and announced that the committee had authorized the manager to purchase longer-term securities. The announcement "went a long way to correcting what had really been a disorderly market" (letter, Hayes to Roelse, Hayes papers, Federal Reserve Bank of New York, correspondence, July 22, 1958).

By the end of the month, the federal funds rate had fallen from 1.32 percent in the week of the crisis to 0.36 percent. The real funds rate was negative; a near-zero nominal rate did not signify a liquidity trap. Yields on three- to five-year Treasury bonds remained at 2.5 percent, a pattern that would be repeated broadly in several subsequent recessions. This suggests that the market did not expect any cyclical reduction in the inflation rate to persist. In fact, the staff reported that markets anticipated higher inflation driven by the high current rates of "time deposit and monetary expansion, the continued ease of bank reserve positions, . . . and the Treasury's large deficit" (FOMC Minutes, July 29, 1958, 5). The staff also reported that preliminary GNP figures for the second quarter showed a modest increase. Foreign economies had strengthened also.

212. In mid-June the Treasury sold $7.3 billion of the 2.625 bonds with seven-year maturity. A popular bond market columnist, Joseph Slevin, wrote on June 19 that the Federal Reserve had ceased efforts to reduce interest rates. Although there is nothing in the record to support Slevin's claim, he was known to have good relations with System officials. The Treasury did not intervene until July 10. The System waited until late in the afternoon on July 18 (Knipe, 1965, 134–35).

213. At a second meeting, on the same afternoon, Rouse reported that the market was disorderly. Bids had dried up. The ten participating members of FOMC agreed to give the manager authority to make additional purchases of government securities without limitation. For the next several days, the FOMC held daily telephone meetings. On July 24, the committee rescinded purchase authority. The System offset its purchase of $27 million of five- to ten-year bonds (most likely seven-years) by a sale of $27 million of over-ten-year bonds. Its net purchase was $10 million of one- to five-year bonds.

Chairman Martin followed the staff reports with a request for recommendations to change the directive. He suggested "absorbing reserves whenever consistent with an orderly market" in place of "contributing further to monetary ease" (ibid., 12). Concern about inflation had to wait, however. The Treasury believed that its latest offering, a 1.625 percent one-year certificate to be issued on August 1, was about to fail. In the week before the meeting, the Federal Reserve departed again from bills-only by purchasing "when issued" securities to support the issue.[214]

Mills argued his usual position: The FOMC had to supply enough reserves to keep the market orderly. President Hayes opposed tightening policy or any major change. The recovery was uncertain; so was the Middle East situation. Unemployment remained high. Hayes wanted to maintain $500 million of free reserves, and favored only a modest change in the directive—removing "further" from "contributing further to monetary ease." Even if the money stock rose 6 percent for the year, average growth for 1955–58 would be a modest 2 percent. Robertson wanted to tighten "to the fullest extent possible" (ibid., 25). Bryan (Atlanta), joined by several others, expressed concern that the budget deficit in an expanding economy would cause loss of confidence "in the future integrity of the dollar" (ibid., 17).[215] The shift from correcting disorder to "the most massive support operations ever undertaken" (ibid., 18) exacerbated the problem. Several spoke of the dangers of inflation, usually mentioning the Treasury's prospective deficit.

Martin gave a lengthy summary. Referring to relations of the Federal Reserve and the Treasury after the summer's problems, he said, "The Committee was dealing with the most difficult problem in political science in the whole world" (ibid., 49). Both institutions had the same goal, and the problems were not all caused by the Treasury. "[I]f the System had not been as intent on following an easy money policy [during the recession] there could not have been the speculative fever that developed and finally culminated in the speculation in the 2.625 percent bonds" (ibid., 50).

Along with some of his colleagues, Martin believed that the Federal Reserve could not treat the deficit as the Treasury's problem. Independence was not absolute. The Federal Reserve was a creature of Congress. Congress created (or permitted) the deficit that the Treasury had to finance.

214. Market yields, though rising, show no reason for concern. For the weeks ending July 26 and August 2, yields were 1.36 percent and 1.49 percent (Board of Governors, 1976, 702). The prediction was accurate, however. Weekly average yields rose above 1.625 in the week of August 9 and continued to rise to a peak of 3.04 percent in early October.

215. This is probably a reference to the $1 billion gold outflow (4.5 percent) in the year ending in July.

The Federal Reserve shared that responsibility, and it had to balance it against its responsibility for preventing inflation. It could not allow the bond market to be disorderly.

The committee did not agree on the wording of the directive. Martin proposed putting off the decision, accepting "recapturing redundant reserves" as a short-term statement of policy, and agreeing on other language at the next meeting. Agreement was again unanimous.[216]

At the manager's request, the FOMC met again in the afternoon. The 3.5 percent bonds of 1990 had fallen to 98. He called the market "disorderly," using the word required for the System to purchase other than bills, and he proposed submitting a few bids, using brokers to hide the intervention. "They did not want to go in, start to buy and create 'an avalanche' of offers" (FOMC Minutes, July 29, 1958, 3). Only Mills favored aggressive intervention. The FOMC decided to wait, but it continued to monitor the market closely and held daily telephone conferences. On July 30, it sold Treasury bills to withdraw some reserves. The market remained stable, so it repeated sales on the next two days. The bill yield remained below 1 percent.

Between meetings, the Board responded to Congressman Patman's complaints by making two moves intended to show its concern about speculation and the growth of credit and money. On August 4, it raised margin requirements for stock purchases from 50 percent to 70 percent, returning to the level prevailing in January. Although stock prices had increased rapidly in July and August, there was neither a sign of increased volume before the change, nor an effect of the change on prices or volume of trading.

The San Francisco bank proposed to raise its discount rate to 2 percent (from 1.75). The directors acted against the advice of President H. N. Mangels, who preferred to wait. Their main reason was concern about inflation and a desire to show that they were alert to the danger (FOMC Minutes, August 19, 1958, 29). Chairman Martin also favored the change, citing the strong recovery and the increase in Treasury bill rates to 1.5 percent. Other members questioned the necessity of the increase or preferred to wait until after the FOMC meeting early the following week. The meeting adjourned without acting. Later that day, after consulting the Treasury, Martin re-

216. The manager proposed increasing the maximum size of the System's portfolio of bankers' acceptances to $75 million. (It had started at $25 million in 1955 and increased to $50 million in 1957.) The aim was to allow the acceptance portfolio to parallel the open market account. Robertson again objected forcefully and at length, arguing that intervention prevented the market from developing resiliency. This was the same argument used to support bills-only. Martin did not join Robertson; the FOMC followed Martin and took no decision.

opened the discussion. He reported that the Treasury did not object. The Board then approved the increase, effective August 15.

The following Monday, August 18, the Board approved a 2 percent discount rate at any Bank that chose to increase its rate. Dallas, Atlanta, and Kansas City responded in the next ten days. All others, including New York, retained the lower rate.

Ralph Young's staff report for the August 18 and 19 meeting warned of the dangers of inflation. He compared the 1957–58 recession to eight previous contractions, concluding (incorrectly) that "it seems certain . . . that the 1957–58 recession will go down . . . as one of the milder recession experiences" (FOMC Minutes, August 19, 1958, 8). Money supply growth had been rapid, up to 8 percent. There was "only one course" to follow (ibid., 9). The System should reduce money growth; the first step should be "to reduce to zero as rapidly as possible the net free reserve position" (ibid., 9). For the future, Young proposed reducing money growth to 2 to 3 percent.

New York remained cautious. In Hayes's absence, Vice President Trieber presented the Bank's statement. He urged that any reduction in reserves be done cautiously. New York opposed a higher discount rate and favored a change in the directive to emphasize fostering growth and recovery. Although Trieber acknowledged Martin's concerns about the deficit and inflation, clearly New York did not share his concerns or want to act on them.

FOMC members divided. Board members expressed most concern about inflation. At least five presidents agreed with New York that fostering recovery should take precedence over controlling prospective inflation. Martin's summary recognized the division. The Federal Reserve could not jeopardize its responsibilities by failing to act when faced with a $12 billion prospective deficit. He favored reducing free reserves, but he would not set a target. The committee changed the directive to call for "fostering conditions in the money market conducive to balanced economic recovery" (ibid., 63).

As often occurred, the manager permitted the three-week moving average of free reserves to decline about a week before the FOMC met. The average fell from about $550 million to about $100 million in mid-September. Brunner and Meltzer (1964, 68–69) date the policy turn toward restraint in mid-August, four months after the cyclical trough. Martin and several of his colleagues seemed determined to act promptly to prevent a return of inflation.

The September 9 meeting was one of the most contentious meetings the FOMC had ever held. President Hayes, back from vacation, commented that "the present is emphatically not the time for backing away from our policy of outright monetary ease" (FOMC Minutes, September 9, 1958, 10). He was troubled by the dramatic increase in interest rates during August, opposed an increase in the discount rate, and favored higher free reserves, perhaps $500 million instead of the $100 to $200 million at the time of the meeting.[217] Hayes recognized the threat of long-term inflation but could not "see any justification for combating this long-term threat by means of a rapid shift in monetary policy" (FOMC Minutes, September 9, 1958, 12). He preferred a government wage policy (ibid., 12–13), a reference to growing interest in wage-price guidelines.

Hayes's challenge to Martin and the majority of the Board drew little support. Bopp (Philadelphia) favored "moderation," and Mills, as usual, expressed concern about Treasury financing and warned that the "System would be ill-advised to be so overwhelmingly concerned with the problem of inflation" (ibid., 24). But even Mills did not support Hayes's easier policy. The rest of the committee remained divided between those who wanted to pause and those who favored greater restraint. Vardaman, Shephardson, and Robertson argued for a more vigorous response to inflation. Balderston criticized New York and several others for failing to increase their discount rate. A split rate made the System look weak and indecisive (ibid., 49).[218]

Lacking a consensus among the very divided members, Martin overlooked New York's criticism and made two characteristic moves. He waited for a consensus to form, and he gave a strong warning about inflation and its consequences. The problem the System faced was "inflation in a bigger way than anything that had been faced in his own lifetime" (ibid., 49). He warned that "he saw certain similarities to 1929," a comment he made again in 1967 (ibid., 50). It was time for the System to "stand up and be counted . . . not dilly-dally about risks" (ibid., 53). An additional increase in the discount rate (to 2.25 percent) was infeasible, so System policy should head toward zero free reserves.[219]

217. Long-term rates at the time were back to the peak levels of the previous year, 3.75 percent for long-term Treasuries. Short-term rates had increased about one percentage point in August, but were below the peaks of 1957. The staff statement pointed to strong increases in credit demand, speculation, and the large expected deficit. The staff described higher rates as "clearly justified" (Recent Financial Developments, Board Correspondence, September 9, 1958, 2).

218. New York, Cleveland, Richmond, and St. Louis changed to 2 percent on September 12. Boston waited until September 23, one day before Philadelphia, Richmond, St. Louis, Minneapolis, and Dallas changed to 2.5 percent. The split discount rate continued until November 7, when all banks had a 2.5 percent rate.

219. Martin's reference to the political infeasibility of an additional increase in the discount rate probably referred to public criticism of the earlier 0.25 increase so early in the recovery. Much public commentary expressed concern that the Federal Reserve would prevent

The following week, Martin found support for his view, but not his policy, at the Federal Advisory Council meeting. The members agreed that business prospects would improve for the next six months and that the recovery was widespread and would continue (Board Minutes, September 16, 1958, 1–2). They agreed, also, that "the feeling that further inflation is inevitable is spreading" (ibid., 19). The FAC cited rising stock prices as evidence that the public expected higher inflation and also mentioned wage increases in excess of productivity growth. The FAC did not, however, mention the Treasury deficit until Martin expressed his concern that the $12 billion expected deficit put pressure on the Federal Reserve to increase the money stock.[220] FAC members praised the System for its steps toward greater restraint, but the majority believed that the System should "provide any reserves that may be required for the forthcoming Treasury financing and for normal seasonal needs" (Board Minutes, September 16, 1958, 27). Martin complained about criticism of the 2 percent discount rate, stating a lesson that would be repeated many times. "Many people . . . are inclined to say that it is fine to go down and that monetary policy must be flexible, but when the reserve bank discount rate was raised by one-quarter of one-percent the view was heard that this would destroy the process of recovery" (ibid., 25). In the 1970s Keynesian economists would repeat the criticisms of early action against inflation. They wanted to wait until inflation appeared.

Disagreement within the FOMC continued. New York recognized that recovery had occurred, but it continued to favor unchanged policy. The Board and its staff warned about inflation. To make the Board's case, the staff presented its analysis of recovery and the inflation problem. The presentation was almost entirely descriptive, a comparison of the movements of principal statistical series in the prewar and postwar years. The report gave "new support to the proponents of the theory of the inevitability of creeping inflation. Once again, as in most of the postwar period, the central problems of the years ahead may well be those of unsustainable de-

---

or hinder the recovery. Martin made only an oblique reference to New York's opposition, warning that if some directors of reserve banks opposed his policy, that was disappointing, but if they interfered in open market policy, changes would be made (FOMC Minutes, September 9, 1958, 51). The implication was that the changes would be in the role of directors. Contrary to earlier belief about political influence, it was the Board, not the bankers, who emphasized inflation.

220. Martin recognized the lags in the response of inflation. "Perhaps the country might have six months or so of happiness, with the recovery not yet having reached boom level, but it would certainly not be a solution simply to take up the check book and print money to the tune of $12 billion" (Board Minutes, September 16, 1958, 23). Purchase of $12 billion was based on the extreme assumption that the Federal Reserve purchased the full amount of the deficit. It would have increased the monetary base by 30 percent.

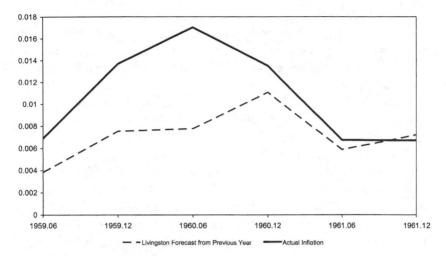

Chart 2.14. Anticipated (Livingston) and actual inflation, June 1959–December 1961.

mands and widespread price advances" (FOMC Minutes, September 30, 1958, 10).

The staff's conclusion was that the FOMC's major problem was to "curb inflationary and speculative developments before they gain headway" (ibid., 12). The FOMC took no further action. Monthly rates of consumer price increase showed no evidence of rising inflation; the twelve-month increase of consumer prices had reached a peak (3.65 percent) in April. By August, the rate of increase had fallen to 2.22 percent. Free reserves remained about $100 million through September and October, and the federal funds rate remained about 1.75 percent. However, the Board again increased stock market margin requirements, to 90 percent, effective October 16. Robertson voted no.

The Livingston Survey of inflationary expectations gave a bit of support to Martin's concerns. In 1958, the one-year ahead inflation forecast began to increase. Chart 2.14 shows that the survey underestimated the change. The forecast did not rise above 1 percent at this time, a modest rate of increase that leading central banks and governments would later dismiss as non-inflationary.

Tensions at the FOMC relaxed after the Treasury's October offerings moved to "substantial premiums." New York continued to favor an easier policy, but all accepted no change in policy at the October 21 meeting.[221]

221. Treatment of Treasury refunding was a major topic at this meeting. The Federal Reserve could not legally buy more than $5 billion directly from the Treasury. Counsel ruled that the limitation did not apply to refunding of expiring issues. Like most regulations, the rule could be circumvented. The Treasury sent a letter outlining two procedures for carry-

Differences arose, however, over a change in the discount rate. Treasury bill yields were almost a full percentage point above the discount rate. Most members regarded a 0.5 increase in the discount rate as a technical correction. New York expressed the concerns of its directors that an increase would be considered a step toward restraint. Only Mills and Mangels (San Francisco) favored delay. Following the meeting, five banks increased the discount rate to 2.5 percent. In the following two weeks, all others followed, with New York acting last, on November 7.[222]

The economy continued to expand and, toward year-end, the unemployment rate began to fall with no sign of rising inflation. The FOMC in November and early December left decisions to the manager's judgment about the "feel" of the market. On December 16, it voted for more restraint over the objections of President Hayes. These meetings were less contentious, but the basic division remained. Most of the Board, and its senior staff, expressed concern about the budget deficit and inflation. New York remained unconvinced.

Woodlief Thomas spoke of the "ominous nature of many aspects of prospective economic developments," citing the budget deficit, the gold outflow, stock market speculation, and "the retreat from fixed return investments" (FOMC Minutes, November 10, 1958, 10). Hayes replied, citing recent moderation and urging continuation of current policy. The only troubling aspect for him was the loss of gold. On a recent trip abroad, foreign central bankers had raised the same issues as Thomas, but Hayes was not convinced. "I would think it unwise to let the gold outflow itself affect our monetary policy directly" (ibid., 15).[223] Chairman Martin, referring back to Thomas's "ominous notes," said that he favored more restraint than the consensus, but left the decision about more restraint to the manager.[224]

---

ing out the exchange, one of which was more favorable to the Federal Reserve than to other holders. The FOMC rejected favorable treatment but accepted its counsel's opinion that the $5 billion limit did not apply to refundings.

222. The staff report called the committee's attention to the sizeable decline in the gold stock. In the year to October, the stock declined $2 billion, 9 percent. The staff report noted a $500 million decline in the most recent three months and estimated future losses at $100 million a month (FOMC Minutes, October 21, 1958, 16–17). The October level was $20.7 billion.

223. Of course, he added words about the "heavy responsibility to encourage confidence in the dollar and the stability of the gold standard," but he did not propose any action (FOMC Minutes, November 10, 1958, 15). Governor Mills referred to "the almost morbid discussions of inflation emanating from financial circles in this country that tended to promote distrust abroad" (ibid., 24–25).

224. The manager, supported by the Board's staff, again requested an increase in the acceptance portfolio to $75 million. He argued that acceptance purchases could be used to influence the loan market and to encourage foreign trade. Robertson, as usual, opposed the increase, citing the shifting arguments, the lack of evidence, the steady progression from an

The manager allowed free reserves to decline and the federal funds rate to rise by 0.5 percentage points in November and an additional 0.25 by year-end. The latter followed an FOMC decision in mid-December to let the market move toward negative free reserves. The committee voted to change the directive to eliminate "recovery" and emphasize "fostering conditions . . . conducive to sustainable economic growth and stability" (FOMC Minutes, December 16, 1958, 43). Hayes voted no.[225]

A new element entered at year-end. The principal European currencies became convertible on current account. The Board and the FOMC did not consider letting their commitment to the $35 gold price under the Bretton Woods Agreement take precedence over domestic policy concerns, as Hayes's November remarks suggest. This seems an accurate reading of congressional and administration sentiment that gave most emphasis to the unemployment rate.[226] The System continued to sterilize gold movements.

By year-end, the federal funds rate and all discount rates were at 2.5 percent, with bill rates 2.75 percent. Several reserve banks discussed raising the discount rate before the Treasury reentered the market, but none voted to do so. On December 29, 30, and 31, the Board voted to renew discount rates without change. Governor Robertson voted with the majority but inserted this statement in the record:

> Failure to act now coupled with an action to increase the rate after the Treasury financing seems to me to be unfair to the Treasury Department as well as to the individuals who purchase the securities that will be issued during the early part of January. (Board Minutes, December 29, 1958, 2–3)

The statement questioned the rationale for "even keel" policies, without saying so explicitly. The policy continued.

Also at year-end, the administration announced that the budget for fiscal

---

initial portfolio of $25 million to $50 million and now to $75 million. Allen (Chicago) sided with Robertson, but the majority voted for the increase (FOMC Minutes, December 2, 1958; Memo Board staff to FOMC, November 17, 1958).

225. On November 30, 1958, Governor James K. Vardaman, Jr., resigned after nearly thirteen years of service. Investigation of "leaks" pointed to Vardaman. This was a serious scandal for the Federal Reserve. Confronted with the evidence by an irate chairman, Vardaman chose to leave. President Eisenhower appointed G. H. King, Jr., to fill the rest of the term.

226. Eisenhower's diary reports his discussions of gold and debt finance in 1958–59. Secretary Anderson "believes that, unless we have a balanced budget, we are going to have very bad effects in foreign banking circles because of diminishing faith in the dollar. Saulnier believes there is very little danger of this at the moment. Moreover, he is not particularly concerned about the accelerated outward movement of gold. . . . [B]oth agree that a balanced budget would have the most salutary effect on our fiscal situation that could be imagined" (Ferrell, 1981, 359).

1960 would have a small surplus instead of a projected $9 billion deficit. Martin's and the Board members' concerns about the inflationary effect of persistent large budget deficits no longer applied. Martin recognized that "some hazards in the situation . . . were not real," but he continued the policy of restraint without apparent change (FOMC Minutes, December 16, 1958, 37). Annual monetary base growth remained between 1 and 2 percent and, as reported at the time, growth of the M_1 money stock slowed after mid-year 1958 (Council of Economic Advisers, 1959, 37).

The staff report for the first meeting in 1959 urged the FOMC to decide "what rate of monetary expansion would contribute best to the sustainability, without inflation, of prospective economic expansion" (FOMC Minutes, January 6, 1959, 5). The report described the long postwar decline in average cash balances per unit of income and the rise of inflationary psychology before concluding that monetary expansion should be moderate.

The recommendation had no visible effect. The FOMC did not define moderate economic growth or constrain its actions to achieve it. Hayes continued to emphasize near-term changes and restored free reserves as his indicator of the System's stance. Although several presidents mentioned an additional discount rate increase, Martin did not believe that would increase saving enough to get the public to finance the Treasury deficit out of current saving. "He hoped that inflation would not get out of hand to such an extent that a very serious price would have to be paid for its correction" (ibid., 37). This explicit recognition that disinflation was costly was not followed by a proposal to take additional actions to prevent an increase in inflation.

This is one of the rare meetings up to that time at which a participant mentioned international considerations. Hayes reported on the first days of convertibility of foreign currencies (on current account) and the devaluation of the French franc as part of the move to convertibility. He favored the change and thought it would "bring significant benefits to the United States in the long run." He did not expect much near-term effect (FOMC Minutes, January 6, 1959, 7). This prediction was soon falsified by increased gold loss.[227] Indeed, at the same meeting, Governor Mills ruminated about whether the System should raise the discount rate and end the policy of sterilizing the effects of gold movements so as to "subject the domestic economy to the discipline that is implicit in the gold outflow by

227. The move to convertibility brought out the major change in New York's role that had occurred since the 1920s when Governor Strong of the New York bank was directly involved in negotiations leading to a return to convertibility. In the 1950s, the Federal Reserve was an observer; responsibility had shifted to the Treasury.

terminating a policy of acquiring U.S. government securities to offset gold withdrawals" (ibid., 18).[228]

The System remained on an even keel through the next two meetings, so the federal funds rate remained near 2.5 percent, and the discount rate did not change. Several members expressed concern about the frequency of Treasury offerings that forced a delay in raising the discount rate.

Pressed by members' comments at the February 10 FOMC meeting, the staff prepared an explanation of policy guides and measures. Of particular interest, Delos Johns (St. Louis) had asked why the FOMC did not use the money stock directly as the main policy guide.[229] His question and others brought forth the most complete statement of operating procedures in many years. Emphasis was on control of money. "The money supply is the principal *quantitative* end of Federal Reserve policy, because System operations exercise their influence primarily through the money supply, although there are broader and more complex ultimate objectives" (Memo, Thomas to FOMC, Board Records, February 25, 1959, 1). The memo went on to explain that both the money stock and reserve measures varied unpredictably, so precise control of money was not feasible. Money stock projections influenced projections of required reserves and, in this way, affected projections for free reserves. The memo added that data on money were not available promptly but "perhaps more attention should be given to the customary broad seasonal changes than has been the practice" (ibid., 4). The memo indicated that control was subject to large errors both because of random fluctuations in free reserves, the variable link between the level of free reserves and the stocks of money and bank credit, and changes in velocity that alter the quantitative relation between money and ultimate goals such as output and the price level.

The memo also discussed the use of free reserves, money rates, and "feel of the market." Free reserves served as both an indicator of the policy and a target, or in Thomas's words, a "signal of policy objectives and an instrument for obtaining them" (Memo, Thomas to FOMC, Board Records, February 25, 1959, 7). They were a measure of the degree of ease or tightness, not an objective. Monetary policy could change the degree of ease

228. See the Appendix for evidence of persistent sterilization of gold movements.
229. Several members asked why estimates of reserve needs made by the Board's staff differed from New York's estimates. The main reasons were that they used different measurement procedures. The Board used seasonal factors based on past history, where New York used predictions of the trend of deposits. Also, each used its own method of projecting Treasury deposits. The memo commented also on the control problem, emphasizing the difficulty of knowing whether a change is a temporary or persistent change in free reserves. Regrettably, this concern was not taken up.

or tightness by making banks borrow or by providing excess reserves. "No other data can so effectively serve this purpose" (ibid., 7). Changes in Treasury bill rates or the general tone of the market provided supplementary information. Often they indicated pressures that would later be reflected in measures of reserves and money. "Feel" may suggest that the distribution of free reserves between country and city banks made the market tighter or easier than suggested by the level of free reserves. The memo then considered the control problem. The manager controlled free reserves within a margin of ±$100 million. Further "response of credit markets to any particular level of free reserves may vary considerably from time to time, depending upon pressures for monetary expansion, shifts in anticipations, and other factors difficult to detect or measure" (ibid., 10).

The March 3, 1959, meeting did not discuss the staff memo. We do not know if members objected to the staff's description, to the emphasis given to money, or to the obvious discrepancy between the factors emphasized in the memo and those emphasized in the regular staff reports at FOMC meetings. Instead, the FOMC turned to its usual business. After the annual ritual of reelecting officers, rotating members and renewing authorizations,[230] the committee took up the decision about the discount rate. Hayes had less enthusiasm for an increase than earlier. He preferred to wait until mid-April, after the next Treasury offering. Others favored an increase for technical reasons—to raise the discount rate above the Treasury bill rate. Mills wanted a higher rate to attract foreign deposits and gold. Martin, concerned about renewed inflation, urged the increase. Recognizing Hayes's reluctance to act, he challenged him directly. Usually the System could rely on New York to lead the increase, he said. Now that was no longer true. "The System either must face up to its responsibilities or take the position that monetary policy could not work in an environment like the present" (FOMC Minutes, March 3, 1959, 56). The Treasury would return to the market in a few weeks. He urged the presidents to act at once, so the higher discount rate would be in effect for two weeks. Addressing Hayes directly, he asked him "to express his [Martin's] personal judgment to the New York Board of Directors" (ibid., 58).

Hayes replied that credit demand had been more modest than he expected. There was no evidence of inflation. He did not think an increase

230. Hayes again voted no on bills-only. He asked again to change "solely" to "primarily" bills, but no one joined him. The FOMC also continued the formula for allocating securities to the reserve banks that had been in effect since June 1953. Each reserve bank received a share based on its share of total assets in the year ending February 28, 1959. Reallocation became effective on April 1. Another of the continuing resolutions provided for succession on the FOMC in the event of war or defense emergency.

was urgent. He preferred to wait until April. If he had to act sooner he would rather vote on March 12 than on March 5.[231]

Martin prevailed. On March 6, New York, Chicago, Philadelphia, and Dallas raised their rates to 3 percent. All others followed within a week.[232] The volume of discounts and the federal funds rate rose immediately, but bill rates remained in the range that had held since January, suggesting anticipation of the change.

The rest of the March 3 meeting was a delayed response to the leaks from FOMC meetings that had precipitated Vardaman's resignation. The number of participants expanded after Martin abolished the Executive Committee and increased the influence of the reserve banks. Members had a lengthy discussion of a proposal to limit the number of observers at FOMC meetings and the number of people who had access to the minutes. Public criticism of leaks from the meeting or the minutes brought the issue to the fore. Malcolm Bryan (Atlanta) argued for a return to the procedures used during the 1930s, a strict following of the statute. Only those who had to vote and their alternates would be present. Staff would be kept to a minimum.

Martin spoke last. He defended the current arrangement. It provided training and developed useful information. He did not want to go back to the System he had inherited, when some presidents did not discuss open market policy with anyone in their bank. The committee deferred a decision to a later meeting.

Treasury operations from mid-March through April kept the Federal Reserve committed to maintaining the same degree of restraint. The manager had considerable discretion. Table 2.4 shows the weekly average federal funds rate, the volume of borrowing, Treasury bill and long-term bond rates for this period. Both controlled and open market rates rose. The data suggest that the manager let the federal funds rate rise to the level of the

231. Martin's response suggested that he wanted to increase the discount rate right away, but the Treasury had "experienced in its refunding what was widely regarded as a failure" (FOMC Minutes, March 3, 1959, 62). Martin's conviction had been strengthened by the response of the Federal Advisory Council (FAC) to a question about the inevitability of further inflation. The members called the inflationary trend "unavoidable" (Board Minutes, February 17, 1959, 15). They mentioned rising wages, continuing budget deficits, increased demand for government projects and services, agricultural subsidies, and stockpiling of materials. They claimed that increased demands for spending were not matched by willingness to pay higher taxes.

232. Minneapolis asked for an increase before it held a directors' meeting, presumably based on conversations with its board members. The Board waited a few days, then approved the change. Robertson dissented. On March 12, the directors met and voted the change. I believe this is the first such incident. Frederick Deming, president of the bank since April 1957, later served as Treasury undersecretary in the Johnson administration.

Table 2.4   Money Market Indicators, March–April 1959

WEEK ENDING	FEDERAL FUNDS (%)	BORROWING (MILLIONS)	WEEK ENDING	NEW ISSUE TREASURY BILLS (%)	LONG-TERM U.S. BONDS (%)
March 11	2.71	506	March 14	3.06	3.92
18	2.86	986	21	2.76	3.92
25	2.93	589	28	2.77	3.94
April 1	2.84	357	April 4	2.84	3.95
8	3.00	775	11	2.95	3.97
15	3.00	918	18	3.08	4.01
22	3.00	1014	25	3.10	4.05

Source: Board of Governors (1976).

discount rate. When the Treasury bill rate remained below the (3 percent) discount rate, discounts fell; when the bill rate rose above the discount rate, discounting increased.

Some of the pressure on the money market reflected loss of gold. During second quarter 1959, the U.S. gold stock declined by $732 million, approximately 3.5 percent of the stock. Nearly half the decline ($344 million) was a payment for a quota increase at the International Monetary Fund. The U.K. withdrew half the remainder ($200 million). The Federal Reserve sterilized the outflow to the extent that it affected the money market, but the manager allowed borrowing and interest rates to increase (and free reserves to decline), so on these measures sterilization was incomplete.

The strong expansion continued. Real GNP rose 5.1 percent in the first quarter and 7.8 percent in the second. The unemployment rate fell to 5.2 percent in April from a 7.5 percent peak the preceding July. Despite the 90 percent margin requirement, stock prices continued to rise at a 25 to 30 percent annual rate. At its meeting with the Board, the Federal Advisory Council described the economy as "moving upward on an expanding front" (Board Minutes, April 28, 1959, 2). Unemployment remained high in some regions. The FAC urged the Board to maintain restraint but not increase it. The members expected strong demands for credit for the rest of the year.[233]

233. In March, the Board had published proposed regulations of credit to brokers and dealers in stocks and to banks lending on margin. On May 1, the Board voted on the proposed regulations. The purpose was to reduce speculation. The regulations prohibited substitution of securities within margin accounts and regulated withdrawal of cash and securities from such accounts. Equity owners and traders would be barred from withdrawing cash (or securities) equal to 90 percent of the value of securities sold. The Board approved limitations on cash withdrawals unanimously, but it rejected, four to three, controls on the substitution of securities within a margin account. Martin, Balderston, Shephardson, and King made up the majority; Szymczak, Mills, and Robertson voted for the new controls. The Board approved some, and rejected other, technical amendments to margin requirements. The new rules took

The May 5 FOMC meeting brought discussion of two new issues. For the first time, a staff member briefed the members on gold flows, balance of payments, and the international accounts. Some members described the recent gold outflow as temporary, but Woodlief Thomas was both correct and pessimistic. He found the origin of the problem in the use of monetary and fiscal expansion to maintain full employment. These policies raised prices and wages and reduced the country's competitive position. A main point of his comment went to the heart of the issue—monetary policy could not achieve two separate goals, one domestic, the other international. This did not evoke any response from the members. They seemed slow to recognize the problem.

The second new topic was the Liberty Loan Act of 1918. The act set a 4.25 percent ceiling on the coupon that the Treasury could offer on long-term bonds. Several issues had reached that range by the spring of 1959. Governor Mills argued that very restrictive monetary policy exacerbated this problem by setting off "a spiral of contractive credit forces" (FOMC Minutes, May 5, 1959, 27). If the policy continued, the banks would have to sell bonds at a loss. Policy was "unnecessarily and unwisely restrictive" (ibid., 26). "[T]he destructive influence of constantly falling prices for U.S. government securities can lead to disorderly market conditions whose correction might defeat the very policy purposes that have been sought after" (ibid., 27).

Mills's demand for an easier policy received no support. Even New York expressed concern about inflation. Inflation was "lurking in the shadows" (ibid., 16). But it was not imminent, so easing policy was wrong but additional restraint could wait. Several members expressed concern about wage increases and the prospect of a steel strike.

Martin and Hayes were absent. Balderston presided and stated the consensus for an even keel until after the Treasury completed its financing. Then he added, "His own personal opinion was that the desk ought to tighten appreciably before the next meeting" (ibid., 42–43). Rouse rejected the suggestion. It would be "pulling the rug from under the money market" (ibid., 43). He doubted that he could tighten, and he was not eager to try.

The mood changed dramatically in three weeks. The main topic at the May 26 meeting was the size of the next discount rate increase. Thomas's staff report favored an increase, citing the rise in stock prices and increase

---

effect on June 15. The discussion, over several months, showed that the real bills tradition had not vanished but it had weakened. Chairman Martin held a mixed view. He did not oppose selective controls or regulation, but he questioned whether tighter rules would be effective. "Governor Szymczak referred to the difficulties involved in administering selective credit controls" (Board Minutes, February 13, 1959, 6).

in the money stock, and for the first time it highlighted a renewed gold outflow.[234] The loss of gold aroused Hayes. He now cited inflationary dangers, especially strong growth of credit and rising stock prices. "[T]he time has come for a decisive signal" (ibid., 17). He proposed a one percentage point increase in the discount rate, if the Treasury would support it, strong statements by the president of the need for non-inflationary wage increases, and a change in the FOMC's directive to recognize "inflationary tendencies" (ibid., 18–19).

Robertson and Shephardson also supported a one–percentage point increase. A smaller increase of one-half percentage point was fully anticipated, so it would have no effect.[235] The FOMC was cautious. Most members favored an increase of 0.5 percentage points, and Martin wanted to move in a "normal way" to avoid a sense of panic (ibid., 49). Only Governor Mills opposed, warning again about the cumulative effect of System policy. He accused the others of having "panicked about anticipated events which had not as yet come into palpable and clear perspective" (FOMC Minutes, May 21, 1959, 35).[236]

Seven reserve banks wrote prior to the meeting to suggest a change in the directive. All of the proposed changes included a statement about sustainable growth and avoidance of inflation (Memo Riefler to FOMC, Board Records, May 25, 1959). Most of the presidents expressed their belief that low inflation contributed to maximum sustainable growth, a position

234. Young mentioned "a deepening concern in foreign circles" about the trend of the United States' payments deficit (FOMC Minutes, May 26, 1959, 6). Arthur Marget, of the Board's international staff, warned that earlier justifications for the payments deficit no longer applied. Europe had recovered. The U.S. was less competitive now, and it had to adjust.

235. Banks had increased the prime rate by 0.50 percentage points. The Board had discussed the size and timing of a discount rate change a week before. Most governors preferred to wait because they did not want to follow the prime rate increase immediately. Governor Mills opposed any change on grounds that it would raise interest rates, forcing banks to sell securities at a loss, weakening the Treasury market, and possibly doing "irreparable" harm (Board Minutes, May 19, 1959, 2). The Board's only action was to recommend a technical change in treatment of outstanding discounts when discount rates changed. It left the policy decision to the reserve banks but it recommended applying the new rate to existing loans.

236. Robertson and Mills almost always disagreed. The disagreement was substantive. Mill's statements suggest that he was very concerned about the ability of the Treasury market to absorb rate increases but also wanted to wait until evidence of inflation became clear. Robertson argued that "for monetary policy to be effective there must be uncertainty in the market place as to the future trend of interest rates. . . . The aim of the Federal Reserve, therefore, should be to foster a level of interest rates that there can be no certainty whether over the foreseeable future, interest rate levels will trend up, trend down, or remain relatively stationary" (FOMC Minutes, May 26, 1958, 36). There was no thought that the System and the market had a common interest in information and in each other's actions. Further, members did not recognize their dependence on the market's responses or that the market's responses depended on its assessment of System's prospective actions.

that they would emphasize in the 1980s and 1990s after neglecting it in the intervening years. None of the proposals suggested a tradeoff between inflation and growth or that inflation contributed to growth, views that became prominent in the 1960s. Without dissent the FOMC changed the directive to call for "restraining inflationary credit expansion *in order to foster* sustainable economic growth and expanding employment opportunities" (ibid., 54; emphasis added).

A few days after the FOMC meeting, New York, Chicago, St. Louis, Minneapolis, and Dallas raised their discount rates to 3.5 percent. Cleveland and Richmond voted to remain at 3 percent. They were the last to change. By June 12, all banks posted the 3.5 percent rate.

Although the FOMC believed it had simply followed the market to a higher level, market rates rose after the increase in the discount rate. By mid-June, the federal funds rate reached 3.50 percent, with Treasury bills at 3.25 percent, and free reserves at −$500 million. The increase in the federal funds rate in the year to mid-June was 2.5 to 3 percentage points, an unusually rapid rise. The proximate cause was a strong recovery and a very restrictive monetary policy. Real GNP rose 8 percent, base money growth 1.5 percent. Interest rates rose, inducing a very sharp increase in monetary velocity. The large increase in real GNP included sizeable accumulations of steel inventories in anticipation of a steel strike beginning in mid-July.

The steel strike came as anticipated, but the rest of the economy continued to expand. Treasury operations prevented any policy change during July. With intermediate and long-term yields near 4.25 percent or above, Congress considered legislation to remove the 1918 ceiling, but it raised the dollar value of the debt ceiling without changing the interest rate ceiling.[237] The Treasury would have to sell short-term securities. These rates had increased. The Board feared that continued increases in short-term rates would spill over to the prime rate and then to the discount rate.

The consensus was to maintain an even keel. Chairman Martin warned, however, that the System had to supply enough reserves to avoid the criticism that System policy made Treasury financing difficult (FOMC Minutes, July 7, 1959, 38). He believed the government securities market "was in a critical state" (ibid., 36).

---

237. Congress was reluctant to raise the 4.25 percent ceiling rate. The House Ways and Means Committee offered to suspend the ceiling for two years, but it wanted to add a section that would end bills-only. Martin sent a letter that described the two-year limit as unsound. He objected in principle to the amendment about bills-only. The legislation did not pass that year. Congress raised the interest ceiling for U.S. Savings Bonds but not for marketable government securities. Martin believed that the main reason for failure to remove the 4.25 percent ceiling was concern in Congress that a higher rate would hurt the savings and loan associations by inducing withdrawals (Board Minutes, July 9, 14, and September 15, 1959).

The FOMC then reconsidered the number of people who could attend FOMC meetings or have access to the minutes.[238] FOMC members, alternates, and other presidents had voted on five options ranging from the very restricted attendance in effect from 1936 to 1939 to the current procedure. Half of the group voted to maintain current attendance, with perhaps minor changes, and three-fourths voted to maintain a broad distribution of the minutes (Memo, Riefler to FOMC, Board Records, July 7, 1959). Martin and Hayes also favored retention of current procedures, so the policy did not change.

A window of opportunity for changing monetary policy opened in August. The Treasury did not plan another offering until late in the month. The steel strike had slowed economic activity temporarily, so the FOMC chose to maintain policy unchanged until September.[239] Despite this decision and a constant federal funds rate, rates on Treasury bills rose sharply in August. By September 1, the rate was almost 0.75 percentage points above the rate at mid-month. The manager described the market as much tighter than expected. The decline in industrial production during the summer was concentrated in the steel and coal industries, entirely the result of the prolonged strike. Major banks increased their prime rates to 5 percent, a new high. The market and the banks did not wait for the steel strike to end. The Federal Reserve believed that it had to wait.

All the usual signals for a discount rate increase were in place. The New York bank warned against an increase while Congress was discussing legislation to repeal the 4.25 percent maximum rate on Treasury bonds.[240] Following the meeting, New York, Cleveland, Richmond, Chicago, St. Louis,

238. The number had increased from about twelve to twenty in 1936–39 to forty to forty-five at the time of the meeting. In 1936, alternate members could attend only if they replaced the regular member. Gradually, attendance expanded to include all presidents and one economist from each reserve bank. Distribution of minutes and materials had expanded also. Up to eighty-five Board and bank employees had access to FOMC records in addition to officers of FOMC (memo on attendance, Board Records, July 8, 1959).

239. The IMF asked U.S. permission to sell $300 million in gold to buy Treasury securities, as it was obligated to do under the agreement authorizing U.S. membership. The Federal Reserve left the decision to the Treasury. The Treasury agreed to purchase the gold with an option to resell it to the Fund. Hayes's main concern was that the gold purchase could be interpreted as an effort to support the dollar (FOMC Minutes, July 28, 1959, 14–16).

240. "If there is still a possibility of congressional action at this session, it would seem well for the Federal Reserve to avoid overt action at this time which might possibly raise extraneous issues and jeopardize the legislation. Since it is generally expected that the Congress will recess within the next couple of weeks, this basis for uncertainty should soon be removed" (FOMC Minutes, September 1, 1959, 12).

Dallas, and San Francisco voted to increase discount rates to 4 percent, effective September 10.[241] The others soon followed. With Governor Mills absent, the first vote was unanimous. The following day Mills said that "the technical conditions in the money market completely justified the increase" (Board Minutes, September 11, 1959, 9). He argued, however, that the Board's policies had increased market rates. He had strong reservations about the cumulative policy action, so he abstained that day on the vote increasing rates at Boston, Atlanta, and Minneapolis. Consumer prices gave no sign of inflation. Prices declined in August, and rose less than 1 percent for the year ending in August. With the strike slowing activity and prices stable, on September 22, the FOMC took a modest step toward ease. It agreed to resolve doubts on the side of ease.

The Treasury was not through borrowing to finance the large deficit. It could not sell bonds, but the 1918 Liberty Loan Act did not restrict interest rates on Treasury notes or bills. In October the Treasury offered a five-year note with a 5 percent coupon, popularly called "the magic 5's." This was the highest yield on a government security since the early 1920s. The strong positive response surprised the markets and the Federal Reserve.[242] Part of the subscription came from time and saving accounts at banks and thrift associations.

Rising interest rates reflected a robust recovery, except for the steel strikes, strong productivity growth (Chart 2.1), and the Federal Reserve's tight policy. Although inflation continued to concern Federal Reserve officials, bankers, and others, actual inflation remained modest. Monetary base growth remained about 1.5 percent for the year to October, the range

241. In August, the FOMC considered the rules for discounting. Some banks acted as "underwriters" for Treasury issues, buying more of the issues than they wanted to hold and distributing the rest. The issue was how much "underwriter" banks should be permitted to borrow from the System while they performed this function. Some banks complained that they did not serve as underwriters because of concern that they would be questioned or reprimanded for borrowing. The Treasury found System policy not helpful. The FOMC agreed informally that each reserve bank should review its procedures and be able to explain them to the Treasury (FOMC Minutes, August 18, 1959, 34–38; Holland memo, Board Records, August 7, 1959). The FOMC's concern was to relate their discount policy to the even keel policy. A side effect of this discussion was a new definition of "even keel" as "no greater ease or tightness at the end of the financing period than at the beginning, with the supplying of only such additional reserves during the period as will take care of the additional drain on reserves caused by the financing itself. Theoretically the amount of such reserves required would be 18 percent of the amount of cash financing taken by the banks" (FOMC Minutes, August 18, 1959, 37).

242. "The market had estimated figures starting at $300 million and then, as the enthusiasm developed, raised the estimates to $500 million and then to $750 million. The actual response exceeded these estimates" (FOMC Minutes, October 13, 1959, 3).

Table 2.5   Loans, Investments, and Interest Rates, Insured Commercial Banks

DATE	LOANS ($ BILLIONS)	INVESTMENTS ($ BILLIONS)	9–12 MONTH RATE (PERCENT)
June 23, 1958	95.5	83.4	0.97
Dec. 31	98.1	86.0	3.18
June 10, 1959	103.3	81.8	3.97
Dec. 31	110.7	78.6	5.00
June 15, 1960	115.2	74.0	3.47

in which it had remained during most of the recovery, and the M_1 money stock rose only 2 percent in the same period (FOMC Minutes, October 13, 1959, 9).

Rising monetary velocity financed much of the recovery. The rise ended, temporarily, during the steel strike, as output declined both absolutely and relative to the money stock. The Board's staff suggested that the postwar rise in velocity had ended (ibid., 10). This proved premature. Continuing strong growth in demand and modest money growth raised interest rates, reduced average cash balances, and restored velocity growth. In the fourth quarter, the government ended the steel strike using a Taft-Hartley injunction. Output and monetary velocity rose.

Public and private demand for credit remained strong. With base growth below growth in credit demand, banks sold Treasury securities to make loans. This was particularly true of the 1959 and 1960 periods. Table 2.5 shows these data.

For the two years that roughly correspond to the expansion, bank loans rose at a 10.3 percent annual rate; bank investments fell at a 5.6 percent rate. These data suggest that part of the sharp rise in interest rates at this time reflected increased demands for credit. The cyclical increase in the nine- to twelve-month rate shown in Table 2.5 reflects the pressure on banks and other lenders to satisfy borrowers wishing to finance increased consumption and investment, while the federal government increased nominal spending by almost 12 percent in fiscal 1959. Most of the increase was for non-defense spending. However, part of the increase in interest rates reflected a rise in anticipated inflation, as suggested earlier by the FAC members. The Livingston Survey, taken at the time, showed an uptick to 1.1 percent in the rate of inflation expected a year ahead. Though modest, the level of anticipated inflation is the highest in the six years that the survey had run. The subsequent decline in actual and anticipated inflation suggests that anticipations may not have been firmly held.

A lesson from the 1958–60 experience was that the Federal Reserve could maintain low inflation (or price stability) despite large government spending and deficits, despite frequent periods of even keel, and despite its contrary belief. It had to be willing to allow market interest rates to increase in the face of criticisms, even mounting criticisms, in the Congress and elsewhere.[243] This was always a difficult choice, made more difficult by the firm belief that the System had an obligation to support Treasury issues. It would take many years of inflation before the System drew the conclusion that to control inflation required independence.

With rates rising, banks preferred to borrow from the System instead of selling securities at a loss. This reduced free reserves to between −$500 and −$600 million. The FOMC rarely permitted free reserves to exceed that range. For this period, free reserves, interest rates, and base growth offered compatible interpretations of the policy stance.

The 1959 increase in interest rates to levels not seen in a generation raised a new issue that would return many times. With open market rates at 5 percent, far above the 3 percent ceiling on time and saving deposits at commercial banks, New York asked again for an increase in regulation Q rates, or a special rate for foreign deposits. Only Mangels (San Francisco) and Leedy (Kansas City) supported the increase. Several presidents reported that the banks in their districts opposed any increase. No one supported an increase limited to foreign bank deposits, and several expressed concern about criticism of a split rate for foreigners. Regulation Q remained unchanged.

The October 13 meeting kept monetary policy unchanged but introduced a new procedure. Instead of Martin ending the meeting by expressing the consensus, the FOMC voted to approve his statement. The committee accepted that the fiscal 1960 budget would be balanced and that the threat of inflation had lessened as a result. They disagreed about whether the threat would reappear once the steel industry reached a settlement. Martin's conclusion called for "marking time." Only Mills voted no. As usual, he wanted to ease.[244]

After 3.5 months, small steel producers reached agreement with the union. A few weeks later the federal government invoked the Taft-Hartley Act to end the strike at larger firms. Industrial production soared, briefly, at year-end. Once again, there was uncertainty about persistence. Hayes re-

243. Secretary Anderson told the FOMC that, during the summer several Congressmen had called the Federal Reserve doctrinaire and inflexible (FOMC Minutes, November 4, 1959, 16). This was a criticism of bills-only.

244. Voting on the consensus started because Mills objected to Martin's statement of a consensus without recording Mills's dissent. Prior to the change, the FOMC had voted only when it changed the directive. Martin responded to the complaints in a letter (October 9) explaining the new procedure. Mills objected to the change but, on the opinion of the Board's counsel that the statute required them to vote, they adopted the new procedure (FOMC Minutes, November 4, 1959, 59–64).

marked that there were "growing doubts as to the vigor and duration of the expansion" (FOMC Minutes, November 4, 1959, 29). Woodlief Thomas expressed similar concerns. The Federal Advisory Council did not agree (Board Minutes, November 17, 1959, 1–2). The FOMC continued to "resolve doubts on the side of ease."[245]

Vault Cash

After many fruitless attempts beginning in the 1930s, the Board considered changes in the rules for reserve requirements several times in 1958. This time it reached agreement. In January 1959, it proposed legislation to (1) permit banks to count vault cash as part of required reserves, (2) reduce the range of required reserve ratios of central reserve city banks to 10 to 20 percent (instead of 13 to 26 percent), and (3) give the Board more power to permit smaller banks in central reserve and reserve cities to carry required reserves at the level specified for reserve city and country banks respectively.

As interest rates rose, the cost of System membership increased. The Board made its first proposal to increase membership by reducing the cost of membership for country banks. These banks, in the aggregate, held $1.3 billion of vault cash, about 4 percent of their net demand deposits. The balances were widely distributed.[246] Large banks could minimize holdings of vault cash, but it was not worth the trouble for small country banks (Memo, Board Records, January 20, 1959).

The third proposal extended the Board's discretionary authority to reclassify banks. At the time, five governors could reclassify a bank in an outlying district of a central reserve or reserve city. The new legislation permitted the Board to reclassify banks in the center of the city.

---

245. Saulnier described the administration's view of 1959–60 emphasizing uncertainty about transitory and permanent changes. Monetary policy was tight. The long steel strike made it difficult to know whether the economy had slowed or how much it had slowed. Inventories surged after the steel strike, but it was difficult to separate the effect of the end of the steel strike from a cyclical decline in spending. The Federal Reserve and the president were both concerned about the dollar, so "there was support . . . for a cautious money policy" (Hargrove and Morley, 1984, 137). Saulnier also minimized the contribution of the $13 billion swing (more than 2.5 percent of GNP) in the budget deficit to the slowdown and recession (ibid., 138). In contrast, Arthur Burns warned Vice President Nixon (and others) in February 1960 that a recession was likely if the Federal Reserve and the administration did not ease policy.

246. Years later, with the introduction of automated teller machines (ATMs), this provision eliminated the burden of required reserves for many banks, particularly city banks with large currency (vault cash) holdings in their ATMs. The 1959–60 change restored a provision of the original Federal Reserve Act. Prior to 1917, banks could count vault cash as part of reserves.

The Board did not ask for authority to eliminate the central reserve city classification, a step urged on it by the Federal Advisory Council (Board Minutes, February 17, 1959, 1–3). Martin told the bankers that the Board would oppose legislation eliminating the central reserve city classification, and it did. On April 2, he wrote to the chairman of the Banking Committee opposing that provision mainly on grounds that it would promote "undue concentration of available reserves in money market centers" (Statement of the Board of Governors in Opposition, Board Minutes, April 2, 1959). The Board cited the 1930s experience with large excess reserves to justify its claim. This was an error. With unchanged interest rates, a reduction in reserve requirement ratios for profit-maximizing central reserve city banks would change the demand for reserves and the effective supply in the same proportion. The principal monetary or credit effect would be a small change in the multiplier of bank reserves. The Board's argument applied only if the banks' minimum desired reserves remained below their required reserves, as happened in some recessions.[247]

In July, Congress approved legislation granting the authority to count vault cash as part of reserves, permitting the Board to lower required ratios for individual banks in central reserve and reserve cities, changing the range for reserve requirements in central reserve and reserve cities to 10 to 22 percent, and eliminating the central reserve city classification within three years. The Board waited the full three years to make the change (Board Minutes, July 29, 1959, 8).

The Board was pleased to have authority to count vault cash as part of required reserves but reluctant to release additional reserves in the summer of 1959. Also, it had previously classified cities and banks according to the percentage of interbank deposits held. The elimination of the central reserve city class and its increased authority to classify banks were reasons to develop new standards. It considered using volume of debits, turnover ratios of deposits, proportion of excess reserves, activity in the federal funds market, and other market measures (letter, Sherman to reserve bank presidents, Board Minutes, July 31, 1959). The presidents' response reaffirmed the use of interbank deposits as the principal measure for classification as a reserve city. They urged the Board to make a "modest start . . . in use of vault cash for reserves" (Statement of the presidents' conference, Board

247. I am indebted to David Lindsey for pointing out when the Board's statement was correct. The Board also argued several times that reducing reserve requirements for central reserve city banks might require an increase in reserve requirements for country banks. This would alter "long-established relationships" (Board Minutes, April 13, 1959, letter, Balderston to Congressman Paul Brown, 1). Congressman Patman objected to the change because it would transfer income to central reserve city banks.

Minutes, September 23, 1959, 7). The presidents opposed increases in reserve requirement ratios to offset the effect of releasing vault cash.[248]

Extensive discussion continued through the fall. On November 30, the Board adopted a modified version of a proposal made by Governor Robertson. Effective December 3, currency and coin at reserve city and central reserve city banks in excess of 2 percent of net demand deposits could be counted as satisfying required reserves. For country banks, effective December 1, currency and coin in excess of 4 percent of net demand deposits could be counted. The Board also changed the dates on which country banks reported reserves and deposits to biweekly from semimonthly.[249] Chairman Martin described his view as "not enthusiastic" but willing to experiment in view of all the discussions. But he wanted agreement to be unanimous (Board Minutes, November 30, 1959, 11). Governors Szymczak and King expressed reservations but agreed to vote for the proposal, and it passed without dissent. A year later, effective November 24, 1960, the Board restored its original rule of 1914–17 that counted all vault cash as part of reserves.[250]

The initial release of vault cash did not bear out the conclusions of the lengthy discussion of consequences. Free reserves fell in November and rose in December to the level reached in October. Country banks increased excess and free reserves. Since the federal funds rate remained unchanged at about 4 percent through November and December, the observed changes in free reserves appear as small random movements largely unrelated to the changes in regulation D affecting vault cash.

The new legislation also increased the Board's authority to reclassify banks in central reserve and reserve cities into categories with lower requirement ratios. Many banks, notably Chicago banks, applied for reclas-

248. The Board regarded the release of vault cash as a major problem because it released very different amounts of reserves at different banks and required some compensating action to avoid an increase in money. Governor Robertson described the problem as "the most important and difficult administrative problem facing the System." Chairman Martin said, "[T]he System was going to . . . start off . . . into uncharted ground" (Board Minutes, September 23, 1959, 11, 13).

249. President Allen (Chicago) raised the only objection. The 4 percent rule did not give much help to country banks. Only about 300 out of 900 non-reserve city banks in his district would benefit whereas 80 percent of the reserve and central reserve banks would benefit (Board Minutes, November 30, 1959, 11). Later, Leedy (Kansas City) reported that less than 10 percent of country banks and 20 percent of reserve city banks in his district benefited (Board Minutes, December 15, 1959, 19).

250. Federal Reserve notes were not legal tender until 1933, so they were not part of reserves at the start of the System. The decision on June 21, 1917, to exclude vault cash from reserves also reduced reserve requirement ratios, more than compensating for the exclusion of vault cash. Country banks lost relatively when the Board excluded vault cash and gained relatively in 1960 when all vault cash counted.

sification.[251] The Board initially decided to have its staff develop criteria for classification, but that took months to complete. The Board spent considerable time discussing criteria, such as the type of business that the bank did, but it relied mainly on bank size measured by total deposits.[252]

The statute required the Board to use "character of the business" as its criterion for classifying cities, but the Board and its staff had difficulty making the criterion operational and applicable to individual banks. Most of the governors' concerns were about individual banks, not cities. Although they did not make their principal concern explicit, they were aware that their criteria would require some large country banks to be reclassified as reserve city banks.[253] A further concern was the probable release of additional reserves at that time.

Discussion by the governors continued throughout the year. The Board did not reach a final decision, but it established some main criteria for classification as a reserve city: (1) presence of a reserve bank or branch, (2) one or two large banks ($200 million in deposits together), and (3) $40 million of interbank deposits. The presidents remained skeptical. Several argued that the formulas seemed arbitrary and had no advantage over the existing rules (Board Minutes, September 13, 1960, 7–8). Board members did not agree on whether to base classification on demand or total deposits, how to treat deposits of branch banks, and what to do if a city qualified as a reserve city but all of the banks were below minimum size.[254]

Board members could not agree on a formula and did not adopt one.

251. Illinois was a unit banking state and Chicago was a central reserve city, so subject to the highest ratios. Chicago had many small banks that could be reclassified under the revised law.

252. Under previous laws and regulations banks in outlying areas of a central reserve city were not subject to central reserve city requirements. Many of the small banks in outlying districts asked to be reclassified as country banks. On January 22 and February 1, 1960, the Board established de facto that banks in outlying regions, with demand deposits less than $43 million, could follow country bank reserve requirement ratios. Small banks in the central city could have country bank status also, if they asked. Banks with more than $70 million in demand deposits would not be reclassified until the Board formulated criteria. The Board treated banks between $43 and $70 million individually (Board Minutes, January 22 and February 1, 1960).

253. The discussion suggests that the Board would have to reclassify cities as reserve cities, then exempt many of the banks from the classification. "[T]here were a number of cities, not presently reserve cities, having one or more banks that would have to be classified as reserve city banks under any standard that the Board might decide upon" (Governor King, Board Minutes, March 14, 1960, 10). Woodlief Thomas reaffirmed King's statement (ibid., 10).

254. In December, Thomas suggested basing the classification on the deposits of all banks in a city instead of the size of the largest banks (Board Minutes, December 7, 1960, 4–5). A problem with this proposal soon appeared: the Board would have to designate a home office city for branch banks. Whether the Board had that power was uncertain.

The Board continued to follow its existing rules. Only five cities changed classification from country to reserve city in the 1960s (Board of Governors, 1976, 609). Effective July 28, 1962, New York and Chicago changed from central reserve to reserve city status as required by law.

Effective August 25, 1960, central reserve and reserve city banks could count vault cash in excess of 1 percent of deposits as part of reserves. On September 1, 1960, vault cash at country banks in excess of 2.5 percent became part of reserves. On November 24, the Board removed the last restrictions; all vault cash became part of reserves.

End of the Expansion

The timing of the initial release of vault cash in 1959 coincided with the seasonal demand for reserves at year-end. The FOMC did not have a firm view of what would happen after the steel strike. Some favored an easier policy. Hayes suggested that the System should seek stand-by authority to impose consumer credit controls (FOMC Minutes, November 4, 1959, 31). The committee kept policy unchanged; Mills dissented because he wanted an easier policy.

The most contentious issue at the November 4 meeting concerned the System's response to the Treasury's refunding offer. The Treasury offered a four-year, 4.875 percent note or a one-year 4.75 percent note in exchange for maturing securities. The System held $5 billion. Taking the four-year note would be inconsistent with bills-only. Treasury Secretary Anderson said he did not care what the System did but, in discussion with Balderston, he reminded Balderston that "many Congressmen of the so-called 'liberal' school [thought] that the Federal Reserve was doctrinaire and inflexible" (FOMC Minutes, November 4, 1959, 16).

Hayes, presiding in Martin's absence, asked the staff for its opinion. Riefler and Thomas opposed taking any four-year notes to avoid conflict with the bills-only policy. Governor Mills thought the System would set a bad precedent if it changed policy (ibid., 15). The FOMC voted seven to four to exchange only for the one-year note. Hayes, Erickson (Boston), Shephardson, and Szymczak voted against.

The FOMC made no changes in policy for the rest of 1959. Chairman Martin described the consensus as maintaining the status quo but giving the manager discretion to adjust to market conditions. "While there were different views expressed there was no real agreement. . . . [W]hat the System did would not really make too much difference" (FOMC Minutes, December 15, 1959, 42). Mills continued to vote no.

The December 15 meeting was the last for Winfield Riefler. He resigned effective December 31. In the 1920s and the 1950s, he had shaped the

System's policies, including bills-only, and its analysis. In January, Ralph Young became Secretary of the FOMC, Guy Noyes took responsibility for the FOMC briefing on the economy, and Woodlief Thomas became adviser to the Board.

Riefler had held a dominant position. Less than a month after he left, members of the FOMC began discussing the directive, the operating target, the role of free reserves, and alternatives. Malcolm Bryan (Atlanta) began the discussion by proposing "total effective reserves," computed by adjusting total reserves for changes in reserve requirement ratios and for reserves released or absorbed by shifts in deposits between banks with different reserve requirements.[255] He presented a chart showing the trend and seasonally adjusted values. The trend was 3.6 percent a year for 1947–59. Effective reserves moved procyclically, generally rising during months of expansion and declining prior to and during the early months of the three recessions after 1947. Bryan used the chart to show that reserve growth had been excessive at the end of the 1957–58 recession, but restrictive policy had eliminated the "reserve surplus" and, with it, the problem of inflation (FOMC Minutes, January 26, 1960).[256]

Two weeks later, the committee discussed Bryan's proposal and a related proposal by the Board's vice chairman, Canby Balderston. The latter related growth of reserves and money to economic growth. If money growth exceeded projections, banks would have to borrow to get additional reserves, increasing restraint in the System's interpretation. In the opposite event, banks would repay borrowing. Balderston proposed that the System offset changes in total reserves resulting from borrowing or repayment (FOMC Minutes, February 9, 1960, 41–47). Borrowing would then change the distribution of reserves, not the total outstanding. As the staff noted, Balderston's proposal differed from the free reserve-operating target by avoiding open market operations to maintain free reserves when reserves rose above target. The Balderston proposal treated an increase in borrowing as expansive because it added reserves. The Board's tradition, based on the Riefler-Burgess analysis of the 1920s, considered borrowing

255. The adjustment follows the procedure discussed in Brunner (1961) and later used by the St. Louis bank. Brunner's paper circulated about this time, but Bryan's proposal may have developed independently.

256. Woodlief Thomas responded to the charts, telling Bryan that the money supply was "in many respects a preferable guide" (letter, Thomas to Bryan, Board Records, February 4, 1960, 1). "Preferable" refers to Bryan's reserve measure. However, for daily or weekly operations, Thomas preferred free reserves because most of the manager's actions offset temporary changes. "From a long-term standpoint total reserves, or money supply, seasonally adjusted, provide a much better guide to System operation than figures for net borrowed reserves. On a short-term basis, however, the latter are probably more satisfactory" (ibid., 3).

contractive. Balderston agreed with the traditional System view that banks would be under pressure to repay borrowing, but he recognized that if repayment induced other banks to borrow, total reserves did not decline.[257] Neither Bryan nor Balderston discussed the speed with which the FOMC would return to the target.

Martin did not believe that rules or formulas could contribute. Hayes expressed polite interest, but he doubted that the System could guide weekly or daily decisions. Martin agreed. He recognized, however, that "there was more concern within the System than for a long time about the question of growth of the money supply" (ibid., 49–50). He preferred to talk about "color, tone, and feel" of the money market. He believed firmly that short-term changes in money were not informative.

Bryan continued to urge adoption of a total reserves target. On March 22, he warned FOMC members that "the recovery is losing momentum, that some massive readjustments are taking place, and others are in prospect" (FOMC Minutes, March 22, 1960, 18). The principal changes were increasing foreign and domestic competition and adjustment by the public from inflationary to non-inflationary beliefs. The latter change was highly desirable, but he warned that the transition could be "gravely troublesome in its economic implications" (ibid., 18). His major concerns included a highly illiquid banking system, the consequence of no growth of reserves in 1959 and declining reserves since year-end. He cited a "highly competent body of monetary theory" as showing that "*some* rate of growth of reserves is necessary to an expanding economy" (ibid., 19; emphasis in original). Bryan added that the money supply had declined also. Then, he warned:

> [O]ur policy, unless greatly ameliorated, will in a matter of time, whether weeks or months, produce effects that we do not at all want . . . [M]onetary policy produces lagged effects. If the effects of an overdone restriction begin sooner or later to be overtly evident, and are unfortunate, as I think they will be, we should not be able to plead ignorance. . . . Let me also suggest, as a sort of aside, that the period we are in is one that illustrates the grave dangers of the free-reserve, net-borrowed reserve concept as a guide to policy. (ibid., 20)[258]

Bryan's statement made little impact. Shephardson questioned the definition of money. Robertson said it was a mistake to overemphasize the

257. Balderston allowed for an increase in currency held by banks and the public and provided for 2 percent annual growth of the money stock, currency and deposits. His rule is a type of total reserve or base money rule that set growth of reserves at $8 million a week (2 percent a year) plus or minus any change in currency demand.

258. Bryan's comment may have been heavily influenced by Milton Friedman's (1961) work on lags published a few years later.

money supply. Leedy (Kansas City) said FOMC could not use a formula to guide policy. Mills and Johns (St. Louis) supported Bryan. Mills argued that rising velocity with declining money supply is not evidence of expansion. It shows that holders of cash balances are strained. Johns recalled that the committee had called for ending the decline in the money supply at its March 1 meeting. But total reserves and money had continued to decline. He urged the FOMC to "reverse the decline in total reserves with a view to reversing also the decline in the money supply" (FOMC Minutes, April 12, 1960, 36). But Martin resisted Bryan's argument. He found short-run changes in money difficult to interpret.

Events soon confirmed Bryan's prediction. The National Bureau dates the peak of the expansion in April 1960, a few weeks after the warnings by Bryan and Johns. The Standard & Poor's index of stock prices had fallen since September 1959. Industrial production began to fall in February, and the unemployment rate started to rise in March. The large, sudden shift from a $12 billion budget deficit to a surplus played a role by reducing spending. As was often the case, the monetary base and free reserves gave different signals. Annual growth of the monetary base fell to 0.25 percent in February, March, and April. Free reserves rose from −350 in January and February to −200 in March and April, mainly resulting from a decline in borrowing. The federal funds rate remained unchanged at 4 percent.

As Bryan, Johns, and Mills warned, the free reserve targets misled the FOMC. With the discount rate about equal to the federal funds rate, financial institutions sold Treasury bills and reduced discounts to avoid the administrative and regulatory costs of borrowing. Free reserves rose, as discounts fell, suggesting incorrectly that policy had eased. The decline in base money growth implied the opposite, as Johns pointed out (FOMC Minutes, April 12, 1960, 36).

The FOMC started 1960 with the belief that, after the steel strike ended, the economy would expand rapidly. The Federal Advisory Council (FAC) held this view in February; they foresaw favorable conditions for the first six months. They tempered this optimism by noting the decline in farm income and stock prices, slower sales of automobiles, and rising unsold auto inventories (Board Minutes, February 16, 1960, 2). Despite the low reported rates of inflation in 1959, the FAC warned that the wage agreement in the steel industry and the government's budget problems raised concerns about long-term inflation. The adverse balance of payments and the administration's efforts to have a budget surplus reduced these pressures in 1960.

As the year progressed, the FOMC recognized that the economy had slowed and that monetary policy was restrictive. In early January, all members except Mills wanted to increase the discount rate, but only one or two preferred not to wait for the end of the Treasury refunding. The main reason for the increase was to realign the discount rate with market rates.[259] Some members wanted a one percentage point increase in February, March, or April instead of 0.5 after the refunding.

Martin opposed the increase. Although he liked to follow the consensus and not dictate to the committee, this was an exception. He had spoken with Secretary Anderson, who did not want to put pressure on the System, but he expected the coming Treasury auction to be difficult and he preferred a delay. Martin then asked all of the presidents not to change their discount rates. The discount rate remained at 4 percent.

By early February, the committee recognized that the economy had slowed. Martin accepted responsibility. He said that Federal Reserve policy had restrained the economy. He preferred an easier policy.[260] Staff reports noted that banks continued to sell governments, investors had become more cautious, and foreigners had purchased both gold and dollar securities.[261] Martin proposed to change the directive, but the committee opposed. Some members said that the directive had little importance. They preferred to change the policy. The FOMC could not reach a consensus; Martin proposed a slight but not visible easing.

Criticism of the bills-only policy in Congress and Riefler's departure began to weaken support for bills-only within the System. Ralph Young pointed out that many outsiders thought the rule was too restrictive. On March 15, the Board received a letter signed by twenty-one senators, led

259. Bryan (Atlanta) said that some banks in the sixth district had used the discount window to supplement their capital. He was considering a progressive discount rate to discourage overborrowing. The only time a reserve bank used a progressive rate was 1921. It proved very unpopular with many bankers and Congressmen.

260. Martin's suggestion to ease policy in the winter partly absolves him from the blame that Nixon placed on him for the recession that, he and many others believed, cost Nixon victory in the very close 1960 election. In March Burns warned Nixon about an impending recession and urged him to press for increased spending and monetary and credit expansion. Andersen and Saulnier were not convinced, and Eisenhower wanted to reduce spending, not increase it (Nixon, 1962, 310). Nixon brought his request to a cabinet meeting on March 25, but nothing was done (Ewald, 1981, 293–96). In 1971, Nixon reminded Burns frequently about the good advice Burns had given in 1960 as a way of urging him not to restrict monetary expansion before the 1972 election.

In Hargrove and Morley (1984, 154–55), Saulnier questions the extent of Nixon's concern at the time. He noted that President Eisenhower told him to brief Nixon about the economy. At the weekly briefings Saulnier explained that "the economy was not growing to the extent we wanted it to grow. . . . Never once did I have a word out of him that he was dissatisfied" (ibid., 155).

261. Governor Szymczak warned that the markets had figured out that the System targets free reserves. He proposed to move the target around to keep the market guessing. Otherwise, it would thwart policy actions (FOMC Minutes, February 9, 1960, 34).

by Senator Douglas, urging the System to adopt four reforms: (1) tighten regulation of government security dealers including margin requirements for their customers, (2) end bills-only, (3) permit the money supply to increase on average at the rate of output growth, and (4) use open market operations (not reserve requirement changes) to provide secular growth of money. The letter suggested that if the Federal Reserve made these changes, Congress would consider removing the 4.25 percent interest rate ceiling on Treasury bonds.

Martin replied on April 14. He rejected tighter regulation of the government securities market, reminding the senators that Congress had considered the issue in the 1930s and exempted the dealer market from regulation.[262] Also, higher costs for government security dealers would reduce participation in the market to the Treasury's detriment. He defended bills-only, assured the senators that the System was not "rigid and inflexible" as sometimes charged. He noted that the System adapted to unusual conditions when it purchased longer-term debt in 1955 and 1958 and when it exchanged for other than short-term securities in the 1959 and 1960 Treasury refundings.[263] He agreed with the third recommendation: "As I have testified to the Congress on various occasions, it is the Board's position that we should provide for such increases in the money supply as can be absorbed by a growing economy without generating inflationary pressures" (Board Minutes, April 14, 1960, 5, letter, Martin to 21 senators). He expressed a reservation, however, about any close relationship between growth of money and output over periods lasting several years, and he explained the slow growth of money in the late 1950s as a reduction in excess money balances accumulated during World War II. He declined to make a commitment to keep reserve requirements unchanged, and he reminded the senators that they had voted recently to reduce reserve requirements in the legislation concerning vault cash.

In a modest step away from bills-only, the staff proposed in February to permit the manager to buy bonds when they became short-term.

262. He referred them to the 1959 Treasury–Federal Reserve study of the dealer market, carried out following the speculation that induced the Federal Reserve to buy long-term securities in 1958. This study is discussed later in the chapter. The Treasury also opposed margin requirements for purchases of government securities. To reduce speculation in new issues, they proposed subsequently to remove "rights" to new issues from holders of expiring securities. The public could then subscribe to a new issue on a cash or exchange basis, with no preference given to current holders (the Federal Reserve, the Treasury trust accounts, and small holders would continue to have preference if they chose to replace existing securities) (Board Minutes, March 29, 1960, 9).

263. At the Treasury's request, the FOMC agreed to help in the April 1960 refunding by exchanging for a one-year bill.

The FOMC would approve each decision. Rouse (the manager) suggested that short-term could include up to two years. As usual, Hayes argued for giving the manager more discretion, but many of the members were reluctant.[264]

On March 1, the committee revised the directive to eliminate the reference to inflation. The new directive called for "fostering sustainable growth in economic activity and employment while guarding against excessive credit expansion" (FOMC Minutes, March 1, 1960, 74). There was general agreement that policy was too restrictive. Martin expressed the consensus as favoring −$250 to −$300 million of free reserves, an increase of $50 to $100 million from the February average.[265]

Several members referred to the decline in the money supply and wanted to end it by using quantitative targets. The manager preferred to concentrate attention on the tone and feel of the market. This tension continued. There was no agreement about how to define and conduct policy. President Hayes proposed more active use of regulation Q ceiling rates to signal the direction in which interest rates should change, and Leedy (Kansas City) proposed using an interest rate target. The FOMC could not reach a consensus. After the March 1 decision to increase free reserves, it took no further action before the recession started, but in April it gave the manager authority to let free reserves fluctuate in a wider band (FOMC Minutes, April 12, 1960).[266]

The divisions within the FOMC covered several dimensions. Some wanted precise quantitative targets to hold the manager to account. Others, led by Hayes but often joined by Martin, favored qualitative targets and managerial discretion. Some wanted to use reserves or the money supply as a target, and many members criticized the use of free reserves. Despite the misleading interpretation of borrowing that Bryan and Balderston pointed out, free reserves remained the most frequent target when the FOMC chose a target. Some thought the economy would continue expanding. They cited consumer surveys and inflationary psychology. Others expressed concern about declining tax receipts, money supply, and credit.

264. Governor King noted that the staff's proposal frequently used the phrase "not the policy of the Committee." He asked, what is the committee's policy?

265. The FOMC voted at the March 1 meeting to distribute the report of its meeting to the Treasury.

266. Brunner and Meltzer (1989, 69) record a decisive move toward easier policy in April 1960 followed by a further move at meetings on May 3 and 24. Free reserves had increased in March but did not change noticeably after the April 12 meeting. Free reserves rose again in advance of the May 24 meeting. One reason often suggested for use of free reserves instead of an interest rate target was concern that Congressman Patman would increase pressure to lower the interest rate target. The System usually denied that it controlled an interest rate.

Table 2.6   Policy Decisions and Free Reserves at Turning Points

| DATE OF TURNING POINT | CHANGE IN POLICY DIRECTION | FIRST INDICATION OF | |
		MAJOR CHANGE IN POLICY	CHANGE IN THE MOVING AVERAGE OF FREE RESERVES (THREE-WEEK)
July 1953	June 11	June 11	May 27
August 1954	December 7	December 7	December 1
July 1957	August 20	October 22	October 23
April 1958	May 27	August 19	August 13
May 1960	February 9	March 1	March 2
February 1961	January 24	December 19, 1961	January 3

Source: Brunner and Meltzer (1989, 71).

President Bryan summarized the committee's position: it had not reached a conclusion about what policy had been, so it was not able to call for a policy change (FOMC Minutes, April 12, 1960, 34). He again predicted trouble ahead.[267]

Differences of opinion about the wording of the directive surfaced again at the March 1 meeting. Chairman Martin had asked the staff to propose changes in the directive, partly to meet complaints that the System was doctrinaire and inflexible. The staff proposed a more flexible alternative that permitted the manager to request permission to intervene in the market for securities other than bills. Also, the proposal introduced "principally but not exclusively" into the bills-only clause (Memo, Thomas, Rouse, Young to FOMC, Board Records, February 5, 1960).

The committee did not address control of policy actions. Vague instructions gave the manager considerable freedom to make decisions or perhaps respond to direction from Martin or Hayes. Table 2.6 shows dates of committee decisions to ease or restrain policy at cyclical turning points and dates for a change in the three-week moving average of free reserves. Two points stand out. First, the committee voted to change policy near the turning points in economic activity, using National Bureau of Economic Research turning points. Although the early change in June 1953 was fortuitous, the Federal Reserve was alert to changes in the economy. The recognition lag was never more than four months (1954) and usually very short. Second, the manager often changed free reserves before the committee acted.

In Executive Session after its February 1960 meeting, the FOMC divided along several lines. No one proposed better control of the manager.

267. Balderston described the economy as in a period of "rolling prosperity," but he was uncertain about the direction in which it was rolling. Martin now defended recent policy as correct, reversing his February comment.

Hayes and Erickson (Boston) favored the staff proposal. Szymczak, Mills, and King preferred the old statement with "primarily" in place of "solely" bills, but Szymczak reminded the members that wartime and postwar pegging began as a policy of maintaining orderly markets for the Treasury. Johns rejected the complaints about inflexibility or rigidity as "a charge brought solely by those who opposed the principles which the statement expressed" (Executive Session, FOMC, March 7, 1960, 4, based on notes included by the Secretary in the March 1, 1960, minutes.)

Seeing no consensus about to form, Martin proposed keeping the existing language temporarily. The committee would revisit the subject at a later meeting.

The decline in inflation in 1959–60 should have added weight to the views of policymakers and others that inflation could be prevented by reducing money growth. They did not draw that conclusion, perhaps because many of them believed that budget deficits or labor unions caused inflation while others doubted that monetary policy alone could slow inflation. Concerns that reducing inflation would increase unemployment played a role also. The shift from a large budget deficit to a small surplus strengthened beliefs about the power of fiscal deficits.

A recession started in 1960. Both presidential candidates and many in Congress and elsewhere blamed the Federal Reserve for sluggish growth and three recessions in seven years. This too reduced the confidence that policymakers might have gained from their success in reducing inflation. In the years after 1965 the members did not look back at this experience as evidence of what they could do.

Regulation Q Again

The Board discussed the competitive position of banks in the market for time deposits many times as open market rates rose above regulation Q ceiling rates. Both the System and the industry had multiple concerns. Large banks in New York wanted rates increased to attract large foreign deposits. Banks facing strong competitive pressures from savings and loan associations also favored higher rates. Banks that did not offer the 3 percent ceiling rate typically opposed higher rates. The Board and the reserve bank presidents reflected these pressures.

The result was much discussion but no action. The Board did not raise the 3 percent ceiling rate until 1962. It considered, but did not adopt, a redefinition of savings deposits and a proposal to offer premium interest rates to foreign depositors. Political considerations dominated economic decisions. Pressure for higher rates came mainly from New York banks. With slow growth of the monetary base, bank credit expansion depended on growth of time deposits. Ceiling rates prevented that growth, reducing bank earnings. Higher interest rates did not appeal to homebuilders, many bankers, and populist members of Congress. Thus, the Federal Reserve took the first steps toward a policy that eventually would have devastating effects on the banking and thrift industries over the next quarter century.

In fall 1958, the New York bank suggested a staff study to determine the principles that should govern changes in regulation Q rates. The conclusion was that regulation Q should be treated as a banking issue and not a monetary policy issue, since the intent of the legislation was to prevent banks from competing aggressively for time deposits. The staff proposed that the Board set the ceiling rate high enough to allow individual banks to change rates up and down. The ceiling rate could be changed judgmentally to meet market rate changes or be set by a formula that provided automatic adjustment.

The decision to treat rate regulation as a banking issue, not a monetary issue, proved to be a costly error. It directed current and subsequent discussion to concerns about the relative position of financial institutions, encouraging banks and non-bank financial firms to base their case on the costs or benefits to them. New York would argue that a higher rate attracted foreign deposits. Regional banks pointed to the cost they would incur by raising the average rate paid to all depositors to attract a small increment of new deposits on the margin. The discussion gave little attention to the effects of disintermediation on the financial system; the System was unprepared for the strong response to ceiling rates in 1966–67 or the financial crisis in 1970. Ultimately, the costs of controls on the allocation of financial assets and the welfare of depositors had to be paid.

The staff described the difference between the economic and supervisory aspects. "From a purely economic standpoint an interest rate ceiling made no sense; but from the viewpoint of maintaining soundness in the asset structure of banks, such regulation had been considered . . . necessary" (Board Minutes, October 6, 1959, 4). The staff cited research suggesting that time deposits responded sensitively to interest rates, but savings deposits did not. Riefler proposed asking Congress to allow the Board to set different rates for different types of banks and deposits and to require that banks hold short-term liquid assets as collateral for time deposits (ibid., 5).[268]

268. Chairman Martin criticized the staff's claim that saving deposits were insensitive to interest rates. "This was a dangerous view for a central banker to take. He noted that there was a time lag between any change in the interest rate and a corresponding change in the over-all supply of savings" (Board Minutes, October 6, 1959, 8). Martin added that it was difficult to estimate the length of the lag, but "sooner or later the rate had an effect" (ibid., 8). He did not favor an increase at the time.

The Board held a cursory discussion. It did not want to draw money from Treasury bills to time deposits or to assist New York banks by permitting a higher rate on foreign time deposits. A decision to pay foreign governments higher rates than domestic savers would arouse criticism that the Board could avoid (Board Minutes, January 16, 1959, 11–13).

New York banks and the New York Reserve bank did not accept defeat. They continued to petition for higher rates on foreign deposits. The Board's only concession was to permit a grace period. Deposits received by the tenth of the month could receive interest from the first (Board Minutes, June 1, 1959, 2–4). The Board's staff generally opposed higher rates. Several questioned whether it was desirable for banks to hold time and savings deposits (Board Minutes, June 30, 1959, 8–9). Most banks, at the time, paid less than the ceiling rate of 3 percent; the average rate was 2.4 percent (ibid., 10).[269]

Governor Balderston recognized the critical issue. If the current increase in market rates was temporary, he said, the Board did not have to increase maximum rates on savings and time deposits. If higher rates were permanent or long lasting, "it would be an anachronism for the System to have retained the present ceiling on savings deposits" (Board Minutes, October 6, 1959, 9). Chairman Martin agreed.

The Board returned to the discussion many times, but it did not make any changes. In December, it discussed its response to a letter from Congressman Patman about payments in kind for demand deposits. The Board's response recalled that the Federal Reserve Act prohibited interest on demand deposits "directly or indirectly, by any device whatsoever." As with any price control, enforcement raised many issues. The rest of the letter discussed the many decisions the Board had to make to specify what was permitted (Board Minutes, December 18, 1959, letter, Martin to Patman).[270]

In February 1960, New York again proposed different treatment for time and savings deposits. The Board decided to follow Balderston's earlier

269. The international staff reported that the funds the banks lost as time deposits went to Treasury bills, so the balance of payments was not affected much (Board Minutes, June 30, 1959, 11). In September, the Federal Advisory Council surprised the Board by favoring higher rates on time deposits held for foreign banks (Board Minutes, September 15, 1959, 14). One of the main arguments by bankers against an increase in the rate paid to domestic savers was that the rise in interest rates had reduced the banks' capital accounts. An increase in rates paid to savers would reduce their earnings and possibly their capital because deposits would not increase enough to cover the higher cost (ibid., 19–20).

270. As examples, the Board permitted omission of a charge for armored car service and free parking facilities, but it prohibited absorption of exchange charges when collecting non-par checks (Board Minutes, December 18, 1959, letter, Martin to Patman).

suggestion. It would change the ceiling rate for savings deposits only after a "fundamental change in the levels of long-term interest rates" (Board Minutes, February 9, 1960, 2). Rates on savings deposits would adjust, after a lag, to changes in long-term government or mortgage rates. Savings accounts belonged mainly to individuals. Many time deposit accounts belonged to corporations, foreign governments, and institutions. New York proposed that these rates should be flexible. The Board could set a ceiling above current market rates for time deposits and permit rates to adjust to market conditions.[271]

Governor Balderston asked why foreign depositors should be paid more than domestic savers. Why not let foreigners buy Treasury bills if they wanted open market rates? Robert Roosa of the New York Reserve bank replied that about two-thirds of the $700 million dollars withdrawn from time deposits at New York banks had gone into government securities. He thought it desirable that the New York banks be allowed to compete, since New York was now the world's banking market.

The following week, the Board again discussed maximum deposit interest rates with the Federal Advisory Council. The Council now agreed unanimously that the 3 percent ceiling rate should remain. New York wanted higher rates for foreign deposits, and the rest of the Council supported the increase.[272] California banks faced intense competition from thrift institutions that offered rates that were unregulated at the time. Its representative voted to maintain the 3 percent ceiling because he believed that non-bank institutions would match any increase by commercial banks to maintain their advantage.

Some large banks pressed the Board to raise ceiling rates. The Board considered a formula that adjusted the ceiling rate to a smoothed average of market rates, but it made no decision. The principal reasons were reluctance to adopt a rule and the divisions within the banking system. The average rate had increased slightly but remained less than 2.5 percent (Board Minutes, May 17, 1960, 1–18).[273]

---

271. Martin asked Hayes whether he would favor an end to regulation of time deposit rates. Hayes replied that he found the "basic idea of regulating interest rates . . . repugnant" (Board Minutes, February 9, 1960, 3). He added that his opinion differed from some of the New York staff. One of the latter responded that there was "a need to protect some of them [banks] against such excesses" of competition (ibid., 3–4).

272. New York banks with branches overseas could pay a higher rate abroad, and most did. Robertson was skeptical that the Board could authorize higher rates for foreign deposits, but the Board's counsel ruled later that the Board could set different rates based on location if there were differences in conditions (Board Minutes, February 25, 1960, 12). A higher rate in New York would attract domestic deposits also to the disadvantage of other banks.

273. Some of the Federal Advisory Council favored removing the prohibition on payment

Aggregate time and saving deposits continued to increase. Most banks did not experience the intense competition for deposits found in California and a few western states. Time and savings deposits at member banks rose at a 7.6 percent average rate from 1955 to 1960. Growth declined to 3.4 percent in 1959, as market rates rose, but increased again in 1960, when market rates fell. By the late 1950s, time and saving deposits approached 50 percent of demand deposits, in dollar value more than $50 billion. A 0.5 percentage point increase in ceiling rates, if generally effective, would have cost member banks more than $250 million in the aggregate, about 17 percent of net income for the year.[274]

In early June 1960, market interest rates fell precipitately, ending any remaining pressure for higher ceiling rates. The Board considered whether it should raise the ceiling to anticipate future increases. Board members discussed many suggestions but did nothing.[275] Governor Robertson reopened the discussion in August by proposing a 6 percent ceiling (or its home state's usury ceiling). He argued that the increase would remove the problem the next time that rates rose. Banks could no longer blame the System for failure to raise rates. His only concern was whether "this would be a wise move in a political year" (Board Minutes, August 19, 1960, 15). Governor King objected that raising the ceiling rate well above market rates was unwise. "Big banks would get bigger and small banks would be eliminated" (ibid., 17). The Board took no action. King offered no evidence, but the discussion ended, and the Board missed the opportunity to establish a policy of allowing banks to respond to market forces.

GOLD AND INTERNATIONAL PAYMENTS

At the time of the Treasury–Federal Reserve Accord, the United States held $22 billion of gold in total, more than 60 percent of the non-Soviet stock. If anyone thought about the possible conflict that could arise from the decisions to ratify the Bretton Woods Agreement and approve the Employment Act, I have not found that their views reached the Truman or

---

of interest on demand deposits, but none favored raising the ceiling on time deposit rates (Board Minutes, May 17, 1960, 17).

274. Banks began to circumvent ceiling rates by compounding interest quarterly but paying interest monthly. Banks in the south absorbed exchange charges for non-par banks as a means of increasing the interest rate (Board Minutes, August 4, 1960, 17–20). Earlier, the Board had ruled against this practice. Costly rules encourage circumvention.

275. In June 1960, the Board agreed to permit the Bank for International Settlements in Switzerland (BIS) to set its interest rates without reference to regulation Q. The Bank remained "in conformity with the monetary policy of the central banks of the countries concerned." The BIS regarded the New York Reserve bank as representative of the U.S. central bank, and New York had asked it in 1951 to follow regulation Q.

Eisenhower administrations, Congress, or the Federal Reserve.[276] The concerns of 1944–45 were opposite. The United States held a disproportionate share of the world's gold. A widely held belief claimed that the international system collapsed in the 1930s because of the maldistribution of gold and would work best if the U.S. lost gold to other countries. A major concern at the time was that the U.S. would return to the deflationary monetary and protectionist trade policies of the 1920s.[277]

This concern soon vanished, replaced by early postwar concerns that growth of dollar balances would be positive but insufficient to finance growth of trade and payments. Higher U.S. productivity and more attractive goods were among the reasons given for expecting a "dollar shortage." Marshall Plan assistance, Korean War expenditures abroad, and currency devaluation by Britain and France ended these issues. Symptomatic of the attitudes during this period was the official reference to the U.S. payments deficit as "net transfers of gold and dollars to the rest of the world" (Solomon, 1977, 19). The U.S. permitted countries to discriminate against U.S. exports and encouraged domestic businesses to invest abroad.

A political agenda guided these policy choices. The United States wanted to restore growth and economic stability in Western Europe and Japan. The cold war strengthened support for these objectives. Also important was the belief, supported by early postwar experience, that European countries would have difficulty competing against the United States for many years.

In the four years ending August 1949, the U.S. gold stock rose more than $4 billion, 20 percent of the August 1945 value, to reach its all-time peak. Table 2.7 shows the local peaks and troughs through the 1950s.

The U.S. gold stock declined slowly at first, but each peak and trough is below the preceding peak or trough. The table shows the major decline during the 1957–58 recession, when interest rates fell. The heavy gold outflow continued after interest rates rose. The proximate reason is that the balance on goods and services declined at the end of the 1950s, whilst U.S. overseas investment increased. The 1958 Report of the President's Council of Economic Advisers expressed little concern about the U.S. international

276. Robert Triffin was the principal exception. Although not directly concerned with the conflict in the text, Triffin was aware of some problems of sustaining the international system. I consider his arguments below.

277. Evidence of this concern is the time and energy that negotiators of the Bretton Woods Agreement spent on the "scarce currency clause" that applied penalties to the U.S. if it followed deflationary policies. The problem did not end there. As late as 1952, Sproul's discussions with German officials showed continued concern about the "dollar shortage" and the importance of the United States moving toward freer trade (European trip, Folder 2, Sproul papers, October 9, 1952, 17).

Table 2.7   Peaks and Troughs in the U.S. Gold Stock, 1949–61 (in $ billions)

PEAKS		TROUGHS		CHANGE
Date	Value	Date	Value	
August 1949	24.77	July 1951	21.85	−2.92
July 1952	23.54	April 1955	21.72	−1.82
January 1958	22.86	February 1961	17.41	−5.45
June 1961	17.60			

Source: Board of Governors (1976).

payments position at the end of 1957. It mentions the French devaluation, Germany's strong external position and its prepayment of long-term
debt. Two years later, the report showed heightened concern but not alarm.
"[C]ost and price disparities may now have developed to the advantage of
these other countries" (Council of Economic Advisers, 1960, 31). Then,
introducing a subject that would be revisited for many years, "[S]erious
contractions [of exports] have been concentrated in a few items. Among
these, automobiles and steel stand out, as they do in the rise in imports"
(ibid., 31). Federal Reserve analysts also viewed the payments imbalance
and gold outflow as arising mainly from loss of competitive position in
selected industries. This is a partial view. The U.S. permitted foreigners to
discriminate against the U.S. in trade, and it provided $33 billion in gifts
and loans from 1946 through 1953, an amount equal to one-fourth of all
U.S. exports (Solomon, 1977, 19–20).[278]

The decline in the U.S. gold stock, the increase in dollar balances of
foreign central banks and governments, and some exchange rate adjustments permitted Western European countries to restore current account
convertibility for non-residents at the end of 1958.[279] By that time, productivity abroad had improved, and a Common Market attracted investment;
Europe and Japan began to close the gap in per capita income with the
United States, a trend that ended in the 1990s.[280]

278. Discrimination took different forms including quotas on imports from the U.S.
Intended to be temporary, they ended for developed countries in 1961. Total foreign aid from
1946 to 1952 came to $41.66 billion, $31 billion economic aid and $10.5 billion military aid.
$13 billion was postwar relief (1946–48), the rest was Marshall Plan assistance (1949–52).
Total exports averaged $16 billion at the time. An interesting sidelight is Sproul's discussion
in 1952 of combining current account convertibility and floating exchange rates. After discussions with European leaders, he called this "a practical near term possibility" (European trip,
Folder 2, Sproul papers, October 9, 1952, 3).

279. Only Germany removed controls on capital transactions in 1959. In 1964, the Japanese yen became convertible for current account transactions. Earlier in the 1950s, Western
European countries cleared bilateral balances through the European Payments Union.

280. German and Japanese export growth reached 40 percent and 35 percent per year

Federal Reserve Actions, 1951–60

The policy of the U.S. government and the International Monetary Fund (IMF) was to maintain the gold price at $35 an ounce and, if possible, keep gold in central banks and official institutions and away from private owners. In June 1947, the IMF urged member countries to prevent gold sales at premium prices. It saw these sales as a threat to exchange rate stability. South Africa did not follow the IMF's recommendations and sold gold at premium prices. By 1951, the IMF did not think itself able to prevent such sales, so it left the decision to member countries. Prodded by the IMF, U.S. policy from 1947 on discouraged participation by individuals, banks, and businesses in gold transactions (Board Minutes, November 15, 1956, 6).

The International Monetary Fund was "considered to be largely immobile" in dealing with European payments and postwar adjustment (European trip, folder 2, Sproul papers, October 9, 1952, 4). Slowly prewar institutions returned. In 1954, the London gold market reopened. South Africa agreed to sell all newly mined gold in that market (Board Minutes, April 23, 1954, 12). In 1954, the Treasury allowed U.S. banks and others to sell in the London market (ibid., December 8, 1954, 17), and the Board was willing to let gold mining companies sell gold at the world market price. Also, the Randall Commission proposed that the Federal Reserve resume its 1920s practice of lending dollars to foreign governments or central banks that desired to restore currency convertibility.[281] At the time, Chairman Martin took "a dim view of the proposal" (Board Minutes, May 18, 1954, 3). The Board believed that loans to restore convertibility should be the responsibility of the IMF or the Treasury. It agreed to make short-term loans to meet seasonal or temporary demands of foreign central banks (Board Minutes, December 6, 1955, 7, Policy on Gold Loans). The term would not generally exceed three months, but the Board could renew the loan. The Federal Reserve used its prevailing discount rate as the interest rate.

The Bank for International Settlements (BIS) received its charter in February 1930. Its main role was to serve as a place for exchange of views

for 1950–52, then 18.6 percent and 10.8 percent in 1952–56. French and British exports rose more slowly.

281. The New York bank made loans to central banks in the 1920s to help countries return to the gold standard. Governments borrowed in the market. At the time the loans were a contentious issue. In 1933, New York lost its exclusive role as agent for the System in international transactions. In the 1950s, the New York bank continued to lend gold and offer participations to the other reserve banks. The loans could not be made without the Board's approval (Board Minutes, September 15, 1955, 8). To prevent New York from proceeding with discussion to a point that would make it difficult for the Board to differ from New York's position, New York agreed to inform the Board about negotiations as they proceeded.

over reparations between the Federal Reserve and European central banks. Congress did not permit the New York Reserve bank to become a member, and the State Department ruled that New York officers could not serve on the board of directors. But New York participated as an observer and remained actively involved.[282] From time to time, the Federal Reserve considered asking Congress to authorize membership, but it never did. Finally, in April 1955, the New York Reserve bank asked whether it could join the BIS. The Board referred the issue to the Treasury department. After almost four months, the Treasury replied that the Federal Reserve should maintain "informal contact" but should not become a member. The Board accepted the Treasury's view (Board Minutes, August 11, 1955, 3).[283]

The New York Reserve bank, with Board approval, also made gold loans to countries to meet temporary payments deficits. At times, the Federal Reserve cooperated with the IMF in its stabilization efforts. An example is a $17 million loan to Argentina to help correct a "structural imbalance in Argentina's foreign trade position" (Board Minutes, December 22, 1958, 4).[284] The Board renewed the loan subsequently.

Except for these occasional decisions, the System paid little attention to the international system until 1958. In that year, it began to include balance of payments, the U.S.'s competitive position, and gold losses as part of the FOMC briefing. International concerns were never a reason in these years for taking, or avoiding, policy action. After the London gold market reopened, the staff studied world demand for gold hoards and industrial and artistic uses relative to gold production (Tamagna and Garber, 1954).[285]

282. The United States' shares were sold to three U.S. banks. This is the origin of the privately held shares that remained outstanding until the end of the century, when the Bank withdrew them (memo, Szymczak to Board of Governors, BIS-FRB participation, Sproul papers, March 15, 1950). Although the Federal Reserve did not join, Gates McGarrah, chairman of the New York Reserve bank, became the BIS's first president.

283. One of the ways in which the New York bank worked with the BIS was making short-term gold loans. The loans were for a maximum of seven days, could not exceed $25 million, and required approval of the New York directors and the Board. New York shared the income with other reserve banks that participated in the loan (Board Minutes, April 28, 1955, 7–11).

284. Governor Mills described the loan as "the kind of transaction undertaken with very little success after World War I by the Bank of England" (Board Minutes, December 22, 1958, 4). This was not the only time the Federal Reserve ignored its rules for gold loans. Often the Board renewed short-term loans. It voted a loan to Brazil in 1959, collateralized by gold, under pressure from the State Department to help an IMF program succeed. The Federal Reserve also bought gold from the IMF, increasing the monetary base. The IMF sold the gold to replenish its dollar balances, after receiving approval for the sale from the Federal Reserve.

285. Before London reopened its market, gold markets functioned in Hong Kong, Tangiers, and elsewhere. None had the volume of trading that London soon developed, and prices often diverged from the official price. The London market had an advantage as a gold mar-

Criticisms of Bretton Woods

The Federal Reserve showed no evidence of concern, but outsiders soon questioned the long-run viability of the Bretton Woods system. Friedman (1953, 157) argued that the fixed exchange rate system "is ill suited to current economic and political conditions. . . . There is scarcely a facet of international economic policy for which the implicit acceptance of a system of rigid exchange rates does not create serious and unnecessary difficulties."[286] He proposed that floating exchange rates replace fixed rates. At the time, and for many years after, bankers, policy officials, and governments gave his proposal little consideration.[287]

Near the end of the 1950s, Edward Bernstein and Robert Triffin separately considered the long-run prospects of the Bretton Woods system, the first of many studies that tried to reconcile a fixed exchange rate system with the domestic employment policies of the United States, the growth of world trade, and increasing capital mobility.[288] Bernstein (1960) blamed the problem on continued trade discrimination against the United States, particularly by the countries of the European Community (later the European Union), and "large US Government expenditures in Europe and for Europe, despite the complete recovery of Europe's capacity to produce and export" (ibid., 5). Bernstein saw the main problem arising from U.S. gold losses as the threat to its ability to follow counter-cyclical monetary and fiscal policies.

Bernstein proposed that the U.S. concentrate on restoring balance to its

ket over New York. In the 1930s, the U.S. Treasury imposed a 0.25 percentage point fee on purchases and sales in the United States. This widened spreads between bid and ask prices relative to London. By the late 1950s, London market volume reached $1 billion a year, but purchases or sales of more than $25 or $50 million in a day were difficult to complete (Coombs, 1976, 47–48).

286. Friedman first wrote his essay in 1950. The policy conflicts he noted included re-armament, trade liberalization, avoidance of direct controls, and harmonization of domestic policies.

287. Canada was an exception. The Canadian dollar had a floating exchange rate from 1950 to 1962.

288. Bernstein had been assistant to Secretary Morgenthau during the Bretton Woods negotiations. He had a major role in developing the U.S. proposal, participated in the Bretton Woods meetings, and was the first research director of the IMF. Triffin, a Belgian, was a Yale professor who had a main role in developing the inter-country settlement system in Europe, known as the European Payments Union, prior to convertibility. Bernstein prepared his paper for the Joint Economic Committee of Congress. Triffin testified before the committee at about the same time. Senator Douglas sent Triffin's testimony to the Federal Reserve and the Treasury and asked for their comments. Douglas described the testimony as "of such outstanding merit and originality as to deserve the most extensive study on the part of responsible officials." The Board's staff described Triffin's proposals as complex. Neither the Board nor the Treasury gave a detailed reply (Board Minutes, November 3, 1959, 2–4).

payments, while helping the development of low-income countries. The "most effective way . . . is to reduce sharply the transfers and expenditures . . . in Europe and on behalf of Europe" (ibid., 6). These adjustments would leave the U.S. in its dominant position in the international economy. At the time, despite its gold losses, the U.S. still held half the world's monetary gold stock. Bernstein believed that with two reserve currencies, the dollar and the pound, portfolio adjustments would go from one to the other instead of from the reserve currency into gold. In several respects Bernstein's views were close to the mainstream views of the time. He did not mention floating exchange rates and did not clearly see the incompatibility of the United States' commitment to full employment, price stability, a fixed exchange rate, currency convertibility, and free capital flows.[289] By 1960, U.S. policymakers became aware that policies to achieve the goals of the Employment Act did not necessarily achieve the Bretton Woods goals.

Solomon (1982, 27–32) reviewed accomplishments and problems as they appeared at the beginning of the 1960s. The main accomplishments were the restoration of a fixed exchange rate system. Countries held their exchange rates within a 1 percent band (or smaller) on each side of its dollar parity. The dollar had become the principal reserve currency; foreigners held $10 billion in dollar reserves and an equal amount in British pounds. Industrial countries had avoided parity changes, with France and Canada the main exceptions after 1949. The IMF had started to take on the role of international lender to countries with a temporary payments imbalance.

The principal problems that Solomon recognized were (1) the lack of an adjustment process to reconcile payments surpluses and deficits, (2) no means of adjusting to large capital flows, and (3) the "Triffin problem." The latter concerned the relation of dollar balances to gold. Since the gold stock grew much less than the volume of international trade, U.S. dollars supplied the additional reserves. As the dollar component of inter-

---

289. Senator Paul Douglas urged the Federal Reserve to favor floating exchange rates. He said he met with "very dubious success" (Joint Economic Committee , 1959, Hearings Part 5, 983). This is an overstatement; the proposal met no response. At the same hearing, Charles Kindleberger pointed out the error in Bernstein's claim that military assistance to Europe caused the gold loss or the payments deficit. Most of the foreign aid to Europe took the form of U.S. exports (ibid., 951). Kindleberger also noted, in passing, that the U.S. had a budget deficit in 1958, and Germany had a large surplus (ibid., 976). Germany could finance the excess of U.S. investment over saving. The hearings also brought out that the creation of the European Common Market lowered tariffs against U.S. exports in France and Italy but raised tariffs in Germany and the Benelux countries. Of course, the Common Market eliminated internal tariffs over time, putting U.S. exports at a relative disadvantage in all six countries (ibid., 997). This encouraged investment by U.S. companies in Europe, increasing the capital outflow.

national reserves increased, the system lost the ability to convert dollars into gold at a fixed gold price.

The Triffin critique. Beginning in 1947, when the System had just started, Robert Triffin warned that the Bretton Woods Agreement had a fundamental flaw: An expanding world economy required increased means of payment or settlement. The supply of new gold was inelastic, so the additions would have to be dollar balances. These balances would, therefore, rise on an inelastic gold base. The general acceptability of dollars, Triffin argued, depended on convertibility into gold. As the stock of dollars rose absolutely and relative to gold, convertibility would go from doubtful to impossible. If the U.S. did not let the stock of dollars increase, trade would grow slowly or not at all. If the U.S. increased the price of gold, it would have to renege on its commitment to convert dollars into gold at the $35 price. Countries would be unwilling to hold dollars, so the system would break down (Triffin, 1947).

Triffin repeated and expanded his argument several times, notably in Triffin (1960, 57). "It seems most unlikely, therefore, that the growth of dollar or sterling balances can provide a lasting solution to the inadequacy of gold production to satisfy prospective requirements for international liquidity in an expanding world economy."

Reasoning from the 1931–33 experience, Triffin suggested that one possibility was a run first from the pound to the dollar, then from the dollar to gold. The system would collapse. Triffin believed the more likely alternative was a slowdown of the growth of dollar reserves, reopening the threat of deflation, devaluation, or payment restrictions (ibid., 70).

Triffin's proposed solution called for expanding the IMF into a world monetary authority capable of supplying a new international medium of exchange. The new IMF would make loans and create reserves under some restrictions on the growth of international money. He opposed both the revaluation of gold and floating exchange rates. His four reasons for not changing the gold price were: (1) the initial change would have to be large, double or triple the $35 price, (2) the initial change would have to be repeated as the world economy grew, (3) increases would produce excess liquidity for a time, and (4) the gains would be distributed unequally, benefiting the Soviet Union, South Africa, and countries with large gold stocks (ibid., 81). Triffin's criticisms of floating exchange rates repeated common arguments: increased speculation would "accelerate and amplify . . . disequilibriating movements without . . . correcting the internal financial policies which lie at the root of the balance of payments deficits" (ibid., 83).[290]

290. Triffin (1960, 85) recognized, however, the "hard core of validity in the theory of

Triffin's argument had great influence on subsequent policies. The influence continued even when it became obvious to all that (1) there was no shortage of reserves, (2) inflation, not deflation, had become a major problem, and (3) countries with sustained payments surpluses remained reluctant to revalue exchange rates out of concern for the effect on their exports. Despite the inflation in the U.S. and abroad by the end of the 1960s, policymakers spent much time, attention, and effort to reach agreement on a new reserve asset to supplement gold and little time on providing an adjustment mechanism.

Three main problems with Triffin's analysis became important. First, he did not appreciate the major political change that had occurred or that the change could not be reconciled with a fixed exchange rate system. Governments and the public disliked inflation, but they disliked recession and unemployment at least as much. Whether it was the memory of the depression or some other reason, governments attempted to achieve high (full) employment. Most accepted inflation, if it remained moderate. Nowhere was this truer than in Britain and the United States, the reserve currency countries.

Second, contrary to Triffin's analysis, once the U.S. removed the option of converting dollars into gold, countries accumulated massive dollar balances. They preferred accumulating dollars to allowing greater appreciation of their exchange rates. A principal concern was to avoid loss of exports and any temporary increase in unemployment. Inflation abroad adjusted real exchange rates.

Third, Triffin erred in arguing against revaluation of gold (depreciation of the dollar against gold). At most, the increased risk of depreciation would induce a one-time reduction in private dollar balances.[291] Tying the price of gold to the growth of trade or to a price index, as suggested by Keynes (1930) and Fisher (1920), would have provided for orderly increases in the value of the gold stock. The expected trend rate of inflation would be reflected in the dollar price of gold and the interest rate on dollar balances.

Triffin's analysis and persuasive arguments misdirected attention. There was never much chance of getting nations to agree on a world central bank, but that was neither a necessary nor a sufficient condition for an efficient

---

flexible exchange rates." It was better to adjust exchange rates than to attempt to hold "unrealistic" rates. The worst solution, he said, was a permanent system of trade and exchange restrictions (ibid., 86).

291. At the time, there was no way to predict what central banks and governments would do. We now know that collectively they held dollars and added to their holdings to limit appreciation of their currency.

solution. Triffin's more persuasive point was the need for institutional changes that would provide more international money. He claimed that adjusting the world price level by increasing international money would solve the problem, but adjusting the world price level by changing the gold price would fail. Others adopted this line of reasoning, most importantly in the United States policymaking group.[292]

The crucial difference between the two policies is not what they would do to the global price level, but what they do to the relative price or exchange rate for the dollar. Raising the price of gold would have permitted the United States to adjust its exchange rate. In addition to providing liquidity, revaluation of gold could have provided much needed adjustment of relative prices or exchange rates.[293] The reasoning at the time neglected relative price, or exchange rate, adjustment. Once again, as in the 1920s, policymakers failed to see the issue as a choice between adjustment of the U.S. price level or its exchange rate.

Triffin recognized correctly that confidence in the fixed but adjustable system had to be maintained. If countries or market participants believed that the Bretton Woods arrangements required long-run deflation, he thought they would not remain in the system.[294] This did not prove to be a problem. Inflation, not deflation followed. Countries did not leave the system. After the system ended, countries continued to acquire dollar balances.

Evolution of the IMF. The Federal Reserve System divided sharply over the Bretton Woods Agreement before it was adopted. The Board supported the administration. New York did not. Allan Sproul, influenced by his adviser, Professor John H. Williams, his directors, and prominent New York bankers, favored a key currency system.[295]

New York lost the battle but won the war. The international system de-

292. The French government argued for revaluation of gold without success. These issues return in chapter 5.

293. Between 1946, when the IMF started operation, and 1960, when Triffin wrote, the real value of gold (fixed at a nominal $35 value) declined 25 percent measured by the U.S. consumer price index (base 100, 1967). Using the GNP deflator, the decline was about 30 percent.

294. Canada floated its exchange rate, but not for this reason. Britain considered floating its currency to avoid adjustment problems and blocked sterling balances (James, 1996, 99). Instead, it received substantial IMF and U.S. bilateral assistance after the Suez crisis in 1956. Corden (1993) and others argue that if the U.S. had devalued, others would have followed, preventing (full) adjustment. I am skeptical of this argument because the facts are opposite. After 1971, the dollar floated down periodically. Major countries did not devalue. They purchased dollars to slow dollar devaluation.

295. See volume 1, chapter 7. Chairman Eccles wanted to fire John H. Williams and force the New York bank to support the System's position in favor of the proposed arrangement.

veloped with many features proposed by Williams. The dollar became the standard, and the United States became the only country that could follow an independent monetary policy (McKinnon 1993, 602–4).[296]

At first, the IMF did very little. That changed. By the end of the 1950s, the IMF had two related achievements. By making a loan that was large at the time, it helped the British through the crisis that followed their aborted effort (with France and Israel) to retake the Suez Canal. Partly as a result, the number and size of IMF assistance programs increased. In 1959, the members agreed to a quota increase that almost doubled the IMF's initial resources. In real terms, deflating by the U.S. consumer price index, the IMF's combined quotas in 1961, when the increase became effective, were 50 percent greater than in 1947 when it began operations. Its membership had increased by 50 percent also. Prodded by the United States, the IMF had started to impose conditions on its loans that eventually became known as "the Washington consensus."

The Diminished Role of Silver

Government silver purchases and pricing had been a major political issue in U.S. history for decades. By the 1950s, the issue had become less important. In 1955, Congress proposed to repeal legislation that fixed the price of silver above the market price, thereby requiring the Treasury to purchase all newly mined silver. Chairman Martin testified that the monetary effect was small and could be offset by open market sales (statement by Chairman Martin before the Subcommittee on the Federal Reserve System, Board Records, July 13, 1955). The Board favored legislation confining silver certificates to $1 and $2 bills, replacing $5 and $10 silver certificates with Federal Reserve notes (Board Minutes, November 5, 1959, 5–6). In the 1970s, inflation raised the market price of silver above the Treasury's purchase price. Silver no longer had a monetary role.

LEGISLATION

In the 1950s, as in other periods, members of Congress introduced legislation to change the structure of the Federal Reserve. Perennial issues included centralization of authority in the Board, a reduced role for the reserve banks, and an outside audit. None of this legislation passed and, usually, it did not get out of committee. Nevertheless, it was a constant

---

296. McKinnon (1993, 602) claims that the critical change resulted from the Marshall Plan and the EPU. The latter solved the payments problem for inconvertible European countries by using dollars for settlement through a multilateral clearing arrangement. The EPU ended in December 1958, when currencies became convertible on current account.

concern for the System and made it wary of Congress, so it increased congressional influence.

The principal legislative change concerned bank holding companies. The Banking Act of 1933 provided for the regulation of bank holding companies, but it did not give the Board the power to approve or limit their expansion. It could limit branching, but a bank could avoid the restrictions by organizing a holding company that owned shares in each of its "independent" branches. The law did not restrict the number of banks a holding company could own or the number of states in which it could own them.

The Board considered the 1933 definition of a holding company inadequate, principally because it did not apply to companies controlling only non-member banks. The Board also wanted legislation to cover the twenty-eight holding companies in business at the time the legislation passed and to give the Board power to approve or reject bank holding companies' decisions to acquire non-bank enterprises.[297]

The 1956 Act

Congress considered legislation for many years before reaching agreement. On May 9, 1956, it approved the Bank Holding Company Act of 1956, placing all bank holding companies (with more than one bank) under the Board's regulatory authority and requiring all bank holding companies to divest interests in non-banking organizations (with certain enumerated exceptions.) A bank holding company could not acquire bank stock without prior approval of the Board. In July, the Board adopted regulation Y, containing the details of its holding company regulations.[298]

Holding company legislation divided the Board. Governors Shephardson, Szymczak, and King interpreted the Board's role as justifying mergers or acquisitions deemed to be in the public interest. Governors Mills

297. A 1950 survey showed that the twenty-eight groups included 367 banks with 1,019 branches. These banks held 12 percent of all commercial bank deposits (Martin papers, letter to Brent Spence, Board Files, April 11, 1952).

298. In the first major case under the new act, the Board heard oral arguments of Transamerica Corporation, an old adversary. The hearing examiner had decided that Transamerica's ownership of Occidental Life Insurance Co. violated the new statute, so Transamerica had to divest its holdings. The Board upheld the hearing examiner. Governor Vardaman voted with the majority but noted that the act treated different types of holding companies inconsistently. In 1948, the Board had issued a complaint against Transamerica Corporation under the Clayton Act to force it to divest ownership in forty-seven banks in five states. Marriner Eccles believed that this action was responsible for his dismissal as Board chairman. The federal appeals court in 1953 agreed that the Board had jurisdiction but rejected the Board's finding of monopoly. The court suggested legislation (Annual Report, 1953, 47–48).

and Balderston wanted only to stop changes they considered undesirable (Board Minutes, February 11, 1960, 15–17). The legal staff sided with Mills and Balderston. On the issue of competition, the legal staff believed that anti-trust legislation did not apply to banking mergers and acquisitions because the effect on competition was not the dominant consideration. Other factors, peculiar to the banking industry, such as capital adequacy, earning prospects, and management, had to be considered.

Congressional consideration of a bank merger bill brought these issues to the fore. After much discussion, the Board voted to treat holding company and merger applications and decisions under separate procedures.[299] The Board opposed legislation bringing bank mergers under the Clayton Act, since that would have made competition the principal basis for permitting or rejecting bank mergers. This issue arose in Congress several times, but it did not pass. The Board retained responsibility for mergers and did not have to get the approval of the Attorney General, a step that some in Congress often proposed.

The new legislation greatly expanded the Board's regulatory reach. With that additional power, it could influence bank policy much more than in earlier years. And it gained a powerful group of potential supporters.

Other Legislation

The Federal Reserve had to defend itself in the 1930s against proposals to restructure the System. These efforts continued in the 1950s and beyond, in part because one of the leading proponents, Congressman Wright Patman (Texas), continued to serve in Congress, and in part because member banks' nominal ownership of the reserve bank shares and service by private citizens as directors attracted populist attention. It is not clear whether Congressman Patman made these proposals with the intention of passing them or saw them as a way of monitoring the Federal Reserve and requiring it to explain its procedures and actions in public. In the 1960s, Patman became chairman of the House Committee on Banking and Currency.

By the mid 1950s, Congressman Patman offered proposals in every session. Some took the form of non-binding resolutions. One such provided that the "Board and the FOMC should support the price of United States Government securities at par, but not exceeding par" (memo, Cherry to Martin, Board Records, January 11, 1955). Another called for an audit of the

---

299. A critical issue was whether the Board should disclose publicly that a holding company had filed an application to acquire a bank. The Board voted five to two to make the disclosure. Governors Mills and King objected that disclosure would permit competitors to oppose an acquisition. They noted that the Board did not publish notices of applications for bank mergers (Board Minutes, March 2, 1960).

Board and the FOMC.[300] The audit proposal alarmed the Board. It saw the audit as a threat to its independence that would expand from an accounting report to an audit of policy actions and decisions.[301] Without waiting for a vote on the resolution, the chairman of the House Committee on Government Operations sent a letter to the GAO requesting them to audit the Board and the reserve banks for the years 1953 and 1954. In response, the Board recognized that it was the "creature of Congress" and subject to any procedures that the Congress adopted. But, the Board said, the proposed audit was "an important departure from long-established practice . . . with far-reaching implications" (Board Minutes, April 20, 1955, 5, letter, Martin to Chairman Dawson, Committee on Government Operations).[302]

Patman's legislative proposals included abolition of the FOMC, transfer of its functions to the Board, and expansion of the Board to twelve members, each with a six-year term. He proposed also that FOMC operations move to Washington from New York. The FOMC considered the last suggestion but did not act on it (Board Records, October 4, 1955).

The use of credit guarantees, subsidies, and other forms of preference appealed to many in Congress as a means of assisting favored groups such as home owners without showing the cost in the government's budget. An example from 1958 called on the System to give financial assistance to small business. The Board offered to give advice and technical assistance

300. The House voted on the audit resolution in 1955. It lost 214 to 178, a result that was close enough to concern the Board (telegram [Walter] Young to [George B.] Vest, Board Records, June 15, 1955). Defending the resolution, Congressman Patman charged that the FOMC "operated in New York City by employees of the Federal Reserve bank who are paid by the reserve banks, [and] that the Board . . . has no control, whatsoever, over the operations" (memo, Cherry to Martin, Board Records, January 13, 1955). This increased the pressure on Martin to change the way the manager was appointed.

301. The 1955 resolution called for an audit of all accounts back to 1913, apparently unaware of the audits done in the early years. The Board had responded to earlier proposals for an audit by appointing a public accounting firm to audit its accounts. Members of the Board did not all agree on the danger. Governor Vardaman objected to an audit by the General Accounting Office (GAO) because it would weaken congressional influence. "[T]here would be a tendency on the part of the Board to pay more attention to the General Accounting Office and less to the Congress" (Board Minutes, February 15, 1955, 23–24). Vardaman mentioned his objection to Congressman Patman and suggested that a subcommittee of Congress do the audit. The rest of the Board wanted to avoid congressional interference as a serious threat to independence. Vardaman's proposal did not attract any support at the Board, but it suggests the degree of his disaffection.

302. The Board's opposition to an audit received support from the Hoover Commission set up to study the operation of the federal government. That commission recommended no changes in the Federal Reserve System. Its report concluded that "[d]uring the 42 years since its foundation in 1913 it has functioned efficiently without a taint of mismanagement or corruption." The Board included that sentence in a subsequent letter to Chairman Dawson (Board Minutes, April 20, 1955, 8).

to an agency that Congress chose for the task. The Board reminded Congress that lending to small business was not a central banking function. It was careful not to state a position on the need for assistance (Board Minutes, May 7, 1958, 5–8).[303]

Patman annoyed the Board by proposing to retire $15 billion of the $25 billion in debt held in the System's account in exchange for a non-interest-bearing Treasury note. The Board's response stated that the proposal "would result in no constructive changes but, on the contrary, might have grave adverse effects on public confidence in the currency" (Board Minutes, February 10, 1960, letter, Martin to Spence). The Board reminded the Banking Committee that the System paid to the Treasury, monthly, all income above operating expenses plus statutory dividends paid to member banks and allocations to maintain surplus accounts equal to subscribed capital. The risk, the Board said, was that issuance of non-interest-bearing securities to the reserve banks would suggest that the government would be able to finance its expenditures by issuing such paper.[304]

During most of the 1950s, the System paid about 90 percent of its excess earnings to the Treasury under a rule adopted in 1947. The payment served in lieu of a franchise tax for the right to issue currency. Prodded from one side by Congressman Patman and other members to recognize that the reserve banks were, in effect, government institutions and from the other side by the Budget Bureau seeking additional revenue, particularly if it could be obtained while placating senior members of Congress, the System reconsidered its accounting rules.[305]

---

303. Preparation for the Korean War brought out many proposals. The Defense Production Act contained provisions for regulation of consumer and real estate credit. The System participated in measures to restore stability following an attack. These measures included back-up records and provisions for replacing leadership.

304. The argument seems to be that interest-bearing debt sold in the market to finance future expenditures would be replaced by non-interest-bearing debt, after purchase by the Federal Reserve. This argument presumes that what matters is the interest payment not the stock of debt. The consolidated balance sheet of the Federal Reserve and the Treasury would not have been altered, since the System's debt holdings vanish in the consolidation. Patman's effort was probably a roundabout way of reducing the System's gross earnings and getting the Federal Reserve to request an annual appropriation from Congress, a proposal he made several times. The System's defense of independence contrasts with its actions in 2008 and 2009.

305. Chairman Martin reminded the presidents and governors that members of Congress had raised questions about ownership, accounting structure and contingency reserves, and that the Budget Bureau's staff had recommended for three years that the government should take all of the reserve banks' accumulated surplus ($800 million) (Board Minutes, September 23, 1959, 21–22). Martin then discussed the possibility of action by Congress and the "serious concern among friends of the System in Congress" (ibid., 22).

Underlying the discussion of accounting lay a much older issue—the character of the System as a mixed public and private institution. The Banking Act of 1935 settled a main part of the struggle for power between the Board and the reserve banks by giving the Board the dominant role in policy. But the banks retained many of the features of private institutions, and these features irritated populist members. The quarrel over accounting was an effort to take another step away from President Wilson's mixed private-public compromise.

In its early years, from 1918 to 1932, the reserve banks paid all net earnings into their surplus accounts until the fund reached 100 percent of a bank's subscribed capital. Thereafter, the banks paid a franchise tax equal to 90 percent of net earnings after dividends. A 1947 decision by the Board levied an interest charge for currency outstanding in excess of gold certificates that it paid to the Treasury. The 1952 Patman Committee questioned the size of the reserve banks' surplus, and Patman frequently questioned Chairman Martin about the reasons for holding more than $850 million as surplus reserves (in 1959). This was more than twice the banks' paid-in capital.[306]

The governors felt vulnerable because, in addition to the large surplus, the reserve banks had allocated more than $100 million as "reserves for contingencies" and more than $60 million additional as allowance for depreciation of buildings and capital assets (Board Minutes, July 15, 1959, 3). The principal rationale was that the banks followed accounting rules similar to the rules followed by private banks, but the Board did not choose to use that argument or to reopen the public-private status of the reserve banks.[307] Even the reserve bank presidents agreed that they could dispense with some of the contingency reserves and pay the past accumulation back to the Treasury.

The Board voted unanimously to pay the accumulated reserves to the Treasury and to discontinue the practice of holding contingency reserves. Over the objection of Governor Mills, it agreed to limit the reserve banks' accumulated surplus to twice the amount of paid-in capital, to pay the Treasury the excess accumulated over 200 percent of paid-in capital, and to pay the Treasury 100 percent of earnings (after expenses and dividends)

306. Between 1947 and 1959 the combined surplus had doubled in nominal value but increased only from 235 percent to 239 percent of paid-in capital. This suggests the dominant role of congressional pressure in forcing the change discussed in the text (Board Minutes, July 15, 1959, letter, Martin to presidents).

307. The Board asked its outside auditor, Price Waterhouse, for an opinion. The auditor expressed doubt about the need for contingency reserves or depreciation by a public entity. It did not express an opinion about the size of the accumulated surplus but was not concerned by the prospect of negative values (Board Minutes, December 17, 1959, 2–3, 9).

once the capital account reached the 200 percent ceiling.[308] These decisions increased the Board's 1959 payment to the Treasury by $261 million, approximately 40 percent more than its scheduled payment of $643 million (Board Minutes, December 23, 1959, 5). Expressed as an interest rate on $26 billion of debt held by the System, the rate paid as a refund rose from 2.5 to 3.5 percent. The Board did not decide to change its depreciation policy or to stop recording depreciation. Mills objected because

> acceptance of the proposal would in effect proclaim that the Federal Reserve banks are no longer the mixed type of private and public corporation that was contemplated by the Federal Reserve Act but, instead, are to be integral and direct appendages of the Federal Government. . . .
>
> [I]t is essential that the Federal Reserve banks represent a corporate financial structure . . . which cannot be done if additions to their accounts from earnings are limited in the manner proposed. (Board Minutes, December 18, 1959, 20)

The minutes contain other less detailed statements pointing to complaints by Congress and the Board's desire to avoid the criticism.[309]

Under the new rules, as under the old, each reserve bank's monthly payment to the Treasury was a charge for issuing Federal Reserve notes based on the daily average of its outstanding Federal Reserve notes not covered by gold certificates pledged as collateral. The interest rate differed between banks and over time because earnings and note issue differed.[310]

The System's concession on interest payments did not remove the issue. Congressman Patman continued to press for legislation to remove 60 percent of the System's interest-bearing debt. The issue became less pressing, however, as members of Congress recognized that the Federal Reserve now returned most of the interest it received.

Congressman Patman used the opportunity presented by the proposed Financial Institutions Act of 1957 to request data and responses to ques-

308. Governor Robertson joined Mills in opposing payment of accumulated surplus in excess of the limit.

309. For example, Vice Chairman Balderston argued that the reserve banks should not accumulate surpluses "that could not be satisfactorily explained to Congress or in other quarters" (Board Minutes, December 18, 1959, 15).

310. The formula for computing the interest rate had as its numerator the net earnings of the reserve bank after dividends and adjustments to keep its surplus at 200 percent of paid-in capital (100 percent of subscribed capital) and as its denominator the average daily amount of notes outstanding net of gold certificates (Board Minutes, February 1, 1960, letter, Sherman to presidents). To supply notes, each reserve bank submitted a request (by denomination) to the Bureau of Printing and Engraving. The notes were shipped to the reserve bank on demand. When small notes were destroyed, no effort was made to record the district that issued the notes, but large denominations were recorded by district when destroyed.

tions about System operations, particularly dealer market operations and fiscal agency operations that the New York bank performed for the Treasury. One result of his inquiries was that the System limited the use of repurchase agreements to New York. The dealer market was located there, and New York had always done the repurchase agreements.

Hayes and the New York officers objected to a provision of the act that the Board supported. It made the bank's fiscal agency operations for the government subject to the supervision and regulation of the Board of Governors. Hayes objected that the proposed regulation would "introduce a lot extra 'red tape' into a series of activities which are in an operating area, or at most an advisory area, rather than consisting of policymaking" (letter, Alfred Hayes to William McC. Martin, Board Records, February 18, 1957).

The Interest Ceiling

In 1918, Congress set a 4.25 percent interest rate ceiling under the Second Liberty Loan Act for Treasury bonds with five or more years to maturity. Intended as a way of holding down the cost of servicing WWI debt, the restriction remained after the war. It was rarely binding until the late 1950s. In 1959 and 1960, the Treasury asked Congress to remove the ceiling so that it could issue long-term bonds and extend the average maturity of the outstanding debt. The Federal Reserve supported the Treasury's request.

Congress did not act. Some members, notably Senator Douglas and Congressmen Patman and Reuss, blamed the Federal Reserve's bills-only policy for the increase in long-term interest rates.[311] To get the Federal Reserve to give up bills-only, they tied the two issues together in a sense-of-Congress resolution lifting the interest rate ceiling for two years and requiring the Federal Reserve to purchase securities of varying maturities, if it increased the money supply during those years. The Treasury, at first, accepted the resolution, but it withdrew its endorsement after hearing the Federal Reserve's remonstrances (Joint Economic Committee, 1959, Hearings 6A, 113–19). The Federal Reserve offered two principal reasons for opposing the part of the resolution treating monetary policy. First, Martin argued that any congressional resolution affecting monetary policy should be offered as an amendment to the Federal Reserve Act, not as an afterthought on a measure before the Ways and Means Commit-

---

311. John Kareken, a professor at the University of Minnesota on leave at the Joint Economic Committee, gave the standard view: "The bills-only doctrine of the Federal Reserve System . . . is one of the contributory causes for the present high level of interest rates but this is mostly crying about spilt milk. Abandonment of bills-only now would nevertheless help in the future" (Joint Economic Committee, 1959, Hearing Part 6A, 125). See also Barger (1964, chapter 7). The memo does not distinguish between real and nominal rates.

tee. The rationale was knowledge, not just jurisdiction. Second, "many thoughtful people, both at home and abroad, . . . [will] question the will of our Government to manage its financial affairs without recourse to the printing press" (ibid., 1288). The second argument annoyed the resolution's author, Congressman Henry Reuss (Wisconsin), who criticized it as metaphysical. Martin held to his position, citing problems of confidence and fear of inflation.

Although no member of the committee mentioned it, the 4.25 percent rate ceiling restricted the Treasury's ability to undo any effect of bills-only on the outstanding stock of debt and relevant interest rates. By selling long-term bonds and retiring bills or short-term debt, the Treasury could alter the maturity distribution of debt and remove the effect of bills-only. The 4.25 percent ceiling also prevented the debt lengthening to which the Eisenhower administration had committed.[312] In fact, average maturity fell almost two years, to four years and four months, between the Accord and 1960. During approximately the same period, the amount of debt ninety-one days and under held by the Federal Reserve rose $4.3 billion. The entire System account rose $4.5 billion. Treasury debt held by the public (including the Federal Reserve) increased $22 billion; without the ceiling rate, additional sales of long-term debt would certainly have been feasible (Board of Governors, 1976, 488–90; Office of Management and Budget, 1990, 144).

In a letter to Senator Harry Byrd (Virginia), the System called attention to a main problem for monetary policy posed by the falling debt maturity. With reduced average maturity, the Treasury had to refinance debt more frequently. Given its even keel policy, frequent refundings (and new issues) restricted Federal Reserve operations to a small part of the year. The problem with this argument was that if the Treasury auctioned its bonds, as the Joint Economic Committee's staff proposed, even keel support would not have been needed. The market would price the bonds at the auction instead of the Treasury announcing a price that the Federal Reserve felt itself obligated to support (Joint Economic Committee, 1959, Part 6A, 1257–58). Martin's concern foresaw the problem that arose in the 1960s. Even keel policy of supporting Treasury issues could create "pressures on the Federal Reserve to supply bank reserves in excess of those consistent with the promotion of economic growth and stability" (Board Minutes, March 3, 1960, letter, Martin to Byrd).[313] In April 1960, the Treasury was

312. Milton Friedman made the point about bills-only in Joint Economic Committee (1959, Part 9A, 3045).

313. The letter to Senator Byrd also responded to the argument that keeping the debt in short-term securities reduced interest cost. The Board rejected this argument, citing experi-

able, at last, to offer a 4.5 percent bond callable in fifteen years. This was the highest coupon since the 1918 act.

EMPLOYMENT, GROWTH, AND PRICE LEVELS

Economic growth averaged 2.7 percent a year for the six years 1954–59, and the deflator rose an average of 2.2 percent. Growth seemed modest compared to Germany, Japan, and other recovering economies. Concerns about growth, productivity, inflation, gold losses, and rising interest rates led Congress to authorize the Joint Economic Committee to undertake one of the most extensive studies of the economy ever done and to hold hearings throughout 1959. Senator Paul Douglas served as the committee's chairman, and Professor Otto Eckstein, a fiscal expert at Harvard, served as technical director.[314]

The staff report shows mainstream academic opinion at the time, mainly Keynesian in its origin. A principal concern was "the slow growth of the American economy of the last six years, which coincided with a rise in the price level" (Joint Economic Committee, 59, Staff Report, xxi). The fault lay in using fiscal and monetary policies to stabilize the price level. "[T]he amount of growth that was surrendered for what at best was a small gain toward stabilizing the price level, was very large" (ibid., xxi).[315] It attacked the administration's concern for avoiding inflation and suggested a permanent increase in inflation would sustain a permanently higher growth rate. "The theory that, in an environment of stable prices the economy will experience sustainable healthy growth is fallacious. The severe, restrictive application of present monetary and fiscal tools which would be necessary to halt the increase of prices would keep the economy in a perennial state of slack" (ibid., 10). In the staff's view, private industry made large investments in 1956 and 1957 to meet high future levels of output, but "[g]overnment stepped too hard on the fiscal and monetary brakes" (ibid., xxv).

The report claimed that lost output in recessions was not made up in subsequent recoveries. If the government chose a policy of facilitating growth and maintaining aggregate demand, the economy could grow at 3.9 percent to 4.5 percent, far above the historic average of 3 percent or

---

ence that year, when the Treasury paid more than 5 percent to borrow. The Clinton administration reopened the issue.

314. The text concentrates on issues related to Federal Reserve actions and policies. The project included studies of pricing, investment, agriculture, taxation, etc.

315. As these quotations suggest, the staff report is highly critical of the Eisenhower administration's emphasis on balanced budgets and the Federal Reserve's concerns about inflation. Less clear is the extent to which the report is a political document prepared for the 1960 election campaign or the mistaken view that policy can increase growth by accepting more inflation.

the lower 1954–59 average (ibid., 8). The report expressed concern about inflation but downplayed the role of monetary policy. Instead, the report highlighted three causes of inflation: instability of output, market "power to raise prices in the absence of excess demand," and rising service prices (ibid., xxii).

Senator Douglas, the committee chair, did not entirely share the staff's view. He frequently expressed annoyance at the emphasis the Federal Reserve, and others, gave to inflation when the reported annual rate of change in the consumer price index remained about 1 percent. As the discussion showed, failure to adjust fully for quality changes gave an upward bias to the index,[316] so true inflation was below 1 percent and probably slightly negative. Douglas's exchanges with some of the witnesses suggest that, although inflation was low or zero, anticipated inflation had increased during the decade. The Eisenhower administration's very large, peacetime deficit in fiscal 1959 (2.5 percent of GNP) aroused concerns. Large budget deficits that had previously occurred only in wartime had now occurred in peacetime.[317]

316. The bias was recognized at the time. Many years later, in the 1990s, economists and officials discussed the bias again and, soon after, the Bureau of Labor Statistics adjusted the index for quality changes and new product introductions.

317. The main argument, made by those who raised concerns about inflation, was that the budget deficit was inflationary. The argument was formalized later as the fiscal theory of inflation. See Woodford (2001). The following exchange between Senator Douglas and Alfred H. Hauser, vice president of the investment division of Chemical Bank, illustrates Senator Douglas's irritation. After Hauser's agreement that principal price indexes showed no evidence of current inflation, Douglas asked: "Do you think that people ought to be more restrained in their talk about how we are being devoured by inflation when as a matter of fact we have had stability in the price level during the last year or perhaps 13 months? . . .

> Mr. Hauser. This is a matter of opinion, but I feel it is necessary for all of us to holler our heads off about inflation all the time.
> The Chairman. Even though it doesn't occur?
> Mr. Hauser. Even though it doesn't occur, because the potential is so great that it could explode at any time if we relax in our diligence and in our efforts to hold it down.
> The Chairman. Do you think we should holler our heads off on the reality of inflation in the last year?
> Mr. Hauser. No, sir. I don't believe in saying anything that is not in accordance with the facts. . . .
> The Chairman. If these hearings have done nothing more than this, to have the eminent financiers of the City of New York say there has been no inflation in the past year, and prices have been steady, we will have served our purpose. . . .
> Would that the newspapers of the city could hear these winged words. Would that the life insurance industry could take these words to heart and cease putting in full-page ads in the newspapers shouting about the horrors of inflation. . . .
> Mr. Hauser. Sir, I do not draw the same conclusions that you do from the concern we have about inflation. . . .

The staff report's principal recommendation for monetary policy was greater reliance on selective controls. "General credit controls have proved to be selective in their effects; in fact generality in stabilization is an illusion" (ibid., xxiv). This claim is based on the more powerful effects on housing, state and local government spending, and small business. The staff's solution was selective controls on consumer credit, inventory investment, residential construction, and fixed investment, although the report recognizes that the last of these would prove difficult to regulate with selective controls. General controls should continue with some changes. To reduce uncertainty, the discount rate should be tied to market rates, reserve requirement ratios should remain fixed, and the Federal Reserve "should abandon the 'bills-only' policy in its present rather doctrinaire form and be prepared to deal in long-term securities whenever the economy would benefit" (ibid., xxxv). The staff favored "turning over the entire administration of monetary policy to a Board of Governors reduced in size" (ibid., xxxv).

Recommendations for debt management included some of the best recommendations in the report: auctioning long-term debt, advance refunding, and purchasing power saving bonds for small investors. Although the staff recognized that the 4.25 percent interest rate ceiling was arbitrary and complicated debt management, the staff took a political position: "modification of the policies that led to the present situation is a matter of much more pressing importance" (ibid., xxxvi–xxxvii). Congress should decide whether it wished to lift the ceiling before other reforms were made. The debt management section repeated the importance of abandoning bills-only. This would permit the Federal Reserve to smooth erratic fluctuations in long-term bond prices.

Two of these recommendations satisfied some of the more active Democratic members, notably Senator Douglas and Congressman Reuss, who wanted an end to bills-only and no further reduction in reserve requirement ratios. They favored holding hostage repeal of the 4.25 percent interest ceiling until the Federal Reserve gave up bills-only.

The staff failed to recommend elimination of regulation Q ceiling rates on deposits or payment of interest on demand deposits. It did not distin-

---

The Chairman. In other words, there is an accumulation of toxic poisons underneath the surface . . . which will undermine the health of the body politic in the future. . . .

Mr. Hauser. The principal one is the deficit which we experienced in the past fiscal year.

The Chairman. That you know is over. Curiously enough it was not accompanied by any increase in prices. The biggest peacetime deficit in history was accompanied with stability in prices. (Joint Economic Committee, Hearings, 1959, August 6, 1959, 1634–37)

guish between real and nominal interest rates when it discussed rising interest rates. As noted above, it claimed that monetary expansion could raise the economy's long-term growth rate.

Pessimism about the effectiveness of general monetary policy for preventing inflation dominated the recommendations about monetary policy. The main reasons advanced for reduced effectiveness were movements in monetary velocity that offset changes in the money stock. Among the causes of offsetting behavior the staff listed were growth of financial intermediaries—savings and loans, mutual savings banks, pension funds, etc.—that remained "outside the reach of Federal Reserve actions" (Joint Economic Committee, 1959, Staff Report, 351). Also, the report described banks as relatively immune to the effects of Federal Reserve policy. "The deposits extinguished by the [Federal Reserve] security sales will largely be idle deposits" (ibid., 348).[318] No basis for any of these claims followed.

The monetary policy chapter was by far the longest and most detailed of the eleven chapters. It occupied nearly one-quarter of the volume, and its main theme could not have been pleasant reading for Chairman Martin and his colleagues. The report repeated several times that monetary policy had slowed the growth of the economy without preventing inflation.

The report did not try to establish that easier monetary policy, perhaps supplemented by selective controls, could achieve the substantially higher growth rates it proclaimed as feasible. It simply asserted this claim. It treated losses of output in recession as permanent losses, never made up in recoveries. Therefore, if recessions could be avoided, the growth rate would increase. The report did not discuss why it rejected the standard view that in the long run money is neutral so that the economy's long-term growth rate is independent of its monetary growth rate.

Fortunately, the importance of this section and its conclusions does not depend on the quality of its analysis. It provided one of the earliest full statements of the prevailing Keynesian policy position that rose to influence in the 1960s—that there is a permanent tradeoff between inflation and unemployment or growth, that the Federal Reserve's concern about preventing inflation permanently lowered either the growth rate or level of output, and well into the 1970s, that the economy could not achieve simultaneously full employment and price stability without government action affecting wage and price changes.[319] A similar claim appears in the 1962 Economic Report.

318. The staff report was written by Warren Smith, who had published similar views about offsetting changes in Smith (1956).

319. The report discusses, and for the most part dismisses, the earlier claim that a large debt makes interest rate changes, especially increases, destabilizing. Long-term interest

Perhaps the report's lasting influence on policy was to raise concerns at the Federal Reserve about the possible political consequences of reducing inflation. The temporary decline in real growth during the transition to lower inflation raised congressional interest in monetary policy and threatened independence. I have found no direct evidence that Martin or his colleagues held this view. There is, however, a distinct difference between the Federal Reserve's response to inflation in 1958–60 and its response the next time inflation rose, after 1965.

The Balance of Payments

Persistent balance of payments deficits had become a policy concern. The chapter on balance of payments problems was both much shorter and made fewer recommendations than the monetary chapter, perhaps because the authors did not favor more restrictive policies. It concluded that the problem was not inability to compete, later called loss of competitiveness. Instability in monetary policy was made partly responsible for the swings in the payments deficit. The report recommended greater reliance on multilateral aid to developing countries to reduce the burden on the United States. It found that non-repetitive, adverse factors contributed to the loss of gold. On the brighter side, it noted that the gold outflow had improved the world distribution of the monetary gold stock.

The Federal Reserve's Response

The 1959 hearings were the first large-scale inquiry into policy procedures in a decade. They came at a time when the Board's staff and its analysis were in transition from the 1920s traditions to the more Keynesian approach of the 1960s. Emanuel Goldenweiser and especially Winfield Riefler had retired, and a new group of economists, trained during the postwar years, occupied many of the junior staff position where drafts of official responses began. Several soon after rose to senior positions

Four main topics interested the Joint Economic Committee's leadership. Their common element was the rise in interest rates. First, reductions in reserve requirement ratios in the 1950s had reduced these ratios for demand deposits from 23, 19, and 13 at the time of the Accord to 18, 16.5, and 11 at the 1959 hearings. The reductions transferred earning assets to banks and deprived government of the additional revenue it would have received had the Federal Reserve bought securities in the open market instead of reducing reserve requirement ratios. Allowing vault cash

---

rates had almost doubled during the decade without major bankruptcies caused by creditors' losses.

to count as part of reserves (approved by Congress) further benefited the banks. Second, the committee's leadership blamed the System's bills-only policy for making long-term rates higher than necessary. The report did not mention higher expected inflation or higher productivity growth in the world economy. Average long-term rates had increased from 2.5 percent at the time of the Accord to between 4 and 4.25 percent in 1959. Rates on five-year notes reached 5 percent or more. Among the public and their representatives in Congress, only those with memories of the 1920s could recall a prevailing 5 percent interest rate. Third, the Treasury wanted to lengthen the average maturity of the public debt, but the 4.25 percent ceiling prevented it from doing so. Fourth, proposals to auction long-term securities did not appeal to the Board or the Treasury. Auctions would have made even-keel unnecessary, because the market, not the Treasury, would set the price. The Federal Reserve would have gained increased opportunity to adjust policy.

Scattered through the hearings and questionnaires to the Federal Reserve and the Treasury were many other topics. Members of Congress did not feel bound by the subject. They inquired about anything that interested them.

Discounting. One set of written questions, early in the year, concentrated on the role of discounting and discount rates. Senator Douglas asked why the System changed discount rates. If the Federal Reserve relied on open market operations and refrained from changing discount rates "interest rates generally would not rise, or not rise as much. . . . [W]ould you agree that this result would be desirable [in recoveries], since higher rates would tend to 'hold back full recovery'?" (Board Minutes, March 17, 1959, 1, replies to Douglas-Patman questions).

The Board's answer showed the gradual evolution from the Riefler-Burgess doctrine that dominated analysis in the 1920s. Discount policy supplemented open market operations, as before. Now it had a larger role. Banks could choose to adjust to tighter policy by reducing liquid assets or by borrowing from a reserve bank. As before, "banks are generally reluctant to become indebted to the Federal Reserve" (ibid., 2). But a new thought entered at this point. "The deterrents to borrowing are greatly weakened if market yields on securities owned become and remain substantially higher than the discount rate. In these conditions, banks may even be induced to borrow for profit"[320] (ibid., 2).

The Board added that borrowing was a privilege and not a right of mem-

---

320. In 1952 Riefler had recognized that banks borrowed for profit when the tax treatment of borrowing made borrowing profitable. That was treated as a special case.

bership in the System. Continuous borrowing was inappropriate under ordinary conditions. The Board quoted from the 1955 revision of regulation A to reinforce these points. Then it added a carryover from the past: "[I]t is of prime importance that the general reluctance of banks to borrow at the Federal Reserve be reinforced by a discount rate with real deterrent power at times when a tempering of bank credit growth is in the public interest" (ibid., 3).

The inconsistency in the Board's analysis of discounting came out clearly when the board explained why it increased the discount rate. Profits came to the fore. "[T]o make the discount mechanism an effective supplement to open market operations the Federal Reserve is obliged [sic] to maintain discount rates not markedly lower than market yields on . . . Treasury bills" (ibid., 3). If it failed to do this, "administering the discount window to prevent excessive credit expansion would become very difficult. In the absence of a rate deterrent to borrowing, Federal Reserve bank officers would be without workable guidelines in acting on a great number of borrowing requests from banks, many of whom would be in a position of profiting directly from the relatively low rate on borrowing" (ibid., 3). In the 1980s, the System ignored this conclusion without causing instability. Banks increased borrowing.

Staff and officers did not take the next two steps—first, recognizing that borrowing added to aggregate bank reserves and bank credit even as it lowered free reserves, and second, distinguishing between changes in discount rates that led and followed the market. It was inconsistent to regard the reduction in free reserves as contractive and the increase in bank credit and bank reserves as expansive.[321] Several of the changes in discount rates came after market rates increased.

Using the presence or absence of a change in the weekly new issue yield of Treasury bills as a measure of response, Table 2.8 suggests that most discount rate changes in the 1950s were not anticipated before they were made. An N in the last column, about one-third of the changes, indicates little or no response. Several times the change in bill yields exceeded the discount rate change.

Role of monetary policy. A questionnaire sent to the Secretary of the Treasury and the Board of Governors provided an opportunity for each institution to give the committee its views on macroeconomic issues. Both agreed

---

321. "Banks are always in a position to supplement their lending capacity by borrowing at the Federal Reserve. It is to keep this source of supplementary lending power under continuous and effective regulation that the Federal Reserve must rely on flexible adjustment of the discount rate" (Board Minutes, March 17, 1959, 5, replies to Douglas and Patman questions).

Table 2.8   Discount Rate Changes, 1953–59

DATE	CHANGE IN DISCOUNT RATE	NEW DISCOUNT RATE	i_t^a	i_{t-1}^a	RESPONSE
1/15/53	+0.25	2.00	2.12	2.09	N
2/4–11/54	−0.25	1.75	1.03	1.57	
4/13/54	−0.25	1.50	1.07	1.07	N
4/13–29/55	+0.25	1.75	1.65	1.23	
8/3/55	+0.25	2.00(2.25)	1.85	1.40	
9/8/55	+0.25	2.25	2.13	1.85	
11/17/55	+0.25	2.50	2.25	2.26	N
4/12/56	+0.25	2.75	2.50	2.17	
8/23/56	+0.25	3.00	2.82	2.24	
8/8/57	+0.50	3.50	3.31	3.24	N
11/14–29/57	−0.50	3.00	3.47	3.52	N
1/21/58	−0.25	2.75	2.59	3.14	
3/6/58	−0.50	2.25	1.35	1.58	
4/17/58	−0.50	1.75	1.22	1.53	
8/14–9/22/58	+0.25	2.00	1.52	0.93	
10/23/58	+0.50	2.50	2.80	2.60	
3/5/59	+0.50	3.00	2.82	2.72	N
5/28/59	+0.50	3.50	2.88	3.10	
9/10/59	+0.50	4.00	3.98	3.04	

Source: Board of Governors (1976).

$^a i_t$ is the yield on new issues at the first auction following the first announced changes in a discount rate; i_{t-1} is the same rate one week earlier.

that monetary policy had been asked to bear too much of the responsibility for stabilizing the economy in the 1950s. The Treasury response blamed the lack of budget surpluses in most years, and their small size in others, for the wide swings in interest rates and problems in debt management. It was not that the "monetary authorities have been overly aggressive in the use of their powers" (ibid., 1720).

The Federal Reserve's response outlined the ways monetary policy affected output. It did not restrict the transmission process to the effect of reserves, interest rates, and availability of credit on bank lending. It cited also "[l]iquidity, capitalized values, and profit expectations" (Employment Growth and Price Levels, Answers to Questions on Monetary Policy and Debt Management, Hearings, Part 6C, 1763). The Board described the inflation process as the cumulative effect of demands for goods and services that can occur "even while the economy as a whole is still rising toward capacity levels" (ibid., 1765). Restrictive monetary policy at such times reduced marginal loan demand, increased saving, and tempered expectations about future earnings (ibid., 1766). The Board's response began to recognize an effect of inflationary expectations on interest rates. Inflationary expectations reduced saving by depreciating its value (ibid., 1767). It did not carry this thought over to recognize that inflation increased nominal interest rates and compensated savers for expected loss of purchasing power, if nominal interest rates adjust freely.

The committee asked about selective effects of general monetary policy. The Board responded at length but not directly or informatively. It emphasized the availability of credit and the level and structure of interest rates, but it did not respond to criticisms of selective effects of monetary policy by explaining why long-lived durable capital responded more quickly and by larger amounts than short-lived capital assets or non-durables to a change in real interest rates. It tried to dodge the question or cloud the answer by telling the committee that "it is impossible to break down the responses of individual sectors of the economy to changes in credit availability and interest rates, so that those attributable to monetary policy may be identified and appraised apart from those due to other market factors" (ibid., 1771).[322]

Chairman Martin's responses to the committee's many questions provide a reading on the System's analysis at the end of the 1950s. Unlike the 1920s, there is no general framework like the Riefler-Burgess version of the real bills doctrine. The Bretton Woods arrangement is mentioned rarely. International effects are mentioned, but they are not part of the general framework.

The most common description highlighted the role of credit availability and interest rates. The two started as inseparable partners, but soon afterward interest rates became less important. "Availability of credit and the level-of-interest rates are twin influences, the significance of which cannot be separated for individual examination. For many purposes, the availability of funds and the terms on which they are available other than the interest rate provisions, are considerably more important to borrowers than interest rates themselves" (ibid., 1771). An outsider cannot know whether statements of this kind reflected staff analysis or Martin's beliefs or an attempt to evade responsibility for the effects of interest rate changes.

Credit availability suggests quantities or aggregates, but neither the responses to questions nor direct testimony attempts to use a quantity-theoretic (or any other explicit) framework. In practice, several members of FOMC compared money growth to output growth as a measure of long-

---

322. The response then considered evidence of effects on state and local expenditures, small business, business in competitive as opposed to oligopolistic industries, residential construction, and public utilities.

term inflation, but this time Martin was not one of them. In his answer, Martin referred to the flow of funds data that the Board collected and published at the time, but this is the only reference, and it responded to a specific question about flow of funds.[323] Martin's response also referred to inflationary expectations. He argued that people who feared inflation would pay less attention to interest rates, but he did not develop the point (ibid., 1777).

The questions then turned to policy instruments and procedures. Martin denied that the System wanted a secular decrease in reserve requirement ratios or that it reduced these ratios to increase bank profits. He turned back a question on the usefulness of consumer credit controls leaving Congress to decide whether such controls would have the public's support.[324] But he opposed direct controls on bank credit, except in national emergencies. Controls would not be effective because substitutes were readily available. Unregulated institutions would supply the loans if the law restricted regulated institutions from lending. Further, "the Board has grave reservations as to the longer run effect of any such direct control on the healthy growth of our free enterprise economy" (ibid., 1782).

As the hearings and staff study neared an end, Martin sent a letter to Senator Douglas, responding to the argument that inflation was mainly the result of cost-push by unions and oligopolistic industries, as the committee staff claimed. He accepted that "there are these imperfections as regards the behavior of individual prices and that they create inflationary pressures or biases" (Board Minutes, December 9, 1959, 1, letter, Martin to Douglas). Then he asked whether monetary policy should be less or more restrictive than if imperfections did not occur. His answer was that the Federal Reserve could not ignore these pressures on prices, called "creeping inflation" in his letter. He gave two main reasons. First, if policy ignored efforts to raise prices and wages, the perpetrators would not stop; they would again try to increase wages above productivity gain and to increase prices to cover the increase in cost.[325] This, the letter said, would bring "all the

323. The housing market was used as an example of how availability affects output. Interest rates and availability change monthly payments, thus the volume of spending on new houses and the relative attractiveness of renting as compared to owning (*Answers to Questions on Monetary Policy and Debt* Management, Joint Economic Committee, 1775).

324. In an earlier, written response to a question from Congressman Reuss, Martin said: "[T]here's little question but that restrictive regulation of the terms offered to installment and mortgage borrowers would effectively reduce the total demand for credit and thus relax somewhat the upward pressure on interest rates." But he left the judgment to Congress as to whether controls should be reintroduced (Joint Economic Committee, Hearings, 1959, July 30, 1490).

325. This argument was common at the time. It did not explain why the monopolists and monopsonists did not extract the economic rent and stop. The entire discussion used the

social injustices that economists universally agree accompany inflation, and it would also disrupt the saving and investment process" (ibid., 2).

Second, Martin's letter tried to establish an effect, through anticipations, of cost pressures on aggregate demand. The link was borrowing, but the argument did not distinguish real and nominal rates. Anticipations of rising prices encouraged borrowing to accumulate inventories (by raising the expected real return) and build plants to profit from the increase. The same anticipations reduced the supply of loanable funds and increased demand (ibid., 3). Hence, interest rates rose. Also, the balance of payments deteriorated because prices rose in home markets, reducing foreign demand.

Market forces of this kind put pressure on the Federal Reserve to increase reserves. It had to choose between sharply higher interest rates or open inflation of the "demand pull variety" (ibid., 3).

The letter was most likely written by the staff. It argued in a way that Martin never did. The proposed solution was to prevent the inflation by limiting credit expansion "to a rate of growth consonant with the increase in the physical output of goods and services" (ibid., 3). Institutional imperfections in the price mechanism "cannot be corrected simply by a sound monetary and fiscal policy; they surely cannot be corrected by an unsound financial policy" (ibid., 5).

The letter summarized some reasons for opposing inflation, asserting a position that the congressional staff rejected and that did not become common until after the Great Inflation. "My interest in a monetary policy directed toward a dollar of stable value is not based on the feeling that price stability is a more important national objective than either maximum sustainable growth or a high level of employment, but rather on the reasoned conclusion that the objective of price stability is an essential prerequisite for their achievement" (ibid., 5). The response did not mention the obligation to maintain a fixed exchange rate.

Martin opposed the report's main proposals—secondary reserve requirements of Treasury bills, real estate credit controls, controls on issuance of state and local government securities, and controls on insurance company lending or lending by other non-bank financial intermediaries. However, his answer did not distinguish between spending financed from saving and money growth. And he failed to distinguish the one-time effects on the price level arising from a change in the community's saving rate and a reallocation of spending financed at an unchanged saving rate.

A series of questions on debt management began by asking whether

---

same term "inflation" to refer to one-time changes in the price level and changes in the rate of price change. This common confusion continues.

Treasury debt management interfered with the execution of monetary policy. Martin named three ways in which conflicts occurred. Most important was that the frequency of Treasury offerings affected the timing of Federal Reserve operations. Martin noted that, on average, the Treasury sold securities other than Treasury bills eight times a year during 1954–58 and eleven times in 1959. The Federal Reserve followed an even keel, at these times, avoiding any overt actions in the money market before, during, and after Treasury operations. "[T]he time intervals during which the Federal Reserve System could appropriately take policy action have been relatively few in number and relatively limited in duration" (ibid., 1785). The only improvement Martin suggested was fewer deficits, but new issues were only half the problem. Refundings of maturing issues were just as frequent.[326]

Martin did not recommend auctioning long-term securities as a means of selling debt. An auction would let the market price the new issue, thereby removing the risk of a failure to sell the issue and, with it, the need for the Federal Reserve to intervene to prevent failure. The problem of not changing market conditions on the auction day would remain, but the long even keel before and after would be reduced or eliminated.[327] The Treasury opposed auctioning long-term securities, and it argued incorrectly that "adoption of the auction technique would, in itself, do nothing to change this [even keel] situation" (Joint Economic Committee, Answers to Questions, 1959, 1739).

Bills only. The committee ended by asking Martin whether the bills-only policy had strengthened the market for Treasury securities in any way. Martin replied that bills-only reduced market uncertainty. The reason he gave was that the bill market was much broader than the market at other maturities, so Federal Reserve operations had less effect on market yields. Martin acknowledged, however, that bills-only had not fully restored "depth, breadth, and resiliency," at maturities over ninety days.[328]

Martin suggested several reasons for the market's weakness. He (or the staff member who prepared it) made one of the first explicit statements of the effect of inflation on interest rates in a Federal Reserve document.

---

326. Between February 1953 and May 1959, the Treasury came to market with ninety-three issues other than bills. It issued forty-six for cash and forty-seven in exchange (Joint Economic Committee, Hearings Part 6A, 1959, July 24, 1105–07). Some were issued on the same day.

327. In the 1970s, the Treasury adopted the auction technique and even keel eventually ended.

328. A market with many orders to buy and sell around the last market price has "depth." If the market draws bids and offers from many sources, it has "breadth," and if the volume of orders increases substantially with a small change in price, the market has "resiliency" (Joint Economic Committee, Answers to Questions . . . , 1959, 1813, note 5).

"This influence [inflation] has tended to diminish the incentive to save and invest in longer maturity fixed income securities in general, including Treasury issues, except at interest rates high enough to cover the forward inflation risk." He then considered three alternatives: the Federal Reserve could purchase and sell long-term securities (1) to smooth the business cycle, (2) to smooth bond prices, and (3) to maintain an interest rate level, or range, believed to be appropriate at the particular time. He described this as a "movable peg."

Martin rejected each of the proposed alternatives to bills-only. His answer recognizes the interaction between policy and market anticipations. The first would encourage speculation and increase volatility of long-term rates. Market participants would observe Federal Reserve actions and speculate on additional changes in the same direction.[329] The second would prevent long-term rates from rising in expansions and falling in recessions by supplying and absorbing reserves procyclically. To counter the procyclical movement in reserves, the System would have to increase the size of counter-cyclical purchases and sales of short-term securities. The third alternative would increase speculation when the interest rate approached its ceiling or floor. Martin's discussion of this alternative anticipated the discussion of exchange rate bands many years later. The answer concluded by invoking the effect on market expectations. If the Federal Reserve adopted one of the three alternatives, the bond market would price bonds according to expected Federal Reserve action and its consequences for inflation. Participants would "turn from observation of basic supply and demand forces for longer-term securities to close attention to Federal Reserve activity in this area of the market" (ibid., 1817). Also, the Federal Reserve's focus would shift from providing the level of cash balances consistent with stable growth to regulation of long-term interest rates.[330]

Martin's testimony emphasized the importance of changes in reserve balances. He listed three channels by which open market operations af-

329. "The mere appearance of official buying or selling . . . would probably produce more extreme price effects than would be justified by the amount of reserves released or absorbed at the time" (Joint Economic Committee, Answers to Questions . . . , 1959, 1816). These effects would be temporary. Like most arguments about destabilizing speculation, this argument is incomplete, as the response soon recognized.

330. Many of the responses to questions about bills-only replied to the committee staff's arguments for and against bills-only. The principal arguments made against the policy were (1) that there were occasional speculative excesses, as in December 1955 and July 1958; (2) that the long-term market does not respond predictably to changes in short-term rates because linkage is weak; (3) that intervention in the long-term market would stabilize security prices and encourage investment; and (4) bills-only denies the Treasury underwriting support (Joint Economic Committee, Hearings 1959, July 27, 1249). Only the third argument supported the staff claim that bills-only had raised long-term rates.

fected interest rates—by changing the volume of reserves, the outstanding stock of securities, and the expectations of professional traders and investors. "Of these effects, the first is by far the most important" (Joint Economic Committee, Hearings, 1959, July 27, 1233).

Typical of Federal Reserve discussions in this period, neither this statement nor others explained how these changes influenced the economy's price, output, and employment objectives. There was usually a suggestion that the long-run inflation path depended on money growth. The committee and its staff concentrated on narrower issues such as operating methods, while suggesting repeatedly that the economy's performance would improve if the Federal Reserve abandoned the bills-only policy.[331]

Congressman Henry Reuss (Wisconsin) questioned Martin about a resolution he had introduced at the Ways and Means Committee stating as the sense of Congress that the 4.25 percent ceiling on Treasury bonds should be removed for two years and the Federal Reserve "should bring about future needed monetary expansion by purchasing United States securities of varying maturities" (ibid., 1241).

Martin had responded in writing to a request from the Republican members. He opposed Reuss's resolution. If Congress wanted to instruct the Federal Reserve about its operations, it should amend the Federal Reserve Act. The resolution did not do that. It simply appended the instruction to debt management legislation. Martin added: "I am convinced that this amendment, when stripped of all technicalities, and regardless of whether the language was permissive or mandatory, will cause many thoughtful people . . . to question the will of our Government to manage its financial affairs without recourse to the printing press. To me this is a grave matter" (ibid., 1287).

Reuss pressed hard against the policy of lowering reserve requirement ratios and in favor of purchasing all debt maturities. Martin could not explain why the instruction to buy and sell all maturities was inflationary or why it destroyed confidence in the government's intention to maintain low inflation.[332] Congressman Reuss pressed him for an explicit response, but he did not get it.

331. One Congressman asked for the definition of a disorderly market. Martin replied that "large sell orders are pouring into the market from sellers who do not need to sell and there are no successive bids" (ibid., 1276). Later, he sent a letter describing how selling "feeds on itself" and the market develops "a trading vacuum accompanied by a buildup in the number and size of offerings and by a disappearance of bids, and a disorganized market psychology" (ibid., 1279).

332. A table in the hearings (ibid., 1261), prepared by the committee staff, showed that average interest costs on the public debt had increased from 2.27 percent to 2.824 percent between 1951 and April 1959. Compared to the changes that came later, the increase is small

The Treasury supported the Federal Reserve's reliance on bills-only. It acknowledged that, at times, departure from bills-only might have helped the Treasury, but the opposite was true also. System purchases or sales could cause transitory price movements that would complicate debt management. The most serious problems would arise when bond prices declined. "When investors expect higher interest rates, an attempt at small-scale support purchases by the System runs the considerable risk of encouraging large-scale liquidation" (Joint Economic Committee, Answers to Questions . . . 1959, 1743). This contrasts with Secretary Mellon's Treasury, which insisted in the early 1920s that the Federal Reserve should not intervene at all.

The Treasury used the same reasoning to explain why it should avoid using its trust funds to support the market. It failed to point out that if Congress removed the interest ceiling, it could offset any effect of bills-only on the composition of the publicly held debt by changing the mix it offered. And neither the Treasury nor the Federal Reserve explained that purchases at the short-end of the market supplied reserves to support Treasury offerings.

The hearings enabled Congress to question the role of bills-only in the 1958 disorderly market. Martin called on Robert Roosa, from the New York bank's staff, who replied that he was more inclined than Riefler to purchase and sell long-term securities, but he minimized the differences with the Board. His main message about 1958 was that "the problems are so complex that it will be impossible not to make a mistaken judgment once in a while" (ibid., 1296).

Auctioning securities. Treasury Secretary Anderson also testified at the hearing and was asked about auctioning long-term debt. He changed the Treasury's previous position by favoring debt auctions in general, but he expressed several concerns. First, auctions would exclude small buyers. Second, there was a risk that a small change in yield would cause large capital gains or losses. Third, the number of bidders would be limited to a few syndicates. Individual buyers would not participate in the auction. With fixed prices, small holders could turn in their expiring security for the new security. In an auction, they would be paid cash, but they would not know the price to bid for the new issue (ibid., 1148–49). He did not

---

indeed. The emphasis given to the change conveys (1) failure to separate real and nominal rates and (2) the intense attention to small changes in nominal rates. At the long end of the market, the increase was from 2.327 percent to 2.619 percent in the same period. On the margin, the increase is larger, about 2.5 percent from the pegged yields of 1951 to the 5 percent notes issued in 1959, but part of the rise is cyclical and part reflects a rise in anticipated inflation.

mention that the Treasury permitted purchasers to buy at the average auction price in bill auctions at the time.

The Treasury also submitted written answers to questions about monetary policy and debt management. One question was whether auctioning long-term securities would remove a constraint on monetary policy operations. The Treasury replied that auctioning would not eliminate the need for "even keel" monetary policy (ibid., 1739–40). Eventually the Treasury adopted the auction method; its concerns proved manageable, and the Federal Reserve eliminated even keel policy.

Other Witnesses

The committee took testimony from economists, government securities dealers, principals in the financial services industry, and officers of the New York reserve bank. Economists' recommendations covered a wide range, representing the differences in academic approaches and personal views.

Sumner Slichter of Harvard was the first witness. He told the committee that slow, creeping inflation is "an encouragement to enterprise. . . . It is a tax that falls on everyone. It is not a bad kind of tax in many respects" (Joint Economic Committee, Hearing, 1959, Part 1, 12).

Richard Musgrave of Johns Hopkins favored discretionary changes in tax rates as a counter-cyclical policy. He also favored adjustment of the tax rate applicable to the first bracket of the income tax. He recognized that his proposal transferred a congressional responsibility to the executive branch. He suggested several additional ways in which fiscal policies could be made more flexible, and he proposed a fact-finding board to recommend price and wage changes (ibid., October 26, 2757–69).

William Baumol of Princeton University proposed basing the tax paid by a corporation on its contribution to economic growth. Firms would get tax exemptions if their sales increased. One possibility that he mentioned made the exemption progressive. This proposal had the odd feature that tax rates would rise in recession, when growth slowed, and fall in expansions. Mergers would not increase the measured growth rate, but firms that had difficulty would face an increased tax rate (ibid., 2792–95).

Robert Triffin of Yale restricted his comments to the U.S. international payments position and the operation of the Bretton Woods system. Triffin offered several suggestions to reduce the current account deficit. His main emphasis was on changes in the international payments system. He proposed an increase in world monetary reserves to supplement the key currencies. The prevailing system required the United States and the United Kingdom to let their short-term liabilities to foreigners rise without limit and much faster than their gold holdings. An international reserve asset, he said, would free the system from dependence on the two countries' balance of payments deficits. To establish the new system, countries would deposit 20 percent of their international reserves at the IMF. To prevent inflation, the charter would restrict the increase in IMF lending to from 3 to 5 percent per annum (ibid., 2927–35). The IMF would function as a world central bank to lend to country central banks.

Walter Heller of the University of Minnesota, and soon to be chairman of the Council of Economic Advisers, addressed two issues, the development of human capital by increasing educational spending and improving stabilization policy by "shifting emphasis from tight money to tight budgets" (ibid., 2988). In office soon after, he abandoned this proposal and favored larger deficits.

Milton Friedman of the University of Chicago emphasized the stabilizing actions of the private sector and the destabilizing actions of government or its agents, particularly the Federal Reserve. He commented explicitly on monetary policy, debt management, fiscal policy, and trade policy (Joint Economic Committee, Hearings, 1959, October 30, 3021–28). His was the only response by an academic that commented on the committee's main concerns—the use of open market operations, relation of monetary policy to debt management, and the role of the rediscount rate. He called for a constant rate of money growth consistent with price stability. He proposed to restrict monetary policy actions to open market operations by removing the power to change reserve requirement ratios and discount rates. Deposits should be subject to a 100 percent reserve requirement ratio, so the banking system could expand only if it received more reserves. He preferred to float the dollar and use monetary policy to maintain domestic purchasing power. Friedman also proposed assigning responsibility for debt management to the Federal Reserve. Even if this were not done, the Treasury should restrict debt issues to a ninety-day bill and an eight- or ten-year long-term bond and sell all securities at auction. The form of the auction should change to allow bidders to present a schedule of quantities they would take at various prices. The Treasury would determine a single market-clearing price and charge all buyers that price.[333]

Friedman's fiscal proposals included integrating corporate and personal income taxation by replacing the corporate income tax with taxation of corporate income at individual tax rates. Stockholders would pay tax as if they directly received their share of corporate net income. He favored

---

333. This auction proposal overcame the Treasury's main objection to auctioning long-term bonds. Friedman's call for a single price avoided the "winner's curse." Many years later, the Treasury adopted single price auctions.

broadening the base and lowering individual income tax rates. His trade proposals included removing tariffs and import quotas.

The recommendations of these and other witnesses covered a wide range. Lack of agreement by the academic witnesses reduced the limited chance that some of their ideas would be adopted.

The Dealer Market

Speculative activity in the government securities market in the spring and summer of 1958 raised concerns in Congress and the administration about the way the market distributed government securities. Much of the attention centered on the dealer market, the seventeen dealer firms that bought and sold government securities. These firms served as a principal buyer of new Treasury issues that they later sold to investors.

The principal concerns were the small number of dealers, the extent of competition, and the profitability of dealer operations.[334] Broader issues included the distribution system itself, whether the Treasury should auction all securities, and whether the institutional arrangements, including bills-only, contributed to the increase in interest rates and the pressures on Congress to remove the ceiling interest rate on long-term issues.

The Treasury and the Federal Reserve's detailed study of market arrangements gave much attention to the 1958 market break. Their joint report concluded that the Federal Reserve did not collect enough information on dealer positions and transactions. Also, the market operated on very thin margins; on average dealer borrowings to finance positions equaled thirty times their net worth (Joint Economic Committee, 1960, 91). The Federal Reserve and Treasury staff report discussed allowing dealers to arrange repurchase agreements with the Federal Reserve, subject to adequate margin, and considered starting a dealer's association to set standards for their operations (Joint Economic Committee, Hearings, 1959, July 24, 1219–20).[335]

The Board and the Treasury considered a proposal to channel all trans-

334. In the 1940s, the Federal Reserve designated recognized dealers. Formal recognition ended in 1953. The Federal Reserve agreed to transact with any firm that "made markets." In practice, this excluded brokers who did not hold inventories. Most of the dealers held only short-term securities in their position at the time. They acted as brokers for longer-term securities. There were a few exceptions, dealers that made markets in long-term bonds.

335. As part of the *Employment, Growth, and Price Levels* study, the committee's staff collected data on positions, transactions, profits, and capital of the seventeen dealer firms. The staff did not use this material. Subsequently, Senator Douglas and Congressman Patman invited Gert von der Linde and me to analyze these data. We interviewed many of the dealers and wrote a detailed description of the market. We found no evidence of the high profitability or lack of competition that concerned Congressman Patman in particular. See Joint Economic Committee (1960).

actions through the New York Stock Exchange so that securities would be purchased and sold in an organized auction market and subject to market rules. The Board's staff concluded that the proposal was not feasible. The exchange required the System to make all open market purchases and sales on the exchange[336] (Board Minutes, October 5, 1959, 3). The remaining recommendations called for increased reporting of dealer information, standardized accounting procedures, and minimum margin requirements.[337] The main change was a decision to collect and publish, with a lag, statistics on dealer financing, short and long market positions, and transactions volume. Dealers had to submit statements of financial condition, but these were not published.[338]

CONCLUSION

The Federal Reserve began to assume its current form in the 1950s under changing perceptions about the influence of monetary actions on economic activity and the leadership of a new chairman, William McChesney Martin, Jr. For most of the preceding eighteen years of depression, war, and postwar recovery, the Federal Reserve had made few policy decisions. Monetary policy became subservient to debt management. The Federal Reserve assisted the Treasury to issue debt at historically low interest rates and advised the Treasury on the type of debt to issue. The Treasury could veto interest rate changes, and it did not hesitate to do so.

The March 1951 Accord with the Treasury changed the Federal Reserve's formal status from subservient to co-equal partner with the Treasury. The Treasury remained responsible for debt management; the Federal Reserve gradually regained authority to change market interest rates, reserves, and money. The two institutions shared responsibility for the success of the Treasury's offerings. The Treasury had to price its issues to attract buyers; the Federal Reserve accepted that it had to assist the Treasury by supplying additional reserves, if offerings failed to attract buyers in sufficient number to sell the issues at the offering price.

336. The president of the exchange also asked for Federal Reserve support of the market and tax exemption for government bonds (Board Minutes, December 30, 1959, letter, Keith Funston to Anderson).

337. One of the dealers, Aubrey Lanston, protested that providing information on positions and transactions to the trading desk would permit the Federal Reserve to trade against him. Riefler replied that the desk could not offer repurchase agreements without information on positions, but it did not require reports on holdings of individual securities (Board Minutes, October 13, 1959, 53).

338. The decision about whether collection would be done by New York or Washington reopened the struggle between New York and the Board (FOMC Minutes, November 4, 1959, 2–11). In the 1920s, an issue of this kind would be quickly resolved in New York's favor. In the 1950s, it took longer, but the New York bank prevailed.

The Federal Reserve's responsibilities to the Treasury were not easy to reconcile with its broader responsibilities or with its independence. Congress gave it two mandates. The Bretton Woods Agreement of 1944 fixed the dollar price of gold and created a system of fixed but adjustable exchange rates. This set a possible external constraint, to avoid a change in parity. The Employment Act of 1946 set the internal constraint as the loose objective of maintaining maximum employment and purchasing power. Given the large U.S. gold stock at war's end, Congress did not explicitly say, or perhaps realize, that the two objectives would often be mutually inconsistent and at times inconsistent also with the budget and debt management. It left the problem to the Federal Reserve, reserving the right to criticize.

The external constraint did not bind for most of the 1950s. With its preponderant share of the world's gold stock the United States permitted countries to discriminate against its producers in trade and to draw gold. This policy, the general prosperity, and economic assistance to promote recovery and military alliances abroad succeeded enough to restore current account convertibility of most West European currencies by the end of 1958. Soon after, concerns increased about U.S. firms' inability to compete effectively in some markets, reductions in the gold stock, and the size of the international payments deficit. These concerns did not lead to action in the 1950s.

In practice, the Employment Act required the Federal Reserve to accept increased responsibility for recessions and unemployment. During the 1920s, it had denied any direct influence of its actions on output or employment. Postwar politics changed the Federal Reserve's objectives. President Eisenhower was the first Republican president since Herbert Hoover. Despite his concern for fiscal responsibility and balanced budgets, he wanted to avoid the mistakes of the late 1920s and early 1930s. The administration took expansive fiscal measures in recessions or allowed built-in stabilizers to increase budget deficits. After 1954 the Democrats controlled Congress, but cooperative working relations between the president and Congress permitted the administration to get agreement on the budget.

The choice of objective made United States monetary policy depend on employment. De facto, the Employment Act made the Federal Reserve responsible for maintaining full employment even if its responses produced mild inflation. The System attempted to use monetary policy instruments to moderate fluctuations in economic activity and employment without causing inflation, but it did not fully succeed. Although there were two recessions in the 1950s and a third soon after, the recessions were shorter in length but not less severe than the 1923–24 and 1926–27 recessions (Zarnowitz and Moore, 1986, Table 7).[339] By the middle of the decade, inflation was 3 percent or more.

The change in objective did not lead to a change in procedures. Federal Reserve staff in New York and Washington continued to use free reserves (excess reserves minus borrowing) or member bank borrowing as their principal operating target, and the FOMC often used a level of free reserves as a quantitative guide for the manager of the System Open Market Account. This is not surprising since principal members of the senior staff—especially Winfield Riefler and Woodlief Thomas—had been active in the 1920s, when the Federal Reserve developed these procedures. The surprising change was that the System, using unchanged procedures, could now claim to affect output or the price level, contrary to their claims in the 1920s.

FOMC members and some staff criticized the use of free reserves at times, and some proposed alternatives. Malcolm Bryan, president of the Atlanta Federal Reserve bank, stands out among his peers. He urged the FOMC repeatedly to adopt quantitative targets for growth of reserves and money.[340] The FOMC ignored his efforts, and Vice Chairman Sproul dismissed Bryan's approach as overly mechanistic. Martin preferred to use free reserves or color, tone, and feel, leaving the trading deck to decide how to implement the FOMC's loose discussion. FOMC members, including Martin, criticized free reserves as an inadequate measure of ease and restraint, and they did not always use it. But they returned to it many times and did not resolve the issue or adopt another target in the 1950s.

In part, free reserves served as a substitute for an interest rate target that many would have preferred. The concern was that Congressman Patman would have urged a lower target, so System spokesmen denied that they controlled interest rates.[341] That was not the only reason. Like many bureaucratic organizations, the Federal Reserve avoided taking responsibil-

---

339. I base this judgment on the decline in industrial production, the maximum unemployment rate, and the decline in real GNP. Zarnowitz and Moore (1986, Table 7) give −4.1 and −2.0 for the decline in real GNP in the 1920s recessions and −3.2, −3.3, and −1.2 for the 1953–54, 1957–58, and 1960–61 recessions.

340. Bryan developed the short-run growth cones later used by the Federal Reserve, when it announced money growth targets in the 1980s and 1990s. The cones showed the growth path and the band or range around the path. An observer could see whether money growth remained above or below the specified path. Hafer (1999) discusses Bryan's efforts. Delos Johns (St. Louis) supported Bryan at times.

341. From 1979 to 1982 the Federal Reserve used reserve measures as the target and claimed that it did not control interest rates. This permitted larger changes in interest rates, and higher rates than the FOMC was likely to vote for, and it permitted the Federal Reserve to blame the market for interest rate changes.

ity. Also, Martin always preferred picturesque imagery to careful analysis or precise instructions. One consequence was that the manager had considerable autonomy. Policy measures such as free reserves often changed before the FOMC voted to change.

The minutes for the 1950s show that Martin, several other members, and principal Board staff believed that to prevent long-run inflation, the Federal Reserve had to keep average money growth close to the average growth rate of real output. They recognized that short-term changes in money and velocity were erratic, so money growth could not be used for short-term money market management. And they had no theory of the demand for money or velocity to help them separate changes in the demand for money from changes in supply. Nevertheless, Federal Reserve statements gave more importance to avoiding inflation by keeping money growth close to growth of output than in earlier or later decades. The policy was generally successful, more successful by far than the alternative policies applied in the next two decades. There is good reason to doubt that the result reflected an intended policy of responding to money growth. There is not much evidence of deliberate decisions to maintain moderate money growth; Chairman Martin did not favor overt control of money.

Romer and Romer (2002b) recognize that the Federal Reserve in the 1950s succeeded in keeping inflation low. They explain this success as the result of applying a well-developed theory of inflation to which it returned in the 1980s. However, the FOMC minutes and other Federal Reserve documents show no evidence that the Federal Reserve developed or systematically applied any explicit theory or framework in the 1950s. On the contrary, there is considerable evidence showing both a lack of agreement about how monetary policy worked and disinterest in developing a more complete understanding. Later, when Governor Sherman Maisel pushed hard for more systematic procedures, the Committee on the Directive that he chaired recognized explicitly the absence of agreement on basic features of the relation between Federal Reserve actions and goals.[342]

An alternative explanation seems more consistent with what the Martin Federal Reserve said and did in the 1950s and why it did not repeat its actions after 1965. Martin and many others believed that budget deficits caused inflation. During the Truman and Eisenhower administrations budget deficits did not persist. Surpluses in 1956, 1957, and 1960 meant that the Federal Reserve had fewer occasions when it felt obliged to

342. This comment and others like it should not suggest that effective monetary policy requires a fully specified model of the economy and its interaction with the world. Rules of thumb such as inflation targeting, a Taylor rule, a monetary base rule, or a Friedman rule may be adequate.

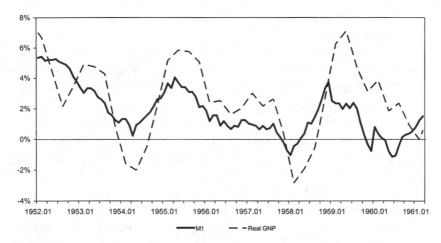

Chart 2.15. Twelve-month moving average of M_1 growth and four-quarter moving average of real GNP growth, 1952:1–1961:1.

support Treasury operations. Base money growth remained low, and the Federal Reserve could slow inflation without raising short-term interest rates above 4 percent. The Johnson administration ran persistent budget deficits: many more periods of even keel not only reduced the time available for restricting growth of reserves and money but required additional reserve injections. Also, nominal interest rates rose with inflation, misleading Federal Reserve officials about the degree of restraint. Chapter 4 develops this alternative.

Although FOMC members did not agree on how monetary policy affected economic activity and inflation, the staff at times showed a sophisticated understanding of the role of anticipations. Their discussion of the transmission process recognized the effects of monetary actions on relative prices and capital values. These statements were far ahead of most academic economic analyses at the time.

Chart 2.15 suggests that trends in money and real GNP were often in the same direction and of similar magnitude, despite frequent, large, short-term changes in monetary velocity. The chart shows that typically money growth was procyclical, rising in periods of economic expansion and falling when output or its growth rate fell. Procyclical monetary policy was a standard feature of policy under a gold standard and for much the same reason: monetary policy restricted interest rate increases during expansions, thereby permitting inflation to increase. In economic contractions, money growth declined. Under the gold standard, the delay reflected the movement of gold. In the 1950s, discretionary actions could have changed the timing of interest rate changes, for example by responding to changes in money growth. However, the Federal Reserve ignored cyclical changes in money growth.

Several features of the Federal Reserve's approach contributed to the neglect of money growth when implementing policy action. First, the FOMC and the staff did not have a systematic way of relating the actions they took in the money market to the longer-term objectives that they often embraced in speeches. The committee met every three weeks soon after Martin took control, and it issued a directive to the manager to guide his actions until the next meeting. There are few mentions of lags between policy actions and their effects or setting an objective to be achieved over time. Occasionally someone suggested that some of the observed changes were transitory and would reverse, but the distinction between persistent and transitory changes rarely affected actions at the time or later. Second, neither the manager nor the committee had developed a systematic way of influencing money growth or goal variables such as prices and output. Operations were more a matter of guess or judgment and trial and error. Third, the Treasury came to market frequently. The Federal Reserve adopted even keel policies from two weeks before to two weeks after Treasury sales. During even keel, it did not implement policy changes; it kept interest rates within a narrow band. Often it had to supply reserves to maintain the even keel, so policy operations yielded to Treasury operations with loss of independence. On two occasions, the FOMC bought long-term issues or new issues to support the Treasury's operation. The reserves they supplied under even keel remained in the market to support a larger money stock. This was a smaller problem in the 1950s than after 1965, when budget deficits rose and even keel became more frequent. Fourth, average money growth remained low after 1954, as Chart 2.15 shows. The Federal Reserve explained the reason for low money growth as an adjustment of cash balances after wartime growth. Although probably correct, the staff did not offer evidence to support this claim. Fifth, money growth and free reserves were not closely related in this as in other periods. Sometimes the two moved in opposite directions as in 1953–54, sometimes in the same direction as in 1958. Control of free reserves did not imply monetary base control. Chart 2.16 shows that from 1954 to 1960, monetary base growth remained low; the compound average growth rate was less than 1 percent a year and, as the chart shows, base growth was rarely above a 2 percent annual rate and not persistently so.[343] Sixth, meeting every three weeks

343. Base growth is based on the Rasche-Anderson (St. Louis) data including adjustment for changes in reserve requirement ratios. Note that base growth declined before each of the recessions.

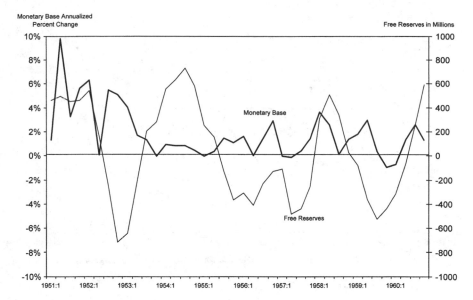

Chart 2.16. Free reserves and monetary base growth 1951–60.

focused attention on short-term changes. Members could wait for another meeting to act. Since there was no agreed framework for interpreting data, action or decisions waited for evidence of inflation or recession. Martin or the Board's staff might predict inflation but Hayes would urge delay.

One of the principal arguments against monetary control was that monetary or base velocity was highly volatile in the short-run. Chart 2.17 shows growth of average cash balance per unit of income, the reciprocal of base velocity growth, at three frequencies. Monthly and annual data show considerable variability. By 1955, the three-year moving average of base velocity growth became more stable although fluctuations continued.

The Federal Reserve under Martin, and Martin himself, wanted to maintain stable prices. In part he believed that low inflation contributed to growth. This view did not gain wide acceptance at the time, but President Eisenhower shared it. By the standards of the 1960s and 1970s, the System did well. Martin often said that the Federal Reserve was the only institution willing to act against inflation. His concern was the budget deficit and the pressure on the Federal Reserve to finance it.

His concern was often overstated. The Eisenhower administration, especially the president and Treasury Secretaries Humphrey and Anderson, also believed that deficit spending was inflationary. The government ran a large deficit in 1959, a result of the 1958 recession, but it closed the deficit quickly at a time when monetary policy tightened, bringing on the

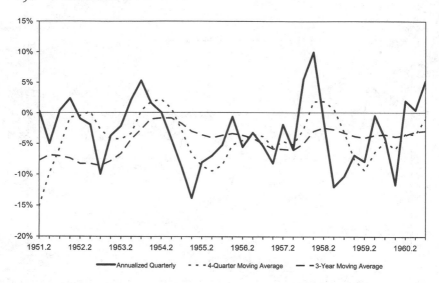

Chart 2.17. Base growth minus nominal GDP growth, 1951:2–1960:4.

1960–61 recession. And the Eisenhower administration achieved a budget surplus in three of its eight years in office. Almost forty years would pass before the Clinton administration would improve on the budget performance. Inflation rose and later fell in periods with sizeable deficits relative to GDP.

The presence of a large outstanding debt was a major difference between the 1920s and the 1950s. At first, many economists claimed that the debt reduced the role of monetary policy. Any change in interest rates would have a magnified effect on the price of long-term debt and, thus, on the wealth of debt owners. This argument can be found as late as 1959 in modified form in the *Staff Report on Employment, Growth, and Price Levels,* where the authors argue that "the growth of the public debt, increased efficiency of the Government securities market, and the expanded role of sophisticated financial institutions have reduced . . . the effectiveness of monetary policy" (Joint Economic Committee, 1959a, 345)[344]

344. A representative Federal Reserve statement describing the views held in the 1940s and 1950s is in Clarke (1970, 5). Higher interest rates "may have brought about grave disturbances in the market for government securities, with damaging repercussions upon our entire financial mechanism as well as serious economic effects upon public confidence in the Government's credit." Total gross debt rose from $270 to $285 billion between 1946 and 1959, but publicly held marketable debt declined from $161 to $148 billion. As a share of GNP, publicly held debt fell from 87 percent to 44 percent. The claim about reduced effectiveness of monetary action was repeated in almost every expansion and contraction for the next forty years. The reason changed. Among the reasons cited have been intermediation, euro-dollars, sophisticated financial instruments, declining relative size of banks, etc.

At the Federal Reserve the opposite argument gained adherents (Roosa, 1951). The existence of a large debt freed the financial system from reliance on the call money market.[345] There was now a market in which the Federal Reserve could affect bank reserves without concern about the size of its operations or not having securities to sell in the event of a gold inflow or a surge in member bank borrowing. Also, the large debt held by the reserve banks removed concerns about reserve bank earnings. All reserve banks shared in the earnings on the open market account and together returned 90 percent of their earnings to the Treasury.

Soon after Martin became chairman, he proposed that, except in the unusual circumstance of a disorderly market, all open market purchases and sales would take place at the short end of the maturity structure. The reasons for the policy included reduced discretion for the manager and the New York bank, but the main purposes were to develop an active private market for long-term debt and end support of a rigid interest rate structure. Martin and Riefler argued that, without bills-only policy, market participants would depend on Federal Reserve intervention to stabilize the market and would expect the Federal Reserve to support new issues if their prices declined. It would be difficult to prevent a return to pegged or controlled long-term rates, with a resulting loss of independence and nullification of the Accord. Their solution was to deal in bills only.

New York opposed the proposal when it first appeared in 1953 and forever after. Most economists who discussed the issue sided with New York, and many members of Congress, including Senator Paul Douglas and Congressman Wright Patman, blamed bills-only for the rise in interest rates during the 1950s.

Martin and the Board's staff had the better economic arguments, but they could not meet the political arguments, especially because long-term rates increased with economic growth and modest inflation. The Federal Reserve had claimed initially that bills-only would strengthen the long-term market, but they had difficulty producing evidence to support the claim, and they did not offer an alternative explanation of the rise in interest rates. Most critics dismissed the fact that, in eight years, the Federal Reserve had to intervene only twice to prevent disorderly long-term markets.

Bills-only was part of Martin's effort to reestablish the independence that the Federal Reserve had lost in the 1930s and 1940s. He succeeded in this aspect during the 1950s. The market for long-term debt absorbed the debt that the Treasury sold without direct support by the Federal Reserve.[346]

---

345. The call money market post at the New York Stock Exchange closed.

346. Direct support meant Federal Reserve purchases of the new issue or "when issued"

The political cost was high. Influential members of Congress blamed the bills-only policy for the rise in long-term rates. The 1960 election brought in an administration staffed with many opponents of the policy. The Federal Reserve ended bills-only shortly after that election. Like most central banks, it continued to operate mainly in the short-term market.

The quarrel over bills-only, and its outcome, suggests some of the complexity attached to "independence." Independence in the 1950s was much different than in the 1920s. Congress held frequent, at times lengthy, oversight hearings at which Martin and others explained and defended decisions and actions. Rumors or evidence of differences between the New York bank and the Board was a call to action by congressional committees followed by a request for Martin, other FOMC members, and outsiders to explain and comment. The Federal Reserve learned that congressional oversight had become, and was likely to remain, a significant means for interested members of Congress to exert much greater political pressure than in the early years. Equally, Federal Reserve statements at public hearings became a more important means of presenting the Federal Reserve's interpretations and positions to Congress and the public, opening the System to criticism but providing information to the interested public and removing some of the earlier secrecy.

Relations with the administration changed also. Gone was the reluctance to question or influence the Federal Reserve, best represented by the apology for asking advice in President Hoover's letters to the Board, when the financial system was under intense strain in February 1933. Commitment to the Employment Act meant to many that monetary and fiscal policy should be coordinated. To Keynesian economists at that time, coordination meant that the Federal Reserve should keep interest rates unchanged to permit fiscal policy actions to have their full effect. The precise meaning of coordination was rarely made clear, but the idea resonated with politicians and some of their advisers.[347] Martin did not oppose coordination, but tried to limit its scope. In keeping with his responsibility, he placed greater weight on price stability. But neither he nor his staff considered how to reconcile independence and coordination with the government's

---

securities. As noted, the Federal Reserve gave indirect support through its even keel policy. Under this policy, the Federal Reserve could, and often did, supply additions to reserves equal to the size of the issue times the average reserve requirement ratio (0.18) times the banks' share of bond purchases.

347. "He [Martin] carried out those responsibilities always on the basis of open discussion and conference with the Council, with the President, and with Treasury. I know of no time when there was any feeling that our interests were in conflict here. True, you could have differences in judgment. . . . Now, do you need common goals? Well, I have testified repeatedly against that" (Raymond Saulnier in Hargrove and Morley, 1984, 157).

fiscal operations. To insulate the Board and the FOMC, Martin acted as a buffer by meeting with the president or his agents, keeping other members informed but avoiding pressure on them.

By the end of the Eisenhower administration, the pattern of coordination for the next decade was in place. Martin held meetings with the president and his advisers, weekly breakfasts or luncheons with the Secretary of the Treasury, and regular meetings with the Council of Economic Advisers. He advised the administration in advance of major changes, for example, by clearing a change in regulation Q with the Secretary on the grounds that it affected the Treasury's savings bond sales. And the Federal Reserve continued to discuss bond issues with the Treasury, although the FOMC ceased advising the Treasury on what it should sell.

Independence no longer excluded consultations and exchange of information. Martin's interpretation of the 1951 Accord went further. He, and most others in the System, believed that the Federal Reserve had a responsibility to assure that Treasury bond issues did not fail. He reasoned that Congress voted the budget that the Treasury had to finance. The Federal Reserve had an obligation to help make the issues succeed in the market, provided the Treasury priced its issues at market rates. It should not refuse to accept the fiscal decision or refuse to assist in financing. Help took two forms: preventing failure of new issues and refundings, and maintaining even keel policy during Treasury operations. Even keel meant that the Federal Reserve supplied enough reserves to permit banks to purchase their share of the issue. This seems a narrow meaning of independence. When budget deficits became large and frequent, independence was severely restricted.

Thus, in the 1950s, independence came to mean that the Federal Reserve could raise interest rates as much as its judgment or analysis required to control inflation if private sector demand expanded. But it limited the increase when the Treasury made large demands on the market. It expected, or hoped, that the Treasury would price its offerings consistent with market anticipations, and usually the Treasury did. But if the Treasury erred, the Federal Reserve would help by buying bills and supplying reserves under bills-only and buying the issue if it judged that the market became "disorderly."[348] Usually, it did not later sell the debt to reduce reserves and money.

Martin borrowed a phrase from Allan Sproul of the New York bank to

348. The minutes suggest that "disorderly" meant that there were few or no bids in the market so that a decline in bond prices induced more supply and additional price decline instead of increasing quantity demanded.

describe the Federal Reserve's role. It was independent within the administration, not independent of the administration. In practice this meant that it was no less responsible for debt management after the Accord than before. The chief difference was that it was not bound to a specific level of interest rates. It could change rates when the Treasury was not in the market or about to enter. But there were often political pressures coming from the administration and Congress when interest rates rose.

But it is also true that the Keynesian analyses of that period gave a modest role to interest rate changes. This was called "elasticity pessimism"; investment was not expected to respond much to interest rate changes.

Soon a new problem appeared. Commitment to discussion and coordination became more problematic when the administration changed. Officials of the Kennedy and Johnson administrations interpreted coordination as support for their fiscal policies. They wanted to use coordination as a way to influence or control monetary policy. In the 1920s, the Federal Reserve limited international policy coordination to periods and operations that would not cause inflation. It was not able to do the same for domestic coordination in the 1960s.

Faced with these explicit and implicit restrictions, it is not surprising that Federal Reserve officials inveighed against deficit spending. No wonder, then, that they believed, and repeated frequently, that monetary policy *alone* could not prevent inflation. No wonder that the Federal Reserve later failed to prevent inflation. It had sacrificed too much of its independence.

The Federal Reserve was much more concerned about congressional oversight in the 1950s than in the 1920s. For example, it wanted its Annual Reports to show that it responded promptly to rising unemployment, as called for by the Employment Act. It chose the wording of its instructions to the manager with an eye on how they would look when the report appeared. Indeed, the committee at times gave more attention to issues of this kind than to the instruction it gave the manager.

Resumption of policy action reopened old antagonisms. The Board and its staff had been in frequent conflict with the reserve banks, especially New York. In the 1920s, the New York bank, led by Benjamin Strong, dominated decisions. New Deal legislation strengthened the Board's role and weakened New York's, but conflict remained.

Martin reshaped the organization, centralizing control in Washington and weakening New York, though it retained its influence and role as fiscal agent of the Treasury. He terminated the FOMC's Executive Committee, where New York dominated, and he increased the number of FOMC meetings from four a year to sixteen or seventeen, one every three weeks. He expected all members to participate actively at FOMC and to state opinions. New York's voice became one among many, although it had more market information and generally spoke before the others. Further, he encouraged, and at times required, discussion of all policy operations, curbing the legal arrangement that put responsibility for proposing discount rates in the reserve banks and responsibility for regulation Q or reserve requirement changes in the Board. The formal structure remained; the operating procedures changed. This, too, weakened the reserve banks by giving the Board a larger voice in discount policy.

The Federal Reserve staff responded rapidly to events in the economy. It recognized quickly the end of expansions and recessions. The FOMC or the Board reversed policy promptly. Although the staff under Riefler did not forecast, their judgments at times proved accurate. As in Brunner and Meltzer (1964), the problem was the reliance on free reserves to judge the policy thrust and the weak relation between changes in free reserves and economic activity or inflation. See also Romer and Romer (1994).

Martin described himself as a "market man." He had little interest in economic theories or analysis of how the changes that the FOMC initiated reached beyond the money market to prices, employment, or exchange rates. Nor did he form a consistent view of how the Federal Reserve could operate best to achieve its objectives. At times, the Federal Reserve changed the discount rate frequently; at other times, it relied mainly on reserve requirement changes or open market operations. Since both Martin and the FOMC were atheoretical, the Federal Reserve did not have a single measure or set of measures by which it judged what had happened or specified what should happen. Free reserves, borrowing, interest rates, color, tone and feel all had their turn. The connection between these measures and more distant goals remained unclear. Martin made no effort to clarify these issues and was uninterested when others tried. On the other hand, Martin avoided the bad advice that economic models of the period urged on the FOMC.

Martin had long-term objectives. He always favored price stability, the $35 gold price and fixed exchange rates, and well-functioning private markets for Treasury debt that operated with little direct intervention by the Federal Reserve. His problem was not uncertainty about his objectives, it was lack of clarity about how the System's actions connected (eventually) to those objectives.

Martin was a patient man who encouraged collective decision making. If other FOMC members did not share his view, only rarely did he speak first to tell them what he wanted the FOMC to do. He would often wait several meetings until a majority agreed with him. Similarly, he tried for several years to get Congress to approve a new Bank Holding Company Act before he succeeded in 1956. He managed also to get Congress to approve counting vault cash as part of required reserves, despite many criticisms of prior reductions in reserve requirement ratios.

The 1950s were the second (after the 1920s) most successful decade that the Federal Reserve had up to that time. Unlike the 1920s, the decade ended with a mild recession, not a major depression. The end of the Korean War brought a recession without postwar deflation. Nevertheless, the Federal Reserve received much criticism, especially criticism from Congress, about three recessions in seven years. Growing balance of payments deficits raised concerns about the "competitiveness" of U.S. industry and the durability of the $35 per ounce gold price.

Martin's successful revitalization and reorganization of the Federal Reserve notwithstanding, the Federal Reserve carried over into the 1960s three issues that would return many times. First was the balance of payments deficit and the viability of the fixed exchange rate system. The Federal Reserve left international policy to the Treasury. Second, problems with regulation Q ceilings rose and fell with market interest rates. The Federal Reserve had not agreed on how to avoid the monetary effects of shifts of deposits to less regulated institutions, when ceiling rates constrained some member banks. Third, the System had not developed an adequate framework for achieving sustained growth without inflation. These problems began in the 1950s but became more acute after the middle of the next decade.

APPENDIX TO CHAPTER 2

Chart 2A.1 shows the relation between the monetary base and its principal sources and the interrelation of the sources. Estimates come from a four-variable vector autoregression using the following order: discounts, gold, base, government securities held by the Federal reserve banks. Data are monthly from July 1951 to December 1960. Estimates are based on 2 lags, 11 seasonal dummy variables, and a constant.

The chart offers a statistical analysis of the policy actions discussed in the text. It repeats for the 1950s the relations shown in the appendix to volume 1, chapter 4 for the 1920s. All of the diagonal elements show the same sign and generally the same configuration in both periods. The negative response of gold to government securities and government securities to discounts are the only statistically significant off-diagonal associations that remain the same in the two periods. Open market purchases induced gold outflow; the Federal Reserve offset the brief aggregate effect of discounting by open market operations. Both responses are consistent with interest rate smoothing.

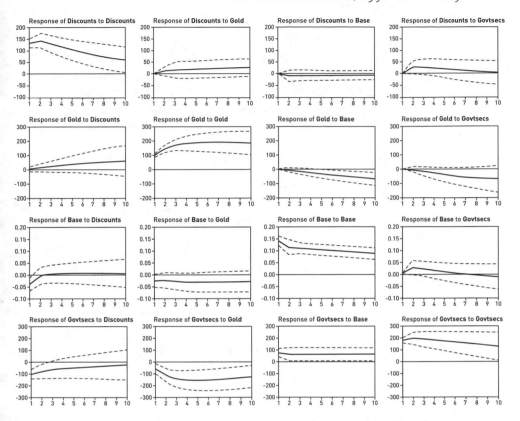

Chart 2.A1. Based on VAR with 2 lags and 11 seasonal dummies. Monthly, July 1951–December 1960.

Four signs change. First, the response of the base to gold is negative in the 1950s and positive, after a lag, in the 1920s. The positive response is expected under the 1920s gold standard, although the Federal Reserve did not always follow the rules. Under the Bretton Woods system, the Federal Reserve offset all but a small initial effect of gold on the base. Second, for the same reason, the response of government securities to gold shows that the Federal Reserve completely sterilized gold movements in the 1950s but not in the 1920s. Third, in the 1950s the Federal Reserve changed the base by purchasing government securities to set free reserves. In Chart 2A.1 the monetary base rises in step with the stock of government securities. Fourth, the response of the base to discounts is significantly negative initially in the 1950s and positive in the 1920s. This reflects the manager's smoothing operations.

The chart shows also that gold outflows followed increases in the monetary base and conversely. Monetary expansion had a significant effect on the gold loss in the 1950s. Much of this reflects the substitution of domestic for foreign sources. This effect is not significant in the 1920s, where the computed response is zero. As in the 1920s, discounts have a brief significant negative effect on the base. In the 1920s, the Federal Reserve countered changes in discounts by changing government securities.

Operating on a free reserve or interest rate target, the Federal Reserve offset discounts and gold movements by changing government securities. The last row of Chart 2.A1 shows these responses. The policy of controlling free reserves surrendered control of the base to the market.

THREE

The Early Keynesian Era:
A Low-Inflation Interlude, 1961–65

*They don't really know what the money supply is now, even today. They print some figures . . .
but a lot of it is just about superstition.*
—William McChesney Martin Jr. (1985)

The 1960s started and ended with the economy in recession. In between, the country had almost nine years of growth, the longest sustained economic expansion up to that time. Industrial production rose 6.4 percent and real GNP 4.3 percent compound average rates. Real per capita consumption increased more than 30 percent. Annualized increases in consumer prices remained below 1.5 percent until the middle of 1965. After five years of recovery, growth, and low inflation, inflation reached 5.5 percent in 1969. The Great Inflation was under way, sustained by rapid money growth to finance the government budget and pay for the Great Society and the war in Vietnam.

This chapter and the next two are a bloc. They discuss the long expansion, the emerging and rising inflation that culminated in peacetime wage and price controls and the August 1971 decision to end convertibility of the dollar into gold. Although not intended to end the Bretton Woods system of fixed exchange rates permanently, efforts at restoration failed. In retrospect, the major policy changes that President Nixon announced at that time ended an era.

The years 1961–71 were a part of the Keynesian interlude dominated by a strong belief that government was responsible for stabilizing an unruly private sector. The distinguishing characteristics were two related beliefs: (1) that policymakers could adjust their actions in a timely way to smooth fluctuations, and achieve full employment with high growth and low inflation, and (2) that policymakers could choose and achieve the right, possibly optimal, combination of inflation and full employment. Keynesian economists called their program "the new economics" to signify the departure from prevailing orthodoxies. They did not concern themselves with the way their prescriptions would work in a political system.

The new economics was not an issue in the 1960 election, but economic growth was. The Democrats criticized the Eisenhower administration's record, three recessions in eight years, and a 2.5 percent growth rate during its term in office.[1] Their platform promised to "put an end to the present high-interest, tight-money policy" (quoted in Kettl, 1986, 97) and to double the growth rate to 5 percent, increase social security payments, raise the minimum wage to $1.25 per hour, and increase housing starts to two million a year using government loans if needed.[2]

When the new administration took office in late January 1961, the unemployment rate was close to 7 percent, near the upper limit of postwar experience to that time. Although the recession soon ended, the unemployment rate lagged behind. In office, the new administration made a determined effort to apply Keynesian economic policies including the relatively new Phillips curve, relating inflation and unemployment.[3] As understood at the time, the Phillips curve implied incorrectly that policy could permanently reduce unemployment by increasing inflation. Instead of aiming for price stability, the government would choose where to set the tradeoff.

1. Per capita GNP from 1956 to 1960 (in 1954 prices) rose 0.6 percent for the United States compared to the following per capita growth rates: Italy, 6.0; Germany, 4.4; France, 3.0; United Kingdom, 1.9 (Knipe, 1965, 149). The comparison suggests one main reason for rising foreign investment by U.S. companies. Soviet growth was also a concern. Stein (1988, 90–92) discusses the campaign's economic issues.

2. The best year for housing in the 1960s was 1963, with 1.6 million starts. Real GDP growth reached 5 percent or more in four years, 1962 and 1964–66. The first of these was a year of recovery. Congressman Reuss later said: "Democrats generally have been quite critical of the Federal Reserve System's performance in the second half of the fifties, and we made a great campaign issue" (Subcommittee on Domestic Finance, 1964, 1206).

3. The Phillips curve was an empirical relation with no formal foundation, but it had great appeal and moved with remarkable speed from the economic journals to the policy process. Samuelson and Solow (1960) estimated the Phillips curve on data for the United States. Both worked with the new administration before the election and in its early years, Samuelson as an informal, personal adviser to President Kennedy and Solow as a senior staff member at the Council of Economic Advisers. Their paper contained a phrase about the relation of inflation to unemployment that they and others chose to ignore: "A first look at the scatter is discouraging; there are points all over the place" (ibid., 188). They recognized, however, that the shape of the curve, hence the tradeoff, depended on the policies pursued. Almost all discussion ignored the fact that most of the data which Phillips used came when the gold standard tied down expected inflation.

The administration soon proposed faster depreciation schedules to increase investment and later reductions in business and personal tax rates as a conscious effort to create a budget deficit to stimulate the economy. During the campaign, John F. Kennedy and his economic advisers promised to end the restrictive monetary policies, especially bills-only, that Democrats had criticized through most of the 1950s. The new presidential advisers wanted closer coordination of monetary and fiscal actions. Some had expressed publicly their desire to replace Martin as chairman of the Board of Governors. Walter Heller, soon to be chairman of the Council of Economic Advisers, spoke to Martin a week before the inauguration. He found Martin "cooperative, open-minded and cordial. He obviously had no intention of resigning" (Oral History Interview, 1964, Heller, August 1 and 2, 186).[4] To show that he intended to cooperate with the new administration, he proposed regular luncheons with the Council of Economic Advisers every two or three weeks (ibid., 186).[5]

The main events of the 1960s that dominated politics and monetary policy were the Vietnam War and the expansion of the welfare state. The last half of the 1960s was a time of major social change. President Lyndon B. Johnson succeeded in passing the landmark "Great Society" legislation that reversed the government's role from enforcing racial laws and restrictions to enforcing equality before the law and, later, giving preference in hiring to groups that had suffered from discrimination. The Great Society

4. The oral history interview took place at Fort Ritchie, Maryland. Heller and other participants read from or used notes and memos made at the time of the event. Paul Samuelson explained that "Kennedy himself was a very cautious temperament and I couldn't imagine him having a showdown on an issue like this [firing Martin]" (letter, Paul A. Samuelson to the author, January 24, 2001). As noted in Chapter 2, Martin considered resigning but did not complete the letter.

5. Martin took up the issue of resigning again at a meeting in 1961 with James Tobin and Walter Heller. He explained that he was a registered Democrat and had voted for Stevenson in 1952. Since coming to the Federal Reserve, he had remained out of politics. In a reference to a January 1961 article by Tobin very critical of Federal Reserve policy, he explained also that he had seen stories in the press that said the new administration wanted him to go. He had been appointed by President Truman. He had offered to resign in 1953 when President Eisenhower took office, but he was asked to stay. "During the [1960] campaign monetary policy was an issue, with the Democrats criticizing tight money. For these reasons Martin felt that a matter of principle was involved, and he decided he should not offer his resignation to President Kennedy" (memo, Tobin to Files, Luncheon Conversation with Chairman William McC. Martin, Heller papers, May 30, 1961, 1). Looking back, Heller said the relation between Martin and the principals in the Treasury, Council, Budget Bureau, and the president was harmonious. He recognized, however, that coordination did not work as he had hoped. He had less influence than he wished. "The Treasury captured . . . control of monetary policy to a very considerable extent by the relationships between [Douglas] Dillon and Roosa on the one hand and Martin on the other" (Oral History Interview, 1964, Heller, August 2, 329). This changed after Dillon resigned.

also initiated and expanded programs in health, education, and welfare that redistributed income, increased social spending, and brought the welfare state to the United States.

Between 1960 and 1970 government outlays doubled in nominal terms and rose 50 percent in real terms. All of the increase in defense expenditure came after the middle of the decade. Its increase, $30 billion between 1962 and 1969, was 60 percent of 1962 expenditure. Spending for education and health and human services other than social security increased five- or sixfold.[6]

President Johnson did not want to choose between war and social programs. In his words, "I was determined to be a leader of war and a leader of peace. I refused to let my critics push me into choosing one or the other. I wanted both" (Goodwin, 1991, 283). Believing that Congress would reduce spending for social programs if he proposed a tax increase, Johnson was slow to raise tax rates to pay for the spending programs and, for a time, hid the true rise in defense spending to mislead the public, Congress, and the Federal Reserve.[7] Budget deficits increased the debt held by the public. Federal Reserve holdings more than doubled.

Financing the war and the president's Great Society by increasing money growth created inflation. Under the Bretton Woods system, foreigners could choose to share the inflation or revalue their currencies. Almost all chose inflation. Although many governments grumbled about "imported inflation," only Germany and the Netherlands agreed to revalue their currencies to reduce the dollar inflow, and their changes were relatively small.

The first half of the decade in the United States was a period of recovery and rapid growth with low inflation. The administration worried about gold losses and the continued international payments deficit, in part a result of strong productivity growth and a high level of employment that pulled in imports, in part a result of foreign loans, grants, and defense spending. In the second half, the problems became more serious. Productivity growth declined after 1965, spending for the Vietnam War and budget deficits increased, inflation rose, and the international payments deficit continued. At first the administration relied on selective controls and ad hoc measures

6. Adjusted for inflation, defense and war expenditures in 1968 were larger than in any year of the defense buildup in the 1980s.

7. Stockwell (1989, 37) wrote: "For both strategic and political reasons, however, this escalation was kept a closely held secret. Along with numerous other government offices, the Federal Reserve was given no information on this buildup [1965] or its likely economic impact." President Johnson apparently believed policy coordination should go one way only. Chairman Martin learned about the 1965 increase independently.

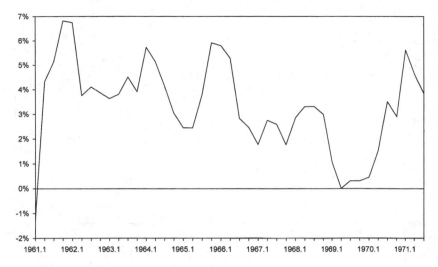

Chart 3.1. Output per hour, business sector, 1961–71. Measured year over year.

to manage the gold loss. Later it avoided gold sales by restricting sales to other than foreign official holders and discouraging purchases by foreign governments and central banks.[8]

Chart 3.1 shows the decline in productivity growth in the business sector beginning in 1966. Productivity rose at a compound annual rate of 4.45 percent from 1961 to second quarter 1966 and 2.40 percent for the remaining quarters. These growth rates include both cyclical and structural changes, so they may overstate the magnitude of the slowdown, but there is no mistaking the change in trend. As always, observers could not at first distinguish between persistent and transitory change. In fact, there was no way to know how long the slowdown would persist, but its persistence presented a problem for monetary policy just at the time that government spending and budget deficits increased markedly. Failure to recognize the persistent reduction in productivity growth was one of the reasons for the major policy errors of the period.

Federal Reserve actions raised the growth rate of the monetary base during the decade from a 4.3 percent average for the first four years to 6.0 percent for 1964 to 1968. By mid-1971 base growth had increased to 7 percent or more. With increased money growth and slower productivity growth, inflation began to rise. Increased money growth was a second

8. This chapter ends in 1965. To compare the earlier and later experience with Keynesian policies, charts in this introduction to the chapter cover the full 1961–71 period up to third quarter 1971.

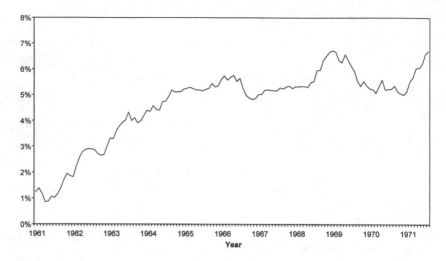

Chart 3.2. Monetary base, two-year moving average, 1961–71.

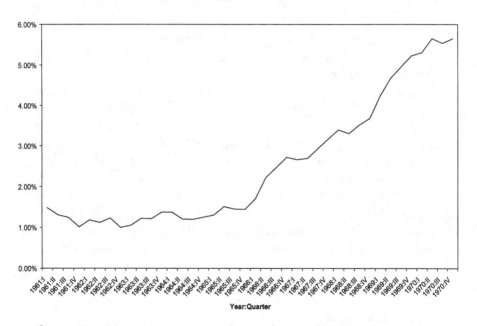

Chart 3.3. Two-year moving average quarterly CPI inflation, annualized, 1961–71.

policy error. By the end of the decade, the inflation rate reached 5 percent. The rise continued. Charts 3.2 and 3.3 show these data.

Chairman Martin disliked inflation and spoke against it forcefully. When he left office the annual rate of increase in consumer prices was 6 percent, a rate that he deplored. A puzzle of the 1960s is that Martin,

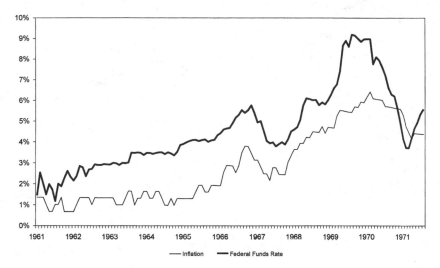

Chart 3.4. Federal funds rate and inflation, 1961–71.

who successfully resisted inflation in the 1950s, permitted and abetted the increase. A principal reason is that he accepted coordination with the administration's fiscal policy even to the point of increasing money growth and lowering interest rates after Congress passed the 1968 tax surcharge.

Policy coordination was the third policy error. Policy coordination and even keel policies permitted inflation to start. Reluctance in Congress, the administration, and the public to permit unemployment to rise made it impossible to reduce inflation permanently once it rose. Analytic mistakes played a role. Both the Federal Reserve and successive administrations professed, and most likely expected, that inflation could be stopped by slowing growth without a recession. After recessions started, policies shifted toward ease. The public soon recognized that inflation would persist.

The Federal Reserve was not passive. As the inflation rate rose, it raised its target for the federal funds rate and reduced free reserves. Chart 3.4 suggests that, after 1965, the difference between the federal funds rate and the maintained (or average) inflation rate narrowed, reducing the real interest rate. An exception was the relatively large increases in the funds rate in 1968–69 that soon reversed as the economy went into recession. The chart shows a major change in 1969–70; the inflation rate did not respond much to the recession, a result explained in part by the unanticipated decline in productivity growth. Reliance on free reserves or nominal interest rates as a measure of policy thrust proved to be a fourth policy error. The Federal Reserve relied mainly on free reserves to judge its policy. This proved to be a poor indicator of policy thrust.

Chart 3.5. Civilian unemployment rate, January 1971–December 1980.

The expanding economy lowered the unemployment rate to levels not seen since the Korean War and not repeated for more than a generation. By 1967, unemployment was half the rate when the new administration took office. Administration economists accepted inflation as the price of lower unemployment and regarded lower unemployment as a significant part of its welfare program. In the 1968 election campaign, President Nixon promised to reduce the inflation rate without causing a recession. This too was a policy error. His administration did not succeed, as Chart 3.5 shows.

Between 1960 and August 1971, gross federal debt increased more than 40 percent, and Federal Reserve holdings increased by $39.5 billion, 144 percent of their holdings at the end of 1960. These purchases were the main source of the increase in the monetary base. They more than offset the nearly $8 billion decline in the gold stock. Table 3.1 shows the stock of debt and its ownership on selected dates.

Between December 1969 and August 1971, foreign holdings of United States government debt doubled and redoubled, as foreign central banks and governments honored their obligations to maintain a fixed exchange rate with the dollar and avoided appreciation of their exchange rates. These purchases raised money growth and inflation abroad. Finally, on August 15, 1971, President Nixon ended the Bretton Woods system by announcing that the United States would no longer sell gold at $35 per ounce.

Table 3.1   Government Debt and Ownership, Selected Dates, 1960–71 (in $ billions)

DATE	GROSS FEDERAL DEBT	HELD BY FEDERAL RESERVE	HELD BY PRIVATE INVESTORS	HELD BY FOREIGNERS AND INTERNATIONAL INSTITUTIONS
December 1960	287.7	27.4	207.5	10.5
December 1969	367.4	57.2	221.2	10.4
December 1970	388.3	62.1	229.1	19.7
August 1971	413.8	66.9	239.6	41.9

Source: Board of Governors (1976, 1981).

This dramatic policy shift recognized formally what had been true for some time. Beginning in March 1968, the United States discouraged gold sales to foreign central banks, and refused sales to others. The United States' gold stock rose modestly for the next two years, but claims against the gold stock continued to rise. This policy enabled the Bretton Woods system to continue for more than three years after March 1968, but it survived only because most countries did not challenge the restriction on gold sales.

The weakness of the original Bretton Woods Agreement is suggested by its duration. If we start its effective operation when major currencies became convertible on current account at the end of 1958 and consider its effective end in 1968, when restrictions on United States' gold sales severely limited the dollar's convertibility into gold, the system lasted only ten years. And it had frequent crises in those years. Its overwhelming weakness was the commitment in many countries to a full-employment policy. The United States would not deflate and, with modest exceptions, surplus countries would not revalue. France favored devaluing the dollar by increasing the gold price, but the United States preferred revaluation by other countries. With memories of the 1930s in the minds of political leaders at home and abroad, no one in authority urged deflation.

The agreement was part of the problem. Britain, mindful of its prewar history, insisted on the right to pursue domestic policies of its own choosing and to devalue if these policies conflicted with its exchange rate. The British position became part of the agreement. In the Employment Act of 1946, the United States accepted an obligation to maintain "maximum employment." Other developed countries, either de facto or de jure, accepted full employment as a principal domestic policy goal. Each of these countries could devalue against gold, the dollar, and other currencies by claiming that its problem would persist. Some did just that.[9] United States policy

9. France, which seems never to have tired of criticizing U.S. policies, devalued its cur-

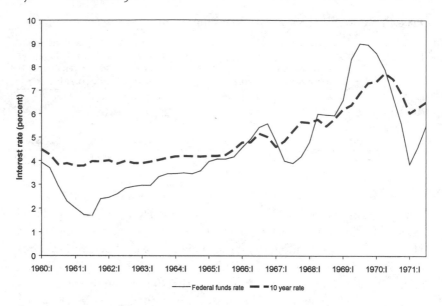

Chart 3.6. Long- and short-term interest rates, 1960:1–1971:3.

officials did not believe they had that option in practice. They considered that the only viable solutions were to: (1) encourage other countries, especially surplus countries, to revalue, (2) put controls on trade or capital flows, mainly the latter, or (3) tighten domestic policy without creating a substantial increase in unemployment. For foreign governments, the choices became revaluation or inflation. Mercantilist attitudes bolstered by concerns about employment ruled out revaluation.

At different times, the United States relied on each of its options. Only Germany and the Netherlands were willing to revalue, and their changes were small. The Johnson and Nixon administrations were reluctant to disinflate domestic prices, since that required slower growth and unemployment. Rising unemployment created demands for expansive policies. It did not take long for markets to recognize that any reductions in inflation and the payments deficit were temporary. By 1965, long-term market interest rates and other prices began to build in anticipations of continued inflation. Chart 3.6 shows the beginning of the rise in long-term interest rates in 1965 and the sustained increase from 1968 to 1970. Consumer prices rose 4 to 5 percent a year in the early 1970s. Recession reduced measured inflation in 1970, but the decline was modest and soon reversed.

---

rency several times. Usually the devaluation undervalued the franc, permitting expansive policies to increase output temporarily.

See Chart 3.3 above. Bondholders expected inflation to continue. Long before economists and policymakers, financial markets recognized that reductions in inflation were temporary, increases persistent. They were not always clear, however, about the distinction or about the degree to which observed changes were permanent or temporary.

President Kennedy and the members of his administration repeated often that they considered maintenance of the Bretton Woods system and the $35 gold price a high priority. Before taking office, Kennedy consulted widely including with President Eisenhower and Treasury Secretary Anderson about the reasons for the current account deficit.[10] President Johnson gave less emphasis to international economic policy. When a problem arose or became acute, he adopted a stopgap that hid or removed the immediate problem.[11] By 1969, when President Nixon took office, the positive balance on goods and services had fallen to $2 to $2.5 billion from $7 to $8 billion in 1964–65. The monetary gold stock was $10.9 billion, far less than foreigners' holdings of dollar claims and only marginally above the level at which professional opinion expected a run on gold that would end the system. Some advisers wanted to suspend gold payments and end the fixed exchange rate, but there was no agreement and, therefore, no action when the new administration took office.[12]

Governments and central banks devoted much time and effort to discussing how the system could be sustained. These efforts culminated in the creation of "special drawing rights," or SDRs, a paper currency intended to supplement the available stocks of gold and dollars as a means of making payments and settling claims between countries or their central banks. The rationale for SDRs was that they could substitute for gold as a means of settlement if central banks and governments agreed to use them. As usage rose, the international system would become less dependent on the supply of dollars and gold. This conjecture proved incorrect. SDRs never become a common means of settlement.

Diagnoses of the international monetary system generally recognized three problems, at the time called confidence, adjustment, and liquidity.

10. President Eisenhower attributed much of the problem to the United States' share of the cost of common defense. He described the European governments as free riders, unwilling to pick up "what seemed to us to be their fair share of the defense burden" (Ferrell, 1981, 382). Professor Paul Samuelson briefed President-elect Kennedy just after the election. After an hour, Kennedy said: "I was a lot happier an hour ago. But thanks for the briefing" (Samuelson, letter to the author, January 24, 2001).

11. These included the interest equalization tax and the voluntary credit restraint program discussed below.

12. Milton Friedman proposed a freely floating exchange rate, but other advisers did not agree. Author's conversation with Professor Friedman.

Confidence referred to the willingness to hold and receive dollars as a means of payment and dollar securities as a reserve, or store of value. Adjustment referred to the mechanism that would restore equilibrium to the payments system, for example by changing prices or real exchange rates to reflect permanent changes in relative position. Liquidity referred to the stock of available means of payment.

In several ways, the 1960s international monetary system repeated some mistakes of the 1920s. In both decades, central banks and governments did nothing to solve the adjustment problem. In the 1920s, after restoring convertibility and fixing the exchange rate, the French franc was undervalued and the British pound overvalued. To restore equilibrium at prevailing exchange rates, France and the United States had to inflate and Britain had to deflate. None of them would do as required. In the 1960s, the dollar and the pound had to depreciate to restore equilibrium, or Britain and the United States had to deflate. Neither country was willing to deflate prices, and the Kennedy and Johnson administrations would not devalue the dollar against gold and other currencies.[13] Again, as in the 1920s, the French government resented the central role of the dollar and the pound as key currencies. It began to convert its dollar and pound holdings into gold, just as it did after 1927.[14] In both periods, failure to solve the adjustment problem by realigning real exchange rates caused the breakdown that central banks and governments wanted to avoid.

The flaws of a gold exchange system, evident in the 1920s, returned in the 1960s. Each country had an interest in claiming gold in exchange for dollars. To weaken this claim, the United States had to either raise interest rates enough to maintain foreign dollar balances, appeal to other countries to cooperate to maintain the system by limiting gold outflows, or use capital controls. As in the 1920s, cooperation faced two problems: (1) national policies limited its extent; and (2) it did not go far enough to address the problem of real exchange rate misalignment.

A new problem arose in the Johnson administration. Policymakers in the United States were much less concerned about international coordination than coordination of domestic fiscal and monetary policies. They believed that domestic policy coordination could harmonize domestic and international concerns while maintaining high domestic employment and economic growth. Unlike the 1920s, the United States had to deflate rela-

---

13. Great Britain devalued the pound twice in the Bretton Woods years. The pound was a second reserve currency.

14. See volume 1, chapter 4. Jacques Rueff, an advocate of the gold standard, was an active policy adviser in both periods. France devalued in 1958 and 1969. Between 1961 and 1968 France bought $3.3 billion, half of the $6.7 billion that the U.S. sold.

tive to foreign countries. But foreign governments objected to the inflationary consequences of the U.S. policy mix for them, particularly after
escalation of the Vietnam conflict. As Undersecretary of State George Ball
predicted in 1962, international policy cooperation to maintain the fixed
exchange rate system and the $35 gold price would not survive "a situation
where we should become more heavily involved in Southeast Asia. . . . [O]ur
European friends would walk away from us . . . [saying] they don't want to
have any part of [financing] it" (Gold and the Dollar Crisis, Kennedy tapes,
Transcript, August 20, 1962, 8). Ball did not anticipate that the war would
raise pressures on the system by increasing the size of the dollar outflow,
especially in 1970–71.

A basic conflict underlay the failure of United States policy to sustain
the fixed exchange rate system. Congress gave two instructions. It ratified
the Bretton Woods Agreement, committing the United States to a fixed exchange rate and the policies to support it. But Congress soon afterward approved the Employment Act with a loose commitment to full employment
and stable prices or purchasing power. Policymakers did not discuss or
even mention the possibility that maintaining the fixed nominal exchange
rate might require deflation relative to foreigners if not absolute deflation.
No one mentioned that the price level adjusted (real) exchange rate would
have to be consistent with real rates of growth and price changes at home
and abroad or that these rates of change might require a temporary increase in unemployment to lower the domestic price level and restore the
equilibrium real exchange rate.

In practice, United States' policymakers put domestic concerns ahead
of international obligations. They told foreign governments and central
banks that they should revalue their currencies. Foreigners, in turn, urged
the United States to stop the flow of dollars that caused "imported inflation." This dialogue, sometimes called the "dialogue of the deaf," continued sporadically until the Bretton Woods system ended in 1971.[15]

The Federal Reserve responded to inflation by repeatedly raising the
federal funds rate and reducing free reserves. As Chart 3.4 above shows,
the increase in the interest rate was often less than the increase in the inflation rate. Taylor (1999) shows that this was true, on average, for the 1960s

15. There were many public and private meetings to discuss what could or should be
done. At one meeting in the Treasury, at which I was present, probably in 1970, Treasury
Secretary David Kennedy was briefed on the balance of payments and the dollar. The meeting lasted most of the day and Kennedy did not get a clear answer about what he should do.
Finally, he told the group that he would soon meet the European finance ministers, and they
would be sure to ask him what he planned to do. No one ventured an answer until Professor
Fritz Machlup said, "ask them what they would do." Kennedy's eyes lit up, and his expression
changed. "Yes, what would you do?" he said.

Table 3.2   Federal Funds Rate 1965–71 (%)

DATE DECEMBER	NOMINAL RATE	CPI INFLATION	REAL RATE
1965	4.17	1.44	2.73
1966	5.56	2.72	2.84
1967	4.17	3.17	1.00
1968	5.92	3.68	2.24
1969	8.94	5.23	3.71
1970	5.57	5.65	−0.08
1971*	5.47	4.92	0.55

*August
Source: Board of Governors (1976, 1981).

and 1970s.[16] Real interest rates declined or remained low, except in 1969. Table 3.2 shows December values for the nominal and ex post real federal funds rate. Although there are occasional comments to the contrary, in the 1960s and some subsequent years, the Board and the FOMC usually failed to distinguish between real and nominal rates. They described their policy as "tight money" and thought themselves bold for raising nominal interest rates as high as they did. This too repeated earlier experience.

Regulations enacted in the 1930s did not work well in the 1960s. Economic growth, rising inflation, and increased wealth and financial sophistication encouraged financial innovation both to increase opportunities and circumvent regulation. The Federal Reserve was slow to respond to the challenge. The Office of the Comptroller of the Currency, in the Treasury Department, endorsed or encouraged reforms by the national banks that it supervised, forcing attention to regulatory changes at the Federal Reserve and other agencies. But interest rate regulation, regulation Q, remained, and its effects on allocation of financial assets began the process that culminated in the massive losses by the savings and loan insurance systems in the 1980s.

The 1960s saw growing professionalization of monetary policy. Economists assumed a larger role, not just as staff members but as Board members and reserve bank presidents. The main factors driving professionalization were the increased demands that governments and the public placed on economic policy, the growing sophistication of financial services and economic analysis, the widespread use of these services, and the frequent crises in the international monetary system. Not to be overlooked

16. Orphanides (2001) challenged Taylor's finding and showed that the marginal response of the federal funds rate to inflation remained about the same, and about 1.5, throughout the Great Inflation.

was the presence of a new generation of economists who had developed Keynesian economics and were eager to use their tools to improve the country's economic performance. President Kennedy brought them into his government, and gradually they or their students rose to positions of influence in the government and the Federal Reserve System.

The Great Inflation caused a significant loss in economic well being. The conclusion to the chapter considers why inflation started and how the Federal Reserve contributed to its start.

KEYNESIAN POLICIES

In 1960, economic policy did not have an explicit framework relating policy decisions or actions to output, prices, balance of payments, and the like. The Employment Act and the Bretton Woods Agreement stated policy goals but did not connect these goals to each other or to policy operations.

Truman administration economists relied mainly on controls and regulation, and the president favored a balanced budget even in wartime. Fiscal discipline and budget balance dominated fiscal discussions in the Eisenhower administration. The president's chief economic advisors, Arthur Burns and Raymond Saulnier, and President Eisenhower himself, favored modest counter-cyclical policy including budget deficits in recession offset by surpluses in prosperous periods. Both economists were pioneers of National Bureau methods of business cycle analysis, which they used in government. This framework tried to isolate statistical regularities based on history. It lacked formal, analytic structure and depended on stability of often tenuous bivariate associations, eschewing attempts to relate the associations to economic theory.

At the Federal Reserve, the only comprehensive efforts to develop a policy framework to that time came in the Board's 1923 Annual Report, in the writings of Winfield Riefler and W. Randolph Burgess, and in Benjamin Strong's speeches and testimony during the 1920s. Vestiges of these efforts remained. Important as they were at the time they were written, they had faded along with the real bills doctrine. They said nothing about the effect of policy actions on output, employment, or prices.[17]

The 1962 Economic Report of the President (Council of Economic Advisers, 1962) introduced a new policy framework based on the Keynesian economics of that time. The "new economics," as it was called, differed markedly from earlier approaches. It proposed activist, discretionary policies aimed not just at smoothing business cycles but at fostering economic

17. See volume 1, chapter 4 for discussion of the Riefler-Burgess framework, the real bills doctrine, and the Board's Tenth Annual Report.

growth.[18] With growth would come resources for reducing poverty, improving health care and education, expanding social programs, and redistributing income. President Kennedy's advisers persuaded him to reduce tax rates in part by explaining that he would eventually have more revenues to finance increased spending (Heller oral history, tape I, 24).

Emphasis on growth was not new. Arthur Burns had worked with a cabinet committee to develop strategies to increase the growth rate (Hargrove and Morley, 1984, 102–3). These efforts were not part of an overall policy plan or tied to the business cycle or a theory of economic policy. Burns did not have a numerical growth target, believing that the growth rate resulted from private decisions to save and invest that he could not forecast. The Democrats' 1960 platform proposed 5 percent growth as a target, although Heller doubted that economic potential could sustain that rate (Hargrove and Morley, 1984, 273–74).

Heller and his colleagues changed the Council and the policy process in several ways. Heller, especially, became a public advocate of the administration's programs. Unlike his predecessors, he appeared on television, gave public speeches, and testified in Congress to advocate administration programs. The Council developed models or frameworks that guided proposed actions and forecast their consequences, particularly fiscal actions. Their early proposals included a request that Congress grant the president limited, discretionary authority to spend for capital improvements and reduce individual tax rates temporarily "to meet the stabilization objectives of the Employment Act" (Council of Economic Advisers, 1962, 72–74). These proposals were bold. They asked Congress to replace some of its constitutional authority to decide spending and tax rates with a veto over presidential discretionary actions. Congress did not take up the proposals.

Discretionary fiscal policy was at the center of the Council's analysis. The 1962 Report introduced the full employment budget surplus as "a numerical measure of the expansionary or restrictive impact of a budget program on the economy" (ibid., 77). In a recession, the current budget might show a deficit, while the full employment budget showed a surplus. The report pointed out that, in this condition, the current deficit should be increased to stimulate growth and a return to full employment. The report used experience from 1958 to 1960 to illustrate the concept. The

18. Walter W. Heller (1966, 28) who served as chairman of the Council of Economic Advisers from 1961 to 1964, described the change in policy. "The patterns of professional thought and practice that prevailed in previous economic policy making had not given full scope to the concepts and techniques of modern economics. Policy thinking had been centered more on minimizing the fluctuations of the business cycle than on realizing the economy's great and growing potential."

Eisenhower administration permitted the deficit to increase during the 1958 recession. It rejected tax reduction during the recession because of its long-term budget effects, and it strove to eliminate the deficit once the recession ended. It succeeded in balancing the 1960 budget, but the economy was far from the 4 percent unemployment rate that the Kennedy advisers regarded as full employment. This, the report said, showed that fiscal policy was restrictive because the budget should reach balance at full employment, not before. The Kennedy advisers wanted to increase the current deficit to reduce "fiscal drag" on the economy.

"Built-in stabilizers" could be counted upon to increase spending and reduce tax collections when income declined or growth slowed, and conversely. This fiscal response was helpful but insufficient. Tax collections began to rise and the budget deficit declined as soon as the economy began to recover. "For these reasons, the task of economic stabilization cannot be left entirely to built-in stabilizers. Discretionary budget policy, e.g., changes in tax rates or expenditure programs is indispensable—sometimes to reinforce, sometimes to offset, the effects of the stabilizers" (ibid., 71).[19]

Monetary policy had to adapt flexibly to prevailing conditions and to fiscal policy. "There is, in principle, a variety of mixtures of fiscal and monetary policies which can accomplish a given stabilization objective.[20] Choice among them depends upon other objectives and constraints" (ibid., 85). As an example, the Council's report cited the balance of payments problem as a restriction on short-term interest rates and money growth during the 1960–61 recession. The reasoning was not obvious. The United States had more than $17.5 billion in gold. Gold that flowed out as interest rates fell relative to foreign rates in recession would return when interest rose in the subsequent expansion, if policy avoided inflation.

Coordination of fiscal and monetary actions under administration guidance diminished Federal Reserve independence. In general, the report treated discretionary choice of monetary policy as similar to fiscal policy. Interest rates declined in recession and rose in expansions without policy action. "Being automatic stabilizers, they can only moderate unfavorable developments; they cannot prevent or reverse them.... Discretionary policy is essential, sometimes to reinforce, sometimes to mitigate or overcome,

19. Heller (1966, 68–69) lists three significant policy changes. "It became more activist and bolder ..., [policy] has to rely less on the automatic stabilizers and more on discretionary action ... less on rules and more on men ..., [and] not only monetary policy but fiscal policy has to be put on constant, rather than intermittent alert."

20. Mundell (1962) formalized the "assignment problem" that fit well with the new Keynesian idea. Soon the Council assigned fiscal policy to domestic expansion and monetary policy to control of the international payments deficit under fixed exchange rates.

the monetary consequences of short-run fluctuations" (ibid., 85).[21] However, the balance of payments problem, and the administration's commitment to slow or stop the gold outflow, restricted discretionary action.[22]

The 1962 report expressed concern about price and wage changes in less competitive industries and found a role for government in moderating the increases by offering guidelines relating wages and prices to changes in productivity (ibid., 185). A major aim was to shift the Phillips curve to get more employment at lower inflation. President Kennedy never endorsed the guidelines explicitly, though he used them to pressure the steel industry to cancel a price increase and at other times. The Council also emphasized the need to improve the functioning of the labor market by increasing the flow of information to shorten the time workers spent unemployed. The report mentioned the need to balance the goals of inflation and unemployment (ibid., 44). It did not mention the Phillips curve by name, but the idea of a short-term tradeoff is present, as is the possibility of shifting the Phillips curve by improving the functioning of labor markets.[23]

21. Heller emphasized many times that he did not neglect discretionary monetary policy. "The economic policy of the 1960s, the 'new economics' if you will, assigns an important role to *both* fiscal and monetary policy. Indeed, the appropriate mix of policies has often been the cornerstone of the argument" (Friedman and Heller, 1969, 16; italics in the original.). Here and elsewhere, Heller criticized Friedman's proposal, calling for constant money growth; but unlike many earlier Keynesian economists, he did not dismiss monetary policy or suggest that the short-term nominal interest rate should be low and constant. Examples of the more extreme view are the survey of monetary theory written for American Economic Association's *Readings in Business Cycles* (Gordon and Klein, 1965) or the association's *Survey of Contemporary Economics* (Villard, 1948). These ideas survived into the 1980s in the writings of Kaldor (1982) and Robinson and Wilkinson (1985). The latter wrote (ibid., 90), "The notion that inflation is a monetary phenomenon and that it can be prevented by refusing to allow the quantity of money to increase is to mistake a symptom for a cause." Gardner Ackley succeeded Heller as chairman of the Council. His textbook, Ackley (1961), is in the older Keynesian tradition, denying any significant influence to money. The Radcliffe Committee in Britain also denied a role to money in inflation (Committee on the Working of the Monetary System, 1959). See Brunner and Meltzer (1993). Friedman challenged Heller's statement about the role of money in the "new economics." He claimed that Heller had changed his opinion based on experience. "I reread the reports of the Council of Economic Advisers that were published when he was chairman . . . I do not believe that anybody can read those reports and come out with the conclusion that they say that money matters significantly" (Friedman and Heller, 1969, 49).

22. "Persistent payments deficits and gold losses have made it necessary for the U.S. government to give greater attention to the net financial outcome of its transactions, and those of its citizens, with the rest of the world. . . . [T]he balance must be under control. . . . Action to safeguard the international position of the dollar is . . . essential" (Council of Economic Advisers, 1962, 144–45). This reflected President Kennedy's concern. His assistant Arthur Schlesinger (1965, 601) reported Kennedy's statement that the "two things that scared him most were nuclear weapons and the payments deficit."

23. At one point, the report distinguished between real and nominal interest rates, but it

The Kennedy administration soon put many of these ideas into practice. Instead of general policies that permitted private decision makers to respond, it offered targeted tax reduction for new investment and more rapid depreciation of capital assets and pressured the Federal Reserve to abandon the bills-only policy and buy longer-term securities. After a few years, it proposed general tax reduction to reduce fiscal drag and stimulate growth. Perhaps most important of all here, it accepted the position that low or moderate inflation would permanently increase employment and that inflation would start to increase before the economy reached full employment. To avoid that outcome, government had to intervene in labor and product markets. This framework dominated policy action and was used to support greater concern for unemployment than for inflation until 1979.

There were four main errors or weaknesses in the policy framework. First, it presumed that economists could forecast with enough accuracy to guide active, discretionary policy changes. There was no sound basis for this optimism at the time or later (Meltzer, 1987). Separating growth of nominal income into real growth and inflation proved inaccurate, in large part because of the inaccuracy of initial estimates of output growth and difficulties of estimating the permanent growth rate (Orphanides et al. 2000; Orphanides, 2001).[24] Implementing the type of activist monetary policy that the "new economics" required for success becomes difficult when forecasts and data are inaccurate. Long after the action, data revisions may show that the action was too small, too large, or even unnecessary. Kennedy's advisers did not address this problem. They acted as if today's errors or excesses could be corrected later. Although they recognized that Congress might be slow to act, they did not connect their desire to give the president (and themselves) authority to change tax rates to their belief in

---

ignored the distinction when it presented and discussed interest rates in three recent business cycles (Council of Economic Advisers, 1962, 86–87, 90). The president appointed a subcommittee on wage and price policies headed by George Shultz with members from industry and labor. The report did not support the Council's proposal. It said: "Private parties will not act against their own interests over any extended period of time, nor would it be desirable for them to do so" (Heller papers, wage price guideposts, August 4, 1961, 8).

24. Arthur Okun, who served as a member (1964–68) and chairman (1968–69) of the Council of Economic Advisers, disliked using the term "fine tuning" or "the new economics" to describe the Council's position. "The switches in policy in recent years have not reflected an effort by economists to keep the economy on some precise, narrow course. We were smart enough to know that we weren't that smart!" (Okun, 1970, 111). Using more technical jargon, James Tobin described the concern about employment as recognition that it takes many Harberger triangles (social loss from inflation) to fill an Okun gap (social loss from unemployment.) See Tobin 1980. This ignores duration. Postwar, cyclical unemployment lasted a few weeks for individuals on average; inflation was far more persistent.

activism. The difficulty encountered in raising tax rates to reduce deficits from 1966 to 1968 must have been an unpleasant surprise.

Second, part of the forecaster's problem is to recognize whether changes are permanent or temporary. Nowhere was this more important than in separating inflation and real growth. The problem arose particularly when productivity or its growth rate changed after 1966 (Chart 3.1), but it was important also in judging whether increases in the price level were one-time changes in level or persistent changes in the rate of change. After several cycles in which the Federal Reserve acted to reduce inflation only until unemployment rose, more of the public became convinced that inflation was permanent and might increase secularly. Once the public perceived increased inflation as a permanent change, long-term interest rates and wage increases did not decline in recessions, reflecting the public's anticipations.[25]

Third, inflation proved unpopular and a political liability. Unemployment was unpopular also. Instead of the stable policy that encouraged investment and growth, policy after 1965 shifted emphasis frequently between these two goals. And since government now accepted responsibility for economic management, advocates of other goals and objectives made their case for assistance. By the late 1960s, the alleged "selective effects" of monetary policy on housing, income distribution, and other concerns made it difficult for the government to pursue, or the public to expect, consistent policies. The result was called "stagflation." Inflation remained positive, and the unemployment rate drifted upward from the 1960s to the 1970s. On average, inflation and the unemployment rate rose together and later declined together, contrary to the Phillips curve reasoning that the Council advocated. The public recognized that the commitment to reduce unemployment dominated concerns about inflation, so any decline in inflation was treated as temporary.

Fourth, perhaps the most serious flaw in the economic analysis underlying policy was the belief that policymakers could maximize economic welfare by choosing the optimal mix of monetary and fiscal stimulus or restraint to achieve the optimal combination of inflation and unemployment.[26] Influenced by early versions of the Phillips curve, economists in the Kennedy and Johnson administrations believed they could perma-

25. Many critics accepted the importance of counter-cyclical fiscal policy but claimed that long-term structural reform was the more appropriate action. Brunner (1986, 109–10) makes this case forcefully.

26. "The economics profession and the nation need better analytical criteria by which to balance the costs of a little more upcreep in prices with those of a little more unemployment" (Okun, 1970, 106).

nently reduce unemployment by choosing to accept higher inflation. Milton Friedman (1968b) pointed out that a permanent or persistent tradeoff of this kind was inconsistent with rational behavior; the long-run Phillips curve must be vertical because inflation is a nominal variable and unemployment is a real variable. Rational behavior required that any influence of nominal variables on real variables last only as long as it takes markets to learn and adjust.[27] Okun (1970, 108) recognized that Friedman's point had "some relevance to the real world." But it should not prevent policymakers from choosing how much inflation and unemployment to accept. "The policy maker must face up to the near-term tradeoff and he must be guided by his perception of public attitudes. It is clear that 4 and 5 percent rates of price increase are intolerable to the American public—whether or not they are likely to speed up to 8 and 10 percent" (ibid., 109).[28]

Later research showed that a discretionary policy reacting to current conditions was sub-optimal. The weight on current concerns, and the discretionary response to those concerns, led policymakers to stimulate the economy when unemployment rose and promise to reduce the resulting inflation later. With discretionary policy, keeping the commitment might not be the desirable option if considered only on the basis of prevailing conditions at the time the commitment came due. Kydland and Prescott (1977) showed that optimal policy required commitment to a rule or known procedure. Failure to follow a rule made policy inconsistent with the promise. The public, on the margin, learned about the inconsistency and disregarded the promise. This very general result applied to promises to maintain low inflation and balanced budgets, main elements in the Council's strategy.

For the Federal Reserve the new approach required closer coordination with other parts of the government followed by increased pressure to allow more inflation with the intent of reducing unemployment. Later it also meant new ideas that put an end to reliance on free reserves as a principal policy indicator and increased attention to a short-term interest rate, the

27. Okun's book appeared after Friedman's paper. Okun (1970, 109) accepted Friedman's logic but denied its general applicability. "We could not escape our current task of searching for a compromise [tradeoff]. The long run is apparently a matter of decades rather than years." This empirical judgment soon proved wrong and costly. President Nixon announced that he would reduce inflation without increasing unemployment (Hargrove and Morley, 1984, 328). Paul McCracken, chairman of Nixon's Council of Economic Advisers, told him that he was mistaken, but the message had gone out and he did not retract it (ibid.).

28. Okun was not alone in rejecting the relevance of Friedman's analysis. Paul Samuelson's popular textbook said: "Even if this pessimistic view were to have an element of truth [sic], no doubt many would argue that, in an uncertain world it is better to grasp the lower unemployment that can be had at hand than to wait for the lower unemployment that . . . can be found only in some future bush" (Samuelson, 1973, 835).

overnight rate on federal funds.[29] Policy coordination also meant direct pressures from the president and his staff to change or modify policy actions to accommodate these pressures. Martin had worked for a decade in the 1950s to restore the System's independence. In the next decade, he sometimes displayed his independence, but he also delayed or avoided actions that he believed necessary or took expansive actions to offset predicted deflationary fiscal actions.[30]

Heller "went to Washington thinking we ought to end the independence of the Federal Reserve, came out after working with the Fed under two presidents with the conviction that it isn't too bad an arrangement, provided there is good will, competent people, and reasonably systematic consultation and presidential participation."[31] He later recognized some of the difficulties he and other economists encountered in a political environment. Perhaps the most important example came early in 1966 (Friedman and Heller, 1969, 35–36). The Council advised President Johnson to reduce the budget deficit by raising tax rates. President Johnson believed that Congress would require reductions in spending; he was reluctant to reduce social spending and redistribution to pay for the Vietnam War (Goodwin, 1991). He also learned from Wilbur Mills, the chairman of the Ways and Means Committee, that a tax increase would not pass in the House (Hargrove and Morley, 1986, 251). More than two years passed before Johnson agreed to reduce spending and Congress agreed to a temporary tax surcharge. Earlier, President Johnson allowed official spending estimates to substantially understate the cost of the Vietnam War and hid the true costs from his advisers.[32]

---

29. Federal funds are the banks' reserve balances, thus part of the monetary base. Chapter 2 discusses the market for these balances.

30. Council chairmen used policy coordination as a way of influencing Martin. During the Eisenhower administration, Martin met with the president or his staff to discuss economic policy thirty-four times, but twelve of the meetings were in 1958. The number of meetings increased to seventy-five in the Kennedy-Johnson years, including eight meetings in which Martin was alone with the president (Kettl, 1986, 94). Gardner Ackley, who succeeded Heller as chairman, described the meetings with President Johnson: Johnson "worked him over on more than one occasion without appreciable results" (ibid., 94). This statement would be more accurate, I believe, if it said without *immediate* result. Martin delayed raising interest rates and he permitted the monetary and credit expansion that produced inflation. Martin (1987, 4) described one such incident.

31. Martin did not mention that the meetings with the president were coercive. He described the meetings as "a very good device to make it possible for me to talk to the President at convenient intervals without being forced into it" (Martin oral history, May 8, 1987, 23).

32. Heller (Friedman and Heller, 1969, 36) treats the problem as unique. "Can you imagine a repeat of the situation in the second half of 1965 when the Council of Economic Advisers and the Treasury . . . were not aware of the Pentagon's expenditure plans?" The precise problem has not occurred, but the Reagan administration's "rosy scenarios" underestimated

The main difference about monetary policy between Heller and his principal academic critics was over discretionary activism versus a rule—a consistent predictable policy.[33] Heller's position on this issue was shared by many of the Federal Reserve's staff and officials, although several disagreed with the judgments, forecasts, and methods of the new Council. Heller said:

> Insofar as the feasibility of discretionary monetary policy is at issue, what matters *most* is whether there is some near-term effect. If there is, then the Federal Reserve can influence the economy one quarter or two quarters from now. That there are subsequent, more pronounced, effects is not the key question. These subsequent effects get caught, as it were, in subsequent forecasts of the economic outlook, and current policy is adjusted accordingly. At least this is what happens in a . . . world where one enjoys the benefits of discretionary policy changes. (Friedman and Heller, 1969, 25; italics in the original)

Heller recognized that discretionary policy would be useful and effective only if economists' forecasts are reasonably accurate six to nine months ahead. Friedman disagreed.

> The available evidence . . . casts grave doubts on the possibility of producing any fine adjustments in economic activity by fine adjustments in monetary policy—at least in the present state of knowledge. . . . There are thus serious limitations to the possibility of discretionary monetary policy and much danger that such a policy may make matters worse rather than better. (ibid., 48)[34]

Heller's focus on current or near-term events fit well with Federal Reserve practice. It too took one step at a time, based on current reports and observed what happened before taking the next step. This too was sub-optimal, as Kydland and Prescott (1977) later pointed out. Further, the Federal Reserve did not have systematic forecasts of future events until the

---

the size of budget deficits in 1982 and 1983 and in several subsequent years, and the Bush administration refused to give cost estimates during the Iraq war in 2003. Martin (1987, 1–2) claimed that it was common to have information not shared between departments.

33. Friedman went further and recommended a fixed rate of money growth, but other rules later permitted activist response to events without discretion.

34. Friedman made clear that the same problem applied to fiscal actions. And he recognized strong political pressure to act even against modest changes. "We can avoid extreme fluctuations; we do not know enough to avoid minor fluctuations" (Friedman and Heller, 1969, 48). Frank Morris, later president of the Boston Federal Reserve bank, commented: "It will be a long time before we again have the complete confidence which we had in the early 1960s—that we knew exactly what we were doing" (quoted in Fuhrer 1994, 14).

mid-1960s and lacked quantitative estimates of the timing and magnitude of the effects of its actions.

Where the Federal Reserve and the Council differed most in the early 1960s was on the reasons for unemployment and the appropriate policy response. Leading Federal Reserve officials thought unemployment was structural, not cyclical. They favored industrial modernization, increased investment, job training, and other structural remedies, and they did not support policies to increase demand because they feared inflation.[35] They differed also on the importance of the balance of payments and in their concern about inflation. By coordinating policy, Martin partly subordinated the Federal Reserve's concerns to the administration's. A principal result was that policy gave greatest weight to unemployment, reinforcing the tendencies brought by the Employment Act. But Martin continued to express concern about inflation and warned President Kennedy as early as second quarter 1961. Heller explained that they began to develop guideposts because any inflation in 1961 "surely wasn't aggregate demand, or demand-pull inflation. . . . And if we are going to deal with cost-push, we ought to have some kind of incomes policy" (Heller oral history, II, 8).

THE COMMISSION ON MONEY AND CREDIT

The January 1957 Economic Report of the President expressed concerns about financial system operations and the system's ability to finance growth. The report, and President Eisenhower's State of the Union message, asked for a commission to study the operation of public and private credit agencies to assess their ability to meet future requirements in a growing economy, finance growth, and control inflation (Council of Economic Advisers, 1957, 49). The Committee for Economic Development, a private group, organized the Commission on Money and Credit. Its twenty-seven members included bankers, business executives, union leaders, consumer and farm organizations, and academic economists.[36] The Commission began

35. Martin later told Heller that he accepted Heller's argument for the tax cut (Kettl, 1986, 102). This was not true at the time.

36. Several of the members had served in previous administrations or at the Federal Reserve. These included Adolf Berle in the Roosevelt administration, Joseph Dodge in the Eisenhower administration, Marriner Eccles, former chairman of the Board of Governors of the Federal Reserve System, and Beardsley Ruml, a former director of the New York Federal Reserve bank and the author of the plan to withhold income tax at the source. Joseph Barr, later a Treasury Secretary, also served. Bertrand Fox of Harvard Business School and Eli Shapiro of MIT served as research director and deputy director respectively. The desirability of a commission to study financial reform had been discussed for several years following the Patman committee hearings in 1952. Showing general concern about the same set of issues, the United Kingdom organized the Radcliffe Committee, and Canada had the Porter Commission at about this time.

its work in 1958 and issued its report in 1961 after nearly three years of meetings and considerable research by its staff, independent scholars, and the staffs of the principal financial institutions. The Commission's report and eighteen supplementary volumes constitute the most extensive study of United States' financial institutions since that of the 1907 Aldrich Commission, which led to the founding of the Federal Reserve.

The Commission attempted to evaluate the contribution that institutions made to the effective conduct of policy. In appraising market and non-market institutions, the Commission reflected contemporary discussion of the causes of a rising average unemployment rate, from 3.7 percent in 1951–54 to 4.9 percent in 1955–58. One view was that higher unemployment reflected insufficient stimulus and inadequate aggregate demand caused by so-called "fiscal drag" and excessively tight monetary policy. The other prominent view claimed structural features reduced employment and cited minimum wages, labor legislation, lack of proper worker training, and mismatch between openings and available skills as examples. While it found much to praise in postwar experience, the Commission noted that growth had slowed, prices had drifted upward after 1952, and balance of payments deficits continued with a loss of gold.

The Commission's report serves as a guide to contemporary discussion of economic policy after a decade of active monetary policy. The Commission accepted that government had a role in achieving three goals: "adequate economic growth, low levels of unemployment, and reasonable price stability" (Commission on Money and Credit, 1961, 12). It accepted the common contemporary claim that "monetary, credit, and fiscal measures alone" would not achieve the three goals simultaneously if adjustment was slow or monopolists maintained wages or prices at "unduly high levels" (ibid., 12).

The Commission defined inflation as "continued increases in the general level of prices" (ibid., 14), but it then went on to describe two causes— "the pull of excessive demand in relation to supply" and cost-push (ibid., 15). The latter could arise from corporate or union market power, higher taxes, or higher import prices.[37] This confused one-time price changes with the maintained positive rate of increase highlighted in the Commission's definition. Discussions of inflation ever after were marred by failure to make this simple, but crucial, distinction.

The Commission did not propose numerical targets for inflation and

---

37. Only two members objected to the idea of cost-push inflation. They argued correctly that any increase of this kind was a one-time increase in the price level or temporary increase in inflation. The rest ignored this point (Commission on Money and Credit, 1961, n. 16).

unemployment. It suggested that the economy could maintain an average annual growth rate above 4.5 percent if government policies removed impediments. This was lower than the rate the Kennedy administration considered feasible, but it reinforced their claim that policies during the 1950s had restricted growth to levels well below potential.

There is little trace of earlier pessimism about the effectiveness of monetary policy. The report suggested that Federal Reserve operations affected interest rates on all classes of securities, and encouraged or discouraged bank lending, mortgage loans, and issuance of corporate bonds. The public chose to hold smaller money balances when interest rates increased, and conversely. The report noted that monetary velocity moved counter to the money stock, but that did not render monetary actions impotent. The report was less certain about the effect on investment (ibid., 52).[38] It accepted criticisms that restrictive monetary policy had larger effects on housing, small business, and debtors than other groups, but it saw "no reason to object to the use of monetary policy relative to tax policy on account of its differential impact among sectors of the economy or size of business, or its indirect income distribution effects" (ibid., 59–60). But the report failed to recognize that the stronger effects on housing reflected the operation of relative prices and interest rate ceilings or that housing expanded relatively at low interest rates.

On the critical issue of deciding between commitment to domestic goals or balance of payments goals, the Commission, without dissent, agreed that the Federal Reserve should subordinate international to domestic objectives.[39] It favored removing the gold reserve requirement behind Federal Reserve notes and bank reserves, a step not completed until 1968.

The Commission endorsed the conventional view that open market operations should remain the principal means of conducting monetary policy. Like the 1959 congressionally sponsored report on employment growth and price levels, it recommended that the Federal Reserve end the bills-only policy, but it claimed that the effect on long-term interest rates would be small (ibid., 63–64). The Commission favored retention of discounting at the discretion of member banks. It opposed automatic adjustment of the discount rate to market rates, but it favored a uniform

38. Karl Brunner's review of the report (1961, 610–11) criticized the Commission for overstating the degree of consensus and the extent of empirically verified knowledge of the transmission mechanism. The report's analysis contrasts favorably with the Radcliffe report in Britain done at about the same time.

39. "Federal Reserve policy should continue to consider the needs of our international balance of payments, but should be governed primarily by domestic economic needs" (Commission on Money and Credit, 1961, 61).

discount rate set nationally. The Commission urged the Federal Reserve to assure the banking system that it would serve as lender of last resort in times of distress (ibid., 65–66).

The Federal Reserve had struggled for decades over the administration of reserve requirement ratios without finding a satisfactory solution. The Commission proposed uniform reserve requirement ratios for all demand deposits, infrequent changes in requirements, reduction of the range within which these requirements could change, and elimination of the statutory reserve requirement against saving and time deposits. The Federal Reserve adopted the last recommendation more than twenty years later, after legislation in 1980 eliminated the requirement.

The Commission differed with several conclusions reached in the *Report on Employment, Growth, and Price Levels*.[40] It did not agree that monetary policy was weak and discriminatory to an important degree. It rejected the alleged tradeoff between inflation and growth for inflation rates between 0 and 6 percent.[41] It could not agree on recommendations about selective controls, so it did not make any, but it recommended making ceiling rates for time and savings deposits uniform across institutions and changing the ceiling from a continuous regulation to a stand-by authority.

The Commission deplored the rising balance of payments deficit, but it opposed devaluing the dollar by raising the gold price or using general monetary and fiscal policies to reduce the deficit by deflation. Instead, it proposed Export-Import Bank subsidies to exports, reduced trade restrictions abroad, possible reductions in foreign aid, and other selective measures. Like many contemporaries, the Commission relied on stopgaps and neglected the adjustment mechanism for real exchange rates.

The Commission endorsed the Federal Reserve's proposal to compel all insured commercial banks to be members. Its reasoning borrowed the Federal Reserve's argument that non-members weakened the effect of monetary policy by permitting some banks to escape. This argument depended on a lending view of monetary policy; bank lending expands and contracts as reserves increase and decrease. The argument is inconsistent with the Commission's emphasis on relative price (interest rate) changes in the transmission of monetary policy. Changes in interest rates and relative prices affect both member and non-member banks and other wealth owners.

The Commission made its boldest recommendations on issues of struc-

40. See Chapter 2 for a summary of the earlier report.
41. "Countries with declining prices or with rates of price increase greater than 6 percent appear to have lower growth rates than those operating within those limits" (Commission on Money and Credit, 1961, 44).

ture and organization. It proposed a central bank with authority over all policy operations, the plan the Republicans favored in 1912. But it adopted Marriner Eccles' 1935 proposal to put responsibility and authority in the Board. Reserve banks would advise on open market policy, but a five-person Board would make decisions. Board members would serve ten-year terms, as in the 1913 act. It agreed to eliminate geographical and occupational qualifications.[42] It replaced the Federal Advisory Council with a new advisory council, representing many groups in the economy (Commission on Money and Credit, 1961, 87–92). It proposed that the Federal Reserve acquire the examination and supervisory responsibilities of the Comptroller of the Currency (national banks) and the Federal Deposit Insurance Corporation (insured non-member banks). Similarly, all federally insured thrift institutions would have a single examining authority (ibid., 174–75).

The report contained many other recommendations for fiscal policy, debt management, government credit institutions, and private financial institutions. Separate volumes contained answers to questions directed to the Board of Governors and the Treasury Department. Trade associations representing groups of financial intermediaries wrote independent reports, but the Federal Deposit Insurance Corporation and the Comptroller of the Currency were not asked about the proposed consolidation of examination and supervision. The Federal Reserve responded to the recommendation by stating pros and cons.

The Federal Reserve's Response

The Commission asked the Federal Reserve twenty-five broad questions about its operations and their effect. The questions and the Board's answers fill nearly two hundred pages. Several of the answers emphasized growth, employment, and price stability as policy goals or objectives.[43]

There are major differences between the Board's answers and the policy

42. President Kennedy recommended that the chairman's four-year term begin on February 1 of the year in which the presidential term began. Interim appointments would complete the unexpired term. This change would give each president the opportunity to appoint a chairman of his own choice. To assure a vacancy, the proposal changed the expiration date for the fourteen-year terms of members from even to odd years. Earlier, Allan Sproul recommended a five-person board with ten-year terms and elimination of geographical limitations (letter, Sproul to Martin, Sproul papers, December 31, 1952).

43. At about this time, the Board's staff published a revised version of its handbook. The new edition claimed that its objectives had always included "sustained high employment, stable values, growth of the country" (Board of Governors, 1961, 1). This is either outright error or intentionally misleading. It ignores policy during the Great Depression. The Federal Reserve did not accept these goals until the 1940s or 1950s and, in the 1920s, explicitly denied that it could affect output or control the price level. See volume 1, chapter 4. When reading the Board's answers to questions, one should remember that these are written by the staff.

framework used by the Council of Economic Advisers. Four major differences of emphasis stand out. First, the Board used rising marginal cost, not the Phillips curve, to explain why prices rose before output reached capacity. Some industries brought less efficient facilities into operation when demand increased; others had idle capacity. The Board's discussion of the interaction of prices and output was much more detailed but less structured than the Council's analytic model (ibid., 26–29). Second, the Board's monetary analysis focused on short-run changes in free reserves and long-run changes in the stocks of money and credit. The Council used interest rates to judge the stance of monetary policy. Third, the Board was more sanguine about the balance of payments than the Council or President Kennedy. Fourth, the Council relied on explicit analytic models relating policy actions to output, prices, and the balance of payments. The Board relied more on judgment and institutional knowledge. These differences often made communication between Federal Reserve Chairman Martin and Council Chairman Heller difficult.

Differences about monetary policy were often sharp. The Board gave pride of place to bank reserves, not interest rates, as the key variable that it controlled. "Through this control, [the Board and the Federal Open Market Committee] exert a strong influence directly on total loans and investments and total deposits of banks and indirectly some influence on spending, investment, and saving" (Commission on Money and Credit, 1963, 3). Effects on interest rates are "intertwined with other market forces, [so] they are not predictable or measurable" (ibid., 3). At each meeting the FOMC decides "the degree of restraint or encouragement that should be imposed on bank credit expansion" (ibid., 4). These decisions are "expressed in general terms" (ibid., 4).

While much of the phrasing was new, the emphasis on bank credit was not very different from that of the 1920s. There are notable changes, however. Free reserves or member bank borrowing received less attention. The Board accepted that it had an indirect influence on economic activity and the price level that it did not acknowledge, or denied, in the 1920s.[44] One constant is the discussion of member bank borrowing. As in the Riefler-Burgess doctrine, banks are reluctant to borrow. Increased borrowing is "a negative element of bank liquidity" because banks want to "get out of debt to the Reserve Banks" (ibid., 7). Discount rate changes raise or lower the degree of restraint that borrowing exerts.

---

44. Free reserves soon enter the description as a measure of primary bank liquidity. Their importance reflects the fact that they are available immediately or can be obtained quickly by using borrowings data from the reserve banks.

These answers differ from the Keynesian views of the Kennedy Council. The Council relied on a model in which an interest rate had the major role in the transmission of fiscal and monetary policy. The Board's answer highlighted quantities. The Council used its model to trace out the expected effects of policy on output, prices, and the balance of payments. The Board did not have a formal model. It saw these connections as loose, variable, and uncertain, dependent on erratic changes in monetary velocity. The Council had started to use the Phillips curve to relate output or unemployment to inflation. Neither the Board nor the reserve banks agreed on a systematic way of thinking about the division of nominal output between real output and the price level. The Board relied on judgment influenced by leading and coincident indicators, time series that typically moved in advance of or together with real output, the price level, or inflation.

A typical passage from the Federal Reserve's response to the Commission's questions described the ways in which monetary operations influenced the economy.

> Even though Federal Reserve operations exercise their influence primarily through the quantity of bank credit and the money supply, policy decisions cannot be made exclusively in terms of the level or rate of change of the money supply. Monetary policy must take into consideration variations in money turnover . . . Variation in money turnover need not be considered as a bar to the effectiveness of monetary policy if policy formulation takes them into consideration, although they may at times complicate its task. . . .
>
> [E]conomic decisions are influenced by all elements of liquidity including holdings of other assets as well as of money balances. . . . Decisions of spenders and lenders are likely to be affected by the degree of their liquidity existing at any point in time and by variations in their liquidity over time. (Commission on Money and Credit, 1963, 10)[45]

The Board's answer emphasized changes in the assets and liabilities on banks' balance sheets and banks' liquidity positions. It neglected the role of relative prices of assets and output. The Board did not neglect interest rates in its response, but it emphasized the costs of borrowing, not the incentives to purchase or sell, save, and invest in response to relative price changes. Further, the Board regarded its actions as "only one supply factor in interest rate determination. [B]ank credit usually comprises only

---

45. The rest of the answer discussed some of the many factors limiting the Federal Reserve's ability to restrict the economy's liquidity. Compare this loose, open-ended description to Thornton (1802), written more than 100 years earlier, described in volume 1, chapter 2.

a small portion of the total [credit supply]" (Commission on Money and Credit, 1963, 14).

The relative price view of monetary transmission makes investment depend on the price of existing assets relative to the price of new production of similar assets. Increases in money initially increase real balances. Excess real balances increase spending on consumption goods and existing assets, raising their prices. Rising consumer spending and higher prices of existing assets induce spending on investment (Brunner and Meltzer, 1993). On this view, membership in the Federal Reserve System is unimportant for the transmission of policy impulses.[46] Bank lending is one way, generally an efficient one, for some spenders to anticipate future income. Readily available substitutes for bank lending include bond markets, commercial paper, and other credit market instruments. Other substitutes include foreign loans and bonds.

Although several members of the FOMC often questioned reliance on free reserves as a measure of policy thrust, the Board's response does not reflect any differences of opinion. In the short-term, the "figure of 'free reserves' or its negative counterpart 'net borrowed reserves' provides a convenient and significant working measure of the posture of policy at the time" (Commission on Money and Credit, 1963, 19).

"The general level of free reserves prevailing over a period of time may be viewed as an indicator of the degree of restraint or ease that exists in the money market. . . . [T]hey must be considered in the context of changes in the total reserve position of member banks. The particular level of free reserves that may be needed to achieve the objective of policy may vary from time to time depending on changing economic conditions. . . . Broader guides to policy operations are provided by the consequences of changes in reserve availability on the amount of total loans and investments of banks and on the money supply. Assumptions or estimates as to these elements underlie the figures for total reserves and free reserves. The Open Market Committee in its deliberations has in mind what conditions with respect to the availability of bank credit and growth in the money supply would be an appropriate end of policy at the time" (ibid., 19–20).[47] Note the absence of output, employment, and inflation.

46. The Federal Reserve was not the only central bank to regard bank lending as central to monetary transmission. The Bank of Japan held this view firmly in the 1990s and was reluctant to increase bank reserves until bank lending increased. This policy stance has much in common with the real bills doctrine that contributed heavily to policy failure in the Great Depression.

47. This seems an accurate description of the procedures at the time. The staff estimated

The Board insisted that it did not control interest rates and did not peg them. "Federal Reserve policies generally are directed toward providing an appropriate volume of reserves and not toward establishing or maintaining any particular level or pattern of interest rates. Such rates are determined by the forces of the market, one of which is the supply of bank credit" (ibid., 21).[48]

Instability of velocity and changes that offset the effect of monetary policy on spending were often used to explain why monetary policy was impotent. The Board's response recognized both arguments. It denied that changes in velocity were sufficiently erratic to make policy operations useless, and it concluded that "the quantity of money can be adjusted to compensate for velocity changes" (ibid., 95).[49] The Board rejected Warren Smith's argument used by the congressional committee in 1959.

The Commission's questions explored other reasons why monetary policy would not work. The Board's answers rejected all of them. The existence of a large government debt "neither 'assists' nor 'hampers' to any significant extent the effectiveness of monetary policy" (ibid., 78). The Board said that the debt helped to transmit monetary impulses across the term structure, and it permitted the System to rely mainly on open market purchases and sales in its operations. The main problem caused by a large debt, the Board said, came from the frequency of Treasury operations. At times, these made the "execution of policy more difficult" (ibid., 79). The Board did not mention that the System could avoid these difficulties if the Treasury auctioned its debt instead of selling at a fixed price and yield.

The Board did not mention the *Report on Employment, Growth, and Price Levels,* but it responded to the call for direct controls on credit. "Selective controls are awkward, costly, and onerous to enforce effectively. When continued over extended periods, moreover, such controls tend to be subverted by changes in credit market relationships" (ibid., 50). Further, direct controls distort demand.

In 1951 the System gave a prominent place to discounting as a monetary

---

the amount of total and free reserves required to support money and bank credit. The reply does not discuss the method of calculation, and there does not seem to have been much effort to improve the estimates.

48. In a final gasp of support for the bills-only policy, the Board added that it conducted its operations to "minimize their influence on the structure or pattern of rates" (Commission on Money and Credit, 1963, 21). The Board's insistence on control of reserves and not interest rates shows continuing concern to avoid pressure from Congressman Patman and others to return to a pegging policy. If they admitted that they controlled an interest rate, he could urge them to lower it and peg it.

49. The answer attributed the postwar increase in velocity to the working off of the large wartime increase in the money stock, firms' resumption of cash management practices used in the 1920s, and the development of credit cards for consumers.

tool. By the 1960s, the Board described the role of discounting much as it had in the 1920s. "Discount policy and open market policy are inevitably integral parts of a single policy. . . . [S]hifts between policies of ease and restraint often do not involve absolute changes in the total amount of reserves available to the banking system, but rather changes in the sources of reserves" (ibid., 118). "Reserves obtained through borrowing are typically accompanied by a spreading atmosphere of credit restraint, as contrasted with the effect of a corresponding amount of reserves injected by open market operations . . . Administrative restraint exercised by discount officials together with the reluctance of banks to borrow make it likely that a bank forced to borrow will in turn search for Federal funds, seek correspondent accommodation, offer securities for sale, . . . and/or curtail its direct loan activity" (ibid., 118).[50]

The Board's response gave the discount rate a larger role than in the past, especially if the discount rate was above the market rate. Elements of the older "reluctance to borrow" view remained, but banks now responded to differences between the discount rate and the market rate. The summary on the discount rate lists three determinants of member bank borrowing— the discount rate or cost, reluctance to borrow or to remain in debt, and administration of the discount window by the reserve banks. The Board continued to reject proposals for a penalty rate that moved the discount rate in step with a prominent market rate, for example the Treasury bill rate.[51] And the statement neglects the effect on banks as borrowed reserves spread through the system. A receiving bank had no way to know whether the reserves it received originated in borrowing or in open market operations.

The Board's reply recognized that ceiling rates for time deposits affected banks' competitive position without any effect on the aggregate amount saved. The clearest case was foreign owned dollar assets. These deposits shifted into non-bank assets, such as Treasury bills, when ceiling rates became binding. Money center banks lost deposits at such times. Other banks were often reluctant to raise time deposit rates to the ceiling. One reason was the prohibition of interest payments on demand deposits. By raising time deposit rates, banks induced customers to shift from demand deposits to time deposits, reducing the average reserve requirement ratio

50. A few pages later, the Board recognized that borrowing increased reserves. "Even though each bank borrows only temporarily, additional reserves are drawn into the banking system providing the basis for credit and monetary expansion" (Commission on Money and Credit, 1963, 122).

51. The Commission asked only one question about reserve requirements. The Board rejected basing reserve requirements on deposit turnover or bank assets. It had considered such arrangements since the 1930s, but seemed to prefer the prevailing system.

but raising interest cost. Although the Board commented on the distortions caused by interest rate regulation, it did not suggest removing the regulation or putting it on stand-by.

The Commission asked only one question about the balance of payments and the influence of international concerns. The Board's response denied any role to international objectives.[52] It recognized the long-run adjustment problem but relied on a strong gold reserve position to maintain confidence during recessions, when there was a balance of payments deficit. And it recognized international considerations as they affected prices and demand in the domestic market. Much of the long-run problem was either non-economic, for example military assistance or foreign aid, or was caused by "shifts in the international competitive situation" (ibid., 176). The Board had an obligation to maintain price stability, but it recognized that stable prices alone would not assure long-run balance of payments adjustment.

The Commission proposed structural changes that removed reserve bank presidents from the FOMC. These angered the presidents. Allan Sproul blamed former Chairman Marriner Eccles, a member of the Commission, who had advocated similar changes in 1935 (letter, Sproul to Hayes, Sproul papers, Correspondence, July 4, 1961).[53] Subsequently the proposal reappeared several times but never gained a following in Congress.

The Administration's Response

The Kennedy administration responded to the Commission's report by appointing two internal committees, one to restudy the role of financial institutions, the other to study federal credit programs. The two reports found no reason either for major changes or for urgent attention to restructuring existing arrangements (Federal Credit, 1963; Financial Institutions, 1963).[54]

---

52. "Considerations related to the international transactions of the United States do not change the underlying objectives of monetary policy, which are to contribute to the maintenance of U.S. financial stability and to sustainable growth in the U.S. economy, they do at times have a bearing on the choice of actions to be taken" (Commission on Money and Credit, 1963, 172). The Board pointed out that in the 1960 recession, it had to consider the effect of lowering interest rates on capital outflows, gold, and confidence in the dollar (ibid., 175).

53. See volume 1, chapter 6. The proposal also raised old internal concerns. William Trieber, New York's vice president, reported that Chairman Martin opposed the proposed change, but "I'm not sure how strongly he'd fight for it [the present structure]" (letter, Trieber to Sproul, Sproul papers, August 11, 1961). Sproul declined to testify in Congress, but he wrote a strongly worded letter to Congressman Patman opposing any change in the membership of the FOMC (letter, Sproul to Patman, Sproul papers August 16, 1961).

54. Meltzer (1964) reviewed the two reports. The summary in the text comes from that review article.

Financial Institutions (1963) proposed (1) basing reserve requirements for demand deposits on volume of deposits instead of location (reserve city and country banks), (2) subjecting member and non-member banks to the same reserve requirements; (3) extending Federal Reserve discount window privileges to all commercial banks; and (4) continuing voluntary membership in the Federal Reserve System for state banks. The Commission on Money and Credit favored elimination of reserve requirements on time deposits and mandatory membership in the System for state banks. Financial Institutions (1963) preferred to equalize competitive position by imposing reserve requirements on shares at savings and loan associations and deposits of mutual savings banks.

None of the recommendations was adopted at the time. In the 1980s, all commercial banks became subject to reserve requirements on transaction deposits (demand deposits, negotiable order of withdrawal accounts) and non-personal time and saving deposits. Personal time and savings deposits became exempt. Congress did not require all banks to become member banks.

On the more critical issue of interest rate regulation, Financial Institutions (1963) made a bold proposal—to replace interest rate ceilings with stand-by controls that could be used in an emergency. Congress did not implement the change.[55]

THE 1960–61 RECESSION

In April 1960 the economy reached a peak only two years after the trough of the previous recession. The recession proved mild. It lasted ten months, but the decline in real GNP, 1.2 percent, was the smallest of the postwar recessions to that time. The unemployment rate rose to 7.1 percent in May 1961, somewhat higher than in 1953–54 because it started from a higher level (Zarnowitz and Moore, 1986, Table 7).

The timing of the recession, and the history of three recessions in eight years, helped the Democrats elect their presidential candidate, John F. Kennedy, on a platform of getting the economy moving. Kennedy blamed the bills-only policy and the Eisenhower administration's policy of allowing the budget to swing from a $12 billion deficit to a $500 million surplus in one year (Office of Management and Budget, 1990, Table 1.1).

Most of the change was in tax receipts that rose with the economy. The Eisenhower administration, and the president himself, could toler-

---

55. Federal Credit (1963) accepted many of the recommendations of the Commission on Money and Credit and discussed implementation. President Kennedy recommended several of the proposed changes.

ate a budget deficit during the recession, but they believed that deficits caused inflation and weakened the dollar. Raymond Saulnier, chairman of the Council of Economic Advisers, explained later that a steel strike in the second half of 1959 left a large inventory accumulation. "It was very difficult in the first half of 1960 to see whether you were dealing with a backlash of the steel strike or whether you had a cyclical problem on your hands" (Hargrove and Morley, 1984, 137). But Saulnier also rejected the claim that the budget was too restrictive.[56]

Although the administration denied a request from Arthur Burns and Vice President Richard Nixon to ask for easier Federal Reserve policy to avoid a recession, Saulnier explained that the administration wanted a more expansive monetary policy than the Federal Reserve in 1960, but the difference was not great.[57] And he agreed with the Federal Reserve's concern about the importance of keeping inflation low to support the dollar. President Eisenhower also believed firmly in the importance of sustaining confidence in the dollar (Stein, 1990, 368).[58]

A major reason for low inflation followed by recession is plainly visible in the slow growth, followed by decline, in the real value of the monetary base, shown in Chart 3.7. The modest decline in ex post real interest rates through most of 1959 and early 1960 was accompanied by a steeper decline first in growth of the real monetary base and later in its level. Annual growth of the nominal base fell from 2.25 percent in December 1958 to 0 in spring and summer 1960. Consumer prices rose modestly, but more than the base.

The 1959–60 policy was the only sustained deflationary action during

56. Saulnier described the Keynesian claim based on the full-employment budget as "an unduly narrow view of the economy" (Hargrove and Morley, 1984, 138). The proper way to judge the credit system, he believed, was to look at the whole credit system—borrowing by households, business, and government. He accused the Keynesians of being "narrow and myopic" (ibid., 138) for concentrating only on the government budget. A few pages later, he attributed the 1959 decline entirely to the effect of the steel strike. "1959 was not a cyclical problem. The steel strike was in 1959, and you can't really discuss anything but the steel strike in 1959" (ibid., 152).

57. "Our position on the question . . . was more inclined to an easing of the situation than his [Martin's]" (Hargrove and Morley, 1984, 137). Later Saulnier defended Federal Reserve policy, noting that free reserves rose from −$500 to +$500 million. Short-term interest rates declined from 4 percent in December 1959 to 2.4 percent in November 1960. There is no evidence that the election influenced the policy change (ibid., 154). Like Federal Reserve officials, Saulnier ignored money growth when discussing policy thrust. This experience heavily influenced Nixon's negative view of Martin and positive view of Burns.

58. "In October [1960], usually a month of rising employment, the jobless rolls increased by 452,000. All the speeches, television broadcasts, and precinct work in the world could not counteract that one hard fact" (Nixon, 1962, 311).

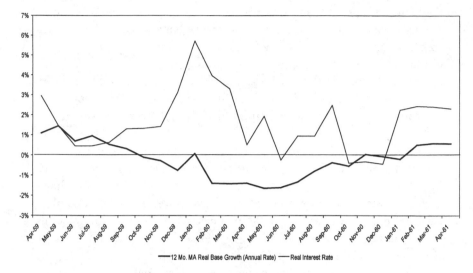

Chart 3.7. Real base growth versus real interest rate, April 1959–April 1961. Twelve-month moving average growth rates.

the Bretton Woods years. It was an unintended consequence of paying attention to free reserves and ignoring money growth. It sacrificed domestic expansion to strengthen the dollar. The short-term effect was negative; the recession lowered returns on domestic assets relative to assets abroad, increasing the capital outflow. There was not enough political support to sustain the program long enough to get the full benefits. Instead, the Kennedy administration introduced a number of actions to stimulate expansion.

Eisenhower's fiscal tightening was planned. The Federal Reserve did not plan a restrictive policy in 1960. FOMC minutes show the members divided on several issues and concerned about whether their usual indicator, free reserves, gave them correct information. The main division was between those who wanted less expansive action to stop the gold outflow and those whose main concern was domestic growth. The committee did not make a serious effort to choose between these goals. The System reduced discount rates twice, but for much of the year it issued vague directions to the account manager that gave him considerable discretion but also exposed him to criticism.

FEDERAL RESERVE ACTIONS
In March 1960 the FOMC voted to increase the supply of reserves. Free reserves rose from −$359 million in February to −$198 million in April, but the federal funds rate did not change. When the FOMC met on May 3,

the members agreed to move free reserves toward zero without changing the discount rate during a period of Treasury borrowing.[59] Free reserves rose as member bank borrowing fell. The Federal Reserve interpreted the change as expansive.

The staff reported that business confidence improved but leading indicators had fallen to levels found at the start of major recessions. The balance of payments position improved also, and there was no sign of inflation.

Malcolm Bryan (Atlanta) noted that total reserves were lower than a year earlier. This level of restraint was "inappropriate and dangerous" (FOMC Minutes, May 3, 1960, 15). He described the economy as expanding slowly with "unutilized and growing supplies of manpower, materials, and plant capacity" (ibid., 15). He called for an increase in bank credit and urged his colleagues to use daily average total reserves as the policy target. As usual, Bryan's remarks drew no response and no support.

Members divided equally between those who favored a more expansive policy and those who preferred to maintain the status quo. Martin said the consensus was to increase free reserves to zero, but he opposed a reduction in the discount rate because the FOMC was not ready to signal a change in the economy.[60]

Bryan gained support at the May 24 FOMC meeting. Several members commented on slow growth of money. Even Chairman Martin wondered why the money stock had not responded to increased ease. He favored a reduction in the discount rate but wanted to delay because of international political uncertainty.[61] Governor Charles N. Shephardson suggested reduction of the discount rate before the next meeting. Alfred Hayes opposed both further ease and a reduction in the discount rate, noting that a majority had spoken against it. Ten days later, Philadelphia and San Francisco reduced their discount rates 0.5 percentage points to 3.5 percent. All other banks followed in the next two weeks.[62]

The May 24 meeting also approved a change in the directive. The new

59. Recognition was rapid. The Brunner and Meltzer (1993, 69) scaling of policy actions assigned $+1/4$ and $+1/2$ to the decisions at the meetings on May 3 and 24, the month following the peak in the economy.

60. Martin reported that the Board's staff was trying to develop a better target than free reserves.

61. The Soviet Union had shot down a U2 plane and captured the pilot, Francis Gary Powers. Following that event, Chairman Khrushchev cancelled a summit meeting with President Eisenhower.

62. The May 17 meeting of the Federal Advisory Council described the outlook as favorable but "not as buoyant as the optimistic forecasts earlier this year" (Board Minutes, May 17, 1960, 2).

directive called for "fostering sustainable growth in economic activity and employment by providing reserves needed for moderate credit expansion." The FOMC removed the clause "guarding against inflationary credit expansion" (FOMC Minutes, May 24, 1960, 54). The manager interpreted the new directive as calling for a further increase in free reserves.

The members and staff recognized slowing growth and acted promptly to ease policy. Unfortunately, their main indicator of ease and restraint, the level of free reserves, misled them. Once again, the problem was the interpretation of reduced member bank borrowing as evidence of greater ease. Growth of the monetary base or the money stock suggested increased restraint. Woodlief Thomas's report discussed at length the problem of finding an indicator of policy thrust and offered several suggestions without accepting any. To increase free reserves he proposed holding the discount rate above the market rate to impose a penalty on borrowing and credit expansion (ibid., 12). This reflected the standard claim that reduced borrowing (increased free reserves) was expansive.

Free reserves continued to rise. In June, the federal funds rate began to decline following reductions in discount rates. The funds rate continued to fall for the rest of the year. In December, the rate reached 1.98 percent, half of its level in the previous January. Partly for seasonal reasons, free reserves reached $682 million in December, more than $1 billion above December 1959.

At the July 6 meeting, Hugh Leach (Richmond), Abbott Mills (San Francisco), M. S. Szymczak, and H. N. Mangels (San Francisco) joined Hayes's call for an end to the bills-only policy, but Martin only said he was "flexible." The reason for the shift in sentiment was the sharp drop in Treasury bill rates in July. The Treasury had reduced its supply of bills, and the System owned about half the outstanding amount. By purchasing from the limited supply, it changed the rate more than usual. The manager began to purchase other short-term securities after checking with the FOMC.

Industrial production fell in July 1960 for the sixth consecutive month. Business inventories rose. Unemployment reached 5.5 percent, a 0.6 percentage point increase since May (FOMC Minutes, July 26, 1960, 4). Stock prices declined sharply. There were signs of strength accompanying the weakness; net exports increased strongly, consumer spending continued to rise, and housing starts were about to increase (ibid., 5).

The staff report on monetary and credit changes recommended a greater than seasonal increase in reserves to offset an estimated $100 million a month gold export and to increase money growth (ibid., 10). The report proposed that an additional amount of vault cash be counted as reserves, and it urged an additional reduction in discount rates. Reflecting the difference between international and domestic concerns, the international staff opposed a reduction in the discount rate.

Several members described the economy as either in recession or on the edge. They favored additional ease but disagreed about whether by open market purchases, by a reduction in the discount rate, or in reserve requirement ratios. Several expressed concern about easing policy a few months before the presidential election. Hayes wanted to do nothing more. Martin favored additional expansion if it were covert, but he did not explain how that could be done. He also favored a discount rate reduction on August 16, after the Treasury auction closed. He expressed the consensus as favoring free reserves at $200 million, about where they were at the time, but he agreed with Bryan that total reserves should increase.[63]

Cleveland did not wait for completion of the Treasury sale. Its directors voted to reduce its discount rate to 3 percent, effective August 12. The Board hesitated to accept the change because it had announced earlier in the week increases in the share of member banks' vault cash counted as reserves and a 0.5 percentage point reduction in the reserve requirement ratio at central reserve city banks to 17.5 percent.[64] This was a step toward implementing legislation in 1959 eliminating the central reserve city classification. Reserve requirement ratios for central reserve city banks remained one percentage point above requirements at reserve city banks (Board Minutes, August 11, 1960, 11–14).

The Board approved Cleveland's decision unanimously and voted to approve the change at any bank that chose the 3 percent rate. By the end of the day, New York, Richmond, and Kansas City joined Cleveland. Others soon followed, but San Francisco and Dallas delayed until September 6 and 8 respectively.

The federal funds rate resumed its decline following these changes, but Treasury bill and bond yields rose. The manager explained that in districts that still had a 3.5 percent discount rate, banks adjusted in the federal

63. The following day the Board reduced stock market margin requirements from 70 percent to 50 percent. Governor Robertson dissented because the change responded to the decline in stock prices, not to the use of credit as the law intended. These technical changes showed recognition of the decline without arousing concerns about influence on the election (Board Minutes, July 27, 1960, 27–28).

64. The vault cash ruling was the second step toward returning to the provision in effect prior to 1917. Effective August 25 country banks could include the excess vault cash over 2.5 percent of reserves as part of reserves. For all other member banks the release date was September 1. They could count vault cash above 1 percent of reserves. On November 24, the Board removed the remaining restriction. All vault cash could be included in reserves. This change later proved to be more valuable than originally conceived. With the development of automatic teller machines (ATMs), banks' demand for vault cash increased so much that reserve requirements were no longer a binding constraint at many banks.

funds market. In the districts that reduced the discount rate, borrowing was profitable, so banks borrowed at the discount window. This again contradicted free reserves doctrine, but no one seemed to notice. The manager added that the Treasury market remained under pressure. Market supply had declined in part because dealers had increased their positions to twice their normal inventories to profit from further rate reductions.

Annual growth of the monetary base increased in August. The staff favored an increase in the money stock, despite a larger gold outflow.

Arthur Marget, head of the Board's international staff, explained that during the first six months, the gold stock declined $125 million. In the six weeks since July 1, the outflow rose to $285 million. Marget objected to press reports describing the outflow as a "flight from the dollar" (FOMC Minutes, August 16, 1960, 10). Much of the outflow was the counterpart of an increased balance of payments deficit. Foreigners had not fled from the dollar; they had acquired gold as settlement of the deficit and had increased their ownership of dollar assets. Marget concluded that international concerns did not call for a more restrictive monetary and fiscal policy. Governor Balderston was the only one to respond to Marget's statement. He expressed concern about the long-run consequences of a continued payments deficit. The only solution he proposed was to bring home the troops, a move over which the System had no control and little influence. The United States should supply equipment, but let foreign governments use their own troops. No one mentioned the Democrats political campaign strategy of blaming the Federal Reserve for tight money and slow growth.

FOMC members and the staff did not agree on whether the economy was in recession, growing slowly, or moving sideways. After considerable discussion, the members voted six to four to change the directive to read: "encouraging monetary expansion for the purpose of fostering sustainable growth in economic activity and employment" (ibid., 55). Governors King, Shephardson, and Szymczak and President Allen voted no. The instructions to the manager did not change. Three months after the peak in the economy, four FOMC members opposed the modest change in wording.

Balderston, acting as chairman with Martin and Hayes absent, expressed the consensus as unchanged from the last meeting but with more discretion to the manager to err on the side of ease. Szymczak reminded them that keeping free reserves unchanged would cancel the effect of the Board's action to count more vault cash as reserves. His statement had no effect on the instructions to the manager.

The meeting also heard a staff report on targeting total reserves instead of free reserves. The conclusion was strongly negative. "It is literally impossible to quantify in advance either the change in total reserves or the volume of System operations which would be necessary to maintain the existing level of the seasonally adjusted money supply or to increase it or decrease it by a specified amount" (ibid., 9). The report concluded that nothing could be gained by estimating the future path of total reserves. The best the staff could do would be to report on actual changes in money. That put aside control of money.

Economic conditions continued to deteriorate at the time of the September 13 FOMC meeting. Consumer expenditures had slowed. The unemployment rate reached a postwar high of 7 percent. Industrial production continued to fall. The FOMC remained divided, but the reason for division changed. Several members, including Martin and Balderston, said that the System had done its best and could do no more. Martin clarified his statement by suggesting that lower interest rates would harm the country, presumably a reference to the gold outflow. Others agreed, but H. N. Mangels (San Francisco) wanted to target free reserves at $500 million, twice the August average. The manager said the level of free reserves did not give useful guidance about the state of the money market. He did not mention an alternative.

The staff report on financial markets concluded that the money supply was a more appropriate indicator of reserve effectiveness when compared with any measure of reserves.[65] These comments displeased Martin, who said there was no shortage of money, but they pleased Bryan (Atlanta), Johns (St. Louis), Fulton (Cleveland), and Shephardson, who wanted increased growth of reserves and money.

Gold outflows received more attention both because they reduced bank reserves and because the gold price had increased to $35.25 an ounce in London and Zurich. This shifted demand for gold to the United States.

Martin had just returned from Europe. He believed that foreigners had not lost confidence in the dollar, as Marget had said, but they watched what the United States did and would regard a Treasury bill rate below 2 percent as evidence of a cheap money policy.

Martin added that the System had been too expansive in 1958. This postponed price adjustments. He did not want to repeat that mistake. He agreed with Mills that monetary and credit policy alone could not manage the economy. Painful adjustments were inevitable.

Less than two months remained before the election. Martin wanted the System to avoid overt action until after the election. The current consensus

---

65. The staff suggested that the "free reserve concept can be a useful indicator to the Manager of the Account . . . if, but only if, the effect of changes in reserve availability on such more fundamental measures as bank credit expansion, the money supply, and interest rates are under constant watch" (FOMC Minutes, September 13, 1960, 9).

was to maintain an even keel during the Treasury funding with doubts resolved on the side of ease.

The Federal Advisory Council also had difficulty deciding whether the economy was in recession. They noted the depressed conditions in the steel industry and the slowdown in home construction, but consumers continued to spend, at a slower pace, and employment remained near record levels. The members anticipated a modest seasonal increase through the fourth quarter, but they were concerned about 1961. Their forecast proved wrong. Real GNP declined in the fourth quarter and rose in first quarter 1961 (Board Minutes, September 15, 1960, 1–2).

Several FOMC members wanted policy to err on the side of ease but to keep market rates above 2 or 2.5 percent to slow the gold loss. They did not say what the manager should do when the two targets gave opposing signals. In mid-October, buy orders flooded the gold markets in London and Zurich. Gold prices rose to $40.00, a 16 percent premium, reflecting concern that, if elected, a liberal Democratic administration would follow more expansive policies to reach the 5 percent growth rate that the Democrats' platform promised. Criticism of the Federal Reserve and increased gold outflows during the fall campaign reinforced these concerns.[66]

During the summer and fall, the manager, staff, and several members commented that free reserves were not a useful target because they did not reflect the position of the money market. Chart 3.8 shows that the response of the Treasury bill rate to free reserves during this period declined. This experience heightened concerns about the reliability of free reserve targets and whether monetary policy had done as much as it could to increase money growth and avoid recession. It suggests also that members used free reserves to proxy for interest rates.

The minutes give several reasons for the absence of a relation between free reserves and the Treasury bill rate in this period. The most plausible reason was the behavior of the manager, who increased or decreased the supply of reserves to maintain the bill rate at 2 percent or above, as Chart 3.8 suggests. The 2 percent rate was said to be the minimum rate that foreigners would accept to hold Treasury bills instead of shipping gold abroad. On this interpretation, the variability of free reserves traces out the volatile demand for free reserves in that period.

At the October 4, 1960, meeting, several members commented on the necessity of a balance of payments policy. Some suggested that higher in-

66. In the week before the election, John F. Kennedy tried to reduce these concerns by pledging to maintain the $35 gold price. For the first time, the Eisenhower administration authorized the Bank of England to sell gold as its agent, and the Bank agreed to lower its discount rate by 0.5 to narrow the spread over the U.S. rate.

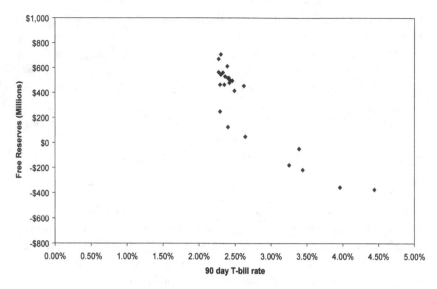

Chart 3.8. Free reserves versus ninety-day bill Rate (auction), January 1960–December 1961.

terest rates abroad restricted the System's ability to reduce short-term rates. Buying longer-term securities, and abandoning bills-only, now seemed more acceptable.[67]

By the October 25–26 meeting several of the members noted that the economy had declined further. Their immediate concern was the balance of payments deficit and the gold price increase. Woodlief Thomas pointed out that several members proposed inconsistent actions. They proposed "purchasing longer-term securities . . . bringing about a desirable downward adjustment in long-term interest rates and stimulating borrowing in that area, and at the same time avoid reducing short-term rates and encouraging the flow of funds abroad. Any such operation would more than likely defeat the purposes for which it was intended. . . . The eventual recipients of the funds determine how they are used. What is desired is for investors to place their funds in longer-term issues, not simply for the Federal Reserve to buy them"[68] (FOMC Minutes, October 25, 1960, 11).

67. The new administration proposed a similar policy after taking office but expected resistance from the Federal Reserve. In October 1960, three-month Treasury bill rates in London and Frankfurt were 5.36 and 4.88 percent respectively.

68. Thomas may have remembered previous attempts to change the slope of the yield curve by selling long-term and buying short-term issues or the reverse. These efforts before World War II and during the early postwar had not been successful. Thomas's statement explained why policy actions had failed to increase money and credit. System actions and a $500 million increase in float supplied about $900 million of additional reserves since early

Thomas warned them that they could not expect to stimulate economic activity by keeping short-term rates from declining "or by artificial action designed to bring about a decrease in long-term rates" (ibid., 12).

Martin summarized the consensus. The manager should supply the seasonal increase in reserves even if interest rates fell below 2 percent. Robert Rouse, the account manager, responded that he understood that he was to keep free reserves between $300 and $500 million. He then asked for permission to deal in longer-term securities, up to fifteen months. The FOMC granted the request, effectively ending bills-only. After years of struggle, New York had a victory.

The committee voted unanimously to change the directive to increase maximum holdings from $1 billion to $1.5 billion and to add to part (b) of the directive the phrase "while taking into consideration current international developments" (ibid., 58). This satisfied the members but left unresolved how, if at all, the new constraint would affect their actions. In practice, the manager ignored Martin's proviso and kept the Treasury bill rate above 2 percent.

The FOMC remained divided about how much to ease monetary policy and how much attention to pay to the loss of gold. Several members urged the manager to keep Treasury bill rates above 2 percent, but the committee did not include that instruction in the directive. The FOMC also divided over whether the manager had followed its instructions.[69] Governor Robertson rebuked the manager both for keeping policy too tight and for excessive use of repurchase agreements at rates below the discount rate. Johns (St. Louis) joined in the criticism, but others, including Martin, praised the manager.[70]

The consensus on November 24, 1960, was to keep policy unchanged, a surprising conclusion since the members did not agree on precisely what

---

August. The reserves financed a $500 million gold outflow, a $200 million reduction in borrowing, and a $200 million increase in required reserves. The last of these supported the 2 percent growth of money. But the money stock was $3 billion less than at its previous peak in June 1959 (FOMC Minutes, October 25, 1960, 10).

69. Some of the suggestions were contradictory, for example calling for targeting free reserves and the bill rate. Several members proposed ignoring free reserves at that time. Earlier the Treasury responded to a question from New York banks about financing gold purchases abroad by United States citizens. The Treasury statement said that "buying or selling gold outside the United States, although permitted by Treasury regulations, was not in the national interest and should not be encouraged or facilitated" (Board Minutes, November 7, 1960, 3). The staff reported that the Treasury had considered amending the regulation to require a license to buy or sell gold outside the country. The Board's staff opposed because the regulation could not be enforced and might have an adverse psychological effect.

70. In early November, repurchase agreements averaged more than $500 million a week, the largest amount to that time.

that meant or whether the manager had followed instructions. Martin commented that the world awaited a clear view of what the new administration would do. He complained that there was a widespread belief outside the System that the budget, the cost-price relationship, debt management policy, etc. could all be solved if the System would just increase short-term rates and cut long-term rates. The System could only target the spread briefly without getting into trouble (FOMC Minutes, November 24, 1960, 41–42). He did not elaborate, but his statement anticipated the pressures that would soon be upon him to "twist the yield curve."

Robertson urged the System to raise the ceiling rate on time and saving deposits high enough to signal their belief that interest rates would never reach that level. Banks could then set their own rates according to local conditions. Bopp (Philadelphia) and Trieber (New York) supported him. "Martin said this was an appropriate subject for discussion . . . [and that] a good case could be made for permitting banks to pay interest on demand deposits" (FOMC Minutes, November 24, 1960, 45). Nothing changed.

Between meetings, the Board completed the release of vault cash to reserves. The reserve requirement ratio for country banks increased from 11 to 12 percent, and effective December 1 the Board lowered the reserve requirement ratios for central reserve city banks by one percentage point to 16.5 percent. The ratios were now the same at central reserve and reserve city banks in anticipation of the elimination of the central reserve city classification in July 1962.[71] The purpose of these changes was to release reserves seasonally without announcing a change in interest rates or in

71. The Board announced the decision on October 26. The staff estimated that the action released $1.3 million reserves; central reserve city banks gained $400 million, reserve city banks $380 million, and country banks $900 million by including all remaining vault cash in required reserves. The increase in the country bank reserve requirement ratio from 11 to 12 percent absorbed $380 million. Country banks held $538 million in excess reserves in October, $200 million above the level of the previous year. The Board's press release reported that the 1959 legislation and the Board's actions reduced average reserve requirement ratios adjusted for the release of vault cash from 14.5 to 12 percent at country banks, 18.2 to 16.5 percent at reserve city banks, and 18.7 to 16.5 percent at central reserve city banks.

The Board also discussed a staff recommendation to reduce float by increasing from two to three days the maximum length of time before granting deferred availability credit in the check collection process. The proposal made this change effective on January 16, 1961. The plan was to use the adjustment of float to remove the seasonal increase in reserves provided by the release of vault cash. Several governors objected to changing the time schedule for deferred availability credit so far in advance or without discussion by the Federal Advisory Council. The Board approved the changes in vault cash and requirement ratios without the change in deferred availability credit. Governor Robertson voted no because he believed the action was taken too much in advance of its effective date, and because reversing a seasonal increase by changing the availability schedule should be announced at the same time. (The deferred availability schedule gave the length of time between a bank's request for check collection and the payment of reserves.)

open market operations. In fact the bill rate remained unchanged at the time of the release.

Treasury bill yields rose in November and December, but growth of the monetary base also rose. The unemployment rate reached 6.6 percent in December, as the rate of decline in industrial production increased. At the November 15 meeting of the Federal Advisory Council, the bankers reported that loans at money center banks were close to an all-time high level. Some of these loans were to finance inventories that would be reduced. The FAC did not think rate reduction or faster money growth was called for[72] (Board Minutes, November 15, 1960, 10–11).

President Hayes (New York) shifted his position at the December FOMC meeting. He favored free reserves at $750 million, $100 million above the level of the previous week. He wanted to use "creative methods" to add reserves so that bill rates would be less affected. Robertson joined him in seeking a more expansive policy, but he also wanted a 0.25 percentage point reduction in the discount rate. Recognizing the income effect of expansion, he favored an overtly expansive policy to show that the Federal Reserve would do as much as possible to strengthen the economy. This would improve the balance of payments, he said (FOMC Minutes, December 13, 1960, 19). With inflation no longer a problem, Robertson became an avid proponent of easier policy.

The conflict between domestic and international concerns or between obligations under the Employment Act and the Bretton Woods Agreement became apparent. Both Mills and Martin wanted to tighten, although Martin recognized that the domestic economy called for ease. Bryan (Atlanta) wanted more attention to domestic problems.[73] In a statement reminiscent of the 1920s, Mills warned against "forced feeding of new reserves into the commercial banking system which policy . . . has been proven ineffective" (ibid., 19). He warned against repeating the mistake of the 1920s, when policy tried to achieve conflicting aims. Martin's consensus statement called for the same degree of ease while keeping Treasury bill rates as high as possible. As on previous occasions, that statement gave no

72. "Chairman Martin expressed the view that the biggest shadow on the domestic business picture was cast by the balance-of-payments problem. . . . There were some suggestions that a reduction in the discount rate to a substantially lower level and a much greater availability of money would do a lot for the economy, but he questioned that reasoning" (Board Minutes, November 15, 1960, 9).

73. Bryan said that total reserves were on a 3 percent growth path, and this was adequate. See Chart 3.7, above, showing that the real value of the monetary base had turned positive. Bryan also reminded the members that when Britain devalued in 1931, the Federal Reserve had protected the gold stock instead of the domestic economy, a catastrophic error. Martin responded that there was now no question about the credit of the United States.

guidance to the manager except to use his judgment as he sorted out the conflicting opinions of FOMC members.[74]

The gold outflow continued at a higher level. Marget's report to the January 10, 1961, FOMC showed sales of $1.2 billion in the fourth quarter (excluding the purchase from the IMF), and $130 million in the first week of January. Almost all the sales were to Europe, principally Britain and Switzerland, where gold markets were active. He now described the outflow as "flight from the dollar," language he rejected earlier (FOMC Minutes, January 10, 1961, 10). Foreign governments had begun to convert dollar holdings into gold using the London and Zurich markets. The change occurred while the deficit on current and long-term capital transactions had fallen to an annual rate of $1 billion.

Few positions on FOMC changed. The consensus was to maintain the status quo without explaining what that meant. Robertson wanted more expansive action, but he did not dissent.

Martin changed the schedule in view of the new administration taking office. The FOMC met again two weeks later. Between meeting dates, President Kennedy signed an order prohibiting United States citizens from holding gold abroad, and the German Bundesbank lowered its discount rate to narrow the interest rate differential with the United States.

The FOMC was almost equally divided between raising short-term interest rates despite the continuing recession and maintaining the status quo, described in various ways. Only Bryan (Atlanta) and Robertson favored more expansive actions. Martin preferred less ease, but the consensus favored the status quo. He added that if the bill rate fell below 2 percent, the FOMC would hold a telephone conference to raise it.[75]

Soon after the new year the recession ended, and the gold outflow abated from $440 million in December to $320 million in January. A staff economist, Guy Noyes, told the FOMC at the February 7 meeting that the recession was near its trough. He anticipated decline for one additional quarter, followed by the start of recovery in the second quarter. Hayes disagreed.

74. The manager reported that the International Monetary Fund sold the United States Treasury $300 million in gold and invested the proceeds in Treasury securities. The New York Federal Reserve acted as fiscal agent with the Board's approval. The Treasury agreed to resell the gold to the IMF at the price prevailing at the time of resale. The IMF did not have earnings sufficient to cover its expenditures. Some Board members expressed concern that the market might interpret the sale as support for the dollar. Previous transactions had been done in 1956 and 1959 (Board Minutes, December 5, 1960, 5–8).

75. President Frederick L. Deming (Minneapolis) reported on his trip to Asia and Europe. Asians were not concerned about the dollar, but they feared a reduction in foreign aid for balance of payments reasons. Europeans were much more concerned, although concern had lessened recently. Confidence was delicately balanced (FOMC Minutes, January 24, 1961, 27–28).

He expected the recession to deepen, and to further put pressure on the dollar, if the budget deficit exceeded projections. In fact, real GNP rose at an annual rate of 4.2 percent in the first quarter. The price deflator was unchanged for the quarter, and the budget deficit was $3.8 billion for the year. FOMC members divided almost equally between those who favored a free reserve target and those who preferred to target an interest rate, usually the Treasury bill rate. Robertson objected to this reasoning. Raising short-term rates harmed the domestic economy. He believed that the capital outflow would reverse when the economy recovered and interest rates moved up, and he was skeptical of efforts to lower long-term rates while raising short-term rates. No one commented on his statement.[76]

Martin said the consensus was to keep the bill rate and the discount rate unchanged. He added that "free reserves may have outlived their usefulness" (FOMC Minutes, February 7, 1961, 41). Robertson dissented from the action. He agreed that Martin's consensus reflected the group discussion, but he disagreed with the decision. Johns (St. Louis) was not a voting member, but he disagreed with the consensus also. He wanted faster growth of total reserves to speed recovery.

Despite the restrictive fiscal policy, the very modest rate of increase in nominal base money, a gradual reduction in short-term interest rates, and a hesitant and divided FOMC, the recession had remained mild. Zarnowitz and Moore (1986) score it as one of the mildest recessions in Federal Reserve history. Although the new administration was slow to recognize its end, the recession trough came in February one month after they took office. By December 1961, industrial production was 10 percent above the previous year.

END OF BILLS-ONLY

Following the election, pressure on the Federal Reserve to abandon bills-only increased. Critics again called the Federal Reserve doctrinaire and gave more attention to this aspect of the System's operating procedure than seems warranted. Some of the pressure to change came from a desire to experiment with a policy of reducing the capital outflow by raising short-term rates while encouraging investment and recovery by lowering long-term rates. The Federal Reserve had taken some tentative steps in

---

76. This was the last meeting for Hugh Leach, president of the Richmond bank. He had served for twenty-five years. He praised the System's actions since the spring then added, "[T]here was much room for improvement in the manner of handling the directive to the New York bank" (FOMC Minutes, February 7, 1961, 30). Edward A. Wayne succeeded him. George H. Ellis replaced Joseph Erickson at the Boston bank, and George Clay replaced H. G. Leedy at Kansas City.

that direction the previous November by buying some longer-term issues while generally keeping the bill rate above 2.25 percent and by formally eliminating the bills-only operating procedures in December 1960, a few weeks after the election.

The timing was not accidental. The Democrats in Congress and Kennedy in his campaign had criticized bills-only sharply and repeatedly. Prior to his inauguration, President Kennedy appointed domestic and international policy task forces, chaired by Paul Samuelson and Allan Sproul respectively. Sproul had opposed bills-only from the start, so it was no surprise that both committee reports favored abandonment. Samuelson's report also favored "operation twist," an effort to change the relation of short- to long-term interest rates by buying one and selling the other and restricting the Treasury to sell only Treasury bills. Sproul's report expressed concern about changing the average maturity of Treasury debt[77] (Oral History Interview, 1964, James Tobin, August 1, 208–9).

The next step was to get an agreement with the Federal Reserve. "Before the inauguration, Kennedy asked me [Heller] to go over and visit with Bill Martin to assess whether he would be cooperative or obstructionist. . . . I met Bill and was just enormously taken with him. He pledged, 'I'm not going to give up the independence of the Fed.' I said, 'Well I'm sure that's not what the President's going to ask you to do.' But Martin added 'There's plenty of room here for cooperation'" (Hargrove and Morley, 1984, 189).[78]

Separately, Treasury Secretary–designate Douglas Dillon told the president-elect about the regular meetings that President Eisenhower held

77. George W. Ball headed a third task force on gold and the balance of payments. "I have always assumed that Bob Roosa got Doug Dillon to get JFK to appoint the Sproul task force. Bob and his friends were afraid about what the Samuelson task force might say about domestic policy and what the Ball task force might say about gold and the balance of payments. . . . I think the idea was to have a sound committee which would reassure the financial community here and abroad. . . . I went to see him [Roosa] at least once in New York at the Fed bank [before inauguration]. He was an old friend and I expected we could work together. But it was soon apparent that he regarded me as an enemy and a threat" (Oral History Interview, 1964, James Tobin, August 1, 208–9). Tobin added these remarks when he reviewed his oral history transcript. My own experience supplements his interpretation. Shortly after the Kennedy administration came into office, Robert Roosa became Undersecretary of the Treasury. He hired me (about February) to serve on his staff to counter the staff work at the Council. I arrived in late May or early June after classes ended. By that time, Roosa was confident of the Treasury's influence in the administration. He did not have much for me to do, so he gave me mail to answer. I had excluded this assignment when I agreed to come. I resigned and became a part-time consultant for a year or so.

78. Heller added that he came to Washington dubious about Federal Reserve independence but came out believing that world was prone to inflation, so it was very useful to have an independent central bank not subject to elections. This is very much in the spirit of Rogoff's (1985) case for a conservative central banker.

with Chairman Martin, the Secretary of the Treasury, director of the Budget Bureau, and chairman of the Council of Economic Advisers. These meetings, without a formal agenda, gave "the President an opportunity to hear at first hand the views of the senior officials of the government most intimately connected with economic problems [and] also served as a mechanism tying the Federal Reserve Board more closely in with the executive branch" (memo, Dillon to Kennedy, Dillon papers, Box 33, January 17, 1961).

In a memo soon after the new administration took office, Heller reminded the president of the proposal. "The current task of monetary policy and debt management is to achieve the credit expansion our domestic economy requires without impairing our ability to hold and to attract internationally mobile liquid funds. Reduction of long-term interest rates relative to short-term rates is within the present capacity of the Federal Reserve System and the Treasury" (Heller to the president, Heller papers, Box 19, January 25, 1961).[79] Martin and Roosa tried to weaken the commitment in the president's statement, and Dillon warned that "there are limitations to what can be accomplished" (memo to the president, Dillon papers, Box 33, January 31, 1961). He reminded the president that the Federal Reserve would make the change; "it would seem advisable to avoid any public implication that they are taking these new steps as a result of outside pressure" (ibid.). President Kennedy did not take that advice. In his first economic message on February 2, he asked for lower long-term and higher short-term rates. Martin had agreed to the language in the statement, although the FOMC had not yet acted (Oral History Interview, 1964, Tobin, August 1, 212).

Martin had to get his colleagues on FOMC to accept the change. He presented the issue in executive session as a political issue. The System was under attack for being uncompromising. It had to show that it was open-minded and willing to experiment "to enable the System to escape from the charge of doctrinaire commitment to a laissez faire, free private market position" (FOMC Minutes, February 7, 1961, 45). He was doubtful about the outcome, but he saw no other way to respond.[80] This was a

79. Heller also proposed that the Treasury should borrow at the short end, that regulation Q ceiling rates should be removed, and that special issues of short-term securities should be offered to foreign central banks and governments. Heller gave Robert Roosa (not James Tobin) credit for proposing the "twist" of the yield curve (Hargrove and Morley, 1984, 190). The New York bank had favored such operations during the bills-only years. Heller reminded the Federal Reserve frequently about the importance of purchasing long-term securities. Apparently, he failed to convince the Treasury. In 1962, they used advanced refunding of debt to lengthen average maturity of the outstanding government debt.

80. *Newsweek* sent one of its editors to question Martin about his commitment to the

step back from his 1953 speech about free markets and further evidence of willingness to reduce independence.

Robert Rouse, the manager, had prepared a report of a subcommittee on these issues. It called for authority to trade in securities of up to 10 years maturity, concentrating at first in the 1- to 5.5-year maturities. Transactions would not affect reserves. He described the actions as an experiment, with quantities limited to "$400 million securities maturing beyond fifteen months and up to five and one-half years, and an additional $100 million securities maturing . . . up to ten years" (FOMC Minutes, February 7, 1961, 50). Rouse suggested that they announce the change "in the light of changes in the international and domestic situations" (ibid.). Ralph Young, a senior adviser to Martin, opposed the change as a return to pegging.[81]

Allen (Chicago) commented first. Since this was an interim report, "he welcomed the opportunity to study the recommendations which he had just heard on such an important subject" (ibid., 51). Martin had made a commitment, however, and wanted no delay; he responded that "a decision would have to be made at the present meeting" (ibid., 51). Allen did not have a vote, but he said he was opposed. He added that if the committee voted to make the change, they should announce it.

Martin spoke early, an unusual step taken only when he wanted a specific action. He favored the change and opposed the announcement. Hayes (New York), Johns (St. Louis), Bopp (Philadelphia), Robertson, and Shephardson favored announcing the change, but Martin resisted with uncharacteristic force. Several of the members expressed doubt that the change would have much effect. No one mentioned that the FOMC in the 1930s had considerable experience with buying long-term and selling short-term securities.

The committee allowed the alternate members to vote. The vote was fifteen to one, with one president absent. Robertson voted no. His principal reason was that the FOMC had based its existing procedures on careful

administration's policy. Martin told him that he took the initiative to cooperate with the administration. "I will wholeheartedly make an effort to see that this new policy is operating. . . . There are 12 bank presidents and six other board members . . . and some of them are quite unhappy about this" (memo to the files, Heller papers, February 23, 1961). Martin said he was not certain that the policy would reduce long-term interest rates, but "he did not want the Fed to be considered 'obstructionist.'" (ibid.)

81. After the meeting, Rouse sent a memo suggesting that the FOMC could control the yield curve (relation of short- to long-term debt.) Young opposed on two grounds. It would become a movable peg, and the relation of investment to long-term interest rates was not as close as Rouse claimed (memo, Young to Martin, Board Records, February 20, 1961).

analytic and empirical work. These procedures worked. By making the change, the FOMC "was asserting, without reason or conviction, that it made a critically incorrect judgment eight years ago and had pursued incorrect operating procedures since" (ibid., 59). He objected, also, that the new procedures gave "practically unlimited authority to the Manager . . . for the stated purpose of affecting rates as distinguished from providing or withdrawing reserves" (ibid., 60).

Martin did not say that the change was made for political reasons. He ruled that the committee would not issue a statement. This was a strange ruling. Once the System bought longer-term securities, or asked for quotations from the dealers, the market would know that a change occurred. Martin may have been embarrassed by his decision to yield to political pressure and therefore reluctant to call attention to the decision. After further discussions with Hayes, Rouse, and Roosa, who favored issuing a statement, Martin reversed the decision so that "all market participants [would] be informed at the same time" (ibid., 62). The announcement referred to conditions in the domestic economy and the balance of payments to explain the change (letter, Rouse to Martin, Board Records, February 20, 1961).[82] It did not say whether the change was temporary or permanent. Probably Martin had not decided.

That brought a formal end to eight years of bills-only. During the next two years, the FOMC purchased nearly $4 billion of coupon securities, mainly securities with one to five years maturity. Table 3.3 shows the detail. Years later, the staff reviewed the experience and the several studies of the effect of intervention. They summarized: the general conclusion drawn from the academic studies was that "even sizeable changes in the term structure of debt exert only a relatively small and short-lived impact on the shape of the yield curve" (memo, "Expanded Desk Buying of Coupon

---

82. The desk filed a report describing the first days operation. They began the operation at 2:30 p.m. to leave only a short time to react before the bond market closed at 3 p.m. The staff chose three issues and asked for offers from the fifteen dealers who traded long-term governments. Only twelve dealers made offers. The desk bought $13.5 million out of $20 million offered. The memo described the dealers' reaction as "routine." There were no comments or "significant questions." The memo compared prices just before the announcement to the prices paid by the desk to show that prices did not increase. After the first purchases, dealers raised market quotations 6/32 in the issues purchased and 18/32 in longer-term issues (memo, Spencer Marsh, Jr., to Ralph Young, Board Records, February 21, 1961). These were large changes at the time. The next day Marsh reported that press reaction was mild. Dealer reaction ranged "from commendation to violent antagonism" (Marsh to Young, Board Records, February 24, 1961). Bond prices continued to rise, reducing yields one to ten basis points for intermediate bonds and three to eight basis points for long-term issues. Short-term rates rose anticipating the administration's program.

Table 3.3   Changes in the Open Market Portfolio 1961–62 (in millions $)

Type and Maturity	1961	1962
Bills	293	−751
Treasury coupon issues of which:	1445	2507
Under 1 year	−874	683
1–5 years	1826	1461
Over 5 years	788	363
Redemptions	−295	

Source: Board Records, May 7, 1975.

Issues," Board Records, May 7, 1975, 16). This was not the view taken by the Council of Economic Advisers at the time.[83]

Martin explained his willingness to change procedures in a letter to a Boston banker. The banker expressed concern that the Federal Reserve might again peg interest rates and asked several questions including whether "pressure was involved [and] how far has the Reserve System lost the independence which it regained in 1951?" (letter, Lloyd Brace to Martin, Board Records, February 23, 1961). Martin's response showed an open mind. He denied that the Federal Reserve was about to peg yields. The reason for the new procedures was to find out "if they can be of some help in dealing with new problems, when the desirability of the result seems certain, even though the possibility of its attainment as yet remains uncertain" (letter, Martin to Lloyd Brace, Board Records, February 28, 1961). The procedural change could possibly answer some of the many questions. "Experience alone can demonstrate what otherwise can only be argued" (ibid.).

Experience did not give strong support to those who wanted intervention. By June 1961, the desk offered its explanation of why the "experiment" had not worked as expected. The System had purchased $1.466 billion of coupon issues plus $1.367 in bills, and it sold $1.903 billion of bills and other short-term securities between February 20 and June 2. The Treasury had purchased $673 million in coupon issues and sold $600 million in short-term securities. At the end, bill rates were 0.024 percent-

---

83. "The idea was to bring down rates for the long-terms because they were the ones that were important for housing, for investment and so forth. That was working fine. But the trouble is that we would have a meeting with Kennedy—and before the meeting Bill [Martin] would be out there buying those long-term securities, but afterwards his buying would flag. It would go up before the meeting and go down afterwards. . . . So I would call a meeting and sure enough the purchases would rise again, and Martin would be able to tell Kennedy, 'We're doing everything we can'" (Heller in Hargrove and Morley, 1984, 191).

age points lower; yields on three- to five-year issues remained unchanged. The System's intent was to twist the yield curve. It had "no intention of dominating the market or of seeking to push long rates in a direction contrary to that indicated by market forces" (Memo, Operations Outside the Short-term Area, Board Records, June 5, 1961, 1). This effort was "seriously hampered by the numerous statements of Administration officials, and also by a great deal of press discussion, suggesting that our intentions are, ought to be, or will be, considerably more aggressive than we know them or want them to be" (ibid, 2). Nevertheless, the staff urged the FOMC to continue the program to supply reserves and avoid downward pressure on short-term rates.[84]

A week before the June 6 FOMC meeting, Heller and Tobin met with Martin for more than two hours. Heller reported to President Kennedy that, though the meeting was friendly, the policy of lowering long-term rates "is in jeopardy" (memo for the president, Heller papers, Box 19, May 31, 1961). Martin, he said, had lost conviction that the policy could lower long-term rates. "He will continue to buy intermediate and long-term bonds, and . . . there will be no reversal of this basic policy. . . . But, he is very pessimistic" (ibid.). He urged Kennedy to have another Quadriad meeting.[85]

Martin told Tobin and Heller that at least seven members of FOMC voted with him against their own conviction. The Federal Advisory Council "was against the new policy from the beginning and at its last meeting suggested that it be abandoned. . . . Many people favor returning to dealing in bills to provide the bank reserves that the Open Market Committee deems appropriate" (memo, Tobin to the files, Heller papers, Box 19, May 30, 1961, 5). Reminded that the president had committed publicly to continued monetary ease, Martin said "he had an equal desire to keep the

84. The same memo noted that market participants used the System's purchases of intermediate- and long-term bonds to adjust their portfolios cyclically. The Treasury started buying dollars forward and gained assistance from the Bundesbank to support the dollar. In 1961, the administration took steps to reduce military spending and get aid recipients to purchase in the United States.

85. Tobin's memo about the same meeting also reports that the meeting was friendly. Martin complained about public statements by Council members that put pressure on the Federal Reserve. He cited Tobin's statement about a reduction in the discount rate and concern about rumors of "severe disagreement" (memo, Tobin to the files, Heller papers, Box 19, May 30, 1961, 2). Martin said the Council had the right to state its position, but the System made monetary policy. On long-term rates, Martin said the Federal Reserve was the "sole buyer in the market. . . . [T]here was a real problem of maintaining government bond prices without engaging in 'pegging'" (ibid., 2–3). Martin thought that market psychology anticipated recovery and possibly inflation. There was no shortage of liquidity with free reserves at $500 million. Tobin wanted a commitment that Martin would prevent an increase in bill rates during the recovery. Martin maintained independence and rejected that proposal (4). It restored pegging.

President from embarrassment" (ibid., 6). He agreed to keep free reserves at about $500 million.

A month later, the desk explained that the FOMC had reduced the volume of purchases and restricted their scope to supplying reserves and offsetting sales of short-term securities. It asked for the right to purchase "when congestion appears to be developing . . . or when market expectations as to the future course of rates seem to be having clearly exaggerated effects"[86] (Memo, Open Market Operations in Intermediate and Longer Term Securities, Board Records, July 7, 1961). The FOMC rejected the request.

By July, several FOMC members decided the new procedure had failed and wanted to end it. Hayes claimed that the international aspect was successful. The gold outflow slowed. Also, he claimed that long-term rates would have increased more than they did. Robertson said that the procedure had made the long-term market "thinner and made Treasury auctions more difficult," the same position that Martin expressed to Tobin and Heller in May. Most of the members took an intermediate position; they were not ready to conclude that the new procedure had failed but were unwilling to expand it. Martin also was not ready to declare the procedure a failure or to end it, but he opposed expanding the manager's discretionary authority (FOMC Minutes, July 11, 6–9; August 1, 1961, 54). He did not mention the commitment he had made to Heller and Tobin, but he agreed to reduce purchases of long-term debt.

Three features of this continuing discussion are representative of the way in which the System made decisions. First, no one suggested a systematic evaluation of the experience.[87] Both proponents and opponents relied on anecdotes or judgments of market participants and foreigners. These

---

86. From February to June, the desk purchased securities other than bills in every week but one. The System stopped adding to reserves in June, and the Treasury curtailed purchases also. Council of Economic Advisers members were not convinced. Heller sent memos to the president in April, May, and June 1961 complaining about the Federal Reserve. (In their internal discussions, they included the Treasury because they believed that Secretary Dillon and Undersecretary Roosa agreed with the Fed.) After one meeting of the four top economic officials, now called the Quadriad, Heller exulted that before the meeting with President Kennedy the Federal Reserve increased its purchases (Monetary Policy, Heller papers Box 19, April 13, 1961). By mid-May, average yields on long-term Treasury bonds had fallen twenty basis points (0.2 percentage points) from their peak in January. By August, they were back above the January peak. For the rest of 1961, these rates remained about 4 percent. Yields on state and local bonds show no effect of the policy change. Corporate bond yields declined more modestly than governments and only from January to March 1961.

87. The desk investigated the use made of the proceeds received by sellers of long-term governments. It concluded, "It is virtually impossible to trace the proceeds of the earlier dealer purchases" (memo, Rouse to FOMC, Board Records August 18, 1961, 1). The effort recalls attempts in the 1920s to control the quality of credit. The staff collected data on net

were as mixed as the members' opinions. Second, the capital outflow and loss of gold were a continuing problem. Keeping the bill rate at 2 percent or 2.5 percent, without changing reserve or money growth, was at best a short-term palliative. Third, most of the FOMC voted to support their chairman. No doubt they recognized the political pressure that he faced, but if a member raised such concerns at the meeting, it did not appear in the minutes. Yet Martin's commitment, of which the members were unaware, to keep free reserves near $500 million tied the FOMC's hands. Nevertheless, the Federal Reserve kept the commitment. Monthly average free reserves remained between $435 and $549 million from June 1961 to February 1962. Martin accepted a Federal funds rate as low as 1.16 percent in July 1961 to implement the policy. Treasury bill rates did not fall below 2.2 percent, however.

Pressure from the administration to increase purchases of long-term debt remained strong. Martin cooperated, within the limits set by his concern about inflation and his beliefs about how monetary policy worked. But he regarded some of Tobin's arguments as "hopelessly naïve" (memo, Tobin to files, Heller papers, Box 19, May 30, 1961, 4).[88]

Table 3.4 shows the changes in the Federal Reserve portfolio under bills-only and operation twist.[89] The large percentage and absolute decline in maturities of ninety-one days to one year in both periods reflects the phasing out of Treasury certificates. As expected, the Federal Reserve acquired bills during the bills-only period. It also acquired one- to five-year securities in an amount equal to 96 percent of its overall net acquisition. During operation twist, the System acquired mainly bills, 72 percent of its net addition, and added substantially to the percentage of short-term bills in its portfolio. It continued to add to its one- to five-year holdings, but the portfolio percentage for this range changed very little. The System added a bit to its holdings of five- to ten-year bonds. These data suggest that the

---

acquisition of various types of assets by groups of lenders, but could not identify the marginal use of long-term funds.

88. The Council discovered also that Martin was morally committed to fight inflation and believed that only the Federal Reserve would do that. Also, he did not share their belief that inflation would not occur until unemployment reached 4 percent. He thought much of the unemployment was structural and technological and could not be lowered by monetary policy (Tobin files, Heller papers, Box 19, May 30, 1961, 5).

89. There is no terminal date for operation twist. I have used the month in which Congress passed the tax cut. President Johnson showed much less interest in meetings of the Quadriad to twist the yield curve or in the balance of payments deficit. When the payments problem worsened, he relied mainly on direct controls. The data in the table are based on Federal Reserve holdings, so they are net of sales and include redemptions and changes in maturity. Table 3.4 shows gross purchases of long-term securities after 1961.

Table 3.4   Federal Reserve Portfolio and Composition (in millions $)

DATE	TOTAL	UP TO 90 DAYS	91 DAYS– 1 YEAR	1–5 YEARS	5–10 YEARS	OVER 10 YEARS
February 1953	23875	584	14208	6655	1070	1358
February 1961	26667	4735	11128	9344	1189	271
Change 53–61	2792	4151	−3080	2689	119	−1087
February 1964	33169	8825	9909	12149	2067	219
Change 61–64	6502	4090	−1219	2805	878	−52
Composition (percentage)						
February 1953		2.4	59.5	27.9	4.5	5.7
February 1961		17.8	41.7	35.0	4.4	1.0
February 1964		26.6	29.9	36.6	6.2	0.6

Source: Board of Governors (1976, 489–91).

pressures on Martin to raise short-term and lower longer-term rates did not have great effect on System policy actions.

END OF THE RECESSION

The National Bureau of Economic Research places the trough of the recession in February 1961. By early March, the Board's staff promptly recognized a slower decline and a month later described the recovery as under way; there were measurable gains in output and employment[90] (FOMC Minutes, April 18, 1961).

The rate of decline of the real monetary base slowed almost a year earlier, in May 1960, but the growth rate did not become positive until January 1961, one month before the recession trough. Real base growth continued to rise but did not reach three percent for more than a year. As on several previous occasions, ex post real interest rates show no evidence of a cyclical decline. Chart 3.9 shows the slight rise in the real long-term rate near the cyclical trough in early 1961. Once again, most of the cyclical action is in real base growth not in the real interest rate.

Monetary expansion received no help from fiscal policy during the recession. The budget had a small surplus in 1960 resulting from $11 billion of increased tax collections and almost $2 billion reduction in outlays. The

90. The Federal Advisory Council did not think the recession had ended until its May meeting, but in February they believed the economy was approaching a bottom (Board Minutes, February 21, 1961, 2). The members considered most of the unemployment as structural, the result of technological change, so they did not favor more expansive policy (ibid., 7). Chairman Martin asked about lowering interest rates. He expressed his view that the Federal Reserve should give highest priority to the domestic economy (ibid., 20). This was a change from 1960.

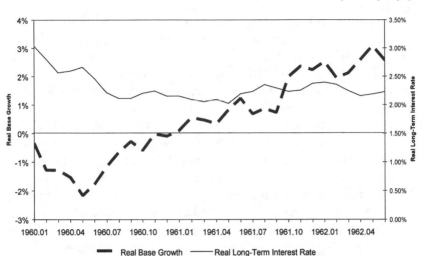

Chart 3.9. Real base growth versus real long-term interest rate, January 1960–June 1962. Real base growth measured year over year; long-term interest rate measured as yield on ten-year Treasury bonds.

budget went back into deficit in 1961 as spending and outlays increased. The increase came after the recession ended, although the public may have anticipated the change after the election.

Real GNP rose at a 5 percent average for the first three quarters of 1961 and at a 9.3 percent annual rate in the fourth quarter. Consumer prices rose less than one percent in 1961. Unemployment reached a peak (7.1 percent) in May. By year-end it had fallen to 6.0 percent.

The recovery occurred during a period of deflation. Consumer prices rose between 0.6 and 1.2 percent from April 1961 to October 1962. Adjusted for the upward bias in the price index, consumer prices declined. This is the last sustained price decline in the postwar years. This experience does not support the prevalent view that monetary policy is impotent in deflation. As in earlier periods of deflation, the economy recovered. The monetary base rose and the federal funds rate declined during the early months of deflation. Thereafter rates rose as shown in Chart 3.6 above.

The FOMC was divided and uncertain about how to give directions in the first half of 1961. Some favored the "experiment" of raising short-term rates and reducing long-term rates, but others opposed any operations in long-term securities. Some continued to use free reserves as the target, but others used an interest rate, total reserves, or the ratio of money to GNP. Chairman Martin had committed to the administration to keep free reserves at about $500 million and to purchase longer-term securities, so discussion of the policy stance or the target had little if any effect on the actions taken. Monthly average federal funds rates ranged from 1.16 to 2.02 percent during this period. Member bank borrowing remained below $100 million throughout.

Through the early months of the recovery, Robertson, usually joined by Bryan (Atlanta), and Johns (St. Louis), wanted a more expansive policy. Robertson urged the FOMC to let the Treasury bill rate fall as much as required to get free reserves up to $650 to $750 million. If gold flowed out when interest rates fell, it would return when rates rose. This reasoning, though correct, attracted little support.[91] Mills placed most emphasis on supporting the dollar. Most others went along with the administration policy of maintaining Treasury bill rates and reducing long-term rates.

Controlling Treasury bill rates proved difficult while fulfilling the conditions on free reserves. Foreign central banks bought heavily in late March, so bill rates dropped to 2.25 percent from 2.45 percent at the previous meeting. At the lower rate, bill rates were the same in New York and London.

At the March 28 meeting, Rouse reported difficulties in buying coupon securities. As Martin had feared earlier, when the desk asked the dealers for quotations and offerings, traders stopped their activity to await the new prices (FOMC Minutes, March 28, 1961). He asked for authority to operate in maturities beyond ten years. Allen and Robertson dissented. Robertson explained that this was a "further delegation of authority to the Manager of the Account without any plan or program to guide him. He did not believe the Manager could be expected to carry out the Committee's unspecified objectives—whatever they were—solely on the basis of his own intuition" (FOMC Minutes, March 28, 1961, 59).

The committee could not agree on a target or state precisely what the policy was. Martin used words like "maintain moderate ease" and left it to the manager to implement as best he could. This grant of discretion pleased the manager and the New York administration. They could now operate as they did before bills-only. Martin, on his side, could take advantage of the FOMC's lack of precision to fulfill his agreement with the Kennedy administration economists. Robertson and Allen (Chicago) continued to dissent at each meeting from authorization to deal in long-term debt.[92]

Foreign support continued. In April, the FOMC minutes report that

91. I made the same argument to Robert Roosa and his deputy Dewey Daane when I worked in the Treasury in 1961. It had the same effect. Policy was firmly in the other direction.

92. At the March 28 meeting, however, Robertson argued that the experiment of purchasing long-term bonds was too cautious. If the System was going to experiment, he said, it should act decisively to show whether it can affect long-term rates. He surmised also that the market remained thin because no one knew the rules for System intervention.

foreign governments reduced their interest rates to support the dollar, despite rising domestic demand. In May, West Germany repaid some of its debt early to reverse the capital flow.

Early in February, President Kennedy repeated his pledge to maintain the $35 gold price. The gold outflow slowed. Following announcements by West Germany and the Netherlands that they had revalued their currencies against the dollar by 5 percent, the gold flow reversed.[93] Between February and June, the United States increased its gold holdings by $191 million, 1.1 percent of the February level. The temporary respite for the United States shifted pressure to the British pound. Despite continued restrictions on capital movements, the pound remained under periodic pressure until its devaluation later in the decade.

The March 7 FOMC meeting renewed the directives and authorizations, as was customary. Robertson continued to argue for free markets with minimum intervention, so he opposed repurchase agreements and intervention in the bankers' acceptance market. The desk had not given evidence that these operations benefited the market, and he doubted that they did.[94]

The April 18 meeting, within two months of the cyclical trough, changed the directive to recognize that the recession had ended. The new statement called for "strengthening the forces of recovery that appear to be developing" (FOMC Minutes, April 18, 1961, 60). Generally, the System changed its policy when it changed its directive. Balderston, Robertson, and Eliot Swan (San Francisco) favored an easier policy, typically $150 million additional free reserves to bring the total to at least $650 million. With Martin and Szymczak absent, the committee voted seven to three to keep the same "degree of ease" with "leeway given to the Manager . . . to accomplish these purposes" (ibid., 60).

Differences of opinion grew stronger. Allen, Irons, Mills, Bryan, Swan, and Deming agreed that targeting free reserves was procyclical, although Swan and Deming did not think that procyclicality was currently a prob-

---

93. The Federal Reserve staff told the members that even if Germany eliminated its surplus, the United States would run a deficit to finance foreign assistance (FOMC Minutes, March 7, 1961, 35). Statements such as this strengthened the belief that the problem was not monetary. From Europe, Allan Sproul wrote that the revaluations revived concerns that par values would not stay fixed. Also, he reported concern that the United States would not control costs and prices (letter, Sproul to Hayes, Sproul papers, Correspondence, May 2, 1961).

94. There was intense concern in the 1950s and early 1960s about the threat of nuclear war. Each year the FOMC authorized system banks to operate autonomously in the event of a defense emergency. An interim committee could decide open market policy and accept a promissory note from a dealer physically unable to deliver securities. The System could purchase directly from the Treasury to supply credit to the Federal government.

lem. Balderston, Hayes, King, Robertson, and Wayne wanted to make full employment a policy goal. Irons, Mills, Shephardson, and Swan strongly opposed.

There were differences of opinion about the strength of the recovery. Guy Noyes, the director of research, noted that the recession was moderate, and the recovery would be moderate. No recovery to that time had been terminated in its early months. Woodlief Thomas pointed to slow growth of money and credit. The money stock had fallen to 28 percent of GNP, almost as low as in the 1920s. With long-term interest rates back in the 1920s range, monetary velocity was in its earlier range also.[95]

OPERATING PROCEDURES AND OBJECTIVES

With the end of the bills-only operating procedure and the increased authority given to the account manager, issues surfaced about the directive, the target, and the objectives of monetary policy. Instructions to maintain the tone and feel of the market, achieve moderate ease, or err on the side of restraint gave little direction even when the members agreed on the action to be taken.[96] When they differed, as in 1960–61, the manager's discretion increased. Often the instructions in the directive and the stated consensus were so imprecise that one member would criticize the manager's actions as inconsistent with his instructions. Another would follow with praise for the manager's performance. Unable to agree on its objectives or how to reach them, the FOMC continued to offer little direction.

The use of free reserves as a policy target added to the dissatisfaction that some members expressed. Free reserves rose when member bank borrowing fell, and conversely. Borrowing rose and fell cyclically, so free reserves moved counter-cyclically. Also, free reserves often moved opposite to or independently of total reserves, the money stock or the Treasury bill rate (See Chart 3.8 above). Concerns about setting interest rate targets were mainly concerns about congressional pressure if the Federal Reserve claimed to control an interest rate.

In November 1960, James Knipe, consultant to the chairman, wrote a

95. This finding continued to hold in later years, strong evidence of the long-term stability of the demand for money. Thomas also made a statement about policy transmission. When the Federal Reserve increased bank reserves, banks invested in securities, lowering long-term rates. Governments and corporations took advantage of lower rates to increase new investment. This is one of the few statements of this kind to that time.

96. Martin explained that "color, tone, and feel" referred to the distribution of reserves among member banks (FOMC Minutes, June 6, 1961, 57–58). Earlier minutes did not define these terms but express a similar point. Country banks may each hold a small amount of excess reserves. The response to a given value of total excess or free reserves would increase if larger banks (reserve city banks) held these reserves.

memo criticizing the instructions that the FOMC sent to the desk. "The directives are cast as such pious expressions of intent that they convey . . . almost no meaning . . . One gets very little sense of progress from one meeting to the next, and not much of an account of what has just been accomplished or what the Committee believes ought to be accomplished during the next three weeks" (Board Records, November 14, 1960, 6, memo, Knipe to Martin). The memo suggested "some use of numbers" (ibid., 6).

A few weeks later, Malcolm Bryan (Atlanta) wrote to Woodlief Thomas: "We can defend the actual policy; what I am afraid we can't do is to explain what we mean by the instructions we give" (Board Records, January 14, 1961, letter, Bryan to Thomas). Bryan continued his effort to improve procedures. In April 1961, he urged the FOMC to "[m]anage the reserve position . . . with a great deal more precision, and with a steadier hand" (FOMC Minutes, April 18, 1961, 22). Bryan argued that total reserves should grow at a 3 percent trend rate based on growth of population and transactions. The chart he presented at the meeting showed that the growth rate fell below trend before each of the postwar recessions and rose above trend during the late stages of economic expansions. Bryan concluded that "we have tended to overstay our position of tightness and to be too tight, and then to overstay our position of ease and to be too easy" (ibid., 22).

Governor King supported Bryan and welcomed his analysis, but Governor Robertson wanted more expansion than 3 percent growth. He argued that the demand for money changed over time, so he opposed using any "historical trend line as a strategic objective of policy"[97] (FOMC Minutes, May 9, 1961, 42). Bryan's proposal attracted support from one or two presidents, but both Martin and Hayes disliked "mechanical rules" and preferred to rely on judgments made at the time.

The directive to the manager usually changed when policy changed. Although the members discussed changes in the directive vigorously, they did not refer to the directive when commenting on policy operations. The directive became public when the Board published its Annual Report, from

---

97. Robertson's argument did not rule out the use of a trend rate. He favored discretion and opposed formal restrictions, but he also opposed loosely worded directives that allowed the manager to make the decision. In an exchange with Szymczak on this issue at the March 7 meeting, he could not contain his irritation, asking why not abolish FOMC and let the manager decide? Hafer (1999) develops Bryan's views and shows his charts and his use of growth rate bands, a technique the System used when it adopted money targets in the 1970s. A year later the FOMC attempted to force "an expansion in demand deposits adjusted and time deposits at an annual rate of 4 percent" (memo, Mills to Albert Koch, April 23, 1962). The memo accepted that growth in terms of the gross national product depends importantly on a constant expansion in the money supply defined to include time deposits" (ibid.). He doubted that the relation was causal and that economic growth could be increased by increasing money growth.

three to fifteen months after the FOMC's decisions. The directive's role was to show that the FOMC responded promptly to changes in the economy. It did not fully succeed.

In June 1 and 2 hearings before the Joint Economic Committee, Congressman Wright Patman (Texas) criticized the directive. "I do not see how the ordinary, average person could possibly interpret what the language means" (FOMC Minutes, June 6, 1961, Attachment A).[98] Robert Rouse, the manager, testified about his role on June 1. He described the consensus reached by the FOMC as "in somewhat more concrete terms [than the directive], but still in a relatively general way" (Board Records, June 1, 1961, 2, Rouse testimony). He added that he relied also on the oral statements made at the meeting, but he emphasized the importance of judgment about market factors such as float, Treasury and foreign accounts, and availability of short-term funds in the country (ibid., 5).[99]

A more substantive problem was lack of continuity and the weak influence of long-term objectives. Each meeting considered and responded to the most recent data. Most members did not have a framework to relate current changes to longer-term developments.[100] Many of the changes to which they responded were transitory, often random movements. Martin

98. Congressmen Patman and Reuss wanted the Federal Reserve to release the 1960 FOMC minutes to the Joint Economic Committee. The FOMC considered the verbal request on June 6. It decided to ask Patman for a letter formally asking for the minutes. It released the 1960 minutes after Patman sent a second letter on June 14.

99. Patman used the question period to claim that having all presidents at FOMC meetings violated the law and over weighted private interests in discussions (memo, Jerome Shay to Martin, Rouse Testimony, Board Records, June 1, 1961, 1). Subsequently, Patman criticized the presence of the non-member presidents because they did not take an oath of office. Patman also asked why changes in discount rates could be announced immediately but not open market operations. The System had no answer. This issue remained until the 1990s.

100. Later in 1961, Governor Balderston made a long statement about the absence of procedures for achieving long-term objectives. He recognized that a series of decisions loosely related to a long-term objective was sub-optimal and used the growth rate of total reserves to illustrate his points. "The guiding philosophy that I favor for the Committee's decision-making is to proceed steadily, week by week, toward whatever goal seems appropriate . . .

"The point I am making is that monetary policy should be flexible but not erratic. . . . [Recently] the Committee may have changed its objective from a 5 percent growth rate to a 3 percent growth rate [of total reserves] without full realization as to what had happened, and since the last meeting the implementation of Committee policy has resulted in a radical departure even from the lower growth rate" (FOMC Minutes, August 22, 1961, 47–48).

When the Board asked the members of the Federal Advisory Council to discuss open market operations in long-term securities, they learned that the bank presidents on FAC thought that the experiment had failed. One thought the Federal Reserve had reverted to pegging interest rates. Another said that most market participants disliked the new policy. Governor Mitchell objected that, although long-term rates had increased, they might have increased more without open market purchases, but his comments and those of other governors did not seem to change any opinions (Board Minutes, September 19, 1961, 15–23).

(and others) recognized that their policy "must be tailored to fit the shape of a future visible only in dim outline" (letter, Martin to Patman, FOMC Minutes, July 11, 1961, 68). They lacked a formal or common means of doing so. Martin always remained properly skeptical about economic models and model-based forecasts, but he did not propose a general guideline as a substitute.

Early in 1961, the FOMC considered a memo suggesting changes in the directive. The memo started a discussion that continued through the year. It showed considerable awareness of the need for change and the reasons for using vague directives. The discussion had two objectives: improving control and public relations. Several members wanted to publish reports of their actions more frequently.

The members debated three substantive issues. First, some FOMC members wanted to remove all standing rules from the directive in the interest of flexibility in operations. They did not make this change. Second, Young and Rouse proposed separating the directive into two parts. One would contain all the standing procedural rules; the other would have only current policy objectives. This, too, was not done.

Third, the FOMC made the current instruction to the manager slightly more explicit by adding a paragraph to the directive. Members of the FOMC, at this time, used different measures or variables to describe the current policy target. Martin did not attempt to reconcile these differences, so the manager (or whoever guided the manager) retained control of policy action.[101] The FOMC did not adopt some of the more explicit instructions suggested by the staff (Board Records, September 6, 1961, Young to FOMC, Attachment II). George Clay (Kansas City) gave the reason: "lack of agreement among the Committee members" (Board Records, November 13, 1961, 2, letter, Clay to Young).[102]

Hayes (New York) favored a proposal by Irons (Dallas) that would allow FOMC members to comment on a "statement of the general economic policy position of the Committee as it developed out of the discussion" (letter, Hayes to Young, Board Records, November 3, 1961, 3). The secre-

---

101. Bryan, Balderston, and Johns favored total reserves. George Mitchell, who joined the Board after mid-year, favored an interest rate target. Others continued to use free reserves or tone and feel.

102. New York liked the suggestion by Carl Allen (Chicago) that the FOMC did not have to agree on a statement of operating procedures because they met every three weeks. "The absence of a public statement of procedures would leave the Committee's hands untied and permit it to take whatever future actions it might indicate as desirable without setting off the magnified and exaggerated reactions in the market and in the press that would ensue if its actions were an exception to a published statement of formal rules" (letter, Hayes to Young, Board Records, November 3, 1961, 1).

tary and the manager would prepare the statement immediately after the meeting. Following a review by the chairman, members would review, approve, dissent, or propose changes. The statement would appear with the policy directive in the record for the meeting. Hayes emphasized that the policy statement would be short, no more than "three or four sentences to express the main points integral to current policy" (ibid., 3).[103]

Eliot Swan (San Francisco) wrote: "We need some economic analysis of policy on a fairly current basis, done within the System, and presented regularly to the public." This would give the public a sense "of what the System is trying to do, how it tried to do it, and what seems to have been accomplished" (letter, Swan to Young, Board Records, November 10, 1961, 3). Swan added that this statement would not be an official statement endorsed by the FOMC.

George Clay (Kansas City) recognized one problem with proposals like Swan's or any attempt to make the directive more explicit. There was a "lack of agreement among the Committee members . . . [E]fforts to be completely explicit may make it more difficult to arrive at a consensus. But a lack of specific directions shifts the responsibility of interpretation to the Trading Desk . . . Attempts to be specific also are hampered by the fact that individual members of the Committee differ in the measures through which they express their choices—using free reserves, interest rates, credit expansion, and other terms that cannot be interchanged" (letter, Clay to Young, Board Records, November 13, 1961, 2).

A remaining problem was to agree on the purpose served by the directive and statement of procedure. Public relations, a public record, and directions to the manager received different weights from each of the members. The more astute members recognized that any substantive statement restricted future actions. Several agreed that procedural rules, such as bills-only or not supporting bond prices, "are unnecessary and can prove to be administratively embarrassing at times" (letter, Deming to Young, Board Records, November 24, 1961, 1). The problem in rewriting explicit rules was that "they may be limiting at times and thus force hard-to-explain deviations; if they are written so broadly as to escape these difficulties, they become almost meaningless" (ibid., 1–2). Deming opposed an explicit target because the FOMC would have to explain why it

103. Hayes attached an example of the type of directive and policy statement he envisaged. The directive maintained the familiar vague language and made no mention of a quantitative target. The general policy statement improved on the old directive. It was similar to the statements issued to the press and public in the 1990s, after the FOMC agreed to announce the reasons for its decision (letter, Hayes to Young, Board Records, Enclosure B, November 3, 1961).

deviated. He insisted that the directive "could not be couched in terms of a guide or guides such as free reserves, money supply, total reserves, federal funds or bill rates . . . I simply do not believe that any one indicator is . . . good enough to use all of the time and I fear that should we attempt to use one (or more) in the directive itself, we will spend a great deal of time subsequently trying to explain why we did not get quite the precise results that these apparently precise indicators would imply we sought. I also feel that an attempt to write directives in specifics would push uncomfortably close to mechanistic policy-making" (ibid., 3).[104]

The letters show clearly that one major purpose that the old flexible and imprecise directive served was covering up disagreements within the FOMC. Bryan and Hayes did not agree about a quantitative target for total reserves, but both agreed with Irons that the FOMC should maintain procedural rules. Bryan differed with several of his colleagues by recognizing the problem that a vague directive posed. Unlike the majority, he believed the FOMC would be well served if it adopted a quantitative target, but he understood that his proposal did not attract much support.[105]

The discussion at this meeting, many subsequent discussions, and failure to adopt a quantitative objective suggest that a majority did not favor precise instructions and explicit objectives. One reason is that ambiguity provided opportunities for Martin, Hayes, or the account manager to change directions. Unambiguous policy objectives and operating procedures to achieve the objectives at lowest cost required a commitment to consistent, predictable behavior that many on the FOMC were not willing to make.[106]

Following the December 19 meeting, Young drafted some suggestions for the chairman summarizing the discussion at the meeting. The proposed directive called for "a somewhat slower increase in total reserves than during recent months. . . . Operations shall place emphasis on continuance of the three-month Treasury bill rate at close to the top of the range recently prevailing. No overt action shall be taken to reduce unduly the

104. Deming favored the type of unofficial explanation by the staff that Swan proposed. Its intent was to provide more information to reduce criticism while avoiding full responsibility for what was said and the difficult process of achieving agreement on what they intended to do. The discussion shows how much the Federal Reserve had begun to change from the secretive central bank of the 1920s to the more transparent bank we find after the mid-1990s.

105. "If we ever attain clear, quantitative directions to the Desk, the present hairsplitting shifts of linguistic emphasis in the directive will be reduced to a lesser and more proper importance, and we shall have a better guide to when a change of language is called for" (letter, Bryan to Young, Board Records, November 24, 1961, 4).

106. Cukierman and Meltzer (1986) and Cukierman (1992) later showed the advantages of ambiguous policy for the policymaker who wanted to fool the public.

supply of reserves or to bring about a rise of interest rates" (memo, Young to Martin, Board Records, December 20, 1961). Martin approved it.

This was a big change from "color, tone, and feel" or "resolve doubts on the side of ease [restraint]," but it did not propose a general policy or strategy. The FOMC adopted the new directive after considerable discussion at the December 19 meeting that put a formal end to the bills-only policy.

Martin spoke first. He offered a political explanation urging an end to bills-only not because it had failed but because they had not made their case to the public. "The System has a public relations problem, and changing words would be more prone to misinterpretation than abandoning the statements entirely" (FOMC Minutes, December 19, 1961, 32).[107] He also proposed continuing purchases of non-bills but renewing the decision at each meeting.[108] He was less certain about making the directive to the manager more explicit. The manager had a great deal of leeway; much of it he thought was necessary, but he acknowledged that the FOMC could make its instructions more explicit (ibid., 33).

The FOMC supported Martin on a twelve to four vote, including the opinions of presidents who were not voting members. The voting members divided eight to four, a rare number of dissents. Governors King, Robertson, and Mills and President Wayne (Richmond) opposed; Martin's efforts to democratize the System encouraged differences of opinion. Several proponents agreed that public relations was the main reason for formally ending the bills-only policy and related statements of procedure.[109] The need for such statements had passed after a decade in which insistence on bills-only attracted much criticism. Opponents included some who wanted operating rules and some (Mills) who wanted the bills-only rule. Robertson gave the best reason for opposing the change: If the FOMC

107. Martin also gave a more substantive reason for the change. He claimed that bills-only had improved the functioning of the long-term market and the market's depth, breadth, and resiliency. Further improvement was unlikely (FOMC Minutes, December 19, 1961, 31–32).

108. Sproul and Hayes had proposed repeatedly that the decision about bills-only be made at each meeting. Martin now adopted both their proposal and their policy. New York would have the discretion it sought. They also won their fight to remove the 1953 statement about operating procedures.

109. These included the commitment not to support any pattern of bond yields or prices, use of open market operations only for monetary and credit policy and correction of disorderly markets, and operations "solely for the purpose of providing or absorbing reserves" (FOMC Minutes, December 19, 1961, 69). The last clause especially irritated Hayes because it emphasized reserves and excluded changes in relative interest rates. This was a peculiar decision since the purpose was to change relative interest rates, but Martin wanted to emphasize that they would not peg rates. Those voting for the motion also wanted a published explanation of the reason for the change from bills-only.

failed to set procedural rules, the desk would have more authority and less guidance from the committee. There would be standard procedures. At issue was who chose them and how explicit they would be.

The committee also adopted the two-part directive. The first part, a statement of continuing authority, set out the quantitative limits on purchases of government securities and bankers' acceptances, authorized repurchase agreements with non-bank government securities dealers (now extended to twenty-four months), and permitted but limited temporary direct purchases from the Treasury (up to $500 million at the time).[110]

The second part contained the economic policy directive. The committee agreed to Irons's proposal with a few changes. Henceforth the secretary, manager, and committee economists would draft a statement to which each of the members could agree or dissent promptly. Some members said that the purpose was more public relations than substance, since the manager heard the discussion at the meeting, but others wanted quantitative targets to increase the committee's control of the manager and the policy action.[111] Hayes, Deming, and Bopp strongly opposed quantitative targets.[112]

For the particular meeting, the FOMC for the first time chose an explicit interest rate target, a 2.75 percent Treasury bill rate. This was probably a move toward the administration's position. Martin began with a looser statement of consensus that did not satisfy the members. Several preferred to reduce total reserve growth to the 3 to 5 percent range.[113] Others had

110. This vote was ten to two. Mills voted no because he preferred the old directive. Robertson objected because the continuing authority included repurchase agreements with non-bank dealers at interest rates at times below the discount rate. Robertson objected also because the directive no longer said that operations were primarily to supply and absorb bank reserves (FOMC Minutes, December 19, 1961, 82–83). This was another victory for New York.

111. Robertson, always alert to expanding the manager's role, objected to the manager participating in the writing. He received no support.

112. George Mitchell recognized the difficulty of agreeing on a quantitative target when members used different measures, but he said that the FOMC should remain in session until they agreed on the target. Thus, he joined Bryan in recognizing this source of the FOMC's problem. Martin did not comment, but he did not believe that a precise instruction was desirable. A few years later Bopp (1965) wrote an essay responding to the Federal Reserve's academic critics. He argued (1) that the FOMC did not know enough about the functioning of the economic system to give precise instructions to the desk and (2) that measures of reserves or money are "influenced by factors over which the manager has no immediate or direct control" (ibid., 15). He did not propose research to improve knowledge, and he did not recognize that the FOMC's unwillingness to adopt a precise directive shifted responsibility but did not avoid it.

113. The closest weekly new issue yield was 2.579 percent. A dialogue between Shephardson and Martin shows Martin's concern about public relations, especially relations with the administration. Shephardson, who favored reducing reserve growth, referred to the action

used a specific interest target in their statements for several months. They did not want to give the manager a range of rates. Martin agreed that it was "wiser to use a T-bill rate as a target rather than reserves growth or the money supply as targets; it's not feasible to pin down the latter" (FOMC Minutes, December 19, 1961, 76).[114]

There was not enough agreement about what the committee intended the directive to do and how it was supposed to resolve contentious issues. The committee revisited these topics several times, using experience with the changes they made to guide additional changes. At the January 23 meeting, the secretary, manager, and economist prepared the directive at lunchtime, so the FOMC could vote at a second session. By March 1962, enthusiasm for quantitative targets had weakened, and free reserves, feel of the market, and slightly less ease reappeared in the directives.[115]

At the December 1962 meeting, Martin reopened discussion of the directive by mentioning two problems: the difficulty the desk had hitting and keeping a quantitative target, and the matter of communicating with the public. Several members agreed that the new directive was an improvement. Only Mills wanted to reverse the changes made the year before. Support for quantitative instructions to the desk was greatly reduced, however.

---

as "tightening." Martin, conscious of the administration's concern, insisted that "trending" was a better term. Shephardson asked why reducing reserve growth was not tightening. Hayes replied that it was a "trend toward tightening." No, Martin said, it's "a trend toward less ease" (FOMC Minutes, December 19, 1961, 78). The FOMC's secretary, Ralph Young, referred to this exchange at the next meeting, when Trieber (New York) criticized the first directive prepared under the new procedure, and Hayes accused Young of taking advantage of the new arrangements to mention reserve growth before "less ease." Hayes thought the consensus called for less ease, not slower growth of total reserves (FOMC Minutes, January 9, 1962, 18–19). Trieber added that the directive should "add clarity . . . without injecting new tests or new interpretations" (ibid., 14). Mitchell responded that if the desk thinks the instructions are inconsistent, it should ask the FOMC to clarify by phone. The exchange suggests that New York viewed the new procedure and its more explicit targets as a renewed effort to reduce its influence. Young noted that each FOMC member used a different phrase to describe his preferred policy. Rouse and Thomas had agreed to include reduced reserve growth in the directive.

114. The vote was eight to four, an unusually large number of dissenters, and a majority of the Board of Governors. Robertson dissented because he did not like to target the Treasury bill rate, Mills because the policy was not sufficiently restrictive, and King and Mitchell because it was too soon to tighten. Martin continued to insist that their action should not be called "tightening." Balderston called it a deceleration of the acceleration (FOMC Minutes, December 19, 1961, 78). The new issue Treasury bill rate did not reach 2.75 percent until mid-January.

115. Martin commented at the January 23 meeting, five weeks after the decision, that use of "concrete figures in the directive has some merit, . . . [but] the directive must recognize the color, tone, and feel of the market" (FOMC Minutes, January 23, 1962, 33). The new procedure accomplished very little of value except perhaps to show why the FOMC issued vague directives.

Only George Ellis (Boston), Eliot Swan (San Francisco), and Mitchell spoke in favor. Swan wanted targets to be "quantitative and prioritized." It was wrong that the manager had to translate the member's statements into a quantitative target; that should be the FOMC's job. Clay (Kansas City) was at the opposite extreme. He could not accept any quantitative target. Bryan (Atlanta) made the greatest change, commenting that quantitative targets were not sufficient; the desk had to use discretion. Deming (Minneapolis) submitted a suggested directive that distinguished between long-range goals and near-term targets. His proposal gave specific objectives but did not use quantitative targets. His was a rare effort to direct explicit attention to the longer-term effects of Federal Reserve actions.

Several members favored quarterly policy reviews, published in the *Federal Reserve Bulletin,* as a way of communicating with the public, particularly academic critics. Martin wanted better communication because he believed the critics were mistaken. He opposed regular quarterly reports, however, because there were times when the FOMC would not want to explain its decision. "Such a review would go beyond the level of disclosure required by the Federal Reserve Act and would cause the press to expect releases on a particular date" (FOMC Minutes, December 18, 1962, 88–89). Martin was willing to consider proposals to release complete minutes after five years. Much later the Federal Reserve implemented this proposal.

Martin accepted a change in the drafting procedure. Instead of having the directive prepared by the secretary, manager, and economist after the meeting, the new procedure required the staff to prepare the directive during a recess, so that the FOMC could vote before leaving. Before long, the directives were as vague as before. The members did not agree on the way to measure policy, so they could not write a precise directive. Martin showed no interest in pushing for more precision or clarity, perhaps because he did not favor it, perhaps because agreement was unlikely, perhaps both.

The problem in choosing targets and deciding where to set them arose in a congressional hearing. Chairman Martin would not give a clear answer when Congressman Patman asked him to "name any reliable barometer or barometers that I could look at to learn just what degree of tightness or ease you are following" (excerpt from House Banking testimony, Correspondence Box 240, Federal Reserve Bank of New York, July 10, 1962). Martin replied that "there is no single barometer or even small group of barometers . . . that can be relied upon at all times and under all economic conditions" (ibid.). He first named total commercial bank reserves, then free reserves, followed by several short-term interest rates and their relation to the discount rate. Later he added growth of bank credit and money. A reader does not learn much from his response. There is no mention of

Table 3.5 New and Retiring Presidents, 1961–62

DATE	BANK	NEW PRESIDENT	RETIRING PRESIDENT	PRESIDENT SINCE
March 1961	San Francisco	Eliot J. Swan	H. N. Mangels	1956
March 1961	Kansas City	George H. Clay	H. G. Leedy	1941
March 1961	Richmond	Edward A. Wayne	Hugh Leach	1936
March 1961	Boston	George H. Ellis	Joseph Erickson	1948
January 1962	Chicago	Charles J. Scanlon	Carl E. Allen, Jr.	1956
October 1962	St. Louis	Harry A. Shuford	Delos C. Johns	1951

the relative weights given to each factor of how he resolved divergent movements. And there is no mention of differences between nominal and real values or international payments.

Martin's answer in one sense seems accurate. Neither he nor most others gave much thought to issues of this kind. As Martin often said, he was a "market man," concerned like them mainly with today's market position.

Personnel Changes

In 1961–62, the FOMC experienced the largest turnover since 1936. Table 3.5 shows the six reserve banks that chose new presidents. Also in 1961, President Kennedy made his first appointment to the Board of Governors and two years later reappointed Martin and Balderston as chairman and vice chairman of the Board.

With the strong support of Treasury Secretary Douglas Dillon, President Kennedy decided to reappoint Martin as chairman without considering opposition by the Council of Economic Advisers (Dillon papers, Box 34, January 16, 1963). He was aware of their opposition but decided that the political cost of replacing Martin was too high, especially because of his own commitment to support the fixed exchange rate system. Kennedy claimed to like Martin's willingness to state an independent view.[116]

Menc Szymczak left the Board at the end of May 1962. He had served since 1933. His successor was George W. Mitchell, also from Illinois. Mitchell completed the remaining months of Szymczak's term, then com-

---

116. Paul Samuelson wanted Martin replaced in 1961, but he told James Tobin that the United States would lose about $1 billion in gold (Oral History Interview, 1964, Tobin, 190). When Kennedy offered Martin reappointment, Martin asked if the offer "was only because it was of political value to his administration. . . . [I]f that I wouldn't like to be reappointed. I have served many years, and I have been ready to go elsewhere for a long time" (ibid., 193; the quotation is from James Tobin reporting on a conversation with Martin in 1964). Kennedy agreed that it would be "embarrassing not to reappoint you. But that is certainly not the only reason. . . . I've found you to be independent-minded. . . . The president needs people like that" (ibid., 193). Martin accepted. After the decision, Gardner Ackley, who disliked Martin's policies, had to write the encomiums for the president to state at the reappointment.

pleted a full fourteen-year term. Mitchell was a tax or fiscal economist who had served at the Illinois tax commission and as director of the Illinois Department of Finance under Governor Adlai Stevenson. Immediately prior to his appointment, he was vice president of the Chicago Reserve bank and an associate economist of the FOMC. He was the first professional economist on the Board since 1936.

Mitchell's appointment was a modest success for the Council of Economic Advisers. They did not trust Martin or the Federal Reserve and saw Mitchell's appointment as a way of influencing monetary policy.[117] Before Mitchell joined the Board in August, Heller sent him copies of the Council's memos on monetary policy, urging an expansionary policy. To the Council members this meant "keeping net free reserves plentiful enough to keep the FF [federal funds] rate below the discount rate . . . This criterion should take precedence over a numerical target for free reserves" (letter, Heller to Mitchell, Heller papers, Box 19, July 18, 1961, 1). Heller urged open market purchases of long-term bonds and a reduction in the discount rate. He closed the letter: "We look forward to talking these matters over with you in the coming months and years" (ibid., 2).[118]

The Council was less successful when the next vacancy opened on the Board of Governors. George Mitchell told them in the spring of 1963 that Governor George King, Jr., was ill and would leave the Board after only 4.5 years. When it happened in September, "Dillon and Martin went directly to the president to tell him about it before we . . . knew . . . that it had happened" (Oral History Interview, 1964, Heller, August 2, 354). Treasury's candidate was Dewey Daane, recently promoted to deputy Treasury undersecretary. President Eisenhower had appointed him to the Treasury, but he remained after the administration changed.[119] Daane had been an economist at the Richmond and Minneapolis Federal Reserve banks be-

117. The Council proposed to Kennedy that Mitchell could be chairman, but President Kennedy did not mention the possibility to Mitchell when he interviewed him (Oral History Interview, 1964, August 2, 352). The Treasury's candidate was Joseph Barr, who became Treasury Secretary at the very end of the Johnson administration. The Council and Paul Samuelson thought that Barr would follow conservative Treasury policies (ibid., 349).

118. The letter describes relations with Martin as "cordial and friendly, and at the moment there is little difference between us on current policy" (letter, Heller to Mitchell, Heller papers, Box 19, July 18, 1961, 2).

119. The Council's candidate was Seymour Harris, a Harvard professor and active liberal Democrat who had been an early Kennedy supporter. "Now there was a bitter battle. . . . [T]here was a great fight for Daane and a great fight against Harris" (Oral History Interview, 1964, Heller, August 2, 357). If Martin had been asked, he would have favored Daane. In the past, the Federal Reserve did not let Harris into their building because he had printed parts of confidential memos when he wrote his book on the Federal Reserve in the early 1930s (ibid., 357).

fore joining the Treasury.[120] Heller and Ackley did not consider him a likely or reliable ally.

Dillon told them he was not against Harvard Professor Seymour Harris. He told the president that appointing Harris to replace King would "be interpreted as a loosening [of policy] and . . . undermining of the soundness of the Federal Reserve Board" (ibid., 359). But if Harris replaced Robertson when his term expired in 1964, that would be "an exchange of one liberal for another" (ibid., 359).

Heller and John Kenneth Galbraith tried to convince the president to appoint Harris to King's seat, then reappoint Robertson in 1964. They argued that by reappointing Martin and Balderston as chairman and vice chairman, Kennedy had satisfied the conservatives and bankers. But Daane got the appointment, and Lyndon Johnson was president in 1964, when Robertson's term ended. He reappointed Robertson.[121] Harris's last chance came in 1966, when Balderston's term as a member expired. Johnson chose Andrew Brimmer, the first African-American to serve on the Board and the FOMC.[122]

Leading members of the staff left in 1962. The account manager, Robert Rouse, reached retirement age in the fall of 1962 but asked to be relieved in the spring. He had joined the System in 1939. The FOMC's economist, Woodlief Thomas, resigned in April to accept an appointment to a World

120. The struggle over Daane's appointment suggests that both sides saw him as more conservative than Robertson. Havrilesky and Gildea (1992, 402) suggest that the two were very close together in the proportion of divided votes that they cast for easier policy. However, Daane dissented only 3 times in 132 votes (about 2 percent) whereas Robertson dissented 23 times in 285 votes (8 percent) (ibid., 414). Many of Robertson's dissents expressed opposition to extensions of the account manager's discretion.

121. Harris was not a finalist in 1966. President Johnson gave the choice between Robertson over Frederick Deming (Minnesota) to Walter Heller. According to Heller's statement in the oral history, he recommended both, but Johnson insisted that he choose. He chose Robertson. Johnson said: "All right, call Robertson, . . . tell him the president said, 'Now I want to be sure that I'm getting a man who, when the president . . . calls the signals, doesn't run to the opposite goal. Do you think you'd be running for the same goal as the president?'

"So I phoned from Minnesota, I called Robertson, and he thought he could run for the same goal. I called the president back and he announced it that afternoon before he ever told Bill Martin about it" (Oral History Interview, 1964, Walter Heller, August 2, 365–66). Deming later became Treasury undersecretary.

In fact, Heller wrote a memo to President Johnson making the case for Robertson's appointment. He described Robertson as a highly respected expert on banking. "He has taken a strong position for maintaining monetary ease to facilitate expansion" (Heller papers, Monetary Policy, Box 20, January 15, 1964). Then he added that another appointment like Dewey Daane would swing the Federal Reserve toward tighter money, limiting the success of the tax cut.

122. Brimmer was an economist who had served in the research department of the New York bank, taught at the University of Pennsylvania, and at the time was an Assistant Secretary of Commerce.

Bank mission to Chile. He had served at the Board in the 1920s. Guy Noyes replaced him as the FOMC economist, and Daniel Brill, Albert Koch, and Robert Holland became FOMC associate economists. Later Brill became head of domestic research and Holland became secretary of the FOMC and still later a Board member.

The Federal Reserve had not engaged in foreign exchange transactions since the 1930s. To implement its decision to actively purchase and sell currencies and currency swaps (see below), it created the position of Special Manager for Foreign Exchange. Martin used the opportunity to reopen the issue about appointment of the open market account manager that he had raised in the 1952 ad hoc report on FOMC operations and on several later occasions. He now proposed to reverse the extant procedure by letting the FOMC choose the two managers subject to veto by the directors of the New York bank. This was a concession. Originally, he had proposed that the manager would work only for the FOMC.

As expected, Hayes objected that Martin's proposal would reduce the manager's responsibility to the New York bank and weaken the directors' statutory authority to appoint officers. New York argued also that Martin's proposal would weaken the regional character of the System and reduce New York's stature.[123]

Martin responded that the existing arrangement arose because of earlier reliance on an executive committee to carry out transactions. In principle, he claimed, the manager could come from anywhere in the System. Hayes accepted in principle that the manager could come from any bank, but he argued that the operating bank has to create an atmosphere in which the staff sees opportunity for promotion. He saw Martin's proposal as another in a series of steps to reduce the role of the regional banks and centralize control in Washington. Hayes ended his remarks by offering to have the FOMC and New York share equally in the appointment decision (FOMC Minutes, April 17, 1962, 13).

The FOMC defeated Hayes's proposal eight to four. All governors voted against, and all presidents expressed some support for Hayes's proposal, but Bryan (Atlanta) voted with the governors. On the next vote, the FOMC accepted Martin's proposal eleven to one, with Hayes the only dissent. Once again, the Board succeeded in its continuing effort to centralize control.

Rouse told Martin about his intention to resign in the summer of 1961,

123. The chairman of New York's Board of Directors made a special plea to retain the long-standing arrangement. He responded to the unspoken argument that the New York directors had the informational advantage of learning about policy actions from direct contact with the manager. The directors only ratified operations after the fact. He said that there had never been a known breach of confidentiality.

about a year ahead of time. Martin reported to the FOMC in January 1962. Since a new arrangement for choosing managers had not been discussed, he appointed himself, Balderston, and Hayes, not the New York bank, to choose Rouse's successor. They considered fifteen possible candidates, mainly senior officers of government security dealer banks and non-banks or former officers of the New York bank. The committee recommended, and the FOMC chose, Robert W. Stone, an assistant vice president of the New York bank, as Rouse's successor. Stone was thirty-nine years old and was the first manager with a Ph.D. degree in economics. He joined the System in 1953 and had worked at the desk since 1958. On his appointment as manager, the New York bank promoted him to vice president, the rank that Rouse held. Rouse became vice president and senior adviser during his remaining months at the bank. All succeeding managers to date have come from the New York bank. New York remains the only place to gain experience in operating the desk, as several members recognized at the time.

The FOMC appointed Charles A. Coombs, also from the New York bank, as Special Manager, Foreign Currency, Open Market Account. Coombs had executed the Treasury's decisions in the year since these operations started. Also, soon afterward, the Board created a Banking Markets Unit to recognize the changing banking structure and the Board's need for better analysis (Stockwell, 1989, 40).

GOLD AND THE DOLLAR, 1961–62

During the presidential campaign, Senator Kennedy committed his administration, if elected, to maintain the $35 gold price. After the election, he learned that the commitment was a costly constraint. United States' reserves declined 10 percent in 1960 to less than $20 billion, the lowest level in more than twenty years.[124] He believed the administration had to act to honor the commitment.

Kennedy renewed his commitment on February 6, 1961, within three weeks of taking office.[125] The speech came in the month that the recession ended. A temporary end to the gold outflow followed for a few months, but

124. Includes reserve position in the International Monetary Fund. Excluding the reserve, the decline was 8.7 percent in 1960.

125. The new administration began planning for the speech before the inauguration. Heller asked Tobin to meet with Roosa, the new Undersecretary for Monetary Affairs. "It soon became clear that as far as he was concerned, this was going to be the most nominal and trivial cooperation" (Oral History Interview, 1964, Tobin, August 2, 169). Paul Samuelson suggested that Roosa may have believed that Tobin held Robert Triffin's view of the problem. Tobin wanted to discuss gold guarantees of official dollar holdings (ibid., 169). This subject returned in 1962.

Table 3.6   Gold Holdings of Selected Countries, 1958–70
(December dates, selected years, millions $)

YEAR	FRANCE	GERMANY	ITALY	JAPAN	NETHERLANDS	SWITZERLAND
1958	750	2639	1086	124	1050	1925
1962	2587	3679	2243	289	1581	2667
Change 1958–62	1837	1040	1157	165	531	742
1970	3532	3980	2887	532	1787	2732
Change 1958–70	2782	1341	1801	408	737	807
Percent of U.S. Sales	24.2	11.7	15.7	3.5	6.4	7.0

Source: Board of Governors (1976, Table 14.3).

the outflow resumed in July. In the two years 1961–62, the gold stock declined an additional 10 percent to $16 billion, two-thirds of its peak value.

The first two years of the 1960s put into place two of the patterns that characterized the rest of the decade. First, the United States introduced a number of expedient measures, but with rare exceptions domestic policy, and later war, dominated international economic policy. Second, European governments, led by France, converted dollars into gold, draining the United States gold stock, threatening and, in 1971, ending the Bretton Woods system.

From the beginning of European convertibility to the end of 1962, the United States' gold holdings declined by $5.32 billion, and the holdings of the countries shown in Table 3.6 increased $5.47 billion. From 1958 to 1970, the United States' gold stock fell by 50 percent, to $11.07 billion, and the countries listed in the table acquired $7.88 billion, 69 percent of United States' sales.[126]

Countries responded in very different ways. Japan had large trade surpluses, held most of its balances in dollars, and bought only $400 million of gold. Germany, another country with sustained trade surpluses, took less gold than Italy. Repeating the pattern of the late 1920s, France took the most gold absolutely and relative to its initial holding. Under the 1920s gold exchange standard, the French government complained that the United States held its reserves in gold while other countries held a mix of gold, dollars, and British pounds. Under Bretton Woods, they had to again accept this distinction, and again France disliked it and converted its dollar holdings to gold. Unlike the 1920s, France did not deflate. During the 1958–70 period, it inflated and devalued the franc several times, cumulatively by 32 percent. This time it did not force deflation on other countries by sterilizing its gold purchases.

126. The linkage is, of course, less direct than the text suggests. World monetary gold increased 4.5 percent in the same period, and gold stocks fell in countries other than the United States, e.g., Canada and the United Kingdom.

Gold and Monetary Policy

Gold and the balance of payments had an important influence on monetary policy in 1961. Despite the early rise in the unemployment rate to 7 percent and subsequent slow decline, the Federal Reserve held the Treasury bill rate between 2.2 and 2.5 percent until December.[127] Average yields on long-term bonds remained between about 3.7 and 3.8 percent early in the year, but rose to 4 percent in August. Annual monetary base growth did not remain above 2 percent until October. In a pattern observed frequently during these years, base growth and monetary growth moved procyclically; as the economy recovered, base growth increased. But base growth remained relatively low in nominal terms, and close to zero in real terms early in the year. Annual consumer price inflation fell below 1 percent in October just as nominal base growth began to rise; real base growth increased (see Chart 3.9 above).

By year-end, the recovery strengthened without inflation. Industrial production increased 12 percent for the year. Real GNP growth reached 9 percent at annual rates in the fourth quarter with an unchanged GNP deflator. In December, the unemployment rate fell to 6 percent, 1.1 percentage points below the April peak.

The balance of payments and the gold outflow were troublesome. In March, West Germany and the Netherlands appreciated their currencies by 5 percent against the dollar to slow the rise in their current account surpluses and reduce imported inflation. The leadership of the Bundesbank favored capital exports and opposed revaluation of the mark (Holtfrerich, 1999, 365). Otmar Emminger, later president of the Bundesbank, was the main advocate of revaluation in the middle 1950s. He renewed his argument in 1960 (ibid., 368, 372). Ludwig Erhard, Economics Minister at the time, agreed. He preferred price stability to exchange rate stability, so he pressed the government to revalue. On March 3, 1961, the cabinet approved a 5 percent revaluation (ibid., 374).[128] The Netherlands followed to keep its currency fixed to the currency of its main trading partner—not to the dollar and gold.

The West German surplus continued following the appreciation. In the second quarter, West Germany repaid a $2.3 billion loan, so the United States had a transitory surplus of $1.6 billion. Increased military spend-

127. In the early months of the 1954 recovery, Treasury bill rates remained between 1 and 1.5 percent and in 1958 between 0.6 and 1.5 percent. Martin stated explicitly that the 1958 policy was too expansive.

128. In the Federal Republic, as in the United States, the government, not the central bank, controlled decisions about the exchange rate.

ing in the summer increased the expected budget deficit and capital outflow.[129]

None of these actions calmed the markets. Rather, the revaluations convinced speculators that rates would not remain fixed. They concentrated their resources on appreciation of the Swiss franc and depreciation of the British pound. After the central banks pledged $900 million in loans to support the pound, speculation slowed. Collective action had damped the currency crisis, but the problems had only begun (Coombs, 1962, 1140).

The Organization for Economic Cooperation and Development (OECD) held regular meetings of the economic officials of the major industrial countries. Working Party 3 of the OECD discussed the fiscal and monetary policies of the member countries and their implications for other countries through balance of payments surpluses and deficits. Many of these discussions emphasized a defect in the Bretton Woods arrangements; surplus countries urged deficit countries to adjust, and vice versa. Sovereign governments remained free to reject this advice, and they usually did. As in the 1920s, countries' willingness to coordinate or cooperate did not include deliberate policy changes to produce inflation in surplus countries or deflation in deficit countries. Under the fixed exchange rate system, foreign governments had little choice. Unwilling to appreciate their currency or devalue the dollar, they complained about imported inflation but could not prevent it. Deflation in deficit countries was a common fear, but disinflation (called relative deflation) was often suggested as a solution for deficit countries.[130]

129. In July, the Soviet Union tried to pressure the United States and its allies to remove troops from Berlin and recognize the East German government. In a televised address, Kennedy asked for $3.2 billion of additional spending and an increase in the authorized size of the armed forces. Tensions of this kind typically strengthened the dollar temporarily.

130. Ralph Young's report on the July 1961 meeting of Working Party 3 and the Economic Policy Committee (of senior officials) summarized the policy discussion that continued throughout the decade: "For convertibility to be maintained . . . surplus countries must allow external surpluses to be registered in internal inflation, i.e., surplus countries must import inflation, while deficit countries must allow deficits to be reflected in deflationary tendencies, i.e., must import deflation. These developments need only be relative . . . If relative adjustment is too slow and too inadequate, convertibility will break down. . . .

"Various delegates took exception to this doctrine and pointed out that there was much that could be done by governments to correct balance-of-payments disequilibria without relative inflation or deflation . . . Deficit countries could encourage export competitiveness, curb imports, and avoid capital outflow and surplus countries could discourage exports . . .

"[T]here were some delegates who contended that governments must retain their ability to alter their exchange values as an alternative to other courses of action. Other delegates, however, argued that . . . recurrent exchange rate alteration was no longer a tolerable alternative to a system of fixed exchange rates with relative inflation and deflation the central reliance for international adjustment" (FOMC Minutes, August 1, 1961, 16–17).

Meetings may perform the useful function of disseminating information and forcing attention to criticism and alternatives. The striking feature of much of the discussion of the OECD meeting was the political difficulty of coordination of sovereign governments through meetings and discussion. Officials who were very aware of political constraints in their own country acted, on occasion, as if there were no political constraints elsewhere. Or they fell back on remedies that at best bought time but did not resolve imbalances.

At the August FOMC meeting, Young reported on a lengthy discussion at OECD of West Germany's persistent surplus. The economic solution required either German inflation, additional revaluation of the mark, or deflation elsewhere. The German delegation rejected inflation and revaluation (FOMC Minutes, August 1, 1961, 14–16). Soon after, the group discussed a British plan to deal with the current British exchange rate problem. In a pattern that countries repeated many times, West German "business and banking circles" reacted skeptically to the British policies. They could not support revaluation of the mark, but they favored devaluation of the pound.

Britain's problem continued. Its gold reserves fell below $2 billion in the third quarter, raising concerns about devaluation. The Federal Reserve discussed the resulting gold price rise on the London market. One proposal called for a gold loan to Britain to be used to stabilize the pound price of gold. Governor Mills expressed concern that the decline in the United States gold stock following a loan would have adverse consequences that would more than offset the strengthening of the British pound (Board Minutes, July 18, 1961, 5–6).[131]

Gold movements and prices in summer 1961 reflected political disturbances about Berlin as well as concerns about the British balance of payments. Tighter British policy worked at the time, and the Berlin crisis ended. The FOMC remained concerned about the dollar but anxious to avoid responsibility. In August, it added "while giving consideration to in-

131. The Board discussed legislation eliminating the gold reserve behind currency and bank reserves. Mills argued for keeping the reserve requirement as a safeguard against excessive expansion. Martin argued that the timing was poor. Robertson said there was never a good time. The currency was a managed currency, and prudence could be exercised without the requirements (Board Minutes, May 15, 1961, 4–7). Nothing happened until the restriction was close to binding in 1965 and 1968. The administration decided against asking for removal of the 25 percent requirement when it took office out of concern that it would be seen as evidence of weakness and that Congress would not go along (memo, Dillon to Kennedy, Dillon papers, May 9, 1961). Dillon's memo urged that Kennedy support a bill by Congressman Abraham Multer to remove the requirement, but the administration did not act. This experience was characteristic of the delay in government response to policy problems.

ternational factors" to its directive (FOMC Minutes, August 22, 1961, 52). Chairman Martin said, "[T]hese words would not put the Committee in the guise of alone being able to defend the integrity of the dollar" (ibid., 52). In his view, foreign aid, military assistance, budget deficits, and foreign lending were the most important factors. Although he did not express it this way, the political system would not tolerate the deflation necessary to reduce the cost of exported goods, and increase the relative price of imported goods, to pay for foreign transfers and loans at an unchanged nominal exchange rate.[132]

Early in October, the gold outflow resumed. In the next thirteen weeks, the U.S. stock declined by $500 million, more than 3 percent of the remaining stock. At this rate of loss, the gold stock would fall below the $10 billion level within five years. This level was considered a critical threshold below which foreigners would demand the remaining gold, ending the system.

Although domestic economic expansion had slowed, October 1961 was one of the few occasions when about half of the FOMC favored a rise in short-term rates to slow the external drain. Bryan (Atlanta) argued that the payments position would not be helped by a small rise in the short-term interest rate, but Balderston and Hayes wanted to take some action.[133] Mills noted that it was "impossible to pursue a 'troika policy' . . . to keep interest rates low while simultaneously trying to raise them and to take a strong attitude toward protecting the dollar" (FOMC Minutes, October 24, 1961, 31–32). The consensus called for resolving doubts on the side of ease. In practice, however, new issue Treasury bill rates and the federal funds rate declined slightly in the next few weeks, then rose.

Governors Mitchell and Robertson ignored the decline and criticized the rise in rates. Rouse explained that the rise was partly inadvertent, possibly caused by the Treasury's decision to issue strips of bills. These required purchasers to buy ten weeks of bills at a time (a strip).[134]

132. At the October 3, 1961, FOMC meeting, the manager (Rouse) for the first time used Euro-dollar rates to compare to rates in other countries.

133. The annual IMF–World Bank meeting had just ended. The press described the meetings as an attack on United States policies. Some countries expressed their doubts about whether the United States had the discipline to follow policies to end the balance of payments problem (FOMC Minutes, October 24, 1961, 13).

134. The sale of ten-week strips originated as part of the effort to raise short-term and lower long-term interest rates. The dealers disliked the strips of bills, so they bid a lower price, raising the stated yield. This pleased Roosa and his deputy Dewey Daane because it raised the quoted new issue bill rate. Along with David Meiselman, who worked with me in the Treasury, I argued that it was a mistaken policy that imposed a transaction cost that the buyers shifted to the Treasury and would have no effect on capital flows or on arbitrage. Rates on bankers' acceptances remained unchanged.

Opinions at the FOMC about the seriousness of the balance of payments problem remained divided with Mills, Hayes, and Ralph Young at one end and Mitchell, Robertson, and Bryan more concerned about the domestic economy. At the December 5 meeting, Young made the strong case for more aggressive action, using phrases such as "breakdown in the payments system" and "end of the faith and credit of the United States government" (FOMC Minutes, December 5, 1961, 48–49).[135]

EXCHANGE MARKET INTERVENTION

In March 1961, the Treasury started to use the Exchange Stabilization Fund (ESF) to purchase and sell foreign exchange in spot and forward markets using the New York reserve bank as its agent. In September, Chairman Martin introduced the possibility that the Federal Reserve would assist the Treasury in these operations. He had prepared the members in June by sending staff memos by Ralph Young and J. Herbert Furth and a response by the New York bank. Martin closed his introductory statement by opining that "the nature of world conditions was such that some activities of this sort unquestionably would be engaged in some manner" (FOMC Minutes, September 12, 1961, 44). That left little doubt about Martin's position and the likely outcome. Five months passed before the FOMC agreed.

Several major issues had to be resolved. First was the legality of foreign exchange operations. Second was the opinion of Congress, possibly its legislated approval and comparison to alternatives such as enlarging the ESF. Third was the way in which the Treasury and the Federal Reserve would work together. Would the Treasury be able to request purchases? Would joint operations be consistent with Federal Reserve independence? Fourth, would the decision to intervene be made by the FOMC, the Board, or some special group? Fifth, would intervention be sterilized?

The Federal Reserve was created when the United States was on the gold standard by men who accepted the real bills doctrine. The idea that it would purchase or sell foreign exchange instead of gold to influence the exchange rate probably did not occur to Congress. The idea that it would initiate purchases or sales of foreign exchange is inconsistent with the real bills doctrine, a basis of the act. Section 14 of the Federal Reserve Act enu-

135. Young's concerns may have reflected the views expressed at the OECD. On December 14, 1961, E. van Lennep, chair of Working Party 3, wrote to Undersecretary Roosa reporting on the U.S. balance of payments position. The report referred to the change in circumstances. The United States' deficit, formerly a source of strength for the world economy, had become a source of concern. It asked for an equilibrium in the basic balance (covering net government purchases and foreign investment) and recommended control of costs and higher interest rates as the economy recovered (Dillon papers, Box 33, December 14, 1961). The recommendations or suggestions remained general.

merated assets that the Federal Reserve could purchase. The list included cable transfers, bankers' acceptances, bills of exchange, gold coin or bullion, and United States government securities. It did not explicitly include foreign currency, although cable transfers were claims to foreign currency. Further, in 1932, Carter Glass, who had a prominent role in writing the act, criticized the New York bank's operations during the 1920s to assist Britain and other countries to restore and maintain the gold standard. The Banking Act of 1933 removed New York's role in the foreign exchange market. Glass's comments at the time opposed actions to support other currencies but did not explicitly oppose actions to support the dollar.[136] In 1933, the Board took a narrow interpretation of the law and advised the New York bank that it could open and maintain foreign accounts only for the purposes mentioned explicitly in section 14. That did not permit currency purchases, but the ESF purchased and sold foreign exchange and gold from 1934 to 1939. The Board had considered the issue on other occasions, but it had not issued a formal opinion. Howard Hackley, the Board's general counsel, remarked, "The Board took a position, which it did not publish, that would preclude this type of program. . . . [T]he Board can reinterpret the law somewhat differently" (FOMC Minutes, September 12, 1961, 48). Later, he did just that, writing an opinion that interpreted section 14 of the Federal Reserve Act to permit federal reserve banks to open accounts at foreign central banks, and vice versa. The Treasury's general counsel, Attorney General Robert Kennedy, and the counsel for the New York reserve bank concurred.[137]

---

136. Howard Hackley, the Board's general counsel, wrote the opinion authorizing Federal Reserve participation in currency stabilization. Hackley's opinion quoted Glass. "For a period of 6 years one of the Reserve banks has apparently given more attention to 'stabilizing' Europe and to making enormous loans to European institutions than it has given to stabilizing America. Accordingly, we have a provision in this bill asserting in somewhat plainer terms, the restraint the Federal Reserve supervisory authority here at Washington should exercise over the foreign and open market operations" (House Committee on Banking and Currency, 1962, 147). Glass's reference was to the $200 million loan to the Bank of England in 1925, when Britain restored gold convertibility. The operation was very similar to the "swap" operations that the System undertook in the 1960s. Britain did not draw on the $200 million credit in the 1920s.

137. Hackley's interpretation relied to a considerable extent on the interpretation of "wheresoever" in the text of section 14(e) of the Federal Reserve Act. The act authorized the Board of Governors "to open and maintain accounts in foreign countries, appoint correspondents, and establish agencies in such countries wheresoever it may be deemed best for the purpose of purchasing, selling, and collecting bills of exchange" (House Committee on Banking and Currency, 1962, 145). If the "wheresoever" clause limited the System to opening only for the purposes named in the clause that followed "wheresoever," it would not permit the action Martin and the Treasury proposed. Note that the wording referred explicitly to bills of exchange reflecting the System's "real bills" origins. Everyone agreed at the time that

Governor Robertson disagreed. *"Nowhere in the Act can authority be found for the stabilization function that is the core of this proposal"* (FOMC Minutes, December 5, 1961, 59; emphasis in the original). Further, Robertson insisted, Congress created the ESF for the express purpose of stabilizing the value of the dollar. If the Treasury needed additional funding, it should ask Congress to increase the size of the ESF.

Several members agreed to approve purchases, if Congress authorized the System to undertake these operations. Although Martin initially agreed, the Board did not ask Congress to legislate or to increase the size of the ESF. The Treasury did not want legislation.[138] It feared opening public discussion at a time when the anticipated balance of payments report would show a large deficit. The Federal Reserve disliked opening broad questions of purpose and authority out of concern that Congress would include amendments that the System did not want (FOMC Minutes, January 9, 1962, 60–62). Martin discussed the Federal Reserve's proposal with the chairmen of the two banking and commerce committees and after the decision to intervene, he included the following statement when he testified at the annual hearing on the Economic Report of the President:

> The System is now prepared in principle and in accordance with its present statutory authority [sic] to consider holding for its own account varying amounts of foreign convertible currencies. Toward this end, we are now exploring with the Secretary of the Treasury methods of conducting foreign exchange operations in convertible currencies with due and full regard for the foreign financial policy of the United States.
>
> These System operations, along with those conducted by the stabilization fund, would have the primary purpose of helping to safeguard the international position of the dollar against speculative flows of funds. They would not, and could not, serve as substitutes for more basic action to correct the deficit in the country's balance of payments. (Joint Economic Committee, 1962, 175)[139]

---

the act did not permit purchases of foreign treasury bills. In 1980, Congress authorized the federal reserve banks to invest in foreign government securities.

138. Congressional committees held hearings on Federal Reserve and Treasury operations without formally approving or disapproving. This is treated as evidence of implied consent, but that is mainly wishful thinking. No committee can bind Congress, and a failure to reject the operation is not the same as approval. Hackley's memo remains as the legal basis of the Federal Reserve's holding of foreign exchange by purchase or "warehousing," i.e., a loan to the Treasury secured by foreign currency. To avoid conflict with provisions regarding loans to the Treasury, the Federal Reserve avoided the word "loan" when describing these operations, hence "warehousing."

139. The only question asked about intervention at the hearing requested an explanation about how the operation would work (Joint Economic Committee, 1962, 181). By citing

The Joint Economic Committee did not endorse the Federal Reserve's decision. Its report took note of the Federal Reserve's announcement and said: "We have doubts that the Federal Reserve should be entering into this field of activity. Responsibility for international incomes and financial policies resides with the President and the Secretary of the Treasury. . . . It would seem undesirable to have two competing and possibly conflicting agencies in this vital area."

Rouse, Trieber, and Hayes stressed the need for prompt action. Martin too called the matter urgent and pressed the case by reminding the FOMC that the System was often accused of being obstructive. It had an opportunity to be constructive. Trieber argued that foreign central banks and governments engaged in these operations. He assumed that these operations were effective and ignored the distinction between sterilized and unsterilized intervention. If the System did not intervene also, the exchange value of the dollar would be "determined exclusively by the exchange authorities of foreign countries" (FOMC Minutes, September 12, 1961, 45). The main advantage of a stabilization policy was that the System could "defend the dollar . . . reduce the drain on gold and . . . promote confidence in the dollar" (ibid., 45).[140] Authorization to undertake operations used similar language, "to help safeguard the value of the dollar in the foreign exchange markets."

At a Board meeting on December 4, Martin expanded the role for foreign exchange intervention that he envisaged. "The System must be prepared to do something, and perhaps this would be more than just facing up to a speculative crisis. Perhaps the operation should be on a reasonably continuous basis" (Board Minutes, December 4, 1961, 11). In effect, the System had found a way to offset the provision in the Banking Act of 1933

"present statutory authority," Martin was less than fully candid with the committee. Hayes mentioned the new program as a possibility in a speech to the New York Bankers Association on January 22, one day before Martin made his announcement to Congress. "We may need to consider, therefore, whether the problems in this area may not require that the Federal Reserve System also enter into foreign exchange operations" (Reprinted, House Committee on Banking and Currency, February 27, 1962, 85).

140. At the time, the Treasury's ESF account had $200 million in capital and $136 million in net earnings over its life (Schwartz 1997, 141). It acquired some gold after President Kennedy approved purchases at a flat $35 price (not $35.20 as before). Also in 1961, the Treasury proposed, and principal countries agreed, to expand the IMF's ability to lend. The General Agreements to Borrow provided $6 billion as lines of credit to assist countries with balance of payments deficits (see text below). At the time, the IMF held only $1.5 billion in convertible currencies other than dollars, (ibid., 141) Also, the Treasury began issuing bonds denominated in foreign currencies and sold to foreign official institutions to reduce their dollar holdings. Austria, Belgium, Germany, Italy, Netherlands, and Switzerland purchased these "Roosa bonds." The total issue between 1962 and 1974 was $4.67 billion (ibid., 143–44). Roosa bonds removed excess supplies of dollars by shifting claims to a future date.

that removed federal reserve banks, particularly New York, from a major role in currency operations. The System would soon authorize currency stabilization agreements between central banks.

Governor Mills expressed immediate concern about Martin's statement. "The operations would constitute a counter-speculation with all of the attendant risks. If the operations were not going to be held down to crisis situations, the temptation toward continuous operation would be endless and the plausible reasons for them would be equally endless . . . [W]hether the System would lose position vis-à-vis the Treasury, which he [Mills] thought quite probable, would have to be seen from experience" (ibid., 12). Governor Robertson was willing to intervene in a crisis, but not otherwise, and Governor Shephardson wondered whether intervention would delay much-needed reforms. Balderston and Mitchell supported Martin at least in part.

Robertson was not satisfied with the legal opinion. He challenged the rationale. The cause of the gold outflow was the excess stock of dollars held by foreigners. The proposal added additional dollars that would be used to buy foreign currencies. "They would merely camouflage the problem" (FOMC Minutes, December 5, 1961, 60). The proper course was to deal with the "cause rather than the effect" (ibid., 62).[141]

Martin showed his usual patience. Although there was little doubt about the outcome, or his own preference, he did not cut off discussion or call for a vote until he wanted to tell Congress that the proposal had been approved. The vote came on January 23, 1962. Governor Balderston proposed that the operation should be an "experiment" that would be evaluated based on their experience. No one suggested evaluating the ten months of Treasury experience or the longer record of intervention by foreign central banks.[142] Balderston's motion also authorized conversations with the Treasury to coordinate operations with the Exchange Stabilization Fund and to establish guidelines for operations.

The FOMC approved the motion ten to two, with Robertson and Mitchell opposed.[143] Six of the seven non-voting reserve bank presidents said

141. The Annual Report (1962, 56–57) described Mitchell's objection as based on a desire for more analysis by outside experts, public discussion, and clarification of statutory authority. Robertson's dissent "regarded the legality of the proposed operations . . . as questionable, inasmuch as the Federal Reserve Act provided no general and positive authorization" (ibid., 56). He favored increased appropriation for the ESF in the event of "dangerously disorderly foreign exchange markets, and undergirded by sound policies designed to eliminate unsustainable deficits in the U.S. balance of payments" (ibid., 57).

142. Later, the Treasury made its records available to the FOMC.

143. Coombs (1976, 74–75) gives main credit for designing the swap arrangement to Julien-Pierre Koszul of the Bank of France. He described a typical operation. The Federal Re-

they supported the motion. President Bryan did not oppose the principle; he wanted to wait until the balance of payments had a surplus. Mitchell and Robertson wanted congressional authorization. Despite the Banking Act of 1933, which transferred foreign exchange decisions to the Board and away from New York, New York had regained a prominent role. Subject to Board approval, it could again negotiate with its counterparts abroad, as in the 1920s.

The arrangements ended formally in 1998, after fifteen years of disuse. After consultation with foreign banks, the FOMC voted to allow the arrangements to lapse (FOMC Minutes, November 17, 1998).

Who intervenes? FOMC approval suggests the Board regarded the FOMC as the proper agency for approving purchases and sales of foreign exchange. They were a type of open market operation. In fact, several Board members argued that the FOMC members did not have much knowledge of international finance and that decisions would often have to be made without time for a meeting. They preferred to leave decisions to a small knowledgeable group.

The Board's general counsel (Hackley) noted that the operations would be like open market operations, mainly purchases and sales of cable transfers, hence under FOMC jurisdiction. Section 14e of the Federal Reserve Act gave the Board the right to open accounts with and for foreign central banks, and section 14g authorized the Board to supervise all transactions (Board Minutes, February 8, 1962, 6–7, memo, Hackley to Board).

Three facts settled the issue. First, the New York bank managed Treasury operations as fiscal agent of the Treasury.[144] It would be odd to establish a separate operation. Second, the FOMC determined open market operations in securities. Although several governors remained reluctant,

---

serve would credit the Bank of France's deposit account for $50 million, advising the amount, the spot exchange rate, time to maturity, and other terms. At maturity, the Federal Reserve cancelled the deposit at the same exchange rate. This was an exchange rate guarantee. At the start, the Bank of France placed the dollar balance in a nontransferable three-month U.S. Treasury certificate of deposit. The Bank could redeem the certificate on two days notice. The Bank of France issued the franc equivalent of a $50 million deposit for the Federal Reserve and entered into a forward contract to reverse the deposit in 90 days. The United States could use the francs to purchase dollars that the Bank of France might otherwise have used to buy gold. Anna Schwartz points out that Coombs should have credited the Treasury staff which designed "swaps" with Mexico in 1936 that were used with other countries later.

144. Chairman Martin referred to this arrangement as a long-standing problem because the Board did not supervise the operations. This is a peculiar argument. New York had served since World War I as fiscal agent for the Treasury without Board supervision. Martin was consistent. He described New York's role as fiscal agent for the Treasury as "a defect and a matter of concern" (FOMC Minutes, February 13, 1962, 65). It set New York apart from the rest of the System; "it was part of a broad problem, involving difficult questions of relationships within the System" (ibid., 65).

the Board decided after much discussion to authorize the FOMC to super-vise transactions with foreign accounts and amended regulation N to that effect. Only Governor Robertson voted against the authorization because he opposed foreign exchange transactions (Annual Report, 1962, 56–57). Third, once the Board accepted that foreign exchange transactions were a type of open market operation, members recalled that they had opposed an Executive Committee arrangement for government securities operations and did not wish to revert to the former arrangement for foreign exchange operations.

Martin reopened the issue with the FOMC using a memo that Hack-ley prepared. The memo did not make a recommendation, but it leaned toward giving responsibility for foreign exchange operations to the Board. The Board "governing these operations would be more defensible from a legal standpoint" (FOMC Minutes, February 13, 1962, 63–64). President Wayne (Richmond) asked whether the law was so ambiguous that either could be responsible. Hackley replied that the Board and the FOMC would have separate roles; the Board would open accounts at foreign banks; the FOMC would execute transactions (ibid., 64). In Hayes's absence, Trieber (New York) argued forcefully for FOMC control on the very reasonable grounds that: (1) the planned operations were open market operations, and (2) section 14 of the Federal Reserve Act explicitly mentioned open market operations in cable transfers, one of the proposed activities. The Board's case rested on its authorized responsibility to open accounts with foreign central banks. The purpose of the accounts was to facilitate open market transactions.

The members divided into three groups. Most presidents favored rest-ing responsibility in the FOMC. Several governors argued for the Board. Robertson, partly supported by Mitchell, argued forcefully that the only reason for Federal Reserve involvement was to augment the funds in the stabilization fund. The Treasury, he said, should ask Congress for the ad-ditional funds or for permission to involve the Federal Reserve.[145]

Martin supported Balderston's position and decided the issue in favor of the FOMC. Balderston argued that domestic and international goals

145. In 1934 the Exchange Stabilization Fund had $2 billion. It contributed $1.8 billion to subscribe to the IMF leaving $336 million in 1961. The Treasury's analysis of its resources reported $222 million in ESF agreements with Latin American countries and spot hold-ings of foreign exchange of about $100 million used as " backing for outstanding forward exchange contracts" of about $340 million (Treasury Memo of February 6, 1962, quoted in Hetzel, 1996, 27).

At the FOMC meeting Fulton (Cleveland) reopened a dormant issue by arguing that the Board was a public body, implying that the reserve banks were not. He favored letting the Board manage foreign exchange operations (FOMC Minutes, February 13, 1962, 75).

are closely related. It would be a mistake to separate them. Martin agreed and added a statement that belied the alleged experimental nature of the proposal. "Ten years from now, foreign exchange operations will likely be as much a part of the System as are open market operations" (FOMC Minutes, February 13, 1962, 78).[146]

The Board provided for crisis response by authorizing the chairman and vice chairman of the Board and the vice chairman of the FOMC to instruct the special manager of foreign exchange operations (FOMC Minutes, February 13, 1962, 85). These operations were to remain consistent with the FOMC's guidelines.

The February 13 FOMC meeting approved the operating rules and rules for coordinating with the Treasury and starting operations.[147] To start operations, the Exchange Stabilization Fund sold the Federal Reserve an initial stock of currencies, mainly $7 million German marks and $1 million each of French and Swiss francs, Italian lire, British pounds, and Netherland guilders (ibid., 93). The initial limit on the account was $500 million, but that limit increased soon after. Within a decade the limit was $20 billion. The Treasury intended to continue its operations, but it now could expand using the Federal Reserve as a funding source without getting approval of its spending from Congress.[148] The two agencies decided that they would make no division between Federal Reserve and Treasury operations while the operations remained "experimental." The Federal Reserve did not

146. The forecast proved incorrect. The Board amended regulation N to recognize the changes. The FOMC approved Charles Coombs as special manager and decided not to publish its actions. Mitchell recorded reservations about the haziness of the relation to the Treasury.

Three weeks later, the staff discovered a memo dated November 20, 1936, dealing with the overlapping responsibilities of the Board and the FOMC in transactions with foreign banks. President Harrison (New York) had proposed that the FOMC "grant blanket authority to the Federal Reserve Banks to purchase and sell cable transfers, and bills of exchange, and bankers' acceptances, payable in foreign currencies in connection with accounts of Federal Reserve Banks established in foreign countries with the approval of the Board of Governors" (FOMC Minutes, March 6, 1962, 15). The March 1962 meeting repealed the 1936 directive.

147. A four-person group from the Board and the Treasury worked out the draft. The Board sent Ralph Young and Charles A. Coombs, a vice president of the New York bank. The Treasury chose Robert H. Knight, Treasury general counsel, and Alan R. Holmes from Undersecretary Roosa's staff and later manager of the System Open Market Account.

148. The Federal Reserve "would stand prepared to purchase currencies of these [the named] countries from the Treasury, either outright or under mutually satisfactory resale agreement, in the event that exchange market developments obliged the Fund to exhaust available resources" (FOMC Minutes, February 13, 1962, 93). The Treasury and the Federal Reserve agreed to get the approval of the National Advisory Council on International Monetary and Financial Policy. This was pro forma. The Council's members included the Secretary of the Treasury, chairman of the Board of Governors, and several cabinet secretaries. It was established under Bretton Woods legislation.

distinguish between sterilized and unsterilized intervention in its discussions, and only a few members mentioned a possible limit on Federal Reserve independence if the Treasury requested intervention.[149] The Federal Reserve could initiate operations in currencies in which the Treasury had not dealt (FOMC Minutes, February 13, 1962, 56). The Treasury could veto any Federal Reserve operation, and the Federal Reserve could refuse to participate in any Treasury operation if it disapproved (Coombs, 1976, 72).

Martin summarized the FOMC's role. Its actions could serve as a "lubricating device . . . [O]perations should not be so large as to aim to correct a basic deficit, but they should be sufficient to give some assistance until fundamental problems could be corrected" (FOMC Minutes, February 13, 1962, 58). Coombs added that the operations would "buy time."[150]

Governor King urged that they agree with the Treasury on risks that would limit the System's obligation. Young responded that the Federal Reserve only had to buy from the ESF if it chose to do so. Robertson asked why, aside from the Federal Reserve's "unlimited pocketbook," two agencies were involved instead of one (ibid., 62). Coombs replied that there was no other reason. King urged again that they clarify how responsibilities would be divided. Martin ended the discussion by repeating that the rules would develop based on experience.

Two weeks later, on February 28, the FOMC approved by telephone vote a three-month $50 million swap operation with the Bank of France. The vote was nine to two, with King and Robertson voting against. Mitchell abstained because the members did not get enough information on the French economic and political situation.[151] King and Robertson opposed because the operation was done so quickly they did not have time to decide.

Coombs used the March 6 meeting to get approval of swap operations with Switzerland and Britain. He said that these operations gave the market confidence that central banks would maintain their exchange rates. In effect the swap operations gave a foreign government a short-term guarantee against devaluation. This substituted for gold and temporarily removed dollars, thereby reducing foreign requests to exchange surplus dollars for gold. Martin recognized that the United States would continue to lose gold

149. The members asked Coombs why the ESF engaged in forward market operations instead of spot. He replied that the Treasury did not have the funds to buy foreign currencies in the spot market and forward markets were thin, so small forward purchases would reduce the implied discount (FOMC Minutes, February 13, 1962, 55).

150. Coombs explained that the main risk of loss arose in case of revaluation. The ESF reduced this risk by getting agreements that countries would give two days notice of revaluations. Two days gave enough time to cover positions. Charles Coombs managed international intervention at the New York bank.

151. Young promised to supply such memos in advance of future transactions.

for a year or more, but he believed swaps slowed the process and made it more orderly. Balderston added that the gold stock would fall to $15 billion from the current $16.7 billion (FOMC Minutes, March 6, 1962).

Coombs also asked for authority to purchase $25 million in marks from the ESF. Several members expressed concern about direct dealings with the Treasury. The law restricted direct purchase of Treasury securities, but Congress had approved limited purchases. Would Congress have to authorize direct foreign currency purchases from the ESF? Hackley said that purchases of foreign exchange were different. In this case, Treasury was not the issuer of the security. It was part of the market, so the purchase was an open market purchase. FOMC approved the $25 million purchase from the Treasury's ESF.

The early swap agreements established the practice but were used only to gain experience. The first use of the swap arrangement to support the dollar came in June 1962. The Federal Reserve used $60 million in Belgian francs and Dutch guilders to buy excess dollar holdings at the two central banks. Soon after, the Federal Reserve used a $200 million swap with the Swiss National Bank to purchase dollars that accumulated following the stock market decline in June and the sharp fall in the Canadian dollar at about that time. Coombs (1976, 80–84) described his operations during these and several subsequent periods of market turbulence.[152]

The General Agreements to Borrow. The Treasury negotiated an agreement with major industrial countries to supplement the IMF's resources by permitting the IMF to borrow currencies and relend them to member countries. The agreement increased available resources by up to $6 billion in the event of a run against the dollar.[153] At the time, deposits of foreign official institutions and commercial banks reached $5.6 billion (House Banking and Currency Committee, 1962, 96). Congress had to approve the new arrangement, submitted as an amendment to the Bretton Woods Agreement Act. The U.S. share was $2 billion.

152. Swaps assisted countries to adjust to disturbances. Coombs explained to Allan Sproul that countries used the dollar to make payments and settle balances. "If money moves from Italy to Switzerland, the Bank of England and the Bank of France wouldn't care less, but we become automatically involved in a problem about what to do about the Swiss dollar surplus and the Italian dollar deficit . . . [T]he adjustment is often effected through debits and credits under our swap network" (Coombs to Sproul, Sproul papers, Correspondence, September 16, 1964).

153. At the time, the United States' quota in the IMF was $4.1 billion. This gave the right to draw $1.7 billion automatically (one quarter of its quota plus an amount equal to the dollars drawn by other countries from the IMF, $600 million at the time). Total drawings could reach $6 billion, but that would require approval by the managing board. The managing director of the IMF would decide whether to use the General Agreements to Borrow before lending most of the IMF's gold and convertible currencies other than dollars to the United States.

Martin used the opportunity to tell the Congress again about the decision to intervene and related that decision to the General Agreements to Borrow. The General Agreements permitted the United States and other countries to borrow for three to five years. Exchange rate intervention would have much shorter duration. He expected in time to ask for congressional legislation once "operating experience under existing authority has provided a clear guide as to the need for it" (ibid.,, 92). Thus, Martin acknowledged congressional authority but dismissed any current need for approval. And he insisted that the new arrangements gave the United States time to adjust its payments imbalance, but he recognized "they will not be substitutes for a basic cure" (ibid., 92).[154] The Federal Reserve never asked for legislation.

Congressman Henry Reuss (Wisconsin) questioned Martin about his claim to have authority to engage in foreign exchange transactions. "You apparently assert the right to do this independently of the President or the Secretary of the Treasury, though you say something about consulting him occasionally. Much of the operation that you are doing under this seems to me to duplicate the foreign exchange stabilization operation that the Secretary of the Treasury has very properly undertaken pursuant to the Gold Reserve Act of 1934. . . . I consider this an usurpation of the powers of Congress. I don't think you are authorized to do this at all, and you give us only the vaguest generalities about what kind of arrangements you are going to make" (ibid., 102). Martin replied that he would be willing to discuss the transactions in executive session at any time and that he proposed to summarize them in the Federal Reserve Bulletin and elsewhere (ibid., 102–3). Reuss later added: "I don't think the Fed has the power to do the things that are in here" (ibid., 128).[155]

The gold pool. Under the Bretton Woods Agreement, gold was the intended nominal anchor of the exchange rate system. Governments and central banks could obtain gold by redeeming currencies. U.S. citizens

---

154. In the hearings Congressman Abraham Multer of New York asked Martin why he did not ask for repeal of the gold reserve requirements on the monetary base. That would make the entire gold stock available. Martin dodged diplomatically by saying that foreign central bankers had no doubts about the exchange rate after President Kennedy's February 6 speech.

155. Congressman Reuss, joined by Congressmen Multer and Patman, continued to question Martin about the legal basis for the operation. Also, Reuss was very critical of the loose statement of purposes and procedures. "You propose to go off on . . . a frolic of your own involving unspecified sums without the slightest statutory guidance as to how you are going to make these, as you call them 'cooperative arrangements'. . . . [Y]ou say . . . you are going to tell us what you think we ought to know, and no more" (House Committee on Banking and Currency, 1962, 140). He did not pursue the subject or insist on greater accountability.

could not hold gold legally or in the United States, or buy it at the Treasury, but, at the time, the law did not prohibit purchases abroad.

The London gold market became the principal market for sales by gold producers, especially Soviet and South African sales. During the first half of 1960, the London price remained between $35.08 and $35.12 with little trading (Coombs, 1976, 48). That changed as the 1960 U.S. election approached. Rumors spread that, as president, Kennedy would follow Roosevelt in 1933–34 by devaluing the dollar. Purchases by central banks and others increased, raising the gold price. An opportunity opened for central banks to buy gold at the U.S. Treasury and resell it at a profit in the London market.

The Bank of England had a limited role as residual buyer or seller. Increased activity by other central banks as buyers left the Bank as residual supplier. It could replenish its gold holdings profitably by selling dollars to the U.S. Treasury at the official price, but it was reluctant to profit from the arbitrage. More worrisome was the market's ability to circumvent U.S. policy of selling gold only to governments (ibid., 51)

The solution in December 1961 established a cooperative arrangement under which the principal European central banks shared part of the responsibility for the London gold market. Seven central banks agreed to commit half of the $270 million subscription to the gold pool. The United States was responsible for the other half.[156] The Bank of England managed intervention, using its own gold. Participating central banks repaid the Bank at the end of each month in proportion to their participation. The aim was to keep the gold price below $35.20, the delivered price of gold purchased in New York and sold in London (ibid., 62). Participating central banks agreed to make gold purchases from the U.S. Treasury or other central banks, not from the market.

Although the agreement fixed shares in the reimbursement, it left the final distribution to the individual central banks. They retained their right to demand gold from the Treasury. Coombs (ibid., 63) wrote: "We hoped that such conversions would not take place immediately after the receipt of dollar proceeds. But it would be entirely within the option of the central bank whether to convert in one week, one month, several months, or not at all." Some held additional dollars. Others converted to gold, so the United States paid for more than half but less than all the gold sold by the pool.

In March 1962, pool members agreed to share the proceeds of purchases as well as sales. The banks relinquished their right to compete

---

156. The commitments (in millions) were: West Germany, $30; Britain, France, and Italy, $25 each; Switzerland, Netherlands, and Belgium, $10 each (Coombs, 1976, 62).

for gold. Thereafter, the principal producers, the Soviet Union and South Africa, faced a single buyer, the Bank of England, acting as agent for the group of central banks. The pool set a maximum price of $35.08 that it would pay. This price was the London price of New York gold after the president agreed to waive the 0.25 percentage point charge on direct sales (Dillon papers, Box 33, May 26, 1961)

The gold pool distributed $650 million in gold to the Treasury in its first twenty-one months of operation. The main reason for the large purchases was a bad Soviet harvest in 1963–64 that required the Soviet Union to sell gold to buy grain abroad. The pool lasted until 1968. While it lasted, it prevented central banks from competing for gold, lowered the price paid to producers, and kept the gold price close to $35. It may have reduced demands on the U.S. gold stock by encouraging countries to hold additional dollars. Like many other measures, the pool may have delayed the breakdown of the Bretton Woods arrangements. It could not prevent it.

During the years that the pool operated, member countries sold gold worth (net) $2.5 billion on the London market. The U.S. share was $1.6 billion (Schwartz, 1987b, 342). During approximately the same period, 1961–67, the U.S. gold reserve declined more than $5 billion, the difference reflecting direct sales from the U.S. gold stock. In the same period, the industrial countries in G-10, especially France, added more than 100 million ounces, $3.5 billion, to their official gold reserves. The purchases by the G-10 equal 97 percent of U.S. sales outside the gold pool. These data suggest that, despite Coombs' claims and efforts, the pool did not function as intended; the G-10 replaced most of their sales from U.S. stocks.

What was achieved? By August 1971, when the gold window closed, Federal Reserve currency swap lines reached $11.7 billion, a long way from the modest experiment, limited to $500 million, only nine years earlier (Hetzel, 1996, 39). Coombs (1976) reports the details of these operations and gives a sense of his excitement and his belief that he prevented many crises. Coombs' book fell short, however, on the analytic side; he did not explain what the Federal Reserve achieved by active intervention beyond possible initial effects. In this, he reflected the almost complete absence of an explanation in the 1961–62 discussions of what Martin and the FOMC expected to achieve by intervention. There are many statements recognizing that currency market intervention could not reduce the payments imbalance. At various times, Martin and his colleagues cited increased productivity, reduced government spending abroad, foreign aid, military assistance, and other real factors as the principal causes of the problem or the sources of potential improvement. And they recognized that currency market intervention was just another type of open market operation.

The only advantage was that the swap arrangement delayed a reduction in the gold stock and reduced dollars held by foreigners. The offset was an obligation to repay the borrowed foreign currency in ninety days, with one possible renewal (Later extended). It differed mainly because it gave a temporary stay to gold sales.

There is a glaring omission from the 1961–62 discussions. The terms "sterilized" and "unsterilized intervention" never appear. In practice, the Federal Reserve sterilized its intervention. It had shifted to an interest rate target some of the time and soon after, most of the time.[157] The special manager withdrew reserves when he sold foreign exchange for dollars. This action increased the market interest rate (and reduced free reserves), inducing the domestic desk to purchase government securities, thereby supplying reserves and reducing the interest rate back to the target. The net effect was to change the mix of assets held by the Federal Reserve and the market. Purchases of foreign exchange shifted the mix in private portfolios also. The market faced smaller exchange risk and greater interest rate risk. Given the large size of the stocks of government securities and foreign assets and the relatively small size of foreign exchange operations, this effect was trivial. Whatever announcement effect it might have on impact, the conclusion of years of research is that there is no lasting effect of sterilized intervention.

Purchases of domestic securities increased reserves and reduced the United States' interest rates relative to rates abroad. The difference in interest rates induced capital to move to the countries with higher relative rates. To effect the transaction, holders sold dollars, bought foreign exchange, and purchased foreign assets. The difference in interest rates just equaled the expected depreciation (or appreciation) of the exchange rate over the term of the securities. All of this worked in reverse following an open market sale of domestic securities.

Federal Reserve staff and officials believed that interest rate differences induced currency movements. They discussed this arbitrage operation many times. No one related interest arbitrage to the role of the special manager or to the expected effect of his operations. To the contrary, no one mentioned that he would not achieve much.

Discussions concentrated on the many legal issues, as we have seen. Concerns for independence from the Treasury surfaced occasionally, but no one recognized that sterilization removed this problem. Neither Ralph Young and the Board's staff nor the staff at New York and the other banks

---

157. A free reserve target was an imperfect substitute. The short-term interest rate moved randomly around the interest rate consistent with the free reserve target.

prepared an economic analysis. Except for George Mitchell, none of the FOMC members had worked as economists, so no one was disposed to ask how the operation would work and what it might achieve. As in the 1920s, efforts to get central bank cooperation replaced careful analysis of what cooperation could achieve. No one asked why it was desirable to delay foreign demand for gold by swaps with three- or six-month duration if the problem arose from continued military or foreign aid that exceeded the private sector's surplus, as many at the FOMC believed.

The payments deficit declined very little if at all during 1961 to 1963. Knipe (1965, 165) suggests that "the full size of the deficits was partially concealed during 1961, 1962, and 1963. This was done . . . by regarding prepayments to the U.S. on loans, prepayments to the U.S. on military exports, and the issuance by the U.S. Treasury of new-type securities to foreign nations, as export-type items." Adjusted for these items, current account deficits were higher by $0.7 to $1.5 billion in each year. Official figures later reported the data with and without the adjustments.

At the Treasury, Robert Roosa worked actively to develop and negoti- ate lending and borrowing arrangements and the gold pool. The Treasury issued some "Roosa bonds" denominated in foreign currency to reduce dollars held abroad. The bonds had longer duration than swaps, but like swaps they were not a solution. The arrangements may have delayed ad- justment. They could not prevent it. Delay was useful if conceived as part of a strategy that permitted lower inflation in the United States to adjust the real exchange rate. By late 1963, this adjustment began to occur. The payments balance fell to $0.5 billion, and the adjustment continued.

What was believed? The problem the System faced in the 1960s was similar in some respects to those in the late 1920s after restoration of widespread convertibility into gold. In both periods, central banks or gov- ernments tried to maintain fixed nominal exchange rates by cooperating and used cooperation in a vain attempt to avoid adjustment of misaligned real exchange rates. In both periods, France cooperated reluctantly or not at all.[158] And in both periods, the main weakness in the exchange rate sys- tem arose because any central bank holding a large stock of dollars could precipitate a crisis by demanding gold. The rules provided no means to adjust to such an attack.

While these flaws in the gold exchange system were common to the two periods, there were significant differences. The United States sterilized

158. In Meltzer (2003, 210), I suggest that the main problem in the 1920s was incompat- ible objectives, not failure to cooperate. Cooperation lessened the short-term problem but did nothing to resolve the longer-term problems—misaligned real exchange rates, (ibid., 178).

gold inflows to avoid inflation in the 1920s. It lost gold because it created inflation in the 1950s and again after 1964. The policies of the 1960s aimed at creating cooperative arrangements in which other countries shared responsibility for maintaining the system. The flaw in any system of this kind was a failure to recognize that cooperative arrangements work in the long-term only if countries have common objectives or incentives to cooperate. The incentives were not absent, but they were often weak.[159] At one point, President Kennedy threatened to take U.S. forces out of Europe to remind France and Germany of their dependence. Later, the Vietnam War muted interest in cooperation because the stock of dollars continued to increase, and the war was unpopular abroad. European governments became reluctant to finance it in any case but especially because financing the U.S. deficit promoted domestic inflation that was also unpopular.

In principle the United States could have adjusted its real exchange rate either by deflating relative to its trading partners or by revaluing gold. The first option worked for a time by creating more inflation abroad than at home. Financing the higher budget deficits used to finance the Vietnam War and the Great Society and slower productivity growth narrowed the difference in inflation rates and reversed the improvement in the U.S. trade balance. Principal policymakers dismissed the second option, either devaluation or floating, as unworthy of serious consideration.

Treasury Undersecretary Robert Roosa set the basic policy early in the Kennedy administration. Roosa (1965, 27) believed not only that fluctuating rates were destabilizing but also that "public authorities then come under pressure to manipulate the rates, and usually do. This leads to competitive devaluation, and on to trade and exchange restrictions." Further, floating exchange rate degenerate into "disorderly chaos if they do not have some fixed point of reference" (ibid., 27). This created a "sense of rubbery unreality concerning the validity of all prices" (ibid., 28).[160]

Under Bretton Woods rules, central banks agreed to keep exchange rates within one percent of their fixed parities. Roosa rejected wider bands to increase flexibility, for example during non-synchronized recessions or

159. In a review of Coombs' book, Jordan (1978, 416) noted its significant flaw: "After relating all his frustrations with uncooperative foreign officials and U.S. Treasury officials, Coombs does not reach the conclusion that . . . a system that was so dependent on the personalities of such a large number of individuals representing such a diverse array of interests was fundamentally flawed."

160. Roosa (1965, 30) did not dismiss fluctuations in forward exchange rates. Instead, he welcomed those fluctuations as a market mechanism that substituted for fluctuations in reserve positions. These fluctuations were limited, however, by the spot rate. If the forward rate rose or fell too far from the spot market rate, it began to influence the spot rate to move toward its upper or lower band.

expansions. These could become a type of "de facto devaluation" (ibid., 31). He regarded convertibility of dollars into a gold as a *"privilege"* that foreign governments retained because they accepted *"responsibility* . . . for the continued smooth functioning of the system" (ibid., 33; emphases in the original).

Roosa initially opposed proposals to augment the gold stock and replace the dollar by creating an international means of settling payments imbalances. By 1965, he accepted the need for a multilateral agreement to augment the supply of gold. The Special Drawing Right (SDR) agreement provided for creating "paper gold" at the IMF.[161]

In 1967, Roosa debated Milton Friedman, the leading exponent of floating exchange rates. As before, he defended fixed rates as a source of discipline on countries' policies, without recognizing that the Employment Act in the United States and similar explicit or tacit agreements abroad necessarily limited the influence of international considerations in policymaking. Domestic policy concerns, especially concerns about unemployment, dominated.[162]

Roosa argued that, under fixed exchange rates, sustained payments deficits or surpluses showed underlying problems that led to correction by market adjustment. Further, "practical considerations . . . render a system of flexible rates unworkable" (Friedman and Roosa, 1967, 31). He rejected "frequent and regular increases in the gold price" or even wider bands (ibid., 35). The wider band idea might someday be of some use; the incremental gold price change would be "an unmitigated disaster" (ibid., 35–36). If exchange rate changes had to occur, rates for countries other than the United States "can and should be changed when there is a persisting disequilibrium under a fixed-rate system" (ibid., 39).

Roosa elaborated. "The most significant overall point to be recognized is that the United States can never expect . . . to bring about at its own initiative any effective change in its exchange rate" (ibid., 54). The reason: other countries would take offsetting action to defend themselves. This argument suggested that other countries would prefer to lend to the

161. In Friedman and Roosa (1967, 10), Milton Friedman predicted that every country "will want a different agreement—one that permits it to borrow much and commits it to lending little. Thus, despite all the appearance of an agreement in principle, no effective agreement will in fact be reached."

162. Roosa raised this point as a criticism of floating rates (Friedman and Roosa, 1967, 83), although he recognized elsewhere that in practice countries could not adjust by creating enough unemployment to reduce wages (ibid., 43). Of course, reducing unemployment was a main reason why the alternatives were floating rates or controls and restrictions to maintain the fixed rate system. As Friedman noted, controls and restrictions introduced uncertainty and costs, removing a main advantage of fixed exchange rates (ibid., 22).

United States rather than adjust. It is noteworthy that this argument was not unique to Roosa. It represented much conventional thinking at the time only three years before President Nixon closed the gold window and forced exchange rate realignment.

Roosa accepted the possibility of a "system-wide change in parities . . . simultaneously against gold" (ibid., 54). Though he did not rule this out, he wrote that it would "undermine confidence for the future in the stabilizing point of reference to which all other elements of the system are hinged" (ibid., 55–56). Later, he changed his mind and opined that the currency problem "cannot simply be solved by a change in the price of gold" (ibid., 64).

Much earlier, Irving Fisher had proposed to adjust the number of grains of gold to keep constant the gold price of a large basket of commodities.[163] If the price level rose or fell the number of grains of gold required to buy the basket would increase or decline to stabilize the gold price of the commodity basket and the purchasing power of money. Benjamin Graham, J. M. Keynes, and others later proposed similar schemes. These proposals gave no reason for loss of confidence in the standard and avoided instability.

The debate established that there was no meeting of the minds. Friedman argued correctly that "*reserves alone cannot do the job.* There must be some adjustment mechanism" (ibid., 11; emphasis in the original.) Roosa rejected all adjustment proposals. The main change he proposed was to augment the supply of reserves.

The French government complained frequently about the special role of the United States based on its ability to balance its accounts by supplying dollars that would be held in reserves by other countries. In fact, United States policymakers did not value the privilege highly. Instead, they took leadership of discussions to create an alternative currency that could serve as a reserve.

Discussion of monetary problems usually ignored the demand for dollars. Demand increased as trade and finance expanded. An overseas market in dollars, called euro-dollars, based mainly in London, arose to avoid U.S. exchange restrictions and satisfy the demand for dollars.[164] Bankers

163. In 1922–23, Congress held hearings on Fisher's proposal but did not adopt it (see volume 1, 182).

164. Euro-dollars are dollar deposits in banks domiciled in Europe (including branches of U.S. banks). The euro-dollar started as a way for the Soviet Union to hold dollar deposits without subjecting themselves to regulation or possible blocking by the United States government. Interest rate ceilings in the United States expanded the market in the 1960s and 1970s.

lent and borrowed euro-dollars in an unregulated market. As in any banking market, producers of euro-dollars depended on a reserve held at a
domestic U.S. bank, but the relation of the euro-dollar loan to the reserve
balance in the United States was less structured than in regulated domestic markets. U.S. banks and corporations both borrowed and lent in the
euro-dollar market. For example, when regulation Q ceilings were binding, corporate treasurers could increase earnings by lending surplus balances in the euro-dollar market. U.S. banks opened branches in London
to service their customers and lend surplus balances at the higher interest
rates available abroad. These actions reduced interest rate differences, so
that euro-dollar rates soon moved to a small premium over domestic rates
(Peter Fousek, "The Euro Dollar Market, Tighter Credit and the Balance of
Payments," Board Records, March 1, 1963, 7).

Much comment suggested that the euro-dollar market was inflationary because it created additional money that the Federal Reserve could
not control. This argument lacked analytic substance. Euro-dollar deposits
depended on deposits or reserves of domestic banks. Banks or financial institutions that created dollar liabilities without any reserve of dollar assets
risked large losses when forced to cover claims. Euro-dollars were simply
another of the many ways that financial markets innovated to better serve
their customers.

Federal Reserve staff did not share the popular view that euro-dollars
represented a net outflow that increased the U.S. payments deficit. Their
1963 report noted that U.S. corporations borrowed in the market and that
foreigners borrowed to finance purchases of U.S. goods, services, and assets. Also the higher interest rates that the market paid induced foreigners to hold additional dollar deposits. "It is not possible to conclude with
any assurance whether the net overall effect so far has been favorable or
damaging to the dollar" (ibid., 10). The report expressed concern that "the
market is developing in a direction unfavorable to the dollar" (ibid., 10).[165]
In fact, much of the borrowing and lending appears to have been used to
finance activities in the United States when regulation Q ceiling rates were
binding. The smallest part of euro-dollar market activities was the use of
euro-dollar deposits as a substitute for deposits at U.S. banks (Bernstein,
1972).[166]

Capital market controls and fear of additional controls encouraged

165. The main effect on the balance of payments came when foreigners borrowed euro-
dollars and invested them abroad.

166. Much of the concern about euro-market activity came from the rapid increase in
euro-dollar deposits—a 37 percent compound rate of increase from December 1964 to December 1969. During the same period commercial paper outstanding in the United States

Table 3.7   Base Growth, Gold Stock, and Outflow 1961–65 (in millions $)

	GOLD STOCK	ANNUAL REDUCTION	GOLD LOSS PERCENTAGE	BASE GROWTH PERCENTAGE
December 1961	16947	857	4.8	2.8
1962	16057	890	5.2	3.8
1963	15596	461	2.9	5.5
1964	15471	125	0.8	5.2
1965	13806	1665	10.7	5.9

Source: Board of Governors (1976), Anderson and Rasche (1999).

growth of the euro-dollar market and other unregulated currency markets. Journalists, market participants, and some central bankers expressed concern that growth of these new credit market instruments seriously weakened monetary control of inflation. This proved to be a false conjecture on this as on many similar occasions. When central banks undertook to control inflation, they succeeded despite continued growth of the euro-dollar market.

Expansion Without Inflation, 1961–65

The years 1961 to 1965 are among the best in Federal Reserve history. The economy grew 17 percent; inflation (deflator) rose at a 1.6 percent average rate and, as late into the expansion as January 1965, the reported annual rise in the consumer price index was only 1 percent. After its usual slow decline, the unemployment rate fell below 5 percent in 1964 and reached 4 percent by the end of 1965. Contrary to administration beliefs, the economy reached full employment with low inflation.

Industrial production and stock prices rose. From the end of the recession in February 1961 to December 1965, both indexes increased 40 percent. Unit labor costs declined more than 7 percent, reflecting the increased productivity growth and low inflation for the period. Partly as a result, the balance of payments deficit fell to $1.3 billion (liquidity basis), the lowest annual value since governments restored currency convertibility.[167]

Table 3.7 shows that the United States continued to sell gold to foreign central banks and governments. The rate of gold loss slowed in 1963 and 1964, then surged in 1965 with slower productivity growth, the reported increase in inflation to 1.9 percent by the end of 1965, and forecasts of 3.5 percent inflation by mid-1966 (Chart 3.3 above). Table 3.7 also shows

---

rose at a 30 percent compound annual rate without arousing similar concerns (Bernstein, 1972, 39).

167. The liquidity measure includes changes in liquid liabilities to foreign official holders and changes in official reserve assets.

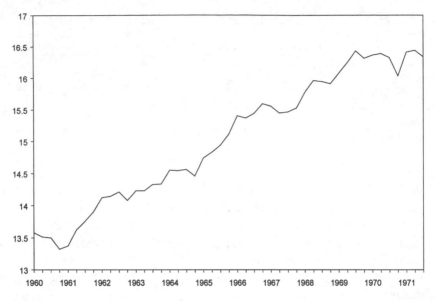

Chart 3.10. Quarterly base velocity, 1960:1–1971:3.

that higher monetary base growth accompanied or preceded higher inflation and the increased rate of gold outflow. Evidence of higher anticipated
inflation also appears in long-term interest rates, shown in Chart 3.6 above.
By the autumn of 1965 these interest rates had reached their highest level
in the postwar years to that time. Base velocity rose, accompanying the
increase in interest rates and anticipated inflation. Chart 3.10 shows the
surge in base velocity beginning in 1965. For the years 1960–64, base velocity rose at a compound average rate of 2 percent. In 1965, base velocity
rose nearly 4 percent. The Great Inflation had begun. Increased spending
for the Vietnam War began the following year, intensifying the inflation
problem.

START OF THE LONG EXPANSION
Despite the relatively high short-term interest rate and rising long-term
real rates, the economy grew more than 6 percent in the four quarters
ending in December 1961. Recovery slowed in second quarter 1962, and
real output fell about 0.7 percent in the fourth quarter. Real GNP fell more
than 2.5 percent below the Council's forecast for the year.

Industrial production fell in the second quarter, then rose slowly for the
rest of the year. The slowdown was not monetary. The proximate cause was
said at the time to be uncertainty generated by a public dispute over steel
prices between President Kennedy and the chairman of the largest steel

company, United States Steel. The president had indicated an interest in wage-price relationships before his inauguration, and the Council of Economic Advisers duly followed up in its 1962 report by setting guidelines for non-inflationary wage-price behavior (Heller papers, Box 4, January 5, 1961). President Kennedy used the guidelines when he wrote to the heads of the steel companies and the union near the end of 1961, asking them to avoid a price increase and an inflationary wage increase. The president thought that he and Secretary of Labor Arthur Goldberg had negotiated a steel wage increase that was within the government's wage-price guidelines based on productivity increase, so there should be no change in steel prices. When the companies announced price increases on April 10, the administration forced them to cancel the announcement by starting an investigation of pricing practices, shifting defense contracts to smaller companies, and issuing statements critical of the increase. Within three days, all companies rescinded the increases.[168] The incident led many to believe that the administration had taken an anti-business tack. Stock prices started to fall before the confrontation. They fell 4.3 percent in the next four weeks and more than 20 percent in the second quarter, more than eliminating the entire gain for the previous twelve months.[169]

Domestic actions. The Federal Reserve undertook few policy actions in 1961–62. Martin had agreed to keep free reserves about $500 million in 1961. The first reduction came in February 1962, following an increase in the bill rate the previous month. In December, the FOMC again reduced free reserves. The Board reduced reserve requirements for time deposits from 5 to 4 percent in late October.

---

168. In addition to threats, the government urged Inland Steel and a few others not to follow the price increase. When these companies agreed, the others withdrew their announced increases. This was the first of many efforts to control inflation by influencing relative prices. In retrospect, Walter Heller concluded that administering the guideposts diverted the Council from its main role of advising the president (Hargrove and Morley, 1964, 183–84). He did not conclude that the effort was based on confusion between relative prices and a general price index.

169. Much of the decline was in real business fixed investment. Real investment fell in the second and fourth quarters. This is the expected effect of a decline in stock prices. The stock market values existing assets. When asset prices rise, the demand for new capital (investment) increases because new capital is a close substitute for existing capital. The FAC met early in May. They told the Board that "the conditions under which the steel companies reversed their decision have caused concern in the business community and may delay future capital investment" (Board Minutes, May 1, 1962, 2).

President Kennedy later worked to restore relations with the leaders of the steel industry by appointing Roger Blough, chairman of United States Steel, to head a commission on foreign trade. Kennedy met with Blough regularly to discuss the Commission's work. Stock prices started to rise steadily in October–November 1962. Real investment resumed its increase early in 1963.

By 1961 most Board members accepted that "price stability is a desirable goal of national economic policy" (Board Minutes, February 14, 1961, 13). Governor Mills objected to including price stability as a goal in the Employment Act because it could require reductions in real growth by slowing money growth. Woodlief Thomas now endorsed the proposed amendment. "More economic growth could be achieved through general stability in the level of prices than if there were wide price swings. Accordingly, he had come to the view that it would be advantageous to have price stability set forth as an explicit goal of government economic policy" (ibid., 4–5). This view did not return for twenty years.

Although the price level remained stable, FAC members expressed concern about inflation throughout the year.[170] In November, they clarified their concern. The economy showed few signs of price increases, and labor costs continued to increase, squeezing profit margins. About half of the FAC wanted tighter monetary policy in November (Board Minutes, November 21, 1961, 5, 12).

FOMC members had mixed appraisals of the attempt to lower long-term and raise short-term rates. Mills said the policy had not worked and only confused market participants. He compared total System purchases of $443 million of securities with maturity over one year (out of $847 million net increase in portfolio) to $10.7 billion of new corporate, state, and local securities. Others pointed out that long-term rates had increased with economic activity, but they might have increased more without intervention. The New York desk reported that offerings of securities over one year had fallen markedly from levels in the spring. In a clear statement that policy actions affect inflation after a lag, Mills described the FOMC as "groping to find a . . . policy" consistent with expansion but without "the danger of generating subsequent inflationary pressures" (FOMC Minutes, August 1, 1961, 40). Martin agreed, recognizing the absence of a systematic policy by emphasizing "groping."

The usual uncertainty under which monetary policy operated increased as the recovery gained momentum. Abroad, the Soviet Union resumed nuclear testing, and tensions leading to the building of the Berlin Wall, separating East and West Berlin, added to concerns. At home, government spending and the budget deficit increased, partly a response to Soviet actions. Prospective labor negotiations and price increases renewed concern

170. "President Livingston [of the FAC] said he regarded this [inflation] as one of the most serious problems facing the country" (Board Minutes, September 19, 1961, 6). He attributed the increase in stock prices and the "lack of interest generally in fixed income obligations" to increases in expected inflation (Board Minutes, September 19, 1961, 6). The FAC did not ask for a more restrictive policy until later.

about inflation. Peacetime budget deficits in a prosperous economy were a relatively new phenomenon to which the public had not become accustomed. Administration forecasts that the economy would grow more than 6 percent in 1963, to $575 billion, added to concerns about inflation.[171]

A few weeks later, the mood changed. The staff reported that business economists had become skeptical about continued expansion based on reported slower current growth of retail sales, industrial production, employment, and personal income. Defense spending now seemed likely to rise more slowly. This is one of many occasions when policymakers found it difficult to distinguish between transitory changes in economic variables, characteristic of a market economy, and the persistent changes that cumulate as business cycle fluctuations. This time the staff ignored the concerns, and the FOMC voted for no change.

Three weeks later, at the November 14 meeting, a split developed. Mills and Hayes dissented because they wanted a higher short-term interest rate to reduce short-term capital outflow. Mitchell argued that the Treasury bill rate had moved up between meetings despite the continued slack in the economy. As long as slack remained, domestic concerns were more important than the balance of payments. Martin could not find a consensus so he chose to maintain money market conditions, but he did not mention his commitment to Heller.

Members divided also on the use of free reserves. A vocal minority preferred to target total reserve growth, but Martin opposed. He said the market had raised Treasury bill rates, not the System. He preferred to let higher rates remain. Several thought it might soon be time for a tighter policy, but the FOMC should wait a few weeks before deciding to act.

Two days later, November 16, the bond market broke on concerns of a repeat of the 1953 experience, when large purchasers of a new treasury issue started to sell in anticipation of faster economic growth and tighter System policy.[172] Long- and short-term rates rose with weekly free reserves at $515 million, slightly above target. The manager asked the Board for

171. The staff gave its perspective on the role of forecasts in setting policy at that time. The FOMC "should not lean too heavily on projections and forecasts. . . . For some sorts of policy planning, estimates or projections . . . are unavoidable. . . . [I]t is futile to speculate now as to whether or not a GNP of $575 billion in the fourth quarter of 1962 is 'inflationary,' and it certainly would be foolhardy to be influenced in current policy formulation one way or the other by such an exercise" (FOMC Minutes, September 12, 1961, 5–6). The staff report added that the "vastly increased liquidity . . . especially in the hands of consumers, constitutes a sort of powder keg of potential spending" (ibid., 6–7).

172. In the week ending November 8, the federal funds rate rose 0.61 percentage points (to 2.75). The Treasury bill and three- to five-year bond rate rose 0.24 and 0.09 percentage points between November 4 and 18. The main policy action was an increase in regulation Q ceiling rates announced on December 1 and effective January 1, 1962 (see text below).

authority to purchase long-term bonds. Martin and Balderston were absent. All the remaining Board members except Robertson voted to permit purchases at Rouse's discretion.

With the end of the automobile strike, output and sales increased rapidly in November, and the unemployment rate fell from 6.8 to 6.1 percent. Inflation did not rise from its low level. Reported money growth reached only 3 percent for the year to November, and the money stock was only slightly above the mid-1959 level. The rising balance of payments deficit continued as a concern.[173]

Free reserves remained about $500 million, as Martin had promised. Hayes commented on the "increasingly widespread notion" that the System was "wedded to a $500 million free reserve target" (FOMC Minutes, December 5, 1961, 14). There was no response and no change. The consensus on December 19 called for an unchanged policy with bill rates held between 2.5 and 2.75 percent. Treasury bill rates increased after the meeting. A three-week moving average of these rates had increased steadily from 2.382 for the week ending November 18 to 2.603 percent in the week ending December 16, just before the FOMC met. In the next five weeks, the moving average rose to 2.737 percent, near the top of the range the FOMC set.[174]

Members of Congress kept watch on the FOMC's decisions and actions. In August 1962, the December actions became the subject of criticism from Congressman Henry Reuss (Wisconsin). Citing changes in free reserves and interest rates, Reuss chided Martin for causing the economic slowdown by raising interest rates and reducing free reserves at the December 19, 1961, meeting.[175] Perhaps influenced by administration economists, Reuss wanted free reserves to remain at $500 million or above, and he pressed Martin to return to the former level of free reserves and remain there until January. Referring to the president's decision not to reduce

173. The staff reported that the data exaggerated the capital account deficit because domestic banks deposited dollars in Canadian banks to lend to domestic borrowers. Hayes replied that the $100 to $150 million monthly flow to Canada was no different from any other outflow. His statement was open to two interpretations. Either the flow to Canada to escape regulation was no different than the flow to other countries, or he denied that regulation had a large effect on the outflow.

174. Trieber now defined "feel of the market" in terms of short-term interest rates, borrowing by member banks, and the cost of dealer financing. This differed from earlier definitions based on the distribution of reserves between New York, Chicago, and other banks.

175. Reuss praised Martin for keeping free reserves near $500 million during most of 1961. "Then on December 19, 1961, a date that will be remembered in monetary history, the Open Market Committee met, and you abandoned that resolution . . . I think it will come to be known as 'Tight Money Tuesday'" (Joint Economic Committee, 1962, 615). Free reserves fell from about $500 million to an average of $410 in December.

tax rates in 1962, Reuss said, "With less fiscal ease, we must have more monetary ease" (Joint Economic Committee, 1962, 616). Martin agreed to deliver Reuss's message to the FOMC. He reported the conversation, but free reserves declined further that same month.

The committee remained divided in 1962. A majority wanted to tighten policy in January to support the dollar. Hayes talked about increasing the discount rate before the forthcoming Treasury auction and, without mentioning Martin by name, proposed that the "System's spokesman should stress to the Administration the seriousness with which we regard the international outlook and . . . urge a more prompt and rigorous concerted Government program" (FOMC Minutes, January 23, 1962, 12).[176] Mitchell directly challenged Hayes, stressing domestic factors. Raising interest rates would not help the domestic economy. Martin tried to balance conflicting pressures by choosing "even keel" and supplying reserves "adequate for credit expansion, while avoiding downward pressure on short-term rates" (ibid., 32). Hayes was not satisfied. He wanted to reverse some of the very slight decline in bill rates during recent weeks, but Martin opposed, saying that "it was easy to see ghosts that might or might not be there" (ibid., 31). After many exchanges, the directive passed with Hayes expressing reservations but unwilling to dissent.

The Federal Reserve held Treasury bill rates between 2.65 and 2.75 percent throughout the winter of 1962. Free reserves declined as banks reduced excess reserves, and growth slowed. The staff remained uncertain about whether the slowdown was temporary, so they proposed no action. The Federal Advisory Council remained optimistic. They told the Board that they expected profits to increase and that there would not be a steel strike (Board Minutes, February 20, 1962, 2). Woodlief Thomas noted that credit and money growth remained sluggish.[177] Governor Mills amplified Thomas's statement. The "theory motivating System open market policy actions postulates forcing an expansion in demand deposits adjusted and time deposits at an annual rate of 4 percent. The theory takes the wholly tenable position that national economic growth . . . depends importantly on

176. On January 23, 1962, President Kennedy asked Congress to raise the pay of the chairman and the governors to $25,000 and $22,000 respectively (from $20,500 and $20,000). In 2000, the equivalent salary would be $142,550 and $125,400, using the consumer price index. The president also asked Congress to make the chairman's term coterminous with the president's term.

177. In March, the FOMC again changed the formula for allocating securities in the open market account to require quarterly reallocation that equalized the average reserve ratios of the twelve reserve banks in proportion to the adjustments required over the first eighty-five days of the preceding three months. The formula allowed additional adjustment if a reserve bank's reserve ratio fell below 30 percent (FOMC Minutes, March 6, 1962, 18).

a constant expansion in the money supply defined to include time deposits" (Mills to Koch, "Open Market Policy," Board Records, April 23, 1962). This is the strongest statement about the role of money in the records to that time. Mills then expressed doubt about the relation during periods of slow growth.

The staff of the New York bank considered several ways of offsetting large temporary changes in float. It rejected frequent changes in reserve requirement ratios, offsetting changes in Treasury balances, and purchases and sales of federal funds. It proposed a new instrument—reverse repurchase agreements with government security dealers. The Federal Reserve could absorb reserves by selling securities with a fixed term for repurchase. This would avoid dealing with individual firms other than dealers.[178] The New York bank would pay interest on the "loan" from the dealers, just as it received interest on repurchase agreements. The New York bank did the transaction for its own account and did not share interest paid and received with other reserve banks.

All the major concerns of 1961 continued in 1962. The FOMC became more divided between those who wanted to tighten and those who favored greater ease. Hayes led the first group. Although people shifted position, usually Deming (Minneapolis), Fleming (Cleveland), Shephardson, and Ellis (Boston) joined him. This group emphasized the balance of payments deficit and the gold outflow. Mitchell and Robertson, later joined by Mills, led the opposition. They favored lower interest rates to stimulate domestic growth. Each side had a legislated mandate, the Bretton Woods Agreement on one side, the Employment Act on the other. Martin tried to balance the two groups, although he often agreed with Hayes's concerns. His own position, stated many times, was that the domestic and international problems were inseparable. The balance of payments problem was "the biggest single shadow looming over the domestic business picture" (FOMC Minutes, December 18, 1962, 61).[179] Greater ease would destroy confidence in

178. The System did not do repurchase agreements with dealer banks, only with non-bank dealers. The latter could recall the securities that the desk repurchased at any time, but the new proposal called for fixed duration of the reverse repurchase agreement. The desk could not use the securities in the open market account since the account was the property of all reserve banks while reverse repurchases were done for the New York bank's own account.

179. Administration economists continued to press Martin for more expansion and more purchases of long-term debt. Early in the year, they forecast 7.5 percent growth of the real economy in 1962. The Board's staff forecast called for 5 percent. Actual growth for the four quarters was 3.2 percent. Note that the Board's staff started to forecast GNP growth and inflation, a marked departure from earlier practice. Although Martin had little confidence in forecasts, he permitted the staff to make them, possibly as a defense against the administration.

the dollar, damaging the economy and reducing employment. Raising the short-term interest rate would improve confidence (ibid., 62).

Some FOMC members shifted sides with changes in employment, output, balance of payments, and factors such as the Cuban missile crisis (October), stock market collapse (May), floating of the Canadian dollar (June), and the president's decision to call for lower tax rates followed by his decision to postpone tax rate reduction until 1963. At year-end 1962, the FOMC remained closely divided. It approved maintaining current policy (status quo) by nine to three on September 11, and seven to five on December 4. The November 13 meeting voted six to five to tighten policy, until Robertson changed his vote to support no change.[180] Five dissents was rare.

Status quo, no change, or slightly less ease did not have a common meaning shared by all FOMC members. Some used free reserves, others interest rates or total reserves. Several used more than one target without mentioning how to resolve discrepancies between them. This left the account manager to decide. "Color, tone and feel" also gave the manager discretion.

If the desk failed to carry out the instructions that the members approved, did a vote for "no change" mean no change from the outcome or no change from the policy that members intended? Martin claimed no change in intention, but Mills thought it should mean no change in outcome (FOMC Minutes, December 4, 1962, 55–56). The difference was large at times because outcomes differed from intentions.

Ambiguities in the discussion and the directive and failure to define terms like "ease," "restraint," and "no change" also gave considerable discretion to the manager. Nevertheless, changes in free reserves remained broadly consistent with the FOMC's intent, and bill rates remained in a narrow range.[181]

Actual policy was a compromise. The narrow range for the Treasury

---

180. At the November 13, 1962, meeting less ease lost seven to four, with Martin, Balderston, Fulton (Cleveland), and Hayes voting for less ease. Martin was in the minority, an exceptional outcome. The next vote was for more ease. It lost seven to three, with one abstention (Bryan). Mills, Mitchell, and Robertson favored greater ease.

181. Treasury bill rates changed very little but in the direction consistent with FOMC decisions. The decline prior to the June 19 meeting reflects possible market response to the large (percentage) stock market decline on May 28 and the manager's decision to let free reserves increase. The decline in the stock market was the largest since 1929, with 9.4 million shares traded. This was considered large volume at the time. The FOMC voted on May 29 to keep policy unchanged. As noted in Brunner and Meltzer (1964), the manager often moved ahead of the FOMC in the early 1960s. On May 29 President Kennedy asked Chairman Martin to reduce stock market margin requirements (FOMC Minutes, May 29, 1962, 39). Martin told Kennedy that the Board had decided the day before to leave margin requirements unchanged. Kennedy accepted its judgment but he asked for a public explanation. The FOMC

bill rate (2.7 to 2.9 percent) reflected the decision to reduce short-term capital outflows, and the positive level of free reserves showed the FOMC's intention to encourage growth of bank reserves, bank credit, and money. Although Martin said that policy wasn't effectively carried out by small and indecisive moves, policy for 1962, using the principal indicators on which the Federal Reserve relied, was both cautious and indecisive. The minutes note, however, that the monetary base and the money stock, currency and demand deposits, rose more rapidly than in the recent past. For the year to December 1962, monetary base growth reached 3.79 percent, the highest annual rate of growth in a decade. The money stock did not increase until the second half of the year, but the rate of increase then reached 6 percent.[182]

Outside the Federal Reserve, many business leaders expressed concern about prolonged easy money. The Federal Advisory Council told the Board to give greater weight to the balance of payments and "the threat confronting the dollar" (Board Minutes, May 1, 1962, 7). The vice chairman of the Dallas Federal Reserve Bank warned the Dallas board and the Board of Governors about excessive ease (FOMC Minutes, June 19, 1962, 14). Comments of this kind strengthened the case for tighter policy without immediate effect. Martin made the same case. "Monetary policy has done what it can do to help the recovery. . . . [I]t was easy to get into a pattern of activity where we think that, by just easing money or increasing expenditures or raising a deficit, we can achieve certain things (FOMC Minutes, July 10, 1962, 42).[183]

By midsummer, concerns about recession began to be reflected in private forecasts and FOMC members' statements. The division between those

---

was reluctant. The Board acted soon after, on July 9, reducing margin requirements to 50 from 70 percent.

182. Opinions about the role of money covered a wide range. Bryan (Atlanta), Woodlief Thomas, and at times others wanted reserves and money to rise at the rate of growth of output. Ellis (Boston) said reserves had increased at an unsustainable rate. Mitchell thought money growth was not important but because people paid attention to it, the Federal Reserve had to be concerned about public relations (FOMC Minutes, December 18, 1962, 39 and 57).

183. Heller arranged a meeting of the Quadriad on July 30, so that President Kennedy could talk to Chairman Martin about Heller's concern that the Federal Reserve had become more restrictive. According to Heller's memo, Martin said that policy had not changed. Later, when asked by the president when the change occurred, Martin said June 19. He explained that European developments had led to a run on the dollar that ended when the president spoke to the Europeans on television via satellite (for the first time.) Martin denied that domestic policy was restrictive and said he was more optimistic than his staff about prospects for the economy (Minutes of the Quadriad, Heller papers, Box 19, July 30, 1962). Heller may have misunderstood Martin because earlier Martin told the FOMC that "there had been a great deal of ease, and . . . lately there had been a little less ease" (FOMC Minutes, July 10, 1962, 42–43).

who emphasized the balance of payments and others principally concerned about the domestic economy prevented any action. Martin argued that easy money could make matters worse by fostering lax loan standards and borrowing for unprofitable projects (FOMC Minutes, July 31, 1962, 34).

Concerns about recession stimulated discussions of a quick tax cut to increase spending instead of a permanent tax cut to expand economic potential. Early in June, President Kennedy announced that he would ask Congress to reduce individual and corporate tax rates.[184] To get support Kennedy met with Congressman Wilbur Mills, chairman of the House Ways and Means Committee, with businessmen and with his advisers. Mills did not support tax reduction, nor did Senator Harry Byrd and many other members of Congress. Mills said he would not rely on economic forecasts but would consider tax reduction if a recession occurred. The businessmen favored higher interest rates to attract foreign capital, tax reduction to increase domestic spending, and a limit on government spending to hold down the budget deficit[185] (Kennedy, 2001b, 337–38). They favored separating tax reform from tax reduction to avoid long delays while Congress debated tax reform. In a television address on August 13, Kennedy retreated temporarily. He withdrew the proposal for a quick tax cut but reaffirmed his request for a permanent tax cut and tax reform in January 1963.[186] The timing would strengthen the economy in the 1964 election year.

184. Kennedy rejected tax cutting at the start of his administration to avoid conflict with his call for sacrifice in his inaugural address. He had not yet accepted the argument in favor of a large budget deficit during a recession. By spring 1962, he reconsidered, and on June 7, 1962, he announced his intention to seek a tax cut that would increase the current deficit. On June 11, at Yale, he accepted the Keynesian logic, taught to him by his economic advisers, arguing that deficits and government debt were not always bad and not to be avoided in recessions (Kennedy, 2001b, 363).

185. The group was led by Allan Sproul, formerly president of the New York Federal Reserve Bank. They told the president that his administration's balance of payments program did "not add up to a program which is easily understood and which gives assurance of strong purpose and ultimate success" (Kennedy, 2001b, 338).

186. In 1962, the administration changed depreciation schedules (Bulletin F) to permit faster write-off of equipment, and Congress approved an investment tax credit to encourage investment by permitting companies that invested to reduce tax payments. These programs added $2.5 to $3 billion to corporate cash flow (Kennedy, 2001b, n. 27). The investment tax credit had not been used before. The Federal Advisory Council was skeptical about the effectiveness of such measures. They explained that most large companies had "a depreciation rate equal to or in excess of that provided by the bulletin. There was not much enthusiasm for the tax credit" (Board Minutes, September 18, 1962, 10). Real investment in equipment rose 12.8 percent in 1962 and 7.2 percent in 1963, but profits rose 10.7 percent in 1962 and 5.7 percent in 1963. The FAC was much more enthusiastic about tax reform and tax reduction (Board Minutes, November 20, 1962, 2). The members preferred tax and spending reduction, but most wanted tax reduction even if the budget deficit increased.

When some Federal Reserve officials argued that monetary policy could do nothing to increase output, they often used a structural argument. Automation and the use of computers left the labor force unable to fill jobs that became available. By extension, the balance of payments deficit resulted from inability to produce exports at competitive prices. Such arguments were very common in the early 1960s. At the September 11 FOMC meeting, President Edward Wayne (Richmond) was explicit. The committee faced less than satisfactory domestic expansion and a persistent external imbalance. The fact that neither problem disappeared meant that they could not be solved by monetary policy. They were "structural elements not susceptible to solution through purely monetary and credit action." Attacking one problem only made the other worse (FOMC Minutes, September 11, 1962, 24–25). Shephardson, Balderston, and King agreed.[187] No one pointed out that the last part of Wayne's argument contradicted the claim that monetary policy would have no effect.

Mitchell, Robertson, and Mills offered an alternative interpretation, one that coincided with administration views.[188] They regarded unemployment and slow growth as a consequence of insufficient demand. They regularly called for more monetary expansion or lower market rates. In addition to this clash of views, a third group led by Hayes, probably reflecting views of principal New York bankers, wanted to give priority to the balance of payments. He regularly called for tighter policy. Martin often joined with him in principle, but he faced opposing pressures from the administration and the Congress.[189]

187. Martin held a different but related view at times. He claimed that the United States was not competitive. The problems were structural and could not be solved by monetary policy, but he often put more emphasis on confidence than on structure. Fulton (Cleveland) "did not pretend to know exactly what was wrong with the economy or the specific cure, [but] the policy that had been followed seemed to be favorable to the general situation" (FOMC Minutes, September 11, 1962, 34). Another remark came from Governor King: "The Committee's policy was to permit a further increase in the money supply, whereas the narrowly defined money supply had been static or contracting. . . . [H]e felt that some change [in the directive] was in order" (FOMC Minutes, October 2, 1962, 19).

188. Heller sent a memo to the president on November 17 to brief him on a meeting the three members of the Council of Economic Advisers held with George Mitchell, described in the memo as "your one-man minority on the Board of Governors" (memo for the president, Heller papers, Box 19, November 17, 1962, 2). Mitchell had provided Heller with a copy of his statement at the FOMC meeting earlier that week in which he warned about the effect of a sudden run on the dollar. Mitchell warned that if the run occurred, the Federal Reserve would tighten credit "drastically."

189. Martin was never doctrinaire and often claimed not to know what to do. He relied on his judgment more than on statistics or economic analysis. And he praised Robertson, Mitchell, and Mills for clear statements of their position, though he did not agree with them. An example is his lengthy statement in FOMC Minutes, September 11, 1962, 41–42. This is a longer version of several statements made at the time.

Chairman Wright Patman of the Joint Economic Committee (JEC) had asked for and, on July 21, 1961, received the 1960 FOMC Minutes. This was the first time the Federal Reserve had released its minutes for a full year. Patman and the JEC agreed to keep the minutes confidential. The JEC hired Professor John Gurley of Stanford University and Asher Achinstein of the Library of Congress to summarize the material.

The *New York Times* obtained a copy of the summary report and published extracts on August 13 and 14. Patman wrote to ask the FOMC to release the minutes so that the JEC report could be released to the press generally. The letter asked for a prompt response (FOMC Minutes, August 21, 1962, 47). The FOMC's response remarked pointedly that the minutes had been released under agreement that they would remain confidential. The FOMC asked for a three-week delay to its next meeting before responding to the JEC request. Although Martin favored publication and spoke in favor of regular publication of the complete minutes after a delay, the FOMC favored independence. It voted ten to one, with one abstention, to refuse the request as not in the public interest.[190] The issue returned in the 1970s.

In October 1962, the staff reported signs of stronger recovery, but it was soon disappointed. Bryan and others who used money supply growth to measure the expansive thrust of policy actions had difficulty most of the year interpreting the much higher growth of time deposits and slower growth of M_1 (currency and demand deposits). They recognized that higher regulation Q ceiling rates had permitted banks to bid for time deposits, but they were uncertain about whether growth of time deposits was as expansive as equal growth of demand deposits would have been. This is one of many subsequent occasions when ceiling rates distorted the money data and confused FOMC members.[191]

On October 18, the Board announced a reduction of reserve require-

---

190. The FOMC voted also that the JEC report "does not reveal a single policy *action* by the Open Market Committee that was not recorded in the Annual Report of the Board of Governors for 1960, along with the economic circumstances of the action, the votes of the Committee members, and the underlying reason why the action was taken" (FOMC Minutes, September 11, 1962, 73). The FOMC added that release of minutes so soon after the meetings occurred would hinder discussion and debate and would not be in the public interest. These discussions show the beginning of awareness that secrecy had costs as well as benefits. Markets had to infer the System's intention, but secrecy had value if members were more candid at the meeting. Much later, "credibility" became an important consideration.

191. Some members expressed disappointment that the president had chosen not to ask for a tax cut. They wanted more fiscal stimulus to reduce pressure on them. Hayes was most forceful at the October 2 meeting. He complained that the Federal Reserve did not comment on fiscal policy actions, but the administration did not hesitate to comment on monetary policy. He wanted tax reduction for domestic stimulus so that the Federal Reserve could con-

ment ratios for time deposits from 5 to 4 percent, effective October 25 at reserve city banks and November 1 at country banks. This was the first reduction in this ratio since 1954. The alleged purpose was to provide a seasonal increase in reserves without lowering short-term rates. It was based on a belief that lowering reserve requirements spread reserves through the financial system more quickly than open market operations (Board Minutes, October 18, 1962, 16–17). The move released $767 million from required reserves but the desk maintained short-term interest rates, so it absorbed the reserves.[192] The manager described the market as uncertain whether this was a first step toward an easier policy.[193] Interpreting data for the period is difficult because President Kennedy told the nation about Soviet missile bases in Cuba on October 22. On November 2, the president announced that the bases were being dismantled. Agreement with the Soviet Union had been reached five days earlier.

During the missile crisis, the Federal Reserve followed a "status quo" policy, but the directive called for a further increase in bank credit and the money supply (FOMC Minutes, October 23, 1962, 55). The precise meaning is not clear. In the two weeks following the announcement, the System increased discounts and repurchase agreements by $290 million and purchased $117 million outright.[194] Float declined more than $800 million, so the monetary base declined by about $400 million from these sources; total reserves increased only $34 million.[195]

---

centrate on the balance of payments by raising interest rates. Without saying so, he accepted the "assignment model" used by the administration, but he made different assignments.

192. The federal funds rate was 2.94, 2.93, and 2.91 in October, November and December. Free reserves were $421, $472 and $312 million in the same three months. The FOMC minutes report the manager's (Stone's) remark that bond prices rose 0.75 from October 1, but the data in Board of Governors (1976, 749) show little change in average yields on long-term debt (3.90 before the announcement, 3.87 after the release). Early in the year, the Board considered again proposals for classifying cities as reserve bank cities. As on all previous occasions, the members could not agree that the new proposals improved on existing procedures, so they did not change.

193. The manager responded to a question by explaining how he and the market measured the policy thrust. If the federal funds rate and the T-bill rate stayed about where they were, that would signal that the FOMC was not moving toward more ease; if the federal funds rate dropped below 2.5 percent, that would serve to confirm recent headlines that the Fed was seeking more ease (FOMC Minutes, October 23, 1962, 14–15). The CEA interpreted the change in reserve requirement as expansive. Heller wrote to Martin: "We are gratified at your projected move in the direction of greater ease" (memo, Heller to Martin, Heller papers, October 18, 1962, 1). He urged the Federal Reserve to do more: "reactivate vigorously the policy of open market purchases of long-term Treasury securities" (ibid., 1).

194. Three weeks later, the desk reported that it purchased Treasury bills from foreign accounts to keep these bills out of the market. The aim again was to supply reserves without reducing interest rates. Foreign banks increased holdings of U.S. time deposits.

195. The System went on alert and asked the regional banks to instruct member banks

In December, the account manager told the FOMC that the Treasury planned to increase its balances at federal reserve banks by $500 million to reach $1 billion. The Treasury had issued excess bills to raise short-term interest rates. Balances were now in tax and loan accounts at commercial banks. Unless offset, this action would reduce bank reserves and raise interest rates just as if the Federal Reserve engaged in an open market sale. The manager intended to offset the effect on reserves. The Treasury would gain, however, from the implicit 100 percent tax on Federal Reserve earnings. This was the main reason given for the change[196] (FOMC Minutes, December 4, 1962, 5–6).

As 1962 ended, the staff worried about money growth of 6 percent since August, twice the staff guideline.[197] Although the FOMC set guidelines for money in this period, it made no effort to achieve them. Stock prices started to rise in October and accelerated through year-end, suggesting that alleged concerns about recession or stagnant growth had dissipated.

Although inflation had not increased, Martin repeated his concern that greater monetary ease would increase unemployment (FOMC Minutes, December 18, 1962, 61). Mitchell urged that FOMC target the covered interest spread relating domestic and foreign interest rates instead of maintaining a fixed level of Treasury bill rates, but no one pursued the idea.

Mills asked Robert Stone (the manager) whether instructions to encourage credit expansion conflicted with maintaining color, tone, and feel. Stone replied that sometimes they did, but not currently. He gave his interpretation of color, tone, and feel, one that differed from previous interpretations. The desk looked not just at interest rates but reserve measures as well, including free reserves and growth of total reserves versus the growth guideline (FOMC Minutes, December 18, 1962, 4). He did not say how he weighed the different measures. His examples suggested that "color, tone, and feel" meant managerial discretion and that he shifted from free reserves to interest rates based on his judgment. The FOMC's instructions at the time remained imprecise, and the discussions at the meetings continued to use different measures and often multiple measures. Martin's statement of the consensus maintained the ambiguity, perhaps because he preferred managerial discretion or doubted that the FOMC could agree

---

to improve their emergency preparedness and maintain duplicate records in safe storage locations.

196. Treasury deposits at reserve banks rose from $472 million to $777 million in January. By April the average reached $917 million.

197. Mitchell dismissed the concern and Robertson said he was puzzled because free reserves had fallen. (Monthly data show no change.) Ellis (Boston) described money growth as "unsustainable."

on a specific target or improve performance by setting and enforcing a more precise target.

As the new year began, a staff member summarized the implications of two guidelines used by FOMC members to gauge the stance of monetary policy. Both money growth and interest rates had increased along with growth of output. The report spoke to the three principal groups on the FOMC and their different prescriptions. If a member

> believes that for support of maximum sustainable growth in economic ac-
> tivity it is necessary . . . for the money supply to increase consistently in
> relation to the advance in activity, then he might well be satisfied with the
> financial performance of recent months. In fact, in the light of the recent
> rapid monetary expansion, he might feel that its pace ought to be tempered
> somewhat. . . .
>
> As another point of view, one's interest might be on interest rates and
> credit availability and their relation to the present state of economic activity.
> Accordingly, he might feel that monetary policy should operate to keep inter-
> est rates, particularly long-term rates, under sustained downward pressure . . .
> until progress toward reasonably full utilization of resources is more clearly
> assured. (FOMC Minutes, January 29, 1963, 4–5)[198]

REGULATION Q

Beginning in January 1961, Governor Robertson proposed that the Board raise ceiling rates on time and saving deposits from 3 to 5 percent for deposits having at least six months maturity. He proposed a ceiling rate of 4 percent for maturities from ninety days to six months and 3 percent for shorter maturities. At the time, six-month Treasury bills yielded 2.4 to 2.6 percent. Once again, Robertson intended to put the ceiling rate high enough so that "each bank could exercise its judgment in the light of conditions in its own area, the competition it must meet, and what it could afford to pay" (Board Minutes, January 19, 1961, 15). Hackley, the Board's general counsel, assured the Board that "there would be no question in his mind as to the legality of the proposed action" (ibid., 15). The law required only that maximum rates be set.[199]

Martin and several other Board members expressed concern that some

198. A third group wanted higher interest rates to reduce the capital outflow. The report indicated that the staff was divided also, but the consensus favored more stimulus.

199. Balderston asked Robertson why he did not seek to repeal the law. Robertson said that, before asking Congress for repeal, it was better to try "every approach possible under the present law" (Board Minutes, January 19, 1961, 15). He did not oppose repeal. Like most Board members, he had considerable reluctance about asking for legislation.

key members of Congress would object to the Board's failure to make the law effective. Woodlief Thomas offered vigorous criticism, citing the need to prevent banks from making risky loans to earn enough to pay competitive rates and pointing out that spillover from demand to time deposits would increase, reducing effective reserve requirements. That was the purpose of the law, and he urged the Board not to neglect that purpose.[200] And Board members knew that higher maximum rates would be unpopular with many bankers who did not want to pay higher rates. These concerns overpowered their support for market competition in setting interest rates, a main reason for bills-only. Martin (Martin speeches, 1953) had presented bills-only as a step toward free markets.

Robertson proposed increasing ceiling rates several times during the year, modifying his proposal to meet some of the objections raised against his previous efforts. In February, Martin expressed willingness to repeal the law, as suggested in the recent report of a committee appointed by President Kennedy. He soon had a partial opportunity. The administration asked for the Board's comments on legislation eliminating ceiling rates for foreign time and savings deposits.[201] The majority of the Board agreed to tell the Treasury informally that they did not object.

The problem of ceiling rates on foreign time deposits first arose in 1959. Some New York banks favored higher rates at that time, while many other banks opposed. The difference by 1961 was that banking deregulation had started under the direction of a new Comptroller of the Currency, James Saxon, who reduced regulations for the national banks that he supervised. Also, President Kennedy mentioned special Treasury issues for foreigners in his February message. Negotiable certificates of deposits at commercial banks of $1 million and above began trading soon after. Regulation Q ceiling rates applied to these certificates. To avoid the ceiling rates, banks

200. This is a throwback to the 1920s experience, when banks encouraged depositors to shift from demand to time deposits, and the argument in the 1930s that competition in banking caused failures. Governor Mills repeated the argument and added that the proposal would force savings and loans to compete by raising dividend rates and buying risky mortgages. Also, higher rates would reduce bank earnings (Board Minutes, February 13, 1961, 23–24). Benston (1964) showed that the 1930s argument lacked empirical support. In a letter to a banker, Hayes pointed out that during extensive Senate hearings on banking problems in 1931, the issue about increased risk did not arise (letter, Alfred Hayes to Joseph G. Mark, Correspondence Box 240, Federal Reserve Bank of New York, December 8, 1961). Congressman Henry Steagall later suggested that the prohibition compensated banks for the cost of deposit insurance (memo, Correspondence Box 240, Federal Reserve Bank of New York, November 28, 1961).

201. President Kennedy proposed the split ceiling rate in his February 6, 1961, speech on the balance of payments. Secretary Dillon argued that the higher rate would reduce foreign governments' demand for gold (Dillon papers, Box 33, March 8, 1961).

with branches in London encouraged their large depositors to redeposit the funds as euro-dollars at their London branches. This increased capital outflow from the United States, and hence interfered with the Treasury's efforts to reduce the outflow.

The Board missed the opportunity to take a strong stand against the ceiling. It did not choose to publicly support or oppose the Treasury's proposal. "The Treasury had made the decision to submit the proposal, and he [Martin] did not think the Federal Reserve should be in the position of undermining it" (Board Minutes, February 28, 1961, 16). The Board decided to have its general council notify the administration informally. Robertson objected. He opposed raising ceiling rates for foreigners but not for domestic savers. When the legislation went to Congress in April, the Board repeated that it would not object, and in July Martin testified in favor of the bill.[202] Congress removed the ceiling for deposits of foreign governments and institutions for 3 years beginning October 1962. In 1965, it extended the separate treatment.

After Governor Mitchell joined the Board at the end of August, he pointed out that "an agency that had been a vigorous proponent of free markets and free competition must appear rather strange to outsiders if it administered a regulation in the manner that Regulation Q had been administered" (Board Minutes, October 31, 1961, 5). Mitchell favored delay, however, because he thought higher ceiling rates would encourage saving at a time when the economy was recovering from recession.[203] He favored removing the ceiling as a constraint in a series of steps starting soon after.

Chairman Martin expressed concern about the flow of deposits to London. He now thought that "timing . . . was the real problem" (ibid., 7). Either British rates would have to go down or United States rates would have to go up. Robertson responded that the ceiling rate had not been binding for many years after it was established. The Board's mistake was failure "to take action earlier . . . What the Board was doing . . . was to run

202. Earlier, he had written to the Senate Banking Committee that "the Board does not object" (letter, Martin to A. Willis Robertson, Correspondence Box 240, Federal Reserve Bank of New York, April 7, 1961). In August, Robertson offered a new proposal that permitted banks to increase ceiling rates based on the length time deposits remained at the bank. Martin again said that he was not sure whether regulation Q promoted sound banking. "Repeal . . . might be advisable" (Board Minutes, August 23, 1961, 10). Balderston and King objected to the timing (early in a recovery); Mills, as usual, more concerned about the cost to bankers than the cost to the public, objected that most banks opposed higher ceiling rates; and Shephardson did not like to tie rates to the duration of the deposit. As before, Robertson argued for competitive freedom—let the banks decide.

203. Mitchell also asked for a quantitative analysis of bankers' need for protection from themselves. Were the portfolios of banks that paid the ceiling rate riskier than other banks? (Board Minutes, October 31, 1961, 5). I have not found a study of this question at the Board.

counter to its general thesis favoring freedom of competition" (ibid., 9). The Commission on Money and Credit had favored stand-by authority. That was what his proposal did. Martin agreed, but King did not think that free competition in banking existed because entry was restricted. He favored keeping the regulation and opposed acting to keep "hot money" from leaving the country. Balderston argued that delay might require acting after the money flow abroad increased substantially.[204] With so little clarity, there was no chance of agreement about removing ceiling rates. Once again, the Board stared at the problem and passed on. It showed more concern for banks than for the public.

On December 1, the Board approved an increase in ceiling rates, effective January 1, 1962. Most of the governors repeated the arguments they made before. Robertson wanted higher ceiling rates than the others, and Mills wanted to raise rates only to 3.5 percent. The compromise was to raise the rate to 4 percent for deposits held one year or longer and to 3.5 percent for deposits held between six and twelve months. Ceiling rates remained 2.5 percent for deposits held from ninety days to six months. Governor King dissented.

Before releasing a statement announcing the change, the Board notified the Federal Deposit Insurance Corporation (FDIC). FDIC agreed to adopt the same rate schedule for insured, non-member banks. The Board's statement emphasized that the change was made to improve banks' competitive position in the markets for savings and foreign deposits, but it was for each bank "to determine the rates of interest it would pay" (Annual Report, 1962, 102).

On December 12, the Board acted to limit the effort by banks to blur the distinction in practice between demand and time deposits. The concern was that banks would attract deposits and reduce their average reserve requirement ratio by offering the new interest rate schedule.

The Board's discussions of ceiling rates are striking for what they omitted. References to free markets aside, most of the discussion is about competitive equity and legality. The staff did not present an analysis of either the aggregate or allocative effects of ceiling rates and, with the exception of Mitchell's statement, the Board neither asked for nor received such analysis.

204. The Federal Advisory Council opposed a general increase in ceiling rates but agreed to an increase in rates on foreign deposits. The view was not unanimous. George Murphy (New York) reported that state authorities had raised ceiling rates for mutual savings banks in New York. He urged the Board to look at the problem from a national perspective (Board Minutes, November 21, 1961, 19). His argument struck home. Martin agreed that there was "a little too much of a popularity basis" in the Board's approach (ibid., 23).

Board members recognized that raising ceiling rates could reduce the capital outflow to the euro-dollar market. The press release mentioned this effect and, with an eye on congressional reaction, suggested a long-run effect on "the savings that will be required in financing the future economic growth that will be essential for expanding job opportunities" (Board of Governors, Press Release, December 1, 1961).

Analysis of the aggregative effects would have found few or none. In later years, the Board defended interest rate regulation as an anti-inflation policy, assistance to the housing industry, and help for the savings and loan associations and thrift institutions. One popular argument was that thrift institutions suffered losses when interest rates rose and the market value of existing mortgages fell. Higher interest rates had to be paid to all depositors, old and new, adding to thrifts' costs without increasing their revenues equivalently. The problem became acute at cyclical peaks when short-term rates rose above long-term.

Regulation could restrict the increase, but it could not keep depositors from withdrawing in search of higher rates. Euro-dollars were one of the first big innovations, but others followed, including money market mutual funds, which grew rapidly in the 1970s.[205] By the 1980s, inflation and the effect of interest rate controls on savings and time deposits penalized, and to a considerable extent destroyed, the savings and loan industry that regulators claimed the controls would protect.

During the months following the increase in ceiling rates, the Board heard that some of the New York banks were pleased by the increase but wanted the ceiling rate raised on short-term time deposits. As expected, many interior banks "raised rates reluctantly and under competitive pressures" (Board Minutes, February 20, 1962, 11).[206] Growth of negotiable

205. Milton Friedman (1969) and James Tobin (1969) analyzed the economic effects of regulation Q ceiling rates. They agreed that any effect on aggregate output or inflation was small. One reason was that substitutes for interest payments in the form of services, in-kind payments, or gifts occurred often. The Board spent considerable time deciding which payments could be permitted. Quantitatively more important was development of unregulated substitutes such as euro-dollars and, later, money market funds. Small and poorly informed depositors bore much of the cost. Later, ceilings were justified as assistance to housing. Tobin (1970, 10) claimed that the main reason for the policy was to permit undistributed profits to increase at savings and loans. Pressure from banks that did not want to pay higher rates was a major factor. Meltzer (1974) found evidence of positive effects of regulation Q on mortgages but not on housing. Housing, a real asset, remained independent of the nominal stock of mortgages.

206. In following months, the Board discussed several issues resulting from the regulation Q ceiling. As always, price controls raised issues that no one foresaw. For example, New York State allowed non-member banks to pay higher interest rates. It had to decide whether banks that absorbed exchange charges were paying interest. This was particularly of interest in districts with many non-par banks. A bank in Chicago permitted depositors to write checks

certificates of deposit concerned some Board members. The Board's counsel said they were legal (Board Minutes, January 15, 1962, 7). Governor Robertson said the certificates were securities, not savings deposits. He proposed prohibiting their use.

Anticipating that market interest rates would continue to rise, the New York bank sent a letter to the Board supporting legislation to change regulation Q ceiling rates to a stand-by regulation above market rates. Until Congress approved that change, it urged the Board to increase ceiling rates for time deposits before deposit rates reached the ceilings. This would avoid the inflexibilities and disruptions that would otherwise occur (letter, New York Bank to Board, Correspondence Box 240, Federal Reserve Bank of New York, June 27, 1963).

The Board did not act at the time. Six months later, the staff at New York discussed the issue again. Peter Sternlight argued for regulation to protect "the large number of commercial banks from mutually destructive competition." One of his main concerns was that banks would invest in "excessively illiquid assets." Others argued that banks performed a useful function as intermediaries. They doubted that many banks invested in illiquid assets. Still others favored stand-by ceilings but expressed concern about appropriate timing (memo, Sternlight to Hayes, ibid., December 26, 1963).

Persistence of disagreement within the System encouraged delay and avoidance of the issue. Many members of Congress, including Congressman Patman, would have opposed stand-by controls in place of regulation. The Board took no action.

The Comptroller of the Currency was less constrained. On January 21, 1964, he objected to the Board's ruling that barred corporations from holding savings deposits and told national banks that the Board's rule could not be enforced.

The Board delayed responding until prodded by Chairman Robertson of Senate Banking. Martin's response denied that the Board lacked power to regulate rates on savings deposits along with time deposits. Then he added that the present time was not an appropriate time to remove or reduce regulation. His main reason was to prevent "competitive escalation" of rates leading to "undesirable consequences in terms of financial soundness and liquidity needs." He favored legislation permitting the Board to

---

to borrow against their savings account. The bank paid the loan with a transfer from the account. The Board ordered the bank to stop. Banks began offering long-term certificates of deposit (CDs) at a fixed rate. If the Board lowered the ceiling rate before the CDs expired, did the bank have to reduce the rate? Some banks gave free printed checks to customers. This was accepted if the checks lowered the banks costs but not if it benefited only the customer!

move to stand-by authority but leave the Board free to choose the time (letter, Martin to A. Willis Robertson, Correspondence Box 240, Federal Reserve Bank of New York, May 13, 1964).[207]

INTERNATIONAL POLICY

Administration and Federal Reserve efforts and increased foreign inflation provided a slight improvement in the payments balance in 1962. The overall balance remained negative but, at about $2 billion, was half the size of the reported 1960 deficit (Council of Economic Advisers, 1963, 96). Much of the improvement reflected accelerated payments by Germany for current and future defense materials, tying foreign aid to domestic purchases, advance debt repayments by other European governments, and sales of non-marketable debt (Roosa bonds) denominated in foreign currency. Without these special factors, the 1962 deficit was $3.6 billion.

The System's experiment with foreign exchange market intervention and currency "swaps" with foreign central banks expanded rapidly. By late May, Coombs had negotiated agreements with West Germany, France, Switzerland, the United Kingdom, Netherlands, Belgium, and Canada (after it returned to a fixed exchange rate on May 2, 1962).[208] The size of the credit lines expanded as well; for example, the swap line with Britain increased in July from $50 to $250 million. The FOMC also approved several special provisions to meet legal requirements on both sides of the swap agreement.[209] By August 1962, total swap agreements reached $700 million, against $19 billion U.S. liabilities to foreign official institutions (OECD, 1990). The plan was to increase swap lines to $2.5 billion from the initial ceiling of $500 million agreed to in February (Kennedy, 2001a, 39, 2).

Members asked questions about some of Coombs's proposals but ap-

207. The Board kept rates extremely low on time deposits with less than ninety days to maturity. The ceiling rate on these deposits was 1 percent in 1964, when the federal funds rate was about 3.5 percent. To circumvent the rate restrictions and avoid reserve requirements, banks began to offer capital notes that were not deposits and thus not subject to regulation. In December 1965, the Board ruled that capital notes were a type of deposit, and therefore subject to its regulations. This is one of many examples showing that markets learn to circumvent regulation.

208. Canada floated its currency in September 1950. Faced with a large capital inflow and a strengthening currency in 1962, the Canadian finance minister described the currency as overvalued. Depreciation was sudden and sharp. Canada stabilized at 92.5 cents per U.S. dollar with assistance from the IMF and the U.S. and U.K. governments.

209. For example, the Federal Reserve could not invest in foreign government bills, and German banks could not offer an interest-bearing deposit. The Bundesbank offered to waive interest payments from the Federal Reserve, if the Federal Reserve made an interest free deposit at the Bundesbank. In May, Coombs reported that Germany changed its law. Also, Switzerland was not an IMF member at the time, so a special procedure had to be established to secure the account. Term to maturity also increased.

proved all of them. The most basic question was what Coombs's very active operations could accomplish. Coombs recognized that swaps and credit lines could not succeed if the balance of payments deficit continued. All that the swap line could do was postpone foreign governments' demands for gold by offering a temporary exchange guarantee on dollars held by foreign central banks. Success in slowing the gold drain, therefore, depended on the willingness of the central bank or government that held excess dollars to accept the temporary swap in place of a more permanent acquisition of gold.[210] Despite its swap agreement, France increased its gold stock by one billion dollars in 1961 and 1962. This was more than half the United States' gold loss for the two years.[211]

Hayes explained that "countries relying upon the dollar as an important part of their international reserve assets are glad to participate in arrangements that reduce the possibility of temporary and capricious pressures on the dollar" (Joint Economic Committee, 1962, 576). Later he added that currency operations "rest upon the assumption that the pressures they have to meet are of a temporary and transitional nature. . . . [A]n indefinite continuation of large U.S. payments deficits would assure that the pressure upon the dollar becomes permanent rather than temporary" (ibid., 576). But neither Hayes nor others wanted to recognize that countries cannot maintain fixed exchange rates, capital mobility, and independent monetary policy. Either monetary policy had to control the exchange rate, or the exchange rate had to adjust, or other countries had to hold more dollars than they wished.

Since swaps were a temporary solution, members also asked Coombs why losing gold in six months was better than losing it at once. Coombs replied that European central bankers became nervous if they saw one country buying gold (FOMC Minutes, October 2, 1962, 56). Yet that was precisely what France did, and most others either did not follow or sought a much smaller gold reserve. See Table 3.5 above.[212]

---

210. The administration did not rely only on swaps. It promoted exports, reduced military spending abroad, made more defense purchases at home, and tied more foreign aid to exports. It sold some foreign currency debt (Roosa bonds) mainly to replace expiring swap links. It got agreement on an increase in IMF quotas to provide the IMF with enough foreign exchange to stop a future run on the dollar. In 1961 preferential trading arrangements for Europe ended. West Germany would not pay for maintaining U.S. troops in Europe, but it agreed to make offsetting military purchases in the United States.

211. In contrast Japan, which did not have a swap agreement, drew only $40 million in gold in the same two years. Japan delayed current account convertibility until 1964.

212. At the October 2 meeting, Coombs proposed a $50 million swap with Austria. Austria would keep its gold purchases to $30 million in 1962 and stretch out gold purchases into early 1963, delaying but not preventing the gold loss. Chairman Martin reminded Coombs

Neither Hayes nor others at the Federal Reserve and the administration had a long-term plan. No one at the Federal Reserve was more concerned about the payments balance than Hayes or more willing to raise interest rates even if that brought slower growth. But though Hayes and others talked about the importance of a more competitive economy, they never discussed deflation, or relative deflation, as a means of depreciating the real exchange rate. They looked to the administration for new initiatives.[213] Robert Roosa, Treasury undersecretary, shaped and guided the policy. He worked on the assumption that short-term measures, stand-by arrangements, and restrictions on government spending abroad would restore balance. While in office, he opposed efforts to supplement or supplant gold or devalue the dollar against gold. Later (Roosa, 1965) he partly reversed his position and favored international creation of money or credit, although he recognized the risk of international money creation.

With hindsight, we know that these and other measures did not restore balance. The financing of the Vietnam War brought more imports, larger budget deficits, and more inflation. Chart 3.11 suggests that without war and inflationary war finance, the current account surplus might have increased enough to balance the capital outflow. In early 1964, the current surplus was more than three times its 1962 low, in part because the United States had less inflation in these years than any of its major trading partners.[214] Solomon (1982, 61–62), who headed the Board's international staff, suggests that the U.S. current account surplus deterred adjustment because European countries were not prepared either to appreciate their

that his proposal violated the guidelines adopted at the February meeting that authorized intervention. Martin proposed changing the guidelines, but Hayes objected that the guidelines were meant to be permanent. The FOMC decided to make an exception to the guidelines but did not change them. At the October 23 meeting, members asked Coombs why he didn't use the same approach with France to delay gold sales. He replied that the Austrians were "agreeable to stretching out contemplated purchases of gold. . . . The French had not indicated that they would be so disposed" (FOMC Minutes, October 23, 1962, 7). In November, Hayes reported that only Austria, France, and Sweden had accumulated significant amounts of uncovered dollar balances. Austria converted all to gold; France acquired gold or prepaid debt; Sweden held dollars.

213. Balderston made one of the very few statements suggesting relative deflation as a long-term solution. After noting that a balance of payments crisis may be near, he expressed concern that foreigners would stop holding dollars. Then he added: "The Federal Reserve System could not, of course, control foreign spending and lending." It could assist in keeping domestic inflation lower than in other countries (FOMC Minutes, December, 1962, 50–51).

214. Several outsiders offered long-term solutions. A summary in Joint Economic Committee (1962, Appendix, 950–51) briefly discussed five proposals including return to a pure gold standard (Jacques Rueff), creation of a world central bank with power to issue money tied to international reserves (Robert Triffin), and letting the IMF create stand-by credits to supplement reserves (several authors). Heller (1966, 48) preferred tying foreign aid and other restrictions as temporary measures. He did not propose a long-term program.

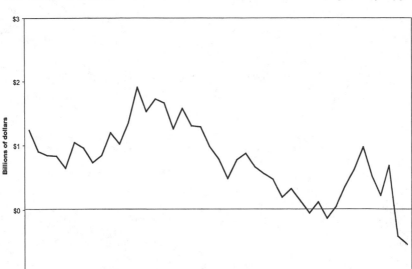

Chart 3.11. Balance on the current account, 1961:1–1971:3.

currencies relative to the dollar or allow the dollar to depreciate while the United States had a large trade and current account surplus. This is clearly mistaken. These countries were no more willing to adjust exchange rates when the United States' current account surplus declined. Also, it neglects the effects of inflation abroad as a way of adjusting relative prices.

Chart 3.12 shows the change in relative prices using consumer price indexes.[215] The current account balance leads the relative price change in 1964 but not in 1968–69. Relative unit labor costs in Chart 3.13 show a similar pattern with different timing. Relative U.S. labor costs reach a low point in the second half of 1965, the beginning of the sharp drop in the current account balance.

Most of the widely discussed proposals for reform both at this time and later concentrated on the Triffin problems—increasing world reserves and replacing the dollar as the principal international currency.[216] Roosa

215. This is not an ideal measure since consumer prices include goods and services that are not traded. Nevertheless, it gives a reasonably accurate picture of the changes in prices over the decade. The trade weighted unit labor cost index uses data from Canada, West Germany, Japan, and U.K. for the denominator.

216. There were notable exceptions. Friedman (1953) made the case for floating exchange rates. Haberler (1965, 46) wrote, "Some of the ingenuity now so lavishly spent on how to guard against the possibility that international liquidity may become scarce could be profitably applied to the more basic and neglected problem of how to improve the adjustment mechanism."

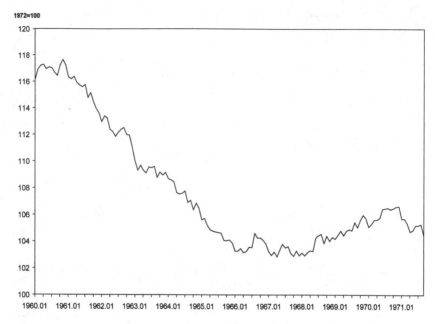

Chart 3.12. Index of the ratio of U.S. CPI to trade-weighted CPI. January 1960–September 1971.

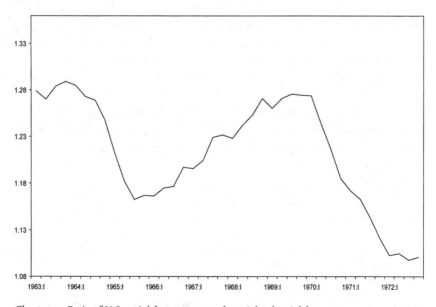

Chart 3.13. Ratio of U.S. unit labor costs to trade-weighted unit labor costs.

opposed both types of changes and also French proposals to increase the gold price. He expected the United States to supply reserves by running a permanent current surplus larger than its capital outflow. "Whether or not there is a corresponding increase in the underlying supply of gold in the world's monetary reserves, additional increases in the supply of dollars can rest upon an accumulation by the United States of incremental amounts of the currencies of other leading countries" (quoted in Solomon, 1982, 64). After leaving office, Roosa, in a major change, supported a proposal to increase reserves by supplementing the dollar and gold with IMF paper, as noted earlier.

Most European governments pursued mercantilist policies, selling exports and accepting dollars. Their suggestions at regular meetings of the Organization for Economic Cooperation and Development (OECD) rarely mentioned proposals that their countries pay a larger share of military and defense spending in Europe. They criticized Federal Reserve policy as too easy and urged the Treasury to borrow at long term to raise long-term interest rates and make the United States less attractive to foreign borrowers. This would help to develop European capital markets. They did not mention that if their proposals slowed U.S. recovery, their exports would decline (FOMC Minutes, December 18, 1962, 24–25).

Federal Reserve concerns about a run on the dollar had some foundation. "In May [1962] rumors reached the President that France—alone or with West Germany—might convert its surplus dollars into gold as a way to pressure the Kennedy administration into changing its European policies" (Kennedy, 2001b, 386).[217] In a conversation with the French ambassador, Kennedy threatened to pull United States troops out of Europe if the Europeans attempted to use their dollar holdings as a threat. The run stopped when President Kennedy in July repeated his pledge not to devalue.

Undersecretary of State George Ball proposed that if NATO countries agreed to hold excess dollars for two years, the United States would use the time to eliminate its payments deficit and to negotiate a new agreement to replace Bretton Woods. The United States would agree to sell $1 billion of gold to participating countries during the two-year period. Ball did not say how the deficit would be closed. In July, the French finance minister (later

217. One May 25, 1962, Secretary Dillon told the president that a Bank of France official had indicated "possible difficulties ahead with France. He said it must be realized that France's dollar holdings represented a political as well as an economic problem" (memo for the president, Dillon papers, Box 289, May 25, 1962). I have found no support for the suggestion that West Germany would join France. Holtfrerich (1999) has no reference to a decision to increase gold and reduce dollar holdings despite 3 percent inflation in 1962–63 and rising unit labor costs. The Bundesbank kept its discount rate close to zero, after adjusting for inflation (ibid., 378).

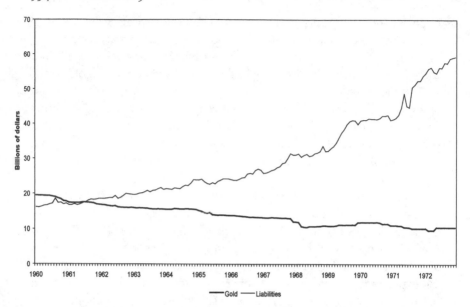

Chart 3.14. U.S. gold reserves and liabilities to foreign central banks and governments, 1960–72.

president), Valery Giscard d'Estaing, visited Washington. He told officials that the dollar's defense against a speculative attack was weak. He offered cooperation "on a grand scale." U.S. officials were uncertain what the offer meant (Kennedy, Oval Office Tape Recordings, Tape 11, August 10, 1962, 2). In a contentious series of meetings, the president's advisers clashed over different proposals.

A proposal supporting Ball's came from the Council of Economic Advisers. James Tobin explained that foreign central banks held $10.3 billion of claims against the U.S. gold stock. Private holders could sell their claims to central banks, and central banks could demand gold. Including these claims give a total of $18.9 billion against $16.1 billion in gold. Chart 3.14 compares the gold stock to dollar liabilities to foreigners. The two lines crossed in July 1961.

Tobin proposed to internationalize the provision of world currency and eliminate the special role of the dollar. Foreign governments would agree to hold a fixed proportion of their reserves in dollars and to hold a fixed proportion of their future acquisition of dollars, whether from existing private holdings or from future payments deficits. In return, the United States would agree to hold the same proportion of gold to total reserves as foreigners, holding the balance in foreign currencies. All countries would agree to compensate other governments for any losses of reserves resulting from devaluation (A Gold Agreement Proposal, Heller papers, Box 19, July 5, 1962).

During the two-year transition period, the United States would treble its swap lines to $2.5 billion to purchase dollars other than those frozen by a multilateral standstill agreement. It would also increase forward exchange market operations to reduce the stock of dollars that private holders offered to their central banks.

The Treasury strongly opposed the program. Secretary "Dillon and [Undersecretary] Roosa contended that the steps they had already taken . . . — swap arrangements, offset agreements, the gold pool operation—were adequate to protect the U.S. dollar and gold supply" (Kennedy, 2001b, 388). They added that the agreement was not needed because most of the support it proposed had already been done (swaps, etc.). The main new element was a commitment to increase the IMF quotas, and this step was under way.

Ball replied, praising Roosa's measures, but told the president, "These are all operations of very short-term" (ibid., 399). He wanted some agreement that required restraint, a type of standstill that limited the claims that foreigners could make and that prevented a run. The Treasury responded that any agreement of this kind would reduce confidence and stimulate what it wanted to prevent.

The idea of a standstill that restricted gold loss appealed to Kennedy. "We are going to be able to get tough about NATO expenditures and all the rest. So that's what we want to do is to prevent a really major run over the next two years. Isn't there any way we can get these countries to agree to hold dollars for this two year period?" (Kennedy, Oval Office tape recordings, tape 11, August 10, 1962, 11). Ball reinforced the argument. "It is only the part of prudence to try to move now towards getting a net under this tightrope on which the Treasury has been performing with such admirable dexterity" (ibid., 13).

Dillon and Roosa continued to argue that a formal agreement was unnecessary and could possibly create alarm that would cause a run on the dollar. Dillon accused Ball and the State Department of "reluctance to squarely tackle the more difficult but necessary job of obtaining a more adequate sharing of the burden of defense (quoted in Gavin and Mahan, undated, 25). Their main argument was that they could expand the length and size of quiet arrangements that countries had agreed upon. The advocates of a formal agreement argued the opposite case. Countries "have the suspicion that we're playing off one against the other. . . . [I]t's not the same thing to have done it one by one as it would be to discuss it all together" (Kennedy, Oval Office tape recordings, tape 11, August 10, 1962, 17).

Carl Kaysen, a member of the National Security Council, urged the Ball proposal in order to reduce "the burdens of running the world's reserve system" (ibid., 19). In contrast to the French complaint that the United States gained great advantage from the dollar's position as reserve currency, Kaysen emphasized only the burden. He did not explain what the burden was or compare it to the benefits. The burden that others talked about was the defense burden, the disproportionate share of NATO costs paid by the United States. This burden did not depend on the exchange rate system.

Paul Samuelson redirected the discussion by asking the Treasury participants if they would accept the proposal urged by Ball and Tobin if the Europeans proposed it. That appealed to the president more than to the Treasury. It spared him from admitting the weakness in the present international arrangements and gave the Europeans the opportunity to appear to lead. The only decision made was to meet the following week.

Almost a week later, August 16, 1962, Kennedy met with Martin to discuss gold and dollar problems and solicit Martin's opinion on the Ball-Tobin proposal. Martin opposed any attempt to get an international agreement to limit gold purchases. He made two principal arguments. First, the negotiations would suggest that the United States could not maintain convertibility into gold. This would reduce confidence and possibly precipitate a run. Second, the United States had made progress, so it did not need the type of "standstill" agreement that Ball and Tobin proposed.[218]

Kennedy expressed his concern vividly: "If everyone wants gold we're all going to be ruined because there is not enough gold to go around. . . . I don't know . . . whether it is impossible to work out an arrangement quickly enough that would be more satisfactory than the one we now have. . . . I am convinced the British, either the government or important influences in Britain, are trying to force us to devalue . . . because they think the pound is going to be devalued or because of their own gold" (Kennedy, Oval Office tape recordings, The Gold and Dollar Crisis, August 16, 1962, 2).

Martin objected. "I think it [a standstill] would be interpreted . . . as receivership on the part of the United States. . . . I think that under the leadership of your administration that it is amazing how much progress we have made" (ibid., 2).[219] Then he added that there was not enough time to negotiate an agreement before the October IMF meeting.

218. Martin praised especially the president's televised press conference in July that was shown via satellite. Kennedy had committed to maintain the dollar price of gold, and he added. "The United States can balance its balance of payments any day it wants if it wishes to withdraw its support of our defense expenditures overseas and our foreign aid" (Kennedy, 2001b, 467 n. 42).

219. Martin added two statements that reveal his thinking: "When inflation gets ahead

Martin urged Kennedy to remove the 25 percent gold reserve behind the monetary base to make the full gold stock available. The timing was not appropriate because of the pressures on the dollar and the reaction of the Europeans. Martin then described how the Europeans had responded to the proposed expansion of the International Monetary Fund. "We were over there [Vienna] negotiating for the first time in my experience where the other people had the cards. . . . [T]he French, and the Italians, and the Germans were more or less jumping up and down and saying well now you're in the soup and we'll go along with you . . . but we want to tell you under what terms we would let you draw if you have to draw" (Kennedy, 2001b, 467).[220]

The president decided to try Ball's plan, if it could be done as a European proposal to the United States. He sent two officials to sound out European opinion. The initiative failed. Soon after, the Cuban missile crisis diverted attention from the dollar and international payments.

The experience recalls French policy after it restored convertibility in 1927–29. Once again, France resented the rules of a monetary standard that asked them to hold dollars or pounds in place of gold but allowed the United States to hold only gold reserves. In both periods, the French government was willing to either destroy the system or force the United States to follow more deflationary policies. This time, they had a stronger case because, as the Kennedy conversations show, the United States did not

---

of you, it leads to deflation. That's the only reason to fight inflation" (Kennedy, Oval Office tape recordings, The Gold and Dollars Crisis, August 16, 1962, 5). Next he accepted Federal Reserve responsibility for the depth of the Great Depression. "I really believed that we could solve everything—all the problems were on the Federal Reserve. I read the records over here today, and I still think they made some grievous mistakes" (ibid., 8). Martin made three additional statements about his firm beliefs. First, referring to Triffin, he said he did not believe there was a gold shortage. Second, "[Congressman] Henry Reuss is always trying to pin me down to 3 percent [money growth] . . . but I think there ought to be steady growth in the money supply." Third, he told the president, "I neither support nor oppose a tax cut" (Kennedy, Oval Office tape recordings, The Gold and Dollar Crisis, August 16, 1962, 8–10).

220. Martin mentioned specifically that Britain, Belgium, and Spain wanted to hold all their reserves in gold. The French had gone from 65 to 75 percent gold. Germany held dollars; its reserves were about 70 percent in dollars. Martin repeated that many in Britain wanted to force the United States to devalue (Kennedy, 2001b, 464). Martin added: "This is a tough, rough mean gang. And there is very little altruism" (ibid., 469). About a year earlier, Jacques Rueff, an adviser to President de Gaulle published a series of letters on monetary issues in Le Monde. He urged de Gaulle to end the dollar's role as a reserve currency by invoking emergency powers to bypass Parliament and take measures to force devaluation of the dollar. He considered the gold exchange system "a prodigious collective error that allowed the United States to avoid the consequences of its economic profligacy" (quoted in Gavin and Mahan, undated, 8). Gavin and Mahan cite other examples of the difficulties and suspicions on both sides of the U.S.-French relationship. De Gaulle did not believe Kennedy would remove the U.S. troops because Europe would be lost and the U.S. weakened, (ibid., 12).

have a long-term strategy in the event that its policy of low inflation, and short-term palliatives did not succeed.

This time, a few other countries joined France in trading surplus dollars for gold. France did not repeat its earlier error of deflating. Instead, it devalued in 1958 and both before and after ran a higher rate of inflation than the United States.[221] As in earlier periods, efforts to coordinate policy failed. A few countries with payments surpluses, at the time notably Germany and Japan, held dollars. But many countries, especially France, did not. They drained gold and pushed the adjustment problem onto the United States.

SILVER

In February 1962, the administration proposed repeal of laws requiring the Treasury to purchase silver at 90.5 cents an ounce.[222] The legislation also authorized the Federal Reserve to issue $1 Federal Reserve notes, and authorized the Treasury to retire silver certificates gradually. Federal Reserve officials had discussed silver many times but had not taken a firm stand. This time was different.

The new elements were the growing difference between Treasury silver purchases and sales and world production and demand for silver. World consumption had reached 300 million ounces, of which the United States used half for industrial use, jewelry, and coinage. Estimated world production remained below consumption by about 65 million ounces at the time, but the gap continued to rise (memo, Dillon to the president, Dillon papers, Box 33, November 27, 1961). Treasury sales from existing stocks filled the gap. From a peak of 174 million ounces in 1959, the Treasury's stock of free silver had fallen to 22 million ounces. The rest of the Treasury's stock, 1.7 billion ounces, served as the reserve behind silver certificates. Replacing the latter with Federal Reserve notes freed the silver reserve for coinage but obligated the Federal Reserve to use more of its shrinking gold stock as backing for the new Federal Reserve notes.

Secretary Dillon proposed to gradually replace $1 and $2 silver certificates and to suspend open market purchases and sales of silver.[223] The

---

221. Rates of change of consumer prices for France are: 1955:1–1958:4, 5.37 percent; and 1958:4–1967:4, 3.54 percent. U.S. consumer prices rose on average 2.04 and 1.73 percent for the same periods. Among other countries—Canada, Italy, West Germany, Japan, and the U.K.—Canada, Italy, and Japan have modestly lower inflation rates in the first period. The United States has the lowest inflation in the second period.

222. See volume 1, chapter 6. Some of the silver purchase laws went back to the nineteenth century, but the government extended these laws in the 1930s. The proposed repeal affected only the silver purchase legislation enacted in 1934, 1939, and 1946. Silver certificates denominated $1, $2, $5, and $10 were outstanding in 1962.

223. The proposed legislation did not replace $2 silver certificates with Federal Reserve

Board accepted the legislation as appropriate but, following objection by Governor Mills, did not request repeal of silver purchase laws. Mills's main concerns were that the legislation required use of gold reserves and, by removing silver backing, reduced the backing for currency (Board Minutes, November 1, 1961, 7). The following year, Congress again considered the legislation. The Federal Reserve supported the change. At the time, the market price of silver had increased to a level that was above the government's purchase price.

Legislation 1962

Most of the legislation in 1962 of specific interest to the Federal Reserve concerned attempts by Congress or the administration to avoid expenditure increases by using credit subsidies in place of expenditures. The Board resisted or opposed legislation to establish a new government corporation to provide a secondary market for industrial mortgages, to permit the Department of Commerce to buy mortgages on industrial property in redevelopment areas, and to liberalize restrictions on financing multiple dwelling units by savings and loan associations.

Of greater moment was the proposal to permit national banks to underwrite revenue bonds. This was one of many steps taken in the early 1960s by the new Comptroller of the Currency, James Saxon, to expand national banks' powers and remove Depression-era restrictions. Publicly, the Board questioned the advisability of the legislation (Board Minutes, August 28, 1962, 7). In fact, the Board divided on the issue. Mills strongly opposed. Martin recalled "the troubles of the 20s and early 30s" (ibid., 11). Mitchell, a former state finance official, favored use of revenue bonds and supported bank underwriting. Other governors were not enthusiastically pro or con.

In September, Congress transferred regulatory authority over trust departments of national banks from the Federal Reserve to the Office of the Comptroller. The Federal Reserve repealed regulation F relating to trusts on October 3 (Annual Report, 1962, 118).

A PLEASANT INTERLUDE

The two and one half years ending in mid-1965 are probably the best years under the Federal Reserve Act to that time and for many years to follow. Unlike the years 1922 to 1929, there were no intervening recessions. Although the period in the 1960s was much shorter, it was part of a long,

---

notes because the law required the Treasury to maintain a certain level of notes. The $2 bills filled the requirement (Board Minutes, February 5, 1962, 4). The minutes do not explain why the Treasury did not seek to repeal the requirement.

sustained expansion. And, unlike the 1920s, the expansion ended with an inflation, not a depression. Of special concern to the administration, the unemployment rate fell from 5.5 to 4.6 percent, the lowest rate since October 1957. The balance of payments deficit (official settlements) declined to a more sustainable level and became a short-lived surplus early in 1966.

The decline in the payments deficit reflected both political and economic changes. The government introduced an interest equalization tax to make it more costly for foreigners to borrow in U.S. capital markets. More foreign aid was tied to purchases in the United States, and the military shifted some of its purchases from foreign to domestic producers.

The economic adjustment process was classical. The outflow of dollars raised price levels abroad, in Europe and Japan as well as elsewhere, relative to U.S. prices. This equilibrating mechanism worked despite European governments' efforts to prevent domestic price increases. Bound by the fixed exchange rate, and unwilling to revalue against the dollar, countries could only accept higher inflation or impose exchange or other controls.[224] Karl Blessing, president of the Bundesbank, recognized that the choice was between revaluation and inflation, but the Bundesbank and the German government disliked both. Like the United States authorities, they relied on selective controls—the interest equalization tax for the United States, a 30 percent reserve ratio for foreign deposits at German banks, and, in March 1965, a 25 percent tax on interest payments by German institutions to non-residents (Holtfrerich, 1999, 378).

The Federal Reserve raised the federal funds rate twice by 0.5 percent in August 1963 to 3.5 percent and in December 1964 to 4 percent. Treasury bill rates followed the earlier change but preceded the later change. These market rates were closely related to discount rate increases from November 24 to 31, the latter taken in response to an increase from 5 to 7 percent by the Bank of England effective November 23.[225] On both occasions, the Board also increased regulation Q ceiling rates by 0.5 percentage points, first to 4 then to 4.5 percent.

None of these changes reduced the reported growth rates of the monetary base and money. Early in 1963 annualized base growth averaged 4 percent, more than double the rate reached two years earlier. By mid-

224. West Germany and the Netherlands revalued in 1961 but did not revalue enough to prevent inflation in costs and prices. German wages rose at an annual 10 percent rate from 1960 to 1962. Unit labor costs rose 14 percent in Germany and 8.6 percent in the United Kingdom and fell 2 percent in the United States (Holtfrerich, 1999, 377–78).

225. Lord Cromer, governor of the Bank of England, proposed that both central banks increase their rates at the same time. Martin explained that coordination of the twelve reserve banks made this difficult but "he personally would favor an increase . . . if Bank rate was raised" (Board Minutes, November 23, 1964, 3).

1965, that average had increased to nearly 6 percent, presaging the inflation that soon brought the low-inflation period to an end.

Members of the FOMC continued to instruct the manager using a variety of targets—free reserves, short-term interest rates, growth of bank reserves or reserves against private deposits, and the inevitable "tone and feel." Often a member would suggest several targets without giving priority to one over another. The account manager, or whoever influenced his decisions, had considerable discretion. If a member complained about the manager's performance, as often happened, the manager could point to some indicator that justified the outcome.[226]

The division continued within the FOMC between those who favored tighter policy principally to slow the flow of gold and dollars abroad and those who emphasized the domestic concerns of employment and growth. An unusual characteristic of the period is the large number of dissents from policy decisions. Chairman Martin liked to achieve a broad consensus and often delayed changes he thought desirable to get broader agreement.[227]

The decline in the outflow of gold and dollars reduced attention in 1964 to external factors. Nevertheless, swap arrangements expanded greatly and were renewed without question. In November 1963, the Federal Reserve began a new "experiment" in "warehousing" to assist Italy to maintain the exchange value of the lira. The new authority allowed the foreign exchange desk at the New York bank to make spot purchases "of currencies in which the Treasury had outstanding indebtedness" (FOMC Minutes, November 12, 1963, 5). The currencies would be sold to the Treasury in exchange for its lira debt. This was called "warehousing" because the intention was to reverse the transaction later. Coombs proposed a maximum of $100 million outstanding and requested authority to purchase above par value.[228] He explained that the Treasury's Stabilization Fund lacked the capital to make the purchases.

Coombs had not asked for general authority and seemed to want only au-

226. Brunner and Meltzer (1964) made this point in a report to the House Banking Committee during this period. Although there is some discussion in the minutes about improving the directive and giving more specific advice, not much changed at the time. Karl Bopp, the president of a reserve bank (1965, 12), gave a more defensive response, dismissing the monetarist approach as "mechanistic."

227. On one occasion, Martin was explicit. According to the FOMC minutes, Martin stated that "[t]he burden of proof was on those who wanted to make a change in policy . . . [I]f he were doing this on his own his inclination would be toward the kind of policy change that Mr. Mills aptly termed 'provisional and probationary'" (a cautious move to tighten) (FOMC Minutes, August 18, 1964, 55). Only six FOMC members spoke in favor of tightening at the meeting.

228. The Bank of Italy elected to defend its parity by purchasing above par value. The U.S. Treasury bought the currency at the price the manager paid.

thority for one operation. The FOMC granted general authority for all currencies in which the Treasury had debts (ibid., 7). Ellis (Boston) suggested that warehousing "might well provide a routine channel for redeeming outstanding Treasury bonds denominated in foreign currencies" (ibid., 7). The FOMC unanimously approved the program "with the understanding that it [warehousing] was experimental" (ibid., 9). It placed a limit of $100 million on the outstanding total, and it did not restrict the operation to the lira. It took no notice of the fact that its "experiment" in swap operations had grown in less than two years to $1.95 billion. Warehousing also rose and fell; by 2000 the maximum reached $20 billion.[229]

At the end of 1964, Martin looked back to appraise their actions. He "recalled that at the preceding meeting he had agreed with a view . . . that the Committee should never be complacent. However, recently he had reviewed the Committee's minutes for the past year and he could not help but feel a sense of satisfaction with the course of monetary policy in 1964" (FOMC Minutes, December 15, 1964, 92).

OUTSIDE APPRAISALS

The year 1964 was the fiftieth anniversary of the Federal Reserve's founding. Congressman Patman held hearings during the winter at which Chairman Martin, other governors, Secretary Dillon, and academic and industry economists testified. Several outsiders were highly critical of the Federal Reserve but did not agree on the source of the problem or its solution. Congressman Patman introduced legislation calling for an increase of the Board of Governors to twelve members, retirement of Federal Reserve stock owned by member banks, transfer of all interest received on government debt to the Treasury, congressional appropriation for the expenses of the Board and the reserve banks, payment of interest on demand deposits, and mandatory support of government bond prices when market yields equaled or exceeded 4.25 percent.[230]

229. The term "warehousing" seems a term of art to circumvent legal restrictions on direct loans to the Treasury. I have not found a study at the Federal Reserve of the "experiment" to evaluate its effects.

230. Karl Brunner and I served as adjunct staff of the committee. The reports that we prepared (1964) were part of the hearings, but Congressman Patman's legislative proposals came from other sources. Based on my conversations with him I do not believe he expected these proposals to be enacted. He liked the exchanges with Martin and others and believed that these exchanges were an important part of congressional oversight. The Federal Reserve had to treat the proposals as serious recommendations though they disliked them. Members of the committee had a similar interpretation. Some members of the Banking Committee also held the view that Chairman Patman did not expect the proposals to become law (Subcommittee on Domestic Finance, 1964, 1206). Stockwell (1989, 41–44) discusses the Board's reaction to these and other congressional hearings.

Governor Daane, however, described the three main points of the hearings as "the relationship and role of the Federal Reserve within the framework of Government, the allegation of banker domination, and the monetary policy process" (Subcommittee on Domestic Finance, 1964, 1192–93). Daane talked about the amicable, cooperative relation between the administration and the Federal Reserve, citing both his earlier experience at the Richmond bank and more recently at the Treasury. "The primary goals of monetary policy are identical to those of Government economic policy: we, too, are governed by the Employment Act of 1946" (ibid., 1193). Recognizing differences in responsibility, "the Federal Reserve is as responsive to the needs of Government finance as it either should be or can be . . . [I]t would be unreasonable to hope for any significant improvement in the technical coordination of monetary policy and debt management through the consolidation of these functions under a single head" (ibid., 1193).[231]

Daane, of course, denied the old charge that bankers dominated the System. Then, turning to the criticism in the staff report, he rejected the charge that the FOMC or the Federal Reserve suffered from what he called "money market myopia" and "overemphasis of short-term factors" (ibid.). "The weakness of the various operational guides, such as free reserves, member bank borrowings, and various short-term interest rates, are well recognized throughout the System" (ibid., 1195). Daane cited a list of the many measures of economic activity, prices, and production, but he did not suggest how the FOMC or the manager connected its money market operations to these measures.[232]

REGULATION

The Kennedy administration undertook major reform of the banking and financial policies independent of the changes in macroeconomic policy. Many of the policies they inherited reflected the attitudes of the Great Depression, when safety became a major concern. Innovation or financing

---

231. Daane does not repeat Martin's statement about independence *within* the government or its implication that the Federal Reserve could not refuse entirely to finance budget deficits voted by Congress. His more cautious statement leaves open what he means by "responsive to the needs of government." He did not mention Bretton Woods.

232. Governor Mitchell, on the other hand, recognized that the Federal Reserve had not connected its actions to economic activity. He welcomed "the vigor with which an increasing number of academic economists, including two who have been serving on your staff, are now analyzing the statistical behavior of monetary magnitudes. . . . I, myself, have recently tried to suggest ways in which the effects of monetary action on spending can be traced. The measurement problems are formidable and . . . we have not come nearly as close to achieving usable results as some of the academic people believe" (Subcommittee on Domestic Finance, 1964, 1185).

growth and expansion seemed less important than preventing additional failures or financial collapse.

By the 1960s early postwar concerns of a return to recession or stagnation dissipated. Growing confidence, helped along by low unemployment and a 50 percent increase in per capita income from the best prewar level, helped to change beliefs about the future. Competition with the reviving European and rapidly growing Japanese economies directed attention to facilitating growth. Concerns about Soviet growth heightened that interest. Growing urbanization and a decline in populist concerns about banks and bankers supplemented these pressures for change. No less important were court decisions bringing bank mergers under the antitrust laws.

The principal agent for change was James J. Saxon, the new Comptroller of the Currency appointed by President Kennedy. The Comptroller regulated national banks under the National Banking Act of 1863 and could expand some of their powers. Research, much of it stimulated by the development of a strong research group at the Comptroller's offices, questioned restrictions on entry, branching, and Depression-era regulation. The Comptroller favored "introduction into the banking industry of new competitive forces with fresh ideas and fresh talents" (Comptroller of the Currency, 102nd Annual Report, 1966, 403). The report viewed regulation as at times preventing the benefits of competition.[233]

The Comptroller's rulings extended the powers of national banks. A more cautious Federal Reserve followed. One result was that banks began to offer negotiable certificates of deposits that permitted their customers to invest surplus funds under more favorable conditions. Later, these instruments were freed from interest rate regulation, a first step toward decontrol. Negotiable certificates later became the basis for money market mutual funds that permitted small depositors to escape interest rate regulation.

Congress also acted in 1960 by establishing criteria for mergers and acquisitions as an amendment to the Federal Deposit Insurance Act. In October 1962, Congress permitted the Federal Reserve to exempt for three years deposits of foreign governments and certain foreign institutions from interest rate ceiling regulations.

233. "Many banks have been barred from the complete realization of production economies, and many communities have been deprived of the broader range of banking services which could have been provided to them" (Comptroller of the Currency, 1966, 419). The report showed the number of banks had declined to about half the number in the 1920s, but the number of banking offices (including branches) was about the same as in 1929 (ibid., 421).

PROSPERITY WITHOUT INFLATION, 1963–64

The country entered 1963 with output rising, inflation low, the stock market soaring and base money growth moderate. Only the unemployment rate, between 5.5 and 6 percent, and the balance of payments deficit disturbed the administration and the Federal Reserve. A three-month average of free reserves had fallen by $100 million between November and February, but the federal funds rate had remained unchanged.

The FOMC began the year by proposing "more moderate growth in bank credit and the money supply, while aiming at money market conditions that would minimize capital outflows" (FOMC Minutes, January 8, 1963, 57). It recognized "the unsatisfactory level of domestic activity, the continuing underutilization of resources, and the absence of inflationary pressures" (ibid., 58). The policy decision kept money market conditions unchanged.

Governor Robertson's dissent reopened discussion. Robertson wanted more effort to "stimulate a lagging economy" (ibid., 66). He opposed maintaining the Treasury bill rate unchanged if it interfered with reserve growth. Ralph Young, who wrote the directive, explained that recently money growth had increased more rapidly than in the past four years. If recent rates of growth continued, "they would result in some kind of explosion at some point" (ibid., 66).

The staff report cautiously favored President Kennedy's proposed tax cut but recognized that the FOMC was skeptical and suggested that "we have some basis for maintaining at least a modicum of skepticism as to whether any likely tax cut will be as efficacious as is contended" (ibid., 15). This reflected Martin's views. He was not enthusiastic about the proposed tax cut when he spoke to the Business Council, a group of chief executives of large corporations. Heller urged the president to encourage Martin to support the administration's program (Heller papers, Box 19, monetary policy, January 27, 1963).[234]

Heller wanted more than Federal Reserve support. At the time, he had little interest in independent monetary actions. To increase his own influence, he urged Kennedy to persuade Martin "to consult with the President and his major economic policy advisers before making significant policy changes" (ibid., 2). Heller recognized that Martin usually informed Secretary Dillon about his decisions, but Dillon often agreed with Martin.

---

234. Frederick Deming (Minneapolis) compared effects on spending to production incentives, later called supply-side effects. He considered government spending and the deficit, not the tax cut, to be the main source of stimulus (FOMC Minutes, January 19, 1963, 43).

Heller wanted more influence for the Quadriad, and he wanted Martin to appoint "one liberal or moderate intellectual" as a director of each Federal Reserve bank.[235]

Martin's four-year term as chairman ended in February 1963. Dillon strongly supported his reappointment. Heller opposed at first, but accepted the outcome because of Martin's reputation in the financial markets at home and abroad. The president told Martin that he recognized that Martin did not always agree with administration policy, but he welcomed his independent views.

The FOMC minutes do not mention administration pressure from meetings of the Quadriad or with officials. Martin may have passed these comments outside the meeting but they do not appear in the minutes. Through the winter and into the spring, the committee remained divided about what, if anything, the System should do. Most members agreed that the balance of payments deficit resulted from foreign aid, overseas military spending, and other non-monetary causes. That did not prevent demands for higher interest rates to squeeze domestic spending. Martin warned of an international crisis if nothing were done within the next three or six months" (FOMC Minutes, February 12, 1963, 48; March 5, 1963, 82). Hayes wanted higher interest rates, despite continued "sluggish domestic performance." The balance of payments situation requires "a more determined attack than any that has yet been undertaken" (FOMC Minutes, February 12, 1963, 20).

Until late March, members believed the recovery remained sluggish. Reports showed industrial production falling in December and January.[236] When the data showed recovery, several members dismissed the evidence as precautionary inventory accumulation in anticipation of a steel strike. The Federal Advisory Council (FAC) noted weak investment, uncertainty about government tax policy and its policy toward business. The FAC expressed concern about the balance of payments, but it favored easier policy (Board Minutes, February 19, 1963, 19).

235. He suggested Robert Solow or James Tobin as examples (Heller papers, Box 19, monetary policy, January 27, 1963). Solow later served as chairman of the Boston Federal Reserve bank. The memo came at about the time that Kennedy reappointed Martin without Heller's support. Heller later said that he came to Washington "thinking we ought to end the independence of the Federal Reserve . . . [but] after working with the Fed under both Presidents [ended] with the conviction that it isn't too bad an arrangement, provided there is good will, competent people, and reasonably systematic consultation" (Heller oral history, tape II, 10).

236. Current data show annual rates of increase in industrial production of 0, 8.75, and 13.63 percent for the three months ending in February. This is one of many occasions where preliminary data misled FOMC members. The staff reported increased production at the April 16, 1963, meeting.

Bryan (Atlanta), Mitchell, and Robertson favored more expansive policies, even if it meant lower short-term interest rates. Bryan dismissed Hayes's and Martin's arguments for higher rates. Using monetary policy to reduce the payments deficit "would require substantial interest rate increases" (FOMC Minutes, March 5, 1963, 51). There was no consensus and no change in policy.

Hayes continued to express concern about future inflation and the payments deficit. He recognized that tighter money has risks, but "they are minor risks in comparison with the growing danger to the dollar's international standing" (ibid., 47). He proposed changing the directive to reflect slightly firmer policy. Mitchell responded that he could accept "any suggestions [for the directive] . . . except those of Mr. Hayes" (ibid., 57).[237]

For the first time since the mid-1940s, the gold reserve requirement behind notes and bank reserves began to bind. In January the System's gold reserve ratio was 32.2 percent, but the Boston bank's reserve ratio fell to 25.7 percent, fractionally above the 25 percent minimum.[238] The rules called for Boston to sell enough of its securities to other reserve banks to bring its reserve ratio up to the System average. To do so, Boston would have to sell $152 million. Boston held only $74.9 million in unpledged securities. If Boston sold all of them, the System would be unable to sell securities because Boston could not participate.

The desk resolved one problem by lending Boston about $5 billion, raising its gold reserve ratio to 28 percent. This violated the allocation rules and pointed to the need for an amendment. In March, the FOMC changed the securities' allocation formula to permit, but not require, adjustments to reach the System average. At the same time, it changed reallocations from quarterly to monthly and permitted the System to allocate more securities to reserve banks with a relatively high proportion of notes to notes plus deposits and offered no securities to a reserve bank if an allocation would create a reserve deficiency[239] (FOMC Minutes, March 5, 1963, 18).

The experiment in foreign exchange market swaps continued to grow. Coombs asked for permission to make purchases or sales up to $25 million in the forward market without the FOMC's prior approval. These op-

237. At the March meeting Hayes gave up the struggle over who appointed the manager. "He saw no purpose in pursuing the matter further. . . . [A]lthough he would go along with the current procedure, he did so with some reluctance" (FOMC Minutes, March 5, 1963, 5).

238. Overall, the System held almost $16 billion in reserves. Dollar liabilities to foreigners had reached $20 billion (Chart 3.14 above).

239. The reallocation would equalize the average reserve ratios of the twelve reserve banks (based on data for the first twenty-three days of the preceding month). Reallocation could not lower a bank's reserve ratio below 28 percent (FOMC Minutes, March 5, 1963, 20–21). The last restriction would soon require additional changes.

Table 3.8   Rates of Price Change, Selected Countries 1960–62 (%)

COUNTRY	RATE OF PRICE CHANGE
Japan	12.5
France	8.3
Germany	5.4
Italy	6.9
United Kingdom	7.8
United States	2.3

Source: Economic Report of the President (1971, 306)

erations would be used to reverse a swap commitment in advance based on the special manager's judgment that an advance purchase or sale was advantageous. Robertson objected to "tinkering with market forces" but did not oppose because the size limit was low (ibid., 34).

The limit on swap arrangements reached $1.3 billion, more than double the initial commitment made a year earlier. Martin continued to refer to swaps as an experiment but did not favor evaluation. Mills questioned the usefulness of the experiment and expressed concern about "the U.S. becoming a handmaiden of assistance to a number of its foreign allies" (FOMC Minutes, March 5, 1963, 15). Robertson concurred. At the time, the French press had the opposite complaint, that a recent increase in the swap agreement was a French loan to the United States (ibid., 30).

The surplus countries had monetized many of the dollars received at their central banks, resulting in higher rates of inflation abroad. Table 3.8 compares rates of consumer price change in the United States and principal foreign countries. These price changes include more than the prices of internationally traded goods, but they suggest that real exchange rate adjustment had occurred.

Young's report of European attitudes and criticisms made at the late February meeting of the OECD mentions concerns about inflation abroad caused by annual money growth rates of 10 to 12 percent; but he did not mention the effect on real exchange rates that moved the system toward balance. He described the meeting as "highly critical of U.S. financial policy" (FOMC Minutes, March 5, 1963, 41). Surplus countries were most vocal, but they offered few useful suggestions. The [OECD] chairman's summary said that "there was agreement that U.S. payments equilibrium had to be reached soon, but without steps that might interfere with domestic expansion or otherwise do harm to the U.S. or the world economy" (ibid., 44). Critics agreed that interest rates should rise, but they differed as to whether the rise should precede or accompany the proposed tax cut.

The United States pressed for a review of capital controls in France, Italy, and West Germany that hindered capital outflow.

The OECD did not consider exchange rate adjustment, so they had to rely on relative inflation abroad to adjust real exchange rates. Devaluation of the dollar would have speeded adjustment. Six continental countries—Belgium, France, Germany, Italy, Luxembourg, and the Netherlands—had formed a common market, the first step toward the later European Union. The Common Market attracted foreign investment, particularly from the United States. Investment abroad joined growing European exports, military spending abroad, and foreign aid to raise the amount of dollar outflow that had to be compensated by changes in relative prices, if exchange rates remained fixed. The surplus countries disliked inflation; neither they nor the United States proposed an acceptable alternative. Discussion had moved away from the threats and counter-threats of the previous summer but had come no closer to a mutually acceptable arrangement.[240]

Attention soon shifted away from the United States to another in the series of British payments problems. Speculation in the press and the market considered the prospect of another British devaluation. The £3.5 billion of foreign balances in London, mostly owed to Commonwealth members and accumulated during WWII, complicated the problem. Devaluation would reduce the value of these claims and precipitate heavy withdrawals. To offset this effect, Britain could increase the size of its devaluation, thereby increasing the foreigners' losses but reducing the British obligation. A larger than necessary devaluation encouraged the expectation that the pound would not depreciate further. A small devaluation followed by the withdrawal of sterling balances was likely to do the opposite.

Many observers urged the British government to float its currency (*Economist*, March 2, 1963, 773–75). Instead, the government raised interest rates to 4.5 percent on advances to discount houses but left the Bank rate at 4 percent. British bill rates rose. The British asked for and received $250 million in loans from other countries; the loans postponed a sterling crisis but did not resolve the long-term problem.

240. President Kennedy appointed a commission, chaired by Roger Blough of U.S. Steel, to recommend ways to reduce the payments deficit. Allan Sproul was a member. The commission proposed that correction be made a national priority and stressed the need to reduce private and public capital outflow, but it opposed controls on private capital outflow. It favored domestic tax reduction to raise rates of return at home, accompanied by reductions in government spending and more European assistance in the defense effort. Kennedy immediately asked about restrictions on foreign borrowing in the U.S. market (letter, Sproul to Hayes, Sproul papers, May 7, 1963).

Policy Evaluation

In March, the staff reported the results of a series of studies requested by Chairman Martin of the effects of policy on the balance of payments and on foreign countries. The studies responded to the growing European demand for higher U.S. interest rates. The common assumptions in the studies were (1) a 0.5 percentage point increase in short-term interest rates achieved over a six-month period, (2) the same or larger increase achieved in three months or less, and (3) a "spectacular program designed to halt a sizeable actual or threatening run on the dollar"[241] (Domestic Effects of Assumed Monetary Policy Programs" Board Records, March 1, 1963, 2–3). The staff memos provide a view of the ways in which key staff analyzed policy actions and reveal many of their concerns about the payments imbalance.

The staff used a simple Keynesian model, starting with changes in cost and availability of credit on particular spending categories and allowing for multiplier effects on other spending categories. The paper expressed uncertainty about quantitative responses to policy actions. As a result, the analysis gave more attention to market mechanics and uncertainty about market responses than to effects of relative price changes on assets, liabilities, output and the balance of payments. Instead, it noted that "opinions regarding the influence of interest rates (and other credit terms) on borrowing and spending have shifted in recent years" (ibid., 17). The Federal Reserve would supply less credit, so "credit-financed expenditures" would decline (ibid., 26). Thus, the domestic economy would decline along with the payments deficits. There was no mention of effects on the price level or on the real exchange rate and thus on exports and imports. The analysis ended with the short-run cost of reduced output and did not consider how a declining price level or lower inflation worked to restore full use of resources.[242]

241. The paper by Robert Solomon refers to expectations of price increases and adds: "This fact in itself tended to elevate interest rates, as lenders demanded higher nominal rates in order to protect real rates of return on credit instruments" (Domestic Effects of Assumed Monetary Policy Programs." Board Records, March 1, 1963, 5). This is the most explicit statement of its kind to this time that I have found in System documents.

242. A separate paper in the study considered the effects on the balance of payments. It mentioned a price level decline as a cyclical response to reduced output but did not analyze the general equilibrium effect. The author concluded that a 0.5 percentage point increase in short-term interest rates would lower the payments deficit by $500 million to $1 billion in a year (Effects on the Balance of Payments, Board Records, March 1, 1963, 37). The author considered only the effects on lending and borrowing. Other papers in the study discussed European reactions to the policy change and the response of the euro-dollar market. One paper concluded that European rates would rise, so the balance of payments response was uncertain. A subsequent paper suggested that the elimination of the deficit would "have to

The memos on domestic and balance of payments effects of higher interest rates served as the background material for the March 25 meeting of the Cabinet Committee on the Balance of Payments. In a separate memo, the Council of Economic Advisers did not oppose higher interest rates, but it urged caution because the domestic economy remained weak. To mitigate these effects, it urged more Treasury borrowing in short-term securities, more Federal Reserve purchases of long-term debt, and an increase in regulation Q ceiling rates to bring more time deposits to banks. The Council recognized, however, that because of "expectations about future changes in interest rates, it might not prove possible to insulate the long-term market fully from the effects of higher short-term interest rates" (memorandum to Cabinet Committee on Balance of Payments, Board Records, March 26, 1963, 5). The Council statement suggests that members recognized that, since long-term rates are an average of expected future short-term rates, twisting the yield curve to lower long rates was not likely to succeed. The memo added, however, that "every effort should be made to do so" (ibid., 5).

Federal Reserve Response

Despite the Council's concerns, the focus given to the payments deficit strengthened Hayes's and Martin's position. In early May, the FOMC voted six to five to tighten policy, and in July the System increased discount rates to 3.5 percent and ceiling rates on time deposits to 4 percent.[243]

The domestic economy had not fully recovered. Unemployment rates remained at about the level reached the previous December and similar to the previous year. Growth in the first quarter at 5.5 percent annual rate included inventory building in anticipation of a steel strike. To spur investment spending the administration rewrote the Treasury's Bulletin F rules to spur investment by increasing depreciation rates, and it introduced an investment tax credit. Mitchell, Bopp, and Robertson urged delay of the rate increase. Swan (San Francisco) in a reprise of the 1920s urged the members to wait for credit demand to increase (FOMC Minutes, May 7, 1963, 30).

---

come gradually . . . mainly through changes in relative prices and costs, and in the relative attractiveness of investment opportunities here and abroad" ("The U.S. Balance of Payments Situation in Early 1963," Board Records, March 25, 1963, 2). It is the only paper that uses that reasoning. The paper notes that French inflation following the 1958 devaluation was likely to reduce the French surplus.

243. W. Braddock Hickman became president of the Cleveland bank on May 1, succeeding Wilbur Fulton. Hickman was a financial economist who had done major studies of bond defaults. His appointment strengthened the group favoring higher interest rates. Although he could not vote at the time, he favored the rate increase.

Pressure from European critics to take more action grew more intense. Young reported on a recent meeting at the OECD. European critics faced with inflation wanted the United States to present a "comprehensive program" for the payments deficit. Forewarned, spokesmen presented a long-term plan that relied on "the work-out of fundamental competitive forces, supplemented by redistribution of aid and defense burdens and gradual reduction of the capital outflow through reciprocal credit and capital market adaptation. For the shorter-run . . . further tying of aid, more stringent control of governmental expenditures abroad, additional debt prepayment and defense expenditure offsets" and other programs in place at the time (FOMC Minutes, May 7, 1963, 21). The Europeans did not hear plans for higher interest rates, and they objected to the pace of change—"two to three years or even longer" (ibid., 21).[244] They did not propose revaluation, and they objected to tying military assistance to purchases in the United States.

There was no time for discussion of the chairman's summary of European recommendations. They agreed to make this topic first on the agenda at the June meeting. This gave the FOMC time to act.

Martin made a strong argument for firming policy. He cited European criticism and his fear of an imminent crisis. To reassure members concerned about the domestic economy, he said that he was not tightening; he was "pulling a little on a rope that was already very loose. . . . [T]he Committee would decide later that this was not the direction in which it should have moved . . . If the Committee waited too long, however, it might have to deal with an active problem of inflationary pressures. . . . [I]nflationary pressures might well undermine the existing level of activity and lead to a decline in employment" (FOMC Minutes, May 7, 1963, 61). Bopp (Philadelphia), Clay (Kansas City), Mitchell, Robertson, and Scanlon (Chicago) voted no. Mills was absent.

The intense debate produced a small change. The directive called for "a slightly greater degree of firmness in the money market than has prevailed in recent weeks" (ibid., 63). The manager reported that interest rates on federal funds were at 3 percent with Treasury bill rates at 2.88 to 2.92 percent. The monthly average of the federal funds rate did not change until August, but Treasury bill rates rose 0.22 percentage points in the next two months. Monthly average free reserves moved down from $350 million in April to between $308 and $318 million for the next three months.

Mitchell attacked the policy change at the next meeting. It was taken

---

244. The European members also criticized use of foreign-denominated bonds instead of borrowing from the IMF and becoming subject to its monitoring.

to "make an overt sign that it [the Federal Reserve] is willing to yield to 'international monetary discipline.' If this was the purpose of the recent action, it seems to me to have been a serious mistake" (FOMC Minutes, May 28, 1963, 38). Most others did not agree. Even those who voted against the policy decision did not want to reverse it.[245]

Proponents of a restrictive policy were dissatisfied also. Coombs wrote a memo to Martin and Hayes making his best case for additional steps. He warned that "we have now reached a critical phase. The dollar has become vulnerable to a break in confidence which might occur almost without warning and with devastating consequences" (memo, Coombs to Martin and Hayes, Board Records, June 12, 1963, 1). The problem as he saw it was that the payments deficit was not cyclical or episodic; it was structural. United States policy did not address the structural problem. Instead, the United States borrowed in various ways, postponing the problem and enlarging it.

Success in managing crises had convinced participants in the foreign exchange market that central bank cooperation would manage the problem. Coombs was scornful. "It would be foolhardy to imagine that we can long maintain this disparity between the surface calm of the exchange markets and the turbulent undercurrents being generated by a continuation of heavy United States payments deficits which Europe is reluctant to finance" (ibid., 5). He favored the usual mix—reductions in foreign aid, military spending, and foreign investment. The Federal Reserve had no responsibility and no authority to act on these measures. Coombs recommended higher long-term interest rates to encourage U.S. companies to finance foreign direct investment overseas and deter foreign borrowing in the United States. Coombs urged higher short-term rates and regulation Q ceilings to reduce the flow abroad and attract foreign deposits.

The Board's staff memo agreed with Coombs's statement of the problem, disagreed with some of his numbers, and doubted the effectiveness of raising short-term rates. "It would tend to mask the U.S. deficit on 'basic' account and thereby make it more difficult to pursue vigorously and consistently policies directed to a fundamental remedy" (memo, Furth to Young, Board Records, June 14, 1963, 2). Short-term improvements, Furth said, convince Congress and others that the problem has lessened. "If drastic monetary measures are deemed too high a price, the solution must be

245. Mitchell noted that long-term rates were historically high and that money growth remained low. He voted against continuing the policy. Mills criticized the policy also, arguing that "the United States was the anchor to which all other economies were tied" (FOMC Minutes, May 28, 1963, 44). But he did not join Mitchell. It was too late to change. Shifting back and forth would be worse.

found in other fields . . . and cannot be sought in modest variations in interest rates" (ibid., 4).

Furth's logical argument did not fully persuade Martin. Although he knew that small changes in interest rates could not solve the problem, he wanted to avoid the crisis that he, like Coombs, believed was near at hand.[246]

In June, Hayes urged increased rates for discounts and time deposits. Mills disagreed. Higher interest rates would require higher rates abroad. "It might offer some temporary relief to the balance of payments problem, but only up to the point that our foreign allies . . . defend their reserves against the losses of gold and dollars" (FOMC Minutes, June 18, 1963, 33). As an alternative, he cited a recent statement by Paul Samuelson in favor of dollar devaluation (FOMC Minutes, June 18, 1963, 33–34). Martin acknowledged "increasing sentiment for devaluation or for credit controls . . . credit controls would spark nationalism worldwide. The United States is the last citadel of non-discriminatory trade and convertible currencies, and its leadership in the world rests on this. . . . Increasing interest rates would boost confidence. Economists . . . had never quite come to grips with the notion of confidence . . . [T]he market is never logical and people are never logical" (FOMC Minutes, June 18, 1963, 54–55).

Policy was too easy, Martin said. Devaluation or credit controls should be a last resort. Something had to be done. Martin, then, made a point that he would make publicly two years later. "It was hardly appropriate to start talking about tight money until net free reserves gave way to net borrowed reserves. . . . No matter whether one looked at the stock market or the real estate market, small business activities or some of the fringe activities of defense operations, there was a speculative movement around the country that was in a way reminiscent of the 1929 period. . . . [Martin] hoped that he was too pessimistic" (FOMC Minutes, June 18, 1963, 55–56).

Many members were skeptical. Others thought higher rates were the wrong remedy either because they believed that the administration had to curtail its foreign outlays or because they opposed slowing the recovery. By a vote of seven to three, they retained the policy directive: "Accommodate moderate growth in bank credit, while putting increased emphasis on money market conditions that would contribute to an improvement in

246. Martin did not accept Phillips curve reasoning. He testified that "there was even serious discussion of the number of percentage points of inflation we might trade off for a percentage point increase in our growth rate. The underlying fallacy in this approach is that it assumes we can concentrate on one major goal without considering collateral, and perhaps deleterious, side effects" (Hearings, Joint Economic Committee, February 1, 1963, 5–6).

the capital account of the U.S. balance of payments" (ibid., 56). Hayes and Balderston dissented because they favored less ease. Mitchell dissented for the opposite reason. He wanted to roll back the tighter policy adopted on May 7.[247]

Martin and Hayes had laid the groundwork for the next move. Pressures from the Europeans supported their arguments. The Bank for International Settlements annual report urged higher rates. At home, President Kennedy planned a speech on the balance of payments in July. Coombs urged the Federal Reserve to show its independence by acting before the speech.

The Federal Advisory Council (FAC) did not expect higher inflation. It favored a gradually more restrictive monetary policy to reduce the international payments deficit during a period of rising business activity (Board Minutes, May 21, 1963, 4). FAC members noted "a growing concern among informed persons . . . regarding the persistence of the deficit in our international payments" (ibid., 13). It favored a higher discount rate. Someone spoke in favor of making the financial market less attractive to foreign borrowers, a proposal that had support within the administration.

Active discussion continued within and outside the System. The staff of the Council of Economic Advisers did not fear higher short-term interest rates.[248] Its chairman was less certain. Heller accepted that the effects would be modest if the Federal Reserve aggressively purchased long-term and sold short-term securities and the Treasury issued mainly short-term debt. He was concerned that this would not occur. He told the president he preferred no change but "if you do decide to say 'yes' on the discount rate boost now, your blessing should be accompanied by an understanding signed in blood that the Fed *will* buy long (real long) and that the Treasury *will* sell and refund short. . . . plus an understanding that if the actions to

---

247. Mitchell bolstered his case by claiming that the Federal Reserve could not change the slope of the yield curve. This statement verbalized the growing belief that the effort to twist the yield curve failed. The slope, he said, depends on the marginal efficiency of capital. Hickman, a long-time student of market rates, corrected him. The marginal efficiency of capital depended on expected future returns. Concerns about the balance of payments altered expected returns. Hickman acknowledged the negative effect on current domestic investment but said the long-term effect would be positive (FOMC Minutes, May 18, 1963, 60–61).

248. A staff memo discussed the proposed increase in discount rates to 3.5 percent as a means of increasing Treasury bill rates to 3.25 to 3.38 percent. The memo suggested that the bill rate would not rise to that level (from 3 percent) without additional action. It proposed additional issues of Treasury bills and System purchases of long-term issues to reduce the impact on long-term rates. The memo anticipated correctly that long-term rates would change very little (memo: "The Domestic Effects of an Increase in the Discount Rate," Heller papers, Monetary Policy, Box 20, June 28, 1963).

boost the bill rate . . . do trigger long-term increases, these actions will be abandoned or reversed"[249] (Heller papers, Monetary Policy, Box 20, July 7, 1963, 2; emphasis in the original).

Payments Problems

Policy coordination had proceeded so far that an administration task force evaluated the Federal Reserve's program and estimated its consequences before it was adopted.[250] It estimated that short-term capital outflows would decline by $250 to $500 million (from $546 million the previous year), with an additional effect from increased confidence in the dollar and the reliance on orthodox policy. Effects on the domestic economy would be modest. Higher interest rates would increase government outlays by $140 to $700 million depending on what happened to longer-term interest rates ("The Effect of an Increase in the Discount Rate," Board Records, July 8, 1963).

The FOMC received the proposed program the following day. The manager, Robert Stone, reported that the program had leaked and markets had revised anticipations. Early in July, newsletters reported the policy change on which the administration and Federal Reserve staff had worked. Ninety-day Treasury bill rates increased to 3.20 percent, and one-year rates were at 3.5 percent, reflecting the 0.5 percentage point increase in the discount rate that the market anticipated.

The leaked information accomplished most of the objectives. Secretary Dillon confirmed market beliefs by testifying in favor of higher rates. All the Federal Reserve had to do was confirm anticipations. Several members opposed the discount rate increase. Robertson called the plan to raise rates "temporary palliatives . . . It will not fool many foreign central bankers" (FOMC Minutes, July 9, 1963, 46).

Robertson countered Coombs's repeated statements about a crisis. He had traveled in Europe, met with officials, and attended meetings at the BIS. "Literally everyone we talked with emphasized the long-run strength of the U.S. economy—its competitive ability, its comparatively fine record of cost and price stability. This meant to them that our balance of payments problem was a relatively short-run transitional thing that could be dealt with accordingly" (ibid., 16).

---

249. Heller added: "I don't view the 'independence of the Fed' as a barrier to full Presidential control of these decisions" (Heller papers, Monetary Policy, Box 20, July 7, 1963, 2). He gave as a reason that the Treasury could take monetary actions through debt management and trust account operations, as Morgenthau had done in the 1930s. Note the indication that the president would decide whether the Federal Reserve raised the discount rate.

250. The memo ended by noting that they did not express a judgment on the desirability of the change and that they might disagree. The memo was signed by Gardner Ackley, CEA; Robert V. Roosa, Treasury; Guy E. Noyes, Federal Reserve; and Charles Schultze, Budget.

Mills thought raising interest rates did "more harm than good" (ibid., 49). He complained that the administration was putting too much burden on the Federal Reserve. Mitchell joined him.

Complaints that the Federal Reserve had been pushed to do most of the work reflected concern that its independence had been compromised. Martin responded by reporting on his activities. He had participated in cabinet-level meetings beginning in April. He had urged changes in military spending and foreign aid in preference to direct controls. A working party had developed the program that had been distributed to them. It relied mainly on Federal Reserve actions supplemented by Treasury debt management operations.

Most of the opponents backed down, perhaps in response to Martin's plea that the System had to cooperate with the administration, perhaps because markets had already adjusted. By a vote of ten to two, the FOMC agreed to "accommodate moderate growth in bank credit, while putting increased emphasis on money market conditions that would contribute to an improvement in the capital account of the U.S. balance of payments" (ibid., 77). Members understood that the reserve banks would raise their discount rates and the Board would raise regulation Q ceiling rates. Only Governors Mitchell and Robertson dissented.

President Kennedy called a meeting of the Quadriad on July 15. The president asked Chairman Martin "whether it was Federal Reserve policy to prevent a rise in long-term rates. Chairman Martin stated 'yes,' Federal Reserve policy would be aimed in that direction; he could not predict with certainty that the effect of the action would be confined to short-term rates, but the Federal Reserve would make a major effort to achieve that goal" (Draft Notes on Quadriad Meeting with the president, Heller papers, Monetary Policy, Box 20).[251]

Seven banks requested discount rate increases to 3.5 percent. With Robertson dissenting, the Board voted to approve the increase effective July 17. By July 26, all banks posted the new rate. On July 17, the Board approved a ceiling rate of 4 percent on time deposits with ninety days or more to maturity. Only four governors were present. All voted for the increase.[252]

251. The president also urged Chairman Martin to announce support for his proposed tax cut. When Martin testified in Congress a few days after the meeting, he made no mention of his commitment to keep long rates down. According to one report, "Heller was furious" (Kettl, 1986, 100). He called another meeting of the Quadriad to reinforce the point and the Federal Reserve's commitment.

252. Robertson approved reluctantly because other rates had increased. Failure to raise the ceiling rate would prevent banks from holding their time deposits, especially negotiable certificates of deposit (Board Minutes, July 17, 1963, 14–15). The Board had considered elimination of the ceiling or setting the rate above the market. Bankers were divided, with

This was the only time since the British devaluation in 1931 that the Federal Reserve raised discount rates solely to support the exchange rate.

Although Martin soon after denied that he had made a commitment to the administration on monetary policy, there is no denying administration involvement in the discount rate increase (FOMC Minutes, July 30, 1963, 55). Even if he did not make a formal commitment, the change had been discussed with administration officials as part of a package before it was brought to the bank presidents. In 1956, Martin had resisted administration pressure to keep the discount rate unchanged, and in 1965 he would resist such pressure again. Now, he sacrificed independence to cooperate with the administration, most likely because he shared its concern about the payments imbalance and used the joint effort to get agreement to both tighten and supplement monetary policy.[253]

The following day, July 18, President Kennedy sent a message to Congress about the balance of payments. He repeated his commitment to freer trade and capital movements, the $35 gold price, and tariff reduction (later called the Kennedy round), and he took steps to reduce the excess cost of freight for exports relative to imports[254] (Kennedy, 1963). The principal action was a request to Congress for an interest equalization tax to raise the cost of foreign borrowing in U.S. capital markets on securities with more than three years initial maturity.[255] Coombs reported that the higher discount rate "brought about a significant improvement in dollar exchange rates on the following day. This favorable reaction has been almost obliterated, however, by the Presidential message . . . calling for

a large majority in favor of the ceiling. This reduced the chance for new legislation (Board Minutes, February 19, 1963, 12). Many bankers complained that raising ceiling rates lowered credit quality because banks would take more risk (ibid., May 16, 1963, 13). Governor Mitchell shared this view (Board Minutes, October 10, 1963, 15). The decision favored the banks, not the public.

253. He resisted the idea that policy was restrictive. "It had recently been following a slightly less stimulative policy" (FOMC Minutes, July 30, 1963, 55). Back in March, he told the FOMC, "If the System does not have the support of the administration we will be defeated psychologically almost at the start on moves that monetary policy might make on the balance of payments" (ibid., March 5, 1963, 84).

254. He also extended for an additional two years the $100 duty-free exemption on tourist purchases abroad. The exemption had been $400.

255. The tax did not apply to bank loans. This omission was corrected in 1965 by a "voluntary restraint program." The president asked to exempt securities of developing countries and Canada. The rate of tax was 15 percent on equity shares and 2.75 to 15 percent on debt, depending on the bond's maturity (Kennedy, 1963). The tax applied to the value or face amount of the issue. A $100 long-term bond provided $85 to the issuer and $15 to the U.S. government. This increased the interest rate about one percentage point. In 1964, legislation required commercial banks to report foreign loans and commitments (Annual Report, 1963, 199–200).

Table 3.9   Selected Balance of Payments Measures (Actual and Proposed)

1960	Expansion of Export-Import Bank lending and guarantees of non-commercial risks.
	Reduction in military dependents abroad (repealed in 1961).
	Reduction in defense and non-defense government purchases abroad.
1961	Offsets for military expenditure in Europe and additional procurement at home.
	Tying development aid to dollar purchases.
	Increased taxes on foreign earnings of U.S. corporations.
	Reduced allowance for tourist purchases abroad from $400 to $100.
	Treasury intervention in foreign exchange markets.
	Repayment of German loans.
1962	Expansion of earlier programs.
	Offset purchases by Germany and Italy.
	Increased borrowing authority for the IMF.
	Beginning of Federal Reserve "swap" arrangements for currencies.
	Treasury issues foreign denominated securities.
1963	An interest equalization tax of 1% on foreign borrowers in U.S. market.
	Additional tying of foreign aid to domestic purchases.
1965	Interest Equalization Tax on bank loans with duration of one year or more made to borrowers in developed
	countries (except Canada).
	Limits on growth of bank lending to foreigners.
	Encourage private companies to increase exports and repatriate earnings.
	Guidelines for direct investment by non-financial corporations to limit growth of foreign direct investment.
1967	Permit tax rates (up to 2%) for interest equalization tax.
	Expansion of lending authority of Export-Import Bank.

Source: *Economic Report of the President*, various years.

an interest equalization tax" (telegram, Coombs to Board, Board Records, July 29, 1963).[256]

The interest equalization tax added a new layer of exchange controls. Earlier, the administration used subsidized loans from the Export-Import Bank, tied purchases financed by military or foreign aid, agreements with foreign governments to make equipment purchases to offset the cost of U.S. troops stationed abroad, and reduced government purchases abroad.[257] Table 3.9 lists some principal measures proposed or adopted in the 1960s.

256. The rest of the telegram is about Coombs's support operations in the gold and foreign exchange markets, often accompanied by foreign central bank dollar purchases. The amounts seem small: $12 million in the Swiss franc market, $4.5 million out of $35 million spent by the Bundesbank, and $12.5 million in France (which failed to keep the dollar exchange rate off the floor).

257. The Council of Economic Advisers (1963, 264) collected data on transfers abroad. From 1946 through 1962, the United States spent $80 billion (net) on foreign assistance programs, an average of $5 billion per year. In the years of concern about payments abroad, 1960–62 inclusive, the average was $4.4 billion. These data include military supplies and

Many of the controls or restrictions were inefficient or could be circumvented. Tying foreign aid expenditures is inefficient and costly, but substitution is limited. Requiring foreigners to purchase military equipment to offset costs of U.S. troops abroad increased exports and reduced capital outflow. Tying foreign aid or military spending also reduced the real value of the spending but may have been offset by increased appropriations so that the actual dollar outflow was not much affected.[258] The interest equalization tax had a strong initial effect but soon shifted lending to banks and foreign markets. But it shifted deposits also. Controls on bank lending to foreigners followed. Foreign interest rates rose relative to domestic rates, so the interest equalization tax had to be raised later in the decade. Eichengreen (2000) concluded that controls were ineffective. He found no evidence of an effect on the speed of adjustment to interest differentials after the controls were in place.

At most controls and restrictions may have given the United States more time to adopt a permanent program. The Kennedy, Johnson, and Nixon administrations never developed policies to sustain the Bretton Woods system. This left the solution to monetary policy, controls, and the market. As prices rose abroad relative to domestic prices, the current balance improved. Foreign governments did not like "imported inflation," but they disliked currency revaluation or slower growth of the U.S. economy even more. Abroad, as at home, maintaining employment and preventing recession had higher priority.

Hayes reported that the interest equalization tax created a boom in foreign term loans instead of securities (FOMC Minutes, July 30, 1963, 6). The staff reported no effect of the policy announcements on covered interest differentials. The foreign press was critical of the tax as not well thought out and full of loopholes.[259]

Members disagreed on whether the attempt to twist the yield curve had failed. Martin expressed skepticism but urged them to continue with the twist, probably for political reasons. Interest rates on long-term Treasury

---

services. Excluding these items, the total transfer was $51.3 billion (excluding currency claims).

258. Fieleke (1969) estimated that buying military equipment at home reduced purchases abroad by $80 million. He makes no allowance for a possible increase in the number of troops abroad.

259. *Economist* (July 20, 1963, 276) added: "It is strains of generosity that afflict the American balance of payments, not any inability to earn a most satisfactory living in trade with the outside world. . . . [I]t took on burdens that some are foolish enough to take for weakness." Balderston agreed that the administration "should impose controls at the point where he thought they would work" on the government's own spending and lending (FOMC Minutes, July 30, 1963).

Table 3.10 Money Market Conditions, 1963 (monthly averages)

	FREE RESERVES (MILLIONS $)	TREASURY BILLS (PERCENTAGE)	FEDERAL FUNDS (PERCENTAGE)
June	138	2.995	2.99
July	161	3.143	3.02
August	133	3.320	3.49
September	91	3.379	3.48
October	94	3.453	3.50
November	33	3.522	3.48
December	209	3.523	3.38

Source: Board of Governors (1976, 600, 695, 689).

bonds remained in a narrow range, 3.99 to 4.07 percent, from July to October. Federal funds and short-term interest rates are shown in Table 3.10. By August the federal funds rate rose to the discount rate. Treasury bill rates at first rose more slowly. The System took no further policy action during 1963.[260] The manager explained the decline in free reserves as a result of a series of missed forecasts. Almost all were in the same direction.

Growth of the monetary base rose to the 4 to 5 percent range, the highest rate of increase since 1952. Chart 3.15 shows the very different movements in monetary base growth and free reserves and the very different readings of policy action. The base suggests more expansive policy in 1963–65; free reserves remain on a plateau in late 1963, a brief pause on a declining trend that suggested to the FOMC that policy tightened.

Repeating a problem of the 1920s, shifts from demand to time deposits reduced effective reserve requirements, permitting banks to expand earnings assets and money plus time deposits (M_2) much faster than base growth. In 1963, M_2 rose 8.4 percent after increasing 8.1 percent in 1962. The increase in regulation Q ceiling rates contributed to the growth after July. The Federal Reserve did not have a consistent view about which growth rate, M_1 or M_2, was most relevant. Some liked the induced shift into time deposits because it increased credit expansion and slowed money growth (M_1) relative to base growth. They disliked ceiling rates. Others thought the ceiling was inflationary. Still others dismissed both credit and monetary expansion. In this, they did not differ from many mainstream academic economists.

The rate of economic expansion increased modestly in second quarter 1963 to 5.7 percent and more rapidly in the third. Stock prices continued to rise at an annual rate of 15 percent, slower than the 20 to 25 percent

260. At the September 10 meeting, the FOMC again changed the allocation formula. The declining gold stock and rising monetary base necessitated more frequent adjustments than the monthly formula.

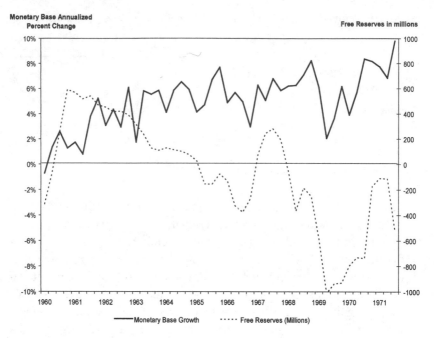

Chart 3.15. Free reserves and monetary base growth, 1960–71.

earlier in the year, but evidence of rising profit anticipations. These and other changes showed no evidence of the modest contraction that Martin and Hayes had worked so hard to achieve. Nor did the balance of payments data show the improvement that a higher discount rate and the interest equalization tax were supposed to bring. Despite an $800 million increase in the balance on goods and services, the official settlements deficit for the year remained above $2 billion, only $700 million less than in 1963. And the gold outflow was the same in the second half year as in the first.[261]

The president's July 18 message accepted the main idea of the Triffin plan. He called for steps to improve the international monetary system by providing additional liquid reserves. At the annual meeting of the International Monetary Fund and the World Bank the following October, G-10 countries undertook the first of many studies of international mon-

261. Knipe (1965, 157) commented that "those in charge of the United States became . . . obsessed with the liquid capital flows rather than with the fundamental need to rectify the basic balance of payments. Oddest of all though, was that the expressions of apprehension brought home from Europe were frequently worded exactly like the expressions which were currently going round in the United States. In many cases this was easily understandable, because the apprehension probably started with the American visitor."

etary reform (Solomon, 1982, 65).[262] The decision taken less than five years after the return of current account convertibility suggests how different was the postwar world from the world envisaged at Bretton Woods. There, the aim had been to avoid deflation, high unemployment, stagnation, and trade barriers driven in part by repeated U.S. payments surpluses. Instead, the main problem was inflation driven by a sustained U.S. payments deficit.

The study group vented criticisms, particularly French criticisms, of the reserve currency system. France proposed ending the reserve currency system by creating a new international reserve asset. The United States opposed the French proposal and agreed only to have a study group consider the issue. The group's report in the summer of 1964 proposed to increase IMF quotas when the issue was to be considered in 1965 but retained the existing system (Solomon, 1982, 69). The State Department was more willing to accept the French position. The outcome would have been different if the State Department had done the negotiating instead of the Treasury.

These discussions repeated several features of the 1920s discussions, with important differences. Again there was no agreement on how real exchange rates should adjust if nominal exchange rates remained fixed. Surplus countries were reluctant to inflate, though less reluctant than in the 1920s. They lacked a better alternative, so they accepted inflation reluctantly and to avoid revaluation and a sudden reduction or loss of their surpluses. As in the 1920s, deficit countries, Britain now joined by the United States, would not deflate. A notable difference from the 1920s was that most of the surplus countries wanted the deficit countries, especially the United States, to avoid deflation for fear of unemployment reaching them.

France repeated its earlier behavior. It devalued in 1958 (as in 1928) to a rate that undervalued the franc. Starting in 1962, it converted the resulting current account surplus into gold at the rate of $30 million a month. Later, it began a more aggressive gold purchase program.

With no solution acceptable to surplus and deficit countries, the United States increased reliance on capital controls. The interest equalization tax and the interest rate increases in July had little immediate success in slowing inflation abroad or improving the balance of payments. In October Coombs reported that speculative gold purchases in London were matched by Soviet gold sales, so the U.S. gold stock remained unchanged for ten weeks. Italian inflation was over 6 percent with wages rising 17 percent,

262. The members of the G-10 (group of ten) were Canada, Japan, Belgium, France, West Germany, Italy, Netherlands, Sweden, the United Kingdom, and the United States. Later Switzerland became the eleventh member, but the name did not change.

and there was a risk of devaluation. West Germany, the Netherlands, Canada, and Switzerland had larger dollar inflows and rising inflation. "In the Netherlands, the wage controls, which many of our European friends had strongly recommended as a model for a U.S. incomes policy, have apparently broken down" (FOMC Minutes, October 22, 1963, 31).[263] France froze wages and prices. Capital outflow slowed in September, reducing concern and pressure for policy changes.

Many bankers and businessmen disliked the interest equalization tax. The Blough commission reported to Secretary Dillon that it favored reductions in tax rates, higher interest rates, and reductions in military aid and other government spending abroad, but it did not support the interest equalization tax (letter, Sproul to Roger Blough, Sproul papers, July 23, 1963). Allan Sproul, a prominent member of the Blough commission, had three complaints about administration policy: (1) "there never was enough power and pressure put behind tax reduction"; (2) it labored under "happy illusions about a reduction in the deficit of the balance of payments during 1962, and its virtual elimination by the end of 1963"; (3) it delayed too long raising interest rates, including time deposit rates (ibid., 1–2).[264]

Coombs next proposed a modest program of "warehousing." To support the Italian lire and other European currencies, the Federal Reserve would purchase lire in the spot market, at rates above par value, and immediately sell them forward to the Treasury's Stabilization Fund to cover outstanding Treasury debt in lire. Like all past programs, this program started modestly. Coombs proposed a limit of $100 million (FOMC Minutes, November 12, 1963, 5–6). The FOMC did not limit the program to the lira and approved unanimously.[265] From its modest beginning, authorized warehousing reached $20 billion in 1995 at the time of a Mexican peso crisis (Schwartz, 1997, 143).

---

263. The October 1 meeting showed an upsurge in concern about the growing size of the swap arrangements. Mills expressed strong opposition and suggested credit controls if the payments imbalance worsened (FOMC Minutes, October, 1963, 44). Balderston was concerned that the government relied too much on the swap arrangements as a substitute for policy. Although the FOMC approved new swap lines as before, there were two objections when the FOMC voted to add Japan to the swap network.

264. Sproul called the interest equalization tax "a mistaken departure from a general policy of non-interference with the international movements of private capital" (notes in preparation for a meeting of the Balance of Payments Committee, Sproul papers, September 19, 1963, 1). Coombs replied to these comments: "I hasten to assure you that neither Al Hayes nor I hatched this 'turkey' . . . but we have been doing our best to minimize . . . its unsettling effects on the markets" (letter, Coombs to Sproul, Sproul papers, July 29, 1963).

265. The main concern was the use of above par value (but within the IMF bands). Coombs explained that the Italians decided to support the currency above par (FOMC Minutes, November 12, 1963, 6).

AN EXPANDING ECONOMY

Expectations improved as the recovery accelerated. In September, the FAC told the Board that it anticipated continued moderate expansion, but the FAC members expressed concern about congressional resistance to the tax cut and the balance of payments as factors weakening the outlook. By November these concerns received less attention; the FAC described the outlook as very positive (Board Minutes, September 17 and November 19, 1963).

The facts support the change of outlook. Growth of real GDP reached 7.2 percent in the third quarter and was above President Kennedy's goal of 5 percent for the four quarters of 1963. Unit labor costs declined, and inflation remained moderate. Treasury forecasts for 1964 became more optimistic. At the BIS and OECD meetings, discussion centered on Italian and Dutch wage increases and concerns about European inflation. For the first time since consultation began at the OECD, "the U.S. balance of payment difficulties were not on the agenda" (FOMC Minutes, November 12, 1963, 10–11). The Europeans recognized that inflation abroad had improved the U.S. position. One report suggested that "the Europeans thought the United States was moving in the right direction . . . and that the crisis might have been passed" (ibid., 14). Chairman Martin, urging an unchanged policy, expressed concern about the start of inflation but optimism about the outlook. "Everything was going in the Committee's favor" (ibid., 59).[266]

Assassination of President Kennedy at 1:30 PM eastern standard time on November 22 caused a surge of uncertainty that temporarily altered expectations. Prices on the New York Stock Exchange fell sharply on volume of 2 million shares in a half hour. Trading on the foreign exchange market in New York halted; trading in Europe had ended for the week. To show the intent to stabilize, at 2 o'clock Coombs offered German marks, British pounds, and Netherland guilders at exchange rates that prevailed before the assassination. The FOMC gave immediate approval to increase the swap agreement with Switzerland to $300 million.[267]

---

266. The FOMC remained divided, but only Mills dissented from the directive. Robertson's statement showed his unhappiness with vague directives. He voted for the directive out of agreement with language; "he expressed some doubt, however, that the directive would be construed consistently with his thinking" (FOMC Minutes, November 12, 1963, 62).

267. Coombs reported that his interventions were successful. "We have subsequently received numerous messages from both the market and foreign central banks that our intervention on Friday afternoon helped considerably to confirm market expectations that the central banks would jointly and firmly resist any speculative developments" (telegram, Coombs to Board of Governors, Board Records, November 23, 1963, 3). This seems an overstated claim. Coombs reports his total intervention in all currencies that afternoon as $23.5 million, mainly in pounds and marks (ibid., 3). At the time, banks reported $2.6 billion of short-term liabilities to foreigners (Board of Governors, 1976, 937). Coombs explained the success of these small operations: "In those days official assurances enjoyed a full measure of credibility"

Heightened uncertainty did not last. Vice President Lyndon B. Johnson became president and made reassuring statements to calm the public. At his first meeting with his economic advisers, Walter Heller warned him that, without the tax cut, the economy could slow or even decline in the second half of 1964. There was no need to point out that this would occur during the election (Bernstein, 1996, 31). Johnson explained that he favored the tax cut and would make it a top priority.

When the FOMC held a telephone conference on Tuesday morning, reports gave no suggestion of market crisis or anxiety. The stock market had started to recover, and currency markets were quiet. The FOMC renewed its directive but inserted "cushioning any unsettlement that might arise in money markets stemming from the death of President Kennedy" (FOMC Minutes, November 26, 1963, 6). At the next FOMC meeting, the staff noted markets' rapid return to normal (FOMC Minutes, December 3, 1963, 13–14). The FOMC retained the clause about Kennedy's death until December 17.[268]

The staff noted in early December that the money stock had increased by $1 billion in each of the past two months, an annual rate of more than 6 percent. Hayes noted a shift of credit expansion into new loans instead of government securities. Martin's concern was excessive exuberance caused by belief that Congress would pass the tax cut. He suggested increasing discount rates even if the Treasury was borrowing. The FOMC took no action.

Russian gold sales had offset U.S. gold sales to France, Argentina, and Austria, so the gold stock had not changed for eighteen weeks. By mid-month Russian gold sales slowed, and the gold stock resumed its decline.[269]

For the first time since the early 1930s, the Federal Reserve had to carefully watch the gold reserve ratios at the individual reserve banks. The cause

---

(Coombs, 1976, 104–5). At 2:08, his offer to sell pounds and, a few minutes later, guilders found no buyers. Further, the following day London reported that it supplied dollars instead of buying dollars to support the exchange rate (telegram, Coombs to Board of Governors, Board Records, November 23, 1963, 4). The Soviet Union sold gold on the London market at $35.10 (ibid., 6).

268. At the December 17 meeting, Dewey Daane joined the FOMC. Daane became a governor on November 29, 1963, replacing George H. King, Jr., who resigned on September 18 for health reasons. Immediately prior to his appointment, Daane had served in the Treasury as deputy to Robert Roosa.

269. The December 3 meeting reopened discussion of releasing the minutes to scholars. Members divided into three groups. Martin and three others favored release after a lag of several years. Martin argued for improved understanding of their decisions. Seven favored a limited release with restrictions; several wanted to limit access to an official historian. Hayes and two others opposed. Hayes, following the tradition of central bankers, said, "The FOMC's deliberations aren't a matter of public concern" (FOMC Minutes, December 3, 1963). He suggested that Martin had responded to political pressure, an issue between New York and Washington dating back to the founding.

was a seasonal increase in currency and deposits during the Christmas season. The Board's first response was to consider assessing a mandatory penalty on reserve banks with deficiencies (Board Minutes, November 29 and December 2, 1963).[270] One of the principal arguments against was reluctance to show reserve deficiencies in the Annual Report.

After meeting with the bank presidents, the FOMC again changed the method of allocating securities. Each week the System shifted securities and gold through the Interdistrict Settlement Fund to equalize the reserve ratios based on the most recent five days of data. During the week, the manager made special adjustments to remove reserve deficiencies. The overall System ratio was about 30 percent, five percentage points above the overall requirement. In March 1965, Congress removed the 25 percent reserve requirement against bank reserves, a step toward ending the gold reserve requirement entirely three years later. Chairman Martin defended the 1965 change as a way of releasing $4.8 billion from earmarked to free gold.

By early 1964 the mood had changed. The Economic Report of the President described as unparalleled the dollar rise in real GNP and labor incomes since the recession ended. Inflation remained low and the balance of payments "is improving . . . sharply in response to measures begun in 1961 and reinforced last July" (Council of Economic Advisers, 1964, 11). The report urged tax rate reduction accompanied by "monetary and debt policy . . . directed toward maintaining interest rates and credit conditions that encourage private investment" (ibid., 11). In the report and elsewhere at the time, President Johnson declared the beginning of the War on Poverty.

The view at the Federal Reserve was more wary. It too noted the smaller payments deficit ($3 billion) and smaller gold sales in 1963. Coombs pointed out, however, that Soviet gold sales reached $500 million in 1963, $300 million more than expected[271] (FOMC Minutes, January 7, 1964, 6–7). He anticipated continued heavy Soviet sales in 1964. Soviet sales allowed the gold pool to satisfy market demand without calling on the United States.

270. The penalty reflected provisions in the original Federal Reserve Act, intended to keep individual reserve banks from extending excessive credit. This kind of autonomy was no longer relevant. Reserve bank expansion depended mainly on its participation in the open market account. Governor Robertson recognized this when he referred to the problem as "bookkeeping" (Board Minutes, November 29, 1963, 3).

271. Hayes reported on the recent BIS meeting in Basel. He described a "general feeling of unease" about the euro-dollar market but no full consensus about what to do (FOMC Minutes, January 28, 1964, 7–8). Many Europeans now favored a multiple reserve currency system to reduce dependence on the dollar. On February 13, 1964, the United States drew $125 million in foreign currencies from the IMF. Foreign central banks sold dollars to the IMF, pushing IMF dollar holdings toward the permitted maximum, 75 percent of the U.S. quota. The U.S. also redeemed the excess dollars.

Hayes remarked that a large part of the improvement in payments position resulted from one-time changes such as repayments of postwar loans and purchases of military equipment. Balderston gave credit to the interest equalization tax and worried that the improvement would end. The staff responded that their projected improvement depended very little on the tax (FOMC Minutes, January 28, 1964, 17–18). Several others commented on interest rate increases abroad. Foreign central banks raised interest rates to support currency parities instead of removing capital controls.

Following the July increase in ceiling rates for time deposits, commercial bank time deposits increased rapidly, so bank credit expanded much more than money (M_1). Since the Treasury was in the market, the FOMC took no action in January.

The Directive Again

Both Mills and Robertson objected that an unchanged directive did not mean that policy had not changed. Both objected that current actions pegged interest rates or the term structure. Robertson added: "Dealer statistics suggest a concentration of private investor sales at times when official accounts are large buyers, with a corresponding thinning out of private selling activity in adjacent periods. Dealers . . . speak of the tendency for prospective sellers . . . preferring . . . to unload on some future official buying orders" (FOMC Minutes, January 28, 1964, 29).[272]

272. The staff produced a report on intervention in the long-term market by the Federal Reserve and the Treasury. It showed that, except for over-ten-year maturities where volume was small, combined Federal Reserve and Treasury purchases were generally less than 10 percent of dealer purchases.

YEAR	OVER I YEAR	1–5 YEARS	5–10 YEARS	OVER 10 YEARS
		Dealer Purchases[a] (millions)		
1961	29,345	22,221	4,316	2,808
1962	30,654	17,707	10,184	2,764
1963[b]	52,350	28,261	17,576	6,513
		Federal Reserve Purchases		
1961	2,556	1,786	641	129
1962	1,883	1,521	326	37
1963[b]	1,453	844	541	68
		Treasury Purchases		
1961	1,002	66	265	670
1962	513	271	119	123
1963[b]	1,939	397	595	947

[a]excludes purchases from other dealers and brokers
[b]through November
Source: Albert R. Koch to FOMC, Board Records, December 19, 1963, Table 1, 3.

The problem for the FOMC was that the more control the System exercised over interest rates, the less information interest rates contained about the market's position. "Instead of the market being a window through which we can observe indications of private actions that might call for policy changes, we have made it—in part at least—a mirror of our own intentions with respect to rates" (ibid., 30). Robertson and Mills urged the FOMC to let market rates fluctuate more freely. Mills urged a return to the bills-only procedures.

Soon after these comments, the Board's secretariat reconsidered the content of the directive and the instructions to the manager. The discussion continued for the rest of the year. The secretariat distinguished between two broad measures—first, money market conditions and, second, monetary or credit aggregates. It then made a very odd distinction. The "first group are of concern to the Committee on two counts: they affect international capital flows, and they are read by the market and the public as 'signals' of current monetary policy." As to the aggregates, their influence was on the domestic economy[273] (quoted in memo F. W. Schiff to Alan Holmes, Board Records, FOMC: General, March 27, 1964, 102).

The FOMC's problems of instructing the manager and directing policy action surfaced again in February. The manager reported that his instructions had proved inconsistent, so he had chosen to ignore the free reserve target. He now gave more attention to the Federal funds rate and less to the Treasury bill rate. He had developed "new contacts that disclosed what was happening with respect to the volume of flows behind the relatively fixed Federal funds rate."

Mitchell was incensed. "Such information may be very useful to the Desk, but the problem remained of how the desk could tell *what objectives the Committee wanted it to pursue*" (FOMC Minutes, February 11, 1964, 15–16; emphasis added). Soon after, he joined with two presidents to express dissatisfaction with the form and content of the directive. It was, they said, "too incomplete to cover the policy decisions, . . . internally inconsistent, . . . [and] too vague to establish Committee authority over . . . the Manager" (draft memo to FOMC from Ellis, Mitchell, and Swan, Board Records, June 2, 1964, 1). They recommended quantitative terms and more specific language whenever possible.[274] Their proposed directive had four

273. "It seems safe to surmise that with respect to the condition of the *domestic* economy, variables in the second group are of more fundamental concern to the Committee than those in the first" (quoted in memo F. W. Schiff to Alan Holmes, Board Records, FOMC: General, March 27, 1964, 1–2). The memo does not offer an explanation. It is an error.

274. In May 1964, in a report to the House Banking and Currency Committee, Karl Brunner and I criticized the Federal Reserve on similar grounds. We knew nothing about the

parts that gave a quantitative and qualitative description of the current economic position, "an analytic statement of recent credit and monetary developments," and "appraisal of the current economic and financial scene" and "the longer run policy intent," and a range for free reserves for the next three weeks (ibid., 3–6). The choice would be conditional on the level or range of interest rates that the market determined. The group proposed use of annual rates of increase of reserves required to support private demand deposits as the indicator of the FOMC's "longer run policy intent" (ibid., 4). This measure excluded Treasury deposits from total demand deposits.

The staff introduced a proposed new directive at the April 14 meeting, offering two choices, one more explicit and quantitative than the other. Those who expressed opinions divided seven to five in favor of the less explicit instructions to the manager. The committee adopted a directive without quantitative targets.[275]

The Ellis-Mitchell-Swan memo, and the lengthy discussion that followed, brought out several perennial, basic problems. One was the prob-

---

internal discussion and relied only on published material and interviews with officials who did not mention it. We showed that free reserves had little relation to monetary aggregates or to output and prices, that the directive was so vague that the manager made many of the decisions, that he often moved ahead of the FOMC, that policy had a procyclical bias, and that longer-term objectives had little if any influence on decisions or actions. We recognized that precise knowledge was not available but criticized the absence of systematic research on these basic issues. Discussion of the Ellis, Mitchell, and Swan memo refers to "critics," suggesting our criticism may have encouraged consideration of procedures (Brunner and Meltzer, 1964). Our study also criticized the absence of research on linkage between policy actions and goals and on the transmission process. The memo refers to some of these criticisms without making specific reference.

Following our report, Congressman Patman held hearings on proposals for changes in the Federal Reserve Act to retire reserve bank stock, retire government debt at the reserve banks, require annual appropriations, increase the Board of Governors to twelve members, eliminate the open market committee, and restore the Secretary of the Treasury to the Board. The more than twenty days of hearings did not support Patman's bills. Many witnesses were critical of the Federal Reserve, but they did not agree on what should be done. One response to the academic criticism was a regular meeting at the Board between Federal Reserve governors and leading academic economists known as the Federal Reserve Consultants meeting. Also, the Board voted to reduce the surplus accounts of the reserve banks from twice paid-in capital to 100 percent of paid-in capital. It voted to return the excess, about $500 million, to the Treasury (Board Minutes, December 16, 1964, 3–9). Mills dissented, and Governor Robertson noted in discussion with the bank presidents that this was a defensive action taken to prevent congressional action that would "diminish the System's independence" (ibid., December 15, 1964, 5).

275. Governor Mills and Presidents Hayes, Irons, Deming, Wayne, and Hickman were particularly critical of the staff proposal. Governor Balderston asked the staff to comment on holding meetings once a month instead of every three weeks. By the 15th or 20th, most data became available. A longer interval might require a more conditional statement. The staff added, "More frequent meetings may tend to focus the attention of the Committee too much on short-run, transitory developments" (Brill to Balderston, Board Records, July 24, 1964, 3).

lem of knowledge. What should the FOMC know to carry out its mandate? What could it know? How important was consensus? Was it better to use vague statements that everyone could accept or to be more precise and report differences of opinion? Underlying much of the discussion was the relative weight attached to public relations and operating instructions to guide the manager.

Ellis, Mitchell, and Swan recognized that the System did not have much knowledge of the linkage between its actions and its objectives. They were less explicit and seem less clear about differences in objectives. Some, like Hayes, placed great weight on the payments deficit and often seemed willing to sacrifice domestic employment for a smaller payments deficit. Mitchell and Robertson took the opposite position. The discussion did not consider this problem.

The memo described the FOMC's solution and its weaknesses. "The Committee does not avoid responsibility for making decisions in the face of uncertainty when it takes this easy road of not specifying its intentions and its instructions in complete, clear, and consistent terms. It does, how-ever, reduce its ability to make the best decisions of which it is capable" (Revised memo, Ellis, Mitchell, and Swan to FOMC, Board Records, June 2, 1964, 13).[276]

Hayes opposed the new directive because the members lacked sufficient knowledge about financial processes and linkage with real activity. He did not suggest steps to improve that knowledge. He did not "share the feel-ing of serious dissatisfaction with existing directives that underlies these new programs" (FOMC Minutes, July 28, 1964, 58). He doubted that the manager could hit a precise target for growth in reserves. Irons (Dallas) thought it was a mistake to avoid "tone and feel" and insist on quantitative targets (ibid., 65). Tow (Kansas City) pointed out the lack of agreement. Some members preferred "a credit and interest rate approach, while others preferred some variant of a money supply approach" (ibid., 71).

Malcolm Bryan, referring to the 1964 hearings, noted the "criticism of the directive by Congress and nearly everyone who testified in front of the Banking and Currency subcommittee" (FOMC Minutes, Septem-ber 9, 1964, 60). He added that the System could not avoid making the decision that Ellis, Mitchell, and Swan proposed. "Those judgments are already being made. If we are fearful in expressing them as a Committee,

276. The memo recognized problems of using free reserves including that "changes in free reserves can be associated with more or less specific degrees, or changes in degree, of 'ease' and 'restraint'" (Revised Memo, Ellis, Mitchell, and Swan to FOMC, Board Records, June 2, 1964, 7). The memo defended free reserves as specific and subject to close control, and because use of free reserves leaves interest rates to market determination (ibid., 2).

then the Manager, whose actions *must* and *do* result in reserve numbers, has to make his decision for us. . . . [H]ave we not delegated, vested, or abdicated—choose the word you prefer—our responsibility?" (ibid., 61).

The committee could not agree because the members could not overcome five obstacles.[277] First, the directive and accompanying material served several purposes ranging from public relations to managerial direction. Explicit instructions, or precise statements about current and future conditions, helped one but hurt the other. Explicit instructions opened the FOMC to criticism. Second, the FOMC did not agree on weights placed on specific objectives or on the way to reach them. Several members recognized that it would be difficult and time consuming to reach agreement on precise quantitative targets. Third, some went further, arguing that no one had sufficient understanding of economic dynamics either to give precise quantitative instructions or to develop side conditions (provisions) that would remain relevant.[278] Fourth, some members saw their task as one of responding to hourly or daily market changes and resetting objectives every three weeks. Hayes was the strong proponent of this view, but he was not alone. Others wanted to set a path for monetary policy to achieve longer-term objectives. Although Bryan and Mitchell did not express this view explicitly, that appeared to be one of their objectives. Fifth, several members recognized that a more quantitative directive would of necessity shift considerable responsibility to the Board's staff. They would not accept the counterargument that an imprecise directive and conflicting statements shifted responsibility to the account manager. Governor Mills rejected interest rate targets as a form of pegging, although that was not part of the proposal.

President Hayes defended the manager's discretionary adjustments, arguing that precise instructions with proviso clauses would lead to less desirable outcomes. "The new instruction would be far narrower than the existing type of instructions, and would necessarily introduce important new constraints . . . [I]n a market that is dynamic and changeable in frequently unpredictable ways, I believe those new constraints would redound to the disadvantage of the Committee in the achievement of its central objectives" (Hayes to FOMC, Board Records, October 15, 1964,

277. Martin presided but did not contribute much substance to the discussion. He may have recognized that the members would not reach agreement.

278. Hickman (Cleveland) praised the recommendation to adopt a range for free reserves. Opponents either feared that the manager would embarrass the FOMC by missing the range frequently or preferred to allow the manager to use his judgment (FOMC Minutes, September 29, 1964, 63). Bopp pointed to lack of knowledge and difference of judgment as the source of differences between FOMC members (ibid., 56). Elsewhere, Bopp (1965) criticized the critics for claiming more useful knowledge than they had.

8–9).[279] Hayes did not believe it was desirable or useful to develop a long-term path. He favored period-by-period reassessment, a procedure later shown to be sub-optimal.

Several members agreed that the first two proposals, describing the economy and financial conditions, should not be part of the directive. Robertson summarized some of the problems. "When do trends begin and when do they end? What changes are temporary and what are permanent? How far ahead do today's actions have an impact?" (Robertson to FOMC, Board Records, October 20, 1964, 4).[280] These issues remain central to a careful analysis. The problem of distinguishing between permanent and transitory changes in trends or levels was usually neglected and has not been resolved.[281]

Tax Cut

On February 26, 1964, President Johnson signed the bill reducing tax rates that President Kennedy had first considered after the stock market break in May 1962. The bill passed the House in September 1963, but the Senate Finance Committee refused to act until satisfied that spending reductions would hold total spending in fiscal 1965 below $100 billion. Johnson brought proposed spending down to $97.9 billion.[282] Actual spending

279. Hayes criticized other parts of the Ellis-Mitchell-Swan proposal also. He doubted that the FOMC could agree on a single long-term target and dismissed reserves against private deposits as inadequate. He saw no advantage in trying to agree on a common assessment of the economic outlook and doubted it could be done.

280. The manager noted some additional problems. During the first thirty-eight weeks of 1964, the first published free reserve figure differed from the final figure by $40 million in fifteen weeks, by $60 million in nine weeks, and twice by more than $80 million. He estimated that "75 percent of the time, the range [for a free reserve target] should be well over $100 million—perhaps more like $150 million" (Stone to FOMC, Board Records, October 16, 1964). Robertson's mention of permanent and transitory disturbances opened an important issue that was never studied by the staff. Muth (1960) gave a general answer.

281. Bremner (2004, 155) reports that Martin was sufficiently concerned about the Patman bills that he asked President Johnson for help. Johnson called the Speaker of the House, John W. McCormick. The hearings ended two weeks later; none of Patman's proposals passed the committee. As part of the hearings, Congressman Patman asked Chairman Martin to release FOMC minutes for 1960–63. The FOMC discussed the request at several meetings before rejecting the specific request. It agreed only to establish procedures that would make available minutes prior to 1961, including the 1960 minutes that the subcommittee had obtained once before. Martin's letter referred Patman to the record reported in the Board's Annual Report. He argued that release would reveal confidential information including plans of foreign governments and restrict discussion at FOMC meetings (FOMC Minutes, April 14, 1964, 68). This is the beginning of the program to make records available to scholars and others that the Board instituted in the 1970s.

282. Johnson should have been aware of congressional demands for spending control when he sought a surtax a few years later. Early in the 1963–64 discussions, Secretary Dillon warned President Kennedy, referring to Senator Byrd: "We do believe you have to put on a

for fiscal 1964 was $96.5 billion, below the budget estimate.[283] The final bill reduced tax rates from the range 20 to 91 percent to 14 to 65 percent in 1965. Corporate tax rates declined from 52 to 48 percent.

A year earlier, Dillon told Kennedy that Martin would be helpful in getting the tax cut adopted (Dillon papers, Box 34, January 16, 1963). Martin did not defend Heller's argument that the tax cut would expand consumer spending, and his support for the policy was modest. He made few references to the administration's proposal and, when he did, it was mainly to the problem of financing the deficit. He did not follow his claim that the Federal Reserve had to help with deficit finance if the Congress approved the budget. Instead, he told the Joint Economic Committee that the Federal Reserve "would be derelict in its responsibilities were it—in the light of a large deficit—to add to bank reserves and to bring about substantial credit expansion solely to facilitate the financing of the deficit. . . . [I]t would be ill-advised to generate the danger of inflation, either long-run or short, by creating redundant dollars, in order to make easier the financing of a deficit" (Martin testimony, Joint Economic Committee, February 1, 1963, 10–11). But he agreed to finance any increase in real output that resulted from the tax cut.

The last quote reflects Martin's non-Keynesian views and his continuing concern that the Federal Reserve would have to inflate to finance the deficits that Congress created. He presumed that interest rates would rise, but they would not increase enough to prevent inflation. His testimony showed him aware of the problem he faced later; his conflict between supporting the tax cut and financing it arose because he believed that the Federal Reserve could not refuse to finance a deficit that Congress adopted. The Kennedy-Johnson tax cut brought this concern to the fore because the administration argued that the deficit was both desirable and temporary. By approving the tax cut, Congress knew that the resulting deficit was not an accident.

---

performance that looks like you're being careful with expenditures" (Kennedy, 2001a, October 2, 1962, 334). Heller's original proposal reduced taxes by $6 to $7 billion and put most tax reduction at lower income levels. The final bill shifted reductions toward corporations and higher income levels to gain business support and Republican votes in Congress, (ibid., 339). The original bill included substantial tax reform that was later eliminated.

283. Heller estimated the total tax reduction as $12 billion. Reductions became effective on January 1, 1964 and 1965 (Stein 1990, 431; Hargrove and Morley, 1984, 200–201). Barro and Sahasakul (1986, Table 2) show a reduction in the average marginal tax rate from 0.247 to 0.212 (14 percent) between 1963 and 1965. Heller had originally emphasized the need to eliminate fiscal drag by reducing the full employment budget surplus. In the first half of 1965, with the tax cut fully in effect, the calculated full employment budget surplus was $7 billion, only $2 billion less than in the latter part of 1962, when Kennedy proposed the tax cut (Stein 1990, 436).

Martin explicitly rejected the idea that policy could reduce unemployment now and respond to inflation later, the Phillips curve reasoning favored by Heller.

> Over the years, we have seen counterposed full employment *or* price stability, social objectives *or* financial objectives, and stagnation *or* inflation. In the last case there was even serious discussion of the number of percentage points of inflation we might trade off for a percentage point increase in our growth rate. The underlying fallacy in this approach is that it assumes we can concentrate on one major goal without considering collateral, and perhaps deleterious, side effects on other objectives. But we cannot. If we were to neglect international financial equilibrium, or price stability, or financial soundness in our understandable zeal to promote faster domestic growth, full employment, or socially desirable programs, we would be confronted with general failure. (ibid., 5–6)

With the tax cut assured of passage, the 1964 Economic Report instructed the Federal Reserve that "[i]t would be self-defeating to cancel the stimulus of tax reduction by tightening money" (Council of Economic Advisers, 1964, 11). Martin recognized the political pressure to avoid increasing interest rates before the election. His early meetings with President Johnson reinforced his belief that Johnson was a populist who supported his personal view with the economic arguments of Heller and others.[284]

The Federal Reserve kept monthly average free reserves between $100 and $150 million most of the time through August. The manager explained the few exceptions as accidents, special events, or a deliberate choice to maintain an interest rate target. Monthly averages of the federal funds rate remained in a narrow band around 3.5 percent until December. Annual growth of the monetary base rose to between 5 and 5.8 percent from about 4.5 percent the previous summer. Thus, the Federal Reserve did what Martin said he would not do, supporting the tax cut with faster money growth, while believing the System had kept policy action unchanged.

Withholding taxes began to reflect lower tax rates early in March, but spending did not respond immediately. Retail sales in March were lower than in February. Auto sales declined (Annual Report, 1964, 81). At the end

---

284. In case Martin forgot, Heller reminded him and urged President Johnson to do the same. For example on March 2, he sent a memo to Johnson stating, "Martin's fears of prospective inflation seem to be mounting to a fever pitch" (Heller Paper, Monetary Policy, March 2, 1964). He urged Johnson to hold a meeting of the Quadriad to increase pressure on Martin. Arthur Okun, later chairman of the Council of Economic Advisers, quotes Johnson's comment on high interest rates: "It's hard for a boy from Texas ever to see high interest rates as a lesser evil than anything else" (Hargrove and Morley, 1984, 274).

of May, the staff reported increased production and sales in April with new orders for durables rising at a 7 percent annual rate (FOMC Minutes, May 26, 1964, 16–17). Further confirmation of expansion came in May with a drop in the unemployment rate to 5.1 percent, the lowest rate since May 1960, but the saving rate remained relatively high until September, seven months after the tax cut passed (Annual Report, 1964, 103). Stock prices continued to decelerate. The peak annual rate of increase reached 20.5 percent in April 1963, fell steadily to 17.1 percent in December and 14.9 percent in May 1964. By October, the rate of increase was below 10%.

In February, the unemployment rate began a gradual decline, and pressure from the balance of payments eased. The first quarter of 1964 had a payments surplus for the first time since 1957. The good news did not continue. By June, Hayes suggested reducing the degree of ease to further improve the balance of payments, but he recognized that with low inflation and an improved payments position his proposal would draw little support. By August, he began to urge a tighter policy more forcefully. Chairman Martin supported him along with Balderston, Hickman, Mills, and Shuford. The vote to tighten was six to five, with Shephardson absent. Some proponents cited the increased payments deficit, others the strengthening domestic economy. Harry Shuford (St. Louis) expressed concern about 8.5 percent (annualized) growth in money in June and July. As was often true, free reserves declined in advance of the decision.

Martin told Heller that the FOMC had reduced the free reserve target to $50 million (from $100 million) in response to the preliminary report of the July balance of payments. "They are going to *keep this very quiet* so that the market won't know that it's being done" (memo to the president, Heller papers, August 18, 1964; emphasis in the original). The move had little effect on short- or long-term interest rates.

Once the election was over, discussion of further tightening increased. Martin joined Hayes in favoring an additional move, and they were joined by four others. There was a stronger sentiment that recent wage increases, continued economic expansion, rapid money growth, and renewed weakness in the balance of payments supported an increase in interest rates. The main reason for delay was Treasury financing. FOMC took no action, however, at its November 10 meeting.

The Federal Reserve again misread the degree of monetary stimulus by concentrating on free reserves and ignoring growth of money aggregates. It missed the opportunity to stop the inflation at an early stage, as Chairman Burns recognized years later. Annual consumer price increases remained in the 1 to 1.5 percent range, but annual base money growth at 5.5 to 5.75 percent suggested strongly that prices would accelerate if money growth continued. By the fall of 1964, wage increases in the automobile industry reached 4 to 5 percent at Ford and Chrysler, and there was a strike at General Motors. This was well above the wage guideline. The guideline proved ineffective before the Great Inflation started. At the September FOMC meeting, Hayes remarked, "The long record of price stability may now be in more serious jeopardy than at any time in recent years" (FOMC Minutes, September 29, 1964, 20).[285] The FOMC ignored his warning.

In a memo to the president, Heller denied that the economy would experience inflation in 1964. "We might not be able to prevent some price-wage creep. . . . [I]t won't be inflation and particularly not the kind that tight money can stop" (memo, Heller to president, Board Records, January 5, 1964.).

Problems with the Pound

Two weeks later, November 24, the U.K. increased its discount rate from 5 to 7 percent to support the pound.[286] The administration wired Prime Minister Harold Wilson that it "had no objection to the U.K. doing whatever it felt was necessary and that the U.S. did not see any reason *on domestic grounds* for raising the discount rate in this country at the moment" (Board Minutes, November 23, 1964, 2; emphasis added).[287] Martin added that a discount rate increase "was not precluded" (ibid., 2).

---

285. Walter Reuther, president of the United Auto Workers (UAW), had rejected the basis for wage guidelines in the Economic Report on two grounds. First, the report compared physical productivity to money wages at several places, suggesting that wages had increased faster than productivity. Real wage increases remained below productivity growth. Second, in a memo that Reuther sent with his note, the UAW staff challenged the measure of trend productivity growth used to set wage guidelines. "Five year moving averages of data . . . fluctuate so widely that consecutive averages of two overlapping five-year periods, having four out of five years in common, can jump by nearly a third—from 2.3 percent to 3.0 percent" (Heller papers, Wage-Price Guidelines, Box 24, January 23, 1964, 3). In March, George Meany, president of the AFL-CIO, attacked the wage guideposts. In May, the AFL-CIO rejected them.

286. The Bank had increased the rate from 4 to 5 percent on February 27.

287. Harold Wilson had been elected prime minister in October. At once, he announced expansive policies and nationalization, but he did not devalue the pound. Within a few weeks, he regretted not having done so. To stem the initial outflow, the government put a 5 percent surtax on imports and sold foreign exchange to support the currency. On November 19, Johnson had a message from Wilson asking for U.S. support. The U.K. had only $300 million of reserves left. Wilson said he planned to raise the discount rate from 5 to 7 percent, but he wanted assurance that the Federal Reserve would not move first. The IMF voted not to lend the U.K. $1 billion. Johnson offered to help with the IMF loan (Johnson Recordings of Telephone Conversations, November 19, 1964, with Don Cook). Johnson later talked to Ackley. Both opposed an increase in U.S. discount rates. If the Federal Reserve acted, they wanted an announcement that it was done for international, not domestic reasons. The administration also got the IMF to make the British loan (Recording of Telephone Conversation, Johnson to Ackley, November 22, 1964).

In fact, Martin told the governor of the Bank of England that he could not commit the reserve banks, but "he personally would favor an increase" (ibid., 3). Over the weekend, he talked to the presidents to tell them about the British decision. Boston and New York planned to raise their discount rates that day. Martin proposed that the Board increase regulation Q ceiling rates. After a lengthy discussion, the Board raised ceiling rates to 4 percent for time deposits with less than ninety days maturity and 4.5 percent for long-term deposits. On a split vote, with Mitchell absent, it kept the rate on savings deposits at 4 percent.[288]

The same afternoon, November 23, the Board approved a 0.5 percentage point increase to 4 percent in discount rates at Boston, New York, Chicago, Philadelphia, and St. Louis. The vote was five to one, with Mitchell absent and Robertson opposed. Robertson said that "he saw no economic justifications for raising the rate in this country. The effect on the domestic economy could be potentially bad . . . [and] would not stem an outflow of funds" (Board Minutes, November 23, 1964, 24). He added that it would have a negative effect, and he accused his colleagues of acting because it was easier to tighten policy at that time. Shephardson and Daane disagreed. The action helped the British, they said; by protecting against an outflow here, it encouraged an outflow from countries with payments surpluses. Within a week all reserve banks were at 4 percent.[289]

288. Earlier the Board missed a possible opportunity to reduce the harmful effect of interest rate ceilings. It replied to a question from Senator Willis Robertson about the Board's response to recommendations made by the President's Committee on Financial Institutions, appointed as part of the administration's response to the Commission on Money and Credit. One recommendation continued the prohibition against payment of interest on demand deposits. The other proposed changing the ceiling rate on time deposits to stand-by authority and extending regulation to other deposit-taking institutions (Board Minutes, April 13, 1964, 8). Governor Mills opposed stand-by authority, and Governor Mitchell thought the timing was bad. The question arose because the Comptroller of the Currency (James Saxon) opposed any controls, including stand-by authority. The chairman of the Home Loan Bank Board opposed any changes that would reduce the advantage of thrifts over banks. Governors Robertson, Shephardson, and Daane favored a stand-by arrangement but did not want to implement it at that time (ibid., April 29, 1964, 11–13). Chairman Martin favored removing the ceiling entirely. He would accept the stand-by authority but not implement it until "the first reasonable opportunity" (ibid., 15–16). The letter to Senator Robertson reflected this hesitation. The Board recognized "the desirability of moving toward freer markets . . . [but also believed] that unrestrained rate competition could, at times like the present, lead to undesirable consequences in terms of financial soundness and liquidity" (Board Minutes, May 12, 1964, letter, Martin to Robertson). Another mistake!

289. House Banking Chairman Wright Patman complained to the president about the increase, but the president dismissed his complaint because the change had been made to support the dollar against a run. The president added: "Of course, I regret any increase in credit costs at this time" (letter, President to Wright Patman, December 10, 1964, WHCF, Box 282, LBJ Library).

International concerns dictated the timing and the magnitude of the rate increase, but many on the FOMC wanted to raise interest rates, as Robertson suggested. However, Daane had voted against any increase only two weeks before the press release and voted yes this time because the public statement attributed the discount rate increase to international concerns. The increase in maximum regulation Q rates was made to assure "that the flow of savings through commercial banks remains ample for the financing of domestic investment" (Board Minutes, November 23, 1964, 2, press release). This was one of very few occasions when the System, acceding to administration urging, announced a discount rate increase for international reasons.

Ackley did not share the administration's view. In a memo to the president he described the increases as "unwelcome," but he gave credit to Martin's "excellent and unprecedented press conference" for limiting the immediate response of interest rates[290] (memo, Ackley to President, Heller papers, November 24, 1964). Ackley added: "Even these small increases in interest rates have some significance . . . [T]he higher discount rate will cost us production and jobs in 1965. . . . Some academic studies suggest that *losses for 1965 could run as high as $1 billion in GNP and 100,000 jobs*" (ibid., 2; emphasis in the original). He urged a more expansive fiscal policy to offset the rate increase. The administration proposed and Congress approved excise tax rate reduction on autos and air conditioners, effective May 15, 1965. And he wanted the Federal Reserve to announce that the discount rate increase was temporary and would be reversed soon (memo, Ackley to the president, CF, Box 43, November 22, 1964, 2).

The rise in the U.K. bank rate and earlier tax increases stopped the outflow temporarily. The Bank of England, Federal Reserve, and the Treasury arranged $3 billion of emergency assistance, announced on the following day (November 25). The funds came from the U.S. Export-Import Bank, ten central banks in Europe, Canada, and Japan, and an expanded Federal Reserve swap line. The new loan was an addition to a $1 billion loan from

290. Gardner Ackley replaced Walter Heller as chairman of the Council of Economic Advisers on November 16, 1964. Ackley had been a member of the Council since August 1962. Ackley's value judgments fit closely with Johnson's. He described his views on inflation and unemployment: "Those who sympathize with the least well off, I expect, put a higher value on employment." He clearly included himself (Hargrove and Morley, 1984, 234). He expressed less concern about inflation. It affected people "whose wealth and income are associated with the ownership of fixed income securities. They tend to be fairly well off" (ibid., 234). (At the time, the steelworkers union pension fund invested all of its assets in government bonds.) Ackley's memo suggests that, despite earlier Keynesian beliefs, he now believed that monetary actions were extremely potent. Martin held the press conference to satisfy President Johnson, who reacted strongly to the news (Bremner, 2004, 158).

the IMF on November 20. This display of international cooperation and support helped the Bank of England stabilize the exchange rate (Solomon, 1982, 88–89).

Once again, the problem remained because cooperation tried to stabilize a nominal exchange rate without recognizing that the real exchange rate was misaligned. The choice for Britain was deflation or devaluation. As expected in these circumstances, success was temporary. The pound experienced repeated runs until Britain devalued in 1967.[291]

In early December 1964 Martin met with Prime Minister Wilson, Secretary Dillon, and President Johnson at the White House. Martin criticized both British and American balance of payments policies, telling President Johnson that overseas commitments would eventually force devaluation of the dollar. He urged the president "to declare yourself [against devaluation] . . . It is important that the whole world know where you stand on this basic question" (quoted in Bremner, 2004, 159). Secretary Dillon surprised the president by agreeing that the United States had not done enough.

The loans and interest rate increases gave the pound a brief period of calm. Some of the November loans came due in May, so speculation resumed in March. Secretary Dillon told the president that speculators believed the Wilson government would not have a contractive budget in April and that the pound would be devalued. Dillon wanted to avoid a British devaluation out of concern for a subsequent attack on the dollar, but he could accept a reduction to $2.50 (from $2.80) because of recent improvements in the U.S. balance (memo, Douglas Dillon to the president, March 27, 1965, Confidential Files, Box 49, LBJ Library).[292] Ackley opposed devalu-

---

291. Less than ten months later, August 5, 1965, Johnson again discussed British problems with Martin. Johnson feared that a British devaluation would put pressure on the United States to devalue.

> Martin: We don't want them to devalue, but we simply can't go on bailing them out if they are not going to actively take steps to help themselves. . . . We have to put all the pressure we can on them, but if they say they can't do it, there is no point in our going to underwrite them without anything to back it up. . . .
>
> Johnson: . . . we have to ask how we can protect the dollar because it became clear some time ago that they are not going to protect the pound.

Johnson, Recordings of Telephone Conversation with William McC. Martin, August 5, 1965. Between 1959 and 1964, prices in the U.K. (GNP deflator) increased by 28 percent, in the United States by 7.7 percent. If the nominal exchange rate was appropriate in 1958–59, it was overvalued in 1964 (data from Federal Reserve Bank of St. Louis, 1978). Consumer prices for 1957 to 1964 show an increase of 18.9 percent for the U.K. and 9.2 percent for the U.S. (Council of Economic Advisers 1971, 306).

292. The U.S. estimated that about this time, the U.K. had $2.5 billion in reserves plus $1.25 billion in dollar securities and a $300 million IMF drawing balance. Against this $4 billion, it had monetary liabilities equal to more than $11 billion. The balance of payments

ation, "It can be avoided. But I see serious danger in telling that it cannot under any circumstances be permitted" (memo, Ackley to the president, July 29, 1965, National Security Files, Box 215, LBJ Library). The danger was that the United States would have to offer "unilateral support of the pound" (ibid., 2). The State Department favored support.

Early in 1965, Dillon resigned. The president appointed Undersecretary Henry Fowler as his replacement.[293] Dillon's departure was a blow to Martin. The two held similar views about inflation and the balance of payments. Both had worked well with President Kennedy, who accepted much of their advice. Dillon's departure and Johnson's manner and attitudes may have made Martin consider his own status. Moreover, Gardner Ackley was a very strict Keynesian who did not approve of central bank independence. On February 8, 1965, Martin prepared a handwritten letter tendering his resignation, but he did not submit it (Martin papers, February 8, 1965). A month later, he told the president that he wanted to leave, but the president said he had lost Douglas Dillon and could not lose him also (Bremner, 2004, 161–62).

End of Non-inflationary Growth

The year 1965 was the transition from one of the best four-year periods in U.S. experience to years of inflation and slow growth. It was the last year of strong productivity growth and the first year of rising inflation. See charts 3.1 and 3.3 above. The four-quarter average rate of increase in the GNP deflator rose from 1.5 to 3 percent. The consumer price index began the year rising at a 1 percent annual rate. It ended at 2 percent: a twelve-month moving average of the CPI rate of increase did not fall below 2 percent in the next twenty years.[294] The unemployment rate fell from 5 percent at the start of the year to 4 percent at the end.

To administration economists with their firm belief in the Phillips curve, the increase in inflation was the price paid for lower unemployment. They were willing to pay the price, reluctant to tighten policy. Martin and several of his colleagues on the FOMC held a very different view. They were more concerned about inflation and the balance of payments.

Until 1965, the United States balance of payments had improved and

---

remained in deficit. The Wilson budget in April 1965 imposed taxes on consumer spending and relied mainly on incomes policy to reduce inflation (memo, the U.K. Balance of Payments Crisis, March 27, 1965, National Security File, Box 215, LBJ Library).

293. Fowler had played an important role in organizing business support for the tax cut. He had served in government in the Roosevelt and Truman administrations.

294. Chart 3.4 above shows that change in the federal funds rate is much smaller than the change in the inflation rate for the next several years. Real short-term rates fell.

not just because of the visible capital controls and military purchases at home. Chart 3.11 (above) shows the increase in the current account surplus. Part of the improvement was a response to the lower inflation rate at home compared to inflation abroad (Chart 3.12). The beginning of domestic inflation coincides with the decline in the current account surplus.[295]

The administration made the first of several errors. Early in 1965 the president's Economic Report and his other messages announced the need for further expansion and proposed a reduction in excise taxes and a "budget that will once again contribute expansionary force rather than restrictive pressure" (Council of Economic Advisers, 1965, 9). This was part of an ambitious program to achieve "the Great Society" by increasing funds for poverty programs, welfare, and training.[296] Monetary policy could contribute by continuing to hold up short-term interest rates to stem a capital outflow, while lowering long-term rates to encourage expansion (ibid., 105–6).[297] The president also asked for repeal of the 25 percent gold reserve requirement against deposit liabilities of reserve banks (ibid., 12).

The administration's concern for fiscal stimulus came despite a decline in unemployment to 4.8 percent in January 1965 and a reported 7.5 percent annual increase in industrial production in 1964, a year with a major automobile strike. These and other signs of strength should have

295. In December 1964, Secretary Dillon sent the president the most positive report on the balance of payments in several years. After reporting about $1 billion smaller deficit in 1964, Dillon wrote: "Our technical experts foresee further limited gains in 1965, bringing the deficit on regular transactions slightly under $2 billion. If realized, that would be the smallest deficit since the balance of payments became a problem in 1958" (memo, Douglas Dillon to the president, December 9, 1964, Confidential Files, Box 49, LBJ Library). Dillon noted that about $1 billion had come from restrictions on purchases—$500 million from tying aid, $300 million from reduced defense spending abroad, and $200 million from reduced purchases by the Atomic Energy Commission. He recommended renewal of the interest equalization tax, continuation of limits on duty-free tourist expenditures, and, as possible further steps, a tax on tourists' foreign expenditures and restrictions on bank lending.

296. Johnson thought of the Great Society as an effort to restructure society "more concerned with the quality of their goals than with the quantity of their goods" (quoted in Goodwin, 1991, 211). President Johnson's ambitions for the Great Society went beyond growth of output or redistribution. Goodwin (ibid., 218) contrasts this elevated aim with the actual accomplishments. "There seemed to be few among the principal officers of government who were trying to determine how the programs could be made actually to work. The standard of success was the passage of the law—and not only within the administration, but in the press and among the public." Goodwin (ibid., 220) added that President Johnson was "unable to foresee the possibility of resentment based, not on objection to his social goals . . . , but on hostility to the implicit assertion of increased central authority to define the general welfare and confer benevolences which . . . should not be imposed by presidential will." Between 1965 and 1968, the government created five hundred new social programs (ibid., 287).

297. The Board's Annual Report gave data on purchases of long-term securities in 1964 as $1 billion. It estimated that this was 2 percent of purchases of long-term securities by all market participants.

suggested that additional stimulus was unnecessary, but administration economists did not interpret them that way.[298] Reports of a large increase in the payments deficit at the end of 1964 gave evidence that the interest equalization tax had shifted a large part of foreign borrowing to banking markets not subject to the tax. The first quarter increase in the deflator, 4.9 percent at annual rate, gave a second warning. This was the largest quarterly increase in eight years. The gold outflow in January gave an additional warning. At $263 million, it was twice the amount of gold sales for the entire year of 1964. Outflows continued in February and March, reaching a record $832 million for the first quarter and $1.664 billion for the calendar year.[299] About half the outflow went to France.

If the push for additional stimulus was the first mistake made that year, it was not the last. More consequential were the effort in midsummer to hide the increase in military spending to support the Vietnam War and, late in the year, public pressure on the Federal Reserve to prevent any increase in interest rates.[300] The Federal Reserve chafed under administration pressure, but it permitted annual growth of the monetary base to reach 5.9 percent by December, the highest twelve-month growth rate since early 1952. Chart 3.16 shows the surge in real output and money. A policy that gave attention to the sustained rate of money growth would have seen the pressure for inflation after 1967.

The Federal Reserve did very little during the first half of the year. Treasury borrowing required "even keel" operations much of the time. That contributed to, but it cannot alone explain, the cautious, hesitant response. Four reasons stand out.

First, Martin wanted the FOMC to reach a consensus before it acted. He often waited, thinking that discussion, events, and perhaps collegiality would help form the consensus. But Governors Mitchell and Robertson persistently opposed tighter policy. On April 30 Sherman Maisel, an economics professor from the University of California at Berkeley, joined the Board, replacing Mills.[301] Maisel usually voted with Mitchell and Rob-

298. A memo from Ackley to Johnson acknowledged the rapid advance, "but *the current strength is partly temporary,* reflecting accumulation of steel inventories and the catch-up in autos. . . . *There is room—In fact, urgent need—for rapid expansion throughout this year* (memo, Ackley to the president, Background for Thursday "Quadriad": the Case Against Tight Money," February 9, 1965, Confidential Files, Box 49, LBJ Library; emphasis in the original).

299. The gold outflow includes an additional subscription to the IMF.

300. Charles Schultze wrote a memo to his staff instructing them not to discuss the budget with Federal Reserve officials. He told the president, "I am afraid that *the budgetary outlook would be used as an excuse to tighten up on monetary policy*" (memo, Schultze to the president, Schultze Papers, WHCF, October 4, 1965).

301. Maisel was the first academic economist appointed to the Board since Adolph Miller, who served from 1914 to 1936. Maisel was an expert on housing finance. He remained until

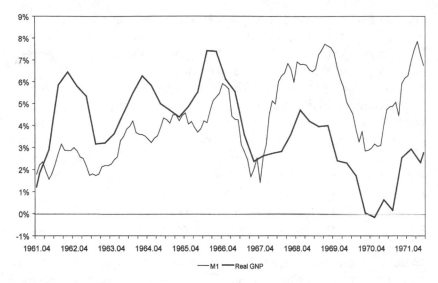

Chart 3.16. Twelve-month moving average of M_1 growth and four-quarter moving average of real GNP growth, 1961:2–1971:3.

ertson. Later, after the president appointed Andrew Brimmer to replace Canby Balderston, Martin was never certain when he would have a majority of the Board. He hesitated to act with a majority of FOMC if it did not include a majority of the Board.

Second, and most important, Martin believed he had a duty to prevent inflation and maintain the dollar's value. This belief clashed with his firm belief that the Federal Reserve was independent within government. If an elected administration proposed and Congress approved budget deficits, the Federal Reserve had to help finance part of them. He did not choose to undermine decisions of elected officials and legislators. Instead, he sacrificed independence.

Third, "policy coordination" added to the problem. Independence "within the government" suggested that monetary, fiscal, and other administration policies should seek the same objectives and attach similar weights to employment, price stability, and the payments deficit. This did not happen. Martin did not accept the mistaken idea that policymakers

---

1972, when he returned to Berkeley. I am greatly indebted to Governor Maisel for giving me use of the private diary that he maintained throughout his tenure at the Board. Other changes at about this time were the appointment of Frederick Deming as Treasury Undersecretary for Monetary Affairs. Hugh Galusha replaced Deming as president of the Minneapolis federal reserve bank. Robert Stone resigned as manager of the System Open Market Account to become an officer of a commercial bank. His successor was Alan R. Holmes, who had worked as his deputy.

could maintain a welfare-maximizing inflation rate that lowered unemployment to the socially desirable minimum. He expressed much greater concern about inflation and the balance of payments than President Johnson or his advisers.[302] When Douglas Dillon left the administration, Martin lost a powerful ally inside. He had earlier lost a president who paid attention to his warnings and acquired one with entrenched populist views who hated "high" interest rates (Bernstein, 1996, 364).

Policy coordination ensnared Martin in administration policy. He willingly sacrificed part of the Federal Reserve's independence for the opportunity to be part of the economic "team," make his views known to the president, and coordinate policy actions.[303] Inevitably he compromised by surrendering some independence of action to coordinate policies. His offer to resign in February 1965 possibly reflected recognition that coordination with President Johnson and his advisers would be costly to Federal Reserve independence and to the country. Although he warned the country about inflation many times, he accepted reappointment in 1967 and remained until his term ended in 1970 without implementing the policy actions that he favored to achieve price stability and protect the gold stock.

President Johnson's main argument in 1965 was that coordination required Martin to wait until he announced the 1967 budget estimates in January 1966, but he refused to give accurate estimates. In November 1965, the working estimate called for $105 billion of total spending in fiscal 1967. By mid-January estimated spending had increased to $106.4 billion for fiscal 1966 and $112.8 billion for 1967, but the 1967 estimate assumed that ordinary spending for the Vietnam War ended in December 1966. That held defense spending to $57 billion.[304] Actual spending was $114.8 billion and $137.0 billion in fiscal 1966 and 1967,

302. During the 1964 expansion without increased inflation, Martin told Heller that he had been wrong to think that the tax cut "would quickly fire up, not to say overheat the economy." According to Heller, Martin offered to "cooperate with CEA—he always has . . . , but [he] was particularly warm and insistent about it" (memo, Walter Heller to the president, July 17, 1964, WHCF, Box 282, LBJ Library).

303. Opportunities for coordination between the Treasury, the Council, and the Federal Reserve at this time included: (1) a Monday lunch at the Treasury with the secretary and Treasury staff followed by an informal meeting between Martin, the secretary, and the undersecretary for monetary affairs; (2) every other Thursday, the secretary met with Ackley, Budget Director Kermit Gordon, and a second member of the Council; (3) meetings of the Quadriad, with the president; and (4) regular meetings of the Cabinet Committee on the Balance of Payments, at which Martin and Governor Robertson participated. Minutes were kept only for the last of these.

304. This was Defense Secretary Robert McNamara's proposal. Johnson complained that the Federal Reserve interest rate increase cost him $600 million, hardly a major item in a $112 billion budget estimate that underestimated spending by $25 billion. McNamara's proposal financed ordinary department spending and all the long lead items for the full

and defense spending reached $58 billion and $71 billion in the two years (Recording of Telephone Conversation with Robert McNamara, December 20, 1965, 9326, Johnson tapes).

Fourth, of lesser importance,[305] the Federal Reserve staff and several of the members denied for several years that inflation had either begun or increased. They did not deny the numbers they saw. Like Gardner Ackley, they gave special explanations. The most common was a relative price theory of the general price level, in effect claiming that the rise in the price level resulted from one-time, transitory changes that they did not expect to repeat. Later, they added other explanations, especially that the cause of inflation had changed from the classic "demand pull" to the new "cost-push." This reasoning at first claimed cost-push effects as a temporary result of slowly adjusting inflationary expectations. Later it exempted the Federal Reserve (and other central banks) from responsibility and suggested that the problem was not monetary. Governor Sherman Maisel (1973, 284), a forceful exponent of this view, presented the main idea:

> In a period of general stability, a strong union or a monopolistic or oligopolistic group of companies may try to increase their income. If they have enough power, they can do so even though unemployment exists elsewhere. It is theoretically possible that other prices would fall as they raise their prices, but this is unlikely in most modern economies, where wages and prices are too rigid to react to minor increases in unemployment. In fact, the opposite occurs. Workers in industries with somewhat lower demand will strive for higher wages also . . . [S]ince profits are generally not that large, over time any increase in wages must show up in higher prices.

The economy had not acted that way in 1961–64. But even if modern economies acted as Maisel described, his discussion explains why the price level would be higher. It does not explain why prices would continue to increase or increase at a rising rate. Failure to distinguish between a change in price or wage level and a maintained rate of change hindered clear thinking about inflation. Sometimes inflation meant any price level increase. Elsewhere it meant a sustained rate of increase. Since one-time price level increases often took place over time, it was easy, but misleading, to mix the two.

---

fiscal year but omitted estimates for increased manpower in Vietnam and other operating expenditures.

305. I regard the interpretation error as of lesser importance because I believe Chairman Martin would not have responded differently if the staff had correctly interpreted price changes. Martin was often considered an alarmist, long before 1965 and after. Despite his concerns and fears, he did not act decisively.

Table 3.11   Interest rates and free reserves, January–June 1965

DATE	FEDERAL FUNDS RATE (PERCENT)	FREE RESERVES ($ MILLIONS)	DATE	TREASURY BILL RATE (PERCENT)	GOVERNMENT BOND RATE (PERCENT)
1/6	4.00	432	1/2	3.87	4.16
2/10	4.00	57	2/6	3.88	4.15
3/24	4.09	−161	3/27	3.92	4.14
6/30	4.13	−82	6/26	3.79	4.13

Source: Board of Governors (1976).

The sustained rate of price increase could not continue without an increase in money or its rate of use (velocity). Maisel recognized that without an increase in money, cost-push price increases were limited. He wrote (ibid., 285) that the principal reason prices continued to increase was "the unwillingness, for valid economic and political reasons, to allow the economy to suffer the necessary recession or depression which would accompany a policy of not expanding money because incomes are being pushed up from the cost side." Then he added a critical sentence (ibid., 285): "The level of unemployment required to stabilize prices . . . is higher than that which the economy finds acceptable."

This popular explanation worked with other features of the Federal Reserve's approach, such as coordination, support for deficit finance, and failure to distinguish between real and nominal rates. No single person may have held all of these views. The ideas worked together to get inflation—sustained rates of price increase—started and permitted it to continue.[306]

FOMC met eight times during the first half of 1965. It voted twice for "slightly firmer" policy, on February 2 and March 23. Governors Mitchell and Robertson opposed both changes, joined by President Clay (Kansas City) in March. Table 3.11 shows that free reserves and the federal funds rate responded to the changes, but other interest rates declined slightly during the first half year.[307]

At almost every meeting, there are references to expanding activity, ris-

306. The cost-push explanation failed to explain why inflation fell in the 1980s and remained low in the 1990s. An alternative explanation does much better. Once the public learned that policymakers would act to prevent a rise in unemployment, they anticipated, correctly as it turned out, that anti-inflation policy would cease soon after unemployment started to increase. Wages and costs became more rigid downward, necessitating a larger and more prolonged increase in unemployment to break the expectation. See Cukierman and Meltzer (1986) for a model of central banking with the appropriate features.

307. Martin described the proposed reduction of $50 million in free reserves voted at the March 23 meeting as "so slight that it was difficult to say whether such a change would have any real effect" (FOMC Minutes, March 23, 1965, 98). At the May 25 meeting, FOMC voted to maintain policy unchanged. Hayes, Balderston, Ellis, and Shephardson dissented. They wanted additional firming. Martin did not support them.

ing prices, rapid credit expansion, or an increasing payments deficit. Difficulties in separating persistent and temporary changes, such as anticipation of rising prices or inventory building in anticipation of a steel strike, reduced the impact of the observations. The administration put on additional controls to reduce the foreign payment outflow, supporting those who wished to put responsibility for the gold loss on the administration and away from monetary policy.

The FOMC remained divided during the spring. At the May 25 meeting, Chairman Martin summarized his policy view. According to the minutes, "His own thinking probably tended in the direction of the group favoring firming, although no one could be sure about the appropriate timing. He was becoming increasingly worried about both the balance of payments and the possibility of domestic inflation. His views were not firm on either point" (FOMC Minutes, May 25, 1965, 62).

His colleagues must have been surprised when he spoke at the Columbia University commencement a week later. His speech compared the economic situation in 1965 to 1928–29. He pointed to similarities and differences. He did not claim that the country faced a serious inflation threat. His concerns were financial weakness and speculation. The press and stock market speculators emphasized the alleged similarities with 1929, not the differences. Industrial stock prices fell 5.4 percent in the next five weeks and did not pass their previous peak for four months.[308]

In the spring, the Treasury was concerned about a possible slowdown of economic growth.[309] During the summer a new problem slowly emerged. Beginning in July 1965, President Johnson expanded the resource and financial commitment to the Vietnam War by announcing the sending of additional troops. The president did not let the members of the Council or Treasury officials know the actual size of planned spending increases.[310]

308. In 1996, Chairman Alan Greenspan gave a speech warning about the risks in the stock market with similar effect. Like Martin, Greenspan took no action suggesting that markets should take the warning as a signal that policy would change. Some main parallels with 1928–29 that Martin criticized were proposals to devalue the dollar against gold and France's reluctance to allow its gold inflow to raise spending and prices.

309. Bach, 1971, 121. Real GNP growth slowed from 9 to 5.9 percent between the first and second quarter! Third quarter growth was 6.5 percent. Heller reported that in June the president, the Council, and others began to discuss "whether we shouldn't have some sort of little income tax cut at the bottom of the scale for the lower income people" (Heller Oral History, tape II, 41).

310. Ackley (Ackley Oral History, tape II, Johnson papers, March 7, 1974, 13–14) denied that President Johnson and Defense Secretary Robert McNamara knew "what it was going to cost and they just weren't telling. It was not a plot to deceive people" (ibid., 14). Later Ackley reconsidered. "There was a period of a couple of months—six weeks maybe—in the summer in which there was, I think, a deliberate effort not to let anybody know what was going on.

Martin learned from Senator Richard Russell, as early as July, that the budget deficit would be much larger than Johnson admitted to the Treasury, the Council, or the Quadriad. "I had better information than the Treasury had. . . . I went to the President, oh, I'd say four or five times and laid them out to him" (oral history, Martin papers, May 8, 1987, 1–2).[311]

Johnson did not want to reduce spending, raise tax rates, or have the Federal Reserve raise interest rates. Martin described the conversation.

<hr />

But the people in Defense knew it, and the people in Budget and the Council did not know it" (Hargrove and Morley, 1984, 249). Johnson (1971, 149) explained the secrecy as an attempt to prevent Russia and China from supplying additional support to North Vietnam. The president told Senator John Stennis, "When you say it is going to cost us $10 billion there . . . the first thing Ho Chi Minh does, he takes your statement . . . and he says to Mr. Kosygin: "Look here's what those damn Yankees are putting in . . . now how much are you going to put in?" (Recording of Telephone Conversation with John Stennis, August 18, 1965, Recording and Transcripts of Conversations, LBJ Library). Califano (2000, 34–36) confirms this explanation and adds the president's unwillingness to open the issue of inflation and price controls when they were not needed. Secretary of Defense Robert McNamara estimated the one-year cost as $8 billion (ibid., 37).

One difficulty with this explanation is that although precise costs were hidden, much of the information about escalation was either publicly announced or known to many people. President Johnson's account of this period (1971, 141–53) describes a press conference in July 1965 at which he announced that, on the recommendation of General William Westmoreland, he was increasing troops in Vietnam to 125,000 (ibid., 153). In April, the authorized number was 40,000 (ibid., 141). Also, in July he met with eleven members of the congressional leadership in both parties and discussed his options in Vietnam and his decision. He told them that costs would increase, although he did not report an amount.

Budget Director Charles Schultze made a determined effort to keep Federal Reserve officials from knowing planned spending and the deficit. "I have instructed my staff *not* to discuss the budgetary outlook with the Fed. Quite apart from security considerations I am afraid that *the* budgetary outlook would be used as an excuse to tighten up on monetary policy" (memo, Schultze to the president, October 4, 1965, WHCF, Box 22, LBJ Library; emphasis in the original). This is a striking example of why "coordination" became a one-way influence on the Federal Reserve to reduce its independence.

311. Senator Richard Russell was chairman of the Senate Armed Services Committee. Martin suggests in his oral history that Russell learned it from the Defense Department. Other sources suggest that Undersecretary of Defense David Packard informed Martin. Both may be correct. Dewey Daane reported, "There was uneasiness [in July]. Martin had some sort of pipeline to undersecretary David Packard. I had a gut feeling that the figures were going to accelerate a lot more and said so at the meeting. Martin called me into his office and said, 'You know, I've been talking to David Packard and you're right . . . These things are going to go way beyond what the administration has admitted'" (Hargrove and Morley, 1984, 249). At about this time, Ackley warned President Johnson that only if defense spending increased by $10 billion should they consider higher tax rates. He described this as "remote" and assured the president that Defense Secretary McNamara assured him that he planned "a gradual and moderate build-up of expenditures and manpower." He concluded: "It is now less likely that you will want to recommend a tax cut next year. But it remains a possibility that shouldn't be ruled out" (memo, Ackley to the president, July 30, 1965, WHCF, Box 23, LBJ Library, 3, 4). A month later, he reported a 1.9% annual rate of increase in consumer prices, but "the evidence does not point to any real inflation in the months ahead" (ibid., August 25, 1965, 3).

> He [President Johnson] didn't want any increase in rates and he wanted
> me to assure him that there wouldn't be. I couldn't do that, of course. I had
> already made up my mind that we needed an increase in rates. So I did my
> best to break this to him as gently as possible but wasn't so very successful
> in that he was absolutely convinced that I was trying to raise the rate and pull
> the rug out from under him. I said "Mr. President you know that I wouldn't
> do that to you even if I could." He said, "Well I'm afraid you can." And I said,
> "Well, I want to tell you right now that if I can [raise the rate] I will, because I
> think you're just on the wrong course. I've been perfectly fair with you. I was
> over here early this year." (Martin papers, Interview I, May 8, 1987, 9).

Despite increases in long-term rates in August and September, no action
followed for several months. In July, Ellis (Boston) dissented because he
wanted a firmer policy. In late August, Trieber (New York) did the same.
Martin "was in complete agreement with the consensus . . . for no change
in policy" (FOMC Minutes, August 31, 1965, 68). Hayes argued for a
tighter policy in September including a discount rate increase. Balderston,
Shephardson, and Ellis (Boston) favored a discount rate increase after the
Treasury completed its financing. Martin did not think the timing was
right. The vote was nine to three for no change. Maisel, Mitchell, and Robertson dissented because interest rates had increased despite a policy of no
change. They wanted policy ease to roll back the increase.

At a Quadriad meeting early in October, Ackley and Fowler urged Martin to delay any increase in interest rates until the evidence was clearer.
Ackley proposed waiting until January, when the new budget data became
available. Fowler argued that "risks of tightening are greater than the risks
of overstaying present policies." He called the danger of overheating "tenuous," and he wanted the administration to oppose changes in the prime
rate (memo, Fowler to the president, October 6, 1965, Confidential Files,
Box 41, LBJ Library, 1–2).

Martin's memo for the Quadriad meeting tried to shift discussion from
interest rates to credit growth. He noted that regulation Q ceiling rates
caused credit to flow outside the banking system, and he warned of "rising expectations, evidenced in financial markets and real investment." A
slight increase in interest rates would help to extend the expansion and
improve the balance of payments (memo, Martin to the president, ibid.,
October 6, 1965).

Martin's views did not prevail. A week later at the FOMC, he read his
memo to the president. FOMC members split. Some agreed with Martin
but wanted to wait for the Treasury to complete its financing. Others opposed because they saw no sign of inflation. Faced with a divided commit-

tee and administration opposition, Martin not only did not insist, he voted against an increase. This was not a new position. He had delayed acting in 1957 to wait for consensus. After warning the committee about the danger of waiting too long, he explained why the FOMC should not change policy. He made no mention of Federal Reserve independence.

> As Chairman, he had the responsibility for maintaining System relations within the Government—for getting the thinking of the President and members of the Administration, and for apprising them of the thinking within the Committee—and he had made that one of his principal concerns during the fourteen years he had held his present office. Last week he had given the President a paper expressing his personal views . . . [H]e had talked with the Chairman of the Council of Economic Advisers, with Treasury officials, and with the President. They had all expressed the view that it would be unwise to change monetary policy now. The President had not taken a rigid position on the matter—he had not suggested that the Committee should abdicate its responsibility for formulating monetary policy . . . At the moment, however, the Administration was strongly opposed to a change in policy. . . . With a divided Committee and in the face of strong Administration opposition he did not believe it would be appropriate for him to lend his support to those who favored a change in policy now. (FOMC Minutes, October 12, 1965, 68–69)

The president was not much concerned about Martin's warnings about spending and the deficit. He spent much of the fall of 1965 pushing enactment of new spending programs for education and the environment (Califano, 2000, 70, 81).

In September, Martin had agreed to let the Federal Reserve staff participate in a joint effort with the staffs of the other Quadriad members to study where the economy was headed.[312] The report in November concluded that the Federal Reserve "should not tighten for the remainder of the year" and reconsider action when the budget and GNP estimate for 1966 became known (Okun oral history, tape I, 24). Monetary tightening should wait for

---

312. The staff members were Daniel Brill, Federal Reserve, Charles Zwick, Bureau of the Budget, Paul Volcker, Treasury, and Arthur Okun, Council of Economic Advisers. Martin not only rejected the report, he suppressed it. Members did not receive copies, and we could not find a copy in the Federal Reserve's records. Okun recorded that Governor Maisel "testified in pain some months later that he'd just found out about its existence, and he had never seen it" (Okun oral history, tape I, 25). Okun records Brill as saying: "'I'll bet we've made monetary policy for the rest of the year. . . . A lot of guys on the Board are predisposed not to take action anyway; it gives them a good consensus excuse'" (Okun oral history, tape I, 25). Maisel's diary (December 3, 1965) records his anger at learning that Martin suppressed the report. He testified at a congressional hearing, angering Martin.

Table 3.12   Growth of M_1 and M_2 in 1965[a] (percent, annual rate)

	YEAR	1Q	2Q	3Q	4Q
M_1	4.8	1.5	3.8	6.2	7.6
M_2	16.0	17.4	11.5	16.8	15.0

[a]preliminary data available at the time.

GNP to reach $720 billion, a 5 percent increase from 1965 and almost two percentage points above the standard forecast (ibid., 24).[313]

Martin knew that the budget estimates understated the increase in defense spending and that Johnson had suppressed the planned increase. He knew also that contrary to standard practice, the Budget Bureau would not discuss the budgetary projections with him or his staff. Martin distrusted President Johnson and was inclined to give more attention to markets than to economists' forecasts.[314] Government bond yields began to rise in August and had increased twenty basis points by mid-November to the highest level since 1960. This was a large increase by the standards of the time.

Too little, too late. On November 4, the Treasury's issue of eighteen-month 4.25 percent notes was not well received, allegedly because of concerns about rumors of increased spending for Vietnam. Between August 1 and December 1, yields on three- to five-year Treasury issues rose forty-two basis points to 4.52 percent (Annual Report, 1965, 190). In the month of November, the System bought $5.5 billion of one- to five-year securities, mainly the new note issue, and sold Treasury bills or let them run off.

The market had signaled that interest rates should rise. With few brief exceptions, the federal funds rate had remained above the discount rate since March. Data available at the time showed rapid growth in the monetary aggregates (Table 3.12).

313. Actual GNP reached $749.9, a 9.5 percent increase of which 5.8 percent was real and 3.8 percent was inflation (deflator). The forecast error was 6 percent.

314. Martin claimed that he liked Johnson but, in his oral history, he said, "He was one of the greatest liars I've ever known, and 'liar' is the only word I can use for it because he would have no hesitation in lying about the most trivial things" (Martin oral history, tape I, 5–6). Bernstein (1996, 364) reports on the Quadriad meeting in October. "Martin wanted to know how much additional the government was going to spend, particularly by McNamara on the war." Johnson mentioned $3 to $5 billion although he knew that this was far below the planned increase. Martin said he was leaning toward higher rates. Johnson opposed an increase, saying it would hurt small farmers and businessmen. Ackley and Budget Director Charles Schultze agreed. Martin looked the president in the eye and said, "If we thought you were right, we'd all do the same thing. But the question is, whose crystal ball is right?" To lower the budget estimates, Secretary McNamara assumed the war would end on June 30, 1967. This avoided budgeting for longer-lived equipment (Califano, 2000, 111). The actual increase in defense spending was $10 billion to a total of $67 billion in fiscal 1967.

Martin had another source warning about inflation, the Federal Advisory Council. Members explained the strength of investment spending as an attempt to substitute capital for rising labor costs (Board Minutes, September 21, 1965, 3).[315] In November, the FAC repeated its September warning: "The Council is concerned with increasing evidence of the development of inflationary pressures, the continued strong demand for bank loans . . . Consequently, we believe the Board should be prepared to move in the direction of further restraint, including a tightening of reserves and an increase in the discount rate" (Board Minutes, November 16, 1965, 22).

Martin was, finally, ready to accept the challenge. The administration remained opposed.[316] At the FOMC meeting on November 23, the staff proposed that if the FOMC tightened policy, it should reduce reserve growth and keep regulation Q ceiling rates unchanged. This would force a reduction in CDs and bank credit. Hayes proposed the opposite, an increase in ceiling rates and the discount rate (Maisel diary, December 3, 1965, 3–4). Nine of the twelve presidents either opposed a discount rate increase or wanted to wait (FOMC Minutes, November 23, 1965). Martin said that the market's "expectations were just as much that the President would not allow any interest rate changes as to the contrary" (ibid., 84). Martin "wanted to raise the discount rate in order to free the interest rates from domina-

315. One member warned: "The banking system might not be able to take care of its share of the job [of lending] unless there was some adjustment in the tempo of the economy or some adjustment in the rate structure" (Board Minutes, September 21, 1965, 9). Some banks had raised prime rates earlier but rescinded the increase under pressure from the president and the Council. The Council was responsible for wage-price guidelines. The banks clearly wanted the Federal Reserve to act so that they could follow.

316. President Johnson and Secretary Fowler continued to oppose the increase. When they discussed the prospective budget deficit on November 28, Fowler warned Johnson that "if the deficit goes beyond the $8 billion level, you've got to very seriously entertain the prospect of monetary action." Johnson then told Fowler that no one knew the correct estimates except himself and Charles Schultze, the Budget Director. Fowler said: "This is the first time I've heard anything beyond $108 or $109 [billion]." Johnson told him that Schultze was trying to reduce spending from $125 to $115 billion with revenues projected to be $107 billion, or a deficit of $8 billion.

Earlier in the discussion, Johnson asked Fowler if he had thought about replacing Martin. Fowler told him that he had considered Paul Volcker, but he was unsure. "We want a sure vote, not a reasonable fellow who will try to steer us down the right path. We'll just want a fellow that just goes along" (Oval Office Conversation, Henry Fowler and Lyndon B. Johnson, tape 6511.08, LBJ Library, November 28, 1965). At about this time, Ackley sent a memo to the president warning him that "too small a budget would invite fiscal drag; one too large could propel the economy forward at a pace threatening inflationary pressures in an economy close to full utilization" (memo, Ackley to the president, November 25, 1965, WHCF, Box 1, 3). The memo also exulted that the economy had expanded more than anticipated. Despite measures of capacity utilization at 90 percent and unemployment at 4.3 percent, Ackley saw no reason for concern about inflation. The most likely reason is that he thought 4 percent was full employment and that prices would not rise until the unemployment rate was below 4 percent.

tion by the President and he was more interested in this than he was in tightening the amount of money" (Maisel diary, December 3, 1965, 15). He opposed an increase in reserve requirement ratios because he did not want to reduce availability. His aim was to show that the System had not yielded to the administration (Maisel diary, January 18, 1966, 2–3).

Maisel warned Ackley that the discount rate would increase.[317] Martin had already told him. The president was at his ranch in Texas recovering from a gall bladder operation. On November 29, the president's assistant relayed an urgent telegram from Ackley to the president in Texas warning that Martin intended to approve a discount rate increase the following week. The telegram quoted Maisel as urging the president to tell Governor Daane to oppose any increase until January (telegram, Califano to President, November 29, 1965, WHCF, Box 50, LBJ Library). A few days later Ackley followed with a memo claiming that he (Ackley) had failed to distinguish between real and nominal interest rates and arguing that the voluntary restraint program on bank lending to foreigners was an effective substitute for higher interest rates in reducing the capital outflow.[318] The president responded by inviting the Quadriad to his ranch the following Monday.

Martin decided to act before the Texas meeting. On December 3, the Board voted four to three to raise the discount rate by 0.5 percentage points at New York and Chicago. In the next ten days, all reserve banks adopted the 4.5 percent rate. Robertson, Mitchell, and Maisel dissented. Dewey Daane cast the swing vote supporting the increase. Following the vote the Board voted to increase regulation Q ceiling rates to 5.5 percent.

The opponents used a number of arguments. Robertson said that inflation was not inevitable. Higher rates might bring on recession and would raise the cost to the Treasury of marketing its debt in January (Board Minutes, December 3, 1965, 2).[319] Robertson proposed instead to (1) slow the

317. Maisel also sent a memo to the Board members opposing a discount rate increase and urging coordination with administration policy. Martin told him that this violated Board norms, a tradition against memos or caucuses outside meetings (Maisel diary, December 3, 1965, 6).

318. "Interest rates today are high—not low" (memo, Ackley to the president, December 2, 1965, WHCF, Box 50, LBJ Library).

319. This is an odd argument for a central banker to make for two reasons. First, central banks are independent to avoid the use of monetary policy to finance the government debt at concessional rates. Second, it is hard to think of any justification for delaying an interest rate increase until after the government sold its bonds. Maisel's diary (December 3, 1965, 9) complained that Martin called the Board meeting suddenly on a Friday afternoon and did not say that the discount rate increase would be on the agenda. He did not have time to prepare. Also, Martin neglected to tell the Board that Ackley had asked him to wait and told him that he would urge the president to support the increase in the State of the Union message. These

issue of bank promissory notes by making them subject to regulation Q ceiling rates;[320] and (2) allow banks to borrow reserves to cover the loss of time deposits because regulation Q ceiling rates were below market rates. In a reversion to Riefler-Burgess notions, he explained that increased borrowing "should serve to moderate somewhat the rate of advance in bank credit" (Board Minutes, December 3, 1965, 3). He also opposed increasing regulation Q ceiling rates.

Mitchell did not agree. He opposed the increase in the discount rate on political grounds. The Federal Reserve "appeared to be on a collision course with the administration" (ibid., 7) He preferred to negotiate a 0.25 percentage point increase with the administration, but he favored an increase in ceiling rates and would support a 5.5 percent rate on all maturities over fifteen days (ibid., 9).

The recovery was Maisel's main concern. He favored incomes policy to control prices and wages. "A discount rate increase . . . could be interpreted only as a vote of no-confidence by this Board in the national goal of growth at full employment" (ibid., 16). He warned the Board that the discount rate at New York had not been as high as 4.5 percent since November 1929 (ibid., 17). He dismissed current concerns about inflation. If inflation rose, the Board could act later.

Daane made the case for higher rates based on persistent price pressures, the risk of more general price increases, and the prospect that an investment boom had started. He mentioned a 10 percent increase in business fixed investment as especially troublesome. He added that he worried about "deterioration in our balance of payments not entirely papered over by changing definitions and some strenuous Governmental efforts to achieve postponement of some scheduled outflows into next year's statistics" (ibid., 11). Then he added that higher interest rates "will contribute to the relative price stability essential to the eventual resolution of our balance of payments problem" (ibid., 11).[321]

---

and other procedural complaints became public in Maisel's testimony at a hearing called by Congressman Patman.

320. The Board had discussed this issue several times. To avoid ceiling rates, reserve requirements, and deposit insurance fees, the First National Bank of Boston issued promissory notes in September 1964. The Comptroller of the Currency ruled that the action was legal. Other banks followed. Robertson proposed redefining deposits to include the notes. The FDIC staff agreed, but the Board delayed because it did not expect the Comptroller to agree, and the Comptroller was also a director of the FDIC. The Comptroller's opposition meant that he would not enforce the ruling against national banks. This would put state chartered banks at a disadvantage. All but one of the reserve banks opposed also (Board Minutes, September 14, 1965, 7–11).

321. Governor Daane's expressed concern for the balance of payments contrasts with the administration's discussions. Fowler, Ackley, and others showed no sign that the improve-

Martin spoke last. He warned about the risk to the System's independence if it acted against the president's wishes. "There is a question whether the Federal Reserve is to be run by the administration in office" (ibid., 28). He believed the Board had to show that it was independent.

The Board's announcement emphasized that it wanted to slow excessive demands for credit and maintain price stability. A news story describing the action said, "The Federal Reserve has no intention of imposing a severe 'tight money' policy that would render bank loans difficult to get" (*New York Times*, December 6, 1965, 6). Nevertheless, President Johnson criticized the decision, publicly expressing his view that it would hurt consumers and state and local governments and complaining that "the decision on interest rates should be a coordinated policy decision in January" (ibid., 31). The *New York Times* editorial supported the president on coordination while recognizing that inflationary pressures had increased and the administration had restricted its efforts to pressuring industries and firms not to raise prices (ibid., 36).

Gardner Ackley, the Council's chairman, used more pointed language (Ackley Oral History, tape II, Johnson papers, 3). But Ackley's concern was as much the breakdown of policy coordination as the increase in interest rates.[322] "The members of the Council were not entirely unsympathetic with Martin's position. We agreed that some kind of restraint was necessary. We would have much preferred a tax increase rather than tighter money. We not only clearly predicted to the President that monetary policy would tighten considerably farther, but I suppose in a sense we also had a certain amount of sympathy with what the Fed was doing, although we didn't always express that sympathy strongly or clearly in the President's presence" (ibid., 4).

Later, Ackley traced policy development under the pressure of war finance as he saw it. Johnson opposed any reduction in spending on his Great Society programs.[323] He disliked higher interest rates. That left a tax

---

ment in the balance of payments reflected the lower U.S. inflation rate and depreciation of the real exchange rate. Ackley seemed to believe that inflation was unlikely and, if it occurred, could be managed by the guideposts. I found no mention of money growth in his discussions of price increases or inflation. Although he does refer to credit growth, the context usually refers to financing business expansion. For the balance of payments, the administration relied mainly on additional "voluntary" controls on bank loans and investment. See below for discussion of voluntary restraint.

322. Ackley describes Martin as "immune to the [Johnson] treatment. He had worked him over on more than one occasion without appreciable results, and he certainly had expected people in his administration . . . to work on Martin and his Federal Reserve colleagues. I guess he came to see that Martin was just there in the way and that there wasn't any way to push him aside" (Ackley oral history, tape II, Johnson papers, 3–4).

323. "Those were his children, his babies—he used that phrase many times. Those were what he'd be remembered for" (Hargrove and Morley, 1984, 247).

increase to pay for rising costs of war and the Great Society programs. By October, Ackley claimed that the Council knew about spending increases. "It is frequently assumed that at this period the Council of Economic Advisers and perhaps other people were misinformed about some of the facts . . . about the size of prospective government expenditures . . . [W]e had all the evidence we needed to conclude without any question, certainly by November or early December, that a tax increase was absolutely necessary if we were going to avoid substantial inflation in 1966. So the proposal for a tax increase was well formulated and strongly supported by Treasury, Council, and Budget Bureau in the late fall and throughout this period" (Hargrove and Morley, 1984, 247–48).[324]

Some of the president's advisers claimed that if Martin had not raised the discount rate, the president might have asked for a tax increase early in 1966 (Okun oral history, tape I, 25).[325] Dewey Daane explained, however, that Martin knew Wilbur Mills well and "never had any sense that there was the slightest possibility of a tax increase from LBJ" (Hargrove and Morley, 1984, 252).[326] Johnson (1971, 444–45) confirms this. For Martin, coordination had become a one-way street; the Federal Reserve supported administration policies but had no support for its own concerns.[327] The president had refused to confirm what Martin knew about the budget. Inflation had started to increase, and the market people whose judgments

324. Ackley then talked about Johnson's discussion in his autobiography. Johnson reprinted one of Ackley's memos about a tax increase if the budget reached $110 or $115 billion. "I am reported as saying that the lower figure . . . very probably would require a tax increase and the higher figure certainly would. But the whole point of the exercise was that we knew damned well that neither of these figures was in the least bit accurate" (Hargrove and Morley, 1984, 248). Ackley's memos in the Johnson Library support neither his claim nor his recollection about timing. The memo to which Johnson referred was sent on December 17, two weeks after the rate increase.

325. This seems improbable. Johnson asked the chairman of the House Ways and Means Committee, Wilbur Mills, whether he would support a tax increase. Mills opposed the increase and said it would be impossible to get it through Congress. Ackley said, "My impression is that Wilbur Mills, in my presence, told him that they would not hold hearings on a tax increase bill" (Hargrove and Morley, 1984, 251).

326. In fact, the budget asked for reinstatement of some of the excise tax reductions approved in June 1965 (automobiles and telephones).

327. It was not just the president. Ackley claimed that he liked Martin, but he did not respect him or his opinions. "Martin was absolutely zero as an economist. He had no real understanding of economics" (Ackley oral history, tape II, Johnson papers, 6). Heller, who continued to advise Johnson after he left the chairmanship of the Council, regarded coordination as a way of influencing, possibly controlling, the Federal Reserve's actions. Ackley did not believe the Federal Reserve should be independent. "I would do everything I could to reduce or even eliminate the independence of the Federal Reserve" (ibid., 6). This attitude, whether or not expressed, was unlikely to make Martin think that the relation was one of equals coordinating their actions.

Martin relied on more than economists' forecasts saw this in the large increase in lending to finance war production. He took a temporary respite
from coordinated policy.[328]

The discount rate increase raised criticisms of Martin and the Federal
Reserve out of proportion to the steps they had taken. Congressman Pat-
man called for Congress to end Martin's power. Senator Paul Douglas (Il-
linois) called the action "as brutal as it was impolite," and Senator William
Proxmire (Wisconsin) said it was a blunder and demanded hearings (New
York Times, December 7, 1965, 1, 74).

The press report of the meeting at the ranch suggested that Johnson
and Martin had a difference of opinion, but the "atmosphere [at the press
conference] was suffused with sweetness" (ibid, 1). Martin's account of the
meeting was entirely different. Johnson accused him of taking advantage
of his illness and harming his presidency. "He was very disagreeable" (oral
history, tape I, Martin papers, 14). But Martin did not yield even when
Johnson swore at him. Martin's account explains why he delayed acting,
despite his June speech and his many warnings about inflation.[329]

The rate increases remained in effect. Under intense pressure, Martin
courageously maintained the Federal Reserve's right to independent action, but the action did not stop inflation or slow growth of the monetary
base. The monetary base and M_1 growth continued to increase rapidly as
the Federal Reserve attempted to moderate the impact on market rates.

Martin had not raised the discount rate to reduce money growth. At
the first FOMC meeting after the discount rate increase his concern was

328. At one point, Ackley described Johnson's attitude toward Martin. "I think in a way
he rather liked Martin, but he didn't think he was a heavyweight and he didn't fully trust him"
(Hargrove and Morley, 1984, 236).

329. Martin repeats his basic story several times. "I went to him in May, I think it was,
of that year [1965] and I said, 'Mr. President, we can't wait any longer. We're going to have
to raise the rate. It'll be too late if we wait beyond that.' He listened to that and he said, 'Well
you'll give me another chance.' I said, "I'll give you another chance but I'm warning you now.
I've got three members of my Board who are in complete agreement with me, so I've got a
majority. I want to get this out of the way. You and I have been playing with this since February. Here it is July . . . and I don't think we can play with it anymore. . . . '

"He said, 'I wanted to tell you I think you were precipitous on this.' I said, 'But, Mr. President, I warned you on this.' He said, 'Yes, you did but I never thought you'd move forward.'
'Well,' I said, 'I told you why. I couldn't wait longer, I would have liked to have raised the rate
in May. You were adamant against it then.' . . .

"And then he said, 'You took advantage of me [when I was sick]. I just want you to
know that I think that's a despicable thing to do'" (Martin oral history, tape I, Martin papers,
15–17).

By late December, the Budget Bureau and the CEA had new budget and deficit numbers.
They recognized that inflation was likely and proposed a tax surcharge delayed until spring
1966 (memo, Schultze to president, CF, Box 42, December 27, 1965).

the shock to the market from the increases in discount and ceiling rates. The FOMC agreed. Part of the market's uncertainty probably came from growing recognition that inflation had returned (Maisel diary, Summary, February 9, 1967).[330] The directive called for moderating the market's turbulence.

Instead of a restrictive policy to stop inflation, "credit was supplied between December and the end of June at record-breaking rates. The rate of increase in total reserves from December through June was at a 6.3 percent annual rate. This was four times as large as the June–November 1965 period. All other aggregate measures showed similar rates of increase" (ibid., 1).

Those who voted for the discount rate increase argued for minor restriction of credit; those who voted against the increase recognized that the administration had left the problem to the Federal Reserve. Although they believed that fiscal restraint was the preferred policy, they saw that it had not happened. They argued for more monetary restriction citing the growth of the aggregates as evidence of the need for restraint (ibid., 3). Martin and other proponents of moderation relied instead on the decline in free reserves and the rise in the federal funds rate and other short-term rates. Once again, these indicators misled them (see Chart 3.15 above).

By March long-term Treasury yields reached 4.7 percent, a 0.35 percentage point increase after the discount rate increase, and the federal funds rate reached 4.63 percent, a 0.5 percentage point increase. Member bank borrowing increased, and free reserves reached −$255 million in March (from $8 million in December). Governor Maisel (1973, 77–79) drew a correct conclusion. "Federal Reserve doctrine was based on a money market strategy. The Fed used money market conditions simultaneously as a target, or measure, of monetary policy and as a guide for the manager" (ibid., 78). Referring to his introduction to FOMC procedures, Maisel wrote: "Nowhere did I find an account of how monetary policy was made or how it operated. . . . Arguments had been strong and quite clear [in 1965] because they were based primarily on ideological views . . . Frequently, members of the FOMC argued over the merits of policy without ever having arrived at a meeting of the minds as to what monetary policy was and how it worked" (ibid., 77–78). This reinforces Hayes's arguments above about the difficulties in trying to write a precise directive to the manager.

The misinterpretation of its actions proved costly. By March 1966

---

330. Maisel did not start keeping a diary at each meeting, although he took notes. The February 9, 1967, summary covers some meetings from December 1965 to October 1966. The text is based on notes made at the meetings.

the twelve-month rate of increase in the consumer price index reached
2.8 percent, the highest rate in eight years.[331]

TOWARD INTERNATIONAL REFORM, 1963–65

President Johnson showed less interest in, and less concern about, the balance of payments and the gold loss than did his predecessor. There were fewer meetings and less discussion, but basic policies were similar. Domestic expansion had precedence. The risk of slowing economic expansion to reduce prices, output, and imports did not appeal to either administration. Both relied mainly on swap lines to alleviate the immediate pressure on the gold stock and specific controls on lending or spending abroad to prevent a crisis. Table 3.9 (above) lists some of the principal controls.

At the Federal Reserve, Martin, Hayes, Balderston, Daane, and a few others expressed much more concern, but Mitchell and Robertson were closer to the administration's position. Most of the time all agreed that the problem was primarily not a monetary problem. FOMC members could agree that the first line of attack should be an administration program to reduce its own overseas spending for defense and foreign aid.[332] Maisel (1973, 224) estimated that during his years on the Board of Governors, international concerns influenced the policy decision in only eight out of more than one hundred directives. In three of the eight, policy remained less restrictive because of concerns for the pound, French franc, and other currencies.

Controls and restrictions relieved pressures temporarily, often by relatively large amounts. The interest equalization tax in July 1963 contributed to a decline in United States purchases of foreign securities, but bank loans to foreigners, not subject to the tax, rose. In February 1965, so-called voluntary restrictions on bank lending and foreign investment by U.S. corporations helped to reduce the officials settlements deficit to $1.3 billion.

---

331. Johnson (1971, 342) wrote, "If I had to do it over again, I would have made the same decision to recommend a guns-and-butter budget to the Congress." He recognized that the guns-and-butter budget created pressure for inflation, but he blamed Congress for inflation because it delayed enactment of the tax surcharge that he requested in 1967 (ibid.).

332. In October 1965, Governor Robertson sent a memo to administration officials proposing extension of the Interest Equalization Tax to most forms of capital outflow and earnings retained abroad. Governor Maisel (1973, 207) wrote that the international payments problems during his term in Washington (1965–72) "was never really faced up to properly." He criticized the Federal Reserve also for supporting "unsound policies" and limiting its activity to swap arrangements (ibid., 207–8). He estimated the cost of slowing the economy as a 10 to 20 percent decline in output to close a $3 billion payments deficit (ibid., 213). Estimates of this kind were misleading. Once the economy recovered, the deficit would return unless prices changed. Maisel (ibid., , 24) estimated that a 5 to 8 percent change in relative wholesale prices would have closed the deficit.

However, foreign direct investment rose to a record level. Evidence suggested these expenditures would increase again in 1966 (Council of Economic Advisers, 1966, 166). The administration imposed a new type of "voluntary" restriction in December. Corporations investing abroad were asked to hold foreign investment and earnings retained abroad in 1966 to 90 percent of their 1962–64 average. Financial institutions were asked to keep their dollar outflow to the 1965 level in 1966 (ibid., 167). Most government spending abroad for foreign aid was either in-kind transfers or tied to purchases in the United States. Military spending abroad increased, however.

The Council's report described the response to existing restrictions as excellent. Secretary Fowler told President Johnson that the voluntary program "is a good in terms of what it accomplishes" (Oval Office Conversations, Johnson Library, November 28, 1965). Johnson was not persuaded. He described the new restrictions as raising "the target a little bit on something that already kind of failed anyway" (ibid.). He blamed the administration's use of guideposts, especially against the aluminum industry, for souring relations with businessmen. He did not expect their cooperation. The Board's staff also doubted the value of the restrictions (Stockwell, 1989, 36).

The most lasting effect on adjustment came through the relative price mechanism. Price stability in the United States and rising prices abroad were major factors reducing the U.S. current account deficit from slightly above zero in 1959 to $6 billion surplus in 1965. During the same years, the surplus of principal industrial countries other than the United States fell from $3.5 billion to $2.25 billion (Solomon, 1982, 51).[333]

A report prepared for the Treasury by outside experts forecast a continued increase in the current account surplus. Based on projections of (1) rising costs and prices in Europe relative to the United States and (2) increased profitability of investment in the U.S. relative to Europe, the report concluded that the United States would go from a 1961 deficit of $850 million to a $2.7 billion surplus in 1968 in its "basic balance" (ibid., 57–58).[334] We cannot judge the projection's accuracy because Vietnam War

333. Politics had a major influence on discussions with the Europeans. They complained about imported inflation resulting from lower U.S. interest rates. The United States countered by complaining about underdeveloped European capital markets that induced them to borrow in the United States. The French, under President de Gaulle, disliked investment by U.S. corporations in Europe but could not get agreement on a policy to restrict it. Solomon (1982, 53–55) presents these positions.

334. The report defined the basic balance as the balance on goods and services and long-term capital both official and private. The report is usually called the "Brookings report." The authors accepted the Triffin argument that world reserves would grow too slowly once the

spending and increased U.S. inflation reversed the rise in the current account surplus (see Chart 3.11 above). Many comments on the report expressed doubts about the optimistic projection. Few favored floating rates as a solution (Solomon, 1982, 66).[335]

The administration recognized that International Monetary Fund rules permitted devaluation of the dollar against gold in case of a structural deficit. Robert Roosa opposed this alternative. His successor on February 1, 1965, was Frederick W. Deming, president of the Minneapolis Federal Reserve Bank. Deming maintained most of Roosa's policies, but he never developed a comprehensive policy. The 1964 Economic Report of the President (ibid., 139) explained that the devaluation option did not exist for the United States. "For a reserve currency country, this alternative is not available. For other major industrial countries, even occasional recourse to such adjustments would induce serious speculative capital movements, thereby accentuating imbalances."[336] This ignored experience with devaluation of the pound, the other reserve currency.

Ruling exchange rate adjustment out of consideration shifted attention away from adjustment back toward a new multi-national reserve asset to replace the dollar and the pound and supplement gold for settling payments. Some of the French favored return to a full gold standard with any new reserve asset tied to gold. Eventually, they relented. In June 1965, Ackley reported the French finance minister, Valéry Giscard d'Estaing, as having said that "France does not support a return to the pure gold standard or any 'appreciable' rise in the price of gold." He opposed any plan centered on the IMF (memo, Weekly Balance of Payments Report, June 19, 1965, Confidential Files, Box 49, LBJ Library).

The United States decided to press the issue. With Roosa retired, the president officially accepted the goal of establishing a multi-national cur-

United States achieved balance. Unlike Triffin, they considered greater exchange rate flexibility as an alternative solution.

335. Ackley gave a different view. Sometime in the 1960s, he recognized that "the dollar was really overvalued and that sooner or later we were going to have to bite the bullet and devalue" (Hargrove and Morley, 1984, 264). He believed that it was a dangerous topic to broach because public awareness that government economists considered floating rates would bring a run on gold. He suggests that he discussed with President Johnson that devaluation "wasn't really the end of the world" (ibid.). Most of the time, "we generally loyally supported the Treasury view about the various kinds of efforts that we made" (ibid., 265).

336. This statement overlooks earlier British devaluation of a reserve currency, devaluation of other European currencies, and revaluation by West Germany and the Netherlands. The argument is a restatement of Nurkse's (1944) claim and ignores Friedman's (1953) reconsideration and rejection of the role of speculation as a destabilizing element. Solomon (1982, 60) notes that few comments on the Brookings report advocated exchange rate adjustment.

rency unit in June 1965 (Johnson, 1971, 315). Several European countries opposed the proposal, arguing correctly that the international system did not require "any further increase in the volume of unconditional or conditional liquidity" (Solomon, 1982, 83).[337]

LEGISLATION AND REGULATION, 1963–65

The System had several continuing regulatory issues during these years. Banks looked for new ways to bypass ceiling rates on deposits. The 1956 Bank Holding Company Act did not apply to one-bank holding companies. The Board tried several times to extend its authority over these companies. The Board had never found the rules for setting reserve requirement ratios satisfactory. It had considered revisions several times in the past without reaching agreement. Requiring non-member banks to meet he System's reserve requirements was a perennial issue. With Congressman Patman as chairman of the House Banking Committee, hearings on legislation changing the System's structure occurred more frequently. Other issues arose periodically.

In response to criticisms at the 1964 Patman hearings, the Board began quarterly meetings with academic economists. The participants varied with the choice of subject matter. Also in 1964, to commemorate its fiftieth anniversary, the Board sent the minutes of FOMC meetings from 1936 to 1960 and supporting documents to the National Archives, where they would be available for research.[338]

Deposit Insurance

In 1963 deposit insurance had a limit of $10,000 per account. The Board opposed a congressional proposal to raise the ceiling to $25,000 at its April 7, 1963, meeting and an administration proposal, as part of a banking bill, raising the limit to $15,000. In May, the Board agreed to support an increase to $12,500 (Board Minutes, May 15, 1963, 9), but it soon reversed its position and accepted the $15,000 limit. Congress did not approve the higher limit (as part of a comprehensive bill). When the issue arose again, the Board approved of the increase with little discussion.

337. International Monetary Fund (IMF) resources increased from $16 to $21 billion, but the G-10 governments did not permit the IMF to have a major role in the liquidity discussions (Solomon, 1982, 83).

338. In March 1964, President Johnson sent Secretary Dillon a note directing him to get the banking agencies to act in concert. Dillon sent the letter to the Comptroller, the FDIC, and the Federal Reserve, asking them to give the other agencies and the Treasury ten days advance notice of any rule change. Martin replied that the Federal Reserve had adopted that policy earlier (Board Records, March 2–5, 1964).

Reverse Repurchase Agreements

The open market desk used repurchase agreements to smooth the money market. The desk provided reserves by purchasing Treasury securities, mainly bills, under an agreement that permitted the member bank to re-purchase the securities at the end of a specified, usually short, period. Sale and purchase prices were set at the start. The difference between them was the interest payment. In April 1963, the desk proposed reversing these transactions to absorb bank reserves when temporarily excessive.

The memo from the New York bank proposing reverse repurchase agree-ments talked about "sloppy" money markets and intra-month changes. Emphasis was much more on the federal funds rate, and less on free re-serves, showing the evolution in operating procedures that occurred in the early 1960s.[339]

The Board's staff opposed on grounds that the transaction constituted a loan to the Federal Reserve from dealers that might be illegal and would be embarrassing. The interest rate might be considered a way of paying inter-est on the dealer's demand deposit (memo, Peter Keir to Robert Holland, Board Records, December 13, 1963, 2). To circumvent these obstacles, the desk proposed to make two simultaneous but separate transactions—a cash sale to absorb reserves and a deferred purchase to reverse the transac-tion. These transactions did not differ from an open market sale and a de-ferred open market purchase. The FOMC subsequently permitted reverse repurchase agreements.

Banking Legislation

Pressed by Comptroller of the Currency James Saxon, the administration proposed to liberalize several of the regulations and prohibitions adopted in the 1930s. The existing rules sought to restrict bank competition for deposits, reduce competition between types of institutions, for example banks and thrift institutions, or commercial and investment banks. Law-yers and bureaucrats make rules; markets learn to circumvent costly rules.

---

339. The problem as seen by the desk occurred during and after a weekend. Weekend dates counted for reserve calculations, so excessive reserve positions on Friday counted for three of the seven days. The desk had difficulty absorbing the excess during the week to make the weekly average target. Reverse repurchase agreements would temporarily absorb reserves on Friday, smoothing the adjustment of reserves with lower variability of the funds rate. The desk claimed that both transactions had to be done simultaneously with the same bank or dealer. Otherwise, they claimed, interest rates would change noticeably (memo, Peter Keir to Robert Holland, Board Records, December 13, 1963, 5). The memo expressed skepticism about the argument and did not endorse the proposal.

Comptroller Saxon supported and encouraged the national banks efforts at circumvention. The Federal Reserve generally opposed the changes.

In addition to increasing the deposit insurance ceiling, discussed above, the administration's banking bill (1) required non-member banks to maintain required reserves on time and savings deposits but permitted them to borrow at the Federal Reserve discount window, (2) authorized the Federal Home Loan Banks to require members to hold reserves with the Home Loan Banks, and (3) permitted the System to put regulation Q ceilings on a permissive and stand-by basis. Board members disliked opening the discount window to non-members. Their main concern was that non-members would gain advantages of membership without having to pay the cost of holding reserves against demand and time deposits at reserve banks. Large state member banks might withdraw. Many had done so because costs of membership rose with interest rates (Board Minutes, May 15, 1963, 5-6).[340] Governor Mills described the provisions as "ominous" (ibid., 7).

The Board supported the legislation. Balderston spoke in favor of the bill, but he wanted to put the reserve requirement legislation in a separate bill. Mitchell supported the entire bill but wanted reserve requirements to apply to demand deposits (ibid., 9). The Board's letter accepted the principal provisions. Mills dissented (ibid., 16). The bill did not pass.

In September, Chairman Martin testified on legislation to (1) permit banks to underwrite and deal in revenue bonds of state and local governments,[341] (2) extend the authority of national banks to make real estate loans, (3) increase the loan limits to a single borrower from 10 to 20 percent of a bank's capital and surplus, (4) permit national banks to increase lending on forest tracts, and (5) broaden the lending powers of savings and loan associations. In 1964 Congress approved more liberalized lending on forest tracts and permitted national banks to lend up to 80 percent of the value of real estate.

---

340. On December 31, 1965, there were 7,320 non-member banks and only 1,406 state member banks, representing 54.9 and 10.2 percent of all banks respectively. Total member banks, national and state-chartered, were 45.6 percent of all banks. The member banks were much larger. Deposit holdings of non-member banks were only 14 percent of total deposits. The number of insured non-member banks rose 5 percent between 1960 and 1965; state member banks declined 14.5 percent in the same period. This was the start of a growing number of banks leaving the System.

341. The bonds differed from general obligations because general obligations were full faith and credit obligations whereas interest payments on revenue bonds came from a dedicated source such as highway or bridge tolls. Revenue bond financing increased markedly in the 1960s, and banks wanted part of the business.

The Comptroller had ruled that national banks could underwrite revenue bonds. The Board's legal staff believed this opinion violated the separation of investment and commercial banking (Glass-Steagall) provisions of the Banking Act of 1933. Charles Partee of the staff explained that critics of revenue bond financing complained that underwriting was subject to conflict of interest because the banks held deposits, provided trust services, and gave advice to the governmental units. Governor Mitchell responded that the problem was no different for revenue bonds than for general obligations that banks could underwrite under existing statutes, and there was no evidence that the problem was important.

Robertson and Shephardson did not see much benefit but also saw no harm. But Martin and Balderston opposed on the principle "that those who advise should not be also selling things that were on their shelves" (Board Minutes, September 18, 1963, 14). Mills opposed also. That made the vote three to three, so Shephardson changed to opposition making the vote to oppose the legislation four to two.

The Board either opposed most recommendations or urged more study of the need for change. Although Martin and most of the Board took pride in the belief that they favored increased competition in the marketplace, they did not vote that way. Many spoke in favor of stand-by ceiling rates instead of actual ceilings, but they favored making the change only "at the proper time." That time never came. Similarly, they could see the risk in less rigid standards for lending and investing activities. Their caution did not stop banking changes. Changes occurred first because of the actions by Comptroller Saxon and later by the market rewarding innovators who found ways to avoid regulatory constraints.

Late in 1964 the Board considered thirteen legislative proposals that it agreed to submit as a package early in 1965. Discussion suggested that it did not expect Congress to act, but it wanted to tell the banking community and the public generally what it favored (Board Minutes, November 18, 1964, 11). The principal legislative proposals recommended broader powers to discount, extension of the Board's powers over holding companies to include one-bank holding companies, and power to invest in obligations of foreign governments payable in convertible currencies and with not more than one year to maturity.

Discounting. Two years before organizing its omnibus bill, a system committee proposed legislation eliminating vestiges of the real bills doctrine that required eligible paper to be short-term self-liquidating commercial or agricultural paper. The staff proposed to eliminate all statements in the law about eligibility requirements for discounts (Board Minutes, July 24, 1963, 7, 10). The Board took their advice and proposed "to make advances to their member banks on any security satisfactory to the Reserve Banks subject to limitations, restrictions, and regulations prescribed by the Board of Governors" (Board Minutes, July 24, 1963, letter, Martin to Senator A. Willis Robertson).[342] The letter noted that in 1932 Congress authorized the reserve banks "to make advances to member banks in exceptional and unusual circumstances on any security satisfactory to the Reserve Banks although at a penalty rate of interest (ibid., 2). Under section 10b, the penalty rate was a 0.5 percentage point increase in the discount rate. Legislation later made the authorization permanent and removed the restriction to "exceptional and unusual circumstances." The penalty interest rate remained.

The Board explained that the "concept of an elastic currency based on short-term, self-liquidating paper is no longer in consonance with banking practice and the needs of the economy" (ibid., 2). It added that the more appropriate principle was (1) "soundness of the paper offered as security" (ibid., 2) and explained that "the nature of the collateral provides no assurance that the borrowing bank will use the proceeds for an appropriate purpose" (ibid., 3). Despite this clear statement, remnants of the real bills doctrine were not dead. The proposed legislation continued to refer to "the maintenance of sound credit conditions and the accommodation of commerce, industry, and agriculture" (Board Minutes, July 24, 1963, Draft of Proposed Bill Regarding Advances). And the draft bill obligated the reserve banks "to keep informed about the general character and amount of the loans and investments of its member banks with a view to ascertaining whether undue or inappropriate use is being made of bank credit for the speculative carrying of or trading in securities, real estate, or commodities, or for any other purpose inconsistent with the maintenance of sound credit conditions" (ibid.). The Board could bar banks that engage in "unsound practices" from use of the discount facility.[343]

When the Board returned to the issue the following year, Governor Mitchell suggested that the System should permit seasonal borrowing for banks that "needed such facilities" (Board Minutes, June 11, 1964, 14). This suggestion was adopted when the Board revised regulation A after extensive study and inability to get legislation passed.

342. The letter is dated August 21, 1963. Senator Robertson was chairman of the Senate Banking Committee. Draft legislation accompanied the letter.

343. Congress did not amend the statute. The Board tried again in 1964, with similar result. It also asked the reserve banks for comments on a revision to regulation A (discounts and advances) in case the legislation passed. The Board's discussion brought out differences of opinion about the relative importance of protecting the assets of the reserve banks compared to providing credit facilities for members and the amount of discretion left to the reserve banks in setting conditions (Board Minutes, June 11, 1964, 8–13).

Edge Act and Foreign Banking

Growth of international trade and foreign investment awakened bankers' interest in opening foreign branches to service their customers. Growth of the euro-dollar market and regulation Q restrictions gave additional incentives. The Board began to consider regulatory changes to expand the powers that U.S. banks could use abroad.[344] The aim was "to free Edge corporations and the Board as far as practicable from an intolerable amount of regulatory minutia" (Board Minutes, January 17, 1963, 16). Chairman Martin explained that existing legislation and regulations did not encourage banks to establish foreign branches. Banks had to request permission to undertake each new activity. As a result borrowers used the Export-Import Bank and international agencies (ibid., 16).

On August 1, 1963, the Board adopted a substantial revision of regulation M spelling out the powers of national banks operating abroad. Over the objections of Governor Mills, the regulation permitted wide powers to foreign branches, including the power to establish branches in a country for which it has been approved by the Board. It had only to notify the Board. The powers granted to national banks under regulation M extended to state member banks under regulation H. Three weeks later, the Board revised and simplified regulation K; Edge Act corporations received powers similar to those approved for banks' foreign branches.

Graduated Reserve Requirements

The President's Committee on Financial Institutions reconsidered the recommendations of the Commission on Money and Credit.[345] Some small banks in reserve cities paid the higher reserve requirements while some large suburban banks paid the country bank requirements. One of its recommendations called for replacement of reserve requirements based on location with requirements graduated by deposit size. The Board had often expressed concern about the inequities resulting from the existing system. It agreed to ask Congress to approve the new system, under which the Board could vary reserve requirements ratios as follows: 5 to 9 percent

344. Discussions began in December 1962 and continued the following month. With staff assistance, Governor Mitchell had revised regulation K (Corporations Doing Foreign Banking or other Foreign Financing under the Federal Reserve Act) and regulation M (Foreign Branches of National Banks). U.S. banks abroad operated under rules promulgated by the Board under the authority of the Edge Act passed in 1927 to permit American banks to operate separate corporations abroad.

345. See discussion of the Commission's report earlier in this chapter.

on the first $5 million, 8 to 20 percent on the next $95 million, and 10 to 22 percent on any excess over $100 million.

Discussion concentrated on a few issues. First, the Board had always favored either extension of reserve requirement ratios to non-member banks or compulsory membership. The Board often argued that existence of non-member banks hampered monetary policy or reduced its effectiveness, but it did not explain why this was true. Governor Mitchell made clear that "he would not attach public policy importance to reaching 100 percent" of deposits in member banks (Board Minutes, August 12, 1964, 9). The discussion brought out that in practice Board members' concerns were that non-member banks had the competitive advantage of lower cost of reserve requirements and, for some, non-par collection fees.

To meet the competition from small non-members, the Board wanted to keep the reserve requirement ratio on the first $5 million relatively low. "The primary reason for classification of banks according to deposit size . . . was to give an earnings advantage to smaller banks" (ibid., 13).[346] Several governors spoke in favor of a uniform reserve requirement ratio for all banks, but they did not adopt it.

The existing range of reserve requirements for time deposits remained 3 to 6 percent. Proposals to apply different ratios for different types of time and saving deposits, within the 3 to 6 percent range, did not attract support.

Problems with Regulation Q

Whenever the Board considered regulation Q ceiling rates, several members spoke in favor of asking Congress to remove them or put them on a stand-by basis. The Board hesitated because the time was not right when rates rose, and no one mentioned the subject when market rates were below ceiling rates. This happened so often that it casts doubt on the statements. The Board members did not propose raising the ceiling and then asking Congress to remove them.[347]

Several bankers who served on the Federal Advisory Council explained two of the problems caused by ceiling rates. First, banks could not be cer-

346. Board members expressed willingness to permit non-member banks to use discount facilities if they became subject to the Board's reserve requirement ratios. The members recognized that Congress was unlikely to approve a proposal extended to non-member banks. The Board had tried several times without success.

347. Economists with very different policy views on some issues agreed that the distortions caused by ceiling rates were costly and that interest rate ceilings should end (Friedman, 1970; Tobin, 1970).

tain whether they could renew certificates of deposit at unchanged rates when they came due. This was a significant source of funds for many banks. If rates rose above the ceiling, a bank would have to adjust to the loss of deposits. Second, one way that they adjusted was by selling municipal securities. This subjected the municipal market to sudden rate changes (Board Minutes, May 18, 1965, 19).

Some banks evaded regulations. Whenever market rates approached ceiling rates, the Board had to consider these efforts to avoid or circumvent regulations. In 1965, the administration proposed legislation authorizing the FDIC and the Federal Reserve to penalize banks that violated the ceilings. The FDIC was eager to enact the legislation. The Board hesitated. Its main concern was the treatment of fees paid to brokers that collected deposits for resale to banks. Proposed legislation gave the Board and the FDIC authority to waive restrictions on fees. Congress did not act on the bill.

To avoid regulation Q ceilings, reserve requirements, and deposit insurance fees, major banks began to increase their liabilities by selling promissory notes. Governor Robertson wanted to classify the notes as deposits to bring them within existing regulations. The Board's legal department ruled that the definition of "deposit" could be extended to include notes[348] (Board Minutes, September 14, 1965)

The Board had a practical problem. The Comptroller would treat promissory notes at national banks as borrowings, not deposits. State member banks would be at a disadvantage. Some argued, however, that this was a clear circumvention of the Board's regulations and should not be permitted. Governor Shephardson responded that "as he had observed on many occasions, particularly in connection with Regulation Q problems, unfortunately the Board was faced with many frustrations in being responsible for administering laws that could not be effectively enforced. . . . Unless the Board was resolved to make a fight on the whole broad spectrum [of evasions], the alternative was to continue along the lines it had followed thus far" (ibid., 21–22). Martin agreed, and the discussion ended.

GUIDEPOSTS

The guideposts first appeared in the 1962 Economic Report of the President (Council of Economic Advisers, 1962) as a general admonition to keep nominal changes in worker compensation bound by productivity changes. Price changes would then reflect costs plus markups. If costs

---

348. The First National Bank of Boston started the practice by selling $1 million of unsecured notes in September 1964. The Board's initial response classified the notes as borrowings (not deposits). Other banks considered following, raising concerns for some Board members. The reserve banks did not favor action.

rose at the trend rate of productivity growth, and markups remained stable, prices would be stable also. The reasoning behind the guideposts is similar to the discussion of price changes in the Joint Economic Committee's 1959 study of 1950s experience, *Employment, Growth and Price Levels*. The job of the guideposts was to remind employers, employees, and the public of this standard.

Behind this exhortation lay a belief that a modern economy could not reconcile full employment and price stability because (mainly) industrial workers demanded wage increases in excess of productivity growth. This was called "inflationary bias," and the claim was that the bias existed in the pricing of both industrial products and workers' compensation. The Economic Report of the President (Council of Economic Advisers, 1966, 88–89) reviewed this argument and recognized other causes including overly expansive fiscal policy. Keynesian economists wrote the report, so monetary policy was not mentioned as a cause of inflation.

The most obvious economic flaws in this argument were failures to distinguish between one-time and continuous changes and between relative and absolute price changes. Labor or producer power could be used once, perhaps a bit more if labor or producers had to discover how much power they had. Inflation bias referred to price changes, not levels. Inflation continued for more than a decade, a fact that was difficult to reconcile with inflation bias. Further, even if guideposts prevented a company or industry from raising its prices, the additional demand created by monetary or fiscal expansion remained. Unless the public added sufficiently to its money holdings, spending on securities or goods and services would not be affected by guideposts. Some individual prices would be controlled, but other prices, and the price level, would rise.

Ackley's messages to the president about inflation often listed the individual commodity or service prices that seemed likely to increase. He believed that "guideposts help put some of the blame for inflation where it belongs. There are always plenty of people trying to put it all on the government" (memo, Ackley to Bill Moyers, June 21, 1965, WHCF, Box 23, LBJ Library, 3). As an alternative to guideposts, Ackley proposed more vigorous anti-trust policy, easing entry into construction unions, and "other highly unpopular measures" (ibid., 5).

The obvious political flaw in the argument was that exhortation and announcement proved insufficient. Enforcement became necessary and, increasingly, required the president to pressure unions and corporations or industries. Ackley acknowledged that in 1965 "service professions had greater wage increases and unions then sought to catch up with non-union labor in 1966, and that's when the breakdown began" (Hargrove and Morley, 1984, 259). This contradicted the claim about inflationary bias by reversing the direction of changes and putting the (largely) non-union service sector first. And Ackley agreed public sector wages rose relative to private sector wages (ibid., 262).

The political problems arose most sharply once the president became involved. Failure forced the president to back down.[349] Looking back, Ackley recognized the political error. "It was a mistake to have this function in the Council of Economic Advisers, and probably a mistake to involve the President in it so closely." He did not recognize that efforts to shift the supply of output or labor would have to be repeated until the administration and the Federal Reserve reduced real aggregate demand to equal aggregate supply.

CONCLUSION: WHY THE GREAT INFLATION STARTED

The years from 1961 to 1965 are some of the very best years in Federal Reserve history. Median income in 1960 prices rose 15 percent, almost 3 percent a year. Until 1965 inflation remained subdued. As the economy recovered from the 1960 recession, the civilian labor force increased 8 percent as unemployment fell and the economy created more than 5 million new jobs.

Fifteen years of inflation and slow growth followed. The mild inflation of 1965 continued sometimes faster, sometimes slower until a reported peak of 13.7 percent in 1980. Another fifteen years passed before the return of above average growth and low recorded inflation.

The Great Inflation started while William McChesney Martin, Jr., was chairman of the Board of Governors. Martin was not a wild radical eager to confiscate the wealth in outstanding bonds and fixed nominal values. He was not a radical of any kind. On the contrary, he was a symbol of conservative fiscal policy and "sound" finance. His contemporaries often portrayed him in caricature wearing a high starched collar and looking like a refugee from the nineteenth century. He gave many speeches warning about inflation and denouncing unbalanced federal budgets, balance of payments deficits, and fiscal profligacy.

Martin seems a most unlikely person to preside over monetary policy at the start of the Great Inflation. Yet until January 1970 he was in a position to stop it. He failed to do so. When he left office, broad-based measures of

---

349. Ackley cites a confrontation with airline machinists that the president lost. "The mistake, I believe, was in building it up as a big issue . . . [W]e would have been so much better off if we had never entered into a public fight. Once we got into a public confrontation with them, we either had to win or we took a very serious defeat" (Hargrove and Morley, 1984, 262). Ackley did not have any attractive proposals for avoiding problems of this kind.

prices had increased 5 to 6 percent in the previous year, an unusually high rate of inflation for a relatively peaceful period.

Inflation increased further in the 1970s, after Martin retired. The reasons for the start of inflation and its later increase overlap to a degree, but it helps to separate them because costs of preventing inflation from starting differ from the costs of stopping an established inflation. This concluding section to the early 1960s considers the reasons the Great Inflation started.

Inflation was not new in 1965, and it was not new to Martin. He had successfully ended the inflation that followed the Korean War. By late 1952, average annual increases in consumer prices reached 1 to 2 percent. Inflation continued to fall until it became modestly negative in 1954–55. Again, in 1959–60, average annual consumer price inflation fell to 0 to 2 percent from 3 to 4 percent in 1957–58.

Terminology about inflation is often confusing. Throughout this text inflation means a *sustained* rate of price increase. Another definition is often found; inflation refers to any increase in the price level. Using this definition, writers refer to cost-push inflation or food price inflation. These usages combine one-time price level changes and sustained rates of change. In both the price level rises. The difference is that one-time price level changes, though they may be spread over time, come to an end without a policy change. Sustained price increases are monetary in origin and end with a reduction in money growth.

The start of the Great Inflation was a monetary event. Monetary policy could have mitigated or prevented the inflation but failed to do so. The intriguing questions about the 1960s inflation are: Why did the Federal Reserve permit inflation to return in 1965? Why did it not repeat the actions that ended inflation twice in the 1950s?

The detail in the chapter suggests not one answer but several. Three seem most important. First is Martin's leadership and beliefs. Second, neither Martin, nor his colleagues in the FOMC, nor the staff had a valid theory of inflation or much of a theory at all. And some of their main ideas were wrong. Third, institutional arrangements hindered or prevented taking timely effective action and increased inflation. Beliefs and arrangements worked together to allow inflation to start and to continue.

Martin's Leadership and Beliefs

Martin was a highly respected chairman. He believed passionately in the independence of the Federal Reserve, and he had the courage to insist upon its independence when pressured by President Johnson or by presidential staff and officials. In his oral history, he described fully and at length the pressure from the president to rescind the discount rate increase in 1965 and his resistance to presidential pressure at other times.

However, at times, Martin responded to administration pressure by hesitating or delaying action. Although he had concluded much earlier that he had to tighten policy to avoid higher inflation, he urged delay in October 1965. His reason was coordination. He told the FOMC that he, as the minutes record it, "had the responsibility for maintaining System relations within the Government . . . and he had made that one of his principal concerns during the fourteen years he had held his present office" (FOMC Minutes, October 12, 1965, 68–69).

He was not confrontational, dogmatic, or unwilling to change his mind. He admitted mistakes and respected Board members who disagreed with him. If a majority did not agree with him about a policy change he would often wait months until a majority formed.

In the System's early years, the Federal Reserve and the government followed classic nineteenth-century practices. The central bank was independent of government, although at times restricted by gold standard rules. The government did not intervene in Federal Reserve decisions despite two members on the Board; the Federal Reserve operated independently and divulged little information.

By the 1950s standards had changed. Central banks controlled one part of the policy "mix" that affected the level of employment, output, and prices. Although no longer represented on the Board, successive administrations recognized that the public expected government to maintain high employment rates and avoid inflation. The Employment Act of 1946 codified this practice.

The meaning of central bank independence changed and with it the goal of monetary policy. In an oft-quoted remark, Martin defined independence indirectly by saying that the Federal Reserve had to take away the punch bowl while the party was getting started. The more formal statement described the Federal Reserve as independent within the government, not independent of the government. To those like Martin, who made that statement, it went beyond recognizing that the Federal Reserve was the agent of Congress—that Congress had delegated its constitutional responsibility to coin money and regulate its value and could withdraw it.

The March 1951 Accord freed the Federal Reserve from Treasury control of interest rate levels but gave it co-equal responsibility for debt management. The Treasury had to price its issues in the light of current market interest rates. The Federal Reserve's role was to prevent the market from failing to accept a Treasury issue; in practice that meant it supplied enough reserves to keep interest rates from rising around the time the Treasury sold its offering. It called the action an "even keel" policy.[350]

Martin explained several times that Congress voted the budget and approved deficit finance. The Federal Reserve was not empowered to prevent the deficit or refuse to finance it. Central bank independence stopped well short of that.[351] Therefore, he complained often about the size and frequency of budget deficits but the Federal Reserve provided the reserves to finance them. And it rarely felt able to remove the additional reserves after it supported the Treasury's offering.

In the early 1960s, Martin regarded unemployment as structural, not responsive to expansive monetary and fiscal policies. Kennedy administration economists blamed restrictive fiscal and monetary policies, including "fiscal drag," the tendency of the budget to reach balance before the economy reached full employment. They wanted permanent tax reduction supported by an expansive monetary policy to finance the deficit. Martin did not agree with the analysis or the policy, and he later accepted that he had been wrong about the stimulative effects of tax reduction. But he agreed that the Federal Reserve should assist in financing the deficit because Congress approved it. Thus, he accepted "coordination." Later, when deficits increased in size and Treasury offerings became larger and more frequent, the Federal Reserve had fewer days on which it could increase interest rates and more debt issues to help manage. Thus it sacrificed operational independence.

Martin often said that monetary policy *alone* could not prevent inflation or achieve balance in international payments. Given his belief that the Federal Reserve shared responsibility for successful deficit finance, his statement was true.

Some of his successors showed that inflation could be reduced *even* in a period with large deficits. In the 1980s, the federal government ran large, persistent deficits. The Federal Reserve had an independent policy and did not assist in deficit finance. One important change in this context was the end of the Federal Reserve's "even keel" policy of holding short-term interest rates constant when the Treasury sold notes or bonds. By the

350. The problem was very apparent in the last half of the 1960s. Precise starting and ending dates for even keel operations are not always given. In the twenty-four quarters from 1966:1 to 1971:4, there are eighteen reported even keel operations, sometimes more than one. Every quarter from 1966:3 to 1968:2 had an even keel operation. Professor William Yohe of Duke found that the FOMC voted for even keel at eleven of eighteen meetings in 1959 and 1964 (letter, Yohe to Meltzer, August 8, 1967).

351. Cukierman (1992) presents several definitions of independence and compares central banks.

1980s, the Treasury auctioned its securities and let the market price them instead of leaving the Treasury to set a price that the Federal Reserve felt bound to support.

Some economists, members of Congress, and congressional staff proposed auctions several times. The Federal Reserve and the Treasury opposed. This was a costly mistake that helped to start the Great Inflation.

The Role of Economics

Martin often began a conversation by saying, "I am not an economist." He had little interest in economic explanations of inflation, claimed not to "understand" the money stock, and did not have much confidence in the accuracy of economic data. He saw, correctly, that measurements of short-term changes were unreliable and were often revised substantially.

Martin did not articulate a coherent theory or explanation of the relation of Federal Reserve policy to economic activity and prices. When pressed, he fell back on an analogy to a river. Policy actions aimed to keep the river within its banks but high enough within the banks that the fields could be irrigated.[352] In his early years he sometimes mentioned money growth relative to output growth as a long-term measure of ease or restraint. When Winfield Riefler and Woodlief Thomas retired from the senior staff, the importance of excessive money growth weakened.

Other members of FOMC held a wide range of views about economics. Several presidents and Board members were practical men without much interest in explanations of inflation or economic activity. Bryan (Atlanta) and Johns (St. Louis) emphasized money growth and at times proposed procedures for adjusting policy to control money growth, but they never received majority support. A few members of FOMC, and a growing number of senior staff members, accepted some version of Keynesian theory. To the extent that there was a dominant view, in the early 1960s, the members favored making judgments for the next three weeks based on observable data. If it seemed appropriate the decision could be revised at the next meeting. This meant that there was no consensus to act against inflation or unemployment until it occurred and was well established. The fact that Chairman Martin was the leading member of this group contributed to its dominance. This approach failed to adjust policy to longer-term movements in output and inflation.

A by-product of this atheoretical approach was the vague instruction

352. Martin used this analogy when I interviewed him as part of the 1964 Patman study and hearings. The analogy appears also in FOMC discussions and his congressional testimony.

given to the account manager. Unable to agree on how their actions affected their longer-term goals, the members could not decide how best to implement policy actions. The manager had considerable discretion and, as the minutes show, members frequently differed over whether the manager had followed instructions. The manager's focus was the money market, so his decisions gave much more weight to current technical details than to longer-range objectives such as inflation. His focus was mainly on transitory movements that affected interest rates. Persistent changes affecting inflation received less attention.

Once inflation started the issues changed. Some members accepted that inflation could permanently lower the unemployment rate. Others were more concerned about the temporary increase in the unemployment rate resulting from actions to slow inflation. Several accepted that little could be done as long as the federal government ran budget deficits. Since there was no generally accepted framework relating unemployment, inflation, budget deficits, balance of payments, and Federal Reserve actions, it was hard to reach agreement about what could or should be done. And most members interpreted the Employment Act as giving primacy to minimizing unemployment, maintaining a 4 percent unemployment rate.

The members recognized that they did not have a common framework. After Sherman Maisel became a Federal Reserve governor in 1965, he tried to make policymaking more coherent and systematic (Maisel, 1973). He soon recognized that there was no basis for agreement; members told him that they were unlikely to find a common framework.

The minutes have an occasional remark about anticipations of inflation. There is little evidence of a general understanding that anticipated inflation raised interest rates. The FOMC did not distinguish between real and nominal rates until much later. At the start of the inflation, and for a long time after, members using nominal interest rates overestimated the degree of restraint. Misinterpretation added to the pressures from President Johnson to keep interest rates from rising. They also overestimated the expected growth of output after productivity growth slowed in the mid 1960s.

One way to avoid responsibility for inflation was to find some other cause. Much public and policy discussion blamed labor union demands for starting inflation, treating these wage demands as autonomous events and not as a response to actual and anticipated inflation. Many at the Federal Reserve and in the administration shared this view. This led to the use of guideposts for wage and price increases. The universal failure of guideposts and guidelines to prevent inflation did not change these views. And it did not remind the proponents that non-inflationary policies would prevent relative price changes from affecting the general price level. Lucas (1972) and Laidler and Parkin (1975) showed that relative price changes would not cause a sustained inflation in the absence of actual or anticipated expansionary policy.

Institutional Arrangements

Two institutional arrangements had a major influence on Federal Reserve decisions. Martin's acceptance of policy coordination with the administration prevented the Federal Reserve from taking timely actions. The System delayed acting in 1965 despite Martin's early warnings about inflation.

Even keel policy also delayed taking policy action, sometimes for months. During even keel periods, usually lasting up to four weeks, the Federal Reserve often added large increments to reserve growth that it did not subsequently reverse. It is, of course, true that the System could have prevented the inflationary impact. It failed to do so because the costs of reversal always seemed large.

Years later Chairman Arthur Burns accepted the importance of even keel policies for the beginning and continuation of inflation.

> While the Federal Reserve would always accommodate the Treasury up to a point, the charge could be made—and was being made—that the System had accommodated the Treasury to an excessive degree. Although he was not a monetarist, he found a basic and inescapable truth in the monetarist position that inflation could not have persisted over a long period of time without a highly accommodative monetary policy. (FOMC Minutes, March 9, 1974, 111–12)

My conclusion is that three factors—Martin's beliefs, the absence of a relevant theory, and institutional arrangements—explain why inflation started. Two other questions remain: Why did the inflation continue as long as it did? Why did it end when it did? These questions are considered in subsequent chapters, after reviewing the decisions and the reasoning.

At the end of the war, the administration and Congress adopted the Bretton Woods Agreement, which fixed the dollar price of gold and committed the United States to keep one fine ounce of gold equal to $35. Throughout the early 1960s, under President Kennedy, the Treasury worked hard to develop controls and arrangements like the gold pool to sustain the fixed exchange rate regime. Higher inflation abroad reduced the real dollar exchange rate and the current account deficit.

These measures were mainly successful. Balance in the current account seemed achievable before the end of the decade. President Johnson gave lower priority to the current account than his predecessor. His administration relied more on controls and crisis management and gave little or no attention to the real exchange rate and low inflation. Their main concerns were domestic equality and the war in Vietnam.

Some commentators on the period point to the international character of the inflation. All countries experienced the start of inflation in the 1960s. All of them were members of the Bretton Woods system, so they either accepted the dollar outflow or appreciated their currency. Few chose appreciation, and some added to their inflation by their own policies. Britain is the best example, but France and later Italy followed inflationary domestic policies leading to devaluation. In addition to the Bretton Woods system of fixed exchange rates, a common concern to prevent increased unemployment contributed to the inflation problem abroad. Laidler (2004) offers an international perspective.

The 1960s began a period of financial innovation. The Comptroller of the Currency, James Saxon, supported and encouraged deregulation. The Federal Reserve was slower to act. Although members sometimes recognized that ceiling rates on time deposits should be removed, they did not agree to do it.

FOUR

The Great Inflation: Phase I

Monetary policy should not, and in fact cannot, be focused solely on interest rate objectives—any more than it can ignore them completely. . . .

The immediate goal of monetary policy should be to provide the reserves needed to support a rate of growth in bank credit and money which will foster stable economic growth. It must take into account the international position of the dollar . . . It must be constantly concerned for the full employment of both human and physical resources. It must take into account price developments and the possibility of inflation, *or the widespread expectation of inflation*, which would do great damage to healthy growth. . . .

All these things, and many others, must be constantly weighed and balanced by the Open Market Committee . . . We cannot produce *through monetary policy alone*, high or low interest rates, balance of payments surpluses or deficits, rising or falling prices, more or less employment, or a sound or unsound financial structure. We do exert some influence on all these things, hopefully in the right direction.

—William McC. Martin, Jr. (memorandum for the president, Martin papers, undated; emphasis in the original)[1]

The memorandum succinctly summarizes Martin's main views about monetary policy. There were multiple objectives that had to be weighed and balanced. Even the best judgment could not achieve any precise goal because many other factors affected prices, output, balance of payments, and interest rates. The most one could do was to do one's best and hope that others would do the same.

By April 1966, Martin had been chairman of the Federal Reserve for

---

1. From references to interest rate levels elsewhere in the memo, it was probably written in 1965, before the increase in the discount rate.

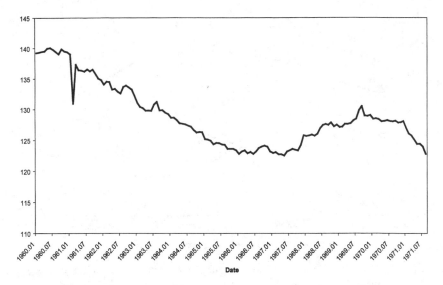

Chart 4.1. Trade-weighted real exchange rate, January 1960–August 1971.

fifteen years, longer than any previous chairman. The economy had entered its fifth year of sustained expansion, much above the National Bureau's thirty-two—month average for peacetime expansions (Zarnowitz and Moore, 1986, Table 3). Consumer price inflation remained below 2 percent. Lower inflation at home than abroad had reduced the real (price level adjusted) exchange rate.

Chart 4.1 shows that the trade-weighted real exchange rate appreciated until the mid-1960s. The main reason was lower inflation at home than abroad. By 1967 the period of more stable prices had ended; inflation reached the 2.5 to 3.5 percent range. Rising budget deficits to finance military, domestic, and wartime spending raised the public's concerns about future inflation. Chart 4.2 compares one measure of anticipated inflation to actual inflation, using the Livingston survey of anticipations. Although the survey systematically underestimated the measured rate of inflation, the survey data show a steady, gradual increase to 3 percent and above by the end of the period.

The current account surplus, though below its 1964 peak, remained large enough in 1965 to cover most capital spending. Chart 4.3 shows that quarterly values of the current account surplus had started a gradual decline that would continue with little interruption for the rest of the decade.

In the 1950s, the Board's senior staff, some FOMC members, and occasionally Chairman Martin relied on the relation of M_1 money growth

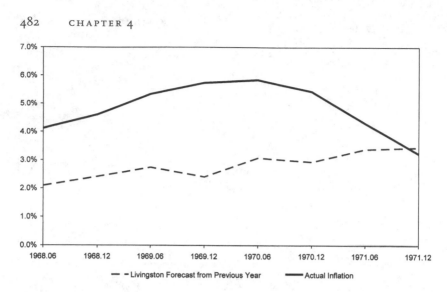

Chart 4.2. Mean inflation forecast from Livingston survey from twelve months prior to actual Inflation, June 1968–December 1971.

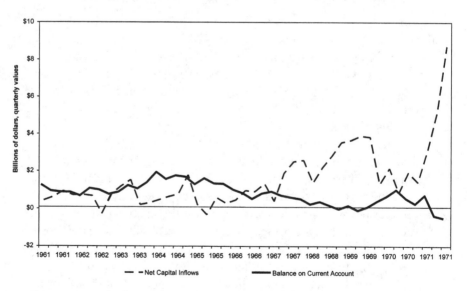

Chart 4.3. Capital inflows and the balance on current account, 1961:1–1971:3.

to growth of real output as a measure of inflation potential. Chart 4.4 smoothes both series to show that in the first half of the 1960s, the two had similar average trends with real growth above money growth. We cannot be sure whether the result was happenstance or whether the FOMC intended to achieve the particular outcome. There is no evidence of any

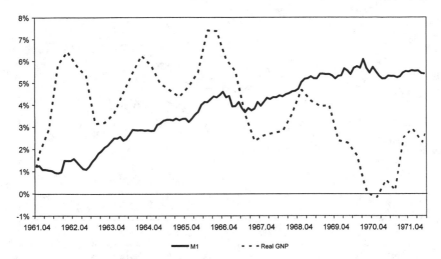

Chart 4.4. Three-year moving average of M_1 growth and four-quarter moving average of real GNP growth, 1961:2–1971:3.

explicit effort, but senior staff members claimed to set reserve targets by estimating money growth.

After 1965, the relationship changed. Real growth slowed with the reduction in productivity growth, shown in Chart 3.1 above, in part the effect of diverting resources from private to public use for war and redistribution. Slower output growth with rising money growth increased inflation and the potential for inflation, supporting the rising anticipation of inflation in the Livingston survey.

Gold continued to flow out, but the Federal Reserve sterilized the outflow. Chart 4.5 shows that, generally, base growth continued to increase after 1964. The peak annual rate of growth for the decade, more than 7 percent, came in 1968. For the five years 1959–64, the base rose at a 3.1 percent compound average rate; in 1964–69, the compound average rose to 5.5 percent despite lower productivity growth.

A common claim is that a budget deficit increases market interest rates. Since the Federal Reserve controls a short-term rate, that rate changed only if the Federal Reserve permitted a change. To prevent a change when the deficit increased, the Federal Reserve permitted an increase in the monetary base or its growth rate.

Chart 4.6 suggests an important difference in deficit finance after 1964. In 1961–64 inclusive, the Federal Reserve increased the base enough to finance 33 percent of the annual budget deficit; in 1965–71, the percentage increased to 50 percent. Despite a small budget surplus in 1969, deficits

Chart 4.5. Annual growth of the monetary base during the 1960s at quarterly dates.

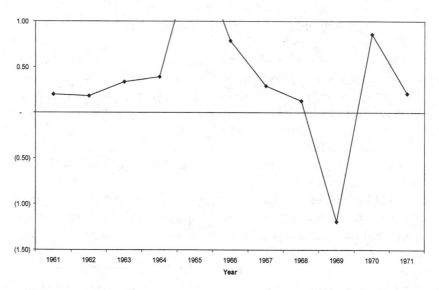

Chart 4.6. Ratio of change in monetary base to federal budget deficit, FY 1961–71.

on average were substantially larger ($8.8 billion compared to $5.3 billion), and the Federal Reserve financed a higher percentage. Money growth rose as a result, and inflation followed.[2]

2. The budget had a surplus in 1969, so the rate is negative for that year. The base increased in 1969 by slightly less than in 1968, a year with a relatively large deficit.

It did not require subtle economic reasoning to know that financing deficits by injecting money was inflationary. This was a commonplace, learned from experience in most wars. Three questions arise, therefore: Why did the Federal Reserve on average finance half the deficits? Why did Chairman Martin, a strong proponent of price stability, continue the policy? And why did the professional economists on the Council of Economic Advisers hesitate to urge higher interest rates?

Experience from 1965 to 1971 suggests two broad answers to these questions. The Federal Reserve accepted its role as a junior partner by agreeing to coordinate its actions with the administration's fiscal policy. Coordination permitted the chairman to discuss the administration's fiscal policy with the president, but he had little effect on decisions. In practice, coordination meant that the Federal Reserve would not raise interest rates much, if at all. Martin's reasons for accepting this role covered a wide range including (1) his definition of independence as independence within the government, (2) failure to distinguish between real and nominal interest rates, and (3) a strong commitment to consensus building within the Board and the FOMC and with the administration. By the late 1960s most of the Board agreed with the administration's policies, not with Martin's warnings about inflation.

Second, the Johnson administration's principal macroeconomic concerns were economic growth and unemployment. Administration economists believed that a little more inflation was the price of permanently lower unemployment. This called for keeping interest rates from rising, a decision that President Johnson favored for populist reasons of his own. Administration economists compounded this error by believing that the main response to inflation had to be fiscal, not monetary, action. They believed that a temporary surcharge would slow inflation; their idea of coordination called for lower interest rates to soften the expected effect of the tax surcharge in 1968.

By the time policymakers recognized that the surcharge and the easier monetary policy had not slowed inflation, the public had learned a different lesson, one that would be reinforced through the 1970s. The public saw that policy responded mainly to actual or anticipated unemployment in 1966–67 in 1968, and in 1969–70. Strong words about the dangers of inflation were not matched by strong actions. They concluded, correctly, that anti-inflation actions would not persist once unemployment increased.

At the end of the decade, the members of the Council of Economic Advisers in the Nixon administration brought different ideas but no less inflation. Nixon's economists, following Friedman (1968b), accepted that any reduction in unemployment achieved by increasing inflation would not persist in the long run. The higher inflation rate would be learned, expected, and impounded into wages, prices, and interest rates. But they continued to believe in a reliable short-run reduction in unemployment achieved by inflating. Further, they put major stress on money growth as a short-run influence on output and long-run inflation.

These analytic changes could have served as the basis for a successful anti-inflation policy, but they were not used for that purpose. The overriding concern remained the unemployment rate. Policy continued to aim at a 4 percent unemployment rate as the attainable equilibrium. As the 1972 election approached, this concern became overwhelming both at the Federal Reserve and in the Council of Economic Advisers. No less important, Arthur Burns, whom President Nixon chose as chairman of the Board of Governors to replace Martin, became convinced that the increase in the unemployment rate required to reduce inflation would be politically unacceptable. He became the leading proponent in the administration of wage-price guidelines and later wage and price controls.

PREVAILING BELIEFS

The Johnson administration's policy views reflected prevailing Keynesian orthodoxy. These views were widely held. To commemorate the twentieth anniversary of the signing of the Employment Act, the Joint Economic Committee invited economists and legislators closely associated with the act to a symposium. Several had served as members or chairs of the Council of Economic Advisers (CEA), which was created by the act. Their views on economic policy, and their differences, summarized the state of opinion among those actively engaged in policymaking or likely to be policy advisors. Their statements covered many issues other than macroeconomic policy, employment, inflation, and balance of payments.

No member of the Federal Reserve Board of Governors presented a statement. Although inflation was an emerging problem in 1966, there was very little attention to money and monetary policy. Most of the comments about inflation discussed fiscal policy, wage-price guideposts or controls.

The main explanations of inflation were either some version of the Phillips curve relating inflation to the unemployment rate, or systemic inflationary bias and the incompatibility of multiple objectives. Kermit Gordon, a budget director in the Kennedy administration, stressed the latter, calling it the "grand dilemma of modern mixed capitalism. As among three basic economic goals that are held in high esteem in our society—reasonably full employment, reasonably stable prices, and reasonably free economic institutions and pressures—it is widely believed that we may attain any two together, but not all three. . . . [W]ages are determined and prices set by groups which possess a measure of discretion in these decisions; and this discretion can be used and has been used to introduce an inflationary bias into wage and price setting at levels of economic activity short of full employment" (Joint Economic Committee, 1966, 60).

Only Paul McCracken, a former member and later chair of the CEA, directly challenged this thesis. After examining non-war data for 1909 to 1929 and 1949 to 1965, he concluded that the central claim was not true. "The record does not seem to suggest that the price level now is prone to rise more rapidly during an economic expansion than in our earlier history. If anything it may be less so" (ibid., 69). Nevertheless, McCracken concluded: "There probably is an element of the market-power phenomenon in the tendency for our price-cost level to edge higher" (ibid.).[3]

Henry Wallich, also a former CEA member and later a Federal Reserve governor, also challenged the persistence of inflation bias, noting that it depended on some type of money illusion. Anticipating an argument soon made famous by Friedman (1968b), Wallich said, "Labor, business, consumers, investors will think in 'real' terms; that is in terms of constant purchasing power. To achieve the same employment effect, inflation would have to be *accelerated* beyond the expected rate, and when that new rate became expected, more acceleration would be needed. . . . I conclude that the possibility of raising employment by accepting inflation exists only in the short run, until people have caught onto the game" (Joint Economic Committee, 1966, 13–14; emphasis added).

Wallich unsuccessfully challenged the prevailing orthodoxy that full employment, price stability, and balance of payments equilibrium involved long-run tradeoffs, such as the Phillips curve tradeoff between inflation and unemployment. "Truly competing objectives are those that make demands upon resources. . . . Full employment, growth, and price stability are not of this sort . . . A rational society should have no difficulty in reconciling them, though the learning period may be painful" (ibid., 15). He criticized the emphasis on demand management in discussions of economic growth and the neglect of supply-side policies to increase productivity and capacity (ibid., 14).

Raymond Saulnier, a former CEA chairman, emphasized the role of combined monetary and fiscal expansion in generating inflation, but he expressed concern about using monetary policy to reduce inflation. "Inter-

---

3. McCracken and other critics did not ask why labor unions that possessed market power did not exhaust their power in a one-time increase in the wage level and similarly for corporations.

est rates are already at levels that are high by all U.S. historical standards" (ibid., 54). Because he failed to distinguish between real and nominal interest rates, he expressed concern that if monetary policy acted decisively, it would disrupt financial markets. Like many in the Federal Reserve, he argued for a more restrictive fiscal policy as the senior partner in an anti-inflation policy under then current circumstances.

As the discussion suggests, one main division was between those who urged fiscal restriction as the primary tool to reduce inflation and those who preferred guideposts for wage and price changes and the use of presidential power to influence individual price and wage decisions. Critics noted that not all decisions were visible, so this policy would fail, but they did not point out that, with unchanged money growth, the policy would not reduce spending unless the public held larger cash balances per unit of income.

Without making the connection to guideposts, Arthur Burns, another former CEA chairman, made the critical point. "Taking the past 20 years as a whole, the administrators of the Employment Act have concentrated on the maximization of employment" (ibid., 28). Other goals—price stability and freedom of contracting—remained secondary. Although administrations had not always succeeded, the primacy given to high employment, or avoidance of recession, was the source of the country's inflationary bias. Although a minority criticized this ordering of goals and proposed greater weight to inflation, the payments imbalance, or poverty reduction, in the political and intellectual climate of the period, the criticisms had limited force. It would take a large and costly inflation—the Great Inflation—to change beliefs or attitudes. In the interim, economic policy put greatest emphasis on reducing unemployment or maintaining the unemployment rate near 4 percent.

Another bias noted in some of the comments was the emphasis on current problems and relative neglect of longer-term consequences. Gardner Ackley, the current CEA chair, agreed that "our horizons need lengthening" (ibid., 129). He noted especially the need for more and better information about "the future impact of Federal programs, especially the new and growing ones" (ibid., 130). Johnson's administration did little or nothing about longer-term consequences. Within a few years, the growth of spending for Great Society programs and the unwillingness to raise tax rates enough to pay for them posed challenges.

Walter Heller emphasized both demand stimulus and, like Wallich, what later became known as supply-side policies. "The discouraging pattern of recessions every 2 or 3 years has been broken, not by simple-minded devotion to demand stimulus, but by a tight coupling of measures to boost demand with measures to boost productivity and hold costs and prices in

check—a combination designed to harmonize the demands of full utilization of our economic potential with demands of high growth, cost-price
stability, and external payments equilibrium" (ibid., 37).[4]

Discussions gave little attention to international issues. Several speakers
mentioned balance of payments equilibrium as one objective that might
be added explicitly to policy goals or written into the Employment Act. But
other speakers made similar arguments for income distribution, poverty
reduction, or cleaner air and water. These differing claims about the use of
real resources or the objectives of government suggest the increased politi-
cization of monetary, or monetary and fiscal, policy. They point up the lack
of consensus about what should be done and how best to do it.

Little more than a year later Paul Samuelson debated the role of guideposts as part of economic policy with Arthur Burns. Samuelson emphasized that he was not "a wholehearted enthusiast for guideposts" (Burns
and Samuelson, 1967, 43). Strict adherence to guideposts everywhere
would freeze the existing distribution of incomes (ibid, 49). Then he repeated the claim about inflationary bias. "Free markets do not give us a
stable consumer price index at the same time that the rate of unemployment stays down to a socially desirable minimum" (ibid., 45).[5]

Samuelson recognized that adjusting wages to one-time price level
changes or adjusting prices to cyclical changes in relative income shares
would cause problems, particularly if the government tried to tie wages
to average productivity growth in a period of high employment (ibid., 53).
But he rejected Friedman's (1968b) argument that claimed that the Phillips curve relating inflation to unemployment was vertical in the long run
(ibid., 65–66). In response to a question, Burns explained that the conventional Phillips curve gave the short-run response, but the long-run effect
would reverse the reduction in unemployment. "You are likely to stir up
inflationary pressures and create other imbalances" (Burns and Samuelson, 1967, 144).[6]

Burns had earlier criticized the guideposts, if enforced on most firms,
as a serious interference with resource allocation (Burns, 1965, 59). He repeated and amplified some of his earlier criticisms. He favored structural

4. Heller criticized the Federal Reserve's 1965 discount rate decision. "The Federal Reserve slipped out of the harness of monetary-fiscal coordination and touched off a wave of
interest rate increases for both buyers and sellers of money, that must be surprising even
to those who initiated the move" (Joint Economic Committee, 1966, 43). Heller called for
temporary tax increases, including suspension of the investment tax credit and excise or
income tax changes.

5. Samuelson attributed the original argument to Peter Wiles, a British economist, but
cited John Kenneth Galbraith as a popularizer.

6. I am grateful to Athanasios Orphanides for insisting on this point.

reforms to improve the functioning of markets and introduce more auto-matic stabilizers and less attention to short-run, cyclical changes. A few years later, as chairman of the Board of Governors, he reversed his position and advocated first guideposts and soon after wage and price controls.[7]

Clearly, issues like guideposts and activist counter-cyclical policy divided economists at the time. Government officials were divided also. Admin-istration economists and policymakers supported the activist approach. At the Federal Reserve, Martin did not accept Phillips curve reasoning, but several Board members did. As the number of Kennedy-Johnson ap-pointees increased, Martin's ability to persuade his colleagues to follow his leadership weakened.

Interpretation of interest rate changes and the importance of separating real and nominal influences divided economists. The Keynesian position at the time doubted that inflation increased interest rates. "This possibility has generally been neglected by Keynesians, but it is in no way inconsis-tent with Keynesian analysis. . . . The probability that nominal interest rates would be pushed above their initial level by this mechanism is very difficult to evaluate, however" (Smith, 1969, 118). Although there are a few references to the influence of inflation on nominal interest rates, neglect of this influence was much more common. Nominal interest rates above 5 or 6 percent were historically high rates and interpreted, incorrectly, as evidence of restrictive monetary policy.

In short, the simple Keynesian model as applied in the late 1960s had three major flaws. It did not generally distinguish between nominal and real interest rate changes. It presumed that the government could perma-nently reduce the unemployment rate by permitting the inflation rate to rise. And it did not distinguish between one-time price level changes and maintained rates of price change. Each of these errors continued through-out the 1970s. Later, the political decision to keep the unemployment rate near 4 percent and to underweight the cost of inflation added to the mis-takes that maintained the Great Inflation in the early 1970s (Orphanides, 2002, 2003a,b).

PERSONNEL CHANGES
Canby Balderston's term as a member and vice chairman of the Board ended in February 1966. Chairman Martin proposed, and strongly urged, the appointment of Atherton Bean as his successor[8] (letter, Martin to John-

7. In the debate Burns did not dismiss any effect. "The net effect of our price and wage guidelines appears to have been slight" (Burns and Samuelson, 1967, 144).

8. Bean was a Minnesota industrialist who had served as a Director of the Minneapolis Federal Reserve Bank. Martin's letter to Johnson indicated that he had discussed the appoint-

son, WHCF, Box 283, LBJ Library, February 2, 1966). Instead, President Johnson chose the first African-American appointee, Andrew Brimmer, serving at the time as an assistant secretary of Commerce. Martin objected to Brimmer as another economist, after three previous economists. He cited Section 10 of the Federal Reserve Act, which called for "fair representation of the financial, agricultural, industrial, and commercial interests . . . of the country." He objected that appointment of another economist "would damage confidence and gravely impair the ability of the Federal Reserve to carry out functions of vital importance to the economy and the government alike" (ibid., 2). Martin stressed that his reservation was to any economist, not specifically to Brimmer.[9]

The president appointed Brimmer as governor and promoted James L. Robertson to vice chairman. Brimmer served 8.5 years until August 31, 1974, and Robertson served until April 30, 1973, completing more than twenty-one years at the Board.

Martin's fourth term as chairman ended on April 1, 1967. His fourteen-year term as a governor ended on January 31, 1970, so he could be renewed as chairman for only three years. At a private meeting with the president, Martin expressed a desire to retire. He had been in the job for sixteen years and, he said, that was "long enough for anyone" (memorandum of a conversation with President Lyndon B. Johnson, Martin oral history, March 14, 1967, 1).

The president told him, "The country has confidence in you and I will state categorically that I desperately need you to continue. I am going to have a very difficult time in the next two years" (ibid., 2). The president swore Martin to secrecy before telling him, "I have decided not to run again in 1968 . . . I am only asking you to stay with me, if your conscience permits, until the inauguration of a new President in 1969" (ibid., 3).[10]

---

ment with the president before writing the letter. Senator Russell Long (Louisiana) wanted one of his friends appointed. When Johnson told Martin, Martin said he would resign because the man was unqualified, "a Chevrolet salesman" (Martin oral history, May 8, 1987, I, 25).

9. The president asked Walter Heller to find out about Brimmer's views. Heller wrote a memo supporting the appointment, describing Brimmer as a "Johnson man" who believed in the "positive use of monetary policy for economic expansion with occasional restraint in tight situations like the present" (letter, Heller to Johnson, Henry Fowler Papers, Box 143, LBJ Library, January 25, 1966). Just to make sure, Johnson had Fowler and Ackley interview Brimmer to hear his view on the December 1965 discount rate increase and on monetary policy more generally. Johnson then conducted his own interview while he was in bed on the afternoon of December 24. According to Brimmer, in both interviews he said he would have supported the discount rate increase. Johnson talked mostly about his aspirations for civil rights (interview with Andrew Brimmer, March 2002).

10. This was a year before President Johnson made his surprise announcement that

Martin made two demands. New civil service regulations required Governor Charles N. Shephardson to retire on May 1 upon reaching age seventy-two. Martin asked that Shephardson be allowed to complete his term ending in February 1968 so that he could continue his work on the Board's new building and other general housekeeping duties. The president agreed to let Shephardson continue as a consultant at an unchanged rate of pay.

Martin then asked for assurance that whoever was appointed to replace Shephardson would be "acceptable to me" (ibid., 5). After much discussion, Martin assured the president that he "didn't want him to be the President's man or my man but to be a man who approached matters with an open mind and with a desire to try to maintain harmony if it was at all possible" (ibid., 5). The president assured him that "he would not appoint anyone until [Martin] gave [his] approval" (ibid., 5). A few days later Martin accepted reappointment.

Shephardson resigned as governor effective April 30, 1967. His successor was William W. Sherrill, who served for only 4.5 years. Sherrill was a Texan and, at the time, a director of the Federal Deposit Insurance Corporation. Responding to Martin's concerns and the president's promise when Martin agreed to stay, Sherrill was not an economist. He had worked in the Houston city government and, later, had developed real estate. The background memo described Sherrill as favoring sound policies "including maximum availability of credit to the public at the lowest possible interest rates" (memo, John W. Macy, Jr. to the president, WHCF, Box 283, LBJ Library, April 19, 1967). Whatever that would mean in practice, the reference to lowest possible interest rates must have attracted Johnson.

This was Johnson's last appointment to the Board and it replaced the last Republican appointee on the Board. Martin now had a Board dominated by Kennedy and Johnson appointees, many of whom were willing to tolerate higher inflation in the belief that it would bring permanently lower unemployment. In this, they shared Ackley's strongly held views.

Sherrill developed a management system and modern budgeting process to improve cost control. This was a response to continued pressure

he would not run. Martin told the president of his desire to retire six months earlier. Some speculated at the time that President Johnson's decision to retire reflected the strength of the opposition in the New Hampshire primary election in March 1968. This suggests that the president had made (or considered) his decision more than a year earlier. The president then told Martin that Secretary Henry Fowler planned to leave by year-end, and that he would appoint Martin as Secretary of the Treasury. Martin demurred, but the president asked him whom he would recommend as his successor as chairman if he later accepted the Treasury position. Martin chose Robert Roosa (memorandum of a Conversation with President Lyndon B. Johnson, Martin oral history, March 14, 1967, 4–7).

Table 4.1   New Presidents 1965–68.

RESERVE BANK	LEAVING	NEW APPOINTEE	EFFECTIVE DATE
Atlanta	Malcolm Bryan	Harold Patterson	October 1965
St. Louis	Harry Shuford	Darryl Francis	January 1966
Dallas	Watrous Irons	Philip Coldwell	February 1968
Atlanta	Harold Patterson	Monroe Kimbrel	February 1968
Richmond	Edward Wayne	Aubrey Heflin	April 1968
Boston	George Ellis	Frank Morris	August 1968

from Congressman Patman to subject the Board's budget to the congressional appropriation process (Stockwell, 1989, 44). It also reflected the increased responsibilities and growing number of employees. Between 1963 and 1968, the Board added nearly 200 employees, an increase from 608 to 790. The number of member banks, however, changed very little, while the number of non-member banks continued to increase.

Between 1965 and 1968, the Board appointed six reserve bank presidents, two of them in Atlanta. Table 4.1 shows these changes. Although Malcolm Bryan and Darryl Francis did not overlap as members of FOMC, they shared a common view that Francis articulated during the Great Inflation.

The Board's senior staff also changed. Ralph Young retired. Daniel Brill and Robert Solomon became responsible for the domestic and international research divisions respectively. Robert Holland, later a governor, became secretary of the FOMC and, subsequently, secretary of the Board. Brill introduced explicit forecasts into FOMC deliberations in 1966 and began staff work on an econometric forecasting model. He was a strong proponent of policy coordination and often aligned his views with the economists in the administration. He later served in the Carter Treasury Department.

THE MINI-RECESSION OF 1966–67

Martin had shown courage and determination by refusing to back down under intense pressure from the president.[11] Then he retreated. Instead

11. Congressional hearings on coordination took the president's position. Senator Jacob Javits (New York) introduced a resolution mandating Quadriad meetings six times a year and requiring the chairman of the Board of Governors to notify the president whenever any reserve bank requested an increase in the discount rate (reductions are not mentioned). Chairman Patman wrote to the president, declaring, "The Federal Reserve Board has seized powers which reside in the Congress and the President as the duly elected representatives of the people. . . . The Joint Economic Committee hearings clearly established that Mr. Martin violated section 2 of the Employment Act of 1946" (letter, Wright Patman to the president, WHCF, Box 50, LBJ Library, December 27, 1965). He, too, wanted the president to mandate regular meetings of an expanded group to replace the Quadriad.

of using the higher discount and ceiling rates as the first step toward price stability, the Federal Reserve allowed monetary base and money growth to remain at a 6 percent average annual rate during the first four months of 1966. The economy started the sixth year of expansion with a 3.8 percent unemployment rate. Industrial production rose at a 9.4 percent average annual rate. Inflation (deflator) rose 4.8 percent in the first quarter.

Sherman Maisel described the positions at the Board and the FOMC.

> FOMC debates revolved around three or four major points. The groupings could be characterized as "hawks" and "doves" with the characterization being almost a complete opposite of the December 3 vote to raise the discount rate. Most of those who voted for the discount rate [increase] then spent the period through June holding that the amount of restriction applied should be minor and should be increased only gradually. On the other hand, those who had voted against the discount rate increase, when they agreed by the end of December that restraint was proper and when they saw that the administration was going to attempt to allow monetary policy to handle the situation rather than using fiscal policy because of the premature monetary action, these doves now became hawks. They urged that the System determine where it wanted to go and move in that direction more rapidly. (Maisel diary, FOMC Summary, February 9, 1966, 3)

Maisel explained what he meant by the last sentence. The doves did not have a strategy for monetary policy. They proposed "raising interest rate cost only gradually with no clear picture of what was expected from net borrowed reserves increase or the interest rate increase" (ibid., 5). They lacked any way of relating their proposed changes to aggregate spending. The hawks related spending to bank credit and total reserves, so they wished to limit growth of reserves and credit.[12]

Pressure from President Johnson continued. One day Martin was asked to come to the White House. The president said, "'I want to tell you that you took advantage of me and I'm not going to forget it because here I am, a sick man. You've got me into a position where you can run a rapier into me and you've run it.' I thought this was just silly. From my standpoint it was." Martin placed the timing in the same year, 1965. Sometime after the president acknowledged that Martin had been right. "'Well, Bill, you know, you are right in your judgment. But I just don't agree with you.' I said 'Mr. President, that's your prerogative. And it's mine'" (Martin oral history, May 8, 1987, I, 16–17).

12. Using data available at the time, Maisel reported that total reserves increased at a 6.3 percent annual rate from December 1965 to June 1966, four times the rate from the previous June through November. Money supply rose at a 7.5 percent rate. Bank loans to business rose at a 34 percent annual rate during this period. Maisel listed as doves Hayes, Ellis (Boston), Irons (Dallas), Daane, and Martin; the hawks were Maisel, Robertson, Mitchell, Shephardson, and Brimmer after he replaced Balderston (Maisel diary, February 9, 1967, 5–6). In June, Darryl Francis supplemented Maisel's statement. The Board had increased

The Federal Reserve recognized the threat to its domestic and international objectives. The minutes report rising prices, reduced idle capacity, upward revision of GNP data, and growth of employment. At its February 8 meeting, it voted to "resist the emergence of inflationary pressures and to help restore equilibrium in the country's balance of payments by *moderating the growth of the reserve base, bank credit and the money supply*" (Annual Report, 1966, 130; emphasis added). The committee voted unanimously to reduce reserve availability gradually. Differences of opinion seem more muted, but Martin and Hayes would not agree to Robertson's proposal to introduce a "proviso clause" authorizing the desk to adjust the free reserves target if reserves increased too rapidly.

The account manager's report designated the February 8 meeting as the start of transition to a firmer policy. Free reserve fell from $8 million in December to −$62 million in January and −$111 million in February. The federal fund rate rose from 4.3 percent in December to 4.6 percent in February. As in many previous and subsequent occasions, these changes misled officials.[13] The change in free reserves was an increase in borrowing; so more reserves became available and monetary base growth continued. The increase in short-term interest rates was less than the increase in the (annualized) inflation rate, so real rates fell. Moreover, the December increase in regulation Q ceiling rates permitted banks to increase time deposits, so bank credit rose rapidly also.

The Federal Reserve persisted in its error. At the March 1 and April 12 FOMC meetings, the members voted unanimously to reduce reserve availability. And again borrowing increased and free reserves fell to −$250 to −$300 million. The federal funds rate rose slightly.

A member of the staff, Charles Partee, later a member of the Board of Governors, summarized the outlook. "Recent rates of gain appear unsustainable in a physical sense and, accordingly, pressures on costs and prices seem to be intensifying" (FOMC Minutes, March 22, 1966, 25).[14]

One reason for caution was concern that higher market interest rates would force the Board to consider another increase in regulation Q ceil-

---

nominal interest rates, but the inflation rate increased also. "When one adjusted market interest rates for the decline in the value of the dollar . . . interest costs had not risen at all" (FOMC Minutes, June 28, 1966, 65).

13. Merritt Sherman (1983, 35) wrote an internal history of the 1960s. Although written long after the events, he described monetary policy in early 1966 as an effort to "blunt the inflationary impact of credit-financed spending." He used the increase in nominal interest rates and the reduction in nonborrowed reserves as evidence.

14. Chief economist Daniel Brill quoted this description of economic conditions. "Prices are up; quality is down. Costs are up; profits are down. Lead-time is long; labor is short. But business is very good" (FOMC Minutes, April 12, 1966, 17).

ing rates. Several believed that a higher ceiling rate would increase bank credit expansion by reducing average reserve requirement ratios and enabling banks to attract time deposits from other thrift institutions. Wayne (Richmond) expressed concern that, if permitted, New York banks "could not be relied on to exercise prudence in setting time deposit rates" (ibid., 61). And Robertson argued that "it may be that only by holding the line on regulation Q that we finally calm down the bank credit expansion" (ibid., May 10, 1966, 93).

Positions changed. Perhaps congressional pressure and the confrontation with President Johnson caused Martin to hesitate to tighten aggressively. He now became even more hesitant, whereas Maisel and Robertson became more willing to tighten. In January, they sent a memo to the president warning him that still higher interest rates were coming. They described the December increase in discount rates, which they had opposed, as "probably . . . not . . . sufficient to cope with inflationary forces. . . . [I]t will be necessary to curb more sharply the availability of money and credit or reduce spending power through taxation" (memo, Sherman J. Maisel and J. L. Robertson to the president, WHCF, Box 50, LBJ Library, January 18, 1966, 3).

Ackley, too, had second thoughts. He continued to criticize the timing and the effects on expectations. But he now concluded that "to help keep prices in bounds while defense spending forges ahead, some further restraint from monetary policy may be needed in the months ahead" (Ackley to the president, WHCF, Box 50, LBJ Library, January 18, 1966).[15]

In March, following increases in open market rates, major banks raised the prime lending rate to 5.5 percent. The president had criticized earlier increases and gotten a rollback. He asked Ackley to render an opinion on whether he should repeat this effort. Ackley asked Governors Maisel, Brimmer, and Robertson. All of them said the president should not comment. Then Ackley added, "All of them felt that monetary policy has now gone as far as it should go in the direction of restriction. As I understand it, this is also the present view of Chairman Martin" (memorandum for the president, WHCF, Box 50, LBJ Library, March 11, 1966). Brimmer and Maisel volunteered that further restriction should come from fiscal policy. Martin shared this view.

As in 1965, coordination had become a reason for not responding promptly to the threat of inflation. Martin and others on the Board and

---

15. It is hard to find much support in the memo for Ackley's earlier criticisms. He noted that corporate and municipal bond yields had increased by 0.02 to 0.05 and that growth of credit had not slowed in December.

the FOMC waited for a tax increase, or other fiscal restriction, that did not come until 1968. Hayes told the FOMC that the threat of inflation called for a coordinated policy involving fiscal, monetary, and wage restraint. "It is clearly undesirable to place too much of the burden on monetary restraint alone, we are justified in moving rather cautiously in the hope that the Administration will decide on more restrictive tax and spending policies. . . . We should not rule out the possibility—particularly if fiscal policy moves are not forthcoming—that a supplementary *voluntary* domestic credit restraint program may be required" (FOMC Minutes, March 1, 1966, 60; emphasis added).[16]

On March 15, 1966, Martin wrote to the president to explain what monetary policy had achieved and to urge him to increase tax rates. But Johnson believed that to get Congress to approve a tax rate increase, he would have to reduce spending on poverty programs and his Great Society. He was not prepared to take that step.[17]

Waiting for a coordinated response was not the only reason for policy failure. Misinterpretations and error played a role also. Most members of the FOMC did not distinguish between real and nominal rates. They thought that at 4.5 percent, the discount rate was a high rate, the highest since January 1930.

16. President Johnson received mixed signals from his advisers. Although back in Minnesota, Walter Heller continued to advise President Johnson and favored an income tax surcharge. A memo on the pros and cons urged a prompt temporary 5 percent increase in tax rates across the board to raise $4 billion (memo, Heller to the president, CF, Box 44, LBJ Library, December 24, 1965). He forecast productivity growth of 3 percent and a 2.1 percent increase in the deflator (memo, Heller to the president, WHCF, Box 23, LBJ Library, December 31, 1965). The results for the year reversed his forecast, productivity rose 2.4 percent and the deflator 2.8 percent (Council of Economic Advisers, 1971). The CEA forecast inflation at less than 2 percent. By March, the CEA wrote to the president, "The economy is breaking all reasonable speed limits. . . . No let-up is in sight on the advance of demand" (memo for the president, "The Economics of a Tax Increase," CF, Box 44, LBJ Library, March 12, 1966). All three CEA members—Ackley, Arthur Okun, and James Duesenberry—signed the memo. It warned that industrial prices rose at a 2.5 percent annual rate from September to January and that "jawboning" could not work without fiscal support. The CEA recommended $4 to $7 billion in additional revenue. Soon after, Secretary Fowler urged a public announcement of the need for additional measures. Most advisers welcomed the discussion but opposed any announcement of the meeting.

17. A memo from budget director Charles Schultze responded to the president's request to reduce spending by $2 billion. Schultze explained that most spending was for fixed commitments, so the $2 billion reduction "would have to fall very heavily on a number of important programs" (memo, Schultze to the president, WHCF, Box 22, LBJ Library, January 24, 1966). Poverty programs were at the top of a list that included construction and work on the supersonic transport (never built). Two months later, the Council of Economic Advisers advised the president that, despite increased military spending, "the fiscal 1967 Budget does not supply fresh new economic stimulus" (memo, Okun to the president, WHCF, Box 22, LBJ Library, March 17, 1966).

Other misinterpretations also contributed to policy failure. Maisel (1973, 77–86) reports on the lack of agreement about the thrust of policy in the winter and spring of 1966.[18] Those who judged monetary policy by free reserves or money market conditions believed that policy had tightened; those who watched growth of money or monetary aggregates drew the opposite conclusion. The discount rate increase "created a rush for credit. . . . Borrowers stormed into banks to obtain money," anticipating additional increases in interest rates (ibid., 78). Maisel explained that the issue was not about whether policy should restrict spending. "I began to suspect that the Fed might be committing some of the errors our critics accused us of. . . . Our problem was to convince the others that the level of net borrowed reserves was not, by itself, an adequate measure of policy; that it had to be supplemented by another measure" (ibid., 82).[19]

Martin yielded slightly to the dissidents at the April 12 meeting by referring to the "trends in aggregate reserves." Instead of setting free reserves, he instructed the manager to follow a proviso clause—tighten "reserve conditions if the aggregates rose sharply" (Annual Report, 1966, 142). The federal funds rate rose briefly following the meeting but then fell back. A sustained increase did not begin until after the next meeting, May 10, 1966.

As a number of young economists filled positions in the growing staff, pressure rose to introduce the methods taught in graduate schools such as econometric forecasts and economic models. Maisel became the spokesman for these methods at the Board. Gradually, Martin yielded.[20] By the spring of 1966, Riefler's rule disappeared; forecasts of economic activity and financial conditions became part of the staff presentations at FOMC.

The administration was not idle, but it was unwilling to take decisive action against inflation. Instead, the president asked businesses to reduce planned capital spending and hinted about a tax increase. He acceler-

18. Maisel (1973, 77) explained that, as a new member in 1965, he received "volumes of documents and descriptions of what the Fed did, but there was no explanation of how monetary policy was made and how it operated." "Members of the FOMC argued over the merits of a policy without ever having arrived at a meeting of the minds as to what monetary policy was and how it worked" (ibid., 78).

19. "At the February 1966 meeting of the FOMC, the directive had been changed. . . . Those of use who were anxious to slow the rapid increase in credit thought the Committee had come around to our view. It turned out we were wrong. The manager continued to furnish reserves, even more rapidly than before. . . . Money market conditions were tighter" (Maisel, 1973, 82).

20. Martin did not accept that these methods improved operations and usually did not give them much weight. Always a consensus seeker, he yielded to pressure from the staff, from the 1964 Patman hearings, and from recognition that models had become the basis for policy discussion in Washington.

ated tax payments and postponed repeal of some excise taxes. President Johnson took personal interest in many issues, including the increase in particular commodity prices. He seemed to believe that he could control inflation by limiting increases in specific prices. When food prices rose in the winter, he noted on a memo: "Get Ackley to list all commodities and elements in price index that may be looking upward and get Wirtz [Labor], Freeman [Agriculture], and Udall [Interior] and Katzenbach [Justice] busy" (memo, Joseph Califano to the president, WHCF, Box 28, LBJ Library, December 17, 1965). A few weeks later, Agriculture Secretary Freeman notified the president that he had suggested that the military reduce use of bacon and other pork products, butter, wheat, and eggs (memo, Orville Freeman to president, WHCF, Box 28, LBJ Library, January 22, 1966).

If there was no risk of general inflation, there was no reason to risk congressional cuts in Great Society programs by asking for a tax increase. Further, a tax increase might strengthen opposition to the war (Hargrove and Morley, 1984, 252). As late as February, with consumer prices rising, Ackley reassured the White House staff that "we are not expecting anything properly called inflation in 1966" (memo, Ackley to Bill Moyers, WHCF, Box 28, LBJ Library, February 14, 1966). By April, he had changed his mind. Ackley warned that he expected additional increases in prices of industrial goods and services. Overall prices would rise by 2.5 percent in 1966, and he expected inflation to increase further in 1967, a year with many wage settlements. Failure to act would turn "creeping inflation into a canter" forcing action and risk ending the "Johnson prosperity" (memo, Ackley to the president, "The Prospect for Prices," WHCF, Box 28, LBJ Library, April 25, 1966).

The preliminary report of first quarter GNP showed the largest increase since the Korean War. One-third of the increase was in the price level. Bank reserves and the M_1 money stock increased at 13.5 percent annual rates in April, and time and saving deposits accelerated also (Annual Report, 1966, 144–45). In early May, prices on the stock exchange fell sharply.

Maisel argued forcefully that despite the call for restrictive policy, since January "each monetary or credit index showed a much sharper growth rate in the past five months than it had in the previous five" (FOMC Minutes, May 10, 1966, 62). He wanted more decisive action and urged the FOMC to state publicly that it wanted to restrain credit but would not raise the discount rate or regulation Q ceiling rates.[21] Martin favored a gradual

21. Maisel's statement included: "When members looked at total reserves or nonborrowed reserves, either of which he took to be the principal measures of the committee's results . . . In the five months since December 1, the committee had poured more reserves into the banking system than were furnished in the [previous] entire year. . . . The committee

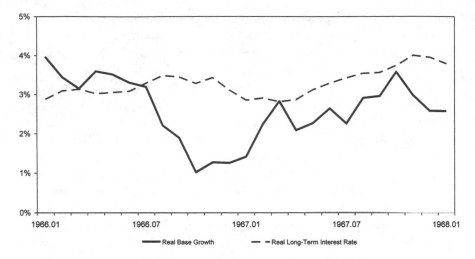

Chart 4.7. Year-over-year real base growth versus real long-term interest rate, January 1966–January 1968. Long-term interest rate measured as yield on ten-year Treasury bonds.

policy and expressed concern about disrupting the money market. The FOMC voted unanimously for Martin's policy, but Martin at last accepted Robertson's proposal to include a proviso clause as a regular part of the directive. If reserve growth (later growth of total deposits) exceeded targets, the manager was told to change the free reserves or money market target.[22]

Annual growth of the real value of monetary base had remained between 3.5 and 4 percent during the first five months of 1966. In June, growth slowed and began a precipitate decline, reaching 1 percent in October. Chart 4.7 shows these data. Anticipated real rates on ten-year Treasury bonds continued to increase until August.[23] During the first eight months of 1966, these yields rose 0.6 percentage points, a 20 percent increase from the January level. Whether judged by growth of real balances or real interest rates, monetary policy tightened decisively in the spring and summer.

Anticipated real rates fell after August. By February–March 1967, this measure had returned to its January 1966 value. The real value of the

had followed . . . feel of the market, net reserves, or the need to offset shocks, and as a result it had moved in a direction opposite to its real aim" (FOMC Minutes, May 10, 1966, 62–63).

22. Maisel (1973, 86) notes that external conditions changed about this time, so the proviso did not restrict actions. Later, "it could have been useful had it been well implemented." In practice the manager ignored it.

23. I used the Livingston survey as a measure of anticipated inflation until data from the SFP became available in 1968. Most of the change is in the nominal interest rate.

monetary base shows a similar pattern easing from 1 percent to nearly 3 percent growth between October 1966 and April 1967. Thereafter, the two series are positively related, the anticipated real rate suggesting less expansion, real base growth slightly more expansion. As on several previous occasions, when the two measures gave different signals, the economy followed real base growth.

Money market measures at first gave similar signals during the summer and fall. Thereafter, measures differed. The manager described the period from the June 7 meeting to September 13 as a time of peak pressure. The federal funds rate rose from 4.98 to 5.80 percent at these meeting dates. It reached a peak in the week ending September 7, before the meeting at which the FOMC shifted from a policy of "supplying the minimum amount of reserves consistent with orderly market conditions" to "maintaining firm but orderly conditions" (Annual Report, 1966, 174, 179). The committee did not approve "the recent tendency toward somewhat less firmness" until the November 1 meeting, when the federal funds rate was back to 5.86 percent. Long-term rates also increased during the fall, from 4.23 following the September meeting to 4.42 in mid-December.

Free reserves and borrowing were the main money market indicators of easier policy. Credit demands slowed with the economy, so banks reduced their loans at federal reserve banks, and free reserves rose along with real base growth. The large increase in free reserves came in 1967. By March free reserves reached +$298 from a low of −$431 in October. The federal funds rate fell gradually to the 4.25–4.75 percent range in March.

With higher and more variable inflation rates, divergence increased between growth of real and nominal values of the monetary base. Chart 4.8 shows these differences. The nominal base declined more steeply in the second half of 1966. The direction of change of the real and nominal base is noticeably different in late 1967 as inflation increased. With that exception, the direction of change is similar, although timing and magnitudes differ.

The Federal Reserve used free reserves or short-term interest rates, not base or money growth, to measure policy thrust. As Maisel called to their attention, the base gave different signals in early 1966, as on other occasions.[24] Table 4.2 shows these differences following the December 1965 discount rate increase.

Table 4.2 shows that during this very brief, but important, turning point for monetary policy, judgments about policy thrusts differed in the spring

24. Here is one example. "Despite a *less* expansive stance of monetary policy, money supply and bank credit grew *even faster* in 1965 than in 1964" ("The Board of Governors of the Federal Reserve System During the Administration of President Lyndon B. Johnson," Lyndon B. Johnson Library, 32; emphasis added).

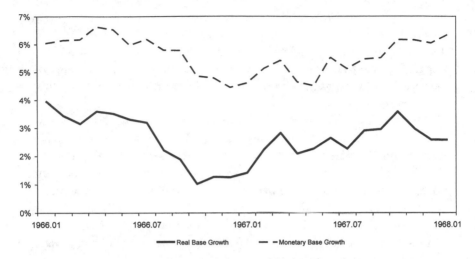

Chart 4.8. Year-over-year monetary base growth versus year-over-year real base growth, January 1966–January 1968.

Table 4.2   Policy Interpretations, 1966–68

PERIOD	NOMINAL BASE GROWTH (PERCENT)	FEDERAL FUNDS RATE
1	Easier: rose from 5.9 a.r. in 12/65 to 6.2 a.r. in 5/66	Tighter: rose from 4.3 in 12/65 to 4.9 in 5/66
2	Tighter: fell to 4.5 a.r. in 12/66	Tighter: continued to rise to 5.77 in 11/66
3	Easier: rose to 6.1 a.r. 11/67	Easier: fell to 3.79 in 7/67; then tighter: rose to 4.51 in 12/67
4	Unchanged: about 6 percent a.r. through 4/68	Tighter: continued to rise to 6.12 in 5/68

of 1966, the summer and fall of 1967, and the winter and spring of 1968. Inflation followed growth of the base and other monetary aggregates, not the federal funds rate.

Policy Decisions and Actions

The December 1965 increase in regulation Q ceiling rates permitted banks to compete more effectively against other thrift institutions. Thrift institutions attracted deposits at short rates and lent on mortgages at long-term rates. As short rates rose relative to long, many found their profits were first squeezed and then eliminated, and their profitable experiences of the early 1960s ended. Some of the largest thrifts had attracted deposits by offering certificates of deposits (CDs) with higher rates than other money market instruments. When open market rates rose, holders withdrew to the higher rates offered by banks and the market.

The thrifts curtailed lending to homebuilders, so building activity declined more than 40 percent, from a peak annual rate of 1.65 million housing starts in December 1965 to a low of 0.96 million in November 1966. The banks acquired many of the deposits that the thrifts lost but did not replace thrifts as lenders to homebuilders. Their loans went mainly to their business customers.

Thrifts and homebuilders can be found in every congressional district. They complained to the administration, Congress, and the Federal Reserve about bearing the burden of war finance and disinflation (Maisel, 1973, 91–93). They did not want to raise their deposit or borrowing rates because the higher rate would apply to new and old deposits and, more importantly, would increase costs more than revenues. Their regulator, the Federal Home Loan Bank Board, reinforced this position by threatening "to refuse loans to associations which pay more than a certain rate" (memo, Ackley to president, WHCF, Box 50, LBJ Library, June 28, 1966). As Maisel noted, the Federal Reserve relearned the problems of credit distribution that had not been prominent since 1928–29. None of the FOMC members mentioned that homebuilding was most responsive to the temporary increases in real interest that occur during a business cycle.[25]

In part to pressure the Federal Reserve into support for thrift institutions and homebuilders, the House Banking and Currency Committee held hearings at which Chairman Martin testified on June 8 and 16, 1966. Martin favored direct injection of funds into the mortgage market by an appropriation of additional funds for the Federal National Mortgage Association, a government-chartered corporation that bought mortgages. He also urged Congress to supplement monetary with fiscal policy and to permit the Federal Reserve to graduate reserve requirement ratios by size of bank. He opposed legislation that would double reserve requirement ratios against time deposits (Martin testimony, House Banking and Currency Committee, June 8 and 16, 1966).

In 1929, the Board wrote a letter to member banks warning them that the discount window should not be used by banks that maintained "speculative security loans with the aid of Federal Reserve Credit" (Board Min-

---

25. Some at the Federal Reserve were not enthusiastic about altering policy to assist the thrift industry. "One can, of course, question the extent to which the Federal Reserve should feel itself responsible for these associations, which, through usage and advertising, have encouraged people to believe they are holding deposits subject to immediate withdrawal" (letter, Hayes to Sproul, Sproul papers, Correspondence 1958–66, July 29, 1966, 1–2). Fortunately, the System as a whole accepted responsibility for the financial system, not just banks. Hayes's letter also took a narrow view of monetary policy, suggesting that certificates of deposit "allowed banks to slip away from Federal Reserve tightening, at least in the short-run" (ibid., 2).

utes, February 2, 1929; Friedman and Schwartz, 1963, 290–91; Meltzer, 2003, I, 237). At the time, the Board believed that by controlling the allocation of credit, it could limit growth of credit without changing interest rates. It was reluctant to raise the discount rate above 5 percent, in part out of concern for congressional reaction to high rates and in part from the belief that higher rates would penalize agriculture and commerce with little effect on stock exchange speculators. Banks sold state and local securities from their portfolios to lend to business customers.

Faced with pressures from Congress, homebuilders, non-bank thrifts, municipal borrowers and others in 1966, several Board members were reluctant to increase the discount rate above 5 percent.[26] Rates on negotiable CDs reached the ceiling. Board members feared that market rates would rise and require an additional increase in the discount rate and regulation Q ceiling rates.[27] Hayes mentioned an increase in discount rates and ceiling rates as a possible move in June, and proposed such a move in July.[28]

Unlike 1929, the Federal Reserve in 1966 decided to use allocation to shift credit away from business borrowers. Martin's opposition ended discussion, but only for one meeting. On July 14, with Martin away for surgery, Vice Chairman Robertson told the Board to expect requests to increase discount rates from several reserve banks. At 5.45 percent, federal funds rates were well above the discount rate suggesting that the market anticipated a 0.5 percentage point increase. Robertson reported that Secretary Fowler opposed an increase and the Federal Advisory Council thought a 0.5 increase would be a "waste of power and serve no purpose" (Board Minutes, July 14, 1966, 9). The FAC believed a one percentage point increase was called for.

26. Joseph Horne, chairman of the Federal Home Loan Bank Board, added to the pressure by criticizing the Federal Reserve for draining mortgage funding from the thrift industry (Bremner, 2004, 176). Many small savings and loans failed or merged.

27. On March 1, the FOMC chose to avoid "further rises in market interest rates to a level that would require consideration of another increase in the discount rate" (Annual Report, 1966, 132–33). On April 12, "relative pressures should not be intensified to the point at which rising market rates would call into question the viability of the current discount rate and the maximum rates permitted to be paid by member banks on time and savings deposits" (ibid., 142). Similar statements occur at other meetings. By June the concern shifted to possible loss of deposits at thrift institutions after the June interest payment date and weakness in housing starts (ibid., 159).

28. The FOMC held a special telephone meeting on July 8 to adopt a policy of smoothing float and reserve flows during a strike by airline employees. New York wanted authority to sell Treasury bills for cash currently combined with simultaneous contracts to purchase the same bills at a specified future date two or three days later (FOMC Minutes, July 11, 1966, 2–4). The main reason for the activity was to avoid the appearance of larger free reserves, suggesting that policy had eased. The committee approved the proposal. Several members were reluctant to adopt a new technique, but they voted for the proposal.

Robertson said he wanted to avoid repeating the December clash with the administration. Daane and Brimmer favored 0.5, Shephardson thought that 1 percentage point would be better because 0.5 was anticipated. The market would expect another increase later. Maisel proposed selective controls as an alternative. He wanted to reject the requests publicly.

The following day, the Board had requests from New York, Cleveland, Chicago, and St. Louis requesting a 5 percent rate. Shephardson opposed because the increase was too small. Daane hesitated on political grounds. "Every economic ground said to increase the rate; his reluctance was because such an action would be harmful to relationships with the Administration" (ibid., July 15, 1966, 3). Maisel opposed. He wanted a coordinated program. Brimmer wanted to delay the increase because Britain had increased its discount rate to strengthen its exchange rate. Robertson opposed any increase. The Board disapproved the requests without objection.[29]

Anxious to tighten without affecting the politically potent housing and thrift industries additionally, the Board wanted to reduce the relative advantage of commercial banks. Increasing reserve requirements on time deposits would raise bank costs, but small member banks would then be at a disadvantage in the market for household deposits that were relatively important to them. They too were politically active and influential. Concerned about increased loss of deposits at either small banks or thrift institutions and possible failures, the Board agreed to serve as lender of last resort to savings and loans, savings banks, and insurance companies. Also, they agreed to lend to the Treasury so that it could relend to the Home Loan Banks to support their members. This is the first explicit recognition that the System was the lender of last resort to the financial system. It was only one hundred years after Bagehot (see volume 1, chapter 2).

Torn between the several competing claims for attention, the Board decided out of political concerns that it needed more powers. The chosen solution was to seek legislation permitting the Board to set reserve requirement ratios according to bank size. On June 27, the Board responded to congressional pressure by raising reserve requirement ratios for time deposits from 4 to 5 percent at all banks with over $5 million in time deposits, effective July 14 and 21 at reserve city and country banks respectively. Smaller banks and all savings deposits remained at 4 percent. At the same time, the Board applied reserve requirement ratios and interest rate ceilings to promissory notes that had been exempt from these regulations.

29. On July 19, it disapproved Boston's request for a 1 percentage point increase, and on July 22 Philadelphia's request for a 0.5 increase.

Effective September 8 and 15, a second increase raised the time deposit reserve requirement ratio from 5 to 6 percent. The Board acted "to exert a tempering influence on bank issuance of time certificates of deposit and to apply some additional restraint upon the expansion of bank credit to businesses and other borrowers" (Annual Report, 1966, 173). The Board's action responded to the increase in yields on municipal and corporate bonds to the highest level since the 1920s and early 1930s and the political effect of reduced state and local spending growth. The Board attributed the high yields to its restrictive policy and the massive selling of municipal bonds by banks. The reasoning remains unclear. Restricting banks' access to time deposits encouraged not fewer but more bond sales.[30]

Instead of increasing the discount rate, the Board repeated its 1929 policy error of restricting access to the discount window. Governor Mitchell asked the Board's secretary, Robert Holland, to rewrite regulation A to state that "the System's discount facilities should not be made available to member banks to make adjustments incident to run-offs of certificates of deposit unless certain management policies were agreed to by the borrowing member bank" (Board Minutes, August 17, 1966, 4–5). The reserve bank presidents objected to the Board's letter, but the Board was under pressure from Congress. It justified its action as a move to remove distortions. It did not consider asking Congress to remove regulation Q (Maisel diary, February 9, 1967, 17).

The Board had maintained that borrowing was a privilege and not a right of membership, and it used persuasion to restrict access by frequent or prolonged borrowers. This action was different in kind. It attempted to control credit and money by restricting its lender of last resort function; in effect, it made CDs more costly to member banks to help non-member thrift associations. Presented as a means of restraining "the growth of credit . . . to fully reach the objectives of current monetary policy, which were of a general tightening" (ibid., August 19, 1966, 14), it did nothing of the kind. It simply shifted expansion from banks to non-banks. Most importantly, it appeased congressional critics.

The Board was now involved in allocating credit to different uses, a policy inconsistent with the fungibility of money and credit. Governor

30. On September 21, 1966, the Board also obtained authority from Congress to raise reserve requirement ratios on time and savings deposits to a 10 percent maximum and to purchase federal agency issues as part of its open market operations. The legislation also permitted the Board to post different maximum rates of interest for smaller time certificates. The Federal Home Loan Bank Board received authorization to enforce ceiling interest rates on deposits at its member thrifts. On the day the president signed the legislation, the Board lowered to 5 percent the ceiling rate for CDs of less then $100,000. The maximum rate for larger CDs remained at 5.5 percent. The legislation expired in one year but was renewed.

Robertson correctly described the aim as giving preferential treatment to banks that did not dump municipal bonds. The draft proposal called for "additional adjustment assistance credit" (borrowing) with extended duration if a bank agreed to restrict its loans (Board Minutes, Meeting with reserve bank presidents, August 23, 1966, 8).

The new regulation brought out the classic split between the market concerns of the reserve banks and the Board's political concerns that was present from the start of the System. President Hayes opposed the Board's recommendation. He recognized the central flaw. If the volume of reserves remained unchanged, credit would be available from other lenders. "Large corporations would be able to obtain elsewhere funds denied by the banking system" (ibid., 7). Further, he saw the proposal as a large, cumbersome scheme that was difficult to administer. He preferred to use open market operations to tighten credit, and he expected discounts to increase if that were done.

Other presidents were also skeptical about the proposal, or regarded it as unnecessary. Several presidents asked how they could distinguish between traditional borrowings under regulation A and the borrowings described in the memo. President Hickman pointed to the "danger in trying to guide the banks too closely in their asset management" (ibid., 24). Most preferred a higher discount rate to a change in regulation A.

Board members emphasized problems in the municipal bond market arising from banks' decisions to sell municipal bonds to supply customer loans. On August 30, Governor Shephardson reported on a telephone conversation with Chairman Martin. Martin, as always seeking consensus, expressed concern about a radical change in regulation A and the split between the reserve banks and the Board (ibid., August 30, 1966, 8). Martin's concern shifted the emphasis to developing a joint program. The result was a program to restrain business lending and a letter on September 1 to all member banks, signed by the reserve bank presidents, announcing the new program. The letter urged banks to reduce loan expansion and hold more municipal bonds. Member banks were told "to use the discount facilities . . . in a manner consistent with these efforts" (ibid., Attachment C, September 1, 1966, 2–3). In effect, the letter warned banks that loans would be available for longer periods than normal only for banks that adjusted by reducing loans instead of selling securities[31] (Sherman, 1983, 39). To reinforce the Board's allocative powers, Congress enacted legislation per-

31. Parts of the letter presumed that bankers knew the use to which credit would be put. This was a reversion to the real bills doctrine that misled the Board in the 1920s. "In considering a request for credit accommodation, each Federal Reserve Bank gives due regard to the purpose of the credit and to its probable effects upon the maintenance of sound credit

Table 4.3   Rates of Price Change in 1966–67 (percent)

DATE	GNP DEFLATOR	CONSUMER PRICES
1966		
1	4.8	3.8
2	3.5	3.3
3	3.5	4.1
4	4.6	2.0
1967		
1	2.3	1.2
2	0	3.3
3	3.4	4.0
4	4.5	3.2

mitting banks and other financial institutions to reduce interest rates paid on certain types of deposits (ibid., 40).

As the economy slowed, the problem ended. On December 23, the Board terminated the restrictions on borrowing. Prime grade municipal bond yields, with maturities from two to five years, had fallen from 4.10 percent in early September to 3.70 to 3.85 in December, 0.4 percentage points. Yields on government bonds of the same maturity declined by 0.67 to 0.72 percentage points. The program probably had little effect.

The main reasons for declining bond yields were slower economic growth and increased monetary base growth. Industrial production reached a peak in October, then declined irregularly until July 1967. The decline was modest. Real GNP growth slowed but did not turn negative. Unemployment rates remained between 3.6 and 3.9 percent throughout the period of slower growth. These were the lowest unemployment rates since 1957.

There is no clear relation between the measures of monetary contraction and the broad measures of real output and employment during this period. One likely reason is that prices adjusted promptly, more promptly than in succeeding downturns. Dating the start of monetary restriction to June 1966 suggests only a six- to nine-month lag before inflation fell. Despite expanding fiscal spending for Vietnam and the Great Society, the rate of price change responded rapidly. Table 4.3 shows the inflation data.

The reversal in policy and inflation was no less rapid. By fourth quarter 1967, Table 4.3 shows inflation had returned to the levels at the beginning of 1966. The turn in inflation followed the turn in monetary base growth by three calendar quarters.

---

conditions, both as to the individual institution and the economy generally" (Federal Reserve Bulletin, September 1966, 1339).

Administration fiscal policy supported the more restrictive policy by withdrawing the 7 percent investment tax credit that had remained in effect throughout the expansion. The aim was to slow investment spending. Wilbur Mills of the Ways and Means Committee supported the change, unlike his response to the surtax. He told Gardner Ackley, "Just have the President tell me what he wants, and we'll go to work" (memo, Ackley to the president, WHCF, Box 1, LBJ Library, August 17, 1966). On September 8, the president requested suspension of the investment credit until January 1968. At the same time, he requested some modest reductions in non-defense spending. Earlier, the administration accelerated some tax payments and increased the payroll tax by $1.5 billion beginning January 1967.

The Economic Report concluded that "after March, monetary and fiscal policy provided adequate restraint" (Council of Economic Advisers, 1967, 50). This ignores the $16.9 billion increase in federal and state government spending, including $10.9 billion in defense spending, between first and fourth quarter 1966. These increases followed increases of $10.7 billion and $5.5 billion in these spending categories during the previous quarters (ibid., 1967, 47).

The president's economic advisers in the cabinet and Council had agreed quickly on repeal of the investment tax credit. They had greater difficulty agreeing on the administration's main fiscal initiative—a surtax on income tax payments. In part, their hesitancy reflected the views of business and labor.[32] Congress was hesitant; and the president remained concerned that Congress would insist on domestic spending cuts as part of any package. Both were reluctant to act based on a forecast.

On May 11, budget director Charles Schultze warned the president that "serious inflation is almost certain unless taxes are raised." Then he added that not raising tax rates would set off "a true wage-price spiral" (memo,

---

32. In a May 5 memo, Ackley summarized the position taken at the President's Labor-Management Advisory Committee. Of the fifteen expressing an opinion, six favored and four opposed or wanted to wait. Five were undecided. Several of the business members said they expected the economy to slow in the second half of the year. Ackley added that a majority of the advisory council would have favored a tax increase "if it were not for resistance from Bill Wirtz and me" (memo, Ackley to the president, WHCF, Box 55, LBJ Library, May 5, 1966). Sproul wrote to Hayes, reporting on the views of prominent businessmen and members of the Labor Management Committee. "Ackley is said to be sort of neutral against a tax increase . . . there is some support in the Labor-Management Advisory Committee" (letter, Sproul to Hayes, Sproul papers, Correspondence 1966, May 6, 1966). Sproul reported that Douglas Dillon, David Rockefeller, and Robert Roosa had urged Secretary Fowler to increase tax rates. Fowler opposed at the time and did not change until the following year. He felt so strongly that he would not sign memos on fiscal policy written as part of the Troika process (consisting of the CEA, the Treasury, and the Budget Bureau) (Okun in Hargrove and Morley, 1984, 301).

Schultze to the president, WHCF, Box 55, LBJ Library, May 11, 1966). Not everyone agreed on the timing. From Minnesota, Walter Heller urged the president to "get ready now" for a temporary income tax boost to be used when the president believed the timing was right.[33]

President Johnson had repeated several times that he was prepared for higher tax rates if military spending increased substantially. Chairman Martin urged him to act, but Secretary Fowler sent a long memo stating the pros and cons but not recommending any action. In August, Ackley began to urge that the administration make a coordination agreement with the Federal Reserve—"get the Federal Reserve on record promising to adjust the monetary policy screws . . . in return for a new fiscal program" (memo, Ackley to the president, WHCF, Box 55, LBJ Library, August 9, 1966, 3). This idea gained strength as time passed, and the housing market remained weak.[34]

In December, the administration had to decide on its policy recommendation for 1967. One internal recommendation called for more stimulus to expand spending and offset the slowdown, which had become very visible.[35] Others favored a delayed tax increase. Finally, the advisers agreed on a mixture of stimulus and delayed restraint. They proposed to reinstate the 7 percent investment tax credit and put a 6 percent surtax on individual and corporate taxes with an exemption for the two lowest brackets of the tax code, effective July 1, 1967.[36]

33. This revived an earlier proposal to give the president limited stand-by authority to change tax rates. Attached to the Heller memo was a copy of a letter to the *New York Times* that read in part, "The Administration feels that, on balance, the signals don't clearly call for early fiscal action" (memo, Heller to the president, CF, Box 44, LBJ Library, May 11 and 13, 1966).

34. Secretary Fowler suggested earlier that the Federal Reserve should reduce regulation Q ceiling rates to 5 percent in exchange for a tax increase (memo, Joseph Califano to the president, WHCF, Box 23, LBJ Library, May 7, 1966, 6).

35. Forecasts and recommendations developed through staff to sub-cabinet officials, then to cabinet-rank officials—the Treasury Secretary, Council Chairman, and Budget Director. A similar proposal came to the president from the National Security Council staff member concerned with economic policy, Francis Bator. A memo to the president summarized the positions of members of the Board of Governors and the Council. Governors Maisel and Mitchell opposed any tax increase. The Federal Reserve staff "strongly opposes a tax increase." Brimmer saw no need but could accept a small ($4 to $5 billion) increase if used to protect the president's domestic programs. Robertson wanted the tax increases and believed it would help ease money. At the Council, Okun opposed a tax increase because he feared a weak economy. He could accept a July 1 increase. James Duesenberry favored a small tax increase. The memo noted that Okun and Duesenberry "each held the exact opposite view a few days ago." The memo reports also that Schultze favored a small increase in July (memo, Califano to the president, CF, Box 44, December 23, 1966). Duesenberry joined the Council in February 1966.

36. Arthur Burns, later chairman of the Board of Governors, was one of several witnesses

In July, both Secretary Fowler and Chairman Ackley lobbied Board members Daane, Brimmer, Robertson, and Maisel not to increase the discount rate. The reasoning emphasized political concerns. With Martin and Mitchell absent, only Shephardson was left to support an increase. The Board voted five to zero to turn down the banks' requests (memo, Ackley to the president, WHCF, Box 50, LBJ Library, July 16, 1966). Coordination now dominated independence for many at the Federal Reserve, so political concerns dominated economics. But they soon found that coordination and politics worked one way. Getting a change to a more restrictive fiscal policy proved more difficult than they expected.

By August, Senators Albert Gore and Russell Long, members of the president's party, denounced the high interest rate policy and the recent increase in bank prime rates. The House Committee on Banking and Currency passed a bill putting a 4.5 percent ceiling on interest paid on time deposits under $100,000 and 5.5 percent over that limit. Higher rates on large certificates could be established only with the president's approval. The bill also increased reserve requirements on time deposits to 10 percent.

The Board was disturbed by the political response and the direct intervention by Congress into its (delegated) jurisdiction. It responded by proposing an alternative to the Senate. Instead of removing regulation Q, the bill extended its reach to include the Home Loan Bank Board and its members. Instead of mandating a 10 percent reserve requirement ratio, it authorized the Board to do so if appropriate in its judgment (H. A. Bilby to Hayes, Correspondence Box 240, Federal Reserve Bank of New York, August 4, 1966). When passed in September, the legislation permitted the Board and the Home Loan Bank Board to set different ceiling rates for small and large deposits. The Board wasted no time in implementing the new legislation by lowering the interest rates on certificates of deposit under $100,000 face value. It left the 4 percent interest rate on saving accounts unchanged despite a strong plea from one of the New York banks to raise the rate (letter, George Champion to the Board, Correspondence Box 240, Federal Reserve Bank of New York, October 19, 1966). Initially temporary, the new rules later became permanent.

The Vietnam War and its financing produced a very different result than Korea. Inflation was much greater. The economic scope of the war was not much greater; government purchases for national defense were

---

at hearings on the tax surcharge. In a preview of his views on anti-inflation policy in the Nixon administration, he said, "Once an inflationary spiral gets underway, I'm afraid there isn't a great deal to be done constructively. A severe recession would bring it to a halt, but no one wants that" (Joint Economic Committee, 1967, 551).

Table 4.4 Economic Data for the Korea and Vietnam War Periods

	KOREAN WAR				VIETNAM WAR		
Date	Base Growth (annual rate)	Free Reserves ($ millions)	National Defense Purchases ($ billions)	Date	Base Growth (annual rate)	Free Reserves ($ millions)	National Defense Purchases ($ billions)
1950:3	1.14	592	14.2	1965:3	6.15	−151	50.1
:4	−4.79	749	17.1	:4	7.62	−77	52.5
1951:1	12.02	461	24.1	1966:1	5.19	−132	55.3
:2	4.50	496	30.4	:2	2.48	−324	58.5
:3	3.08	452	37.7	:3	5.93	−373	63.3
:4	6.23	460	42.1	:4	2.99	−273	65.6
1952:1	5.39	544	42.5	1967:1	8.07	72	69.9
:2	1.84	159	45.7	:2	4.24	247	71.9
Average	3.68	489	31.7		5.33	−126	60.9

twice as large in the Vietnam period, but GNP had increased 2.3 times between 1952 and 1967. A more important difference is the more rapid growth rate of the monetary base. Judged by free reserves or nominal interest rates, monetary policy was much more restrictive during the Vietnam War. Ackley explained to the president, once again, that interest rates on government and corporate bonds were close to the peak 1921 rates, but he neglected to mention that in 1921 the economy was in deflation, not inflation, so real rates were much higher in 1921. Judged by monetary base growth, policy was more inflationary than during the Korean War. Table 4.4 compares data for the two wartime periods.

Fiscal policy contributed to the inflation in two principal ways. President Truman was a fiscal conservative who insisted on budget balance and managed to achieve either a small deficit or a surplus by raising tax rates. The Federal Reserve had smaller deficits to finance and pursued a less inflationary policy. President Johnson ran large deficits in 1967 and 1968. Under the "new economics" of coordinated fiscal and monetary policy, the Federal Reserve would not raise interest rates enough to keep inflation low, so the larger deficit was financed by higher money growth.[37]

The Federal Reserve began to lower interest rates in the fall. It reduced the ceiling rate for time deposits to 5 percent on time deposits of less than $100,000 but left the rate at 5.5 percent for longer-term deposits. By a 10 to 2 vote on November 22, it changed the directive from "maintaining

37. The difference in inflationary effects of the policy showed up with a lag. By 1953, consumer price were rising at 1 percent or less. In 1968 they rose at 4 percent or more.

steady conditions" to seeking "somewhat easier conditions." Free reserve rose and the federal funds rate fell.[38]

Governor Robertson took the lead. "A number of key increases of business activity are softening. Much of this slackening is probably the direct or indirect consequences of restrictive monetary public policies . . . [W]e have had no net growth in bank credit or money supply for three and six months respectively" (FOMC Minutes, November 22, 1966, 86).[39]

Chairman Martin remained cautious. He favored a change to show that the FOMC "was aware of a change in the basic elements of the economy" (ibid., 90). Unemployment remained low, and the first decline in industrial production came in November, so it was not known at the meeting. However, stock prices had fallen in nine of the previous eleven months.

President Hayes and Governor Daane dissented. They saw no reason for an overt policy change. They agreed that the economy had weakened, but they cited rising defense spending, rising inflation, and a growing balance of payments deficit. The FOMC had adopted a proviso clause per-

38. The effort to adjust maximum ceiling rates responded to a sharp increase in yields on longer-term securities during the summer. One reason was that banks sold municipal bonds to satisfy loan demand. Since they were normally large buyers of these bonds, and the new supply continued to increase, there were reports of unsettled conditions and days on which there were no bids in the secondary market. On August 3, President Johnson asked for a 10 percent tax surcharge, effective October 1 to reduce the budget deficit and the size of new Treasury issues. On September 13, Congress approved the Financial Institutions Supervisory Act of 1966. The Federal Reserve received authority to buy and sell all federal agency obligations to assist the mortgage market. The act also extended interest rate ceilings to all financial institutions supervised by federal agencies. In the hearings leading to the act, members of Congress and the heads of other agencies criticized the Federal Reserve for failure to give advance notice or coordinate policy with other financial regulatory agencies (House Committee on Banking and Currency, 1966, 280–81, 556). The result was a coordinating committee that included representatives of the Federal Reserve, the Comptroller, the Home Loan Bank Board, and the FDIC.

Federal Reserve officials did not welcome permission to buy agency issues. When Sproul criticized the proposal in a letter to Hayes, Hayes replied agreeing with Sproul. "Some of its proponents undoubtedly think of it as a means of pressuring the System to support the market for this type of obligation. I can assure you that there is no disposition whatever in the System to accept an assignment of this kind, and I hope and trust that we can resist any efforts to change our mind" (letter, Hayes to Sproul, Sproul papers, Correspondence 1966, August 25, 1966). No one mentioned that trying to adjust relative rates of interest was unlikely to have much effect.

39. Beginning with the November 22 meeting, I had the use of Sherman J. Maisel's diary written at about the time of each meeting. Maisel served as a governor from April 1965 to May 1972. He reconstructed notes for the meetings he attended prior to November 22. The diary is a valuable supplement to the minutes and other official materials. I am grateful to him for making these materials available. After using them, I deposited them at the Board of Governors.

mitting the manager to adjust his money market targets to larger than anticipated changes in the bank credit proxy—total bank deposits. Both dissenters believed that was sufficient.[40]

Despite the sharp decline in housing, reported GNP growth increased in the third quarter and inflation rose. In November, the credit proxy (total deposits) declined at a 3 percent annual rate. The FOMC divided eight to four at its December 13 meeting. The majority recognized the rising balance of payments deficit but preferred to rely on the voluntary guidelines for investment and asset acquisition. Shephardson and Irons (Dallas) joined Hayes and Daane in dissent. They expressed greater concern about inflation and the payments imbalance. A more contentious issue arose over a proposal by Mitchell, Robertson, Brimmer, Maisel, and Hickman (Cleveland) to target a moderate rate of increase in the money and bank credit aggregates. "Chairman Martin objected strongly to this proposed amendment. . . . [They] had to use a money market directive" (Maisel diary, December 13, 1966, 6). Maisel urged that the FOMC vote on the proposal, but Martin refused. Martin also refused to let the public know that policy had eased. "Brimmer made the point that policies of the System ought to be open and published and not told to a few select bankers" (ibid., 7). The chairman's view prevailed.

By early January 1967, the federal funds rate was 5.14 percent, 0.82 percentage points below its high in mid-November. Free reserves were in the −$800 to −$900 range, usually considered restrictive. As shown in Chart 4.7 above, growth of the real monetary base began to increase, and the index of stock prices rose in November and December.[41]

Chairman Martin reported these developments to the Joint Economic

40. At its November 1 meeting the FOMC authorized the manager to make repurchase agreements using government agency securities. The committee proposed further study of open market purchases of agency securities. Martin notified Gardner Ackley of the change the next morning. Ackley told the president that perhaps "if we do more on taxes the Fed is ready to move on money" (memo to the president, WHCF, Box 282, LBJ Library, November 23, 1966).

41. Urged by the Council, the Board of Governors withdrew the September 1 letter restricting use of the discount window (memo, Ackley to the president, WHCF, Box 282, LBJ Library, December 23, 1966). Bankers on the Federal Advisory Council (FAC) disliked the restrictions on discounting. The rules were uncertain. "The concern was whether the city banks could depend on the Federal Reserve if they needed money in a situation such as seemed likely to occur in the next few months" (Board Minutes, September 20, 1966, 8). Bankers on FAC gave examples of national companies coming to regional markets to borrow and borrowers offering government securities as collateral. If the banks restricted loans, the borrowers would sell the securities; they claimed this would defeat the program. The bankers also complained that the program reduced business lending for new capital spending, so there would be less production in the future. Selective controls had thrown "the whole interest rate structure out of balance" (Board Minutes, November 15, 1966, 23).

Committee, emphasizing the economy's resilience and the need to restore full use of resources and price stability (Martin speeches, February 9, 1967). Market opinion, reinforced by a small uptick in the federal funds rate, emphasized Martin's concern about inflation. Long-term rates rose. To counter this interpretation, the Board appeased populist members of Congress by reducing reserve requirement ratios against saving accounts from 4 to 3 percent for banks with less than $5 million in deposits, effective in March (Maisel diary, February 28, 1967, 5). Large banks remained at 6 percent. Robertson explained that one reason for limiting the reduction to small banks was to avoid increasing the capital outflow. If large banks received the additional free reserves, they "might be inclined to pay off borrowings from their foreign branches" (ibid., February 28, 1967, 12). This would appear as a reduction in liabilities to foreign institutions. In mid-March, the FOMC lowered the federal funds rate target to 4.5 percent over Hayes's objection.[42] Robertson and others argued that the move would signal the market and change market expectations. Martin warned about trying to manage expectations. "The real question was the availability of reserves. He would like to have more available" (Board Minutes, February 27, 1967, 27). By reducing the federal funds rate and increasing free reserves, the Board maintained easier policy.[43]

The easing policy continued until May. The FOMC then shifted to a policy of maintaining money market conditions but not easing further. Chairman Martin described the FOMC's actions during the winter as seeking "an easier, but not an easy, policy" (FOMC Minutes, January 10, 1967, 76). Governor Maisel raised two issues. First, he proposed to reverse procedures; the FOMC should choose credit and reserves as its primary targets and make interest rates a subsidiary guide. "By adopting interest rates or money market conditions alone, the Committee was likely to pay too much attention to most recent events" (ibid., 47). Second, Maisel asked whether FOMC should give more attention to interest rate levels or changes.

Maisel's effort to focus on medium- to longer-term goals drew little re-

---

42. President Johnson reappointed Martin as chairman. The Board requested that he waive the requirement that Governor Shephardson retire at age sixty-five, but the president did not do so. He kept his commitment to Martin by permitting Shephardson to remain at the Board to continue planning a new building (later called the Martin Building) at unchanged salary. The same arrangement had been used for Adolph Miller in 1936. Subsequently, the president appointed William Sherrill to fill the unexpired term. Ackley supported Martin's reappointment because "the policy of the Federal Reserve would be determined by the majority of the Board" (Maisel diary, April 4, 1967, 1).

43. For once a member of the staff made the point explicit. "If a reduction in reserves required against savings deposits was simply offset by open market operations, nothing would appear to be gained" (Board Minutes, February 27, 1967, 32).

sponse. Mitchell dismissed it with a peculiar argument that supported the opposite conclusion from the one he drew. "He thought the basic problem lay in the short-run because the lags in transmitting the effects of policy changes . . . were rather substantial" (ibid., 51).

Martin described the members "for the most part to be in agreement" (ibid., 76), but three members—Trieber (New York), Irons (Dallas) and Shephardson—dissented from the decision, citing weakness in the balance of payments and uncertainty about the administration's fiscal policy. The dissents reflected different weights on objectives. The staff report showed inflation slowing as measured by falling wholesale prices and a 0.1 percent increase in consumer prices. The main evidence of continuing inflation was a rise in unit labor costs, attributed in part to slower productivity growth (Annual Report, 1966, 95). The main reason for greater ease was the near-term prospect for the economy. The dissenters agreed on the near-term outlook but noted that "longer-run prospects for the economy were not weak" (ibid., 100).[44]

Free reserves rose following the meeting. This was the only sign of increased ease in the data that the staff monitored.[45] The federal funds rate remained unchanged, but the inflation rate for February was below the January rate, so the real (inflation adjusted) federal funds rate rose.

The proviso clause was one way of imposing longer-term aims of monetary policy on daily or weekly operations.[46] Beginning in 1966 the staff began to provide the members with forecasts of output, inflation, and other variables, and estimated the volume of total deposits (credit proxy) associated with the forecast and the equilibrium interest rate consistent with the forecasts. Brill's memo suggests that the staff was highly uncertain about the relationships and the accuracy of their estimates and forecasts. He recognized that bank credit could change because of reallocation from other types of credit, that short-run changes could reverse quickly, and that many of the variables of interest could be measured inaccurately or not at all

44. In January, Secretary Fowler proposed to the president that the administration ask again for relaxation of the 4.25 percent ceiling rate on government bonds with five years or more to maturity. He rested his case on the desirability of extending average debt maturity, then less than five years. Ackley agreed with the desirability of extending average maturity but opposed the proposal because the timing was wrong (memo, Ackley to the president, WHCF, Box 51, LBJ Library, January 26, 1967).

45. Growth of the monetary base and the money stock increased after January.

46. Brunner and Meltzer (1967) opened the analytic issue of choosing the optimal intermediate indicator to judge whether policy deviated from the path consistent with the long-term objectives of maximum output growth consistent with price stability under the uncertainty that policymakers faced. The bank credit proxy attempted to provide an intermediate indicator of that kind (memo, Directives and Staff Projections, Daniel Brill to George Mitchell, Board Records, October 11, 1967).

for the three-week period between meetings (memo, Directives and Staff Projections, Daniel Brill to George Mitchell, Board Records, October 11, 1967). Instead of searching for more stable long-term relations, the Board's staff concentrated on developing data on balance sheet changes (the flow of funds) and estimating a large-scale econometric model to exploit these data and forecast future values.[47]

George Ellis (Boston) opened discussion of a discount rate reduction in February, by suggesting that the discount rate had become a "prop holding up market rates" (FOMC Minutes, February 7, 1967, 47). Martin opposed a reduction. Overreaching "could be self defeating" (ibid., 80). A reduction might have to be reversed soon. He also opposed Maisel's proposal to substitute medium- and long-term interest rates for the credit proxy in the proviso clause. Maisel's proposal received no support from other members.

Boston reopened the discount rate issue by voting to reduce its rate from 4.5 to 4.25 per cent on March 27. The Board could not decide whether a 0.25 percentage point reduction was enough, so it postponed the vote until after the April 4 FOMC meeting. Martin spoke in favor of 0.5 percentage point reduction to 4 percent, but if the directors voted for 4.25 percent, he could accept a split rate temporarily.[48] Following the meeting, ten banks voted to reduce the rate to 4 percent. Atlanta asked for 4.25 percent, and St. Louis kept its rate at 4.5 percent. Governor Brimmer said he would not approve a 4.5 percent rate, and several other governors agreed (Board Minutes, April 6, 1967, 7). The Board approved the 4 percent rate and deferred approval of Atlanta and St. Louis. Within a week all banks posted the 4 percent rate. The federal funds rate fell from 4.55 to below 4 percent following the announcement. West Germany and Canada followed the reduction immediately.

At about this time, Homer Jones, first vice president at the St. Louis bank, wrote to Robert Holland, secretary of the Open Market Committee. For the first time since the early 1930s, someone in the System pointed out that interest rates could decline because of low demand for credit. A decline of that kind should not be confused with easier policy.[49] A few weeks

47. The econometric model was a joint product of members of the Board's staff and Professors Franco Modigliani of MIT and Albert Ando of the University of Pennsylvania.

48. Among the reasons for Martin's changed position was the rise in market rates at the end of February. On February 24, bill rates were 0.14 percentage points above January–February lows, but Aa corporate rates and new municipal bond yields rose 0.26. Ackley told the president that "they all seem to favor giving some signal to show that they are still moving toward easier money" (memo, Ackley to the president, WHCF, Box 51, LBJ Library, February 25, 1967). The administration restored the investment tax credit in March. Martin testified for restoration of the credit.

49. "I fear that all our resolves to ease money market conditions may be no more than

later, Sherman Maisel proposed lengthening quarterly FOMC meetings to provide more time for discussion of economic forecasts or projections and "to get a clear picture of various views on where the economy was going and what proper goals for System policy ought to be during the coming period" (S. J. Maisel to the Board, Board Records, May 29, 1967). This was one of several efforts that Maisel made to develop a more explicit, more coherent policy framework that looked beyond the money market and the next three weeks. The Board approved the proposal for further discussion at the FOMC. No action appears to have been taken.

In April and May, monthly consumer prices rose at a 2.4 and 3.6 percent annual rate, and unit labor costs were 4.7 percent above a year earlier, the largest increase in almost a decade. Productivity growth had slowed to about 2 percent from the faster growth earlier in the decade, so the implied inflation rate was about 2.5 percent (see Chart 3.1). "In contrast to the developments in short-term markets, long-term interest rates had risen considerably . . . reaching levels well above the highs of late February" (Annual Report, 1966, 124). The staff interpreted the rise in yields as a response to the volume of new bond issues and optimism about recovery. There is no mention of inflationary expectations affecting interest rates and the volume of long-term borrowing. There is discussion of the rapidly rising budget deficit.

The spread between short- and long-term rates increased, surprising and puzzling the staff and most of the members. Their main explanation was that the borrowing had increased because corporations believed that the cyclical lows had been reached.[50] Chart 4.7 above suggests that, although nominal rates increased, real long-term rates declined with actual and anticipated inflation. The System's rapid response to recession contrasted with its sluggish and hesitant response to inflation. When policy started to ease in February, the unemployment rate was 3.8 percent, considered low, with consumer price inflation at 2.8 percent, considered high at the time. The System's actions may have been appropriate based on their forecasts and projections, but the asymmetry in their response gave a warning about their priorities.

Citing "even keel" considerations, the FOMC took no action on May

---

keeping up with the deterioration in the demand for loan funds—that all the declines in interest rates reflect this deterioration of demand rather than anything we are positively doing" (letter, Homer Jones to Robert Holland, Board Records, March 9, 1967). There is no sign that the letter affected policy interpretations.

50. The Treasury again asked Congress to raise the ceiling on bonds with over five years original maturity. Maisel accused them of neglecting the economic consequences and the expectations aroused by their request (Maisel diary, May 24, 1967, 2).

2. Three weeks later, the members expressed concern about continued increases in long-term yields, despite "some dampening of earlier market optimism" (ibid., 30). The staff reported rapid growth of the money stock and anticipated further increases. The committee agreed to purchase long-term securities, instead of bills, to reduce bond yields and, perhaps, raise short-term rates "for balance of payments reasons." But it voted to keep money market conditions unchanged. Between April and November 1967, it increased its holdings by almost $6 billion, 12 percent of the existing monetary base.

Darryl Francis (St. Louis) dissented, citing the highly stimulative monetary and fiscal policies. He told the committee that "with total demand at a high level and likely to increase rapidly in coming months, with fiscal actions so expansionary, and with recent large increases in supplies of money and credit, he felt it was time to avoid overreacting to the pause in total demand of last fall and winter" (FOMC Minutes, May 23, 1967, 81). No one joined him.

A few days later, Ackley and Arthur Okun met the governors at their regular luncheon at the Board. Ackley described the Board as "as troubled as we are about what has been happening to long-term interest rates and the threat that housing will be clobbered again" (memo, Ackley to the president, WHCF, Box 51, LBJ Library, May 26, 1967). The Council members came "prepared to push them hard on why they weren't buying long-term bonds and whether they shouldn't consider reducing the discount rate" (ibid.). Ackley was delighted to learn that they had started buying long-term bonds that week and had considered reducing discount rates. He told the president that the Board thought that "the market is convinced a boom is coming and that no tax action will be taken" (ibid.). The Board wanted the president to call at once for a tax increase in the fall.[51] Maisel conjectured that if Congress approved the tax surcharge, four or five Board members "would be willing to see monetary policy eased as soon as the tax increases passed" (Maisel diary, June 20, 1967, 7).

In June, money growth reached a 13 percent annual rate. "In the six months through June 1967, time deposits had risen at an annual rate of 17 percent, the money supply almost 7 percent, and the bank credit proxy, 12 percent" (Annual Report, 1967, 147). The staff expected the proxy to in-

---

51. At the time, the unemployment rate was 3.8 percent. It remained at 4 percent or less for the entire slowdown. Stock prices had increased for seven months and were 20 percent above their previous low. Prices had risen, and money growth was excessive, but Ackley wanted more stimulus. The sustained low unemployment rate suggests that business managements did not expect a prolonged slowdown. The Freedom of Information Act now required the FOMC to publish its decisions within ninety days.

crease at a faster rate from June to July. "In the course of the Committee's discussion considerable concern was expressed about the recent high rates of growth of bank credit and the money supply, particularly in view of the prospects for more rapid economic expansion later in the year" (ibid., 147). Forthcoming Treasury operations suggested an even keel. The main issue about policy was whether the directive should call for continued purchases of coupon securities. The vote was seven to three to remove the reference, with Brimmer, Maisel, and Mitchell in the minority and Martin and Daane absent.

Hayes recognized "the strong underlying case for some firming of policy in the light of inflationary risks, the balance of payments situation, and the need to moderate the growth of bank credit and deposits" (FOMC Minutes, July 18, 1967, 55–56). In Martin's absence he stated the consensus as keeping policy unchanged. He gave four reasons. First, excessive growth of demand was "only a forecast rather than a present reality; second . . . even a modest firming of policy would run the risk of a dangerous overreaction in financial markets; third, it would . . . disturb the prospects for quick action on taxes; and, finally, . . . insufficient time to change policy . . . before even keel considerations become a factor" (ibid., 56). Even keel prevented any action, but the majority agreed on a one-way proviso clause. The desk would permit slower growth of credit and money, if it occurred.

On August 3, the president requested enactment of a 10 percent tax surcharge, effective October 1. Congress delayed nine months before passage. By that time the annual rate of consumer price increase had reached 4.5 percent, on its way higher. Monetary base growth was above 6 percent. The unemployment rate soon reached 3.4 percent, the lowest rate since 1951–53. Unemployment did not approach that level again until 2000.[52]

The reasons for the delay in getting the surtax approved show three major obstacles to using fiscal policy for short-run stabilization. First, the policy advisers had to be convinced about the need for restraint and the appropriate timing. Ackley and his colleagues vacillated, as did others in the administration. A strong, consistent message from all of his advisers might have moved the president to be more forceful, but that strong consensus was slow to form.[53] Second, Wilbur Mills, chairman of the House

52. Ackley recognized the policy error. He explained that Chairman Mills of the Ways and Means Committee would not accept forecasts that the economy would pick up in the second half of 1967. His later recollection was that "we never backed away from our recommendation; but it was not the best time to be going public with this fight." Then he added, "I guess we were not pushing very hard" (Hargrove and Morley, 1984, 257).

53. "In that period, [1966] Fowler was not signing Troika memos, not signing memos jointly with Ackley urging tax increases" (Okun, in Hargrove and Morley, 1984, 302). Even in 1968, the advisers divided. Okun described Fowler as willing to take "any cut in domestic

Ways and Means Committee, was reluctant to introduce the bill partly because it lacked support and partly because President Johnson would not agree to the spending reductions that Mills believed necessary to get enough votes to pass the bill. Third, President Johnson hesitated to cut back his Great Society programs. "The President was entirely convinced that he couldn't get it, that it would be a mistake to ask for it, and that it would boomerang in terms of substantial cuts in his social programs. . . . [H]e believed he couldn't afford to lose a major battle on a major issue of policy" (Ackley in Hargrove and Morley, 1984, 254).[54]

In retrospect, several of the principals joined others in blaming the inflation on President Johnson's secrecy about the increase in expenditures for Vietnam. The claim is that they would have urged the president to request the tax surcharge. The record shows that even after the increased spending was known, Congress was unwilling to increase tax rates, and the president was unwilling to reduce social spending.

These were not the only reasons. The FOMC and the administration economists gave excessive emphasis to the budget deficit and too little attention to money growth. Despite unemployment below 4 percent, they were not willing to insist strongly on the need for restraint. Their analysis was wrong, and their policy and recommendations reflected the error. And, as usual, they ignored both real interest rates and money growth.

Delay in getting a tax increase and commitment to policy coordination had decisive influences on Federal Reserve decisions. In September, Martin told the FOMC: "With fiscal policy strongly stimulative pending action on the President's tax program, the simple logic of the economic situation implied the desirability of changing monetary policy, as it probably had as much as two months ago. But the overriding need at this point was to get some restraint from fiscal policy through a tax increase, and in his judgment *that would be less likely if Congress came to believe that adequate restraint was being exercised by monetary policy.* . . . [A] modest operation would not result in any major gains; at the same time its significance was likely to be greatly exaggerated, thus *exposing the System to misrepresenta-*

---

spending to get the tax increase. . . . Zwick really was dragging his heels on any significant expenditure cut . . . [T]he agency heads whose program would have been gored by a spending cut did not see the same urgency in the tax surcharge that Fowler and I did" (ibid., 303) Charles Zwick replaced Charles Schultze as budget director.

54. One of Mills' ways of pressuring the president and the administration was to open hearings, hear witnesses, sense the atmosphere, and shut down the hearings if he didn't believe the bill would pass without more concessions from the administration. Both Okun and Ackley describe the president as unusually passive about the bill, leaving the negotiations to Secretary Fowler. Passivity seems not correct. Califano (2000, 112) reports that Congressman Mills and Senator Russell Long told him that a tax increase could not be passed..

tion of its position on the question of the appropriate mix of fiscal and monetary policy (FOMC Minutes, September 12, 1967, 73–74; emphasis added). A majority of the FOMC agreed with Martin's position.[55] Policy coordination worked perversely.

At the time of the September meeting, the staff reported that industrial production had recovered its modest loss during the slowdown. Unemployment fell; housing starts rose strongly in July, and the outlook called for a strong expansion in GNP. Inflation continued to increase. Nevertheless, the FOMC followed Martin and voted nine to three for no change. Hayes, Francis (St. Louis), and Scanlon (Chicago) dissented but did not agree on the alternative. Francis said that fiscal stimulus would remain strong even if Congress passed the surtax. He wanted "significantly firmer money market conditions" (Annual Report, 1966, 166). Hayes and Scanlon wanted a small first step toward "moderately less easy conditions" (ibid., 166).[56]

The following day, Martin testified for the surtax before the House Ways and Means Committee. There can be no doubt that he saw the risk of inflation. On this occasion, as on several others for the next four months, he warned Congress about the dangers of inflation, strains in the international monetary system and in the mortgage market (Martin speeches, September 14, 1967, 11–12).

The FAC favored a "considerably less expansive" fiscal policy achieved mainly by reducing spending but they did not oppose a tax increase. They wanted less expansive monetary policy but expressed concern about another credit crunch (Board Minutes, September 29, 1967, 27).

Expansion and inflation continued. The FOMC voted to maintain prevailing money market conditions, and Francis continued to dissent at the next two meetings. Others recognized the inflation risk, the strong recovery, and the balance of payments problem. At the October 3 meeting, Hayes stated the consensus. "Most members seemed to believe that there

55. Maisel described the division within FOMC. By maintaining rapid growth in money and credit, the economy would grow at 8 percent in 1968, 5 percent real and 3 percent inflation. With more restrictive policy, real growth would fall to 2 to 3 percent and inflation to 2 percent. A slight majority of the presidents would choose slower growth and less inflation. A majority of the Board preferred higher growth with higher inflation (Maisel diary, August 15, 1967, 6). Despite the surcharge actual growth, fourth quarter to fourth quarter, was 3.6 percent with inflation 5.8 percent.

56. The start of an automobile workers' strike was one reason for some of the votes for no change. Maisel's diary (September 13, 1967, 4–5) reported that the division of opinion was much closer, six to five against a tighter policy, before Martin spoke. Four of the presidents favored a tighter policy, and five of the Board opposed. Again, coordination and political concerns got in the way of appropriate monetary policy. Martin argued that the president would feel "betrayed" if the FOMC tightened. Mitchell and Swan (San Francisco) shifted their votes.

were strong economic grounds for taking some firming action today. It was clear, however, that after weighing various other considerations the majority thought it would not be desirable to change policy at this time" (FOMC Minutes, October 3, 1967, 99).[57]

The reasons for not acting covered a wide range. Some cited the auto strike, near-term Treasury financing, and "the highly critical position of sterling" (ibid., 45). The reasons always included "the extent to which action by it [the Federal Reserve] may enhance or impede the chances of getting a tax increase" (ibid., November 24, 1967, 33).

Francis pointed out that even keel policy led to excessive money growth. "Failure to restrict the present excessive expansion of money and bank credit was sometimes justified on the grounds that there must be no interference with Treasury financing. To his mind, this was a pernicious doctrine. . . . [I]t meant that when the Federal budget was excessively stimulative and was running deficits, . . . monetary actions were also excessively stimulative" (FOMC Minutes, October 24, 1967, 34). Francis did not take the next step by recommending securities auctions instead of fixed price issues. Even keel would then be unnecessary.[58]

Martin recognized the problem but would not do anything to relieve it. For him, the deficit caused inflation, not the Federal Reserve. "Large deficits in the budget are rapidly generating inexorable forces that might prove more important than any decisions the committee would take" (ibid., 66). He also feared a return to conditions in the summer of 1966 and wanted to avoid a repetition, particularly the political response by the thrift institutions, the homebuilders, and their representatives in Congress. Although he spoke in apocalyptic terms, as in most of 1965, he favored a policy of no change.[59]

57. By this time, Secretary Fowler was pressing hard for the surtax. On October 19, he warned the president that "without the tax surcharge interest rates will rise markedly above today's already high levels. . . . It is difficult for me to understand why anybody who was concerned with high interest rates last year can do anything but strive for the early enactment of your tax proposals this year" (memo, Fowler to the president, WHCF, Box 51, LBJ Library, October 19, 1967). But Congressman Mills and Senator Long remained unconvinced about the need for higher tax rates; Mills preferred spending reductions, particularly spending on the Great Society programs.

58. Francis also commented on some of the other reasons for delay. He recognized the critical problems of the British pound. The best policy for the United States was to have a long-term strategy to lower interest rates in the U.S. instead of preventing an increase for the next few weeks. He also rejected the argument that tightening in 1966 produced severe problems for the construction industry. The Committee "had done a good thing that should be repeated as called for, not . . . a bad thing which must be avoided at all costs" (FOMC Minutes, October 24, 1967, 35–36). These arguments did not persuade the other members to vote with him.

59. An example is "The moment of truth for Federal Reserve and Governmental policy

In late October, renewed weakness in the pound gave a new reason for delay in raising the short-term rate. The market did not wait. Convinced that Congress would not pass the tax bill and that the Federal Reserve would not act, investors in long-term bonds raised rates nearly 0.5 percentage points in three months, suggesting that the market expected inflation to increase. The only action the Board took aimed at speculation; it tightened stock market margins by including convertible bonds under margin requirements.

By December 12, the automobile workers had a new contract, the British had devalued the pound by 14.3 percent on November 18 to $2.40, and the GNP deflator was rising at a 6.5 percent annual rate for the quarter. The federal funds rate had remained at about 4 percent since April, but long-term bond yields had risen by 60 basis points to 5.4 percent. This was the highest average yield on government bonds since 1920.

The Federal Reserve increased the discount rate by 0.5 percentage points on November 18 in response to the British devaluation. The discussion divided those who wanted to increase the rate by 1 percentage point from those who wanted 0.5. The Board rejected New York's request for 1 percentage point. New York agreed to the smaller increase "with a strong protest" (Maisel diary, November 20, 1967, 6). Open market rates rose following the discount rate increase and some rates on large bank CDs were back at the 5.5 percent ceiling.

Martin at last conceded that he had waited too long for the surtax that had not come. He repeated some of his earlier arguments. The proper time for an increase had been months ago but that would have made "Congressional action on taxes less likely" (FOMC Minutes, December 12, 1967, 97). It was too late to prevent inflation. "The horse of inflation not only was out of the barn but was already well down the road" (ibid., 98). Coming into an election year, Congress increased social security benefits and raised the minimum wage and federal pay.

The reason for acting in December was to show the market that the FOMC "was not unwilling to act to resist inflationary pressures. That, to

<hr/>

was approaching" (FOMC Minutes, October 24, 1967, 66). A few weeks earlier, Martin and Robertson told Secretary Fowler about pressures to tighten from the regional federal reserve banks. "They further indicated their judgment that it would be a mistake to . . . change from a policy of monetary ease at this time" (memo, Fowler to the president, WHCF, Box 2, LBJ Library, October 9, 1967). Fowler's response included some market commentary that read in part that the House Ways and Means Committee "'temporarily' tabled the tax proposals and decided that 'further consideration [will] be deferred until such time as the President and the Congress reach an understanding on . . . more effective expenditure reduction and controls as an essential corollary of a tax increase.'" The vote for Congressman Mills's motion was twenty to five.

his mind, was more important than the matter of the scale of the action" (ibid., 97). The FOMC voted for only slightly firmer conditions fearing repetition of the effects on housing and the need to increase regulation Q ceiling rates.

This time the bank presidents favored higher rates; the Board members, except Martin, were opposed but unwilling to dissent (Maisel diary, December 12, 1967, 4). The vote was ten to one. Daane was absent, and Maisel dissented. Although the directive called for "moving slightly beyond the firmer conditions that have developed in the money markets" (Annual Report, 1967, 204), Maisel feared that "growth in member bank reserves and bank deposits would be slowed too abruptly, and perhaps succeeded by contraction" (ibid., 205). In the event, base growth continued to rise at a 6 percent annual rate, and the federal funds rate rose about 0.5 percentage points to about 4.5 percent. Consumer prices rose at a nearly 3 percent annual rate.[60]

Lessons From 1966–67

Though mild and brief, the 1966–67 slowdown was a turning point. There is no sharp demarcation of before and after, but the response to the slowdown and the rise in inflation anticipations changed both at home and abroad. The slow and hesitant response of the Federal Reserve to rising inflation and its prompt response to the mild slowdown suggested to many that policy was asymmetric; policymakers were more responsive to unemployment than to inflation. Also, the burden placed on homebuilding and the congressional response remained a concern for the FOMC that it tried to avoid repeating. This too made for delay and hesitation.

Market participants recognized the hesitation to act against inflation. At one point, Martin insisted on taking a restrictive step just to show that they were aware of the problem and could act. Foreigners recognized that the United States would not curtail output or risk recession to prevent a capital outflow and continued gold loss. The 1967 British devaluation (see chapter 5), the clear reluctance of the president and Congress to agree on a tax increase or expenditure reduction, rapid money growth, and the public's experience with past wars raised concerns about the stability of the internal and external value of the dollar.

In the nine months ending September 1967, the United States' gold stock declined by $158 million. In the next three months, it fell an additional $1012 million. And the rate of outflow increased in the early months of 1968.

---

60. The Board replaced Howard Hackley as Board counsel and Merritt Sherman as Board secretary. They became special assistants. Ralph Hexter and Robert Holland replaced them.

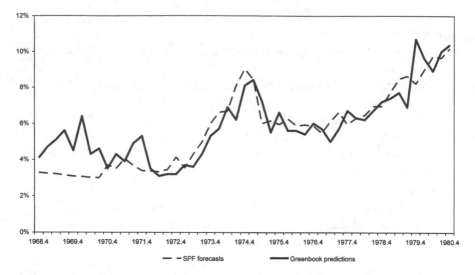

Chart 4.9. SPF vs. green book forecasts of GNP/GDP implicit price deflator, annualized quarterly growth, 1968:4–1980:4.

Martin was not surprised by the asymmetry. He testified, "The zeal with which policies were adopted to deal with a flagging economy has not been matched by commensurate zeal in coping with the emergence of economic overheating" (Martin speeches, Joint Economic Committee, February 14, 1968, 2). Later he added, "It is clear that we have, as a Nation, greater readiness to combat recession than to cope with inflation, despite the grave consequences that failure to restrain inflation could have for our economy, both domestically and internationally" (ibid., 11). Instead of reducing money growth, he urged Congress to pass the surtax.

At home, forecasts of inflation increased. By late 1968, when published forecasts became available, both the Federal Reserve and the Society of Professional Forecasters (SPF) anticipated continued inflation of at least a 3 percent annual rate. These anticipations eventually reached 10 percent or more. Chart 4.9 shows these data.[61] As in most other periods, Federal Reserve internal forecasts are close to the SPF forecasts.

FOMC minutes comment on the surprising rise in long-term rates and the faster increase in wages than in productivity. Both suggest that anticipated inflation had increased and that trend real growth had slowed,

61. The SPF initially provided annual forecasts with quarterly forecasts beginning in 1970. A 3 percent annual rate was considered a high rate of inflation at the time. The green book contains staff forecasts.

although neither change was recognized as evidence of inflation anticipations at the time. There were ample warnings from Presidents Hayes and Francis especially. Chairman Martin was certainly aware that he was in danger of failing to maintain the domestic and international value of the dollar.

Martin and the Federal Reserve made four principal errors.[62] First, the Federal Reserve tried to coordinate policy with the administration and persisted in doing so long after it became a serious impediment to carrying out its responsibilities. Even when Martin recognized that a tax increase was unlikely, he resisted even mild steps toward restriction, in part because Congress might use tighter monetary policy as an excuse for not raising tax rates.

Coordination was the enemy of central bank independence; the Federal Reserve would not raise interest rates high enough or fast enough to prevent inflation. The administration found it easier to finance its deficits at prevailing interest rates.

Second, under the pressure of events, the Federal Reserve accepted too many objectives as within its responsibility. Housing, the thrift industry, credit, and income distribution became matters of political concern and, in turn, Federal Reserve concern.[63] The objective of protecting the internal value of the currency gave way to new and diffused objectives. There were always reasons for delay to avoid one or more of the costs of disinflation. And some of the injured groups were politically active and able to bring their concerns to the Congress and thus to the Federal Reserve.

Third, the Federal Reserve had a short-term focus. It considered action every three weeks, so unpleasant decisions were easily postponed. More importantly, it pursued a money market strategy that responded to most short-term changes and neglected the longer-term effects on the economy. After the problems experienced in 1966, the FOMC adopted a proviso clause intended to limit longer-term effects by having the manager adjust the money market to large changes in money or bank credit. But the

62. Okun praised their performance as "*the* virtuoso performance in the history of stabilization policy. It was the greatest tight-rope walking and balancing act ever performed by either fiscal or monetary policy" (quoted in Maisel 1973, 88; emphasis in the original).

63. "The July and September [1966] actions marked a watershed in Federal Reserve policy. Blind faith in the market as a method of properly distributing funds was discredited. . . . Traditional channels of lending exist which cannot be overturned in short periods" (Maisel, 1973, 105). At one point, the Board and other regulators considered an additional reduction in interest rates on small certificates because many savings banks reported losses (memo, Fred W. Piderit, Jr., to Hayes, Correspondence Box 240, Federal Reserve Bank of New York, February 1, 1967).

manager generally ignored the proviso clause, as the System eventually recognized.[64]

The FOMC lacked an effective means of controlling the manager. It did not have an analytic framework because members did not agree on how its actions affected its goals, and some did not believe that such a framework was possible. In seeking consensus, it gave weak and ambiguous instructions to the manager. Stephen Axilrod, charged with developing better methods and later Chief of Staff at the Board in the 1970s, described the loose controls.

> What were money market conditions? The dealer loan rate this week, the three-month bill rate that week, free reserves the other week. . . . And he [the manager] would come before the committee and say: "It got a little away from me. It was a bit tighter but after all the dealer loan rate went up, or there was a shift in distribution away from the big city banks." . . . What do you know when you have a different starting point for what's tighter? (Axilrod, 1997)

The consequence was that the manager had substantial control, and his focus remained on the money market and excluded longer-term objectives.

Assigning the short-term focus to the manager overstates his role. He did what he was trained to do—smoothing the money market for banks and financial institutions. Some members of FOMC, Maisel and Francis especially, complained about the lack of control and the absence of a strategy, but influential members like Martin, Hayes, and several others did not share these concerns. Furthermore, the FOMC permitted money and credit to grow rapidly during even keel periods, when it supported Treasury financing. The short-term increase in reserves became a long-term increase in money and credit. The System could have proposed security auctions, but it didn't. Those who pointed to the divergent information in interest rates and money remained a minority. They could not influence policy decisions because the majority either did not believe money could be controlled or would not focus on the longer-term implications of the policies they approved.

Fourth, within the Federal Reserve and outside, many economists accepted the idea of a reliable long-run Phillips curve tradeoff. By accepting higher inflation, they believed they could get persistently lower unemploy-

---

64. As Maisel wrote, "The staff considered that, although the proviso clause had constrained the degree of accommodation to some extent, its effect in practice had been rather minor. The proviso clause never led to any substantial change in money market conditions." He concluded, "The movements [of money and credit] were not sensible in terms of the policies the Federal Reserve said and thought it was following" (Maisel, 1973, 230–31).

ment. And reducing inflation meant, to them at the time, not just a temporary increase in the unemployment rate, but a permanent or persistent increase.[65] At the Board, Maisel and Mitchell accepted this idea, and Robertson at the time gave priority to low unemployment, so he voted with them. By 1967, Martin could count only on Shephardson, who left in the spring of that year, and sometimes Daane or Brimmer. The chief economist, Daniel Brill, and many of the staff shared the new view. At the Council of Economic Advisers, Gardner Ackley had a simple Keynesian-Phillips curve view. The president detested "high" interest rates. Ackley had a less subtle understanding than either his predecessor or his successor as chairman, Walter Heller and Arthur Okun. Leading members of Congress, Wright Patman, Henry Reuss, and William Proxmire, differed on many points but not in their aversion to high or rising interest rates. Moreover, members of the administration, the FOMC, and the Congress were slow to distinguish between real and nominal interest rates. At the Federal Reserve this error combined with a reluctance to raise interest rates above 6 percent, carried over from the 1920s, and the Federal Reserve was unwilling to ask Congress to eliminate regulation Q.

As Martin put it, the Federal Reserve had let the horse of inflation out of the barn. With strong opposition to raising interest rates and unemployment, it would be difficult to get the barn locked with the horse inside.

Martin was an excellent example of "the independent, conservative central banker" appointed because his greater concern about inflation would discipline society (Rogoff, 1985). Unfortunately, Martin did not succeed because, despite his concerns, his style was to seek consensus and avoid confrontation as long as possible. He was always willing to give the president and others his views about appropriate policy. If they did not agree, he was willing to wait before acting. In dealing with his colleagues at the Federal Reserve and the administration, he waited too long to stop inflation, against his own judgment.[66] He probably could have had majority

65. Orphanides (2003b, 17 n. 24) gave an additional reason for the failure of the Phillips curve based on measures of the "gap" between actual and potential output. "The analysis failed to take into account that, in real time, gap-based forecasts of inflation are largely uninformative and often misleading." At the time, the misuse of potential output changed when productivity growth slowed, but the decline in long-term growth was not discussed and probably not noticed until much later.

66. The delay in tightening in 1965 and 1967 are examples. In both cases, policy eased too much soon after the Federal Reserve tightened. The Federal Reserve responded to the 1964 House Banking hearings by appointing an academic advisory committee. At a meeting in the fall of 1967, I recall Milton Friedman pleading with Martin to slow money growth and not restart the inflation that he had recently stopped. Martin listened politely, nodded, but did not respond. Martin was not persuaded by economists. No notes were kept at these meetings. There was rarely agreement among the academics about what should be done, reflecting the

support on the FOMC by relying on the presidents, but that was not his way of making decisions.

As a consensus seeker, coordination had great appeal on both analytic and practical grounds. Martin had often said that the Federal Reserve was independent within the government. To him that meant that the Federal Reserve could not raise interest rates high enough to finance the government deficit without inflation. Congress had approved or permitted the deficit, so the Federal Reserve had to assist in its financing.[67] Since he believed budget deficits caused inflation, it made practical good sense to him to try to influence decisions about tax and spending policies, even if it sacrificed some independence. He had decided, moreover, that his initial concerns about the 1964 tax cut had been wrong, and Heller had been right. He never reported looking back to see that he had adjusted the Federal Reserve's actions to the administration, but they did not adjust their policies in a coordinated effort to slow inflation. He had waited for that to happen, but in 1967 he waited in vain.

Furthermore, Martin said repeatedly that monetary policy alone could not achieve low inflation. Others on the FOMC shared that view. The most likely meaning was that the required increase in interest rates would be too large to be acceptable politically. Except for a brief and much criticized use of progressive discount rates in 1920–21, the Federal Reserve had never posted a rate above 7 percent (Meltzer, 2003, 105–7). Martin had ample reason to believe that President Johnson and key members of Congress would not support a substantial increase in interest rates.

The principal reasons for central bank independence are to protect the central bank from political pressures to finance the public sector deficit or support an administration politically. Policy coordination sacrificed independence by strengthening the pressures that independence weakened, and the even keel policy implemented deficit financing by the Federal Reserve.

Two popular beliefs added to the Federal Reserve's concern about using monetary policy forcefully. First, many economists inside and outside government believed that fiscal actions were powerful and monetary actions relatively weak. Second, many believed that some inflation was endemic in

---

divisions within the academic profession at the time. The division weakened the influence of the monetarist critics.

67. The concern that stopping inflation would require very high interest rates was widely shared. In July 1966, the president asked several people to comment on a criticism of administration policy by Congressman Al Ullman. Sherman Maisel wrote, "Interest rates except at a disastrously high level cannot halt inflation" (Maisel to the president, WHCF, Box 24, LBJ Library, July 13, 1966). Citing the rapid growth of money, bank credit, and business loans, Maisel added that monetary policy had not been "as tight as most believe" (ibid.).

a modern economy with unions and monopoly elements in key industries like steel, autos, tires, and durable goods. This was a main reason given for guideposts. The record of high growth and low inflation from 1961–65 showed the opposite (as happened again in the 1990s). The 1961–65 evidence did not alter this popular belief.

Policymakers learned three additional lessons. First, Martin, the administration, and many others, mistakenly believed that exhortation and threats to enforce guideposts for wages and prices were a useful tool to reduce inflation. Experience after 1965 changed some minds. In Hargrove and Morley (1984, 263) Ackley responded to questions about the use of guideposts. "The basic failure of the guideposts is that they were dreamed up by some economists who said: 'Here it is, boys,' and we expected people to pay attention to them. It's a ridiculous way to try to get people voluntarily to adopt them." But Ackley saw the failure as an inability to get people to follow guideposts when it was not in their private interest.[68] He did not see that controlling selected individual prices could at most change the rate of price change temporarily unless fiscal and monetary policy became more restrictive. And he and others did not distinguish one-time changes from the persistent rate of change caused by monetary policy.

Second, both the Federal Reserve and the administration economists failed to distinguish between real and nominal interest rates. They considered interest rates high. In their memos to President Johnson, who disliked high interest rates, they never explained that interest rates had increased, in large part, because the public expected inflation to persist and could be reduced by lowering inflation permanently.

Third, the 1964 tax cut was a major policy victory for the "new Keynesian economics" and the belief that short-term macroeconomic management—often called economic fine-tuning by its critics—could control inflation

68. In the same passages, Ackley lists some of the tactics used against business such as threats of anti-trust action, imports, and opposition to government contracts. He is critical of the lawyers' use of some of these threats but not all. The administration sold 300 thousand tons of aluminum from federal stockpiles to force Alcoa to rescind its price increase. To get a rollback of copper prices, it sold 200 thousand tons of copper and sent Averell Harriman to Chile to ask President Eduardo Frei to keep the copper price unchanged (Califano, 2000, 100–102). The administration put export controls on hides to prevent an increase in shoe prices, (ibid., 137). Califano (2000, 137) gives several other examples: color TVs, lamb, household appliances, paper cartons, newsprint, men's underwear, and others. The president was unable to convince, or successfully threaten, New York Mayor John Lindsay, who settled a transit strike by agreeing to wage increases far above the guideposts (ibid., 118), or to get the machinists' union to settle for less than a 4.9 percent increase, far above the 3.2 percent guidepost (ibid., 146). The union president boasted that the settlement destroyed the guideposts. The steel industry soon followed. President Johnson had his staff explore his authority to impose mandatory controls (ibid., 146–47).

and maintain high employment perhaps aided by guideposts for wages and prices. The long delay in enacting the surtax, and the weak response of inflation to the surtax, severely eroded these beliefs. Reducing tax rates is much more popular politically than increasing rates. Both Congress and the president hesitated or refused to act based on economists' forecasts of what would happen.[69] Congress held asymmetric views about taxes. Okun quotes congressional responses to the dire warnings coming from the Council and the Treasury. [Can I] "tell my constituents back home that I did them a favor by taking money out of their paycheck?" (Hargrove and Morley, 1984, 306).

An interviewer asked: "Given these difficulties with Congress, how do you come down on the feasibility of pursuing a counter-cyclical fiscal policy as a stabilization device?" Okun replied: "Well, it's limited." Then he added that "we don't know as much as we used to think we knew" (ibid., 311)

AN INFLATIONARY EXPANSION

Industrial production began to increase after July 1967. By January 1968, annual production growth reached 3 percent. Measured by growth of industrial production, the expansion was moderate. Real GNP growth reached 7 percent in second quarter 1968, however, with the unemployment rate at 3.5 percent of the labor force.

Consumer price inflation rose from zero in early 1967 to a local peak of 7 percent annual rate in June 1968. The GNP deflator rose 7.9 percent in first quarter 1968. Annual base money growth remained between 6 and 7 percent. The administration's forecast called for a four-quarter growth of 4 percent and a 3 percent increase in the deflator. The actual values were 3.6 and 5.8 percent.

The Federal Reserve responded by raising the federal funds rate and reducing free reserves. By May, the monthly average funds rate reached 6.12 percent, the highest rate recorded to that time and 1.50 percentage points above the previous December. But the annual rate of consumer price inflation increased 1 percentage point, so the effective change and the real level were much smaller than perceived.

---

69. Arthur Okun's summary describes President Johnson's views. "He kept telling us he was for a tax increase at the earliest possible moment he thought it conceivably could be taken seriously, that you couldn't sell it on the basis of a forecast, that you had to wait for a little bleeding to take place before you volunteered to sew up the wound" (Hargrove and Morley, 1984, 302). Chairman Mills of Ways and Means held this position strongly. Califano (2000, 244) held a more cynical view. "Most members of Congress preferred cuts in spending for the poor (most of whom don't vote and none of whom have excess money to contribute to political campaigns) to increasing the taxes of the affluent (most of whom do vote and many of whom make political contributions.)"

The Federal Reserve responded slowly. It was not from lack of knowledge about inflation or balance of payments outflows. At the January 9, 1968, meeting, the staff warned that "prices were rising at a substantial rate; and with demands strong and costs increasing, inflationary pressures were expected to increase in the period ahead" (Annual Report, 1968, 108). Further, the staff expected output to accelerate early in the year.[70]

Hayes favored additional restraint but thought it should come from fiscal policy. The Board had voted in December to increase reserve requirement ratios for demand deposits at banks with more than $5 million by 0.5 percentage points. The change became effective at reserve city banks on January 11 and at all other banks on January 18.[71] Martin opposed additional restraint. The System thought it had done its part. With Treasury bill rates above 5 percent, Martin wanted to avoid repeating the December 1965 conflict with the administration.[72] Despite the relatively large rise in inflation and loss of gold, the FOMC decided to wait for the forthcoming budget message and hope for a tax increase.

By the time of the February meeting, several members led by Hayes, Francis (St. Louis), and Maisel had become disturbed by the continued rise in inflation and the System's failure to slow or stop the rise. Francis asked for "an immediate and substantial move toward restraint" and a reduction in money growth from 6 to 3 percent despite Treasury financing operations (FOMC Minutes, February 6, 1968, 59). Maisel wanted more specific language and a more coherent plan.[73] His statement was far ahead of its time in recognizing the role of market anticipations. The term "firm," he said, "had to be interpreted in terms of . . . market expectations. . . . The Committee should make up its mind as to where it hoped to go over a considerable period in advance . . . He thought the Committee should set goals in terms of expansion of total reserves or of bank credit" (ibid., 73–4). He preferred to set a target for deposit growth. Interest rates reflected "both

70. The staff estimated the liquidity measure of the balance of payments deficit as $3.7 billion in 1967 compared to $1.4 billion in 1966. The liquidity measure reported changes in U.S. reserves net of liquid liabilities to all foreigners. On January 1, President Johnson announced a new program of mandatory and voluntary controls on capital movements. Once again the administration responded with a stopgap instead of a policy to lower inflation.

71. The staff proposed the change at a Board meeting on December 20. The Board divided between an increase applicable to all demand deposits or only to deposits above $5 million. It voted for the lesser change on December 27, 1967.

72. Any increase would "carry implications for the tenability of present regulation Q ceilings, and he would not want to have the question of a possible increase in those ceilings raised at this time" (FOMC Minutes, January 9, 1968, 81).

73. Maisel urged "better quantitative predictions . . . related to a three to six month projection" and a more specific directive including quantitative targets (Maisel diary, February 23, 1968, 9).

the demand and supply of funds. That was why he would reject interest rates as a goal" (ibid., 75). "The Committee is torn. A majority feel that money should be tighter. They are not clear what this means or how far tightening should go" (Maisel diary, February 23, 1968, 9).

Committee members recognized the source of some of their problems, but it lacked leadership to correct them. Clay (Kansas City) commented on the excessive growth of reserves during even keel operations. And Galusha (Minneapolis) called for increasing regulation Q ceiling rates, when the Treasury completed its financing.

Martin summarized the consensus. He was pleased that many "would have preferred a firmer monetary posture than had prevailed in the recent period" (ibid., 107). He thought it was important to "continue to press for a tax increase, however questionable the prospects were." The president had asked again for a 10 percent surtax effective January 1 for corporate taxes and April 1 for personal taxes. Although the staff recognized that the prospective budget deficit would be large even if the tax bill passed, the FOMC voted unanimously to maintain money market conditions. It added the proviso clause that permitted the manager to tighten if bank credit expanded at the projected 7 to 10 percent annual rate.

As in the Great Depression, some members of Congress expected more of the Federal Reserve. Led by Congressman Henry Reuss, they had become alarmed by the rising inflation rate and the Federal Reserve's vague directives. In March 1967, the Joint Economic Committee wrote:

> The committee urges that the monetary authority adopt the policy of moderate and relatively steady increases in the money supply, avoiding wide swings in the rate of increase or decrease . . .
>
> Such rate of increase should be more or less consistent with the projected rate of growth—generally within a range of 3 to 5 percent per year. (Joint Economic Committee, 1968, 16)

The committee repeated and amplified this recommendation the following year. It recognized that exceptions should be made and that the guidelines were not rigid directives (ibid., 17). But the exceptions should not distort seasonally adjusted quarterly averages. "A 3-month period is sufficiently long to allow abnormal and extreme temporary movements to be absorbed in an average" (ibid., 17).

The report proposed that the standard against which Congress should appraise Federal Reserve actions was a 2 to 6 percent annual rate of increase in the M_1 money stock. "On occasions when the increase was outside this range, it would be wise for the Congress to take a prompt look at the Federal Reserve System's actions" (ibid., 17). The 2 to 6 percent range was not fixed permanently. The range would change with technological progress in the financial and non-financial sectors and in the public's decisions about the allocation of their wealth between money, other financial assets, and capital.[74]

Unfortunately, the report had little effect on either the subsequent behavior of the Federal Reserve or congressional monitoring. Congressman Reuss complained that the Federal Reserve ignored the committee's recommendation. "Was the Fed continuing to create money at the rate of 9 percent—in the face of Joint Economic Committee's 3 to 5 percent 'advice'—because of Treasury borrowing, the level of production, expectations about future tax increases, worries about residential construction, or what? What weight was assigned to these factors? We are not told" (Joint Economic Committee, 1968a, 44).[75]

The Federal Reserve could not answer Reuss's question because they did not assign weights to the various factors. They simply controlled interest rates and money market conditions and acted as residual buyer to clear the money market at the interest rate they (or the manager) chose. The FOMC made no effort to estimate explicit effects of the various factors affecting interest rates when setting the directive.

Policy differed from the period of pegged rates from 1942 to 1951 by allowing the Federal Reserve to change the interest rate that it pegged. Any peg was temporary and subject to change. But the effect was similar, though

74. The committee criticized the System for imprecision in its instructions to the manager, failing to have clear objectives, and neglecting to audit its performance. By default, judgments about policy were left to the manager (Joint Economic Committee, 1968, 10). The committee concluded that imprecision was not willful but "an inherent imprecision in the objectives, policy standards, and operations themselves" (ibid., 14).

75. A survey of economists by the House Banking Committee showed the majority in favor of the Joint Economic Committee's rule (Bach, 1971, 141–42). The Council of Economic Advisers, the Treasury, and, of course, the Federal Reserve opposed the rule. Reuss sent a letter to the Board asking for a response to his proposal. Martin's response avoided an answer but sent some staff papers opposing the proposal. The staffs of the banks and the Board had considered monetary control. The report was not one to convince skeptics to make the change. The account manager pointed out that the aggregates "are not controllable in the short-run," and he added that "market participants would not know how to adjust to what was happening" (memo, Brill to FOMC, Board Records, May 16, 1968, 2). He favored a proviso clause based on bank credit, although he usually ignored it in practice. Others proposed using a moving average to damp fluctuations. Stephen Axilrod emphasized that the main difference in operation would be larger fluctuations in interest rates and fewer in reserves. "The odds favor a better policy with continuation of something like present form of doctrine than with the proposed form" (ibid., 10). John Kareken thought that the proposed policy could be destabilizing under certain (unspecified) conditions (ibid., 16).

not identical, because the interest rate could change. The Federal Reserve held the interest rate below the market-clearing rate consistent with price stability. Hence money growth and prices rose in both periods.

At the March 1968 meeting, Hayes and Francis pressed again for restraint. Others suggested specific actions, such as changes in the discount rate or regulation Q ceilings. Martin was cautious. He acknowledged the "unanimous view of the members today that greater monetary restraint was desirable. . . . Personally, he was not prepared at the moment to advocate an increase in the discount rate of either one-quarter or one-half of a percentage point. He would want to increase restraint gradually and unaggressively while watching developments closely" (FOMC Minutes, March 5, 1968, 117).

The federal funds rate ended the week 0.07 percentage points above the previous week, but it reversed the following week falling to the lowest weekly average in two months. Two events surrounding this meeting make Martin's hesitation puzzling. Both events reflected the severe gold drain that followed the British devaluation in November 1967, the Federal Reserve's failure to stop inflation, and the administration's inability to increase taxes and unwillingness to reduce spending. First, Congress eliminated the 25 percent gold reserve requirement behind Federal Reserve notes, to free the remaining gold stock for sale but severing the last vestige of the gold reserve requirement in the 1913 Federal Reserve Act. The bill passed on the last day; on the next day, the Federal Reserve would have been forced to suspend the gold cover and impose a tax on the reserve banks (Maisel diary, March 15, 1968, 24). The president signed the bill on March 18. The Treasury had only $3.5 million of free gold left. Second, the members of the gold pool met in Washington to end the crisis in the gold market by ending the gold pool.[76] Thereafter, central banks and monetary authorities would buy and sell gold to each other from their existing stocks. All other gold, including newly mined gold, would be traded at market prices without intervention by central banks. The gold exchange standard and the Bretton Woods system of fixed exchange rates was now in its last phase. Although the central bankers pledged to maintain fixed exchange rates against each other, the public could not impose discipline by demanding gold from a central bank in exchange for paper money.

Within two weeks of the FOMC meeting, Martin spoke to the Economic Club of Detroit. The speech barely mentions Federal Reserve inaction or the run on gold. The problem was fiscal profligacy, perpetual deficits, "a

76. France left the gold pool in the summer of 1967, so it was not represented at the meeting.

very sad progression toward undermining the currency" (Martin speeches, March 18, 1968, 7). The country was "overextended and over-committed" (ibid., 8). He cited the military commitments but did not mention the expansive domestic Great Society programs except to say that "it's time that we stopped talking about 'guns and butter'" (ibid., 8).[77] If "the central bank prints money, there's only one answer: rising prices and continuing deficit. . . . [T]he monetary system has a responsibility at least to bring this to the attention of people" (ibid., 10).

Effective on March 15, the Board approved a 0.5 percentage point increase to a 5 percent discount rate at ten of the reserve banks. New York and Philadelphia followed within a week.[78] A month later, New York, Philadelphia, Minneapolis, and San Francisco increased discount rates to 5.5 percent. By April 26, all banks had the 5.5 percent rate. With the higher discount rate and a federal funds rate of 5.7 percent in mid-April, the Board raised the regulation Q ceiling rate on CDs of $100,000 or more on a schedule rising from 5.5 percent for 60 to 89 days to 6.25 percent for 180 days or more. Long-term rates remained in the range from 5.2 to 5.5 percent that they entered in early March. These rates were now above the 1966–67 peaks. In the secondary market Treasury bill rates reached 5.25 percent, close to the postwar peak. New issue Treasury bill rates and the index of stock prices continued to increase.

With consumer price inflation at 4 percent, Arthur Okun, the new chairman of the Council of Economic Advisers, explained the Federal Reserve's actions to the president but did not criticize them.[79] On this and many other occasions, he warned the president about possible serious consequences unless Congress approved the tax surcharge.[80] Okun described

77. Later in his speech, Martin endorsed the Great Society but added that "we don't have the self-discipline, we don't have the capacity to govern ourselves in such a way that we can be great" (Martin speeches, March 8, 1968, 13). Martin also recognized that a tax increase was unpopular. His mail ran 15 to 1 against (ibid., 15–16).

78. Chicago asked for 0.25; six banks asked for 0.5. St. Louis and Dallas asked for 1 percent, New York asked for 1.5 percent to show its commitment to defend the exchange rate system. New York would not accept less than 1 percent. After some discussion, Martin prevailed on the Board not to impose a lower rate.

79. Okun had been a Council member since 1964 and before that a staff member. He served as chairman from February 15, 1968, until the administration ended on January 20, 1969. He also served as a member of the new Cabinet Committee on Price Stability, established in February 1968. The committee considered price and wage controls, but Okun convinced them to reinvigorate guideposts (Hargrove and Morley, 1984, 269).

80. Almost every memo Okun wrote to the president urged a tax increase, often in detail. One memo, in May 1968, sketched the development of a possible world financial crisis including a run on gold, end of the gold-exchange system, failure to maintain a solemn pledge to pay gold, and political consequences at home including loss of employment, rapid decline in stock prices, and a conservative attack on all government spending. Okun opposed efforts

his "main professional concern [as] seeing that the war was financed responsibly and sensibly, and it wasn't financed responsibly and sensibly until we got the surcharge enacted" (Okun oral history, tape II, third attachment, undated, 5).

The FOMC continued to vote for slightly firmer conditions. Free reserves turned negative in the winter and reached −$415 in April. Annual growth of the monetary base rose, however, from 6 to 6.5 percent. Bank credit growth slowed until the Board raised the regulation Q ceiling.

The FOMC gave three reasons for following a policy that it described as cautious. First was an improved prospect (in April) for fiscal action by Congress. Second, a "considerable degree of monetary restraint had already been achieved, the effects of which were still unfolding" (Annual Report, 1968, 140). Third, concern about a shift out of commercial bank time deposits would set off disruptive shifts in asset allocation and require an increase in regulation Q ceilings (which occurred soon after). It did not mention a political response but it was surely conscious after its 1966–67 experience that such a response could occur.

The Big Error

Through May and June, the FOMC maintained its policy stance, but it did not increase interest rates or reduce free reserves further. Finally, on June 21, almost three years after discussion started, and eighteen months after it was first proposed, Congress approved a 10 percent surtax. The final vote was not close, 268 to 150 in the House and 64 to 16 in the Senate. President Johnson signed the bill on June 28, 1968. The new law raised tax rates retroactively to January 1 for corporations and to April 1 for individuals.[81] The surtax was temporary; it expired on June 30, 1969, unless renewed.

To get the surtax passed, the president had agreed to reduce spending by $6 billion in fiscal 1969.[82] Congress found it much easier to agree on the principle of reduced spending than to implement it, and "Johnson declined to make any reductions above those passed on Capitol Hill"

---

within the Council to warn the president about the economic effects of continuing the war. "I felt that he would not at all be receptive to such an obviously hortatory position . . . and that this might very severely prejudice his confidence in us" (Okun oral history, tape II, third attachment, undated, 6). Okun described his relation with President Johnson as not close.

81. Unlike all other tax legislation, the surtax began in the Senate as an amendment to a revenue measure approved in the House. Chairman Mills accepted this departure from established procedure in exchange for larger reductions in spending.

82. Califano (2000, 244–46, 284–88) describes some of the difficulties encountered in getting Congress to agree to the tax increase and the president to agree to the spending reductions. By the time the bill passed, the Kennedy and King assassinations, riots in many cities, the Vietnamese Tet offensive and Johnson's decision not to run for reelection had fostered a sense of crisis.

(Califano, 2000, 288). Cuts in programs amounted to less than $4 billion. In the aggregate, spending increased by $2.7 billion in fiscal 1969 compared to $18.7 billion in 1968. Most of the reduced growth came in defense spending; spending on human resources, including most of the Great Society programs, rose $7 billion in fiscal 1969 compared to $8 billion in 1968.[83]

The surcharge set up the big error of the late 1960s. The error had two parts. As soon as the surcharge passed, Okun, the Council, Federal Reserve staff, and others began to worry about "fiscal overkill." As in 1967, action to prevent a slowdown in real growth came promptly, in contrast to the very slow response to inflation. The contrast between the two responses, and the weights on the two concerns, was not lost on the market. This was the origin of what came to be known as "stagflation." Anti-inflation policies that increased unemployment could not be expected to persist, so inflation would persist. The public came to believe that any reductions in inflation induced by policy action would prove transitory. Hence prices, wages, and long-term interest rates were slow to adjust downward. Wages and many prices would seem rigid downward, or more rigid than earlier. Costs of disinflation would be large, therefore, and disinflation would be politically unpopular.

The second part of the error combined an analytic error and a forecast error. Keynesian economists at the Council and on the Federal Reserve staff believed that the temporary surcharge would have a powerful effect on consumer spending. Friedman's (1957) analysis of consumer behavior predicted the opposite; a temporary tax increase would fall mainly on saving, not consumer spending. The Council and the Federal Reserve forecast using their Keynesian models, so they forecast a large response, hence "fiscal overkill."[84]

Four days before the president signed the tax bill, Okun completely shifted his position. Instead of the dire consequences of the budget deficit, he now warned the president about the serious consequences of the ex-

---

83. During Johnson's administration, spending for human resources increased from 5.6 percent to 7.1 percent of GNP. These expenditures were programmed to continue increasing in later years. By 1985, they reached 11.9 percent of GNP.

84. A month before Congress approved the surcharge, Franco Modigliani, a leading Keynesian economist, told the Joint Economic Committee based on his own more sophisticated work:

> If the people know that taxes are going to be put up for just 3 or 6 months, chances are that there will be little change in their consumption because they would look forward to being able to recoup later. Therefore, I think that attention should be given to finding measures that have the right incentives. (Testimony, Joint Economic Committee, 1968, 63)

pected budget surplus and the swing from a prospective $10 billion deficit to a surplus at the annual rate of $5 billion in the first half of 1969.[85] He offered no explanation, in the memo, or elsewhere, about why he had not mentioned his concern earlier and urged the president to reduce the size of the surtax. He told the president:

> Real growth over the coming year will probably be at only a snail's pace, less than half as fast as in the past year. Unemployment is likely to rise above 4 percent in early 1969.
>
> Indeed there is a risk that we will slow down too much unless the effects of fiscal restraint are cushioned by an upturn in homebuilding activity later this year. (memo, Okun to the president, WHCF, Box 2, LBJ Library, June 24, 1968)[86]

On July 18, Okun overstated the power of the surcharge. He projected a 1 percent increase in real GNP in the last half of 1968 and a slight decline in the first half of 1969. He forecast inflation at 3 percent in June 1969 and the unemployment rate at 5 percent instead of the 3.7 percent in June 1968. These estimates were much too pessimistic about unemployment and output growth and too optimistic about inflation. Actual values reported at the time were 5.2 percent for the deflator in second quarter 1969, 3.1 percent real growth in the first half of 1969, and a 3.5 percent unemployment rate in June of that year (Maisel diary, July 16, 1968, 9).

To assist housing, Okun wanted the Federal Reserve to reduce interest rates.[87] In numerous conversations with the president in the three years of discussion about budget finance, Martin had told the president repeatedly that interest rates would be higher without the surcharge and lower with it. His statement was open to three interpretations: (1) The Federal Reserve

85. He compared the estimated $15 billion swing to the sharp change from 1959 to 1960 and reminded the president that the Democrats had campaigned against fiscal drag at the time.

86. Okun was cautious about the projected fall in inflation. He forecast 3 percent inflation by spring 1969 from the 4 percent rate at the time. In fact, consumer prices rose at about 5.3 percent in spring 1969 and the unemployment rate declined from 3.7 to 3.4 percent between June 1968 and early 1969. Real GNP growth for the four quarters ending in June 1969 was half the growth rate of the previous four quarters, as Okun forecast. One reason is that fourth quarter 1968 had negative growth. The SPF have quarterly forecasts beginning in late 1968. In fourth quarter 1968, they forecast a rise in unemployment to 4 percent by second quarter 1969.

87. Okun was moderate. He recognized that "confidence in the dollar generated by the tax bill might be dissipated by a drastic monetary easing that seemed irresponsible" (memo, Okun to the president, WHCF, Box 2, LBJ Library, June 24, 1968, 4). The Federal Advisory Council also believed that growth would slow following the surtax. They did not expect recession (Board Minutes, June 4, 1968).

Table 4.5 Interest Rates Before and After the Surtax, 1968 (percent)

	JAN.–FEB. LOW	MAY 21–24 HIGH	JUNE 21 AFTER TAX BILL	JULY 12	DEC. 28
3-month bills	4.82	5.90	5.20	5.38	6.22
3–5 year issues	5.43	6.17	5.56	5.53	6.17
Long-term bonds	5.08	5.54	5.12	5.10	5.82

Source: Columns (1) to (4) from Memo, Okun to president, WHCF, Box 2, LBJ Library, July 15, 1968; Board of Governors, 1981, 706, 755.

would act to lower interest rates; (2) it would not prevent a decline in interest rates caused by reduced government borrowing and slower economic growth; or (3) interest rates could rise but would be lower than without the surcharge.[88]

At the last FOMC meeting before the surcharge, June 18, the Federal Reserve recognized that interest rates had fallen "substantially" in the previous three weeks in anticipation of fiscal restraint. Increased borrowing had reduced free reserves, so the manager considered the markets to be "tight" despite the decline in rates. Table 4.5 shows the changes in interest rates.

Passage of the surtax brought long-term rates back to their lows for the year. Short-term rates remained considerably above early levels but below the May readings. The Federal Reserve concluded that it should permit rates to fall. "The Committee concluded that if Congress acted . . . open market operations should seek to accommodate any resulting declines in short-term rates and to cushion any upward pressures on such rates that might emerge subsequently" (Annual Report, 1968, 165–66). The staff expected much slower growth in real GNP but not much immediate change in inflation or wage increases if the tax increase passed. Nevertheless, some members, fearing excessive restraint, favored easier policy. The unanimous decision was to resist any upward pressure and accommodate any decline.[89]

By July 15, a day before the next FOMC meeting, long- and medium-term rates were little changed from June. Short-term rates had increased. Okun told the president that the FOMC was split. Some "recognize that,

88. Okun quotes Martin as repeatedly telling the president "If you can get the tax bill, I can back off on interest rates. I can't do it until you do" (Hargrove and Morley, 1984, 304).

89. At the June 18 meeting, Martin voted to break a tie between those who favored allowing rates to move with the market, even if they moved up and those who favored intervention to assure that rates declined. In the end, all the committee members agreed to the more activist policy (Maisel diary, June 19, 1968, 12–15).

if they wait for really hard evidence that the economy has cooled off, their easing may be too late" (memo, Okun to the president, WHCF, Box 2, LBJ Library, July 15, 1968, 3). Joseph Califano, the Domestic Policy Adviser, explained to the president that "there is no point in talking to Martin until we have done something about prices and wages" (Califano to the president, CF, Box 43, LBJ Library, July 18, 1968). Another group expressed concern that "overt monetary easing might offset the big boost to world confidence in the dollar. . . . They also fear that a drastic easing would be *viewed as undoing the anti-inflationary effect* of fiscal restraint" (ibid., 3; emphasis added). Califano would have liked a discount rate cut, but he expected no more than a modest increase in free reserves.[90]

The July FOMC meeting began with the usual discussion of foreign operations and pressures. Neither Coombs nor the members mentioned the tax surcharge or cited any evidence that the surcharge had changed the international position of the dollar. The discussion focused on recent French riots, France's gold losses, and its sudden willingness to expand its swap line with the United States.[91]

The staff's domestic report emphasized uncertainty about strikes and the effect of the tax cut. It suggested "a sharper slowing of economic activity for the remainder of the year" than foreseen earlier (FOMC Minutes, July 16, 1968, 31). The current forecast called for growth to stop and unemployment to rise (ibid., 32) with no increase in consumer or investment spending and a sharp reduction in inventories. Then the staff added: "at a minimum, it now seems *certain* that the restraints on aggregate demand will act to preclude any further upward twist in the inflationary spiral. In fact, the prospects for some slackening in price pressures seems favorable" (ibid., 33; emphasis added.) The report pointed to the 1966 decline in inflation to support its forecast.

The report concluded with a warning intended to change policy. "The prospective economic picture strongly suggests that the present fiscal-monetary mix could lead to an abrupt halt in the expansion of production, incomes, and employment" (ibid., 34). The report proposed to stimulate construction by reducing interest rates (ibid., 34, 37, 39). It urged the committee to change policy to keep "faith with Congress and with its previous commitments" (Maisel diary, July 16, 1968, 4–5).

90. Johnson returned the memo to Califano with a note telling him to have Okun talk to Fowler to get Fowler to talk to Martin.

91. The riots in Paris threatened at one time to bring down the government. Between March and December 1968, France had to sell $1.4 billion of gold, about one-fourth of its stock, to defend the franc parity. On August 10, 1969, after selling an additional $33 million, France devalued the franc about 12 percent, from 5.55 to 4.94 per dollar.

Hayes (New York) urged caution. The response to the surcharge depended on whether it fell more on consumption or saving. He spoke of the "vital necessity, on both domestic and international grounds, of checking the rampant inflationary forces . . . and accordingly I conclude that we should not change policy at this time" (ibid., 47). He added that a slowdown might come but a recession was doubtful. "All of us have worked long and hard for a sound fiscal program. Now, we have it, let's stop, look and listen before altering course on monetary policy" (FOMC Minutes, July 16, 1968, 49).

The committee divided. Francis (St. Louis) and Kimbrel (Atlanta) wanted a tighter policy. Brimmer, Maisel, Mitchell, Galusha (Minneapolis), and Robert Black (speaking for Aubrey Heflin, the Richmond president) wanted some version of easier policy. The most Keynesian members, Brimmer and Maisel, strongly favored ease. The rest wanted some version of no change with qualifications to lean one way or the other. Martin's consensus was for no change while accommodating less firm conditions that developed in the market. Hayes agreed reluctantly.

The principal intellectual difference was between those who favored policy coordination and those who wanted to reinforce fiscal tightening. Francis (St. Louis) made a strong statement for reinforcing the fiscal change. He did not accept the claim of fiscal "overkill," nor did he "believe that the new fiscal program was restrictive enough to bring an end to the inflationary spiral unless the rate of monetary expansion was significantly abated" (ibid., 50). He predicted that if 7 percent money growth continued, nominal GNP would rise 9 percent to about $925 billion in second quarter 1969.[92] Then he added the first clear statement in the minutes relating nominal interest rates to anticipated inflation and real rates to productivity growth. "The level of nominal interest rates depended to a great extent on expectations regarding inflation. If the public anticipated future price rises of 3 percent a year, then nominal interest rates of 7 percent meant real interest of 4 percent, a very low rate in view of the current high productivity of capital" (ibid., 53).[93]

Maisel argued forcefully for coordination. "The largest fiscal restraint package in history had just been passed. It did not make much sense to him to vote for the same monetary policy after that package had passed as was voted before. A no-change decision today would make superfluous all the Committee had said about the necessary relationship between

92. His forecast was much closer than the staff's. Actual GNP was $923.7 billion, with M_1 growth of about 6.5 percent.

93. Like many others at the time and later, he neglected the effect of taxes on interest rates. Feldstein (1982) brought out these effects.

monetary and fiscal policy" (ibid., 64). To counteract the restrictive effects of the fiscal package on the economy, he suggested that total deposits
should grow at an 8 or 9 percent annual rate. He considered that a neutral
monetary stance (ibid., 65). The staff proposed two options. One kept the
federal funds rate at 6 percent. The other lowered it to 5.75 percent. Maisel
wanted 5.5 percent followed by a 0.25 percentage point reduction in the
discount rate.

Galusha (Minneapolis) openly recognized political pressures on the
Federal Reserve. Usually such pressures were not admitted. He thought
it would be "unwise . . . both economically and (perhaps more important)
politically" (ibid., 83) to delay easing.[94] More than other presidents, he
wanted to lower rates. The Board would soon use this argument to push
through a discount rate reduction.

The FOMC held its regular meeting on August 13 and six days later a
special telephone meeting called by Hayes in Martin's absence. The August 13 meeting voted to keep money market conditions unchanged unless
growth of bank credit exceeded projections. The staff raised its forecast
for the third quarter but continued to believe that the economy would slow
"considerably in the months ahead as a result of the new fiscal restraint
measures and a marked reduction in inventory accumulation" built up
for a steel strike (Annual Report, 1968, 179). The report noted, but downplayed, recent increases in inflation.

The manager had responded to the rapid growth of the bank credit
proxy by tightening the money market. Bank borrowing reached $670 mil-
lion, an exceptionally high value. The staff expected the recent 16 percent
rate of increase to slow to about 6 percent.[95]

Several Board members used the August 13 meeting to urge the presi-

---

94. The committee had an intense discussion of the practice of announcing the interest rate at which the New York bank would do repurchase agreements (RPs). With some
objections from Hayes (New York), the FOMC voted to set the RP rate at the discount rate
and reduce the manager's discretionary authority. The FOMC voted at the July meeting to
reduce the RP rate to 5.5 percent, the current discount rate. In April the Board had approved
an experimental program permitting the account manager to set a flexible rate on repurchase agreements with non-bank dealers in government securities. The next month, at the
urging of Governor Robertson, the Board's staff evaluated the experiment. Instead of tying
the RP rate to the discount rate, the manager fixed the rate 0.25 below the federal funds rate
as a general rule but varied it on occasion. The staff report found that market participants
interpreted changes in the RP rate as policy actions. This raised an issue about whether the
manager should have authority to adjust a rate perceived as a policy change without approval
by FOMC (Board Records, April 26 and May 29, 1968).

95. President Clay (Kansas City) pointed to a recurring problem. "The System seemed to
lose control of bank reserves and credit expansion during such periods [of Treasury financ-
ing] and the result sometimes deviated sharply from what was intended" (FOMC Minutes,
August 13, 1968, 56).

dents to reduce discount rates. Martin made the odd claim that "he was concerned as other members were about the high current rates of bank credit" but the discount rate was "out of line" because the market expected greater monetary ease (FOMC Minutes, August 13, 1968, 82). Brimmer and Maisel wanted a 0.5 percentage point reduction in the discount rate. Others favored only 0.25.

For the first time in many years, there was a clear division between the reserve banks and the Board that was reminiscent of the System's early days, when the Board forced changes in the discount rate in 1919 and 1927. Then members of the Board viewed the reserve bank governors as bankers, and the reserve bank governors viewed the Board members as motivated by politics. In 1968 political concerns had a role, but the major difference was the weight given to inflation and prospective unemployment.[96]

One bank president who voted, Galusha (Minneapolis), had pressed for greater ease. The Board sent Governor Daane, a former vice president of the Minneapolis bank, to the bank's meeting on August 15 to encourage the directors to vote for a lower discount rate. The directors voted for a 5.25 percent rate instead of the 5 percent rate that Martin and Daane proposed. Despite the Board's pressure, directors at Philadelphia and New York voted to keep the rate unchanged. At Philadelphia, some directors "indicated that they would be willing to countenance a certain degree of economic downturn in order to bring inflation under control" (Board Minutes, August 15, 1968, 2). This was heresy at the Board. The New York directors also put most stress on the continuing inflation.[97]

Martin, Maisel, and Brimmer wanted a 5 percent rate, but the Minneapolis directors had voted for 5.25, and a four-to-three majority of the Board favored that rate. Martin asked for, and got, unanimous approval of the 5.25 percent rate, effective August 16. Richmond followed three days later,

96. Governor Mitchell "did not feel any action was really required." If the discount rate was reduced, he preferred a modest reduction of 0.25 percentage points to 5.25 percent (Board Minutes, August 14, 1968, 17–18). This differed from the administration's position. Okun told the president: "Some of the district banks were clearly dragging their heels. Moreover, none of them was prepared to move more than a quarter of a point even though the Fed Board had invited a decline of half of a point" (memo, Okun to the president, WHCF, Box 51, LBJ Library, August 31, 1968). Okun praised Martin for "his unusual ability to achieve a consensus among often widely disparate views" (ibid., 2). He urged President Johnson to consider reorganization to either vest all authority in the Board or subject the bank presidents to the same appointment and confirmation procedures as Board members. This was not the first or last time that an administration official wanted to reduce independence to increase administration influence over monetary policy.

97. Maisel attended the Philadelphia meeting. He urged a reduction, but President Bopp opposed it. The bank's board members thought that inflation was the more serious problem (Maisel diary, August 16, 1968, 9).

but two weeks passed before Atlanta, New York, St. Louis, and San Francisco voted for the reduction. Later, Martin blamed the staff forecast. "That was the days of the quadriad, and the staff was too much involved with the administration. And I don't think Martin was too forgiving" (Axilrod, 1997).

The press interpreted the move as modest because New York and Chicago did not participate. Market and press reaction irritated some Board members. On August 27, with four banks holding out, Brimmer urged the Board not to approve a rate differing from current policy or allow an old rate to continue indefinitely "because the banks failed to act" (Board Minutes, August 27, 1968, 9). His position drew no support from the other governors. Martin argued that it was a System, not a centralized organization. That imposed costs, but it had benefits also. He preferred the decentralized system and was reluctant to "down grade the job of the directors" (ibid., 11).

Although only two small regional banks had reduced discount rates by August 19, the FOMC voted to "facilitate orderly adjustments in money market conditions but did not use its power to force recalcitrant banks to lower their discount rates" (FOMC Minutes, August 19, 1968, 20). The FOMC expected rates to fall. Uncertainty surrounding the Russian invasion of Czechoslovakia pushed rates higher.

With consumer prices rising at a twelve-month rate of 4.2 percent, more than 1.5 percentage points above the previous August, the discount rate reductions gave a clear signal that the System would not follow an anti-inflation policy. Market rates did not respond as anticipated to the reductions in the discount rates.[98] The FOMC staff interpreted the increase in rates as evidence of market disappointment at the small reduction in the discount rate. They neglected the effect of rising prices on interest rates and the fact that consumer prices increased at the highest rate since 1951. Most of all, they misinterpreted the effects of their actions; they ignored arguments for more restrictive policy from Francis (St. Louis) and Coldwell (Dallas). Based on their Keynesian beliefs, they chose to prevent the anticipated recession.

In September, the FOMC attributed a rise in market rates to disappointment about the size of the discount rate change and speculation by government security dealers. In October, they said increases in interest rates showed disappointment that most banks had reduced the prime rate only by 0.25 percentage points to 6.25 percent (Annual Report, 1968, 199).

---

98. New issue Treasury bill rates rose 25 basis points from August 10 to August 31, after all banks had acted. Government bond yields rose also. By late October, bills yielded 5.4 percent, about the same rate as in April before the tax surcharge was expected to pass.

Bank credit continued to rise rapidly. Although free reserves increased from
− $415 in April to − $120 in September, the federal funds rate was the same
in both months. Annual growth of the monetary base reached 6.5 percent
in October, the largest annual rate of increase since January 1952.[99]

The Board and the administration had similar forecasts for the second
half of 1968. The administration forecast, prepared by the so-called Troika
process, predicted real growth at a one percent annual rate for the second
half of 1968 and zero for the first half of 1969.[100] With that forecast, unemployment would increase to 4 percent in fourth quarter 1968 and as
much as 5 percent in second quarter 1969. Inflation would fall gradually
to about 2.5 percent by mid-1969. The memo emphasized the need for
monetary accommodation to avoid a recession. Lower interest rates would
stimulate housing and maintain economic activity (memo, Troika to the
president, CF, Box 3, LBJ Library, August 5, 1968). A letter from Martin expressed general agreement but differed on the increase in housing starts,
the reduction in government spending, and the decline in inflation. In
each case, the Board's staff was less optimistic than the administration. But
they agreed on the direction: slower growth, rising unemployment, and
lower inflation. Maisel (1973, 189) reports the Board's forecast for nominal
GNP growth as 6 percent annual rate for the second half of 1968.

Actual results reported at the time differed markedly from the Troika
forecast. Real GNP grew at annual rates of 3.4 and 2.4 percent in the two
half years following the surtax. The GNP deflator rose at rates of 4.5 and
4.8 percent, and the unemployment rate remained at 3.4 percent, then
rose very modestly to 3.5 percent in June 1969. Nominal GNP rose at a
7.8 percent annual rate in the second half of 1968 (Council of Economic
Advisers, 1971).[101]

At the September FOMC meeting, Martin gave his reason for a more
pessimistic outlook on inflation than the Troika. He said that the admin-

99. At the IMF–World Bank meeting at the end of September, European participants
complained that "inflation would not be stopped unless the Federal Reserve kept the creation
of the money supply or bank credit much more severely in hand" (Maisel diary, October 9,
1968, 4).

100. The Troika process combined efforts of the Budget Bureau (later the Office of Management and Budget), the Treasury Department, and the Council of Economic Advisers. It
had three stages. The three professional staffs prepared a forecast that was approved or adjusted by the agency deputies and, finally, by the principals. This became the administration
forecast and was used in the spending estimates.

101. Revised data show real GNP growth slowing to 1.4 and 2.4 percent in the two periods
and the deflator rising to 5.4 and 5.2 percent. Lagged reserve accounting became effective in
September 1968. Banks based required reserves on deposits two weeks earlier. This eased
the banks' problem but made short-term control of monetary and credit aggregates more
difficult.

istration and the Federal Reserve had delayed too long in responding to inflation. "He thought it would be asking too much of the available tools of monetary policy to expect them to deal with the inflationary psychology that had resulted from that delay" (FOMC Minutes, September 10, 1968, 68). Nevertheless, he thought the current stance was "about right" (ibid., 69). He continued to believe that interest rates would fall.

By October, Martin's policy had lost some adherents. Hayes urged "a check on credit growth . . . to bring it back down to a rate of about 6 percent per annum" (FOMC Minutes, October 8, 1968, 33). Hickman (Cleveland) and Kimbrel (Atlanta) joined him in dissent. Martin was not persuaded. "It was his impression that monetary policy had been about as effective as could have reasonably been expected" (FOMC Minutes, October 8, 1968, 75). He favored an unchanged policy. "A move toward firming now, on the eve of a Treasury refunding, was likely to be misconstrued and to set in motion a train of events that could be difficult to cope with. . . . [T]he less the Committee did by way of overt action at this time the better it would be" (ibid., 75).

There are two possible interpretations of Martin's statement. The first puts more weight on a possible concern that the economy would slow too rapidly. His letter to the president commenting on the Troika forecast expressed doubt that the economy would achieve the low real growth rates or reduction in inflation in the administration forecast. Although he did not mention recession, this seems a likely concern. The second interpretation is a political concern. The administration, particularly Okun, kept reminding Martin of the need for a more expansive policy and possibly suggested a change in the Federal Reserve Act. Martin had agreed many times that the surcharge would lower interest rates. Raising rates, even under the changed circumstances, would appear to break a quasi-commitment just before the presidential election. Thus, torn between his long-standing concern about inflation and his political concerns, he favored no change.

The next meeting came when the Treasury was in the market. Bank credit growth had remained strong, and the manager had responded by letting the funds rate rise. The staff forecast called for continued rapid credit growth. Hayes opposed Martin. On five occasions in recent years, the FOMC had acted during a Treasury operation. His proposal to tighten received support, but the FOMC would not abandon or modify its even keel policy. Hayes's was the only dissent.

Maisel (diary, October 9, 1968, 8–9) states the two main positions at the FOMC. On his interpretation, the difference perhaps reflected values but more certainly reflected differences in analysis. Both groups wanted the same result, lower inflation; they differed on the conditions for obtaining it.

At the moment, a majority of the Committee would accept a 4.5 percent unemployment rate and would recognize that it might take two years or more
to get down to a 2 percent growth in the consumer price index and relative
stability in wholesale industrial prices.

I think the people who want to tighten now . . . would be willing to run at
unemployment of between 5 and 6 percent for quite a period in the hope that
this would slow the price increases down to the 2 percent cpi, flat industrial
price index within six or nine months rather than the two years or so which
might be possible under the lower rate of employment.

Notable in his statement is the acceptance of 2 percent inflation, the same
goal the Federal Reserve and some other central banks accepted in the
1990s.

In November, the staff reported that the strong expansion continued.
Surveys indicated a higher rate of increase in capital spending in 1969
than in 1968. Even keel had ended. Still Martin hesitated. "He thought
a good case could be made for firming. But he had concluded—with
reluctance—that policy should not be firmed now because he thought it
was too late for such action. It would be asking too much of current monetary policy to expect it to deal with the inflationary psychology that had
resulted from the cumulative heritage of past failures of public policy"
(FOMC Minutes, November 26, 1968, 91–92; emphasis added.). This time
four members, all presidents—Hayes, Hickman (Cleveland), Kimbrel (Atlanta), and Morris (Boston) dissented.[102] The meeting summary reported
that the majority still expected the economy to slow. They were concerned
also about turbulence in the foreign exchange market. The British pound
was under pressure again, and the German government had recently announced that it would lower the border tax rebate of the value added tax
to reduce exports but would not revalue (see Chapter 5). The dissenters
emphasized both domestic credit growth and inflationary pressures and
the need to strengthen the dollar.

One reason for Martin's hesitation to act was overt pressure from the
administration. At Okun's suggestion, President Johnson appointed a task
force to consider changes in the Federal Reserve System. The task force's
report in early November 1968 proposed to weaken the role of the reserve
banks by excluding them from the FOMC, as suggested earlier by the
Commission on Money and Credit and by Eccles in 1935. With the Board
members much more amenable to persuasion, the administration would
gain influence over monetary policy.

102. Frank E. Morris replaced George Ellis as president of the Boston bank on
August 15, 1968. He served until 1988.

Hayes chaired the December 17 meeting in Martin's absence. The staff now estimated that real GNP growth would slow less than previous forecasts for the fourth quarter, and inflation would rise. Unemployment was reported at the lowest level in fifteen years. The staff continued to forecast slower growth in 1969.

Market interest rates "had risen sharply further . . . as the steady stream of statistics reflecting strength in the economy heightened concern about inflationary pressures and enhanced expectations of a firmer monetary policy" (Annual Report, 1968, 221). Banks had not waited for the Federal Reserve to act; they increased prime rates to 6.5 percent, reversing reductions in September. Bond yields rose to new highs. Estimated growth of money and the credit proxy reached 11.5 percent (annual rate) in November. Annual growth of the monetary base reached 7.15 percent in December. The market expected the Federal Reserve to respond.

Prior to the meeting, nine federal reserve banks voted to increase the discount rate. Board members indicated that they expected to increase the discount rate by 0.25 percentage points following the meeting. The FOMC then voted for firmer money market conditions. The federal funds rate reached 6 percent for the week ending December 18, an increase of 0.16, and 6.25 percent the following week. These were the highest nominal rates since the Board began collecting data in August 1954. With 4.6 percent reported inflation, real interest rates remained modest.

The Board received requests for a discount rate increase on December 12 but postponed action until after the FOMC meeting. Chairman Martin reported that he warned President Johnson that an increase was imminent. The president had indicated that he preferred that no action be taken. Some members wanted to increase reserve requirements at the same time.

Governors Daane, Maisel and Sherrill favored an increase of 0.25 percentage points to 5.5 percent; Robertson, Mitchell, and Brimmer believed that this would not signal a policy change. They believed the circumstances called for a larger increase (Board Minutes, December 16, 1968, 12–15).[103]

The Board learned that British reserve losses were likely to force the pound to float. This concern supported those favoring the smaller change in the discount rate. A majority did not support higher reserve requirement ratios. The Board approved the 5.5 discount rate unanimously, effective December 18. Governors Robertson, Mitchell, and Brimmer noted

103. Maisel was very critical of the handling of international policy. "Coombs is given almost complete discretion. He reports after the fact to the Board and does not give any explanation as to what he is attempting to do" (diary, December 13, 1968, 7). Maisel added that Coombs supplied reserves to ease the euro-dollar market when the Board tried to tighten domestically.

that they voted for the small increase because no other change could pass. Martin was absent and did not vote.

Trading Employment for Lower Inflation?

The SPF regular report became available in fourth quarter 1968. It showed no decline in the inflation rate expected one quarter ahead until the second half of 1971. The S&P index of stock prices reached a local peak in December 1968 that it did not surpass until March 1973, despite a nearly 50 percent increase in nominal GNP during the interval. By June 1969 it had declined 13 percent. This suggests expectations of lower real earnings growth not lower inflation.

In Hargrove and Morley (1984, 307), Okun explained the failure of coordinated policy action.

> I would still say that the big error we made at that point was in assessing the strength of the underlying state of private demand rather than in underestimating the danger that the fiscal program would put on or in underestimating the stimulus that would be provided by monetary policy. . . . [T]here was much more vigor in the capital boom than we had anticipated. We were wrong.
>
> [Morley:] "Were you and the Fed coordinating your policy? You were in agreement with what they were doing?
>
> [Okun:] If anything, we were pushing them harder for more easing, and we were off.
>
> [Morley:] So the idea was to touch the brakes and then let the economy go on.
>
> [Okun:] . . . Yes, this was a big change in fiscal restraint. . . . It did appear as though that would permit a further easing of monetary policy and still give us a slowdown. We got a slowdown in real economic activity. We didn't get as much of a slowdown as we expected.
>
> The more significant link of the chain, which became evident in 1969 and 1970 more than in 1968, was that a slowdown and even a recession didn't do much to slow inflation, and that was the bigger surprise.

There is no doubt that the forecast was too confident about the effect of a temporary increase in tax rates accompanied by lower interest rates. Maisel (1973, 189–91) claimed that the error that the Federal Reserve made was coordination and policy procedures, not mainly forecasting.

> In the fourth quarter, the economy was 1 percent higher than expected, but this amount was critical to an economy balanced on the knife edge of infla-

tion. Instead of the predicted 3.9 percent unemployment rate, unemployment fell to 3.4 percent, which was enough to send the economy into an inflationary spiral.

While the forecast was certainly one of the factors that influenced monetary policy in the wrong way for the next four months, I doubt that it played as important a role as many believe. Even without it, monetary policy would have relaxed some, partly because there was an implicit agreement with the Administration, Congress, and the concerned public that this time fiscal policy would carry the ball. . . .

With hindsight, it is evident that measurement problems again plagued the Fed during this period. Most of our discussion was still centered on money market conditions. . . . The fall in the funds rate seemed insignificant; they hovered near 6 percent, whereas they had been 4 percent only a year before. . . .

Even though bank credit grew considerably faster than my target, I failed to fight to curtail it because I mistakenly ascribed its growth to data that were erratic and which I thought would reverse.

Maisel summarized the lessons learned from the experience (ibid., 191–92). First, forecast errors are unavoidable and are large relative to the changes that are reported. "Failure to develop the necessary policy flexibility and response to forecasting variance can lead to unfortunate results" (ibid., 191). Second, little progress had been made in developing a better measure of policy thrust. "There was still only slight agreement on a proper set of targets or measures. . . . [T]he Committee and the markets still concentrated most of their attention on money market conditions" (ibid., 191–92). Third, "There was a failure to develop operating procedures and guides that would have made it possible to reach the selected targets" (ibid., 192). He could have added the problem of identifying permanent or persistent changes.

Both Okun and Maisel omit the most basic failure—economics is not the science that provides reliable quarterly forecasts. Economists could not accurately adjust the economy using a simple Keynesian (or other) model to coordinate policy actions to move along a stable Phillips curve. Not only were the forecasts inaccurate and control imperfect, the expectations set off by the policy action worked against the attractive but unattainable goal in practice of slowing the inflation rate without causing a recession.[104] The

104. The 1969 Economic Report (7) described the policy objective: "Enough restraint must be provided to permit a cooling off of the economy and a waning of inflationary forces. But the restraint must also be tempered to ensure continued economic growth." Critics called this "fine-tuning" and denied that it could work in the current state of knowledge.

evidence from 1966 through 1968 showed that the Federal Reserve responded promptly and decisively to a threat of recession or higher unemployment and slowly and hesitantly to observed increases in inflation. This asymmetry was reinforced by the short-term nature of policy actions and relative neglect of their long-term consequences.

Fifteen years later, with some of the participants at the time still present, although several in different positions, an exchange reopened these issues prior to the August 23, 1983, FOMC meeting.

> Mr. [Henry] Wallich. Well, if one could engage in some fine-tuning, one could say we'd raise the rate of money growth for a year because the tax increase will have some downward impact on the economy. The decline in interest rates that comes from that will not completely offset it, so there is some net downward response by the economy. If one dares to fine-tune, monetary policy can offset that [response]. But we must not get trapped into a permanently higher rate of money growth. Everybody understands that that means more inflation. . . .
>
> Mr. [J. Charles] Partee. This can get to be very complicated though, Henry. It depends on the kind of tax increase. You remember in 1968 when we very, very desperately wanted a tax increase to help finance the war in Vietnam, we got a 10 percent surtax in the middle of 1968 and then the Chairman or the Board or the Committee—I'm not sure who—came as close as they could to promising a reduction in interest rates if that 10 percent surtax went in. It went in and I'll be darned if interest rates didn't start to go up rather than down. And it was a great, great political problem. So, we do have in modern history a representation of the kind of trap that I'm sure Paul Volcker has very much in mind.
>
> Mr. [Lyle] Gramley. And the worst part of that story is that we led the parade with a decline in the discount rate. We kept—
>
> Mr. Partee. We went out to Minneapolis and got them to cut it.
>
> Mr. Gramley. We kept trying to pump in enough money to make sure that interest rates didn't go back up. The 10 percent surcharge had no fiscal restraint effects at all. The monetary stimulus had a lot. We ended up with the worst of all possible worlds. (FOMC Minutes, August 23, 1983, 33–34)

This was the precise point made by the Andersen-Jordan article (Andersen and Jordan, 1968), to which the Board's staff reacted very negatively. The paper estimated the relative responses to money growth and budget spending and tax changes. It found much stronger and more reliable responses to money growth. This supported the monetarist position and irritated Keynesian economists at the Board and elsewhere.[105]

Using a short-run, fixed Phillips curve, Okun described the policy objective as gradually slowing the economy down to about "2 percent growth for a couple of quarters . . . [keeping] the unemployment rate 4.1" (Hargrove and Morley, 1984, 308). The means of achieving lower inflation was to move "down that curve [a Phillips curve relating unemployment to inflation] just as we went up that curve. Why can't we get back to where we were in 1965, the good old days? That's exactly what we thought would happen. That's exactly what didn't happen" (ibid., 308).

This was not the last time that policymakers would make a major error by relying on the stability of the short-run Phillips curve relation. The principal reason in this period was that the public had learned that policymakers placed greater weight on avoiding a rise in unemployment than avoiding higher inflation. The experience in 1965, the Federal Reserve's response to the tax surcharge, and administration rhetoric about "fiscal overkill" strongly suggested that policy would not tighten enough or remain tight long enough to reduce inflation permanently. Whatever modest decline in measured inflation occurred, the public now expected it to be temporary. The long-term inflation rate was expected to persist and might even rise if monetary stimulus increased.[106] This change in expected inflation shifted the Phillips curve, contrary to Okun's forecast for the Council.

Policy failure in this period was not entirely the result of staff errors. Chairman Martin did not put much credence in economists' forecasts; he probably gave little weight to them at the time. Chart 4.10 shows that free reserves rose after June 1968, but the rise was modest, about a $300 million increase from the April low point to the local peak in September. This was much less than in 1967. Martin believed the Federal Reserve had eased, but not aggressively. We know from Okun's comments that Martin resisted pressures for greater ease. No less important was the implicit commitment

105. Some Board staff members—Frank deLeeuw and John Kalchbrenner—published a paper directly critiquing the Andersen-Jordan paper (deLeeuw and Kalchbrenner 1969). This was the first time such a critique had been written by Board staff about research at a reserve bank (interview with Jerry L. Jordan, December 16, 2002). At the time of the interview, Jordan was president of the Cleveland Federal Reserve Bank. In 1970, the FOMC discussed the conflict between St. Louis's emphasis on money growth and other views within the System. Although some Board members deplored these differences, most favored competition in ideas (FOMC Minutes, June 23, 1970, 26–28).

106. Brunner, Cukierman, and Meltzer (1980) later showed the importance of the distinction between permanent or persistent and transitory or temporary changes in inflation for "stagflation," the coexistence of inflation and unemployment. The Board staff did not recognize this source of error.

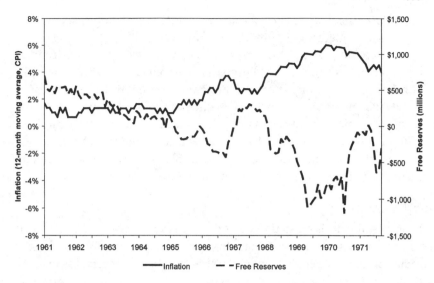

Chart 4.10. Free reserves and inflation, January 1961–September 1971.

Martin had made to President Johnson to continue policy coordination by easing to prevent recession and offset fiscal overkill.

Behind the commitment lay a belief that the public, the administration, and Congress would not accept a significant increase in unemployment to reduce inflation. Dislike of inflation was not yet strong enough to induce the public or the political parties to pay much cost to reduce it. As President Eisenhower remarked in the 1960s, Republican administrations had to avoid repetition of the Great Depression. Democratic administrations placed more weight on temporary job losses than on permanent reductions in inflation. Much academic literature supported that view by claiming that the only cost of inflation was the loss in value of cash balances and the increased frequency of financial transactions. This ignored the costs of inflation resulting from the tax system and other institutional arrangements. Fischer (1981) later developed these costs. See also Feldstein (1982).

Further, staff forecasts were not the only source of information. Darryl Francis (St. Louis) warned repeatedly about the inflationary consequences. Although not a voting member, Francis took an active part in policy discussion at the time. At the August, September, November, and December meetings, he warned that monetary policy was overly expansive.[107] Despite

107. Examples from the August and December meetings suggest the strength and prescience of Francis's remarks. "The view that the recently adopted fiscal package would, by itself, adequately restrict total demand and cure the inflationary problems was overly optimistic. Monetary actions had continued to be excessively stimulative, negating the desirable anti-inflationary impact of the fiscal package" (FOMC Minutes, August 13, 1968, 75). He rejected

these warnings, Martin and most of the FOMC remained focused on free reserves and interest rates, not on money growth.

Was it simply chance that the Federal Reserve waited until December to tighten policy? The Federal Reserve is often reluctant to act decisively in either direction during the months before an election. By December 1968, the FOMC knew that there would be a different political party in the White House. Its actions could not change the political result, and the incumbent Johnson administration was less concerned about the consequences of a more restrictive policy whose effects on employment would not be felt on their watch. The new administration would have to deal with that.

A Policy Change

Following the decision to tighten at the December 17 meeting, the Board voted to increase the discount rates to 5.5 percent. This reversed the August reduction of 0.25 percentage points. It is the shortest interval between a discount rate change and its reversal in Federal Reserve history up to that time, a tacit recognition of a policy error.

The Federal Advisory Council had warned the Board in September that the "recent [August] reduction in the discount rate might have been 'premature'" (Board Minutes, September 17, 1968, 32). Two months later, the FAC warned that it could see little evidence of response to the tax surcharge. Governor Maisel reported that some businessmen believed that the unemployment rate would have to reach 5.5 percent to bring inflation under control (Board Minutes, November 19, 1968, 26). He asked for their views. The FAC members divided. Some agreed, but several said that an increase of that magnitude was "unacceptable" to the public and to both political parties (ibid., 26). They did not urge a more restrictive policy.

Most of the reserve banks had resisted the discount rate reduction in August. By December, they were ready to reverse the reduction or do more. On December 12, Richmond, Chicago, and Dallas voted to restore the 0.25 percentage point reduction, and St. Louis voted to increase by 0.5 to 5.75 percent. New York indicated a strong interest in joining, if the Board approved an increase.

Martin notified President Johnson of a coming discount rate increase.

---

the conventional view. "The greater concern about a possible recession than about present and prospective inflation seemed unwarranted" (ibid., 77). "Mr. Francis commented that inflation was continuing at a 4 percent annual rate, and expectations of future inflation appear to be heightening. . . . There seemed little question that a restrictive monetary policy had to be pursued. . . . But an apparent conflict arose between the desirability of taking effective action against inflation and the desirability of preventing a further rise in interest rates" (FOMC Minutes, December 17, 1968, 51–52).

With about a month remaining in his term, Johnson did not object. His last Economic Report continued emphasis on coordination of fiscal and monetary actions, but now the aim was to slow the economy by extending the tax surcharge for another year and a monetary policy of moderate restraint (Council of Economic Advisers, 1969, 9–10).[108]

The weakness of the pound remained a concern. The staff reported that the British had large reserve losses. An increase in the U.S. discount rate might require them to float. Coombs believed that the British could stand a 0.25 percentage point increase and Governors Daane, Maisel, and Sherrill favored a 0.25 increase. Robertson, Mitchell, and Brimmer wanted stronger action, including an increase in reserve requirement ratios. The only decision at the December 16 meeting was to delay a decision until the FOMC met on the following day. The only agreement was for a 0.25 increase in the discount rate. The announcement noted that the 5.5 percent discount rate was the highest rate in nearly 40 years, but it failed to note that the 12 month inflation rate had reached 4.6 percent, and both the SPF and the CEA expected inflation of about 3.25 percent in the coming year.

The CEA forecast called for growth to slow to 3 percent from more than 4 percent in 1968.[109] In the Council's view, monetary restraint had now joined fiscal restraint. Industrial production slowed at the end of 1968, and real GNP declined modestly in the fourth quarter, so there was some reason to believe that policy would soon lower the inflation rate and increase unemployment.

Governor Daane asked the key question: Was the market convinced that the System would continue its policy of restraint? Would the FOMC persist? Holmes's answer was disquieting. He said opinions were divided. Some believed that once the economy slowed, the System would ease and not carry the policy through (FOMC Minutes, January 14, 1969, 18). As if to support the skeptics, Frank Morris (Boston) dissented from the policy of "maintaining the prevailing firm conditions" because "it could be [sic] compatible with an unduly restrictive monetary policy" (ibid., 76–77). By unduly restrictive, he meant bank credit growth of zero to 3 percent instead of the 5 to 7 percent that he favored.

---

108. The Johnson administration proposed extending the surcharge after discussions with the incoming administration. Nixon campaigned against the surcharge but decided to leave the option open.

109. The CEA expected growth to fall to 1 percent in the first half, then recover sharply under the impact of a federal pay increase and an easier monetary policy. The Board's staff agreed on the first half, not the second (FOMC Minutes, February 4, 1969, 19–20). Okun estimated that a full year with the 10 percent surtax would produce $8.5 billion of additional revenue and a $1.9 billion budget surplus (Okun to the president, CF, Box 5, LBJ Library, December 2, 1968).

The January 1969 meeting was the last FOMC meeting before the new administration. President-elect Nixon had criticized inflation during the campaign but had not proposed a definite program. Stein (1990, 138) described Nixon as not very interested in economic policy. "He did not consider economics as an area of his major competence." He found it boring and believed that the public was concerned about inflation but unwilling to accept higher unemployment to lower inflation (ibid., 134–38).[110] President Johnson agreed. He told his aide, Joseph Califano, to invest in land. "This Nixon knows nothing about the economy and it's going to go to hell" (Califano, 2000, 337).

President Nixon told Stein at their first meeting that "we must not raise unemployment," still only 3.4 percent (Stein, 1990, 135). In part, this reflected his experience in the 1960 election, when, he believed, rising unemployment cost him the presidency in a very close election. But it also reflected residual concerns about the blame that President Hoover and the Republican party bore for the 1929–33 depression. The Federal Reserve believed it now had an administration more willing to sustain an anti-inflation policy provided the unemployment rate did not rise precipitately or remain above 4.5 percent. As Orphanides emphasized (2001, 2002) the prevailing belief among Federal Reserve staff and administration economists was that a period of unemployment somewhat above 4 percent would gradually reduce the inflation rate. The new Council's projections no longer were concerned about "overkill." They showed inflation (deflator) falling from 4 percent in 1968 to 3.5 percent in 1969 at the cost of unemployment reaching 4.4 percent by mid-1970 (Matusow, 1998, 17–18).[111] This policy was called "gradualism" in order to distinguish it from a more decisive effort to end inflation quickly and accept a much larger temporary increase in unemployment.

Through June 1969 the FOMC continued to vote for maintaining the same policy stance subject to provisos about credit growth or Treasury financing. Morris (Boston) continued to express concern about excessive

110. Herbert Stein became a member and later chairman of the Council of Economic Advisers in the Nixon administration. His Ph.D. dissertation and later work developed the idea of built-in stabilizers to shift the budget from surplus to deficit and vice versa as the economy expanded and contracted. Later, this idea led to the so-called full employment budget surplus or deficit used to justify actual deficits when the economy operated at less than full employment. Like the Johnson administration, Nixon's economists continued the error of setting 4 percent employment as their measure of full employment.

111. Matusow (1998, 18) reports that President Nixon "distrusted his policy of gradualism in part because it assigned to the Federal Reserve and William McChesney Martin the main responsibility for slowing down the economy." In fact, the president offered Martin the position of Secretary of the Treasury so that he could appoint Arthur Burns in his place. Martin declined. Brimmer (1966) reported that Martin told the Board at the time that he had rejected the president's offer.

restraint, and Francis (St. Louis), often joined by Governor Robertson, favored increased restraint.[112] But even those who favored a firmer policy opposed any increase in regulation Q ceiling rates. Daniel Brill, the Board's chief economist, explained that markets would "mistakenly regard an increase in ceiling rates as an easing, rather than a tightening, action" (FOMC Minutes, February 4, 1969, 28).[113]

Brill noted this was a confusion caused by concerns about bank credit growth. Higher ceiling rates would permit banks to supply more credit absolutely and relative to other lenders, such as the commercial paper market, and shift more deposits from demand to time accounts. Its principal expansionary effect resulted from the difference in reserve requirement ratios for the two types of deposits. The statement ignored the banks' response to regulation. They bought financial paper through their holding companies or borrowed euro-dollars. Nevertheless, some members frequently repeated the statement associating higher ceiling rates with monetary or credit ease.[114]

Throughout this period, members expressed concerns about a renewed "credit crunch," reminiscent of 1966, and market anticipations of future policy. Reports showed that market participants had accepted that policy would remain restrictive near-term, but many remained skeptical about whether the policy would avoid a "credit crunch" and how long the Federal Reserve would continue the policy in that event or if unemployment rose. FOMC minutes for 1969 contain many statements about the difficulty of convincing the public that the System would persist until the inflation rate fell. Owens and Schreft (1992) discusses credit crunches in these years and banks' use of non-price rationing.

112. In February, Francis said that for four years the FOMC had been led into "unintended inflationary monetary expansion while following interest rates, net reserves, and the bank credit objectives" (FOMC Minutes, February 4, 1969, 47). Robertson favored an increase in reserve requirements, open market sales, and a discount rate increase, a policy very different from gradualism.

113. The Treasury faced another of its recurrent problems of getting Congress to approve an increase in the debt ceiling. The FOMC discussed actions it would take to help if needed and decided it could make available to the Treasury some of the warehoused foreign currencies it had acquired. This seems a violation of the spirit of the provision barring direct loans to the Treasury.

114. Like most price control programs, practice raised many issues. Should gifts paid to a new depositor be counted as interest? The Board decided no because it was a one-time payment. What should be done about commercial paper that banks used as a substitute for negotiable CDs? The Board extended regulations to commercial paper. In October 1969, the Board proposed to extend regulation to other "non deposit funds" (memo, Proposed rule making regarding certain borrowings by bank affiliates, Correspondence Box 240, Federal Reserve Bank of New York, October 31, 1969). There was, in addition, a regular stream of decisions about what constituted interest, what restrictions to impose on compounding, and what constituted a deposit.

Although the FOMC voted repeatedly to keep policy unchanged, the federal funds rate rose steadily from a monthly average of 6 percent in December 1968 to 8.9 percent in June 1969. During this period free reserves fell from −$290 to −$1042 million, and annual growth of the monetary base fell from 7.2 to 5.7 percent, then to 5 percent in July. It continued to fall.[115] Warning of an expected decline in output and profits, the S&P 500 index greeted the new administration by falling 4.2 percent in January, reducing the twelve-month rate of change to −1 percent. By June, the twelve-month rate of change was −13 percent, and the index continued to fall.

Real GNP rose 5.7 percent in the first quarter but slowed to 0.5 percent in the second. The unemployment rate remained 3.4 percent through May and 3.5 percent through August. Consumer price inflation continued to increase. By June the annual rate of increase reached 5.3 percent from 4.6 percent in December. It was well above the 4.5 percent rate that administration economists had agreed to tolerate. The SPF began to increase the expected inflation rate.

Gradualism, if that's what it was, did not support the presuppositions of the economists in the new administration. They had expected a less decisive move toward monetary restraint, supported by fiscal tightening to a budget deficit of $500 million for fiscal 1969 (ending June 1969) from a $27.7 billion deficit the previous year. The Johnson surtax provided a large part of the change. Although candidate Nixon criticized the surtax, his advisers convinced him to renew it for another year.[116] Congress remained under Democratic control, so it exacted a price. It approved a 10 percent

115. Within a few weeks of the new administration's start, the CEA warned the president that because the Federal Reserve did not use its power to control money, growth the administration should not trust its statements. The memo suggested that the administration could challenge the Federal Reserve's independence (memo, Stein to the president, Communications with the Fed, Nixon papers, February 15, 1969). This lack of trust continued. A CEA staff memo said, "The Federal Reserve's operating concepts *threaten* our stabilization program just as they did in every postwar recession and inflation" (memo, Leonall Andersen to Paul McCracken, Communications with the Fed and Burns, Nixon papers, May 1, 1969; emphasis in the original). The memo described the principal source of errors as reliance on money market conditions and the accommodation principle. The latter meant that the Federal Reserve interpreted changes in money as the result of shifts in the demand for money that the Federal Reserve accommodated by leaving the interest rate unchanged.

116. President Johnson announced the proposal to extend the surtax on January 14, 1969. President-elect Nixon issued a statement tentatively supporting the decision as a part of his program to reduce the budget deficit and the inflation rate. A higher budget deficit would add to borrowing and raise interest rates. The statement then added, "If an attempt were made to avoid the rise in interest rates, the result would be more inflation, and this would subsequently *cause* (as it has in the past) still higher rates" (preliminary draft, statement by President-elect Nixon, Nixon papers, undated; emphasis added). This appears to be the first explicit statement from an administration recognizing the positive, causal relation between inflation and market interest rates.

surtax for six months, but only 5 percent for the following six months. It also removed the investment tax credit, increased taxes on the oil industry, raised the capital gains tax, and removed income taxes from low-income taxpayers. The net effect was a deficit for fiscal 1970 instead of the surplus that the administration hoped to spend or use for its preferred form of tax reduction in election year 1970. Instead, the budget deficit reached $8.7 billion in fiscal 1970 and $26 billion in 1971.

Both the administration and the Federal Reserve had mixed and incompletely formed ideas about how to achieve the common objective of reducing inflation without causing a large recession. Administration economists stressed control of money growth. The chairman of the Council of Economic Advisers, Paul McCracken, hoped to have a fiscal surplus and a tight monetary policy, so he favored a tax increase and the introduction of a value added tax to offset the budget deficit. Arthur Burns, at the time counselor to the president, and Labor Secretary George Shultz opposed any tax increase. They wanted a smaller government. They favored reduced monetary growth and tighter monetary policy to offset easier fiscal policy. McCracken favored a continuation of coordination; if fiscal policy had eased and no tax increase was forthcoming, monetary policy should tighten (Matusow, 1998, 51, 58). The president said that his "concern must not be inflation but recession" (quoted in ibid., 55). Early in 1969, the president promised George Meany, president of the AFL-CIO, that his administration would slow inflation without increasing unemployment (Hargrove and Morley, 1984, 328).[117]

At the first meeting of the Quadriad on January 23, most of the discussion concerned steps to gradually reduce inflation while minimizing the effect on unemployment. Chairman Martin said, "The System had pulled a boner after the tax increase last year by pursuing for a time an easier monetary policy. This decision heavily reflected projections of their staff that the tax increase might produce an overkill effect, causing substantial slack in the economy. In retrospect this evaluation of prospects was in error" (meeting with the Quadriad, Nixon papers, January 23, 1969). Martin said that policy was now less expansive to achieve approximately 7 percent money growth.[118]

To the extent the new administration started with a framework and consensus about how to reduce inflation, it differed on only a few points from

117. McCracken explained to the president that "it was not going to happen" (Hargrove and Morley, 1984, 328; Stein 1990, 143). All his economic advisers considered President Nixon to be knowledgeable about economics but not much interested. Herbert Stein said, "He would rely more heavily on others in the case of economic policy . . . He also didn't believe it was a terribly interesting subject to the country" (Hargrove and Morley, 1984, 365).

118. A brief discussion of the international position focused on continuing control of foreign investment.

the previous orthodoxy. The new administration gave much greater importance to money growth as the factor driving excess aggregate demand and inflation, but like its predecessor it accepted 4 percent unemployment as full employment (ibid., 3, 5), making no adjustment for the age and sex composition of the labor force, the marginal tax rate, and other factors. Both relied on a short-run Phillips curve to show how much the unemployment rate would rise as inflation fell. And both believed that the adjustment to lower inflation could occur within a few months or a year without a recession.[119] Where they differed most was on the value of guidelines or guideposts to improve the Phillips curve tradeoff by lowering inflation.[120] The Nixon administration disavowed guideposts.

There were three difficulties in implementing the program. First, the administration relied heavily on slower but steadier money growth, but it did not control money growth. Martin remained as chairman until the end of January 1970, and he did not agree about the importance of money growth or the System's ability to control it.[121] Arthur Burns, who took his place in February 1970, wanted to adjust money market conditions to the fiscal deficit, not money growth (Matusow, 1998, 51). This continued the coordination policy of the past. Second, both the administration and the Federal Reserve were surprised by the very slow response of inflation. Both failed to recognize that the 4 percent unemployment rate was no longer a relevant target. Like most academic economists at the time, they did not recognize that previous failures to stop inflation strengthened beliefs that the administration would not persist when unemployment rose, especially

119. Okun and Stein use almost the same words to describe their surprise at learning that "we don't have an adequate inflation theory or inflation forecasting mechanism within the profession" (Hargrove and Morley, 1984, 307, 364). McCracken expected "possibly a mild decline in the economy, . . . [and] an upturn somewhere around the second quarter or the middle part of the next year" (ibid., 342). Lower inflation would take longer.

120. The new administration had a very different idea about the role of government. Instead of seeing government policies as a way of disciplining an unstable private sector, President Nixon and his principal economic advisers talked about government policy as a destabilizing element in a relatively stable private economy. This had two direct consequences. First, the administration initially opposed pressures for intervention in price and wage setting processes. Second, the new administration eschewed efforts to use policy actions to make frequent policy adjustments, called "fine-tuning" by McCracken (Hargrove and Morley, 1984, 323).

121. Burns believed that monetary velocity was unstable, a view held by many at the Federal Reserve. "I wish the world was as simple as the Friedmanites and Keynesians wish to make it, but it never has been and, I dare say, it never will be" (letter, Burns to Edwin Nourse, January 30, 1970, quoted in Wells, 1994, 25). Burns was a highly respected developer of a business cycle analysis that was atheoretical. He and his associates at the National Bureau of Economic Research had studied the statistical properties of hundreds of time series and analyzed their comovements, leads, and lags.

before an election. Third, by rejecting price and wage guidelines, the administration gave an easy target to critics who claimed that ideology prevented it from using techniques that reduced the cost of lowering inflation. Critics brushed aside McCracken's claim that the evidence from all developed countries showed that guidepost policies had not worked (Hargrove and Morley, 1984, 347). The administration retreated from this position gradually by acting in the construction industry, with chain store executives, and on copper and steel prices. But the president faced dissension within his cabinet and from Arthur Burns, his counselor at the time, for rejecting more general measures (Wells, 1994, 40).[122] Attention to guideposts focused attention away from the requisites of an effective program.

Guideposts and controls grew in popularity. Businessmen wanted the government to reduce wage growth and labor costs. Unions and many consumers wanted price controls. Congress responded in August 1970 by authorizing the administration to impose mandatory price and wage controls at the president's discretion.[123]

Federal Reserve Discussions, 1969–70[124]

The FOMC gave more attention to total deposit growth, called the bank credit proxy, in this period than earlier or later. It could not decide how to respond if it missed the current target or objective. If the proxy grew

122. As noted earlier, Burns had been an outspoken critic of the Kennedy and Johnson guidelines. In the White House, and even more at the Federal Reserve, he irritated President Nixon by becoming a leading proponent.

123. Inflation was not high among the problems mentioned by the public to pollsters. Starting in 1970 the Gallup organization asked regularly what respondents regarded as the most important problem facing the country. Data from early 1970, with annual CPI inflation at 6 percent, show that only 14 percent named inflation or "the high cost of living" as one of the most important problems. The percentage rose and fell with inflation in the 1970s. It did not remain persistently above 50 percent until 1980–81. I am indebted to Karlyn Bowman for supplying these data.

124. At a Board meeting in early January, an extraordinary discussion took place in which Martin discussed problems at the Board and the policy failures of the past few years. Maisel started by criticizing the way the Board dealt with international monetary policy. He said that Daane and Solomon acted without instructions, and policy was not discussed. Martin responded by describing his "feeling of difficulty and frustration in coordinating the Board. . . . ([H]e said that I [Maisel] had been characterized as a doctrinaire liberal.) . . . He also indicated that he felt there were major problems with the Board. Governor Brimmer gave too many speeches, Governor Robertson was too adamant in his views and stuck to them too strongly. . . . He indicated that probably he should have gone off the Board in '67. . . .

"[H]e felt that Burns was too inflexible. . . . [H]e felt this was true of all the economists on the Board. . . .

"Martin said he thought the Treasury team would be better than the last. He had a low opinion of the knowledge and job performance of Fowler, Barr, and Deming even though he liked them all personally. He felt that, too, had diminished his historical stature by the part he had had to play in the gold negotiations and at Bonn" (Maisel diary, January 24, 1969, 20–22).

faster than the target, action reducing its growth raised concerns about a credit crunch. Failure to act raised concerns that the System was about to ease policy and lowered its credibility[125] (FOMC Minutes, March 4, 1969, 47–48). This was the wrong time to make this choice. With interest rates at the regulation Q ceiling, data on time deposits were distorted, as Governor Mitchell recognized (Maisel diary, January 24, 1969, 10). Banks lost large certificates of deposit but acquired euro-dollars to maintain lending.

By late February, the Board had to consider raising the regulation Q ceiling. At the FAC meeting, the large banks supported an increase. They had no liquidity and would soon have to sell long-term securities at a substantial loss in order to service their customers. Smaller banks feared that the large banks would use the increased ceiling to draw deposits from them. The Board feared a return of the 1966 credit crunch if banks began to sell municipal bonds. Perhaps for this reason, Martin favored an increase in the ceiling rate (Maisel diary, February 20, 1969, 30).

The Board received conflicting advice from all sides. It remained uncertain about next steps. Mitchell favored more attention to money growth because "market psychology and the market's interpretation of System policy seemed increasingly to be influenced by changes in M_1," (ibid., 49). The manager denied the claim and repeated that money was hard to control in the short run. Several members, including Martin, urged the FOMC to be patient.[126] He told the Joint Economic Committee that he was now optimistic that inflation would be controlled (Martin speeches, February 26, 1969, 1).

The administration was concerned but willing to wait. A staff memo

---

125. The System was aware that its credibility was at stake. Businessmen made the point frequently and, on occasion, someone would refer explicitly to credibility. For example, Chairman Martin mentioned the government's "credibility gap." At the February meeting of the FAC, the members' statement said, "Businessmen wanted to see tangible results rather than to hear promises, which they found largely unfulfilled in recent years" (Board Minutes, February 18, 1969, 4). In response to a question about time certificates of deposit, the FAC complained about the speed with which the Federal Reserve had tightened (raised interest rates). But it favored continued restraint. Three months later the FAC said, "There is a continuing skepticism in the business community that the objective of price stability will be accorded priority if unemployment should increase significantly" (Board Minutes, May 20, 1969, 7).

126. "Holmes replied that in his opinion it was not feasible to attempt direct control of short-run movements in the money stock . . . [E]fforts at close control . . . could involve drastic medicine" (FOMC Minutes, March 4, 1969, 50–51). Other members of the FOMC expressed concern that the manager ignored the proviso clause requiring a change in money market conditions if the credit proxy deviated considerably from its desired range. A study by the Board's staff found that the proviso clause had caused a change by the manager on seven occasions between May 10, 1966, when the FOMC first used the clause, and December 1968. On two occasions in 1966, the manager eased. On the other five, all in 1968, he tightened (memo, Normand Bernard to Robert Holland, Board Records, March 20, 1969).

prepared for a Quadriad meeting in March was one of several memos at the time arguing the need for patience, while suggesting further reductions in government spending and renewal of the surtax. Even with these changes, the projected inflation rate (deflator) would fall only from 4 percent at the end of 1968 to 3.5 percent in fourth quarter 1969 and a bit lower in 1970. At the meeting the president agreed to request renewal of the surtax.

In testimony to the Senate Banking and Currency Committee, Martin at last recognized that "the way to get interest rates down is to end the inflation that has been raising them" (Martin speeches, March 25, 1969, 1). He then reversed course, attributing the rise in interest rates to the "high rate of technological progress occurring in both the U.S. and abroad" (ibid.). However, he returned to the effects of inflation by concluding that "expansive monetary policies may not [sic] lower interest rates; in fact they may raise them appreciably. This is the clear lesson of history that has been reconfirmed by the experience of the past several years" (ibid., 9).

The Board was not willing to raise the regulation Q ceiling rate to reflect inflation out of concern for political pressures from regional banks, savings and loans, and Congress. Large banks borrowed euro-dollars to support loans. The Board was divided about what should be done. Brimmer wanted to put reserve requirements on euro-dollars. Remembering 1966, Martin viewed euro-dollar inflows as a safety valve for the large banks as suppliers of bank credit. At one point, with a majority of the Board in favor of raising reserve requirement ratios, he adjourned the meeting without taking a vote (Maisel diary, March 7, 1969, 37).

Through April, the FOMC found few signs that its policy was working to slow the economy and reduce inflation. Heavy borrowing by U.S. banks in the euro-dollar market promptly transmitted domestic policy to other countries. These countries complained about the increase in interest rates, their inability to control domestic money growth, and the reflow of euro-dollars that they expected when rates fell in the United States (ibid., April 29, 1969, 38). They were learning the hard way about the policy trilemma; countries could not expect to control inflation, fix exchange rates, and permit capital flows. It would take a while before they agreed to give up fixed exchange rates.

To convince skeptics that the Board intended to maintain its restrictive interest rate policy, eleven reserve banks increased their discount rates to 6 percent for the first time since 1929, effective April 4. Boston followed a few days later. At the same meeting, the Board increased reserve requirement ratios on demand deposits by 0.5 percentage points, to 17.5 and 13 percent at reserve city and country banks respectively but retained a 0.5 percentage point difference for banks with deposits under $5 million.

Changes became effective on April 17. Governor Maisel dissented, citing the slow growth in monetary aggregates and the rise in interest rates during the year. Maisel (1973, 243) explained that many of those who voted for the change believed that they could affect expectations without changing interest rates or monetary aggregates. With the interest rate unchanged, the change in required reserves would be matched by an increase in total reserves.[127] They expected the market to get an announcement effect that would convince it that the Federal Reserve would stay the course.

The Board had discussed a discount rate increase since January 24, when the St. Louis bank first requested the change. St. Louis renewed its request several times. It was rejected or not acted upon on January 27 and February 17 and 24. In February, Dallas requested a 5.75 percent rate, and in March Richmond and Kansas City joined St. Louis; Chicago requested 6.25 percent. With the federal funds rate at 6.3 percent in January and 6.79 percent in March, the discount rate increases seem pro forma, but the Board did not act at first, out of concern for the effect on regulation Q ceilings and the political consequences.

Discussion of the discount rate change showed several different approaches to the inflation problem. The staff proposed an increase of 0.5 percentage points to 6 percent, citing rapid growth of the credit proxy, with no change in reserve requirement ratios or regulation Q ceilings. Governors Mitchell and Daane wanted an increase in reserve requirement ratios, regulation Q ceilings, and the discount rate for its "psychological" or announcement effect. Mitchell believed the Board had a credibility problem; the public did not believe that it would persist in its anti-inflation policy (Maisel diary, April 3, 1969, 51). Maisel opposed; he disliked substituting psychological for economic arguments. The monetary aggregates had grown appropriately for several months and projections showed that they would continue to do so. He was "unwilling to accept the psychological feeling of bankers and the investment community as a proper goal. . . . [I]t seemed to me that the Board was changing its strategy . . . by attempting to act on psychology directly" (ibid., 52). Brimmer wanted higher reserve requirement ratios and discount rates but not an increase in regulation Q ceilings. Sherrill wanted to only raise the discount rate. Robertson was eager to raise reserve requirements but was reluctant to raise the discount rate. Since ten banks had asked for an increase, he said the Board had to agree. He did not want to raise regulation Q ceilings.

127. CEA staff noted that the change in reserve requirements increased required reserves by $660 million for the week ending April 23, 1969. The System supplied $900 million (seasonally adjusted) mainly by open market purchases and increased discounting (memo, Andersen to McCracken, Communications with Fed and Burns, Nixon papers, May 1, 1969).

Table 4.6   Annual Growth Rates of Money and Credit Aggregates (percent)

MONTH	BASE[a]	MONEY[b]	BANK CREDIT[b]
December 1968	7.2	6.5	11.4
January 1969	6.9	3.8	0.9
February	6.8	0.6	0.0
March	6.4	2.5	2.8
April*	5.7	10.0	5.0

*estimate

[a] Anderson and Rasche 1999; [b] McCracken to the president, Nixon Papers, April 26, 1969.

Chairman Martin's statement took a strong stand but did not lead. He said that the Board had to fight inflation and "take all necessary action until the inflationary psychology was halted. . . . [T]here was a credibility gap on the part of the Board and the administration—neither was willing to take the hard action required if inflation was to be stopped" (ibid., 53). Then he retreated a bit. Since a majority opposed raising regulation Q ceilings, he favored only the discount rate and reserve requirement increases. The proposed action did not match his statement.

The Board found it easier to agree on the increase in reserve requirement ratios than on the press release. The stumbling bloc was whether the action changed policy. The discussion brought out that the members did not agree on whether this was a policy change. Press interviews confirmed that the Treasury did not regard the action as tightening policy; "if it had meant more tightening, the Treasury or the Administration would have opposed the change, but they did not do so since it was purely psychological" (Maisel diary, April 7, 1969, 57). Writing in the *New York Times,* Erich Heinemann interpreted the change as a shift from "gradualism." He thought that was an error because it neglected the lags in response to slower monetary growth. As Board members noted, growth of the monetary aggregates had slowed.

For the April 29 Quadriad meeting, the CEA staff prepared a table for the president showing recent money and bank credit growth. Table 4.6 supplements these data with annual growth rates of the monetary base.

Base growth showed gradual deceleration, but the other aggregates did not. As the Federal Reserve soon learned, money and credit could change over a large range in the short term with changes in Treasury deposits, float, and other temporary changes. In addition, both bank credit and money were affected in different ways by the regulation Q ceilings. With market rates at the ceiling, banks lost time deposits to their foreign branches and foreign banks and to non-banks at home. This had a large negative effect on credit growth and a smaller positive effect on growth of demand deposits and money. Banks had to buy back their deposits by issuing commercial paper and acquiring euro-dollars. Raising the ceiling rate would have avoided these changes.

Members were confused. Some feared that increased growth of time deposits would suggest that policy had eased, so they hesitated to make a desirable change. Faulty reasoning or excessive concern for cosmetics prevented appropriate action. In a reversion to the discredited real bills doctrine, Morris (Boston) and Coldwell (Dallas) wanted the Board to urge banks not to lend for corporate acquisitions because the loans were not productive credit. Bopp (Philadelphia), Kimbrel (Atlanta), and Francis (St. Louis) said that this decision was up to bankers, not the Board, and that "productive" credit was not a useful concept (Maisel diary, April 29, 1969, 61).

Soon afterward, the Federal Reserve again discussed restrictions on commercial paper and euro-dollars to limit this substitution.[128] In May, Governor Robertson urged the Board to expand the definition of "deposit" to include any funds borrowed by a member bank. The Board soon thereafter considered Robertson's proposal and a proposal to put the commercial paper purchases by bank affiliates under regulation Q. Legal counsel cautioned that the proposal had uncertain legality. Robertson and Brimmer were eager to act. Sherrill argued that Board policy was working and they should not change the regulations (Board Minutes, June 23, 1969, 10–16). The next month the Board took the first step; on a six-to-one vote it amended regulation Q "to narrow the scope of the repurchase agreement exemption from the definition of deposits" (ibid., July 24, 1969, 9). Mitchell dissented.[129]

This step did not satisfy Board members concerned about banks "evading monetary policy" by issuing commercial paper (Board Minutes, October 22, 1969, 4). The Board did not discuss removal of regulation Q ceilings to restrict rapid growth of commercial paper. The Board's Legal Division had found a way to make regulation Q applicable to "certain funds obtained by a member bank through issuance of commercial paper" (Board Minutes, September 18, 1969, 11). Discussion proceeded about how this could best be done.[130]

128. Anyone who added bank related commercial paper to bank loans would not be fooled by the substitution. Several bankers made this point at the May FAC meeting: "Chairman Martin said . . . the real question was whether banks were using these methods to thwart the current restrictive monetary policy. Mr. Graham [a FAC member] said . . . these devices were more alternative than additional sources of funds" (Board Minutes, May 20, 1969, 23).

129. Growth of the M_1 money supply had fallen to 3 percent in 1969 to May. Projections suggested that with unchanged policy, it would continue at that rate. Board members became impatient and wanted more evidence of lower inflation. Overreaction was a frequent fault in this period.

130. The Board's data on bank-related commercial paper outstanding begins in April

On October 29, the Board issued for comment a proposal to apply regulation Q ceilings to interest rates on commercial paper issued by a bank or its affiliates. The Board also discussed applying reserve requirements to commercial paper, but Governors Mitchell and Maisel wanted to obtain legislation before acting because they doubted that the Board's powers permitted this step.

The Board did not implement any proposals at the time. In response to banks' concerns, it delayed its decision until January 15, 1970, then delayed again. A majority wanted to apply regulation Q ceilings, but the members could not agree on reserve requirements, in part because the Legal Division was not fully convinced about the Board's authority.

The Board agreed to increase ceiling rates on time deposits and issue a statement for comment on a 10 percent reserve requirement ratio for commercial paper. Congress had removed the legal issue by granting authority on December 23, 1969. Announcing the change on January 20, the Board took account of Congressman Patman's telegram expressing concern about a large increase in rates that would hurt non-bank thrift associations.[131] Governor Robertson dissented because the higher ceiling rates would allow bank credit growth to increase. He wanted a quantitative restriction on the amount of the increase. Without it, the action would be considered expansive for bank credit.

By May 1969, members began to express doubts about "gradualism" openly.[132] They rejected the stable Phillips curve. Some favored a "credit crunch." Banks tried to avoid monetary policy by using letters of credit, selling assets with puts attached, selling to foreign branches, and issuing commercial paper. Hayes was "convinced that a business slowdown of some considerable duration may be needed if we are to make any real

---

1969 at $200 million, less than 1 percent of total outstanding commercial paper. By October, it had grown to $3.7 billion, 11 percent of outstanding paper. On September 10, 1968, a Deputy Comptroller of the Currency had informed a bank, by letter, that regulation Q did not apply to bank subsidiaries (Board Minutes, November 4, 1969, 5). A letter from a leading banker cautioned that euro-dollar rates started to rise in anticipation of the regulation (letter, George Moore to Hayes, Correspondence Box 240, Federal Reserve Bank of New York, November 24, 1969).

131. Patman's telegram along with telegrams from various trade associations for the thrift industry called attention to competitive aspects. Patman and others in Congress were very sensitive to effects on housing and mortgage lending. The Board's announcement said that the "revisions were held to moderate size so as not to foster sudden and large movements of funds" (Board Minutes, January 20, 1970, press release). Rates for thirty to eighty-nine days increased 0.5 percentage points to 4.5 percent. Rates for consumers' one- and two-year CDs rose 0.5 and 0.75 to 5.50 and 5.75 percent. Large CD rates (over 100,000) increased 0.75.

132. Daniel Brill announced his intention to resign to take a position in the private sector. J. Charles Partee replaced him as research director.

progress on the cost-price front" (ibid., May 27, 1969, 37). Kimbrel (Atlanta), Robertson, Daane, Mitchell, and Coldwell (Dallas) agreed that a firmer policy was needed. But Martin urged them to wait until July before changing policy.[133]

The CEA's concern was that the Federal Reserve would undermine administration policy by not controlling money growth. Stein described the Federal Reserve's view as a possible threat. The Federal Reserve, reacting to the administration's spending, said that the principal reason for inflation in the late 1960s was a large budget deficit. "Moreover the large budget deficit prevented the Federal Reserve from pursuing an even more restrictive policy, because to have done so . . . would have caused intolerable interest rates and credit stringency" (Stein to the president, Nixon papers, WHCF, Box 34, Correspondence, February 15, 1969). This was a variant of the standard Martin explanation that the Federal Reserve had to finance much of the budget deficit that Congress approved. Stein then suggested that "skepticism is growing in the financial community and the lack of confidence is spreading in the Congress. Accordingly the Federal Reserve will be sensitive to the danger of finding itself far out of line with the administration" (ibid.). The threat proved empty.

The St. Louis bank wanted a more aggressive program to stop inflation. Beginning in May, the bank repeatedly requested a 7 percent discount rate, a one percentage point increase. It was not alone. In June, Boston requested 6.5 percent; in July and August, Kansas City and Chicago joined in the request. Despite average federal funds rates of 8.61 and 9.19 percent in July and August, the Board would not approve the changes. Instead, it asked the reserve banks to prevent "inappropriate borrowing." Maisel claimed that Martin urged rejection of the requests "probably partly for political reasons" (Maisel diary, June 26, 1969, 80).

The Board considered it inappropriate for a bank to borrow from a reserve bank and sell federal funds in the same week. This was borrowing for profit. Discounts reached well above $1 billion. Instead of increasing the discount rate, the Federal Reserve returned to the type of policy action—moral suasion or pressure—that had failed in 1929 (Board Minutes, August 13, 1969, 11). This experience demonstrated again that the System's claim was false; when the opportunity arose, banks borrowed for profit.[134]

133. The FOMC considered whether to undertake open market operations in agency securities to assist the housing market. The members were skeptical about whether this was the proper time to undertake such an experiment. However, they feared that Congress would mandate action (FOMC Minutes, May 27, 1969, 87). Martin was "saddened by the fact that the System was involved in a political matter whether it liked it or not" (ibid.).

134. The Board again came under pressure from Congress to buy agency issues to sup-

With money growth continuing to rise, the staff proposed that the FOMC should choose a quantitative target, preferably total bank reserves. They too were divided. Stephen Axilrod's report supplemented interest rates with quantitative measures; he suggested that policy was too restrictive (FOMC Minutes, July 15, 1969, 34). Governor Maisel, later joined by Francis (St. Louis), believed that maintaining current policy would further increase interest rates. This policy, he said, was unsustainable; he dissented from the decision to maintain money market conditions and complained that the manager ignored the proviso clause. The bank credit proxy had fallen much more than anticipated, but the manager ignored it, as usual (FOMC Minutes, June 24, 1969, 80).

Some of the control problems resulted from the mistaken policy of holding regulation Q ceiling rates fixed. This distorted the credit flows and possibly altered credit allocation. Many at the Board shared Maisel's view that "raising Q would mean less restraint since we would furnish more reserves and interest rates would fall" (Maisel diary, July 16, 1969, 86). On the contrary, the principal benefit would come from improved allocative efficiency, achieved by an increase in the cost banks paid to acquire CDs. Banks would demand more reserves to cover increased required reserves. The FOMC could choose whether or how much to supply additional reserves.

The monetary aggregates fell sharply in July. By August, the staff suggested that a recession was possible later in the year. It proposed lowering the funds rate from 10 to 8.5 percent, but Hayes disagreed. Suggestions of a slowdown "were disturbingly premature" (FOMC Minutes, August 12, 1969, 30). He opposed an increase in the discount rate, but he favored getting rid of regulation Q ceilings for large denominations. Morris (Boston) disagreed. Policy was not gradual; it was restrictive and likely to produce a recession in 1970 (ibid., 35). Most members disagreed, but Mitchell supported Morris. Continuation of the "current sharp declines in monetary aggregates . . . could lead to disastrous consequences" (ibid., 54). Mitchell feared also that, if the desk eased, the market would conclude that the System would not maintain its anti-inflation stance.[135]

---

port the housing industry. Robertson, Mitchell and Maisel were sympathetic; the other members agreed that if purchases were made, they should not be used to assist the housing market. A staff memo pointed out some difficulties: many small issues, difficult to resell or trade, and possible legal problems in rolling over such securities at maturity. The Board reached similar conclusions in 2000, when there was concern that the budget surplus would eliminate Treasury debt outstanding (memo, Holmes to FOMC, Board Records, June 18, 1969). In 2008, it appeased Congress.

135. Maisel describes the struggle within the FOMC at this period (Maisel's diary, August 13, 1969, 03–05). At the May meeting, the staff predicted that growth would slow almost to zero

The members remained divided. Some favored more restraint, usually gradual restraint. Others sided with Morris and Mitchell. Martin, remembering his 1968 error, favored no change at that time. "It was important for the System not to get into a position of validating the expectations of numerous skeptics who believed the System would ease its policy as soon as it heard the words 'recession' or 'overkill'" (ibid., 78).

By August, several new divisions had opened. Some wanted the Federal Reserve to tighten more, but "the majority of the FOMC remained gradualist" (Maisel, 1973, 245). The gradualists split into two factions. The larger group wanted to maintain, but not increase, pressure on banks and the money market. Maisel and Mitchell wanted "a midcourse correction" to avoid a recession or reduce its risk (ibid., 245–46). They feared that a recession would shift the majority to favor easier policy, reducing the chances of lowering the inflation rate. "Money market conditions as a target were leading to too tight a policy. Soon it could become too accommodative. The System should shift to monetary aggregates to avoid whip lashing the economy" (ibid., 246). To avoid misinterpretations, they favored an announcement saying that policy would henceforth target the monetary aggregates. They could not convince Martin, but in a few months Arthur Burns became chairman and adopted some of their proposals.[136]

(0.4 percent) in fiscal 1970, and they maintained the forecast of recession or near recession throughout. They forecast inflation of 4 to 4.5 percent (Actual growth was −0.8 with inflation at 5.4 percent). Hayes, Coldwell (Dallas), Brimmer, and Clay (Kansas City) were willing to accept a serious recession to fight inflation (ibid., 103). "They continued to call for continued tightening and restraint in every meeting through February 10 . . . they made it clear that there was no way of avoiding sacrifices in terms of lost jobs, lost output, and lost income in order to hold prices down" (Maisel diary, February 16, 1970, 23). Maisel and Mitchell wanted money growth, M_2 minus CDs, at a 3 percent rate, to avoid a credit crunch and gradually reduce inflation. They argued that money market conditions had to move more than in the past to maintain proper growth of the monetary aggregates and the flow of credit. Robertson leaned toward the inflation hawks. The other members of the committee fell somewhere in between. A principal concern for several members was that the market would interpret reduction in short-term rates or increase in free reserves as retreat from an anti-inflation policy. In the language prominent in later years, the System lacked credibility.

Chairman Martin did not provide leadership. "He frequently did not speak up. He indicated throughout the earlier period that he was in favor of more restriction. During the summer, he shifted saying that he did not want to show any sign of ease. . . . By the beginning of January, he wanted to move, particularly on Q, but also to make a minimum move through open market conditions" (ibid., 24). In Martin's view, "the Committee shouldn't think about the aggregates at all. It should only think about money market conditions and their impact on psychology in the financial markets and, therefore, in the real market" (ibid.).

136. The background memo for the August 28 Quadriad meeting noted that inflation and growth continued. Consumer prices had increased 6.3 percent (annualized) for the year to date. Nevertheless, the memo said: "We may not be too far from the time when economic policy should be relaxed" (agenda for the Quadriad, Nixon papers, August 28, 1969).

Martin believed that a shift toward ease would compound an earlier error and convince the market that inflation would remain or rise. The System had "been misled into premature easing in 1968 by an overemphasis on technical considerations at the expense of proper attention to the psychological environment. Too much emphasis was placed on the prospective $25 billion turnaround in the fiscal position of the Federal Government and not enough on the underlying inflationary expectations which had been building up over an extended period. The mistake had subsequently been compounded for a period of several months by the rationalization that some moderation of the inflationary pressures was imminent" (FOMC Minutes, August 12, 1969, 77–78). The staff concluded that "the majority of the Committee was willing to see considerably more ease as long as the change did not show too clearly in the market!" (Maisel diary, August 14, 1969, 106).

At the time, Burns expressed concern about any additional restriction that reduced real growth below the projected 1 percent or that increased the unemployment rate above a projected 4.5 percent (Maisel diary, August 14, 1969, 107). About this time, the FAC and the Board's academic consultants were as divided as the FOMC. Some favored a strong anti-inflation policy. Others preferred a more gradual approach (ibid., September 17, 1969, 116).

By September, signs of slower growth had become apparent. Industrial production declined slightly. After rising in October, production began a sustained decline. The unemployment rate reached 3.7 percent, but there was no sign of slower inflation. The GNP deflator reached an annual rate of 6.2 percent for the quarter. Consumer price inflation was 5.6 percent. The staff expected a mild recession in the first half of 1970.

Long-term government bonds reached 6.9 percent in mid-August and were only slightly below that level in mid-September. The federal funds rate remained between 9 and 9.5 percent, well above the inflation rate. The Board's staff recognized the slowdown as it occurred. They were not alone. The Federal Advisory Council expected growth to continue to slow (Board Minutes, September 16, 1969, 2). The System now faced a test. Would it continue to press for lower inflation or would it shift its policy to prevent a possible recession?

Opinion divided. The FAC by a large majority favored continuing but not increasing pressure, but two members favored a move toward ease. The beginning of a shift in attitudes appeared in the suggestion that moderate inflation of 3 percent might be better than paying to reduce inflation to 1 or 2 percent (ibid., 13). Chairman Martin ended that discussion with the optimistic statement that reducing inflation would not require a large increase in the unemployment rate.[137]

The FOMC continued to call for an unchanged policy, with dissents from Governors Maisel and Mitchell in September and Maisel in early October. Although the committee voted to keep policy unchanged, the October 7 meeting had a much more intense discussion than usual. Two issues remained contentious. One was the meaning of unchanged policy. The second was growing support for the use of a monetary aggregate target and continued opposition.

Governor Mitchell pointed out the committee had voted several times for "no change." He then read a list of six monetary aggregates and concluded that "every aggregate listed showed deterioration in the third quarter" (FOMC Minutes, October 7, 1969, 59). Declines were large. Turning to interest rates, Mitchell reported that fourteen of the twenty-three securities listed in the staff report reached peak rates in September, including all the intermediate- and long-term issues. This was "incompatible with the Committee's stated posture of 'no change'" (ibid., 60). Mitchell concluded that "if monetary policy continued to tighten as it had recently the result was likely to be a major recession in 1970" (idem.). He too departed from the Keynesian Phillips curve by suggesting that it might require stagnation in real activity to bring inflation down.

Martin was in the last months of his term. Although he had opposed inflation in his public statements, he faced the prospect that he would leave office with inflation above 5 percent, the highest rate since the Korean War. It seems likely that he tolerated, perhaps encouraged, the much more restrictive policy hoping to reduce inflation before he left office.[138] There is no direct evidence to support this conjecture aside from the continued increase in interest rates and decline in free reserves under the "no change" policy that he supported and the committee approved.[139] Martin's comments at the time are difficult to interpret. He did not believe "that the real impact of monetary policy was that important . . . [but] its psychological impact is critical" (Maisel diary, October 8, 1969, 3).

Philip Coldwell (Dallas) made some of the case for those who opposed

137. Nearly the entire FAC favored an increase in ceiling rates on large certificates of deposit (over $1 million) and the elimination of ceiling rates on these CDs (Board Minutes, September 16, 1969, 22). But there was less agreement about rates on smaller time and saving deposits.

138. Consumer price inflation reached 6 percent in January 1970, the last month of his term. The peak came in February at 6.16 percent. The GNP deflator reached a peak of 7.1 percent in first quarter 1970.

139. Free reserves were less than −$1 billion in October, a reduction of $700 million under the "no change" policy.

using monetary aggregates to guide policy decisions. Coldwell emphasized two points. First, interpretation of monetary aggregates or interest
rates depended on expectations. "With each passing month the force of
expectations of further inflation brought potentially disruptive factors
closer to the economic horizon" (ibid., 53). Monetary aggregates did not
take account of these forces. Second, bank reserves had fallen, but "the
impact of that development was mitigated by the rise of the large nonbank
credit accommodations and the shift of funds from bank time deposits to
direct investments and indirect support of the euro-dollar and commercial
paper markets" (idem.). This statement reflected a firm, but erroneous,
belief that many held. They thought that growth of credit (lending) outside the banking system showed that the financial sector escaped from
restrictive policy. In this view, monetary aggregates did not capture these
changes, hence they were misleading or inadequate. That these changes
were sustained by ever-increasing interest rates showed not an escape, but
the spreading effect of monetary restriction.[140]

In late October, Maisel made a detailed statement of his alternative position, separating the problem of writing an instruction for the manager
from the more serious problem of introducing longer-term considerations
into the directive and the FOMC's actions. Maisel noted that growth of
the bank credit proxy fluctuated considerably in the short-term because
Treasury financing operations moved deposits from private to Treasury
accounts. "Thus, for November, a fairly sizeable increase in the proxy was
projected, even though November was the middle month of a quarter in
which no increase at all was expected on average" (FOMC Minutes, October 28, 1969, 70). He proposed less "stop and go" and more attention to
deviations from projected trend.[141]

140. Coldwell's were not the only criticisms. The manager said frequently that he could
not control short-run changes in the aggregates without permitting large changes in interest
rates. He believed that the demand for reserves or base money was very interest inelastic in
the short run. Coldwell was mistaken also in his statement about expectations. Persistent
high money growth was a main reason for expecting continued inflation. The manager's
explanation of the reasons for not using a monetary target are in Holmes (1969, 71–77).

141. At the October 28 meeting, Martin reported that the president had appointed Arthur
Burns as chairman and that Burns had asked him to tell the FOMC that "he would not feel
bound by any of its decisions made before his term" (FOMC Minutes, October 28, 1969, 2).
Martin had argued against the appointment with President Nixon on grounds that Burns
lacked administrative and personal skills and, as an economist, lacked sufficient breadth
about banking and financial markets. He repeated this to Burns. Martin and the president
agreed to look for other people. The president asked Gabriel Hauge, who declined for personal reasons. "Martin says that if Nixon had twisted hard enough, he could have gotten him"
(Maisel diary, October 22, 1969, 1). Martin urged other names, but the president appointed
Burns. Martin also said that "he blamed Brill and Okun for the overkill scare in 1968 . . .

Heflin (Richmond) opposed further ease as "fine tuning." He voiced the thoughts of several others by arguing that the System had to change antici-pations. This required a firm policy. Francis (St. Louis) replied that if the money stock continued unchanged for another three months "the rate of increase" in total spending "would probably experience such a decline that real production would decline unnecessarily and regrettably" (ibid., 86).

Francis urged 3 percent money growth starting at once. Martin opposed any change toward ease. "He did not agree that the consequences of deviat-ing significantly from some preferred rate [of money growth] for a period of time would be as disastrous as the monetarists believed" (ibid., 90).[142] At the next meeting, Francis responded to the argument by Martin and several others placing principal weight on the need to control expectations. "The conduct of monetary policy by attempting to control public psychol-ogy directly rather than through control of financial magnitudes had not and would not be successful" (FOMC Minutes, October 28, 1969, 56). The committee should instead take three steps: "resume moderate monetary growth; raise the discount rate in line with market rates; and lift regulation Q ceiling rates, especially for large CDs" (ibid.). Any adverse psychological effect could be dispelled by announcing that the System would maintain moderate growth of money.[143]

Governor Daane explicitly rejected Francis's proposals. "There was no basis for relaxation of policy at this point. . . . He felt that fiscal policy is on the verge of a large shift towards expansion" (ibid., 71). Apparently some FOMC members had learned about the risks of policy coordination. He

and said 'see don't trust economists and statistics'—he had done so unwillingly and now regretted it" (ibid., 2).

142. Over the objections of Robertson and others, the FOMC voted to permit the manager to lend securities to government securities dealers. The Treasury was willing to authorize such lending by the Home Loan banks and other agencies but would not lend unissued securities. Robertson pointed out that this removed the finding of necessity.

143. Some Board members and administration officials expressed concern about the dis-tribution of credit. Maisel was most outspoken: "Since we were in an inflation that was caused primarily by corporate spending and corporate price policy, the one area that we should try to hold down was large corporate investment" (Maisel diary, November 13, 1969, 2). He wanted to get more credit to the housing industry by raising ceiling rates. He was concerned about the distributive effect of monetary policy on different sectors, and he complained that Martin ran the System as "a major lobby for hard money" and to favor large banks (ibid., 7). Banks used the commercial paper and euro-dollar markets to support lending. This drained deposits from thrift institutions. The Coordinating Committee of regulators could not agree to raise interest rates because many of the institutions did not want to pay higher interest rates (ibid., December 10, 1969, 7). Congress pressed for action to assist homebuilders by considering legislation that, in Martin's words, "would provide direct access to Federal Re-serve credit to those agencies without limitation as to amount—an unlimited line of credit at the central bank that our laws have denied even the U.S. Treasury" (Martin speeches, October 6, 1969, 3).

no longer wanted monetary actions to offset the effects on interest rates of increased government spending.

The staff forecast a recession. No one challenged the forecast. But a majority was unwilling to ease monetary policy. Thus, policy actions were procyclical, as was often the case under a free reserve or interest rate target. The difference this time was that a majority agreed for different reasons to reject increased ease.

The dominant new element at the November meeting was evidence of slower growth in consumer spending. Bopp (Philadelphia) expressed the modal interpretation of rising interest rates despite slower spending growth. "Financial markets are clearly registering doubts about the Committee's ability and willingness to maintain the restraint necessary to stop inflation. . . . A policy of restraint severe enough and held long enough to shift expectations might prove too much to avoid a recession. On the other hand, if the Committee were to ease visibly now, he felt certain that inflationary forces would be even more difficult to cope with. . . . [H]e failed to see what the Committee could do now that would not make for difficult times ahead." Nevertheless, he believed that continuing under the current restraint was less dangerous than moving to ease (FOMC Minutes, November 25, 1969, 79–80). Martin concurred. He had "reached the conclusion that there was no way out of the present situation that would not involve serious difficulties" (ibid., 89). This was a decided change from his position six weeks earlier.

Hugh Galusha (Minneapolis) questioned the Board's announcement of its proposal to apply regulation Q to commercial paper sold by bank holding companies. "The System had already gone rather a long way in restricting banks in their historic role as financial intermediaries. And to what end had never been clear, at least to him" (FOMC Minutes, November 25, 1969, 64). Galusha's statement challenged those who claimed that commercial paper, euro-dollars, and other unregulated instruments weakened monetary policy. None replied.

The FOMC had lost much of its innocence. It now recognized the mistakes it had made by permitting rapid monetary expansion in 1967 and following the surtax in 1968. Policy coordination had worked for the political benefit of the Johnson administration but not for them. The members saw more clearly than ever before that inflationary anticipations affected interest rates. And several saw clearly that there was no easy, painless, low-cost way of reducing inflationary expectations. Past mistakes would prove costly to correct. Failure to pay the cost now would defer the cost and probably increase it.

The learning from these experiences would soon be tested. The November meeting was the last meeting before the economy reached a peak. Many of those, like Bopp and Martin, who insisted on maintaining a very restrictive, procyclical policy would soon have to decide how to respond to the recession that their actions helped to bring on.[144]

THE 1969–70 RECESSION

The National Bureau puts the peak of the 106-month expansion in December 1969. By the time the FOMC met that month, the economy was about to start an eleven-month recession. The Bureau graded the recession as mild, about the same as the 1960–61 recession that preceded the long expansion. Industrial production fell 6.8 percent, 1 percentage point less than the average postwar mild cycle. The unemployment rate rose to 5.9 percent, 2 percentage points above the rate at the NBER peak. Consumer price inflation declined only 0.50 percentage points. The Federal Reserve had not learned that a temporary policy change would have little effect on inflation, but the public apparently had learned to wait for evidence that anti-inflation policy would continue.

Real base growth had fallen for a year prior to the start of the recession. It turned negative in July 1969. Real interest rates, adjusted by anticipated inflation, rose on average from 3.4 percent in January 1969 to 5 percent a year later. Unlike many previous recessions, both series showed policy tightening until the new year, then easing. Although real base growth remained negative until August 1970, by early 1971 both series had returned to the levels of January 1969. Chart 4.11 shows these data.

Policy action, judged by real monetary base growth, began to ease after January 1970, very soon after the start of the recession. Despite the many protestations and commitments to stay the course until inflation fell, policy change was neither hesitant nor slow to arrive. Within a year nominal monetary base growth doubled, from 4 to 8 percent. This brought it back to the level at the start of tightening. Chart 4.12 shows that nominal and real base growth changed together; the inflation rate changed very little. Officials were aware, and had repeated many times, that an early shift to an easier policy would reinforce beliefs that they would respond more aggressively to unemployment than to inflation. In their words, market psychology would sustain inflation. This was obfuscation; their policy action

144. Martin asked the bank presidents to comment on the Board's proposal to place bank-endorsed commercial paper under regulation Q ceilings. Those who spoke opposed or asked for a delay. Scanlon (Chicago) said that the proposal would induce banks to "increase their euro-dollar borrowings to offset commercial paper losses" (FOMC Minutes, November 25, 1969, 67). He urged the Board to raise interest on large-denomination CDs if they approved their proposal.

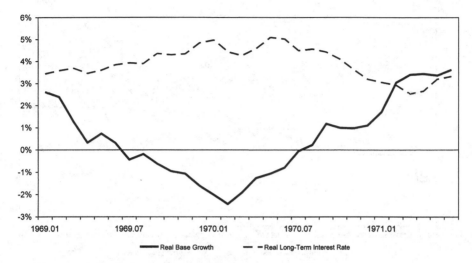

Chart 4.11. Real base year-over-year growth versus real long-term interest rate, January 1969–June 1971. Long-term interest rate measured as yield on ten-year Treasury bonds.

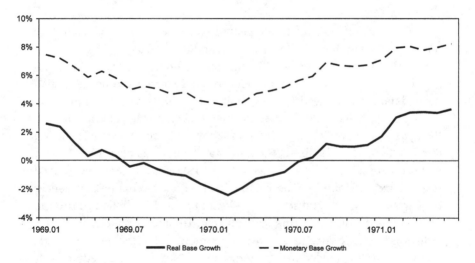

Chart 4.12. Year-over-year monetary base growth versus year-over-year real base growth. January 1969–June 1971.

sustained inflation. Interest rates show the market's skepticism. Although the federal funds rate fell from 9 percent to 4.8 percent a year later, long-term Treasury yields fell only to 6 from 7 percent.

The decline in short-term rates eased the problems caused by the large gap between market rates and regulated rates. The inflow of dollars borrowed in the euro-dollar market reversed. Chart 4.13 shows the sizeable

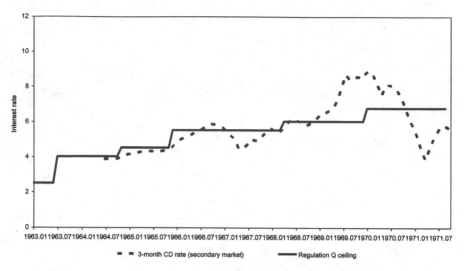

Chart 4.13. Three-month CD secondary market rate and regulation Q ceiling. 1963:01–1971:09.

change in market rates relative to ceiling rates that induced banks to first borrow heavily in the euro-dollar market and then repay.

The January 15 meeting was Martin's last. He retired at the end of January after nearly nineteen years as chairman. Two of his major aims had been to maintain domestic price stability, or low inflation, and to preserve the $35 gold price and the fixed exchange rate system. He failed at both. Although the SPF predicted 3 percent inflation for 1970; the actual inflation rate was 6 percent; the fixed exchange rate system was near its end. Gold had been embargoed for all but central banks and they were discouraged from converting dollars. The balance of payments remained in deficit; the surplus on goods and services had fallen from $8.6 billion in 1964 to $1.9 billion in 1969, Martin's last full year. Inflation was a major factor reducing the trade surplus and the adjustment of the real exchange rate that would have extended the Bretton Woods system. Acknowledging this at a farewell luncheon with the Board, Martin said, "I've failed" (Bremner, 2004, 224). After President Nixon floated the dollar, he said: "It represents a failure of United States economic policy—a failure to restrain inflation and failure to improve the balance of payments" (ibid., 235).

Despite his earlier insistence on the importance of maintaining a restrictive policy, Martin used his last meeting to respond to the recession by proposing an easier policy.[145] The staff report recognized that the economy

145. Maisel's diary (February 16, 1970, 26) reports that a move toward easier policy would

had not grown at the end of 1969. It predicted sluggish growth in spending and a further decline in inventories during the first half of the year.

Divisions in the FOMC remained. Robertson wanted to continue the anti-inflation policy. In a prophetic statement, he told the committee that "if we give in too soon, we may well find that we have to begin the whole painful inflation-fighting job over again" (FOMC Minutes, January 15, 1970, 99). Several members recognized that they could not count on fiscal restraint. Galusha (Minneapolis) and Hayes were most critical of the administration's failures to reduce current and prospective deficits. Hayes blamed "fiscal actions taken and initiatives not taken" (ibid., 47) for growing cynicism about the administration's commitment to reduce inflation. The reference was to his belief that the administration would not keep tight control of spending in fiscal 1971 and its acceptance of a reduction in the surtax rate from 10 to 5 percent for the second half of fiscal 1970. In February, after the administration announced its 1971 budget, his concerns eased.[146]

After considerable discussion, the FOMC voted unanimously to maintain firm conditions in the money market. For the first time it adopted growth in money as a policy indicator and instructed the manager to change money market conditions if monetary growth deviated from a 2 percent annual rate (Maisel diary, January 15, 1970, 5). Hayes, Coldwell (Dallas), and Clay (Kansas City) continued to oppose any change. Daane and Brimmer wanted tighter policy despite the recession and the staff forecast of zero real growth and rising unemployment in the first half of the year (ibid., 4, 6). Martin agreed to the change. "Since it was his last meeting, he would look for a way of unifying the Committee" (ibid., 6). The agreement called

---

have been made at the December meeting but Martin had "just talked to President-elect Nixon and the Quadriad and had urged on them the need for tighter fiscal policy. Therefore, he had to say wait." Maisel does not comment on the difference between Martin's views following this meeting and his response in 1968 when tighter fiscal policy called for easier monetary policy (lower short-term rates). In December 1969, Hayes wrote to Board members about the deposit outflow and expected increased outflow of deposits from thrift institutions. He urged an increase in ceiling rates (letter, Hayes to Board of Governors, Correspondence Box 240, December 19, 1969). At about this time, the Board supported an increase in deposit insurance to $20,000 per account (from $15,000). Also, the Board sent a letter to all reserve bank presidents telling them to extend emergency credit assistance to non-member banks, mutual savings banks, and thrift associations, in some cases directly and in others by lending to the Treasury for relending to the Home Loan Banks (letter, Robert Holland to Hayes, Correspondence Box 431.2, Federal Reserve Bank of New York, December 24, 1969).

146. The Tax Reform Act of 1969, enacted on December 30, increased personal exemptions from $600 to $625 in 1970 and to $650, $700, and $750 in the next three years, increased the standard exemption from 10 to 15 percent in the three years starting in 1971, reduced the maximum tax rate on earned income to 50 percent, but repealed the investment tax credit. President Nixon and his advisers could not get congressional support for their attempts to reduce the deficit (Matusow, 1998, 53–54).

for a two-way proviso clause aiming at 2 percent money growth for the quarter.[147]

The Board continued its concerns about deposit losses at small banks and thrifts and the use of commercial paper to circumvent regulation Q ceilings by large commercial banks and bank holding companies. Congressional pressure heightened their concerns. A letter from Congressman Emanuel Celler accused the Board of "discriminating against bank subsidiaries and in favor of bank parent companies" and called the alleged discrimination "intolerable" (letter, Celler to Martin, Correspondence Box 240, Federal Reserve Bank of New York, January 8, 1990). Celler urged the Board to delay regulation of commercial paper for ninety days.

Two weeks later the Board raised ceiling rates but postponed regulation of commercial paper, as Celler and others had urged. The Board's press release emphasized the desire to bring bank deposit rates into closer proximity to open market rates and to limit the change to "moderate size so as not to foster sudden and large movements of funds" (Press Release, Board Records, January 20, 1979.). The increase was 0.5 for thirty to eighty-nine days for consumer accounts and 0.75 percentage points for large certificates. The new rates on these certificates ranged from 6.25 percent for thirty to fifty-nine days to 7 percent for six months and 7.5 percent for one year or longer.[148] This was the first increase in the rate on passbook savings since 1964.

Personnel Changes

Arthur Burns became chairman of the Board of Governors on February 1, 1970. He served two terms as chairman. Although six years of his

147. Maisel commented: "The debate was so confused that the Manager felt that he did not have to try for an expansion through any change in money market conditions as long as some of the estimates showed that the money supply was rising. . . . The staff was mixed . . . as to whether the FOMC wanted conditions changed affirmatively." The money market remained tight (Maisel diary, February 16, 1970, 26).

148. Maisel's diary (January 15 and 20, 1970) describes the difficulty in reaching agreement among the members of the Board and between the Board, the Home Loan Bank Board, and the Federal Deposit Insurance Corporation (FDIC). The Home Loan Bank Board wanted to delay any change, while the FDIC wanted higher rates than the Board proposed. Within the Board a main issue was whether to use their new power to subject bank-issued commercial paper to time deposit reserve requirements under regulation D. Robertson wanted to include euro-dollars with commercial paper, but the Board did not agree. He dissented, an unusual action on a vote of this kind.

Brimmer and Robertson wanted to put commercial paper under regulation Q ceilings. According to Maisel (diary, February 16, 1970, 27), they wanted to tighten more. Mitchell and Maisel opposed because they wanted to ease, not tighten, and "because we thought it was wrong" to use reserve requirements instead of regulation Q ceilings. Martin wanted to act because he had told Chase Bank and some others that "he would see that the other banks didn't do it [issue commercial paper]" (ibid.).

fourteen-year term as a member remained in 1978, he left the System on March 31, 1978, when President Carter did not reappoint him as chairman. He was the first economist to serve as chairman, a recognition of the growing complexity of monetary policy and the increased professional role in policy. He also had a close relationship with President Nixon.

Burns was a distinguished economist. His major work on business cycles with Wesley C. Mitchell was a statistical and atheoretical study of the interrelation of numerous economic time series to detect patterns of cyclical coherence. He told Edwin Nourse that he was neither a monetarist nor a Keynesian (Wells, 1994, 25). He suffered from the arrogance of the distinguished academic; he knew what was right. He had little patience with interpretations that disagreed with his, but he was willing to change his long-standing positions when it served his purpose. The prime example was his advocacy of price and wage guidelines, and his support of price and wage controls, despite his earlier writings and speeches opposing such policies and explaining why they would not work.

This was not his only error. He failed to control inflation. Of the ninety-eight months that he served as chairman, the measured twelve-month average rate of consumer price change fell below 3 percent in only three of them, all months in which measurement was distorted by price controls. A year later consumer prices rose more than 7 percent on their way to a maximum of 11.5 percent during his term. He left the System with the consumer price level rising at 6.3 percent, about where it was when he began. Part of the blame for increased rates of price change came from oil price increases and dollar devaluation that were not under his control.

Burns's aides and senior officials describe him as a dominant chairman who left no doubt about who was in control (Guenther, 2001, 12). But he was open to discussion. He would, however, disagree with other members and correct them when he thought they were wrong. That was a marked change from the Martin era (Brimmer, 2002, 17).

One of his contributions at the Federal Reserve was improved data. As an atheoretical economist, he relied on his interpretation of a large number of data series. Burns's failure as chairman came despite his understanding of economics and business cycles. He accepted the chairmanship of the Committee on Interest and Dividends, during the price control period, aware of the conflict of interest with his responsibility for controlling money growth and inflation. And he acquiesced in the view that the public would not accept a deep recession if required to end inflation. This was a political decision that led to the choices that sustained and increased inflation. Burns was unwilling to use the independence of the Federal Reserve for its intended purpose, refusing to finance government deficit spending with additional money growth to avoid inflation.[149]

Martin worked with the administration to coordinate monetary and fiscal policy, and he did not become deeply involved in administration decisions outside this sphere. Burns returned to the Eccles tradition of advising President Nixon on all phases of economic policy, especially macro-economic policy. "He saw the Fed's role as one of innovator, supporter, and pleader for good macro policy" (Maisel, 1973, 121). He participated in the deliberations at Camp David in August 1971, when the administration floated the dollar, imposed a surtax on exports, revised the tax system, and imposed price and wage controls. Burns was a principal advocate of controls, and he became an adviser to the Cost of Living Council, which administered the control program.

Although Burns spent considerable time advising the president, he resented administration advice about monetary policy.[150] He received such advice regularly during the Nixon years, but not during Gerald Ford's presidency (1974–76). In Burns's words: "Mr. Nixon tried to interfere with the Federal Reserve both in ways that were fair and in ways that by almost any standard, were unfair. Mr. Ford on the other hand was truly angelic. I met with President Ford frequently, alone in the privacy of his office. . . . He never even remotely intimated what the Federal Reserve should be doing. . . . Mr. Carter had a good record but not a perfect one" (Burns, 1988, 136–37).

Burns's chairmanship brought major procedural changes. Burns was autocratic, not collegial as Martin had been. Often Martin achieved agreement and influence by speaking last and stating a consensus. Burns often spoke first to focus discussion on his proposal. He eliminated the recitation by the presidents of regional conditions (memo, Burns to FOMC, Board Records, March 2, 1970). Also, he reduced the number of meetings from seventeen to twelve or thirteen, and used the Federal Bureau of Investigation to investigate leaks to the press by the members or the staff. Maisel, who served during Burns's term as chairman described him as "not believing that anyone who disagreed could be right" (Maisel, 2003). At times, he embarrassed members by challenging their statements.[151] In

149. Burns was sworn in as chairman in the White House. President Nixon remarked that the Federal Reserve was an independent agency, but he hoped the chairman would independently decide to act as his president suggested.

150. When the president's Domestic Policy Adviser, John Ehrlichman, came to Burns's office to discuss monetary policy, Burns phoned the president to tell him that if he came again he "would physically throw him out" (Brunner, 2002, 24).

151. Jerry Jordan, senior vice president at St. Louis from 1972 to 1975, described Burns at FOMC meetings. "His style at the table was sometimes combative. He would question

short, he had the right personality to make large errors. The staff worked for the chairman, so he was able to control some of the information available to the other members.

Burns recognized that short-term economic control could not be exact, but he could not accept the loose arrangement existing between New York and Washington. He wanted better control of policy actions. To improve operations, he favored more research on monetary policy and more precise instructions to the manager. Tone and feel ended forever as an instruction soon after Burns arrived. The manager lost much of his previous autonomy, and New York lost more of its special position.[152]

The Phillips curve relating the inflation rate negatively to the unemployment rate was part of mainstream economic thought at the time and later. Some thought of the tradeoff as a long-run effect. Others, following Friedman (1968b), believed any tradeoff was temporary. Burns and the Nixon Council accepted Friedman's analysis, but they were not at pains to make that clear. When making the case for wage-price controls or guidelines, Burns claimed that reducing inflation would require a socially (or politically) unacceptable short-term increase in unemployment. In his confirmation hearings, however, he explicitly rejected the tradeoff (Senate Committee on Banking and Currency, 1969, 23–24).

> Chairman [Proxmire]: Let me ask you about your views on the Phillips curve . . .
>
> Burns: I think even for the short-run the Phillips curve can be changed. I think we ought to be able in the years ahead to pursue when we need to a restrictive financial policy without significantly increasing unemployment.

---

people . . . interrupt their prepared remarks, and throw them off balance sometimes by asking questions they were unprepared for. . . . After a statement was made by one of the presidents or governors, he would pointedly take issue with them and say I don't recall that or I don't agree with that" (Jordan, 2002).

152. Maisel's diary (February 10, 1970, 16–18) describes Burns's first week. He wanted to reduce Board meetings from daily to three times a week. He wanted to end the procedure of having each person make a statement at FOMC. Even more contentious was his decision to shift representation at the Bank for International Settlements (BIS) from New York to the Board. He chose Governor Dewey Daane as the System's representative, the first time that the representative had not come from the New York bank in the forty years since the BIS started. And he indicated that he was "concerned with the New York travel budget as well as with other budgets of the System" (Maisel diary, February 12, 1970, 20). Burns recognized the contentious aspect of these issues by discussing them only in executive session of the Board.

After Burns presided over his second FOMC meeting, Maisel wrote: "As in the Board meetings, Chairman Burns had taken a more aggressive position in shaping the debate . . . He said that the Committee would have to vote his position up or down" (Maisel diary, March 10, 1970, 33).

Table 4.7   New Presidents 1970–71

BANK	PRESIDENT	DATES OF SERVICE
Philadelphia	David P. Eastburn	3/1/70–1/31/81
Chicago	Robert P. Mayo	7/29/70–4/1/81
Minneapolis	Bruce K. McLaury	7/1/71–2/28/77
Cleveland	Willis J. Winn	9/1/71–4/30/82

Here Burns's belief seems close to Okun's position at the time—that the cost of reducing inflation would be small. Either he ignored heightened expectations of inflation or he believed these would reverse at low cost.[153] And he did not mention that the 4 percent unemployment rate at which they aimed was below the rate needed to stabilize inflation.

Four reserve banks changed presidents in the next nineteen months. Karl Bopp, a career Federal Reserve official, retired as president of the Philadelphia bank at the end of February 1970.[154] W. Braddock Hickman (Cleveland) died in late November 1970, and Hugh Galusha (Minneapolis) died in late January 1971. Charles J. Scanlon (Chicago) retired on April 15, 1970. Burns did not leave the choice of presidents entirely to bank committees, as had been customary. He intervened frequently. The successors at the four banks are shown in Table 4.7.

Eastburn and McLaury were economists. Winn was dean of the Wharton School at the University of Pennsylvania. Mayo served as director of the Bureau of the Budget at the start of the Nixon administration. He was a protégé of David Kennedy, Nixon's first Treasury Secretary. According to Safire (1975), Nixon did not like working with him and wanted him out. He left when the Budget Bureau was reorganized as the Office of Management and Budget with George P. Shultz as director. Shultz was also

---

153. Hetzel (1998) develops Burns's views in more detail.

154. Bopp's statement at his last meeting included a strong critique of the System's understanding. "Mr. Bopp believed that the System should allocate significant resources to developing knowledge and comprehension of the linkages among financial and real economic variables. As of today, however, its ignorance was colossal" (FOMC Minutes, February 10, 1970, 54). This is a remarkable indictment of an institution in its fifty-seventh year of operation.

Maisel briefed Burns on the inchoate state of policymaking. "There was no good definition of monetary policy now. . . . [A] majority really didn't have a clear view . . . of the relationship [of monetary policy] to actions in the Committee room" (Maisel diary, January 15, 1970, 8). Maisel also told him about the work of the committee on the Directive and explained difficulties with the staff of the Board's Legal Division. The division presented the Board with a narrow interpretation of the law instead of addressing the entire regulatory problem and presenting pros and cons of alternative decisions to the Board, (ibid., January 15, 1970, 7; January 20, 1970, 9–10).

Secretary of Labor at the start of the administration, later Secretary of the Treasury, and in the Reagan administration Secretary of State.[155]

Targets for Money and Bank Credit

At his first meeting as chairman of FOMC, Burns instructed the members on the need for longer-range planning. This attempt to look over a longer horizon recognized that monetary policy actions operated with a lag. Controlling inflation required the FOMC to gear policy changes to the future conditions they foresaw, "to attend to today's problems and to those of the future as best they could be discerned" (Burns statement, FOMC Minutes, February 10, 1970, 3). "[Burns's] own thinking on monetary policy . . . tended to focus more on bank credit than on the money supply because the former was subject to closer control by the System" (ibid., 92). In his first year, he told the FOMC members several times that policy should not change frequently.

Maisel (1973, 169–78) reports some of the reasons that, at the time, led many FOMC members to oppose using quantitative targets or to make the instructions to the manager more precise. He discussed six principal objections but did not endorse them.

(1) Monetary policymaking is an art rather than a science; precise instructions crowd out the manager's judgment of events.

(2) Closely related is the belief that knowledge of monetary transmission is too uncertain to provide reliable guidance.

(3) "Attempts to quantify monetary decision making will diminish the intuitive skills and judgment necessary for the best decisions" (ibid., 170–71).

(4) Data are imprecise and subject to revision. The FOMC and the manager may learn after the fact that money or credit growth was faster or slower than reported at the time.

(5) Quantification encourages neglect of useful non-quantitative information. "An experienced observer can often spot movements and dangers before they appear in the statistics" (ibid., 173).

(6) Public statements become commitments. If the Federal Reserve announced a target, it would be reluctant to change if it made an error.[156]

155. Shultz held four cabinet positions, equaled only by Eliot Richardson in U.S. history.
156 Maisel (1973, 173–75) presented the arguments used against announced objectives and policy changes. By the 1990s, influenced by the literature on credibility, many central

Several of these comments are correct. Data are imprecise and some are revised later. Economic theory has not produced persistently reliable forecasts of short-run changes. Qualitative information can provide useful input into activist policy decisions. Announcing a target focuses public anticipations. None of these arguments alleviated the need for more precise control, but they raised an issue that, to my knowledge, was never discussed: Why not adjust policy decisions to coincide more closely with the time frame for which information is more reliable and economic models more useful?

Not only are new data often inaccurate and subject to revision, users cannot distinguish between persistent and temporary changes as they occur. The number of observations to make accurate judgments depends on relative variability of the persistent and transitory components. Frequently this will require several observations and considerable time. Reacting to changes too quickly can produce major mistakes.

Through the Great Inflation and afterward the Federal Reserve failed to distinguish between temporary or one-time changes in the price level and changes in the persistent rate of price change. One-time changes can be caused by excise tax changes, currency revaluations, changes in productivity, and many similar factors. Prices rise or fall and changes may continue for a short time, but they do not persist if not financed by monetary policy.

Table 4.8 shows the forecast errors for various periods. During the Great Inflation, the average absolute forecast error was about 3 percent for real growth and more than 1.5 percent for inflation. Errors in forecasts four quarters ahead were smaller than quarterly errors for real growth but not for inflation. These data suggest that focusing on short-term changes was unlikely to succeed. See Orphanides (2002).

Operating Procedures

Several of these issues came to the fore as part of extensive staff research on the consequences of using monetary aggregates in place of money market conditions. In October 1968 Chairman Martin appointed Governor Maisel as chair of a three-person committee (with Presidents Morris and Swan) to reconsider FOMC operating procedures and the instructions given to the account manager. Background papers discussed the deficiencies in policymaking procedures including lack of clarity about objectives, short-term focus, the manager's autonomy, and excessive concern for money market changes.

---

banks adopted explicit inflation targets. The Federal Reserve did not, but in 1994 it began announcing interest rate targets. None of the concerns about market reaction to announcements proved correct.

Table 4.8   Forecast Errors, Growth and Inflation (percent)

A	68.4–95.4	68.4–71.3	71.4–80.4	81.1–95.4
Mean error in SPF RGNP growth forecasts:	−0.265	0.878	−0.743	−0.199
Mean absolute error in SPF RGNP growth forecasts:	2.600	2.813	3.421	2.051
Mean error in SPF deflator growth forecasts:	−0.170	−1.653	−1.093	0.696
Mean absolute error in SPF deflator growth forecasts:	1.220	1.716	1.583	0.896
Mean error in SPF RGNP 4Q growth forecasts:	0.117	0.532	0.281	−0.037
Mean absolute error in SPF RGNP 4Q growth forecasts:	1.516	0.756	1.782	1.457
Mean error in SPF deflator 4Q growth forecasts:	−0.158	−1.408	−1.743	0.985
Mean absolute error in SPF deflator 4Q growth forecasts:	1.382	1.408	1.946	1.031

Source: Society of Professional Forecasters.

A lengthy, very perceptive, forthright paper by Stephen Axilrod (1970a) began by noting that the first paragraph of the directive described economic conditions in a way that did not permit readers to understand the analysis that lay behind the FOMC's instructions or the tradeoffs between competing objectives (ibid., 3–4).[157] System policy accommodated all changes in the money market until the introduction of the proviso clause in 1966 directed the manager to alter money market conditions if the bank credit proxy rose or fell more than anticipated. "In practice, this [the proviso clause] has represented a rather minor element of constraint, partly because the Committee has been willing to tolerate wide swings in bank credit and partly because the proviso clause has not in application been taken as a strong target of policy" (ibid., 9).[158] "No large change in money market conditions has ever been undertaken in connection with the proviso clause" (ibid., 11).

Use of targets for monetary aggregates required reconsideration of

157. "The vagueness of the statement of goals when limited to ultimate objectives of policy may reflect the inability or unwillingness of the FOMC itself to take, or make known, a position on the trade-off problem, thereby possibly reflecting a gap in the discussion of policy and in the formulation of the directive" (Axilrod, 1970a, 5). Axilrod noted also that it was difficult to relate the FOMC's goals to its instructions (ibid., 6).

158. Deposit data were available daily. Axilrod does not mention the problem of separating temporary from persistent changes in bank credit. Accommodation of such changes dates back to the start of the Federal Reserve in 1913, when the gold standard served as a constraint. Also, generally, the staff projected bank credit only one month ahead.

"even keel" policy. Staff analysis suggested that the meaning of the term was imprecise. Axilrod (1969) studied empirical data for 1966–68 and concluded that the most consistent effects were on the federal funds rate and free reserves. He noted that typically even keel extended from "a week before the announcement of terms [on a Treasury issue] to a week after settlement date" (ibid., 4), but he observed variations in practice. The reason for intervening was to "help underwrite Treasury issues . . . with a short period of time in which market forces rather than new monetary policy decisions are the main factors affecting interest rates" (ibid., 2).[159]

Axilrod noted that typically the System did not use even keel policy when the Treasury issued bills. He gave four reasons: (1) the Treasury auctioned bills but not coupon securities; (2) coupon issues were generally larger, and the Treasury required payment for bills in a week but gave ten to fourteen days on coupon issues; (3) rate fluctuations have a larger effect on the value of coupon issues because of their longer maturity; and (4) if the Treasury issue failed to attract the requisite amount of sales, the Federal Reserve would have to buy the issue. He recognized (Axilrod, 1970a, 12) that the System could reduce its use of even keel by getting the Treasury to auction coupon issues.

During the three years studied, even keel remained in effect 40 percent of the time (ibid., 6). One result was that "in such periods the Federal Reserve has permitted somewhat more expansion in monetary aggregates than it might otherwise in order to keep interest rate fluctuations more damped than they otherwise would be" (ibid., 13).[160]

Soon afterward, a staff study reconsidered even keel after few months of experience with money or credit targets. This time the staff recognized more fully the market's problems: (1) government security dealers, acting as underwriters, would experience large losses or gains if expectations changed during a period when they had to distribute Treasury coupon issues; and (2) they would not know whether changes in money and short-term rates represented random fluctuations or a persistent policy change. As a result, "the commitment [to even-keel] will still have to be defined

---

159. "Even keel" replaced the policy of pegging interest rates to specific pre-announced ceilings. It has a loose relation to an investment bank's policy of maintaining a market in newly underwritten issues for a period following initial sale.

160. "The major impact of even keel is that the System refrains from changing its constellation of money market conditions in a period of Treasury financings, whereas it would not refrain from doing so in a period of particular corporate or state and local government financing" (Axilrod, 1970a, 13). This formulation is very similar in its implication to Chairman Martin's interpretation of independence within the government—that the government had to be financed; the System could not refuse to assist in its financing at or near current interest rates (see Chapter 2).

largely in terms of maintaining a reasonably flat trend in day-to-day money market conditions during the Treasury financing period, even when the monetary aggregates are given top billing as operating targets" (Staff study, "Even-keel and the Monetary Aggregates," Board Records, July 17, 1970, 10). The study recognized the implication: control of monetary aggregates would have to take place outside even-keel periods (ibid., 15).

The manager's autonomy. In the 1950s and early 1960s, the account manager received vague instructions from the FOMC, and there was little correspondence between the members' suggestions, so the manager could exercise considerable judgment. Efforts to increase the committee's control led to the publication of the "Blue Book," containing staff projections of bank credit, deposits, money, interest rates, and other variables. The projections assumed some set of money market conditions: prevailing, easier, or tighter. Axilrod (1970a, 15) recognized that "given the multiplicity of variables, the manager has considerable scope to play off one variable against another . . . so long as at least some key variables remain within specified ranges."

In practice, FOMC members often rejected the constraints that associated one set of money market conditions with values for money or credit growth. Instead, they chose a different money stock growth rate at a given interest rate or a different interest rate for a given money growth rate (Lombra and Moran, 1980, 44). James Pierce (1980, 83) described the FOMC's procedures as similar to choosing from "a menu in a Chinese restaurant: We will have one item from alternative A, [tighter] one item from B [unchanged] and split an item between B and C [easier]. The choices were often 'wish lists,' i.e. a low federal funds rate was selected along with slow money growth."[161]

Pierce (ibid., 82) summarized the outcome:

> If one examines data for that period, one notes that an interesting phenomenon surfaces. Each month the FOMC set ranges of tolerance for the federal funds rate and for growth of the monetary aggregates. After the fact, *the funds rate was always in the targeted range, while money was rarely in its range.* The reason is that the FOMC was not using M_1 as a target. M_1 was to be achieved *provided* the federal funds rate did not stray outside its allowable range. . . .
>
> The implications of pegging money growth was explained time and again to the FOMC, to individual Federal Reserve Board members, and to Reserve bank presidents. Despite these explanations, the FOMC *chose not to change its operating procedures.* (emphasis added)

---

161. During the period they discussed, Lombra and Pierce were members of the Federal Reserve staff. Pierce had a major role in preparing material for the forecasts.

Axilrod (1970a, 19) gave two reasons. First, use of money market conditions provided a target that the manager could hit daily or weekly with little difficulty. Second, setting the federal funds rate or free reserves accommodated short-term changes in demand. As a principal example, he used seasonal changes in the demand for currency. He recognized, however, that a money market target provided or absorbed "bank reserves, credit and money in a pro-cyclical fashion" (ibid.) Here Axilrod accepted that Federal Reserve actions frequently reinforced cyclical changes in output and inflation instead of damping them.[162]

Axilrod's lengthy discussion recognized fully that "an increase in inflationary anticipations . . . will increase the interest rate premium demanded by investors and will make borrowers more willing to pay it. Similarly, an abatement of inflationary expectations will have the reverse effect" (ibid., 27). The FOMC was slow to make this proposition an integral part of its analysis, and discussion and staff briefings did not make the distinction consistently. Consequently nominal rates were often considered "high" even if real interest rates were negative.

Effects of a money target. Axilrod recognized also that "the System in the past has appeared reluctant to change money market conditions by more than small gradual amounts. Such short-run and longer-run goals for the money market can often interfere with the attainment of the longer-run interest rate, bank credit, and money objectives of policy—all of which appear to be more closely related to economic activity than are money market conditions themselves" (Axilrod, 1970a, 32). Axilrod took a long step toward the critics' position. He recognized the value of smoothing the money market to avoid wide swings in interest rates and possible liquidity problems, but he concluded that "more fluctuation in money market conditions than has been permitted seems to have desirable aspects" (ibid., 35).[163] Once the market became accustomed to fluctuations in short-term rates, it would not respond by changing credit conditions, and it would

162. This was a standard complaint of the Federal Reserve critics called monetarists. Axilrod (1970a, 31) accepted that opening the discount window and letting the discount rate adjust freely to market rates, as proposed by Brunner and Meltzer (1964), would accommodate these demands with much less intervention. In a classic paper, Poole (1970) analyzed the choice problem under uncertainty. He showed that the proper choice of money or an interest rate depended on the principal source of variation in the economy. A money stock target lowered expected loss if most of the disturbances came from the real economy. If most disturbances came from shifts in the demand for money, an interest rate target was more appropriate.

163. Pierce (1970) did simulations as part of the staff study supporting the work of the Committee on the Directive. He concluded that the FOMC could improve its success at achieving long-term goals if it permitted more short-term fluctuation in market rates to achieve more control of money growth. The policy simulations used the Board's new MPS econometric model with 125 or more structural equations.

learn not to interpret all such changes as policy changes. This was very different from the traditional answer (Roosa, 1951) that assigned responsibility to the System for smoothing the market.

A main conclusion is that by attempting to hit a money growth target, the FOMC would change the relation between short- and long-term objectives. Market rates would fluctuate more, at least initially. Once the longer-term trend became clear, some of the instability in short-term rates would moderate. Greater attention to achieving money growth targets would increase control of "financial variables that more directly affect changes in the public's spending propensities" (Axilrod, 1970a, 55).

The committee and staff reports. The final staff reports appear in the appendix to the Report of the Committee on the Directive, dated March 2, 1970. The committee report recognized parts of the problem. It called for a change in the target from money market conditions to one or more monetary aggregates; it attempted to shift attention from short-term changes in the money market to longer-term changes in aggregate demand, economic activity and prices; and it recognized that there was very little relation between money market changes and longer-term policy goals. These are the principal criticisms by Brunner and Meltzer (1964) in their report to the House Banking Committee.

The report of the Committee on the Directive, prepared by Governor Maisel, chair, and Presidents Morris (Boston) and Swan (San Francisco), did not try to decide which aggregate would make the best target. Instead, it chose a total reserve target that could be consistent with different intermediate objectives such as money or credit growth or some broader measure of money. Each monthly meeting could reset the target, based on new information, but the presumption was that policy would change infrequently.

With Martin gone, the report accepted some of the principal criticisms of the procedures that developed during his tenure, particularly the weak connection between money market conditions and final goals and the absence of procedures that looked beyond the short term. "The weakest sector of the FOMC directive operations has been the Committee's formulation of the role and posture of monetary policy for the immediate period which stretches between the current month's targets and the ultimate goals. . . . [T]he specification of what monetary policy the Committee desires and the relating of such a policy to the Manager's operations and the Committee's goals remain critical problems" (Report of the Committee on the Directive, Board Records, March 2, 1970, 5).

Procedures had changed substantially in the five preceding years, partly responding to outside critics and partly to members' and staff criticisms, particularly criticisms from Governor Maisel. Until 1965, the Board and the FOMC operated under the "Riefler rule," a prohibition against forecasts.[164]

By 1970, for each meeting the staff prepared a "green book" containing economic forecasts for six to fifteen months ahead and periodically made projections of money, credit, and interest rates believed consistent with the forecast. The two forecasts or projections were independent and unrelated. The committee report wanted the staff to relate proposed changes in the directive to anticipated changes in money, credit markets, and the economy.

The "blue book," containing inter-meeting changes in interest rates and monetary aggregates, accompanied the green book. Blue book projections had been extended to a quarter, so the manager knew the staff forecast of reserves and money market conditions for a rolling three-month period.

The staff report was unanimous that "primary focus in the directive on money market conditions . . . can lead and often has led to inappropriate policy" (ibid., 7). The committee agreed and accepted that "financial markets are sufficiently resilient to offer scope for wider week-to-week fluctuations, and intermediate target changes, in money market conditions than has generally been permitted in the past" (ibid.). The report identified the problem as unforeseen changes in aggregate demand or demand for money that caused policy action to change in ways different from those desired by the FOMC without inducing sufficient FOMC response.

The committee recommended that the staff use a variety of methods, including judgment, to forecast the principal economic variables three times a year and relate their projections to movements in monetary aggregates and interest rates assuming unchanged policy. In addition, the staff was asked to project the same variables based on alternative policies. This is the origin of the three alternatives—tighter, easier, unchanged—that the staff provided at subsequent meetings. The FOMC would decide on a total reserves target for the next three months, expressed in qualitative terms in the directive and quantitatively in the instructions to the manager.[165]

The staff recognized that the proposed procedure would not be easy to implement.[166] Its memo supported the proposed change, however. Both

164. Riefler left at the end of 1958, but the rule remained. It is hard to know what the rule meant in practice, since the FOMC recognized recessions and recoveries promptly. The rule banned econometric models but was silent about judgmental forecasts.

165. The staff would base its forecast or projection on seasonally adjusted data but use its seasonal factors to give the manager a seasonally unadjusted number for total reserves. This required a forecast of member bank borrowing and excess reserves as well as estimates of float, Treasury deposits, etc. The committee recognized that much was unknown or subject to error, possibly large error.

166. "We have not progressed to the point where an econometric model can be the foun-

the staff and the committee either neglected or underestimated the difficulties in using money market conditions—for example, a daily or weekly short-term interest rate—to hit a target for a monetary aggregate three months ahead. First, the staff recognized that it had not developed a procedure for estimating borrowed reserves. The staff assumed that expected borrowing would remain at the average level of recent weeks. This was not helpful and created a problem at the time and again in 1979–81, a later attempt to use a reserve target. Second, the staff left to the manager to decide whether a change in reserves or money was permanent or transitory. Neither he nor they had much basis for making the judgment, but it became important. Under the money market procedure, the manager supplied all such changes, in effect treating all changes as transitory. The FOMC could then make a change at the next meeting. The new procedure required the manager, perhaps assisted by the staff, to make these judgments as they occurred. This, too, proved to be a problem. Muth (1960) showed that the size of the adjustment depended on the relative variance of permanent and transitory components, but the staff did not use this analysis. Third, neither the report nor the appendixes discussed what would replace the even-keel procedure. None of the material suggested auctioning all government securities to permit the market to set the price. Fourth, the FOMC had adopted lagged reserve accounting. Member banks held reserves based on deposits two weeks prior to the settlement date. This change fixed the amount of required reserves, reducing flexibility and making control of monetary aggregates difficult.

International aspects of policy did not appear in any of the documents. Although there was a short reference to euro-dollar flows, the effect of improved control of monetary aggregates on the capital account and the value of the dollar received no mention. This suggests the limited attention these matters received at the time.

The report to the FOMC. Maisel's opening statement to the April 1970 FOMC meeting recognized that in January the full committee had adopted some of the proposed changes. He asked, in addition, that the FOMC issue an explicit statement explaining the change and agree to devote more time and attention at FOMC meetings to longer-term objectives and how to achieve them. The report criticized the use of money market conditions— "particularly net borrowed reserves and the Federal funds rate"—because

---

dation of our projections; indeed, we may never do so. . . . [S]taff projections for the year ahead are based on many hours of judgmental forecasting" (Appendix B to Report of the Committee on the Directive, Board Records, March 2, 1970, 3). The staff expected to continue to rely mainly on judgmental forecasts for a year ahead, supplemented by model forecasts for longer periods.

they "often led to inappropriate policy, particularly in periods of rapidly shifting demands for credits" (FOMC Minutes, April 7, 1970, 71).[167] The report added: "On too many occasions, and for too extended a period of time, the amount of money and credit has grown at a rate far greater or far smaller than would have been desirable in the economic circumstances" (ibid., 72).

The Maisel committee proposed that members state their objectives for aggregate demand (neutral, stronger, or weaker than projected) and the quantitative condition they believed would achieve their objective over time. The manager would then "specify desired changes in total reserves for the next three months that are consistent with the consensus of the FOMC's views about desired financial conditions" (ibid., 72). The committee proposed including a total reserves path for the next four weeks.[168] At each meeting, the FOMC could adjust the three-month path in the light of new information. Maisel recognized that the federal funds rates would fluctuate over a wider range. To prevent the market from misreading these fluctuations, he wanted the FOMC to announce that the four-week average growth of total reserves was now the target.

Morris noted that the committee had chosen total reserves because members who wanted to control bank credit or money could agree on the growth of total reserves consistent with their different objectives. "There was a wide degree of agreement that the Open Market Committee's shift

167. Many of these criticisms are similar to an earlier report for Congress (Brunner and Meltzer, 1964) and a 1964 internal report by a committee consisting of Governor Mitchell and Presidents Ellis and Swan. Neither the Committee on the Directive nor these reports recognized that frequent changes in the federal funds rate that prevented excessive or deficient growth of money or base money over six months or a year would achieve many of the objectives that these reports favored. President Scanlon (Chicago) reminded Maisel of a main point in the FOMC's 1964 report. "The Committee is not really concerned about short-run developments in the money market except as these affect the Manager's ability to achieve longer-run goals, and it is these longer-run effects on monetary aggregates that are closely linked [sic] to desired trends in real economic variables. . . . The essential element of this approach is . . . that the committee set a specific desired rate of change in an aggregate monetary variable with maximum freedom for the Manager as to the methods employed in reaching it" (letter, Charles J. Scanlon to Sherman J. Maisel, Board Records, January 12, 1970, 3). Scanlon further urged "detailed elucidation of the FOMC's conception of the monetary process," (ibid., 4). He included the "trade-offs or Phillips curve relationships among them . . . the interrelationship between monetary and fiscal policy," (ibid., 4). This went much further than the Maisel committee ventured and was never adopted.

168. The committee chose total reserves because "it would be difficult for the members of the FOMC to agree on a specific theory of monetary policy, on the relevant variables, or on the relationship between possible variables and desired results. . . . Thus, the FOMC must be able to agree on desired reserve movements, even if it is fragmented in its individual views as to how such operations are expected to influence monetary policy and how such policy will influence the economy" (FOMC Minutes, April 7, 1970, 73).

toward aggregative targets thus far in 1970 had been a desirable development and that the Committee should continue to pursue such targets."
But agreement was neither strong nor deep. Burns's summary of the consensus said that the directive committee should continue to function informally, but the FOMC would not take any additional steps and would not
issue a statement about the change. The FOMC rejected the reserve target
and chose three-month averages for both money and bank credit growth,
but it retained money market conditions as an operating target and did
not decide what to do if money and bank credit diverged. In practice, the
manager and the FOMC were supposed to emphasize money growth. The
FOMC would now specify a level of the federal funds rate believed to be
consistent with its money growth target, and the manager would adjust his
operations to achieve the money target.

Maisel described the most important change as "the agreement, which
the market would understand, that a movement in money market conditions would not mean that monetary policy had changed. Policy was
to be measured by movements in the monetary aggregates" (Maisel,
1973, 254).

Maisel's proposal did not really change much. Pressures to concentrate on short-term changes remained strong.[169] Adjusting fully to short-
term movements in money growth or bank credit required frequent, large
changes, up and down, in market rates, larger changes in interest rates
than the FOMC would accept.

One of the more puzzling decisions was to avoid any announcement. If
implemented as proposed by the Committee on the Directive, participants
in the market for federal funds and other short-term securities would at
once observe larger daily and weekly changes in market rates. Failure to
explain the procedural change would increase uncertainty, misinterpretation, and speculation that would work against successful implementation.
The lack of announcement underscores the ambivalence that Chairman
Burns must have felt about the proposal. He would pay some lip service to
the aggregates when it served his purpose, but he would not implement
the recommendations.

At a broader level the decision not to announce the change shows the
lingering effect of traditional central bank secrecy. The Federal Reserve,
and other central banks, did not yet accept that well-informed market participants could help to implement policy smoothly and efficiently. A broad

169. Pressures from the Joint Economic Committee of Congress to maintain money
growth in the 2 to 6 (or 3 to 5) percent range are not mentioned by Maisel or the FOMC, but
they may have played a role in getting to an agreement or in getting Chairman Martin to accept an aggregate target at his last meeting (see Joint Economic Committee, 1968).

understanding of the mutual interdependence of the market and the central bank remained a missing element in the theory and practice of central banking.[170]

Policy Action in the Recession

Maisel (1973, 250) described discussion at the February 10 meeting as "the most bitter debate I experienced in my entire service on the FOMC." He might have added that it initiated a period of confusion and uncertainty. This was Burns's first meeting, so he had not established a leadership position. Most members recognized that the economy was in recession, but members differed about its anticipated duration and depth. Hayes called a decision to ease "premature and unwise" (FOMC Minutes, February 10, 1970, 45). He wanted the System's main goal to be lower inflation. Robertson, Brimmer, and Coldwell (Dallas) sided with Hayes. Burns thought a depression was possible, a gross mischaracterization of a mild recession. He wanted moderate growth in money and credit. On a vote of nine to three, the FOMC chose "somewhat less firm conditions in the money market" with a proviso to resist any significant change of money and credit "from a moderate growth pattern" (Annual Report, 1970, 105). Hayes, Brimmer, and Coldwell dissented, citing "the strength of inflationary expectations" (ibid.).[171] The core issue in the policy debate was between those who wanted counter-cyclical policy in part because they believed that failure to respond to rising unemployment would jeopardize anti-inflation policy later and those who, remembering the promise they made

170. The change would become apparent in the Board's 1970 Annual Report. In October, Stephen Axilrod prepared an essay for the *Federal Reserve Bulletin* to explain the changed procedures. He minimized the extent of the change by making it appear as another step in the evolution of operations that began in 1966 with introduction of the proviso clause or that had long existed because of the System's recognition that money, bank credit, and interest rates were all relevant. He noted, however, that the new procedures lengthened the time horizon over which money market changes affected changes in the monetary aggregates. The time horizon was now longer "than simply the interval between FOMC meetings" (Axilrod, 1970a, 12). Axilrod's essay also alluded to a possible shift from procyclical to counter-cyclical actions. "An unexpected and undesired shortfall in business and consumer demand for goods and services would be accompanied in the short-run by a greater decline in interest rates than would otherwise be the case" (ibid., 14). He recognized the main point, stressed by Poole (1970), that the best response to a shift in aggregate demand was to induce an opposite shift in aggregate demand by changing money. And he recognized that open market policy must "evaluate the extent to which such shifts are transitory or more permanent" (ibid., 16). Regrettably, the FOMC did not make the change to a counter-cyclical policy or regularly distinguish permanent from transitory changes for many years.

171. Burns rejected both directives proposed by the staff. Instead of changing wording, as Martin had done, he wrote his own, intermediate between the two (FOMC Minutes, February 10, 1970, 83). On February 20, the Board again delayed regulations affecting commercial paper. This time the reason given was to avoid further tightening.

in the fall, wanted to continue anti-inflation policy even if it required a deep recession.

Paul McCracken, chairman of the Council of Economic Advisers, believed that continuous adjustment, fine-tuning the economy, built instability (Hargrove and Morley, 1984, 323). Burns agreed. He thought "it was undesirable in general for the Committee to shift its policy stance from month to month on the basis of the latest readings of uncertain indicators" (FOMC Minutes, April 7, 1970, 52).[172] To those who wanted to tighten policy because of rising inflation, Burns warned that Congress was about to act against "the problem of recession in the economy and of depression in the housing industry . . . [I]t would only be a matter of time before the Federal Reserve would find itself in the position of some Latin American central banks" (ibid., 52). Burns's statement broke the policy logjam. Some went along reluctantly, but a majority supported the new chairman. Once again, the FOMC responded to the slowing economy by abandoning its anti-inflation policy, reinforcing the belief that inflation would persist. Markets now had evidence from 1967, 1968, and 1970 under two administrations and two chairmen that preventing inflation had lower priority. The action in February 1970 repeated the 1968 policy error.

An unusual feature of open market operations during this period was acceptance of the relatively large weekly variation in the federal funds rate under the policy of trying to maintain moderate growth of monetary aggregates.[173] Monthly changes in the monetary aggregates varied widely, however. The money stock rose at an annual rate of 11.5 percent from February to March and 12.5 percent from March to April but less than 3 percent for the first quarter average (computed from the mid-point of the previous quarter). Total deposits, the bank credit proxy, showed a similar pattern— large monthly variation around a relatively modest quarterly growth rate (Annual Report, 1970, 117, 124).

At the April 7 meeting, Burns criticized Hayes and others who wanted stronger action against inflation. He claimed inflation came from "cost-push," mainly from wage increases that reduced supply and raised prices. Presaging his later insistence that the old rules no longer worked, he absolved the Federal Reserve (and himself) from responsibility and favored

172. Early in March, the manager reported on six months experience lending securities to dealers. He concluded it strengthened the market for government securities and proposed increasing the limit on borrowing by a single dealer.

173. There were several large swings. For example, the weekly average funds rate declined from a peak of 9.39 percent on February 18 to 7.45 percent at the end of March. By late April, the rate increased a full percentage point to 8.43 before falling in May to 7.64. Long Treasury rates also shifted up and down but by smaller amounts: February 14, 6.48; April 4, 6.32; May 30, 7.21.

less use of monetary policy to reduce inflation. "It was a mistake for the Federal Reserve to attempt to deal with cost-push inflation through monetary policy. He said that either the country learned to live with cost-push inflation or direct controls would have to be used to get rid of it" (Maisel diary, April 7, 1970, 36).[174]

The reference to price and wage controls follows Governor Robertson's comment that "if there were a resurgence of inflation it would probably prove impossible to cope with it through general stabilization policies, and direct controls would be required" (FOMC Minutes, April 7, 1970, 48). Burns agreed. "Excess demands had largely been eliminated and the inflation that was occurring . . . was of the cost-push variety. That type of inflation, he believed, could not be dealt with successfully from the monetary side. . . . One had either to live with it or begin thinking along the lines Mr. Robertson had mentioned" (ibid., 50–51).

A few days earlier, Burns received a summary of the replies to a letter he sent in February to all reserve bank directors. Most expected inflation to continue at a slower rate. "The most frequent reason given for expecting a continuation of inflationary pressures was the belief that union leaders would continue to press successfully for wage increases with the consequent cost-push effect on prices" (memo, Summary of responses to Chairman Burns's letter, Board Records, April 2, 1970). Only about 10 percent believed that reducing inflation required wage and price controls.[175]

At its April meeting, the FOMC held a lengthy discussion about whether reserve or monetary growth measures should be treated as projections or targets. If treated as projections, the manager would use the federal funds rate as a target and presume that the projected reserve or money growth would be reached. He would adjust the federal funds rate only if money growth deviated by more than one percentage point from projections. If reserve or money growth became the target, the manager would change

---

174. Burns responded to Robertson, Daane, Hickman (Cleveland), Swan (San Francisco), Kimbrel (Atlanta), and others who complained about the budget deficit that they "were looking at the wrong figures" (Maisel diary, April 7, 1970, 36). He told them that the proper measure of fiscal stimulus was the full employment budget and that it was appropriately stimulative during the recession but would turn restrictive in 1971. He later reverted to the standard central bank position.

175. At about this time, in an effort to increase control, Burns sent a memo to members of the Board noting that the Board's Rules Regarding Employee Responsibilities and Conduct did not apply to Board members. He proposed a committee to develop guidelines for "the content and circumstances of public speeches, . . . relations with the press, maintaining the confidentiality of inside information" etc. (memo, Guide to conduct for System officials, Board Records, April 7, 1970). He suggested a voluntary agreement by Board members and reserve bank presidents.

the federal funds rate when he missed the target. The federal funds rate would be an instrument and reserve or money growth the target.

The FOMC divided, but Burns decided to use money and bank credit growth as targets. Staff forecasts of weekly growth rates for the next six weeks, then monthly for the quarter, were available in the blue book. Now, the FOMC had an objective that went beyond the next meeting, although the committee could change the projected path at that meeting. As noted, the FOMC did not vote to announce the new procedures. However, Hayes gave a news conference soon after. He warned that the money market rates would vary more than in the past but that movements would be contained.

The System began the new procedure by raising the federal funds rate, perhaps the first time the manager decided on an overt change explicitly to control money and bank credit growth. This effort came at a time of new military operations in Cambodia that set off riots on college campuses and increased uncertainty in financial markets. The System ended by supplying more reserves, in part to prevent failure of a Treasury financing.[176] Monetary base growth rose to a 7.4 percent annual rate, substantially above the 4.8 percent twelve-month rate. The decision to abandon the target suggests that Burns was unconvinced about the desirability of the new procedures, and it supported members who believed the target had to be a money market variable.

The FOMC soon took a step back from monetary control. It changed the directive issued at the May 5 meeting to "clarify the Committee's intention that . . . deviations from the expected paths of various aggregative reserve measures was to be used as a supplement to—but not as a substitute for—data reflecting money market conditions in making decisions" (Annual Report, 1970, 125).[177] Francis (St. Louis) dissented.

176. "When it became apparent soon after the April 7 meeting that both money and bank credit were expanding more rapidly on the average than desired by the Committee, System open market operations were directed to achieving somewhat firmer conditions in the money market. Later . . . it was found necessary first to moderate developing tendencies toward undue firmness and then to calm market unsettlement" (Annual Report, 1970, 124).

177. The minutes hint at the way the manager implemented the policy of targeting monetary aggregates. "A reference to 'bank reserves' as well as 'money market conditions' is suggested in the statement of instructions to help make clear that in reaching his operating decisions the Manager is expected to keep an eye on the path of changes in the whole family of reserve aggregates. The staff understands that deviations from the path are expected to be used as information supplementing—not substituting for—developments in money market conditions as a guide to possible Desk operations" (FOMC Minutes, May 5, 1970, 50 n. 1). The problem that the manager and the FOMC faced arose from the short-term focus. Growth of the monetary aggregates have relatively large weekly and monthly variances. The manager would have to vary interest rates up and down to adjust to weekly deviations of money growth

The principal reason given for the change was the "spectre of possible financial panic in the eyes of some market observers" (FOMC Minutes, May 5, 1970, 14). The concern had multiple causes, but the important new elements included the president's decision to extend military operations to Cambodia and the response at home and abroad. As in 1953, heightened uncertainty came at a time when bond dealers had relatively large holdings of government securities in anticipation of falling interest rates. Borrowing in the long-term market remained heavy, putting upward pressure on rates. Release of the FOMC's January minutes added to the uncertainty by creating "puzzlement over the market implications of greater reliance on monetary and credit aggregates"[178] (ibid.). To meet the aggregate targets, the manager had increased the federal funds rate by 0.5 percentage points. Coming at a time when dealers expected interest rates to fall, "a very substantial interest rate reaction occurred" (ibid., 15).

The FOMC would not agree to issue a statement explaining the new procedures. Dealers asked whether even keel was still in effect and what would be done during a Treasury financing. The only answer was a suggestion that the staff write a report that, if approved, would appear in a future Federal Reserve Bulletin. The FOMC did not make a decision at the time. This exacerbated the uncertainty that an announcement of the new procedures, and their limits, could have avoided.

Several members were pleased by the manager's response to slow growth of the aggregates. Burns criticized the members for giving "insufficient attention" to unemployment (ibid., 45). At 4.8 percent the unemployment rate already was above the 4.3 percent average the Council of Economic Advisers predicted for the year. Although Burns had voted in April to target reserve growth and money, he disliked the result and did not want to accept higher interest rates and higher unemployment to reduce inflation. "He thought it would be a disastrous mistake to tighten monetary policy at this time, but . . . relaxing would also be a serious mistake" (ibid., 46).[179]

The annual index of stock prices declined beginning in January 1969.

---

from target, annoying market participants and increasing their costs. This was not likely to last, and it did not.

178. The FOMC was prepared to make longer-term (weeks) loans direct to the Treasury, if the market remained in flux. In the recent sale of an eighteen-month note, attrition was 50 percent of the issue. The manager said that attrition would be above 50 percent currently. Attrition of this magnitude was always a concern.

179. Soon after, Burns changed the weighting and now disregarded his opposition to frequent policy changes. "The greatest danger we could face would be in a relaxation of policy" (FOMC Minutes, May 5, 1970, 46). He referred to concerns that the administration would give up its anti-inflation policy.

By January 1970, these prices were 21 percent below the level of the previous January. They continued to fall at a slower rate until May. The Cambodian incursion, expected inflation of 6.2 percent, continued recession,[180] and other uncertainties reduced the Standard & Poor's index by 12 percent in May to a level last seen seven years earlier, when consumer prices were 20 percent lower.

Stock market margin requirements had remained at 80 percent since June 1968. Board members reached general agreement that only initial margin requirements should be lowered, but timing was a problem. Brimmer and Robertson thought the move was inflationary and would undercut their efforts. Mitchell and Maisel did not want to suggest that the Board feared a stock market panic. Burns pointed out that many stock exchange firms faced insolvency as their assets declined in value. Poor psychology dominated sound economics four to three, so the Board did not act on May 4. It decided to wait for the FOMC meeting the following day.

The presidents divided also. Burns wanted to make the change. After the FOMC meeting, the Board met to lower stock margin requirements to 65 percent. The stock price index continued to fall on average until July, but the major move had occurred.

The stock market and the economy were the main topics of discussion when the Board had its regular luncheon meeting with the CEA. Two CEA members wanted faster money growth and lower interest rates, but Hendrik Houthakker disagreed. The meeting also discussed Chairman Burns's speech urging voluntary wage and price controls. He received no support from the CEA members, but some suggested that the president could do more to hold down wages and prices in specific sectors, especially construction and energy (Maisel diary, May 21, 1970, 56–57). Whatever Burns meant by cost-push inflation, his speech claimed that voluntary controls could reduce this source of inflation.

Faced with the many problems and uncertainties, the System ignored targets for money and credit, supplying reserves to assist the Treasury financing (even keel) and satisfy the increased demand for money. The main issue at the May 26 FOMC meeting was whether to remove the bulge in bank reserves and money and, if so, how soon. "Burns spoke up in a very emotional manner" warning of a financial crisis and urging attention to the liquidity problem and the possible crisis (Maisel diary, May 27, 1970, 61). "It was necessary temporarily to put aside the objective of moderate growth in the monetary aggregates and to undertake the classical func-

---

180. The forecast is from the SPF for second quarter 1970. The Board's staff forecast 5 percent inflation for the year with recovery starting in third quarter 1970.

tions of a central bank when a crisis existed—or was near at hand" (FOMC Minutes, May 26, 1970, 28).

Not all of the members agreed that a crisis was near or on the policy action to be taken if one were. The committee went back to doing what it had done before. It granted discretion to the manager to moderate pressures in financial markets. It made one change, mainly cosmetic, by instructing the manager to recognize the committee's longer run objectives for money and credit growth. On the central issue of what should be done about the bulge in reserves during the May Treasury financing, there were many opinions but the only firm decision came from the manager's statement that the sense of the meeting was to do nothing at the time. The issue of how to deal with temporary (positive and negative) deviations from a projected path was a critical part of achieving long-run objectives.[181] The System had not decided how to treat these bulges in reserves, and again it did not consider auctioning securities to avoid the problems arising from even keel operations to support the Treasury market.

Between December 1969 and June 1970, the unemployment rate rose from 3.5 to 4.9 percent. The staff predicted a continued rise to 5.6 percent in fourth quarter 1970 and 5.9 percent in first half 1971. The actual rate was 5.8 for the fourth quarter, and 6.1 in December 1970. The rate remained between 5.9 and 6.0 percent in the first half of 1971. "Burns felt this unemployment rate was not satisfactory—it was too high—and he wanted to get greater monetary ease" (Maisel diary, June 12, 1970, 64).

At Burns's request the staff proposed to reduce reserve requirement ratios for time deposits but to offset some of the reserves released by putting reserve requirements on bank-issued commercial paper. Mitchell proposed to remove regulation Q ceilings on CDs over $100,000. Only Burns supported him. Neither proposal could overcome opposition from those concerned about the unsettled state of the money market and those who did not want any increase in ease.[182]

181. Much of the bulge came as discounts and advances. Between May 1 and 20, discounts increased $405 million to $1.27 billion. This seems an appropriate response to a temporary increase in demand that would reverse when market conditions improved.

182. Maisel's diary (June 12, 1970, 67) concluded that the Board would have voted to put reserve requirements on bank-issued commercial paper but hesitated because of concern about the announcement effect. Maisel reported on the views expressed at the academic consultants meeting on June 19. The prevailing view was that once the unemployment rate rose above the full employment rate of 4 percent, inflation would fall. Gardner Ackley and Herb Stein agreed that with unemployment at 5 percent at the time, "there was no advantage in any increase in unemployment with respect to future price decreases. . . . [P]rices would come down just as rapidly with a minimum excess of unemployment as they would with a much higher unemployment rate" (ibid., June 19, 1970, 70–71). This seems a peculiar version of a Phillips curve, but Maisel reported it was widely accepted. In fact, inflation increased from

Reflecting on its experience in the spring, the Board asked for a staff report on the use of even keel in a monetary targeting regime. The staff report, "Even Keel and the Monetary Aggregates" (Board Records, July 17, 1970), recognized that dealers and other market participants would have to distinguish between policy changes in interest rates and changes resulting from the new operating procedure. Also, the manager would have to learn how quickly or slowly to adjust the money stock back to its target. The fact that the FOMC used more than one aggregate target raised additional issues; they often moved in different directions in weekly or monthly data.

The staff recognized a divergence between current and longer-term consequences. Inflation or aggregate demand depended on trend growth in the aggregates, but dealers held large volumes of debt during Treasury financings. Debt prices would fluctuate with short-term interest rate changes. The rationale for even keel was to prevent (or minimize) these fluctuations. This problem could not be avoided, but it could be reduced if the Treasury used more auctions for longer-term debt (ibid., 11).

The staff concluded that the FOMC should continue even keel operations. At later meetings, it would have to adjust the growth paths of the monetary aggregates by adjusting money market conditions. During discussion at the July 21, 1970, FOMC meeting, Axilrod proposed permitting greater flexibility in the use of even keel. Some members agreed, but Burns was cautious. There was a risk that a Treasury financing would fail.

The FOMC did not make a decision and did not change policy. The Treasury gradually shifted to auctioning medium- and long-term maturities in 1972. Auctions let the market choose a market clearing rate. Gradually even keel operations ended (Garbade, 2004).

THE PENN CENTRAL FAILURE

Events intervened to change positions on regulation Q and the Federal Reserve's role as lender of last resort. The System's responsibility as lender of last resort had led in December 1969 to an agreement on the use of emergency credit to assist mutual savings banks and savings and loan associations that were not members of either the Federal Reserve or the Federal Home Loan Bank System. For members of the Home Loan Bank System, the Reserve Board limited its responsibility to "conduit loans"—loans to Home Loan Banks that these banks would relend to "individual savings and loan associations when the inability of those associations to meet . . . withdrawals appeared to threaten a run that might have more gen-

5.43 to 5.97 percent between October 1969, before the recession, and May 1970. During the same months, the unemployment rate rose from 3.7 to 4.8 percent.

eral spillover effects on the financial system" (Board Minutes, January 8, 1970, 6). The Home Loan Banks would secure the loans with government or federal agency obligations. The agreement was temporary but the Board renewed it several times.

The agreement anticipated failure of some large thrift institutions. That didn't happen at the time. However, the discussion created a general understanding that the Federal Reserve had a broad responsibility in a crisis to sustain solvent but illiquid financial institutions, not just its members. It was not about to repeat the errors made in the banking crises of 1929 to 1933.[183]

It was also not yet ready to accept much risk. The first test came as a mixed package early in June. The Penn Central Railroad, then the seventh-largest corporation in the United States and a principal means of transport in the northeast and midwest, was unable to rollover its outstanding commercial paper liabilities. The Federal Reserve did not feel obligated to support non-financial institutions; its concern was the $40 billion commercial paper market. Bank affiliates had issued $7.5 billion, enough to threaten the solvency of major banks if there were many defaults.

The government's first effort was to stretch the authorization in the Defense Production Act of 1950 to make loans to defense contractors unable to obtain commercial credit. The railroad did not have a defense contract, but it moved military equipment, supplies, and personnel. A consortium of banks would make a short-term loan of $250 million, if the Federal Reserve guaranteed the loan. The System would in turn get a guarantee from the Navy Department. Later, this loan would be replaced by a longer-term loan arranged by the Department of Transportation. The effort failed when the Defense Department decided not to issue the guarantee.

On June 21, the Penn Central filed for reorganization under the Bankruptcy Act. It had paid off $100 million of its $200 million in outstanding commercial paper, but it could not obtain credit without a guarantee, and none was forthcoming.

The New York bank anticipated two main consequences. First, as commercial paper matured, banks would be pressed to lend directly to corporations and issuers of commercial paper. Since there were no reserves against commercial paper, substitution of loans would increase the demand for reserves, tightening the market. Second, some borrowers would not find loans. The bank estimated that replacing commercial paper with

183. Pierce (1998, 1–2) recalled meeting with the discount officers of the reserve banks at the time. "The fascinating part of it was that I discovered the real bills doctrine lived. The discount officers did not want to lend to the banks because . . . if they couldn't borrow they would be bankrupt. . . . Burns was there. He had to yell at them and tell them lend. Just lend."

bank loans required as much as $7 to $10 billion of additional reserves, as much as 16 percent of the monetary base. New York had told the large banks that the discount window would be open for temporary loans to assist banks during the adjustment. It suggested that the Board suspend indefinitely ceiling rates of interest on large certificates of deposit and supply the reserves required by the increase in CDs.

Chairman Burns noted that Penn Central had also borrowed heavily in the euro-dollar market. He feared that the firm's failure would reduce the willingness of foreigners to lend or invest in dollar assets. To keep them from selling required confidence. He was uncertain how to do that.[184] He reminded the FOMC on June 23 that financial crises followed major financial failures in the past, citing the Baring Bank, Knickerbocker Trust, and the First and Second Banks of the United States as examples. Burns "was the prime mover in the administration to try to get the government to guarantee Penn Central's cash needs" (Maisel diary, June 24, 1970, 73). He had the support of the Treasury but not the Council of Economic Advisers or George Shultz, newly appointed as director of the Office of Management and Budget.[185] At the Board, Robertson and Brimmer "saw no reason to save the Penn Central" (ibid.). Congressman Patman disliked what he regarded as a close relationship between the Penn Central and the Pennsylvania Republican Party.[186]

Burns had only modest support for removing regulation Q on large CDs at the June 22 Board meeting. Mitchell was the only one who fully shared his view. He had always favored removing regulation Q ceilings. As often happens, members gave ample reasons for delay. Robertson and Brimmer

184. The *Wall Street Journal* printed a front-page article on June 12 discussing the spreading liquidity crisis. In addition to Penn Central, it mentioned two industrial corporations, LTV and Lockheed, and cited statistics showing a relatively low ratio of cash and government securities to current liabilities of corporations. The article cited the decline in growth of reserve bank credit at a time of rising demands for credit.

185. George Shultz moved from Secretary of Labor to become first director of the new Office of Management and Budget (OMB). He became a principal presidential adviser with an office in the White House west wing instead of at OMB. Shultz described the president as wanting "to be sure that I knew what he was thinking" (interview with George P. Shultz, November 10, 2003). "The previous budget director acted as though it was his budget, not the president's budget" (ibid.). Shultz opposed Burns's policy of bailing out Penn Central. "It sends a wrong signal for people who mismanage. They should fail" (ibid.). Of course, Burns received staff memos and pleading from the financial markets about the risks of a spreading financial crisis (memo, Effects of a possible default by a major corporation, Burns papers, Box B-20, June 3, 1970).

186. Congress was asked to vote a $500 million loan as part of the defense loan. Maisel and Shultz claim that the loan collapsed because Penn Central hired President Nixon's former law firm as special counsel who had been active in the Republican Party (Maisel diary, June 24, 1970, 74 and June 26, 1970, 88; Shultz Interview, November 10, 2003).

favored waiting to see if a crisis occurred. Acting hastily might suggest a crisis when none was imminent. Sherrill could agree to a temporary change. Daane expressed concern about the effects on the exchange rate, and Maisel wanted to coordinate any action with the FDIC and the Home Loan Bank. Burns's strong case for restoring confidence had a four-to-three majority, but the Board waited to act until they coordinated decisions with other agencies (Board Minutes, June 22, 1970, 23).

Frank Wille, chairman of the FDIC, wanted to delay for a few days to see what happened. Preston Martin, chairman of the Federal Home Loan Bank Board, expressed concern that removing ceiling rates would let large banks compete with the commercial paper market and hurt the weaker issuers of commercial paper (Maisel diary, June 24, 1970, 79). Their support was weak at best.

Burns and Mitchell prevailed the following day. On June 23, the Board voted to suspend ceiling rates on CDs of $100,000 or more issued with thirty to eighty-nine days maturity. Citing "uncertainties," the press release noted that there could be unusual demands for short-term bank credit. It made no mention of Penn Central, but it explained that the action permitted substitution of bank credit for other forms of credit and did not constitute a relaxation of restrictive policy. Robertson dissented, citing lack of evidence of a crisis and expressing skepticism about whether there would be a large runoff of commercial paper. He expressed concern, also, about a "sharp net expansion of total bank credit" (Board Minutes, June 22, 1970, 38).[187]

No one mentioned one of the major effects of eliminating the ceiling rate. CDs of $100,000 or more could now be bought and subdivided to offer small savers a better return than regulated rates. It did not take long for investment companies to recognize the opportunity. Money market funds began soon after. In little more than a decade, Congress removed regulation Q ceilings on all maturities to stop the drain of funds from thrift associations restricted to offering ceiling rates. The eventual cost, however, was large. Regulation and inflation destroyed much of the savings and loan industry leaving a large debt for taxpayers in the 1980s.

In the immediate aftermath, problems continued in the commercial paper market as lenders left that market. The Board considered direct lending under section 13 of the Federal Reserve Act, which authorized such

187. Ceiling rates for CDs with more than 89 days to maturity remained unchanged. Before the change, the highest rate, 7.5 percent for a year or longer and 6.75 percent for 90 to 179 days compared to 8.25, 8.09, 9.60, and 7.5 to 8.0 percent on four- to six-month prime commercial paper, three-month CDs in the secondary market, new 30- to 89-day CDs, and three month euro-dollars respectively.

loans to solvent businesses unable to obtain loans from standard sources. Authorization for section 13 loans was granted in 1932 as a depression measure but little used.[188] The 1970 problem reopened the issue of when the central bank system should make direct loans to supplement its lender-of-last-resort function. By law, a super-majority of five had to approve the loans and the staff had to approve the collateral.[189]

By July 1, Robert Holland, the Board's secretary, could report that the market situation had improved. Several large holders of commercial paper continued to have difficulties, and outstanding commercial paper continued to decline at a rate of $200 million a day. The Board discussed several contingencies but agreed only to develop tactics for managing future crises. On July 21, Burns noted that the limited suspension of regulation Q ceilings had been "timely and salutary" (Board Minutes, July 21, 1970, 1). A bailout of Penn Central had not been necessary to prevent a financial panic.

Results of Crisis Management

The System's response to the Penn Central crisis was appropriate, much better than actions in some earlier crises but not without some weaknesses. Prompt System action permitted the market to adjust, and limited the extent and duration of the problem. The principal weakness was a confusion between supporting the failing firm and preventing the crisis from spreading by supplying reserves to the market. The initial reaction by the administration, to prevent the railroad from failing, confused the role of lender of last resort to the financial system with responsibilities to individual firms.

Despite bankruptcy of the seventh-largest domestic corporation, prompt announcement by the Federal Reserve that it would open the discount window forestalled a possible financial crisis. The Board limited the announcement's effect by deciding not to make it public. It told the reserve bank presidents who, in turn, told the principal banks. The news undoubtedly spread, but the terms, conditions, and duration of the loans was less clear than it might have been.[190] This was a step back from the more forth-

188. From 1932 to 1936, the System made 123 loans valued at $1.5 million.

189. This provision mixed the responsibilities of the Board and the reserve banks. The loans would have to be made by the reserve banks and included in their portfolios. Aside from Maisel and Mitchell, there was little enthusiasm. Governor Sherrill opposed bailouts of individual firms (Board Minutes, July 1, 1970, 3).

190. Bagehot's ([1873] 1962) classic statement of principles for a lender of last resort criticized the nineteenth-century Bank of England for failing to announce its policy, not for having the wrong policy (see Meltzer, 2003, chapter 2). The Board had not fully learned this lesson in the Penn Central situation.

Table 4.9   Advances, CDs, Loans, and Commercial Paper, 1970 ($ millions)

A. WEEKLY REPORTING BANKS			
Date	Discounts	Large CDs	Loans[a]
6/17	273	5966	79914
6/24	613	5982	79564
7/1	671	5984	80094
7/8	1402	5992	80013
8/26	941	9752	79219

B. COMMERCIAL PAPER		
	Total	Bank Related
May	40906	7600
June	38952	7603
July	38133	7820
December	33071	2349

[a]Commercial and industrial loans.
Source: Board of Governors (1976, 282–87, 719).

right statement that the System made in 1939 at the start of the European war (Meltzer, 2003, 551).

Member banks increased their borrowing but did not promptly increase the volume of negotiable CDs. Bank loans show a modest increase in early July, much of it a shift from commercial paper. Table 4.9 shows these data.

Borrowing provided the safety net. Aside from the greatly increased bank borrowing from the Federal Reserve, the principal changes occurred slowly. By late August, banks had increased outstanding negotiable CDs more than 60 percent, partly to replace bank-related commercial paper. The latter began a precipitate decline in the fall, accounting for two-thirds of the decline in total commercial paper outstanding by the end of the year.

By claiming a crisis, the Federal Reserve was able to relax regulation Q ceilings. Restricting the change to CDs with thirty to eighty-nine days' maturity encouraged substitution of short for longer maturity CDs. In October, Burns asked the Board to suspend ceiling rates for CDs of $100,000 or more for all maturities over twenty-nine days. Several governors objected. The Board did not make the change until March 1973 (Board Minutes, October 19, 1970, 3–5).[191]

Schwartz (1987a, 284) argued later that the Penn Central's failure did

191. Congress granted authority to put regulation Q ceilings on temporary stand-by for large CDs in the fall of 1966 and extended the authority several times. A staff memo prepared for the October 19 Board meeting recognized that removing the ceiling rate would improve monetary control by eliminating abrupt changes in the effect of the ceiling rate. The memo argued, however, that removing the ceilings would shift the burden of restrictive policy more

not create a crisis. Claims to the contrary required that the market was unable to distinguish between the few commercial paper issuers that had problems and those that did not. The CEA (Council of Economic Advisers, 1971, 169–78) found that few corporations suffered from a liquidity squeeze at the time. Removing regulation Q ceilings did not cause an immediate surge in bank CDs and credit, as would have been the case if demands for credit had been subject to severe restrictions.[192]

During the next few months, the Board considered several times how to conduct future lender-of-last-resort operations. Discussion centered on two supplements to discount window operations. The first would provide conduit loans; a reserve bank would lend to a member bank that would relend to a troubled corporation. The second provided direct loans to corporations under section 13 of the Federal Reserve Act. The issues included when the loans would be made, to whom, for how long, and under what restrictions.

Robertson and Brimmer opposed such lending. "Corporations that were in trouble were probably there because of their own faults. It was not up to the Federal Reserve to rescue any of them" (Maisel diary, July 2, 1970, 91). Maisel argued that the System controlled credit conditions and reserve and credit availability. It could change banks' decisions to lend by changing market conditions, and it had an obligation to prevent unnecessary failures. Mitchell supported conduit loans but opposed direct loans to corporations. Reserve bank officers were not trained to evaluate firms or their loan applications. Other members were in between.[193] After further discussion, the Board agreed unanimously to develop a contingency plan that mainly used conduit loans to supplement open market and discount operations.

The rationale for this program was not made clear. If the Federal Reserve used open market operations and discounting to increase reserves in the economy, the market distributed the reserves to banks. Discounting extended credit to banks that have collateral. There was no need for additional channels. Moreover, the discussion ignored a key political problem. Once

---

toward housing and state and local government construction, sectors it described as social priorities (memo, Staff to Board of Governors, Burns papers, Box B-B92, October 16, 1970).

192. Calomiris (1994, 50) found a significant effect of the Penn Central's problems on highest rated commercial paper issuers. These problems appear to have improved after the Federal Reserve opened the discount window.

193. Detroit's Bank of the Commonwealth had borrowed more than $100 million from the Chicago reserve bank. The reserve bank requested that it reduce the loan by $15 million for eight weeks. Bank of the Commonwealth had $1.5 billion of assets, but the requirement to repay the loan threatened its solvency at a time of heightened uncertainty. The bank had invested heavily in municipal bonds. When interest rates rose, it had large portfolio losses. The Board agreed to assist the bank "with all the money it needed to stay open" on condition that the principal stockholders leave the management and the bank commit its cash flow to increase its liquidity (Maisel diary, July 21, 1970, 95).

the Federal Reserve began to rescue banks and firms, it would be difficult to avoid pressures to bail out all large or politically connected failures.

The Board resisted these pressures later in the year when Senator Warren Magnuson, chairman of the Commerce Committee, suggested that the Federal Reserve should lend to the Penn Central to provide operating expenses. The Board approved Burns's letter rejecting the request on grounds that the Board's only authorization for direct loans, section 13b, permitted ninety-day loans on good collateral to creditworthy corporations. The Board had not used the authority since 1936 and did not believe it was the appropriate vehicle for Penn Central. Nevertheless, the letter said, there was a public interest issue, since continued operation was essential to the northeastern economy. Burns's letter endorsed legislation that provided federal guarantees of private sector loans. The proposed legislation applied only to railroads. The Board suggested broadening the program to create an Emergency Loan Guarantee Board (Board Minutes, November 24, 1970, letter, Burns to Magnuson).

Conflicts at the FOMC

Conflicts within the FOMC broke into the open at its June 23 meeting. Canada had floated its dollar on June 1. It immediately appreciated more than 3 percent and continued to rise. By December, it was 5 percent above its May value. The manager, Charles Coombs, a strong proponent of fixed exchange rates, reported that the Europeans believed that the United States was trying to force other countries to revalue to prevent a dollar devaluation. "Coombs said he felt this was terrible and that we ought to try to get everyone to agree that we should fight speculators at any cost" (Maisel diary, June 24, 1970, 82). He found no support. Trieber, substituting for Hayes, wanted to support the dollar by reducing inflation but chose to leave interest rates unchanged to achieve increased money growth.

"Mitchell raised a major attack on St. Louis" after Francis (St. Louis) opted for slower money growth (ibid., 82). Mitchell did not want to abandon money growth targets, but he criticized the short time periods that Francis used to measure growth rates. He said the six-month growth rate was 4.5 percent, an appropriate rate. The three-month rate of 9 percent that Francis used was misleading. Brimmer joined Mitchell but also attacked the framework that St. Louis used. Burns then criticized Brimmer for making public forecasts more pessimistic than internal forecasts but interpreted widely as the committee's view.[194]

---

194. Earlier Burns included "the content and circumstances of public speeches" in the guidelines for conduct (memo, Guide to conduct of System officials, Board Records, April 7,

The committee chose to concentrate on the money market and instructed the manager to keep the interest rate at or below recent levels (8 percent) and seek a 5 percent growth in M_1, slightly above the second quarter rate.

Through the summer, the Board's staff continued to forecast slow recovery, rising unemployment, but lower inflation.[195] Burns remained pessimistic about the unemployment rate and the recovery. He joined a minority including Daane, Sherrill, Maisel, and Galusha (Minneapolis) that favored money growth at 6 to 6.5 percent instead of the consensus rate of 5 percent. Francis, Hickman (Cleveland), Brimmer, and Trieber wanted 5 percent or less. They remained disturbed by fear of inflationary expectations. Kimbrel (Atlanta) and Clay (Kansas City) could not vote, but they preferred less than 5 percent money growth. Morris (Boston) and Robertson were in the middle, favoring the 5 percent money growth rate projected as consistent with prevailing money market conditions.[196] With Mitchell absent, the committee voted eleven to zero for the 5 percent growth rate. It recognized that the change in regulation Q returned more credit to the banking system, so it accepted a very high, but uncertain, growth of the bank credit proxy.

Burns wanted more stimulus. After the vote on the directive, he asked for a second vote to instruct the manager that he should not prevent money growth above 5 percent. The FOMC supported his position in a seven-to-three vote (Maisel diary, July 21, 1970, 100).[197]

Greater attention to the monetary aggregates reopened issues about measurement and control. The internal discussion gives insight on the staff's understanding. A memo to Burns discussing time deposits argued that regulation Q was powerful for controlling bank credit expansion. The memo recognized that part of the increase substituted non-bank for bank credit or conversely, but it dismissed this substitution by concluding that

---

1970). This may have been a reference to Brimmer's speeches. Evidence suggests that the two did not get along well.

195. Their forecast in July 1970 predicted unemployment at 5.8 percent and inflation at 2.8 percent in second quarter 1971. Actual unemployment was 5.9 percent, up from 5 percent at the time of the forecast. Inflation (deflator) was far away from the forecast at 7.6 percent in second quarter 1971, up 1.7 percentage points in a year. This suggests a possible large problem with the model used to forecast inflation.

196. Burns told Maisel that "the crew around the President all watched M_1. . . . They had Nixon watching week-to-week movements in the St. Louis figures and Burns had told the President to forget it. Short-term movements meant little" (Maisel diary, July 21, 1970, 99).

197. The Record of Policy Action in the Annual Report does not mention this vote. The staff proposed a definition of "even keel" as no change in Federal Reserve policy between Treasury announcement of financing terms and payment for the securities. The FOMC accepted the definition but did not inquire how it should measure Federal Reserve policy.

full offset is "extremely unlikely" (memo, A. B. Hersey to Burns, Board Records, April 17, 1970). It offered no evidence, and the staff did not all agree with the conclusion, as the memo noted. The memo failed to note that removing regulation Q ceilings would smooth adjustments instead of forcing discrete jumps and avoidance of controls through the euro-dollar, commercial paper, and other markets.

Lyle Gramley, later a Board member, explained why the staff preferred to focus on reserves instead of the monetary base. The main reason was that the base included currency, and the staff "did not know much about the sources of short-run changes in currency demand" (memo, Lyle Gramley to Burns, Board Records, March 30, 1970).[198]

Milton Friedman, Burns's long-time friend, wrote to Burns frequently, at times suggesting procedural changes to improve control of money growth. One letter criticized the use of shifting base periods from which to measure growth of monetary aggregates and proposed using an initial base period uniformly. Governor Mitchell's responses rejected that proposal because the aberrations in the data were not promptly and easily recognizable (Burns papers, Box B-K12, July 6, 1970). Later, Friedman made several suggestions to reduce variability in money growth—elimination of lagged reserve accounting, calculations of required reserves on a five-day week (instead of seven days with Fridays receiving the weight of three days), and use of staggered settlement periods with one-fifth of the banks settling each day (letter, Friedman to Burns, Burns papers, Box B-K12, August 11, 1970). The staff response dismissed Friedman's suggestions as unimportant (Stephen Axilrod to Burns, ibid., August 20, 1970).

On August 17, the Board voted reserve requirements for commercial paper issued by bank affiliates. Burns proposed that the ratio be set at 4.5 percent for both commercial paper and time deposits at banks with time deposits totaling $5 million or more. The reduction from 6 to 4.5 percent on time deposits would release $750 million from required reserves, but the new requirement for commercial paper would add $90 million. Net reserves would rise mainly at New York City banks.

Mitchell did not want to lower reserve requirements at country banks. He preferred a major reform, discussed many times before, to base reserves requirements on bank size instead of location in reserve city or

198. This is a common misstatement. The source of the monetary base is the total emission by the central bank for open market operations, gold flows, and several other, mostly minor, sources. Reserves and currency are uses of the base. The sources can be controlled completely by controlling open market operations. Shifts in currency demand can be satisfied by allowing banks to borrow or repay. For a full description of the base see Meltzer (2003, 267–70, appendix B to chapter 4).

country banks. The staff showed that about thirty country banks would have higher reserve ratios if the Board set the ratio by size of banks. Burns rejected the idea because of the political pressures that the thirty banks would generate before the November election.

All Board members except Burns did not want to announce that additional reserves would become available, so they preferred to set both requirements ratios at 5 percent. Burns resisted, but lost. The Board approved the 5 percent reserve ratio on deposits effective October 1 and on commercial paper two weeks earlier.[199] The staff estimated that the action released millions of reserves, but monthly average reserves rose much less. The Federal Reserve offset part of the addition, but it no longer held the funds rate constant, so the action was a small move toward easier policy.

The staff memo for the August 17 meeting at which the Board made its decision argued that additional stimulus was desirable because the economy was "on dead center." (Real GNP growth was 5 percent for the third quarter after −0.3 percent in the second.) The difference in existing reserve requirements (6 percent and 0) gave commercial paper a 0.5 percentage point interest rate advantage, encouraging credit expansion outside the banking system or through affiliates (memo, J. Charles Partee to Burns, Burns papers, Box B-B93, August 12, 1970).

New Efforts to Ease

The mild recession continued until November but did little to reduce inflation. There is no evidence suggesting movement along a short-run Phillips curve. In July 1970 consumer prices rose at an annualized rate of 4.1 percent. The twelve-month sustained rate, 5.7 percent, was only 0.2 percentage points lower than at the start of the recession. By the same month the unemployment rate had increased from 3.5 to 5.0 percent. Base money growth, after a brief decline, increased at a twelve-month rate of 5.5 percent. Real base growth turned positive for the first time in a year (see Chart 4.12 above). And real interest rates started to decline (see Chart 4.11 above).

Monetary indicators such as base growth and real interest rates suggested that policy had become more expansive. Those who expected the rising unemployment rate to reduce inflation were disappointed. They had

199. The Board acted under the authority granted by Congress on December 23, 1969, authorizing reserve requirements on commercial paper. The Board considered the issue several times in the nine months after Congress acted but could not agree. Part of the disagreement concerned the announcement effect of releasing reserves and the possible interpretation of the move as a step to ease policy. Usually only Robertson supported Burns. Brimmer was most opposed because he wanted a tighter policy. By June, Burns was annoyed enough by the delay to warn that the issue would continue on their agenda until it was decided.

assured themselves, and others, that a modest increase in unemployment would lower inflation. After more than six months, many began to doubt. Arthur Burns, especially, proclaimed at an FOMC meeting in June and in congressional testimony in July that the old rules no longer worked as they had before. Once a principal critic of the idea that price and wage guidelines could shift the Phillips curve, thereby changing the tradeoff between inflation and unemployment, Burns now became a prominent advocate of the need to change the short-run tradeoff. He had delivered M_1 growth of 3 to 5 percent in the first two quarters of his term and seemed to expect a more prompt response than he achieved. By the time the inflation rate began to fall, early in 1971, Burns was committed to price-wage guidelines as a necessary adjunct to monetary and fiscal policy.[200]

The CEA continued to press for expansion. In October, Paul McCracken wrote to Burns urging faster money growth to get "an increase of 12 to 13 percent in real GNP between mid-1970 and mid-1972. . . . [T]his probably means an increase of 17 to 19 percent in money GNP" (Draft letter Mc-Cracken to Burns, Paul McCracken, Box 45, Nixon papers, White House Staff Memos, October 9, 1970).[201] McCracken defended his position by claiming that the benefits of lower inflation achieved by delaying the return to full employment "would not be worth the cost" (ibid.).

At each FOMC meeting from August to November, the directive said: "promote some easing of conditions in credit markets."[202] Hayes, Brimmer, and Francis dissented in August, and Hayes dissented alone in September and October to record opposition to easier policy. Maisel dissented in November because he regarded as too low the objectives for growth of money and credit that the FOMC chose.[203]

200. Burns stopped talking about the prospects of a depression, but he continued to press for more expansion. He annoyed or angered several members in August by changing procedures in an attempt to get his way in a divided committee. The compromise called for M_1 growth of 5.5 percent and a federal funds rate of 6.5 percent, a 0.25 percentage point reduction.

201. I have not found that McCracken sent the memo, but it was typical of the recommendation that McCracken and Stein made at the time.

202. Relations between Burns and the president waxed and waned. In September the president invited Burns to join his trip to London. Burns declined because it was an election year. "Some members of the press continue to believe the Fed is under White House control" (Burns to President, Burns papers, Box B-N1, Sept. 16, 1970).

203. The inelegant term "stagflation" came into common use to describe simultaneous occurrence of unemployment and inflation. For Burns, the CEA members in the Johnson and Nixon administrations, and many others, unemployment and inflation should not coexist, at least not for long. Increased unemployment should lower inflation toward zero. This neglected the role of expectations, forcefully pointed out in Friedman (1968b), a paper well known to economists at the time. Later Brunner, Cukierman, and Meltzer (1980) pointed out that temporary efforts to restrain inflation would fail until the public became convinced that

A strike at General Motors caused additional uncertainty in October. The staff urged greater ease and lower interest rates to increase demand for housing and spending by state and local governments. The FOMC remained evenly divided, but the difference was typically small—a choice between 5 or 5.5 percent money growth. This probably understates differences of opinion because Burns, Maisel, Mitchell, and several others who pushed for 5.5 percent preferred faster growth while Hayes, Brimmer, and some others who urged 5 percent would have accepted less expansion if it had been feasible to get agreement. The first group gave priority to recession and unemployment, the second to inflation, actual and expected.[204]

Expected inflation kept long-term rates from falling. Ten-year constant maturity Treasury yields were higher during the summer and early part of 1970 than at the cyclical peak in November 1969. One proposed solution to the expectations problem was to initiate purchases of longer-term securities. This had modest support at the November meeting. A second was to lower the discount rate. The Board voted for a 5.75 percent discount rate on November 10, a 0.25 percentage point reduction. Philadelphia was most reluctant, but it joined the others on December 16. Most of the governors recognized that the move followed the short-term market. Those who favored expansion favored a 5.5 percent discount rate, but others feared announcement effects—a concern about inflationary anticipations. The expansionists prevailed three weeks later. On December 1, the Board reduced the discount rate to 5.5 percent, again following the short-term market. Burns pushed the change hard at the November 17 FOMC meeting, telling the presidents that one bank had requested 5.5 percent so "they had better make it clear to their boards of directors that the Board would shortly take up the question" (Maisel diary, November 17, 1970, 124). Presidents Hayes, Hickman (Cleveland), Eastburn (Philadelphia), and Kimbrel (Atlanta) said they did not want an additional discount rate cut, but five banks supported Burns, so the others fell in line. Bond yields declined following the discount rate changes.

At the November 17 FOMC meeting, the staff urged the members to

---

the authorities would tolerate unemployment and persist in restrictive policy until inflation ended. The movements of long-term interest rates, inflation and money wages during this recession suggest little conviction about the administration's willingness to tolerate rising (or perhaps high) unemployment as the cost of ending inflation. Repeated discussion of inflationary expectations at FOMC meetings also suggests that the public remained skeptical about the permanence of the restrictive policy, as well they should since policy was expansive. The Board's staff attributed continued high long-term interest rates to demands for credit and not to skepticism.

204. Maisel's diary (November 17, 1970, 122) describes Brimmer as saying that "we ought to take as much depression as necessary to stop prices from rising."

undertake a much more expansive policy by lowering the federal funds rate enough to get 7 to 8 percent M_1 growth in first quarter 1971. Only Mitchell, Morris, Maisel, and Burns favored the staff recommendation, but there was additional support from some non-voting members. The directive called for moderate growth in money. Maisel dissented because he wanted faster growth of money and credit.

Concerns about unemployment overcame anti-inflation policy. Successive moves toward ease lowered the federal funds rate from 7.8 percent in mid-June to 5.2 percent in late November. At year-end the rate was 4.8 percent. Long-term Treasury bonds fell much less, from 7 percent in mid-June to 6 percent at year-end. Free reserves rose to −$60 million, the highest level since early 1968. Money growth also rose; for the two halves of 1970, M_1 growth was 3.5 and 6.5 percent at annual rates.

With the end of the two-month General Motors strike, industrial production surged in December. Stock price indexes increased also, continuing the rise that began in July 1970. It took more than an additional year before the nominal S&P index surpassed its previous peak in December 1968. This suggests that the outlook for profits and expansion remained modest. The Board staff forecast called for modest growth also.

Most of the Board's academic consultants wanted more rapid growth in output and money. There was general agreement that unemployment would increase in 1971. James Duesenberry (Harvard), James Tobin (Yale), Franco Modigliani and Paul Samuelson (MIT), and Robert Gordon (Northwestern) urged the Federal Reserve to adopt a target of about 9 percent for nominal GNP growth to get 5 percent real growth. They wanted 7 to 9 percent M_1 growth whatever the interest rate might be.[205] Milton Friedman (Chicago) warned that the proposed policy would fail because inflation would increase. The result would be only 3 percent real growth and 6 percent inflation. He urged slower money growth, equivalent to less than 5 percent M_1 growth (Maisel diary, December 2, 1970, 135).

205. The belief that inflation would be lowered without a recession was held widely at the time. Governor Brimmer reported on the November 16 and 17 meeting at the OECD. The OECD's staff reported that the inflation problem affected all member countries. (They had a fixed exchange rate.) It had proved "more difficult to stem, particularly through demand-management policies, than would have seemed likely on the basis of experience in the earlier part of the 1960s. . . . A permanent and significant rise [in unemployment] would not be acceptable; nor would it necessarily be an effective barrier against inflation over the longer run" (memo, Brimmer to the FOMC, Board Records, December 4, 1970, 2). The memo then turned to the importance of lowering inflationary expectations. It concluded that "there was general agreement with the broad lines of the Secretariat's inflation report" (ibid., 3). Of course, the secretariat did not explain how countries could lower inflation expectations while acting to reduce unemployment.

Tobin's argument was close to mainstream academic views at the time. The reason he wanted 8 to 10 percent money growth was to reduce long-term rates. He made no mention of inflationary expectations preventing a decline in long-term rates or precipitating an increase on the reasonable belief that the System had abandoned its effort to reduce inflation. Instead, he urged that unemployment above 5 percent "should in the long-run bring prices down to growing by 2 percent or less. . . . Unemployment above 5 percent should cause prices to fall even as output rose" (ibid., 136).

Samuelson, Gordon, and Friedman agreed on one point: "Employment should not be sacrificed for the exchange rate parity." This was a critical point because European officials complained that as domestic interest rates fell, New York banks repaid euro-dollar credits, increasing the dollar outflow and making it difficult for them to control near-term inflation. European complaints resonated at the Board and the FOMC. The Board discussed several proposals to restrict euro-dollar repayments by offering to auction repurchase agreements with payment only in euro-dollars, or marginally lower reserve requirement ratios for banks that held euro-dollars, and other inducements to encourage banks to hold their euro-dollars. The Board made no decision at the time (ibid., 129–30).[206] A few days later, on November 30, it raised reserve requirements against future euro-dollar deposits from 10 to 20 percent and increased lending ceilings for a few banks so they would not have to repay euro-dollars. This reduced euro-dollar repayments temporarily, but it did not stop European inflation.

With Francis dissenting, the December meeting shifted back to money market conditions. The ostensible reason was that end of the strike made the monetary aggregates harder to interpret, but Daane, Hayes, and others always preferred the old procedure that gave more discretion to the manager and required less variability of short-term interest rates.

A more basic problem concerned information and timing. The manager could see the interest rate at any moment during the working day. The number was not subject to revision, seasonal adjustment, or changes in its components. The money stock was available weekly, subject to seasonal correction and revision. Furthermore, the manager knew what to do when transitory changes in currency, Treasury balances, or other variables pressed for a change in interest rates. He supplied or withdrew reserves and allowed money growth to change. If he mistook persistent changes as transitory, money growth rose. Monetary policy became more expansive

206. The U.S. payments deficit was $3 billion in the quarter and $9.8 billion for the year. Nearly 70 percent appeared as an increase in West Germany's reserves.

than intended. Targeting money growth resolved that problem in principle but created another bigger problem for the account manager—deciding how much of the money stock change to offset.

The basic problem was the difference in relevant time frames, as Axilrod's paper on the directive had recognized. The manager's time frame was the very short-term market period. The relevant period for money growth was longer because many short-term changes reversed soon after. The manager was trained to deal with all transitory market fluctuations; only the persistent changes in money growth were relevant. The manager could understand and implement an even keel policy that called for a constant market interest rate during Treasury financing. He supplied any addition to reserves that the market demanded. No one told him exactly how to implement even keel policy with a money growth target. Keeping reserve or money growth constant was not a close substitute for the manager.

The proviso clause attempted to solve the problem by letting the manager adjust for persistent deviations in money growth from a chosen path. He never developed the requisite tools or procedures, and the FOMC did not supply them. The FOMC debated actively whether it wanted money growth at 4.5 or 5 percent, but it spent almost no time on implementation.

Despite these unresolved problems, the manager came close to the preferred growth rates at quarterly frequency. Table 4.10 shows forecast and actual growth rates reported in the FOMC transcripts for the period in 1970 when the FOMC set money growth targets and the revised growth rates reported subsequently. Except for the third quarter, when the Board suspended regulation Q ceiling rates for thirty to eighty-nine days on CDs over $100,000, the manager maintained quarterly money growth rates close to forecast where we have comparable data.

The monetary forecasts were more accurate than the inflation forecasts. The staff predicted inflation of 3.9 in 1970. Actual inflation was 5.1 percent (Lombra and Moran, 1980, 21).

The year ended with further evidence of the division within the Board between those who wanted more expansive policies to reduce unemployment and those who wanted less to reduce inflation. As market rates fell, Boston requested an additional discount rate reduction, to 5.25 percent in late December. The Board declined, partly responding to the discontent of the New York officers and directors over the two previous reductions. The reduction to 5.25 percent was made early in January 1971 (Maisel diary, December 21, 1970, 149).[207]

---

207. At year-end, the Board also considered steps it might take to encourage banks not to let euro-dollar holdings decline. The Board had tried exhortation with modest success. Inter-

Table 4.10 Predicted and Actual Money Growth 1970 (percent)

DATE	FORECAST M$_1$	FOR PERIOD	REPORTED RATE	REVISED[a] RATE
February 10	3–4	Q1		
March 10	2	Q1		3.6
	3	Q2		
April 7	3	Q2		
May 5	4	Q2		
May 26	7	Q2		
	4	Q3		
June 23		Q1	3.8	3.5
	4.5	Q2		
July 21	5	Q3		
August 18		Q2	4.2	3.8
	4–5	Q3		
September 15	5	Q4		
October 20	5	Q4		
November 17		Q3	5	8
	4	Q4		
December 15		Q4	5	5

[a]St. Louis Reserve Bank data base.

The main reason for the January 7 reduction in the discount rate was that the Board followed the market down. Between December 20 and January 7 open market rates had declined so that "almost all boards of directors agreed that it was a proper move simply keeping up with the market" (Maisel diary, January 13, 1971, 4). Soon after, Boston asked for another reduction to 5, again following market rates down. The Board hesitated because it was only eight days since the previous changes. Nevertheless, the gap between the discount rate and the market rate was wider than eight days earlier. Those who opposed agreed that if market rates declined further, the change would be appropriate. "While we were still debating . . . [One of the staff] brought in a ticker item indicating that the prime rate had been moved down by Citibank" (ibid., January 15, 1971, 15). The Board reduced the discount rate to 5 percent effective January 19 at seven reserve banks. The others soon followed.

Market rates continued to fall. Effective February 13, the Board reduced the discount rate for the fourth time in three months. The rate was now 4.75 percent, one percentage point lower than in mid-November. The initial vote was four to two, with Sherrill absent. After further reflection the vote was unanimous.[208]

---

est rates had fallen in the United States both absolutely and relative to Europe. Hence banks reduced euro-dollar borrowing, increasing the capital outflow. The Board discussed some proposals to subsidize banks that held euro-dollars, but it did not adopt any.

208. Initially, Daane dissented for balance of payments reasons. He left the meeting to

PRESSURES FOR WAGE-PRICE POLICY

Shortly after Arthur Burns became Federal Reserve chairman, he began to talk publicly about wage-price policy. As time passed, qualifications about possible ineffectiveness disappeared from his speeches, and institutional mechanisms took a larger role. It seems odd that Burns would abandon his long-standing opposition to wage-price policies, particularly since the change occurred within a few months of his accession to the chairmanship. He noted that unemployment had increased but wage rates and commodity prices continued to rise. Burns had spent his life as an empirical economist, but he offered little evidence to support his position that the economy had changed. An alternative explanation was that the so-called natural rate of unemployment had increased from the 4 percent level assumed at the time. Orphanides (2003a, 656–59) makes this argument persuasively.

His new belief was that so-called cost-push inflation, resulting either from union pressures or more general social pressures, was a new source of inflation and inflation bias. Burns (1978, 92–93) at first joined those who attributed the bias to "social aspirations" for high employment, sustained growth, and rising government spending. A main difficulty with this reasoning was that the Eisenhower-Martin policies in 1959 had brought inflation near zero in 1961–62. Thereafter, inflation remained low for several years. The cost was a peak unemployment rate of 7.1 percent. Both Nixon and Burns believed that this policy cost Richard Nixon electoral victory in 1960. Both wanted to avoid repetition in 1970 and especially in 1972. Burns was reluctant to repeat the experience. The reason was entirely political.

> In February 1961, economic expansion resumed and the administration's expectation of an early upturn was vindicated; but before this happened, *the nation's electorate decided in a close presidential election to entrust power to the Democratic party.* (ibid.; emphasis added)

Burns later offered an explanation of his changed view.

> An effort to offset, through monetary and fiscal restraints, all of the upward push that rising costs are now exerting on prices would be most unwise. Such an effort would restrict aggregate demand so severely as to increase

---

speak to Treasury Undersecretary Paul Volcker, who said "it would be good for balance of payments reasons for Daane to dissent . . . [but] would not be good for domestic reasons. He would get himself into trouble with the Administration. Therefore, it was up to him to decide for himself." The other dissent was from Brimmer, who did not want to remain the sole dissenter (Maisel diary, February 23, 1971, 23).

greatly the risks of a very serious business recession. If that happened, the outcries of an enraged citizenry would probably soon force the government to move rapidly and aggressively toward fiscal and monetary ease, and our hopes of getting the inflationary problem under control would then be shattered. (Burns, 1978, 98)

Burns did not simply opt for the neo-Keynesian position of the Kennedy-Johnson or Nixon CEAs. He rejected their idea that a slight reduction in growth would lower inflation. He thought he had to avoid as counterproductive a "serious business recession." Although in May he recognized that at home and abroad wage-price or income policies "have achieved relatively little success" (ibid., 99), he soon dropped that cautionary note. By December, and perhaps before, he no longer mentioned past lack of success. His suggestion was to establish a "high-level price and wage review board which, while lacking enforcement power, would have broad authority to investigate, advise, and recommend" (ibid., 114).

In a December speech, Burns explained his new reason for choosing incomes policy. "We are dealing, practically speaking, with a new problem— namely persistent inflation in the face of substantial unemployment—and that the classical remedies may not work well enough *or fast enough* in this case" (ibid., 114–15; emphasis added). To amplify "fast enough," Burns referred to "the limits of our national patience" (ibid., 115). Further, the problem was not due to excess demand; it resulted from rising wage demands that raised costs and prices.

McCracken and Stein at the CEA emphasized what Burns now neglected—that income policies of various kinds had failed everywhere they had been tried in the 1960s. But they made no response to Burns's main political point—that the public would not accept a sizeable increase in unemployment to reduce inflation substantially. Nor did they say that the administration would accept responsibility for whatever unemployment rate was required to bring inflation down. When they spoke about unemployment, they wanted more monetary growth, not less.

The public's concern about inflation waxed and waned with the unemployment rate. When inflation was relatively high and unemployment relatively low, public opinion showed support for anti-inflation policy. Once recession started, unemployment became a more important concern for the public and their representatives in Congress. This shifting lexico-graphic ordering of priorities continued through the 1970s.

Pressure for administration action on wages and prices came from many quarters. Large corporations with a unionized labor force wanted the government to "discipline" labor. Many groups complained about the construction unions.[209] Business hoped that government policy would control wages more than prices, eliminating or reducing what they regarded as cost-push inflation. Labor union spokesmen argued for better control of price increases that eroded nominal wage gains. The Democratic Policy Council, chaired by Gardner Ackley, wanted more stimulus and wage-price guidelines. Congress added to this pressure in August 1970 by authorizing the president to impose formal wage-price controls at his discretion.

As several economists noted at the time and afterward, there was little theoretical foundation and no empirical support for wage-price policies as a way of reducing the loss of employment (see especially Laidler and Parkin, 1975). The response to such criticisms was to insist that ideological bias was the principal, and perhaps the only, explanation of the unwillingness of the president and his economic advisers to embrace such policies. Burns, and most other proponents, did not address the issue of how guideposts and guidelines could be enforced.[210] What would happen if unions, workers, and firms did not follow the guidelines? The Kennedy and Johnson administrations used sanctions and threats of reprisal to punish offenders, often with little effect. How could a wage-price board survive if it had no power to enforce its standards?[211]

Burns's speeches added the voice of a conservative economist and a close adviser of the president to the rising demand to do something more

209. Burns (1978, 112) mentions a 7 percent average rate of increase in compensation for 1970 and a 10 percent increase in wages in newly negotiated contracts with inflation in the 5 percent range. But construction unions received a 16 percent average rate of increase over the life of the contract and 22 percent in the first year. Burns blamed "speculative exuberance" for some of the changes (ibid., 104).

210. Some writers proposed changing taxes selectively to enforce guidelines.

211. None of these criticisms of guideposts or a review board surprised Burns. He heard them frequently from George Shultz, Herbert Stein, and Paul McCracken. Stein's notes for a meeting with Burns accuse Burns of "contributing to the common idea that there is a simple way out of our economic difficulties which the Administration for some mysterious reason refuses to take" (Stein, Notes for Discussion with AFB, Nixon papers, WHCF, Box 34, Agencies Files, December 11, 1970, 3). He accused Burns also of frightening the public "without firm evidence about the inflationary consequences of an expansive policy" (ibid., 1). But he did not ask for monetary restraint. Instead he said: "We intend to get a strong recovery of the economy and believe that a strong recovery can be achieved while continuing to make progress on the inflation front," (ibid.). We don't have Burns's response, but we know he dismissed such statements. Shultz had sponsored a conference in the 1960s, edited a volume, and concluded that guidelines could not work without enforcement (Shultz and Aliber, 1966). He had not changed his mind in government (Shultz, 2003, 3). He described a meeting of the Business Council, made up of CEOs of major corporations. He opposed guidelines in his speech. "The CEOs railed against me, took a vote and only two opposed controls" (ibid.).

to reduce inflation while lowering the cost of doing so.[212] As pressure mounted from Burns, Congress, some academicians, and many business-men, the administration retreated. In December 1970, the president an-nounced steps to roll back an oil price increase by importing more oil from Canada, and he proposed steps to centralize bargaining in the construction industry. In January, he pressured the steel companies to reduce a price increase from 12 to 6 percent. In February, he suspended the Davis-Bacon Act, which required union wages on government construction projects whether or not workers were unionized. The interpretation of the law at the time shows the confusion between high wages and rising wages. The government could reduce its construction costs by suspending Davis-Bacon. Any effect on inflation would be limited to the financing of a smaller budget deficit. Pressures to do more continued to build.[213]

At about this time, the president announced that John Connally, a con-servative Democrat, would become Secretary of the Treasury. Connally was much more forceful than the incumbent, David Kennedy, and had greater concern for the political process. Most comments noted that Connally did not have preset positions or commitment to any particular beliefs about economic policy. He is often quoted as saying "I can sell it square or I can sell it round," conveying that he would implement whatever policy the president wanted and would not be bound by the administration's re-luctance to use wage-price policies. Among the strengths he brought to the administration were a bipartisan appeal, a forceful personality, and an excellent ability to handle press conferences effectively. He became the ad-ministration's spokesman on economic policy and a favorite among many of the president's advisers other than Burns.

Arthur Burns spoke frequently and testified in Congress, advocating a review board for prices and wages. The entire Board of Governors voted several times to support some type of incomes policy and a review board (Board Minutes, February 17, 1971, and March 30, 1971). At the time, and in retrospect, claims proved wrong that guideposts could work without

212. Some in the administration suggested that Burns's conversion to guidelines was taken to gain support among congressional Democrats (Matusow, 1998, 71).

213. Press speculation at the time suggested that Burns had agreed to a more expansive monetary policy in exchange for President Nixon's agreement to adopt guidelines (New York Times, December 9, 1970, 93). Burns explained to the Board that he had not made any com-mitments and the president had not asked for any (Maisel diary, December 9, 1970, 142). The president had taken several previous steps to reduce wage increases in the construction industry and had acted to lower meat prices in the winter of 1970 (Matusow, 1998, 65–67). Wells (1994, 40 n51) claims that the president's earlier reluctance to challenge construction workers' wage increases reflected their support of his policy in Vietnam.

any enforcement other than the president's "bully pulpit." When the subject came up, President Nixon cited the difficulties he encountered as a young lawyer administering World War II price controls to explain why he did not want the country to repeat that experience. Pressures to do something more about inflation without increasing unemployment remained and grew. As the election approached, price and wage controls grew more appealing to him. The Democrats in Congress had challenged him to use controls, certain that he would not. He expected them to use his unwillingness as a campaign issue; they would claim that he could have lowered inflation with less unemployment if he had not rejected guideposts or controls for ideological reasons.

The approaching election was important, but it was not the only factor. Administration economists were disappointed by the very limited progress toward lower inflation. Paul McCracken described a view that others shared: "If you look[ed] at the rates of increases in hourly earnings and compensation . . . , those weren't showing the kind of deceleration that we would have pointed to as evidence that the strategy was working" (Hargrove and Morley, 1984, 344). Twelve-month hourly earnings rose 6.35 percent in January 1969, when the administration took office; two years later the rate of increase was 6.16 percent.

McCracken explained that President Nixon did not believe that guideposts would work. "In the early part of 1971, I can recall him saying, 'we're not going to go to an incomes policy. You and I know that won't work anyway. If I have to go, I'll go all the way.'"[214]

Those who favored the policy of gradual disinflation without wage-price policy lost ground in the spring of 1971. They could point to progress, but real growth remained slow, inflation relatively high, and unemployment at 6 percent. In July and August 1971, industrial production was about where it had been when the administration took office in January 1969. Consumer price inflation had fallen from its peak, above 6 percent, but remained above 4 percent. Private sector hourly earnings growth showed little change.

At a Quadriad meeting in June, McCracken told the president that the administration's policies had reached a critical juncture. After describing

214. William Safire (1975, 587), a presidential speech writer, says the president made the statement at a cabinet meeting on March 26, 1971. McCracken presented some alternative policies, including a review board as proposed by Burns. "The President gave a clear indication that he would not move halfway. . . . 'The idea of a wage-price review board is wrong,' Nixon told his Cabinet flatly. 'I will not go for something so temporary. Either we bite the bullet or else.'" President Nixon often used a football metaphor to express his views. He did not want "four yards and a cloud of dust." He wanted to throw the long pass (McCracken in Hargrove and Morley, 1984, 345).

the slow and uncertain progress to date, McCracken wrote: "With no joy, I have concluded that we must even be prepared at a suitable time to invoke wage and price controls" (McCracken to the president, Nixon papers, June 14, 1971).

Burns had, of course, reached the conclusion about the need for wage-price policy much earlier. He told the president that "it is doubtful we have made any progress in moderating the pace of inflation" (letter, Burns to the president, Burns papers, Box B-B90, June 22, 1971, 1). Burns explained why he believed administration policy could not succeed. Workers were less concerned about prolonged unemployment and businessmen about a sustained decline in sales. "Wage and price decisions are now being made on the assumption that governmental policy will move promptly to check a sluggish economy" (ibid., 2). He went on to cite other factors such as public sector unions, expansion of welfare programs, and firm expectations that inflation would persist.

After repeating his proposal for a wage-price review board, Burns added for the first time: "in the event of insufficient success . . . [it should be] followed—perhaps no later than next January—by a six month wage and price freeze" (ibid., 8). Burns added that with controls in place, confidence would improve, inflationary psychology would abate, "and perhaps leave elbow room for a more stimulative fiscal policy to hasten the decline of unemployment" (ibid., 9). This last suggestion spoke directly to President Nixon's main electoral concern—not inflation but unemployment.[215] Meeting with the president a week later, Burns drove home the point. He warned the president that it was too late to increase spending or change tax rates, and he urged the president to freeze prices and wages.

> You've got to get at the inflation problem to get the economy going. . . . I am uncertain that any fiscal solution can do any good at this stage." (White House tapes, conversation 531-16, June 28, 1971)

The president responded by rejecting proposals for a price-wage freeze. Less than two months before the wage-price freeze, he rejected controls. But he left an opening to change his mind.

> I am not going to—and this is against all the recommendations that I take very much to heart—I am not going to go on the wage-price board, and I'm

215. Burns added: "My omission of any reference to a more stimulative monetary policy is deliberate. Monetary policy, I feel, has done its job fully" (letter, Burns to the president, Burns papers, Box B-B90, June 22, 1971, 9). The letter referred to Burns's presentation at the June 14 Quadriad meeting.

not to go on the wage-price freeze. . . . I'm not going to say never . . . but I've
got to indicate, Arthur, that right now this is what we're going to do. (ibid.)

He urged Burns to support his position, but Burns declined. He told the
president that when he testified the following week, he would have to remain consistent with what he had said many times.

The president repeated this message firmly to the cabinet a few days
later, but accepted "jawboning," as he told Burns he would. Then he warned
them not to disagree. As he often said, "there must be certainty." And he
told them that Connally was the spokesman. "Everybody in this room will
follow the line announced by the Secretary of the Treasury" (Haldeman,
1994, 308).

Less than a month later, the president met with John Connally and Peter
Peterson, his assistant for international economic policy. Connally proposed wage and price controls, closing the gold window, floating the currency, and shocking the system out of its current lethargy. He had talked
to Shultz, who agreed. Peterson suggested an export rebate. The president
urged that the proposals be kept secret, known only to Connally, Peterson,
McCracken, Burns, and Shultz. He was most anxious to get Burns's agreement because he did not want him to criticize the program publicly, and he
knew that Burns opposed closing the gold window and floating the dollar
(White House tapes, conversation 547-9, July 27, 1971).

By August 2, the new policy was set. A major change replaced the proposed export rebate with a 10 percent import tax and the addition of some
fiscal measures, including a 7 percent investment tax credit (Haldeman,
1994, 340). They set no date, but the earlier discussion suggested a delay,
perhaps until January, in case the program developed problems.

The president shifted position. He now opposed *permanent* wage and
price controls (White House tapes, conversation 67-11, August 5, 1971).
Soon after timing became firm, Connally called from his vacation in Texas
to warn the president, according to Haldeman, that "we had a bad day in
the gold market yesterday and another bad day today, and he anticipates
a really bad one tomorrow. . . . There's no panic, but it is getting worse
and worse, and we're losing the initiative" (Haldeman, 1994, 340). He
returned to Washington, met with the president who decided to "go ahead
on the whole move on Monday" (ibid.) after spending the weekend at Camp
David with Burns and key Treasury and economic officials to work out the
details.

The actual gold loss was small compared to 1968. By March 1971 the
gold stock had fallen $1 billion from a local peak of $11.9 billion in September 1970. Following the German decision to float the mark in April,

the gold stock declined by $500 million through July. In August, the gold loss was $250 million. As Connally recognized, the greater the decline in the stock, the more likely others would convert dollars into gold.

AFTER THE RECESSION

The National Bureau chose November 1970 as the end of the recession, but the auto strike makes the timing uncertain. Industrial production surged 27 percent (annual) rate in December, but part of the surge made up for strike-related declines in October and November. January 1971 had a 9.2 percent increase, before production fell in February and March. The twelve-month average rate of increase did not become positive until May.

Real GNP fell in fourth quarter 1970, rose 11.2 percent (annual rate) in first quarter 1971 but was stagnant in the second quarter. The unemployment rate remained at 5.9 or 6 percent throughout the spring and summer, and the S&P 500 average did not increase until July. For an administration that had been willing to tolerate unemployment of no more than 4.5 percent to reduce inflation, the outcome suggested failure.

The data support those who claimed the recovery was sluggish. The deflator was even more discouraging, rising at 6.7 and 7.6 percent annual rates in the first two quarters of 1971. And despite the slow growth, the current account deficit increase added to the general sense that administration policies were not solving the nation's problems. Monetary base growth rose in the spring of 1971, and the Federal Reserve increased the federal funds rate beginning in April 1971. The monthly average rate reached a cyclical low of 3.7 percent in March. By July, the rate was 5.3 percent.

As the year 1971 started, the administration recognized that something more had to be done to lower the unemployment rate to 5 percent or less in time for the 1972 presidential election (Maisel diary, January 13, 1971, 3). President Nixon adopted an unbalanced budget with a $15 billion projected deficit. The actual deficit was $23 billion. Like President Kennedy in 1962, his advisers brought him to accept the full employment budget deficit, not the actual deficit, as a proper measure of fiscal position. To make his conversion clear, the president announced that "we are all Keynesians now." The president's advisers explained to Burns that they had to run a large deficit because money growth was not sufficient (Maisel diary, June 13, 1971, 3).

At a meeting with the president's economic advisers, Maisel asked for the administration's forecast for 1971. Although the official forecast called for GNP to reach $1065 million by the fourth quarter, Herbert Stein privately expressed considerable skepticism. He expected that a fiscal policy that produced the $15 billion deficit they planned would bring nominal

GNP to $1050 million, not $1065.[216] To get to $1065, Stein explained, would require more expansive monetary policy, but he was "unwilling to specify what monetary policy they believed was necessary to get on this path" (ibid., 13).

President Nixon was not so constrained. At meetings with his principal advisers, he brought up monetary policy repeatedly, often questioned Burns's commitment to the administration's objectives, and made threatening statements.[217] He urged Secretary Connally to find "an opponent of Arthur Burns" to fill the next vacancy (Ehrlichman notes, Box 5, July 9 and 20, 1970). The president was upset particularly by Burns's statements about a wage-price review board. At one time, he refused to have further contact.[218]

The first half of 1971 was an example of how not to conduct monetary policy operations. The System had several objectives, and the members had different priorities. Some expressed greatest concern about inflation; some gave more attention to unemployment and slow economic growth; some wanted to lower money growth to bring down inflation or respond to the growing balance of payments deficit and complaints from abroad; some wanted to shift emphasis back to money market conditions; and some wanted tighter control of money growth or monetary aggregates. With the FOMC divided along several dimensions, agreement could be obtained only, if at all, by making small changes that accomplished none of the objectives. Adding to the System's woes were administration complaints that unemployment and inflation were both too high and, if they were receding, they were doing so much too slowly.

Members of the administration blamed the Federal Reserve for the unsatisfactory outcome. Relations declined. Federal Reserve meetings with the Treasury or the CEA became infrequent or ended temporarily. Burns's insistence on advocating price-wage guidelines, with Board support, exacerbated the bad feeling.

216. The $1065 forecast was based on work by the new chief economist at the Office of Management and Budget, Arthur Laffer. Work at the CEA (and elsewhere) cast doubt on his methods and results.

217. John Ehrlichman's handwritten notes of these meetings contain many statements such as "time to take the Fed on," "give Fed a good kick," or "I'll unload on him." Ehrlichman was Domestic Policy Adviser in the White House. The president was less belligerent when he spoke directly to Burns. In a White House tape, Nixon says, "I think that interest rates going down . . . would be something most people would appreciate. People are saying there just isn't enough demand for money." Burns responded that they needed to increase money growth but that faster money growth does not guarantee increased spending (White House tapes, conversation 454-4, February 19, 1971).

218. Entirely apart from Burns's relationship to the White House, the administration had no meetings of sub-cabinet and Federal Reserve officials (the junior Quadriad) from the summer of 1969 to 1971.

Without much understanding of why inflation declined very slowly and unemployment remained unchanged, many accepted that the problem came from cost-push. Those taking this position could point to unemployment, or the gap between actual and potential output, to persuade themselves that inflation could not result from excess demand. Hence, they said, it must come from unions and large corporations exerting their monopoly power. They recognized that long-term interest rates remained high, and even rose. They attributed that to increased credit market borrowing and did not connect increased borrowing to expected inflation. They recognized that the balance of payments deficit had increased. They attributed the increase to an overvalued dollar, and they saw the balance of payments and the exchange rate as entirely administration problems, reflecting mainly large fiscal deficits.

As in the Great Depression, the Board and the FOMC lacked a coherent framework and a coherent explanation of what was happening. By this time the staff had a multi-equation econometric model, but there is not much to indicate that it had an important influence on decisions. Although FOMC members recognized that inflation and unemployment would not be greatly changed in the near-term by their decisions, they continued to operate from meeting to meeting making (usually) small adjustments. Only Maisel and Brimmer proposed working out a consistent, coherent program and agreeing on a sustained policy. Most of the members did not support them.

The problem was easier for market participants. As the minutes noted on several occasions, they observed money growth and the budget deficit. They observed also that both the administration and the Federal Reserve were unwilling to accept a temporary rise in unemployment sufficient to bring down inflation. To the contrary, policy actions showed what policymakers' words often denied; they would accept inflation, even higher inflation, to bring the unemployment rate down in time for the election. President Nixon was often explicit about his belief that incumbents lost elections because of unemployment, not inflation.

What was true of the group of policymakers was not true of all of its members. Within the administration, views differed not only about the policy but about whether it was working. These differences would, at times, become public. That too contributed to the uncertainty about what would be done.

Table 4.11 gives an indication of policy and market actions in the first half of 1971. Most of the time after March, the FOMC was torn between preventing high money growth and permitting interest rates to rise. In the spring, the committee wanted to act against the wider spread between

Table 4.11   Interest Rates, Money Growth, and Inflation January–July 1971 (percent)

MONTH	MONEY GROWTH (1)	FEDERAL FUNDS (2)	5-YEAR TREASURIES (3)	SPREAD 3–2 (4)	MONTHLY CPI INFLATION
January	7.8	4.14	5.89	1.75	1.0
February	8.9	3.72	5.56	1.84	2.0
March	7.2	3.71	5.00	1.29	4.0
April	7.1	4.15	5.65	1.50	4.0
May	10.9	4.63	6.28	1.65	6.0
June	7.6	4.91	6.53	1.62	6.9
July	8.0	5.31	6.85	1.54	3.0

Source: Board of Governors (1981).

short- and intermediate- or long-term rates, but it was uncertain whether that required more monetary expansion or less. It decided to purchase intermediate-term securities, briefly lowering their rates and narrowing the spread, as shown in the table. Annualized consumer price inflation rose until July, but the unemployment rate remained either 5.9 or 6 percent throughout.

Early in the year, the System considered two issues. First, money growth had slowed in fourth quarter 1970. Should the System compensate by expanding more rapidly in the first quarter? Second, should it reduce the discount rate to follow market rates down? Or would that signal imply that the Federal Reserve had ended its anti-inflation policy?

Burns warned that the "administration's confidence in the System was weakening as a result of the shortfalls that had occurred in the rates of money growth. He was not concerned so much about the loss of System prestige and credibility as he was about the possible impact on other government policies" (FOMC Minutes, January 12, 1971, 37). The reference is to the president's announcement that he was not concerned about the actual budget deficit as long as the budget remained balanced at an assumed full employment. Burns argued that to restore credibility, the FOMC should ease to make up the shortfall in money growth. Charles Partee, director of the Division of Research and Statistics, supported his chairman by arguing that "the existing slack was so great that reducing it was not likely at this point to add to inflationary pressures" (ibid., 27).[219] Data revisions later showed that the slack was much smaller than Partee believed.

The FOMC wanted 5.5 percent M_1 growth. To make up the shortfall, Burns wanted 7.5 percent growth in first quarter 1971 and 6 percent for

219. This was a strange argument from a staff that used a Phillips curve relating unemployment and inflation to forecast inflation.

the year.[220] The committee divided. The compromise called for reducing the federal funds rate from 4.5 to 4.25 percent, a shift back to money market conditions with the expectation that money growth would increase at lower interest rates. The vote was eleven to one, with Francis (St. Louis) dissenting because he wanted 5 percent money growth. Maisel recorded that the actual division was much wider. Francis, Eastburn (Philadelphia), and Clay (Kansas City) wanted a more restrictive policy to reduce inflation. The latter two were not voting members at the time. But Swan (San Francisco), Trieber (New York), Heflin (Richmond), and Robertson shared this view. Galusha (Minneapolis) and Morris (Boston), usually joined Maisel and Mitchell in supporting faster money growth. At the January meeting, Brimmer joined this group. That left only a few voting members in the middle with Burns.

Between January and July, the Board approved four changes in the discount rate: three reductions and one increase. Generally, it followed bank rates such as the prime rate or open market rates. On three occasions, it rejected requests for a change in the discount rate. All changes were 0.25 percentage points.

Maisel reports that on several occasions Daane talked to Undersecretary Volcker before voting. Volcker usually voiced his opinion but could only give a Treasury opinion if he spoke to Secretary Connally. Burns disliked Connally, envied his position with the president, and did not want the Board to consult him. Furthermore, he did not want more input and influence from the administration than he already had. The decisive facts in February were that, although the discount rate typically followed the market rate, market rates had fallen steeply, and eleven of the twelve banks had voted for lower rates.

On May 6, the New York directors responded in a classic way to the large outflow of dollars and the decisions by West Germany, Switzerland, Belgium, Netherlands, and Austria to allow their exchange rates to float. New York explained its request for a 0.5 percentage point increase in its discount rate (to 5.25 percent) as a signal to foreign countries that the United States intended to defend the fixed exchange rate system. Coombs (special manager) wanted Germany to maintain its exchange rate and use exchange controls (Maisel diary, May 7, 1971, 37). This seems rather late in the day for a decision to begin using monetary policy to defend the dollar exchange rate.

Although Burns told Nixon that the United States would not practice

220. Maisel reports that Burns believed the manager was too much influenced by the New York bank (Maisel diary, January 12, 1971, 5).

"benign neglect" of the balance of payments, he did not urge the Board to raise discount rates. He warned the president that short-term rates would rise, but he thought this action would lower long rates (Ehrlichman notes, Box 5, April 14, 1971). The president gave his view earlier. He told Burns, "You are not going to sit there and save the dollar and let the country go to hell" (White House tapes, conversation 462-13, March 5, 1971).

The Board preferred to have New York withdraw the request, leaving no record. By telephone, New York explained that its directors supported Coombs's negotiations with the West Germans and preferred to have the request rejected. The four Board members present voted to reject the request.

The next month, June, the Board approved an increase in the discount rate to 5 percent effective July 16. Continuous high unemployment was the main reason given by those who wanted to reject the June requests. The surge in inflation in May and June (Table 4.11 above) and sustained high money growth convinced Burns and others to show independence by signaling their concern about current and prospective inflation.

Burns valued the Federal Reserve's independence, but neither he nor others on the Board believed that independence permitted them to work against administration policy. They could criticize and suggest alternatives. As we know, Burns worked actively to change the president's opposition to an incomes, or wage-price, policy. He offered advice on a wide range of other policies, but he complained about the pressure he received from the administration about money growth.

Maisel's discussion of independence elaborated the view established since Sproul and Martin.

> It is up to the President and Congress to determine the national economic goals. While the President is considering these goals, it is proper for the Federal Reserve Board through the chairman or individuals in their speeches to point out the logical policies as they see them to deal with the question of trade-offs, the problem of whether a path is too rapid or too slow, and similar matters. . . .
>
> However, if the Congress and the President agree on the national economic goals then it seems clear that the Federal Reserve has to agree to furnish the necessary sums of money and credit. . . . [E]ven in this case, the Federal Reserve as an independent agency has to make its own determination of how monetary policy can best hope to achieve its goals, but there is a commitment by the Federal Reserve System to help achieve these goals and not try to impose its own goals or to sabotage the goals set by the rest of the government in any form. (Maisel diary, January 14, 1971, 11)

This statement elaborated on "independence within the government, not independence of the government." Like earlier statements, it left open the choice of interest rate (or money growth) at which the Federal Reserve would direct its actions to achieve the politically agreed objectives. And it was the rate of money growth that was an almost constant issue between Burns and the president or his staff and advisers. Burns's "clear feeling which he has expressed that the President has gone all out to be re-elected in 1972. As a result he has subordinated inflation control to this idea" (ibid., 10).[221]

Meeting alone with the president in March 1971, Burns complained about leaks from the administration to the press complaining about him and Federal Reserve policy. Then he insisted on his loyalty to the president. They discussed monetary policy in a way that is hard to reconcile with Federal Reserve independence.

> I am a dedicated man to serve the health and strength of our national economy and I have done everything in my power, as I see it, to help you as president, your reputation and standing in American life and history. I've never seen a conflict between the two, but I want you to know this . . . the moment a conflict arises, I'm going to be right here. I'll tell you about it, and we'll talk it out and try to decide together where to go next. (White House tapes, conversation 470-18, March 19, 1971)

He told the president that interest rates were lower, 3.2 percent compared to 8.1 percent a year earlier. They could be reduced more but, he told the president, "We run the risk of accelerating an international monetary crisis." Then he turned to domestic policy.

> If interest rates go down further through my actions . . . the probability, as I see it, is that they will go up later in the year. In 1972, housing, which is recovering very nicely, would go into a tailspin in 1972. Where would we be as a country, as a party, and you personally? I think it is stupid. (ibid.)

The president talked about their long relationship and urged Burns to meet with Connally. Then he added:

> The key to this is first you [Burns] and I stand close together, which we will do. Second, on the Quadriad that . . . [we] knock down discord. . . . I don't mean that you have to get to 3 percent unemployment.

221. Chairman Burns testified before the Joint Economic Committee that the FOMC "would make all the money necessary to ratify the $1,065 [million] goal," although they doubted that it would happen (ibid., 24). Arthur Laffer's forecast of $1,065 assumed 6 percent money growth. Burns statement was a commitment to inflation if necessary that he probably did not intend.

Burns replied, "The direction has to be right" (idem.).

Faced with the pressure from the administration, Burns and the FOMC yielded. Money growth remained above the level that would reduce inflation and above the rate that they set. The FOMC raised its federal funds rate target gradually in 1971 (Table 4.11 above) but not enough to slow money growth. As in many committee actions, no single motive can explain the result. Some may have wished to support the president's goals; some put greater weight on unemployment than inflation; some went along with the chairman or the majority; and some hoped that they would avoid the consequences or reverse their actions before inflation rose. Those holding the last of these views thought that with unemployment above 4 percent, inflation would not increase because of the slack in the economy, and if it did increase, it resulted from cost-push, not from anything they did.

At the February FOMC meeting the directive called for "resumption of sustainable long-term economic growth, while encouraging the orderly reduction in the rate of inflation and the attainment of reasonable equilibrium in the country's balance of payments" (Annual Report, 1971, 124). What concerned the members most was whether to lower the federal funds rate by 0.5 percentage points to get money to grow faster than the 6 percent proposed for the year. Hayes, Brimmer, Daane, Robertson, and Francis opposed the reduction. Burns expressed concern "about the political pressure the Board would be under if we didn't get a 6 percent growth rate and, therefore, felt that we had to make up for shortages" (Maisel diary, February 10, 1971, 21). The compromise was to keep the 3.75 percent funds rate for a week; if money growth was below the 6 percent path at the end of the week, the funds rate would be reduced to 3.5 percent. They agreed to call a special meeting if money growth was below the target after two additional weeks. Only Francis dissented because, as before, he did not want money growth above 5 percent. To reduce intermediate- and long-term rates, the FOMC instructed the manager to purchase coupon issues.[222]

Money growth rose, so the federal funds rate remained unchanged on average in March. Yields on intermediate-term Treasuries moved down sharply. Much of the move was probably a speculative response to sizable System purchases that soon reversed (Table 4.11). Long-term yields rose slightly. The minutes explain higher yields on corporate and municipal new issues as a response to the "heavy calendar of new offerings" and

222. Burns asked Maisel how the committee could control the manager. The manager "was more concerned about day-to-day movements in the money market" (Maisel diary, February 10, 1971, 22). Maisel suggested setting a reserve growth target with an interest rate proviso clause. The FOMC did not make this change.

made no mention of borrowing to anticipate higher inflation (Annual Report, 1971, 128).

FOMC members could not agree about the response of long-term rates to higher short-term rates. Some thought an increase in short-term rates would lower long-term rates; others argued that long-term rates would rise (ibid., 129–30). The Board's Annual Report showed a unanimous vote for no change. Maisel (diary, March 12, 1971, 28) reported the actual vote as eight to four, with the minority in favor of tightening. Burns got unanimity by putting a very wide band, plus or minus 4 percent, on money growth.

The March meeting reopened an old issue, bankers' concerns versus political or national policy. Daane said that at Basel "the central bankers . . . were very much concerned with the ease of money here" (Maisel diary, March 12, 1971, 26). Soon afterward, "Brimmer, Holmes [the manager], and Kimbrel [Atlanta], all indicated that they were told by their banker friends as well as some other observers that we were moving too fast. Interest rates were too low. The bankers were afraid they could not take additional lowering of interest rates. In addition the balance of payments situation was bad and the Committee ought to do something about it. . . . [Presidents] Mayo, Coldwell, and Francis indicated that they too had been under the same pressure and more or less agreed" (ibid., 26).

This was not what Burns wanted to hear or do. Burns responded that "we had to beware of banker opinion. We had to consider the total economy, its growth and particularly unemployment" (ibid., 27). Having expressed his priorities and allied himself with the president, he "made the strongest statement on the balance of payments that I [Maisel] had heard pointing out that basically we were not charged with solving the balance of payments problem. . . . [H]e recognized that we had some marginal things we could do in the balance of payments field but that we ought to recognize that it was not a major responsibility of the Federal Reserve" (ibid., 27).

Burns did not favor floating the dollar. Like Martin before him, he wanted the administration to act. They had no interest. At a meeting later in the day, Maisel asked Herbert Stein about the Council's view of the balance of payments. "Their feeling was that we should not worry. We would be better off suspending payments and let the dollar or other currencies float. . . . He also indicated that he had talked to Connally, . . . and Connally felt even more strongly that this was true. He felt that we ought not to let foreign central banks dominate our internal situation" (ibid., 28).

In short, neither the administration nor the Federal Reserve intended to honor the commitment to the $35 gold price. There is no evidence in the record that word of this discussion became known, but during the next few weeks, flight from the dollar increased. On April 6, Coombs reported that $4.5 billion had been acquired by foreign central banks in the four weeks since the March meeting. The pace of dollar inflows to foreign central banks increased. On Friday, April 2, the flow was $1 billion. "Corporation treasurers and other traders were now beginning to hedge against the risk of parity changes" (FOMC Minutes, April 6, 1971, 3).

Burns now reversed the position so forcefully offered at the previous meeting. He favored an increase in the funds rate of 0.5 or 0.6 percentage points above the directive at the March meeting: "He was doing this primarily for balance of payments reasons" (Maisel diary, April 9, 1971, 32). The manager had permitted half the increase before the meeting, so the actual increase was small, too small for Presidents Hayes and Kimbrel (Atlanta). They dissented, Hayes citing "inadequate recognition" of international financial events. Kimbrel wanted slower money growth to avoid "rekindling inflationary expectations" (Annual Report, 1971, 140).

Yielding to pressure from some members of Congress, Burns proposed purchases of government agency issues to assist housing finance. Hayes objected for principled and practical reasons. Yielding to congressional requests to aid a particular sector would "expose the Federal Reserve to strong pressures to provide similar assistance to other sectors" (FOMC Minutes, April 6, 1971, 39). Furthermore, agency securities sold in "highly fragmented" markets. This made operations in these markets difficult.[223]

Dollar outflow slowed for a few weeks, then resumed. Coombs told the May 11 FOMC meeting that $4 billion had moved abroad in two days, the largest movement to that time. The West German Economics Minister, Karl Schiller, called for a floating rate for the mark.

The New York directors had voted to increase the discount rate to show that the United States intended to defend the dollar exchange rate. Burns thoroughly opposed floating rates, but neither he nor the administration wanted to sacrifice domestic expansion. The Board rejected the discount rate increase, signaling that the United States would not defend the ex-

223. The proposal was one of several to assist the housing market. On March 31, Burns testified on a Senate bill that (1) extended the authority, first granted in 1966, for flexible rates on time and savings deposits and coordination with other regulators, (2) extended the president's authority to impose mandatory controls on wages, prices, rents, and salaries, (3) renewed authority granted in 1960 to impose selective credit controls, and (4) authorized the Board to require member banks to maintain supplemental reserves against assets to increase credit to six sectors, including housing. The Board unanimously endorsed Burns's statement favoring a wage-price review board instead of mandatory controls (Board Minutes, March 30, 1971). It did not reject mandatory controls, but it suggested they be used as a last resort. Burns testified against asset reserves, but he continued to receive pressure for assistance to housing. Housing starts had fallen from a local peak of 1.8 million annual rate in January 1969 to less than 1.1 million a year later, but they recovered to 1.9 million in the month he testified.

change rate.[224] Some European countries joined Germany in a float; others appreciated their exchange rates. See chapter 5.

At the May 11 FOMC meeting, the staff reported rapid wage increases and, despite the rise in interest rates, rapid money growth. Reported money growth for the first quarter reached 8.9 percent, more than making up for the shortfall at the end of 1970. The report for April was 10.9 percent, not the 7 percent now shown in Table 4.11. The staff projected 9 percent for the second quarter if money market conditions remained unchanged. To slow money growth to about 6 percent in the second and third quarters, the staff estimated that the FOMC would have to increase the funds rate from 4.5 to between 6 and 8 percent (Maisel diary, May 11, 1971, 41). That destroyed any chance of majority support.

The usual split reoccurred. To resolve the issue, the FOMC gave "more than the usual degree of discretion" to the manager (Annual Report, 1971, 146). He allowed the funds rate to rise modestly. The market did not perceive a change to a less inflationary policy. Long-term rates rose and inflation increased to a 6 percent annualized rate in May. Stock prices fell, no doubt influenced by the uncertainty about the exchange rate system and higher inflation.[225]

Maisel described three main control problems of that time. First, they did not know where the equilibrium interest rate was. Second, "what premium should be included in the nominal long-term rate over real?" Third, "we can't explain why M_1 has risen so fast in the past six weeks. We don't know if this is temporary or permanent" (Maisel diary, May 21, 1971, 47). At the time, estimated M_1 growth for May reached 17 percent.

Burns too recognized that the forecasts of money growth were inaccurate and misleading, that control was poor, and that as measured at the time, money growth was 11 percent for the year to date, twice the average rate the FOMC wanted. Although he did not believe that money growth affected inflation as long as there was excess capacity, he disliked the criticism by those who believed otherwise. To improve control, he turned again

224. Maisel (diary, May 7, 1971, 37) described his view: "This was not a proper use of the discount rate; the domestic cost might be very high." Burns believed that "the New York directors and the New York Bank believed in high interest rates. They wanted them to go up and were willing to use this as an excuse to get higher rates" (ibid.).

225. The manager faced a dilemma. "He doesn't know whether the aggregates are temporarily high. On the other hand, he knows that if he is very active trying to keep the federal funds rate high, the long-term market might even become disorderly" (Maisel diary, May 21, 1971, 44). To help the Treasury through the period of market turbulence, the System purchased short-term securities directly from the Treasury. The maximum amount was $610 million on June 10 (Annual Report, 1971, 157). The Board voted in June to support legislation authorizing direct purchases up to $5 billion (Board Minutes, June 15, 1971).

to Maisel and the Committee on the Directive, proposing that they consider reviewing the proposal to control reserve growth instead of a money market rate that he had rejected earlier.[226]

Excessive money growth was not Burns's major concern. The recovery was "not robust and much higher interest rates might cut it short" (Maisel diary, June 8, 1971, 52). He favored a slow, gradual increase in rates and opposed any change in the discount rate. Burns expressed his belief that the rules had changed; "it would take much more unemployment now to hold down wages and prices than had been true in the prewar period or even in the immediate postwar period" (ibid.). He mentioned 10 percent unemployment as a possibility. This was unacceptable, so the only solution was an incomes policy.

Maisel then summarized current thinking. "It is clear that the Board as a whole agrees that monetary policy is not responsible for prices. On the other hand, a fair percentage of the presidents probably feel the opposite" (ibid., 53).

At the June 8 FOMC meeting Burns made a full statement of his own belief that "the old rules were no longer working" (FOMC Minutes, June 8, 1971, 50). He did not accept the Phillips curve tradeoff the staff used. It implied that inflation could be reduced by higher unemployment. Citing experience in the United States, Canada, and Great Britain, Burns argued that the old forces that lowered inflation during recessions remained but were dominated by new, stronger forces. He discussed three. First, expansion of public sector trade unions willing to strike against the government. Frequently, their demands had been met. "It was judged that the Government lacked the power or will to curb abuses in the market place. Hence, the trade unions have become bolder" (FOMC Minutes, June 8, 1971, 50). Second was the greater scale of welfare payments. The government allowed these payments to subsidize strikers. Third, with high inflation, union demands for cost-of-living adjustments to compensate for inflation gained

226. Stephen Axilrod on the staff made the suggestion, and Burns endorsed it. He received the same advice from Milton Friedman, who urged him to improve monetary control procedures. Friedman described efforts to control money by concentrating on interest rates as "a Central Bank delusion . . . there is no more certain route to erratic and unwise monetary policy" (letter, Friedman to Burns, Burns papers, Box B-K12, April 26, 1971). Burns replied a few days later agreeing to most of Friedman's points. A few days later he received a letter from Senator William Proxmire, chairman of the Senate Banking Committee. Proxmire enclosed a Friedman column from *Newsweek* criticizing rapid money growth and placing responsibility on controlling interest rates and money market conditions. Burns denied Friedman's claim. He explained rapid money growth as due mainly to "the temporary surge in demand for cash balances to accommodate enlarged transaction needs" (letter, Burns to Proxmire, Burns papers, Box B-K12, May 14, 1971). This is similar to the argument used by the German central bank during the 1920s hyperinflation.

moral force. "In his view, monetary policy could do little to arrest an inflation that rested so heavily on wage-cost pressures" (ibid., 51).[227]

When the FOMC met on June 29, the morning news reported that,
after meeting with his advisers, the president had rejected any change in
policy. Secretary Connally announced three nos: no tax reduction, no additional spending, and no wage-price review board or wage-price controls.
In addition, the president intended to veto a $5.6 billion public works bill.
This was a victory for George Shultz, who favored "steady as you go" and
believed the economy was recovering.[228]

Shultz was not alone. Darryl Francis (St. Louis) reported on a meeting
with twelve top executives of major companies in St. Louis. "To a man . . .
the participants reported that their businesses had been strengthening
rapidly in recent months, and they all expected a continuation of growth of
sales through the balance of this year" (FOMC Minutes, June 29, 1971, 47).
Citing rising government spending, none expected inflation to slow.

In May and June, new housing starts rose above a 2 million annual rate
for the first time. The staff maintained its forecast of real growth for the
year and forecast 4.1 percent real growth in 1972, rising to 5.1 percent in
the second quarter. They expected unemployment to reach a peak at the
end of 1971, but it would be over 6 percent at mid-year 1972.[229]

The FOMC turned to its decision. Governor Daane asked whether the

227. A striking feature of Burns's analysis is the total absence of both inflation anticipations and the credibility of government policy as a principal determinant of anticipations.
Burns's statement is representative of a large number of others he made at about this time.
This was not true of the staff. Partee, the research director, told the FOMC that "the amount
of attention given to the monetary aggregates by outside observers posed a problem in terms
of expectations. . . . [T]he market was simply responding to a particular theory of the monetary
policy process—a theory which, incidentally, had had a relatively good forecasting record over
the past few years. If that theory was wrong—and he was not sure it was—the market could
be weaned from it only by a long educational process or by a clear demonstration of failure"
(FOMC Minutes, June 29, 1971, 45). Burns himself argued that interest rates had increased
in the spring because of inflationary expectations resulting from "very rapid expansion in
M_1," (ibid., 37). But he did not relate this to his explanation of inflation. Governor Daane, on
the other hand, said the FOMC placed "too much emphasis on the aggregates" (ibid., 43). The
market and the public generally paid attention because the FOMC did.

Minutes for the period also suggest that the belief was widely held that the administration
had abandoned its anti-inflation policy and focused on unemployment to win the 1972 election. One of many examples is the February meeting of the Federal Advisory Council (Board
Minutes, February 5, 1971). Less clear is whether support for wage-price policy would have
been as widespread if the public believed the administration and the Federal Reserve would
follow an orthodox anti-inflation policy.

228. Burns said he had been at the meeting. "He and the Council had both argued for a
more activist policy" (Maisel diary, June 30, 1971, 67).

229. This forecast came from the judgmental exercise. The econometric model was less
optimistic, and the staff argued for more fiscal stimulus and 8 percent money growth.

manager could suggest any operational measures that would encourage a decline in long-term interest rates. Mr. Holmes replied that "there was very little the Desk could do in that regard" (FOMC Minutes, June 29, 1971, 58–59).

The majority agreed that they wanted to slow growth of the monetary aggregates. The issue was how much to raise interest rates and how fast. Once again, the compromise was a modest increase that left the federal funds rate in July below the annualized inflation rate for the month.[230]

Between meetings, the Board approved a 0.25 percentage point increase in the discount rate to 5 percent to bring it closer to market rates. Also, the Secretary announced publicly, for the first time, that the United States supported a wider band on the exchange rate. And Daane reported that at meetings in Europe, "all of the Europeans except France had agreed that a wider band would be better and . . . that occasional floats for brief periods to change rates would be all right" (Maisel diary, July 16, 1971, 69).

On July 23 Burns testified to the Joint Economic Committee. His comments offer a slightly softer version of remarks that he made at FOMC and Board meetings. Although he recognized that "expectations of inflation thus permeate the gamut of private decisions to spend and invest" (Burns, 1978, 118), he explained that interest rates had increased "despite rapid monetary expansion" (ibid., 117), and that "despite extensive unemployment, wage rate increases have not moderated" (ibid., 118). This showed that "the rules of economics are not working in quite the way they used to" (ibid.).[231] After expressing concern about the budget deficit and reminding the committee about the "substantial contribution it [monetary policy] has made to stimulating economic activity" (ibid., 122), he turned again to his explanation of the reasons economic rules changed (ibid., 126–27). First was the commitment to a full employment policy. This encouraged a "general expectation on the part of both business and labor that recessions, if they occur at all, will prove brief and mild; and this expectation has influenced both the strength of wage demands and the willingness of

230. Between meetings Maisel met with the staff to get them to improve estimates of money growth. He charged them with failing "in their responsibility . . . by not putting enough resources in this area" (Maisel diary, July 1, 1971, 60). The principal tasks he proposed were: (1) improve seasonal adjustment, (2) estimate the tradeoff between reserves and interest rates for money growth, and (3) develop a better analysis of the reserve flow into various aggregates. He also met with the staff at the New York bank to get suggestions for giving instructions to the manager that would improve monetary control.

231. It seems out of character for Burns to accept the alternative—that the rules worked but he did not understand that wages, interest rates, and prices reflected concern that his policy raised the anticipated rate of inflation. He did, however, acknowledge that the FOMC permitted too much money growth in the spring (Burns, 1978, 123).

management to accept them." Second was the "intensity and duration" of the previous period of excess demand." Third was the catch-up of money wages to compensate for previous inflation. Fourth, as before, he cited increased union militancy in the public and private sectors and the growth of welfare programs used to sustain striking employees.

Burns called again for a wage-price policy to control cost-push inflation. This time he did not deny that fiscal and monetary policy could reduce inflation. The problem was that these policies cannot work "as quickly as the national interest demands" (ibid., 127).

This casual empiricism is surprising, since it came from a careful empirical economic scientist. It claimed that in practice a private market economy could not reconcile price stability, full employment, and free markets. Claiming the economy had changed, it disregarded the period of high growth and low inflation prior to 1966, when unemployment remained between 4 and 5 percent with inflation below 2 percent. It dismissed, also, the substantial reduction in inflation after policy changed in 1966. And subsequently, it was falsified by the changed experience in the United States, Great Britain, and elsewhere when the public relearned that sustained inflation was neither inevitable nor likely under prevailing policies.

Burns's testimony said little or nothing that he had not said on previous occasions. What annoyed the president and his staff most was the use made of it by congressional Democrats and the press. Senator Proxmire called the administration's refusal to use incomes policy "inexcusable" (Wells, 1994, 72). The press picked up the dispute and spread it widely. Even Republican senators introduced bills requiring the president to stop increases in wages and prices (ibid., 73).[232]

232. *The Wall Street Journal*, July 29, 1971, 1, described the president as "piqued," and he complained to Haldeman and Charles Colson of his staff. Colson asked a press staff member to put out some negative commentary on Burns. The story on July 27 reported that advisers had urged the president to double the size of the Federal Reserve Board and to reject Burns's request for a $20,000 annual pay raise. Since Burns complained regularly about excessive union wage increases, he was embarrassed by press reports claiming that he asked for a large increase. Burns told William Safire that he was "deeply offended." The story was false. Burns had rejected a wage increase. He encouraged Senator Sparkman to hold hearings on his competence as chairman, and he told the Board that he had checked with Connally, Shultz, and Stein. All three disclaimed involvement or advance knowledge (Maisel diary, July 29, 1971, 73). Safire (1974, 442) claimed that the president was unaware of Colson's action, but Haldeman (1994, 332) claimed the opposite. News about the budget and payments deficits and the appearance of a fight between the president and the Federal Reserve induced a sharp decline in stock prices. The president backed down, denied that Burns had asked for a raise, and praised him as "the most responsible and statesmanlike of any Chairman . . . in my memory" (quoted in Matusow, 1998, 112). Burns then wrote a letter, pledging his strong support and thanking the president for words that "were generous as well as kind" (Burns to the president,

The July 27 FOMC meeting was the last meeting before the president adopted what he called a New Economic Policy. Unaware of the new policy, the staff raised its forecast for the year; existing policy appeared to them capable of generating strong expansion.[233]

Burns's principal concern was to slow money growth, contrary to his claim that it would not work. Despite Treasury financing and presumed even keel policy, he wanted to increase rates. He deplored the necessity of increasing rates, but rapid money growth was a bigger threat (FOMC Minutes, July 27, 1971, 47). He told the committee that "rapid rates of growth in the monetary aggregates—together with the larger Federal budget deficit—had alarmed many people and had been widely interpreted as indicating that the Federal Reserve had joined the Administration in pursuing a highly expansionary economic policy. Interest rates had risen in large measure because of the resulting expectations of renewed rapid inflation, so that the Federal Reserve was in part responsible for their rise"[234] (FOMC Minutes, July 27, 1971, 77). Hayes and Maisel opposed, citing even keel and the risk to the new issue and the market if the dealers dumped their unsold securities. But Robertson and Daane supported Burns (ibid., 69, 77).

Burns could not get support for an increase in the funds rate from 5.5 to 6 percent, so he took a vote on 5.75. The FOMC divided six to six. He then proposed a range of 5.375 to 5.75. This passed on a seven-to-five vote. The directive called for more moderate growth in the monetary aggregates and directed the manager to "achieve bank reserve and money market conditions consistent" with the FOMC's objectives. The published vote was unanimous (Annual Report, 1971, 167).

Two weeks later, the Board received requests from Dallas and St. Louis to increase the discount rate. Dallas initially proposed a 1–percentage point increase, from 5 to 6 percent, but reduced its request to 0.5, the same as St. Louis. The Board rejected the request because it came from two banks whose presidents wanted the System to "tighten as much as possible" (Maisel diary, August 13, 1971, 77). Furthermore, the proposed change was made to strengthen the dollar, under growing pressure in the exchange markets. The five Board members present agreed that "the discount rate would not be used for balance of payments purposes. . . . The discount rate

---

Burns papers, Box B-N1, August 4, 1971). He told Maisel (diary, August 13, 1971, 80) that if the Board kept good relations with the White House, it would shift to an incomes policy.

233. They now projected 3.8 percent growth in second half 1971, 0.5 percentage points above their earlier forecast, and 5.3 percent in first half 1972.

234. This is a very different explanation from what he had said many times before. It may reflect his recent return from a vacation at his summer home in Vermont. Milton Friedman was his neighbor there. The argument very much reflects Friedman's influence.

would only be used if it were necessary for domestic policy reasons" (ibid., 77). This decision came just as the fixed exchange rate system was about to end. Clearly, the Federal Reserve was not concerned to save it. Maisel refers to the "growing belief that the dollar was overvalued" (ibid.).

Maisel, in discussion with Burns, critiqued Burns's view that the money growth of more than 10 percent in the first seven months of 1971 "had raised expectation so rapidly that they were having an inflationary impact on the economy and they were raising interest rates. Therefore, if the rate of [money] growth was slowed down, interest rates would fall" (Maisel diary, August 13, 1971, 78–80). Maisel argued that this was monetarist reasoning and "now known to be wrong."

Maisel's explanation was that until recently business and the administration "had improperly assumed that there was no cost-push and that, as a result, when demand-pull disappeared, prices would come down rapidly. The inflation would be ended. . . . [T]he experience of the past six months had shown business that this was wrong. . . . [P]art of the increase in inflationary expectations had simply been a recognition of this fact now by investors and business who had not recognized it previously" (ibid., 78–79). This explanation allowed wage-price policy to lower expectations by lowering inflation. It could explain an additional increase in inflation and expectations only by assuming that unions or workers had not yet used all their market power.

Maisel told Burns that a 6 percent average money growth rate was too low. If the System didn't expand money enough "to take care of wage-price push, you would get high nominal and high real rates . . . with a great deal of unemployment" (ibid., 80).

Maisel did not report that Burns either accepted or rejected his reasoning. He thought that Burns " partially buys the monetarists' views that money must come out in prices rather than the opposite view that the increase in money may be demanded by the increase in prices"[235] (ibid., 79). The only agreement that he reported was that the administration "will attempt to blame the Federal Reserve for whatever happens in the economy particularly if inflation is continuing" (ibid.). The last was a continuing concern.[236]

235. The latter was the argument used by officials of the German Reichsbank in 1922–23, when they generated hyperinflation.

236. At about this time, the Lockheed Aircraft Company faced bankruptcy. Burns feared that Transworld Airlines, Eastern Airlines, and others would follow. Both had made substantial deposits for delivery of a new Lockheed plane. Burns proposed a permanent $2 billion fund to guarantee corporate loans up to $250 million (Wells, 1994, 69). The Board endorsed Burns's proposal for a permanent agency but did not take a stand on the narrower proposal (Board Minutes, July 3 and August 3, 1971). Congress passed a narrow proposal, a $250 mil-

REGULATORY AND ADMINISTRATIVE ACTION, 1965–71

The years of rising inflation were also years of increased regulation. The relation was not entirely accidental. Many of the regulations responded to consequences of rising inflation. The Board was slow to increase ceiling rates on time deposits, as shown in Chart 4.13 above. Banks developed new ways to borrow that avoided both ceiling rates and reserve requirements. Increases in ceiling rates enabled banks to compete more effectively with other thrift institutions for time deposits, so in 1966 regulation spread to savings and loan associations. Laws against payment of interest on bank reserves and bank deposits became more costly to depositors as inflation rose. Banks and their customers had a common interest in economizing on cash balances and bank reserves.[237] Banks responded also by withdrawing from Federal Reserve membership.

Growth and development of financial institutions created new opportunities for political intervention and new problems. The Federal Reserve returned frequently to consider regulatory changes to rein in growth of commercial paper and euro-dollars. Trade expansion and increased overseas investment by U.S. corporations induced banks to establish branches abroad. Government programs to restrict capital outflow added to the Board's regulatory burden.

After many years of effort by System officials, Congress gave the Board power to regulate one-bank holding companies. Between 1956 and 1970, the number of holding companies increased from 428 to 895 and the number of their branches increased from 783 to 3260 (Board of Governors, 1976). In the same period, the number of banks rose from 11,815 to 13,100, but the number of member banks fell from 6456 to 5773, reflecting higher costs of membership in an inflationary era. The Federal Reserve was successful in reducing the number of banks that charged check collection fees to their customers; the number of non-par banks fell from 1754 to 501.

---

lion guarantee for Lockheed, by a margin of only one vote in the Senate. Wells (ibid., 70) reports that the experience changed Burns's view about bailouts for large corporations. He served on a three-person board with the Secretaries of Treasury and Commerce. "He became unhappy with Lockheed, which missed its timetable, fell short of performance goals, and became involved in a scandal" with the Japanese government. Haldeman (1994, 335) reported that Governor Reagan of California supported the assistance because "if we lost the vote, it would be critical to our chances in California in '72."

237. Axilrod explained that the staff and some of the members believed that controlling money meant control of credit and that regulation Q kept bank credit under control. "There was a body of opinion that was fairly strong for a long time that what was important wasn't the money supply, what was important was bank credit" (Axilrod, 1997).

Release of Information

To commemorate its fiftieth anniversary in 1964, the Federal Reserve began to deposit records of the FOMC from 1936 through 1960 at the National Archives. Other records followed as part of a program to make available to scholars and other interested parties information on central banking. This first step was a notable departure from traditional central bank secrecy.

Two years later, Congress approved the Freedom of Information Act (FOIA), which opened to the public the files and records of many government agencies. The Federal Reserve wanted to be exempt from FOIA, but it did not fully succeed. The law permitted exemption for national defense and foreign policy. The latter permitted the System to exempt international transactions. Special treatment of commercial information allowed the System to delay release of domestic open market information for several weeks. A court ruling eventually supported this argument.

The Board was able to exempt large parts of its information about individual banks obtained by examiners or personnel, or contained in interagency or intra-agency memoranda. In a break with the past, it agreed to release more promptly the material on open market operations and foreign currency transactions that had hitherto appeared in the Board's Annual Report. Release would be made ninety days after a meeting.

The reserve banks are not part of government, so they are not subject to FOIA.[238] Reserve banks have records and information about open market operations and other activities that involve the Board. Each bank established procedures for separating requests for the two sources (memo, Alan Holmes to Securities Department, Box 007973, FOMC, New York Reserve Bank, July 5, 1967).

Regulations Q and D

As the cost of interest rate regulation rose, banks and financial institutions sought ways to circumvent the rules without violating them. Lawyers and bureaucrats make regulations. Markets decide if and when to circumvent them. The Board soon found that it had to use time and other resources to resolve many issues. The Board was aware that money market funds by-

238. In the San Francisco National Bank case, a judge ruled that the Federal Reserve Bank of San Francisco was not liable for damages arising from the bank's failure. The judge ruled that the Federal Reserve Bank was an agency of the federal government under the Tort Claims Act. The reserve bank had loaned more than $9 million to San Francisco National. Out-of-court settlement prevented the appeal from being heard (Board Minutes, February 19, 1968, 3–8; October 28, 1968, 5).

passed their regulations. It took small steps to help the banks and thrifts, but it did not step back to consider the general problem (Brimmer, 2002, 18).

Time deposits were subject to regulation Q ceilings and to reserve requirements under regulation D. To avoid these costs, banks began borrowing on promissory notes. Since the notes were not time deposits, they were not subject to regulations D and Q.

To close what it regarded as a loophole, the Board proposed to amend regulations Q and D to define promissory notes and other forms of indebtedness as deposits. If the note had an original maturity within less than thirty days, it was deemed a demand deposit. No interest could be paid. Discussions with the Interagency Coordinating Committee, consisting of the Federal Reserve, the Treasury, the Federal Deposit Insurance Corporation (FDIC), the Comptroller of the Currency, and the Federal Home Loan Bank Board (FHLBB), began in January 1966. The Comptroller objected to proposals that would make promissory notes subject to deposit regulation. He told the group that if a national bank challenged the ruling, he would join with them against the Board.

The rule as written at the time would include repurchase agreements and promissory notes. Alan Holmes, the account manager, objected that the proposed rule would be disruptive because it would eliminate payment of interest on any debt with maturity of less than ninety days. Banks would have to refinance $2 billion of repurchase agreements. The legal counsel, Howard Hackley, pointed out that promissory notes and repurchase agreements were different instruments serving the same purposes. It would be difficult to write rules prohibiting one and permitting the other (Board Minutes, January 11, 1966, 2–22).

The Board tried to resolve the issue by regulating promissory notes explicitly. On June 24, the Board raised reserve requirements on time deposits in excess of $5 million at any bank and, effective September 1, 1966, included promissory notes as deposits. On August 17, the Board increased the reserve requirement ratio to 6 percent.[239]

"To help forestall excessive interest rate competition among financial institutions," on July 15, 1966, the Board lowered the maximum rate on multiple maturity time deposits. A deposit issued for (say) 90 days and renewable at the same interest rate for another 90 days could receive a

239. The new regulation was only a few months old before a bank attempted to circumvent it. The Edge Act (foreign) subsidiary of Morgan Guaranty Trust (New York) issued promissory notes in exchange for foreign loans. The bank endorsed the notes and sold them under repurchase agreements. Morgan Guaranty claimed that these were not deposits under the new regulation, and therefore not subject to reserve requirements. The Board rejected the claim (Board Minutes, March 27, 1967, 10).

5 percent interest rate compared to 5.5 percent on a 180-day certificate. If the renewal lender had the option of calling for payment in 30 days, the rate dropped to 4 percent (Board Minutes, July 15, 1966, press release).

Apparently the Board had not yet learned that each new regulation encouraged search for ways to circumvent it. The Board's early (1922) definition of a deposit distinguished only between deposits, trust funds, and capital. Funds received in trust or as capital remained free of reserve requirements. The September 1966 redefinition of "deposit" to include promissory notes reduced banks' reliance on such notes. The new definition included all "funds to be used in its banking business, except any such instrument (1) that is issued to another bank, (2) that evidences an indebtedness arising from a transfer of assets that the bank is obligated to repurchase, or (3) that has an original maturity of more than 2 years and states expressly that it is subordinated to the claims of depositors" (memo, Definition of "deposit" in regulations D and Q, Correspondence Box 240, Federal Reserve Bank of New York, February 3, 1969, 1–2.).

The first two exceptions provided opportunities for avoiding regulations Q and D. One of the New York banks began issuing "participation certificates" that gave the holder claim to a share of the bank's loan portfolio but guaranteed to repurchase the certificate. This met the second exception, so the bank could offer interest rates above the regulation Q ceiling. In September 1968, the Board redefined deposits to cover these transactions. Banks purchasing the certificates would be deemed to hold deposits (ibid., 2).[240]

In 1966, the Board also requested new legislation to permit it to set different ceiling rates for different classes of accounts, for different amounts, different maturities, "according to the nature and location of the institutions, or the account holders, or any other reasonable basis" (ibid., 2). The legislation would apply to the Federal Deposit Insurance Corporation, the Federal Home Loan Bank Board, and the Board of Governors.[241]

The Board returned again to consider reserve requirements graduated by size of deposit instead of the bank's location. The Board had considered this topic since the 1930s without adopting it. This time proponents wanted to slow credit expansion at large country banks. Population move-

240. Exemption of foreign branches of U.S. banks created difficulties also. Banks opened branches in the Bahamas and elsewhere; the Board required banks to stipulate that the branch would not be used to transfer deposits from the United States.

241. At one point, the Board considered defining a time deposit by the size of the deposit because it wanted to regulate large deposits separately for political reasons. Legal counsel explained that the Board did not have that authority (Board Minutes, March 25, 1966, 4–5). In addition to problems arising from the number of instruments that would be affected by any new regulation, the Board learned about laws of several states that would affect banks in the state adversely.

ments had encouraged economic and bank expansion in formerly rural areas, but a principal reason for using graduated reserve requirements by size was to lower the cost of membership for small and intermediate banks.

Congressman Patman, chairman of House Banking, introduced legislation to prohibit insured banks from issuing negotiable certificates of deposit, or similar negotiable instruments, and prohibiting these banks from issuing time deposits in amounts less than $15,000. The aim was to channel more savings into savings and loan institutions faced at the time with large outflows.[242] The Board wrote a letter opposing the legislation and calling it " unwise" (Board Minutes, May 17, 1966, 4). It did not send the letter, and softened its stance, when the Treasury proposed to permit different rates of interest on time deposits depending on whether the deposits were insured.

The Board continued to oppose the Patman bills. It said that the bills circumscribed competitive pressures (Board Minutes, May 23, 1966, 3). It welcomed the Treasury proposal as one way to increase flexibility, but it expressed concern that changes often had unforeseen consequences. It favored exploring the "ultimate as well as immediate effects" (ibid., 3).

On June 2, the Board agreed on steps to increase the flexibility of its control procedures. It favored: (1) "any legislation which would expand their flexibility in setting reserve requirements"; (2) graduated reserve requirements applicable to all (member and non-member banks); (3) "a minimum maturity of time deposits for a year or even six months" (Board Minutes, June 2, 1966, 1–6). Legislation permitting increased flexibility in setting ceiling rates became law in August.

The legislation extended ceiling rates of interest to savings and loan associations and insured non-member commercial banks. The Federal Home Loan Bank Board and the FDIC received authority to set ceiling rates for their members. Coordination with other deposit regulators by the Federal Reserve became mandatory. The new legislation also called on the regulators to reduce interest rates to the maximum extent feasible, regulated the compounding of interest, and required the reserve banks to accept agency securities as collateral.

The requirements were temporary, terminating in one year. In April 1967, the Treasury proposed to make the legislation permanent. Several Board members objected but, as a staff member reminded them, "it did

242. Housing starts fell more than 20 percent in 1966 as mortgage rates rose above 6 percent for the first time since the 1930s.

not seem reasonable to expect that Congress would repeal a clause in favor of low interest rates" (Board Minutes, April 24, 1967, 7). Chairman Martin disliked the legislation, but Governors Robertson and Maisel found it a useful tool. The Board decided to ask for a postponement of the legislation until it could study its experience.

One main purpose of the discussion was to respond to pressure to help the housing industry by changing reserve requirements and interest rates. In his testimony to the House Banking Committee on June 8, Chairman Martin said that most of the proposals were less effective than an increase in funds available to purchase mortgages by the government mortgage agencies. The common presumption was that more mortgage finance would increase housing production. Evidence to support this conclusion was lacking at the time (Meltzer, 1974). None of the officials suggested that the decline in housing starts resulted from reduced demand instead of constrained supply.

A second purpose was to limit credit expansion. The Board divided on whether increases in time deposit reserve requirement ratios were more effective than open market operations. Governor Robertson was the chief proponent of increased reserve requirement ratios. In August, he urged his colleagues to raise from 5 to 6 percent the requirement ratio for time deposits at banks with more than $5 million of deposits. Only Governor Shephardson supported his motion, so it failed.[243]

After 1966, the law regulating rates on time and savings accounts at banks and other financial institutions permitted savings and loans to offer an interest rate 0.75 percentage points higher than banks. Banks in competitive markets tried to find ways to compete. In 1967, some banks offered "golden passbook accounts," a time deposit using a passbook similar to a savings account, with a rate of 4.5 or 5 percent depending on location. These accounts were more competitive with thrift institutions. Congress, always concerned about complaints from thrift institutions, questioned the legality of the accounts. The Board assured them that the accounts met the requirements of regulation Q. This was one of many incidents involv-

243. Among the more flexible rules was a decision by the Board to reclassify Christmas club deposits as saving deposits not time deposits, so subject to lower reserve requirements. The FDIC objected because that would lower the ceiling interest rate. The agencies retained the time deposit classification but lowered the reserve requirement ratio for these accounts. In February 1967, the Board proposed legislation changing reserve requirement ratios for demand deposits to a system graduated by size of deposits. There were three brackets with graduation at $5 million and $100 million. Requirements would apply to all insured banks. In return, banks would get access to the discount window. This was the first time the Board made a legislative proposal for this change (Board Minutes, February 20, 1967, 13-15).

ing efforts to improve competitive positions. Offering "free" merchandise premiums was one of the most common (Board Minutes, October 18, December 15 and 22, 1967).[244]

At the same time that the Board acted to prevent domestic depositors from receiving market interest rates, it supported legislation permitting foreign governments, central banks, and international financial institutions to receive market interest rates. The justification was the financing of the balance of payments (Board Minutes, January 18, 1968, 7–16). Until October 1968, the Board required that the interest rate paid on foreign official deposits revert to the ceiling rate if the original holder sold the certificate to a non-exempt holder. In October 1968, the Board waived the restriction (ibid., October 7, 1968, 6–7).

Brokers found new ways to avoid regulation Q ceilings. The broker deposited a customer's funds at the ceiling rate. In return, the bank made a loan to a specified borrower. The borrower paid a fee for the loan. The broker shared part of the fee with the depositor. The broker advertised a 7 percent interest rate, when the ceiling rate was 5 percent. The Board, the FDIC, and the Home Loan Bank Board added a provision to their regulations that prohibited advertisements of this kind. Enforcement proved difficult at times (Board Minutes, October 3, 1969, 5–8).[245]

Congress approved legislation on December 23, 1969, permitting the Board to regulate commercial paper issued by bank affiliates. The Board discussed interest rate ceiling and reserve requirement ratios on January 13, 1970, but could not agree on the timing of interest rate ceilings or the applicability of reserve requirement ratios. Eventually, ceiling rates became applicable, as discussed in the section on domestic policy.

The Board continued to request legislation authorizing reserve requirement ratios set by size of deposits. Congress continued to ignore the requests. Members especially disliked proposals to apply the requirements to all insured banks (letter, Burns to Sparkman, Burns papers, Box B-B93, May 21, 1971).

By the summer of 1971, several FOMC members wanted to remove regulation Q ceiling rates from all large negotiable certificates of deposit.

244. The maximum rate on a $100,000 CD was 6.25 percent in spring 1968. What if several persons pooled their deposits to buy a single CD? The Board told the bank that pooling was not illegal but they would amend the regulations to prevent it (Board Minutes, May 7, 1968). The Board could not prevent money market mutual funds from taking comparable action after these funds started in the 1970s.

245. Other devices used included soliciting deposits for branches of U.S. banks in Puerto Rico and the Virgin Islands. These branches were not subject to regulation Q. Banks also transferred funds to foreign branches to avoid reserve requirements (Board Minutes, June 3, 1969, 4–8; July 24, 1969, 8).

Burns raised the issue at the June 29 FOMC meeting. The New York bank supported the change. It wrote expressing doubt about the effectiveness of ceiling rates. "A major impact of Regulation Q ceilings on large CD's, during periods of restraint, has been to force credit flows away from the domestic banking system and into channels—such as the Euro-dollar market and the commercial paper market—over which the Federal Reserve System has no direct control" (letter, William Trieber to Board of Governors, Federal Reserve Bank of New York, Correspondence File 240, July 18, 1971). The letter pointed out also that substitution of this kind distorted the data on which the System relied, and it urged suspension of the ceiling for CDs of $100,000 or more. Several other reserve banks wrote similar letters. The Board did not act.[246]

Lagged Reserve Requirements

An Ad Hoc Subcommittee on Reserve Proposals recommended a change in the timing of reserve requirements in 1966. Instead of maintaining requirement ratios based on current deposits, banks would use deposits at an earlier period to compute the requirement. The aim of the proposal was to reduce volatility of excess reserve holdings and to reduce uncertainty about the volume of required reserves. Banks with many branches had difficulty knowing the volume of deposits and reserves until after the settlement date for reserve balances.

Critics soon pointed out[247] that the proposal restricted monetary policy operations because the System would have to supply a fixed volume of reserves either through discounting or open market purchases (including repurchase agreements). Nevertheless, the Board adopted the proposal in 1968 as part of its reappraisal of discounting. Under the new arrangement, banks would calculate weekly average required reserves based on average deposits two weeks earlier. Vault cash two weeks earlier would replace con-

246. The reserve banks undertook an extensive System-wide study of regulation Q. One paper by Philip Davidson and Robert McTeer of the Richmond bank challenged the basis for the regulation. They pointed out that the claim that competition drove up interest rates and induced banks to take excessive risk was false. Another paper by Max Klass of Philadelphia discussed the complexity of the regulation and the difficulty small banks had in interpreting the rules and complying. The System committee recommended the "eventual elimination on interest rate ceilings on thrift deposits" (Preliminary Report, Correspondence Box 240, Federal Reserve Bank of New York, undated).

247. Memo George Kaufman to Ernest Baughman, Federal Reserve Bank of Chicago, June 13, 1966. I am indebted to George Kaufman for furnishing a copy of his memo. Axilrod (1997) pointed out that lowering membership cost was a main reason for the change. "It was my first big Board presentation on a major issue. I hinted strongly that maybe, this wasn't the wisest thing. At the end Bill Martin first said that it was a very good presentation, then said 'we ought to go ahead.'"

temporaneous vault cash when calculating reserves held to satisfy requirements, but current reserve balances would continue to be used. Banks could carry forward up to 2 percent surplus or deficiency.

President Black commented that the main benefit would be in the "bank relations area" (Board Minutes, January 25, 1968, 8). No one made any claim that the step effected an important change in monetary policy. The proposal received few comments or suggestions for changes, so it was adopted in April 1968 and implemented on September 12. Governor Brimmer said banks could always go to the discount window if they had problems with reserve volatility. He saw no reason for the proposal. The staff, too, thought the proposal unnecessary (Board Minutes, April 23, 1968, 6–9).

At the time, the System used an interest rate or money market target. It responded to changes in demand for reserves by supplying reserves. A few years later, and again in 1979–82, the System set targets for money growth and bank reserves. Lagged reserve requirements made it harder to control reserves and money growth. Nevertheless, the Board retained lagged reserve requirements throughout those periods. It reverted to contemporaneous reserve requirements in 1984, after its policy of controlling reserves ended, and it returned to lagged requirements in 1998.

Discounting

In 1968 a System committee consisting of four Board governors and four reserve bank presidents, headed by Governor Mitchell, proposed changes in discount regulations and the operation of the discount window. The stated purpose was to use discounting to facilitate short-term adjustments of bank reserves.[248] "A more liberal and convenient mechanism should enable member banks to adjust to changes in fund availability in a more orderly fashion and, in so doing, should lessen some of the causes of in-

248. Governor Mitchell's testimony brought out the reasons for considering major changes in discounting at that time. First, the 1966 period of restrictive monetary policy affected the savings and loan industry heavily. The Senate came within one vote of authorizing the Federal Reserve to lend to the Home Loan Banks. Second, the borrowing line and seasonal adjustment credit assisted small, rural banks. Many had left the System. Mitchell testified that between 1957 and 1967, membership declined from 48.8 to 44.9 percent of commercial banks (Joint Economic Committee, 1968, 20). Third, the proposal kept the discount rate closely related to market rates and avoided announcements effects when the discount rate changed. This part of the proposal was not implemented; changes in the discount rate remained infrequent and often gave rise to announcement effects.

In internal discussion, Governor Mitchell added a fourth reason: borrowing had fallen to very low levels. Much of the decline resulted from uncertainty about what the 1955 revision of regulation A permitted after the Board's ambiguous September 1966 letter restricting discounts (Board Minutes, May 28, 1968, 2).

stability in financial markets without hampering overall monetary control" (Board of Governors, 1971, 3). The report envisioned a system in which open market operations supplied a volume of reserves and the discount window (along with federal funds transactions) adjusted the distribution of reserves for individual banks.[249]

The committee proposed two principal changes to meet these objectives: (1) "more objectively defined terms and conditions for discounting"; and (2) designing arrangements for borrowing to "provide credit for a specific type of need" (Board of Governors, 1971, 3). The categories were short-term adjustment credit, seasonal credit, and emergency credit. Each bank would have a "basic borrowing privilege" that gave it automatic access to assistance. The reserve bank could supplement the basic credit at its discretion. The revised system remained in effect until 2003.

Use of words like "borrowing privilege" reinforced the long-standing Federal Reserve claim that borrowing was a privilege, not a right, of membership, a claim that the System had worked to inculcate in its members. In a break from the past the Board staff made the amount borrowed depend on the interest rate or the spread between the discount rate and the market rate. The staff's work recognized that cost mattered as did frowns at the discount window. Heretofore, System orthodoxy was that banks did not borrow for profit but only reluctantly and for need. The Board in 1955 had issued regulation A, which maintained a "considerable reluctance to borrow from the central bank" (ibid., 8). Assigning a borrowing line returned to the very earliest days of the Federal Reserve System.

The report recognized that banks had invested heavily in mortgages and municipal obligations to supplement loans. Markets for these assets were not as well developed as the government securities market, so banks were less able to adjust flexibly to adverse conditions. Also, administration of regulation A varied widely from one district to another. "A key objective . . . is to formalize the terms of limited and temporary access to the [discount] window" (ibid., 10). The report envisaged greater use of the discount window by banks needing temporary accommodation. Evidence suggests increased discounting especially in 1969, 1973–74, and thereafter.

The committee recommended setting the basic borrowing privilege for each bank as a percentage of the bank's capital stock and surplus. To give greater relative assistance to small banks, the proportion of capital and surplus declined as the value of a bank's capital and surplus rose. The basic credit was a privilege of membership, but it was subject to restriction if

---

249. Brunner and Meltzer (1964) proposed this arrangement to eliminate many of the so-called defensive operations.

a bank was in poor financial condition. Also, banks were told not to sell federal funds while in debt to the Federal Reserve.

A bank could borrow more than its basic credit line on request. Decisions would be subject to the same procedures developed after the 1955 revision of regulation A.

The report next considered revisions to two traditional Federal Reserve functions, providing seasonal credit and lender of last resort (provider of emergency credit). To assist banks, particularly rural banks, with financing seasonal demands, the committee proposed to establish "a seasonal borrowing privilege" for each bank. The reserve bank would extend credit for a longer term, more than four weeks and up to nine months in unusual circumstances. The report suggested that it expected banks to borrow for ninety days under this privilege. To prevent banks from speculating on rate increases by borrowing at a discount rate that they expected to rise, the report proposed charging higher rates on existing borrowing.

"Emergency Credit Assistance" offered borrowing facilities to "a troubled member bank, after having obtained the assurance of the chartering authority that the bank is solvent and that steps are being taken to find a solution to its problems" (ibid., 19). The report distinguished this part of its lender-of-last-resort function from the general assistance provided to the banking system through open market operations. It did not give an illustration of the circumstances in which a bank would be solvent but sufficiently illiquid to require this form of assistance. Although the report recognized that the "System should not act to prevent losses and impairment of capital of particular financial institutions" (ibid.) it provided no means to prevent such bailouts and, as future experience showed, the emergency credit facility was used for that purpose.

A landmark change came near the end of the committee report when the committee recognized explicitly that the Federal Reserve was the lender of last resort to the entire financial system, not just member banks or commercial banks.[250] It limited its responsibility appropriately by restricting assistance to non-member institutions according to the "probable

---

250. The Board discussed emergency credit facilities for mutual savings banks during the credit crunch in 1966 (Board Minutes, June 27, 1966). A staff memo recommended special attention to mutual savings banks because they experienced relatively large deposit losses and did not have a lender-of-last-resort facility. The proposed assistance could be direct, or indirect by collateralized lending to a member bank that would relend to the mutual savings bank. The Board "should not insist on repayment terms so strict as to require unnecessary short-term adjustments in borrower activity" (memo, Staff to Board of Governors, Board Records, June 27, 1966, 3). Later that summer the Board offered similar arrangements to the Home Loan Banks, but they were not used.

impact of failure on the economy's financial structure" (ibid., 20). Then it limited its responsibility further by noting that the Federal Reserve Act placed "stringent limitations" on the collateral it could accept—only "direct obligations of the United States" (ibid.). The report proposed to circumvent this limitation by lending to a member bank, on acceptable collateral, that would relend to the non-member institution. A federal agency such as the FHLBB, with lending authority and appropriate collateral, could replace the member bank. Loans would be made "at a significant penalty rate vis-à-vis that charged member banks" (ibid., 20). The report softened these restrictions by noting that in "an extreme emergency" consideration would be given to opening the discount window to non-member financial institutions offering to sell state, local, or government securities (ibid., 21). The Board used this provision to offer discount facilities during crises in 1987 and 1998.

The report also called for more frequent changes in the discount rate. It codified prevailing practice, not always observed, of setting the discount rate below the market rate in periods of restraint and above the market rate in periods of ease. Ease and restraint appear to refer to levels of interest rates. The committee did not explain why it retained procyclical fluctuations in the discount rate with a penalty rate limited to periods of ease. The only comment was reference to "instability in the structure of market rates" caused by "too frequent or poorly timed changes" (ibid., 22).

Within the System, most presidents supported the report. Francis (St. Louis) thought the report was too complicated and would make little difference, but he did not oppose it. Hayes (New York) reacted most negatively. He disliked the proposals to change discount rates frequently and by small amounts, and he agreed with Francis that the proposed borrowing lines did not simplify discount window administration. He argued also that the proposed arrangements made money market control more difficult, but he did not support the argument (Board Minutes, May 28, 1968, 9).

The Joint Economic Committee reported its view of the proposals (Joint Economic Committee, 1969). It commended several of the proposals, but it objected to the restrictions placed on loans to non-members, especially savings and loan associations. The Joint Economic Committee recommended that the Federal Reserve delay any changes until further study by the Banking and Currency Committee of Congress.

Subsequently, the Board made two main changes. It provided the seasonal credit facility for rural, mainly agricultural, credit. And it acted as lender of last resort to the financial system without adopting an explicit proposal. In October 1970, it made some technical changes recommended by the Presidents' Conference to eliminate old forms and to make procedures and administration of the discount window more uniform.

The first opportunity to use its broader role as lender of last resort came at about the time of the Penn Central crisis. On May 25, 1970, the Board discussed problems at some major brokerage houses following steep declines in share prices (Board Minutes, May 25, 1970, 1–3).

Consumer Affairs

Senators Abraham Ribicoff (Connecticut) and John Sparkman (Alabama) introduced legislation to create a cabinet-level department, the Department of Consumer Affairs. Sparkman was chairman of the Senate Banking Committee and interested in regulating standards for issuing credit cards and limiting a consumer's liability arising from unauthorized use of credit cards.

The Board did not support the legislation. Its draft reply said that "protection of consumers was not consistent with effective performance of the Board's responsibilities in the field of monetary policy" (Board Minutes, March 19, 1969, 4). Mitchell objected that credit cards were a substitute for money and therefore of concern to the Board (ibid., 6), but Sherrill objected that if it accepted responsibility for non-bank credit cards, it would be "verging on responsibility for total credit control" (ibid., 7). The 1968 Consumer Credit Protection Act included "truth in lending" legislation. The Board became responsible for policing the provisions.

An issue that bothered Congress was unsolicited mailing of credit cards. Robertson said that Congress should not regulate this practice separately; it could prevent use of the mails if it wanted to prevent the practice. But Martin expressed concern that banks solicited users at a time (1969) when the System wanted to restrict growth of credit and money. Of course, banks could create money only if they held reserves. By restricting reserve growth, the System limited growth of money and credit.

By December, the Board changed its mind. It supported legislation restricting unsolicited mailing of credit cards and a limit of $50 on liability for unauthorized use of a credit card (Board Minutes, December 17, 1969, 6–7).

The Board received several requests in the late 1960s to comment on legislation permitting banks to operate mutual funds. The Board concluded that the benefits to the public from increased competition more than offset the risks to banks. They favored regulation by the Securities and Exchange Commission, not themselves or the Comptroller. Senator Sparkman preferred the Comptroller of the Currency. That agency was subject to oversight by his committee.

Organization and Administration

Issues continued to arise about the legal status of the reserve banks, the organization of the System, the division of responsibilities between the reserve banks and the Board, and the relation of monetary policy to the administration's economic policy. Congressman Wright Patman continued to press for changes in the Federal Reserve Act to require an outside audit of the System's accounts,[251] the retirement of all government debt held by the System (to force the System to request appropriations from Congress) and other actions that would restrict independence. Patman never had sufficient following in Congress compared to the Federal Reserve, so he could not get his proposals enacted. Nevertheless, they made the Board conscious of the possibility of change and anxious about their legislative success. That may have been their purpose.

In 1968, the Johnson administration considered proposals to strengthen coordination of System and administration economic policies. The memo accepted the familiar language about "independent *within* but not *of* the administration," but it did not offer an explicit meaning for that phrase (memo, Warren L. Smith to Larry Levinson, White House Confidential Files, Box FI9-1 LBJ Library, November 4, 1968; emphasis in the original). The administration was about to leave office, so it is hard to accept the proposals as a serious effort.

The memo credited Martin with "successful coordination" with administration policy (ibid., 3) but noted that Martin's term ended in little more than a year. The problems Smith considered were familiar from discussions going back to 1935. Presidents voted on monetary policy but were not subject to presidential appointment and Senate confirmation. The FOMC was too large to be efficient. The chairman's term should be coterminous with the president's term or nearly so. He proposed to reduce the statutory length of terms to seven years with possible reappointment and put control of all policy instruments in a single entity, either the Board or a revamped FOMC. The memo also suggested reducing or ending geographical limitations so that more than one Board member could come from a single district.

The most radical proposal called for a restructured Board of Governors consisting of a chairman and two members in Washington with the four

---

251. The Board was willing to have its income and expense accounts audited by an accounting firm. It opposed an audit by a government entity, the General Accounting Office, especially an audit of the System Open Market Account. In a letter to Congressman B. Fletcher Thompson, the board argued against the view that the debt they held was distinct debt effectively retired from circulation while at the same time arguing that approximately 90 percent of the interest they received was returned to the Treasury (Board Minutes, June 6, 1967).

remaining members assigned to four super-regions. Each of the twelve reserve bank presidents would report to one of the four regional Board members. The presidents' advice on monetary policy actions would be indirect.

The last proposal changed the basic compromise under which Congress agreed to create the System as a mix of public and private interests, and it reduced the role of the reserve banks. Two years earlier, Congress approved legislation permitting the Board to move in the opposite direction by increasing the reserve banks' responsibilities by delegating some Board activities.

The Board approved the first list of delegated responsibilities in June 1967. The list included: (1) authority to approve domestic branches of state-chartered member banks, (2) extensions of time for registration by a bank holding company, and (3) extensions of time for registration of securities of state member banks. The Board retained authority to review decisions if there were complaints (Board Minutes, June 5, 1967, 14–16).

This was the first of many delegations to reduce the Board's activity and recognize the additional responsibilities Congress had given it in the 1960s. In 1970, the Board extended the staff's responsibility for bank mergers when the staff members agreed unanimously. And it gave advance approval of reserve bank discount rate schedules that called for renewal unless the Board had approved a change elsewhere.

At a time of increased government regulation, issues arose about the applicability to the Board and the reserve banks of new regulations of employment practices, release of information, and privacy of personnel information. The System had developed rules requiring senior staff and consultants to report confidential information on outside employment, business activities, and financial interests. Bank examiners had to report their indebtedness. The Board wanted these rules waived. The rules did not apply to the reserve banks because they were not considered federal agencies (Board Minutes, February 15, 1967, 13–16).

Board members and staff were not consistent as to whether the reserve banks were federal agencies. Discussing application of the 1964 Civil Rights Act, the Board's counsel said that they were divided on whether the reserve banks were agencies for the purposes of the act (Board Minutes, May 26, 1965, 11–20). Board members divided also, but they did not want to raise the issue for discussion by Congress or the administration.[252] Re-

252. After much active discussion, the Board decided to avoid the issue and rejected the application of Title VII of the Civil Rights Act on other grounds. Governor Robertson dissented. No one doubted that Title VII, making discrimination based on race illegal, applied to the entire System and to member banks. In a suit tried in San Francisco concerning five

serve bank counsel agreed unanimously that the banks were not agencies of the federal government.

Debt and Dealers

Some issues returned several times. Members of Congress pressed the Board and the FOMC to conduct open market operations or do repurchase agreements in federal agency securities, particularly securities of the housing finance agencies. The Board objected to mandates of this kind but did not object to legislation authorizing purchase of agency securities at its discretion. Congress approved legislation in 1966 authorizing open market operations in direct obligations of any federal agency.

The FOMC voted on October 7, 1969, to permit the manager to lend securities to government securities dealers. The purpose was to reduce the number of transactions in which one party failed to deliver securities to complete the transaction. The problem arose because the FOMC had begun again to use longer-term securities in open market operations. Loans were usually for one to three days. The initial program was for six months in order to learn how it worked. In March 1970, the FOMC renewed authorization (memo, Alan R. Holmes to FOMC, Board Records, March 4, 1970).

Late in 1968, the SEC delivered a report to the Board on the use of advance information on a Treasury financing in 1967. It found that the employees of a government securities dealer had access to such information (Board Minutes, December 2, 1968; February 13, 1969).

The Glass-Steagall Act (1933) separated investment and commercial banking. As the economy expanded and borrowing increased, banks pressed to remove many of the 1930s regulations and legislation. The Board considered making a recommendation in its 1966 Annual Report to permit commercial banks to underwrite state and local revenue bonds, but it decided against doing so. The Comptroller ruled that national banks had the authority, but in a lawsuit brought by an investment bank, the court ruled against the Comptroller.

Congress responded by introducing legislation permitting banks to underwrite revenue bonds. Banks had retained authority to serve as underwriters of state and local general obligations. The Senate committee asked the Board and the Comptroller to conduct a study to estimate the cost saving to state and local governments from extension of authority to revenue bonds. The study found that underwriting costs would decline.

---

large depositors in the failed San Francisco National Bank, the federal district court dismissed charges against the San Francisco reserve bank on grounds that it was an agency of the federal government (Board Minutes, April 29, 1966, 6).

The Board divided on the desirability of legislation. Five members favored the bill. Governor Daane opposed because he liked the separation of commercial and investment banking and did not want "a continuing erosion of barriers" (Board Minutes, August 18, 1967, 15). Chairman Martin was ambivalent at the time. He was concerned about conflict of interest by banks, but he liked the idea of lower costs to state and local governments. The following year, Martin changed his mind, and the Board supported revenue bond underwriting (ibid., March 6, 1968, 5–7). Congress approved the change.

One-Bank Holding Companies

The Board inadvertently failed to include one-bank holding companies under the 1956 Bank Holding Company Act. It took fourteen years to remedy that oversight, but Congress approved legislation in 1970 authorizing the Board of Governors to regulate these companies. The legislation also defined a bank as an institution that received deposits and made loans.

Several issues about holding companies remained contentious before the legislation passed and even after. Principal among these were limits on the scope of bank holding companies, such as whether they could include commercial and industrial activities or, more broadly, precisely the type of activities that could be specified in the legislation. The Board tried several times to draw up a list of activities that it would approve, but it could not agree. The Board also could not agree on whether a grandfather clause should protect arrangements reached before the legislation. Robertson opposed a grandfather clause, and both he and Brimmer insisted that only one agency should regulate holding companies; they preferred the Board, of course, but they did not say that in the Statement of Principles prepared for Congress[253] (Board Minutes, February 20, 1969). After considerable discussion, the Board prepared a list of eleven activities that bank holding companies could do, then added a twelfth that gave it authority to approve activities "functionally related to banking" (Board Minutes, May 13, 1969, 2, letter, Robert Cardon to House Banking Committee). The legislation did not adopt a list; in the end it reused but modified the language of the 1956 act setting standards for approval.[254]

253. By December 1970, the number of bank holding companies was 11.8 percent of all commercial banks. They held 16.2 percent of deposits. Passage of the amendment increased the percentages to 36.2 and 55.3 percent respectively in the first year (1971). By 1979, the percentages reached 52.8 and 67.8.

254. Maisel wrote that despite many previous discussions, the staff did not have a firm idea about what the regulations should cover. The staff proposed that the Board use the list it

The Board eagerly accepted authority over holding companies. Regulatory authority strengthened its control of banks' expansion, thereby strengthening the System's support for its actions by an important group. That group was likely to support the System in issues with the Congress.

Other Regulations, 1965–71

Despite its name, the voluntary credit restraint program required the Board repeatedly to issue regulations specifying what it permitted. For example, in 1965, the Board discussed whether the System's acceptance portfolio should reduce its holdings of acceptances of foreign banks. Other regulations of international transactions included making more routine the approval of Edge Act corporations (foreign branches of domestic banks) to reduce the Board's workload following the expansion of such branches (Board Minutes, January 7, 1969, 6–10). Activities of the growing number of foreign banks in the United States also raised new issues. Among them was whether to exempt such banks from regulation Q ceilings on payment of interest to their employees. The Board, acting under congressional authority, suspended regulation Q ceilings for time deposits of foreign governments and monetary authorities.

Several of these examples show that, as is often the case, regulation created two incentives. One was for the regulated to invent arrangements that avoided the regulation without violating the law. The second was for the regulator to develop exceptions that suited some of its purposes. And of course, the two interacted. New exceptions created potential opportunities to avoid regulation. The Board was asked by Congress to report on or stop particular practices of this kind. One of many examples was the use of branches in Puerto Rico or the Virgin Islands to attract corporate deposits by paying above regulation Q ceilings. This problem largely ended after June 1970, when some CDs of $100,000 or more became exempt from ceiling rates.[255]

In July 1971, First National City Bank proposed that the Board eliminate reserve requirements on euro-dollar loans made to U.S. corporations by overseas branches of U.S. banks. The Board's staff concurred. Regulation M

---

had sent to Congress as the basis for hearings. At the hearings, banks or others could comment on the list and propose additions. A unique feature of Maisel's proposal was that the hearing officers "have a good economic background" and, before proceeding, should take a training course. The Board adopted his proposal (Maisel diary, January 13, 1971, 9–10).

255. One of the stranger administrative issues was a request from the Bank of Canada that the Board's Annual Report for 1966 avoid showing that it had drawn on its swap lines in September and repaid in November. The Board's monthly numerical data would show that a transaction occurred. The Board demurred (Board Minutes, February 23, 1967, 5–8).

had been amended in September 1969, when the Board wanted to restrain euro-dollar borrowing. Relaxation of regulation Q for large CDs led to reduced reliance on the euro-dollar market to support bank lending.

After President Nixon embargoed gold sales, the restrictions lost their original purpose. The staff memo noted also that the rules had become complex and difficult to administer. It recommended repeal. "The banks would be pleased to see that the System could remove a restriction once it has outlived its usefulness" (memo, Regulation M, Correspondence Box 240, Federal Reserve Bank of New York, September 14, 1971, 4).

Senator Gordon Alcott (Colorado) wrote to the Board in 1965 inquiring about his request that a new Federal Reserve district be created in the mountain states. Most of this area was in District 10, with headquarters in Kansas City. A new district would have required legislation enlarging the number of districts; the original act specified a maximum of twelve districts. The Board replied that the costs involved in creating a new district exceeded the benefits (Board Minutes, August 9, 1965, 11–12).

Banking supervision and regulation was an issue from the past that would return many times. In the 1930s Eccles tried several times to get President Roosevelt to concentrate all regulation and supervision at the Federal Reserve (Meltzer, 2003, 487). He never succeeded. The Comptroller of the Currency in the Treasury Department continued to supervise national banks. Because the Federal Reserve did little in 1931–33 to prevent failure of a large part of the banking system, the Federal Deposit Insurance Corporation now supervised (and insured) a large number of banks.

In 1965, members of the House Banking Committee introduced legislation creating a banking agency that would centralize all federal bank supervision and regulation. The proposed legislation abolished the Office of the Comptroller of the Currency and transferred its functions to the proposed banking agency together with the supervisory functions of the Federal Reserve and the FDIC. One bill would have put the banking agency in the Treasury Department. Another would have created an independent banking agency. Authorizing the Treasury to directly supervise banks was an invitation to get more banks engaged in campaign finance and possible corruption.

The Federal Reserve always claimed that bank supervision and regulation were essential for effective conduct of monetary policy, but it rarely offered reasons that convinced most outsiders or its staff that its argument were valid or persuasive. Many countries separated bank supervision and monetary policy without experiencing difficulties.

One of the Board's main contentions was that the discount function could be administered properly only if the Federal Reserve had continuing contacts with banks eligible to discount. Other arguments were even weaker. Governor Daane argued that the Federal Reserve was responsible for "sound credit conditions," so it had to be concerned about individual bank positions (Board Minutes, April 5, 1965, 13). This reasoning overlooked the fact that many banks were not members of the Federal Reserve System and, of those that were, the *Comptroller's* office regulated, supervised, and examined national banks. The Federal Reserve received data from the *Comptroller's* office.

Governor Shephardson added that the System implemented monetary policy "through the commercial banking system. The Federal Reserve should have close relationships with the commercial banks and an opportunity for close observation of activities within the banks" (ibid., 16). The examples he gave were the regulation of time deposit interest rates and the quality of credit, but only the second would seem to be relevant. The second is a throwback to early mistaken concerns about real bills and speculative credit. Shephardson did not remember that the use of credit and the type of borrowing or collateral securing the credit were not the same.

Governor Robertson, often the maverick, disputed these claims. First, "he did not believe that any Board member or Reserve Bank president made a judgment on monetary policy on the basis of examination reports. . . . [Second,] all the information needed by the Federal Reserve would be obtained through access to reports of examination plus the right to require any information it desired from banks coming to the discount window" (ibid., 17–18). Then he added that giving the Federal Reserve responsibility for examinations risked raising pressures to adjust examination standards to support monetary policy. However, he shared Daane's concern that, if the federal government took responsibility for all banking regulation, it risked becoming absorbed by the executive branch (ibid., 19).

Daane probably expressed the more serious concern when he said that, if the Federal Reserve lost its supervisory and regulatory functions, "it would be more vulnerable to a move to bring monetary policy matters within the sphere of the Executive Branch of the government" (ibid., 12). He did not explain why this was likely. The most plausible reason is that the System relied on the membership for political support. Once it lost direct contact and close relations with the member banks, and the right to approve mergers, branching, and acquisitions, it could not count on their political support for an independent monetary authority. Banks and the Federal Reserve had a common interest in low inflation, so it is hard to know how much weight to put on this argument.

Governor Robertson favored an independent banking agency, and Governor Mitchell was not averse to that solution, although he preferred to have the Federal Reserve perform the function. He was most explicit about citing the problems in the current arrangement. The current regulatory "setup was working less and less effectively. . . . [T]he situation had become intolerable" (ibid., 13). Banking was changing rapidly, and regulation had not changed with it.[256] The legislation did not pass, but it returned several times.

The 1960 Bank Merger Act required bank regulatory agencies to consider the competitive effects of bank mergers and acquisitions. In some cases after the Federal Reserve approved a merger or acquisition, the Anti-Trust Division of the Department of Justice acted to overturn the merger even if the banks had consolidated or started to consolidate.

Congress considered legislation in 1965. Members of the Board believed that the Department of Justice should have only a limited time, perhaps ten days, after the Board's decision in which to notify the banks that it proposed to go to court to stop the merger as a violation of anti-trust legislation. The proposed legislation required the Justice Department to act within thirty days of the Board's decision. Chairman Martin wanted to support the legislation but also suggested changes that, if adopted, would reduce the Department's role. The Board approved his suggestions.

In 1918, the Federal Reserve began issuing notes denominated at $500, $1000, $5000, and $10,000, to be used principally for settling interbank balances. It stopped printing these denominations in 1946 but continued to pay out the stocks on hand. By 1969, the stocks had diminished to the point where additional notes would have to be printed. Banks rarely used the notes for settlement.

The Reserve Bank Presidents' Conference recommended in March 1969 that the Federal Reserve request the Treasury to authorize it to stop issuing notes in these denominations. The Board had first made this recommendation in 1946 (Board Minutes, May 6, 1969, 7–10). The Board's letter to Secretary David Kennedy noted that an earlier effort to eliminate those notes had claimed that most of the notes were used for illegal transactions. The Board and the Treasury had no evidence to support the claim, so it reversed a 1964 decision ordering the large-denomination notes withdrawn.

The Board did not repeat the claim. It suggested that production of additional notes would require new plates and that the cost of producing the plates exceeded the benefits. The Treasury accepted this reason. On July 14,

---

256. A staff member raised a question about capture. Would a single banking agency be more open to capture by the industry? Governor Robertson acknowledged the point but did not see why it would be more true of a single banking agency (Board Minutes, April 5, 1965, 22).

1969, the Federal Reserve and the Treasury issued a joint statement ending issuance of the four denominations. The $100 note was the largest remaining denomination.

The Federal Reserve returned the remaining unissued large-denomination notes to the Treasury for destruction. As outstanding notes returned to the Federal Reserve, they were destroyed also.[257]

Concerned by the rising number of bank robberies, Congress passed the Bank Protection Act directing the banking agencies to agree on regulations that recognized differences in the types of banks that were most subject to holdups. Governor Robertson was the Board's representative on a committee to coordinate regulation by the different agencies. The original proposal by the Board's staff was highly specific and detailed. Although Maisel and Mitchell objected, the Board issued the regulations for comment. "The comments received were quite devastating. . . . [T]he Federal Reserve had made itself appear unbending, adamant, and pig headed . . . whereas the other agencies had been able to arrive at a proposal that indicated a more flexible solution was possible" (Maisel diary, January 10, 1969, 2). After further efforts, the Board's staff accepted a proposal similar to the other agencies, and the Board voted regulation P to implement the proposal.

CONCLUSION: WHY DID INFLATION CONTINUE?

The Great Inflation that began in 1965 was not inevitable. It could, and should, have been prevented by the Federal Reserve in the interest of preserving money values and avoiding costly disinflation. Like the Federal Reserve's other great mistake, the Great Depression, it began and continued because of mistaken beliefs about the obligations and responsibilities of a central bank. The Federal Reserve was not alone in these mistakes. They were widely shared. And, for the Great Inflation, the costs of ending inflation loomed large. Burns (1987) gives several reasons for permitting inflation to continue.

There were two kinds of cost. One was the social cost, approximately measured at the time by the unemployment rate or lost output that society would pay during the transition to price stability. Second was the political cost to the administration in power from recession or slow growth, particularly if the transition to lower inflation occurred in an election year. The second was often more relevant to the officials who made the decisions.

Set against these costs were the gains accruing to the government from

257. In the last half of the 1960s Congress passed several bills providing for civil liberties, equal protection of the laws, equal employment opportunity and non-discrimination in lending. The Board developed rules and procedures for implementing such legislation even if, as an independent agency, it was not covered by the legislation.

the inflation tax; inflation reduced the real value of the government's monetary liabilities, and unanticipated inflation reduced the real value of the government's debt. The nominal value of the government's promises to pay remained the same, but the real value that holders of debt and money received was less than the nominal amount. The difference accrued to the government; hence it was a type of tax.

The government's gains from inflation took other forms as well. Income tax rates did not adjust to inflation at the time, so taxpayers moved into higher tax brackets as their nominal incomes rose with inflation. Depreciation of fixed capital also was not adjusted to inflation. The replacement cost of capital rose with inflation, but depreciation was tied to original cost, so the replacement cost exceeded the accumulated depreciation of existing capital. Inflation also transferred wealth. Ceiling rates of interest prevented owners of time and demand deposits from receiving interest payments that compensated for inflation. Banks that issued these liabilities received the transfer. Member banks held non-interest-bearing required reserves. Homeowners who issued fixed-rate mortgages received transfers from lenders. Fischer (1981) discussed these and other costs and gains of inflation. See also Cukierman and Wachtel (1979), Cukierman (1984), and Feldstein (1982).

Theoretical economic analysis emphasized the tax on cash balances and ignored most of the other costs, perhaps because most could be prevented by institutional changes such as indexing depreciation or tax brackets to inflation or removing regulation Q ceilings. The loss from inflation was typically described as the cost of more frequent adjustment of cash balances. Frether (1981) noted that this cost was estimated at about 0.7 percent of GDP, not negligible but a small part of the cost that the public bore in practice.[258] A large part of the true cost was the efficiency lost by obscuring the allocative signals sent by relative price changes and the redirection of management efforts away from the search for productivity and efficiency gains.

We have no evidence that the tax on cash balances or similar gains influenced either policymakers or the public. It is never mentioned in Federal Reserve discussions. Federal Reserve and administration records suggest

258. An influential paper, Tobin (1980) compared this cost of inflation (called a Harberger triangle) to the loss from unemployment (called an Okun gap). Tobin justified opposition to anti-inflation policies by pointing out that the Okun gap was larger than the Harberger triangle. This is an invalid comparison because the loss from unemployment was a transitional cost with little or no permanent effect. (The qualification recognizes possible hysteresis arising, say, from loss of skills during unemployment.) The loss from inflation that he used considered only the steady state costs of a fully indexed and fully anticipated inflation. For a more complete criticism, see Brunner and Meltzer (1993, 187–88).

that the 1946 Employment Act, and the ideas that gave rise to that act, were much more important. The imprecise language of the act, calling for maximum employment and purchasing power, became a commitment to full employment, in turn translated to mean avoiding unemployment above 4 percent. In practice, the act became an argument for an activist policy to reduce the unemployment rate. And although the 4 percent rate was not a constant, the records show that it was treated that way for many years.

Versions of the Phillips curve used from the early to the late 1960s reinforced the belief that policy could permanently reduce the unemployment rate by accepting more inflation. The choice was seen as a social judgment; at the cost of a small additional tax on cash balances, society could employ more people, especially people with low marginal productivity and little education and skill.[259]

Though advanced by many academic economists and policymakers in the Kennedy and Johnson administrations, there is not much evidence that President Johnson or Chairman Martin accepted this reasoning. Johnson was an old-time populist who disliked "high" interest rates and used his famous persuasive skills to prevent or delay interest rate increases. Martin was a committed anti-inflationist who made many speeches about the dangers of inflation. Yet consumer prices rose at a 6 percent average rate in the last twelve months of his term. This was the highest inflation rate since the Korean War nearly twenty years before. And contrary to the original Phillips curve, the unemployment rate had started to rise also.

There is ample reason to believe that Martin disliked this outcome and truly wanted to prevent it. The longer he and his colleagues at the Federal Reserve allowed inflation to persist, however, the more firmly held the anticipations that made it costly to end. The Federal Reserve and the administration were aware of the inflation. Why did they permit it to continue once it had started?

Martin's beliefs, the absence of a relevant theory, errors, and institutional arrangements explain why inflation started. The first two eventually changed, but inflation continued; thus, the reasons it continued are separate from the reasons it started. Two main institutional arrangements contributed to inflation under the circumstances of the 1960s.[260]

259. At the time, empirical estimates suggested that the Phillips curve was relatively flat; small increases in inflation generated relatively large reductions in the unemployment rate. As inflation rose, estimates of the tradeoff became steeper. The likely reason is that at the low inflation rates of the early 1960s, the public was not very concerned about inflation. David Lindsey pointed out that by 1971 or 1972, the Board's staff estimated that the sum of lagged inflation on wage increases reached unity. Inflation could not permanently increase employment by reducing real wage growth.

260. The rest of this section draws on Meltzer (2005).

First, even keel policy caused the Federal Reserve to delay taking appropriate policy action, sometimes for months. I noted in chapter 3 that even keel became very frequent in the late 1960s. During even keel periods, usually lasting for two to four weeks, the Federal Reserve often permitted large increases in reserve growth that it did not subsequently remove. It is, of course, true that the System could have prevented the inflationary impact. It failed to do so because the cost of reducing reserves (or reserve growth) always seemed large. It could have eliminated even keel by auctioning securities, as it eventually did.

Several years later Chairman Arthur Burns accepted the importance of even keel policies for the beginning and continuation of inflation.

> While the Federal Reserve would always accommodate the Treasury up to a point, the charge could be made—and was being made—that the System had accommodated the Treasury to an excessive degree. Although [Burns] was not a monetarist, he found a basic and inescapable truth in the monetarist position that inflation could not have persisted over a long period of time without a highly accommodative monetary policy. (FOMC Minutes, March 9, 1974, 111–12)

Second, Martin's acceptance of policy coordination with the administration prevented the Federal Reserve from taking timely actions and contributed to more expansive policies than were consistent with price stability. The System delayed acting in 1965 despite Martin's early warnings about inflation; it eased policy in 1968 to coordinate with fiscal restriction, and it again delayed acting in 1970. Despite well-known arguments from the permanent income hypothesis, Arthur Okun and the Board's staff expressed concern in 1968 about fiscal overkill from the surtax. Martin had promised President Johnson that passage of the temporary tax surcharge would lower interest rates. The Board moved to ease policy by encouraging reductions in the discount rate against the wishes of most of the reserve bank presidents. Output continued to rise and unemployment to fall. By December 1968, the annual rate of CPI increase was 4.6 percent, 1.8 percentage points higher than a year earlier. The unemployment rate was 3.4 percent, the lowest since 1951–53. Monetary base growth for the year reached 7.15 percent.

Martin acknowledged the error in easing policy. Reversing the error proved costly. As Okun eventually recognized, we could not "get back to where we were in 1965, the good old days . . . That's exactly what we thought would happen. That's exactly what didn't happen" (Hargrove and Morley, 1984, 308). Expected inflation shifted the Phillips curve on which he relied.

The Nixon administration had a different analytic framework. It accepted the vertical long-run Phillips curve and paid attention to money growth as an indicator of future inflation. Initially, it chose a gradualist policy and, in its internal memos, was willing to tolerate an unemployment rate as high as 4.5 percent. By the end of the 1969–70 recession, the unemployment rate reached 6 percent with annual CPI inflation of 5.4 percent. The administration shifted its concern from reducing inflation to increasing employment.

Arthur Burns, the new chairman of the Board of Governors, decided that inflation could not be reduced at a politically acceptable unemployment rate. He told President Nixon: "Wage and price decisions are now being made on the assumption that governmental policy will move promptly to check a sluggish economy" (letter, Burns to the president, Burns papers, Box B-B90, June 22, 1971, 2). He also blamed cost-push factors, the power of labor unions, and welfare programs, along with expectations that inflation would persist. By mid-1970 he argued that inflation had become entirely cost-push, independent of previous excess demand. Soon thereafter, he claimed that the rules of economics had changed. Standard macroeconomic policies were virtually impotent against inflation. He favored controls or guideposts to break expectations. As the 1972 election approached, President Nixon accepted that advice. The administration chose political benefit over economic fundamentals.

Inflation continued because of the unwillingness of policymakers to persist in a political and socially costly policy of disinflation. During the 1960s, and afterward, there was little political support for an anti-inflation policy in Congress and none in the administration, if it required unemployment much above 4 percent. Polling data show that inflation was not named by many people as "the most important problem facing the country." Beginning in January 1970, the number of respondents that named inflation never exceeded 14 percent; during the rest of 1970–71, it was usually well below 14 percent. Often it came fourth or fifth on the list of most important problems.[261] Without political support, the Federal Reserve was back in a position similar to 1946–50. It had greater independence on paper; it had not committed to maintain interest rates at or below a fixed ceiling, as it had in 1942–50. The unemployment rate functioned in much the same way, however. It limited the extent to which the System would persist in a policy to end inflation or reduce it permanently. Soon after unemployment rose, the administration and the Federal Reserve shifted

261. I am greatly indebted to Karlyn Bowman of the American Enterprise Institute for retrieving the Gallup data.

their operations and goal from lowering inflation to avoiding or ending recession and restoring full employment.

In several papers, Athanasios Orphanides attributed continued inflation to a mistaken estimate of 4 percent as the unemployment rate consistent with non-accelerating inflation. This encouraged policies that proved excessively expansive. I am persuaded that he is correct in pointing out this error (see especially Orphanides, 2002). But inflationary policies persisted in the Carter administration after recognizing that the 4 percent rate was too low. Also, there is considerable evidence that neither the administration nor the FOMC was willing to accept a large temporary increase in unemployment to achieve a permanent reduction in inflation.

Andrew Brimmer, a Board member from 1966 to 1974, explained that employment was the principal goal. "Fighting inflation, checking inflation was the second priority" (Brimmer, 2002, 22). The FOMC never took an explicit vote to order these priorities, but the decisions taken at critical times support Brimmer's interpretation.

Reversals had lasting effects. Inflation fell quickly in 1966–67 without a recession but with major disruption of the housing market and strident opposition from Congress and the politically powerful thrift and home building industries. The public learned from this attempt to reduce inflation that anti-inflation actions did not last once unemployment (or other costs) started to rise. The policy focus then shifted, reinforcing the public's growing belief that inflation would continue and even increase. These beliefs made it harder for the Federal Reserve to persuade the public that it would persist the next time it tried.

The next time was 1969–70. A new administration was in power. The principal economic policymakers did not subscribe to the idea of a permanent tradeoff between unemployment and inflation. They accepted the logic of Milton Friedman's (1968a) analysis showing that any reduction in unemployment achieved by increasing inflation was temporary. It persisted only as long as the inflation was unanticipated. But the public and Congress were unwilling to accept the temporary increase in unemployment that would substantially lower or end inflation. Officials learned subsequently that by refusing to pay the costs of transition to lower inflation, they increased the costs they would face subsequently by reinforcing beliefs that the public held.[262] They called this mixture of inflation and un-

---

262. I suspect that at least some of them would have paid these costs if they would not go on too long. By the time they generally recognized that their policy was working very slowly, the presidential election was less than two years away. President Nixon was not inclined to sacrifice his second term to end inflation and probably not convinced that his advisers and

employment "stagflation" and found it puzzling and mysterious because they ignored the anticipations that the policy actions fostered.

Once inflation became entrenched, it required a more persistent commitment to end it. Martin, the Federal Reserve, and administration economists were aware of the cost paid to end a modest inflation after 1958. After four years of stable prices, why did they let inflation continue after it returned?

Bad luck contributed. Growth of output slowed after 1966, just as the money growth rate increased. Many officials continued to believe that higher growth would return. Other beliefs played a larger role. Some of the same factors that contributed to the start also contributed to persistence. Until the Treasury began to auction notes and bonds after 1970, even keel operations contributed to inflation and made disinflation difficult.[263] George Mitchell, a member of the Board from 1961 to 1976, told Congress that if the Treasury sold short-term debt to the banking system, "we have to supply reserves to the banking system . . . The success of this operation depends on how much pressure the banking system is under. If it is not under much pressure, it would continue to hold the securities and therefore the money supply would rise" (Joint Economic Committee, 1968, 134). He did not say that if banks were under pressure, they would sell the securities and make loans.

At the same hearing, senators tried to get the Federal Reserve to control money growth within a range of 2 to 5 percent. Mitchell denied that money growth was excessive.

> Senator [Jack] Miller. I have heard criticisms of the Federal Reserve Board for being responsible for the inflation, as a result of the excessive expansion of the money supply. . . .
> Mr. Mitchell. . . . Our conviction is that we have not overused this tool.
> Senator Miller. If you have not overused the tool, then where does the inflation come from? . . .
> Mr. Mitchell. I think it really comes from the government deficit. (ibid., 135)

Later in the same hearing, Senator William Proxmire questioned Mitchell about the procyclical behavior of the money stock, citing declines in four postwar recessions. Mitchell would not accept the conclusion (ibid., 140). Martin, like Mitchell and many others, claimed that budget deficits

---

the Federal Reserve could deliver. He believed that he lost the 1960 election because of rising unemployment and was determined to not repeat the experience.

263. Brimmer (2002, 25–26) did not recall any discussion about changing even keel policy.

Table 4.12   Deficits and Inflation, 1966–69, 1982–85.

YEAR	DEFICIT ($ BILLIONS)	DEFICIT (PERCENT GNP)	PRICE DEFLATOR (CHAIN-TYPE)
1966	3.1	0.4	0.8
1967	12.6	1.6	3.1
1968	27.7	3.3	4.3
1969	0.5	0.1	5.0
1982	120.0	3.8	6.1
1983	208.0	6.3	3.9
1984	185.6	5.0	3.8
1985	221.6	5.6	3.0

Source: Fiscal year deficits from Office of Management and Budget (1990); calendar year inflation from Council of Economic Advisers (2004).

were the principal cause of inflation. At times, the statement of this belief suggests that the inflationary effect of the deficit depends only on the size of the deficit and is independent of deficit finance and money growth. Experience in the 1960s and 1980s can be looked upon as an experiment that tests this proposition in a simple, direct way. Table 4.12 shows that the much smaller budget deficits of the 1960s occurred with rising inflation rates, and the larger deficits of the 1980s accompanied falling inflation rates. A major difference was that the Federal Reserve did not believe it was obliged to finance the 1980s deficits, and it did not do so. Neglecting or ignoring the effects of policy actions on money growth and inflation was a major error in the 1960s and 1970s.

Federal Reserve decisions in the Martin era were made every three weeks. Much time was spent on what had happened or what might happen before the next meeting. There is no evidence that the Board or the FOMC had an organized way of thinking about the more distant future, as senior staff recognized (Axilrod, 1970b; Pierce, 1980; Lombra and Moran, 1980). Until 1965–66, Chairman Martin followed the Riefler rule that prohibited forecasts. When forecasts began, they often had large errors, discrediting them. Also, the members of the Board and the FOMC did not have a common framework or way of thinking about monetary policy. Neither Martin nor Burns made any effort to develop an agreed-upon way of thinking about how their actions influenced prices, employment, and the balance of payments. Sherman Maisel argued frequently for a more systematic approach without much success. The members did not agree on elementary propositions.

Even if these problems had been resolved and a common framework developed, as Burns (1987) notes, the absence of political and popular support would likely have prevented the System from continuing decisive action. A more appropriate common framework would have avoided the large policy error in 1968 when the Federal Reserve eased policy and increased the inflation rate because it accepted the Keynesian claim that the temporary surtax was "fiscal overkill." But it is also true that the Johnson administration and the Federal Reserve were willing to undertake anti-inflation monetary policy only after the 1968 election, when the effect would be felt under the Nixon administration.

Martin believed he could maintain Federal Reserve independence while coordinating policy actions with the administration. Although he warned about inflation in 1965, he encouraged no action against it until late in the year because he and his colleagues hoped that President Johnson would raise tax rates instead. Three years later, he eased policy to offset the surtax, a step that he later recognized as an error. Some of his senior staff agreed.[264]

Martin was not alone in these errors. He had the support of most of his Board and much of the academic profession. He made little effort to lead the Federal Reserve away from coordinated policy. And there is no evidence of coordination working in the opposite direction—administration policy adjusting to the Federal Reserve's responsibility for inflation.[265]

Policy coordination was not the only error in 1968. Administration and Federal Reserve forecasts attributed a powerful effect to the $10 billion temporary tax surcharge. They could have known better. Economic analysis had established that the main effect of a temporary surcharge would be on saving. A prominent Keynesian economist, Franco Modigliani, testified to that effect a month before the surcharge passed:

> If the people know that taxes are going to be put up for just 3 or 6 months, chances are that there would be little change in their consumption because they would look forward to being able to recoup later. Therefore, I think attention should be given to finding measures that have the right incentives. (testimony, Franco Modigliani, Joint Economic Committee, May 8, 1968, 63)

Partly as a consequence of policy coordination, but also in response to political and public pressure, the Federal Reserve accepted responsibil-

---

264. "Question: Do you think it was a mistake for the Fed to be that closely involved in administration policy? Answer: Yes, because you become less objective" (Axilrod, 1997, 17–18).

265. The House Banking Committee asked economists and policy officials for their opinions on mandating policy coordination, a policy rule, or the present regime. Replies came from 69 respondents. Most (42) favored a coordinated program; 13 favored a monetary rule of some kind; 14 favored no change. I interpret that to mean that the group members did not oppose coordination but did not want it made mandatory. Chairman Okun of the Council of Economic Advisers voted for mandatory coordination. Chairman Martin and Secretary Fowler voted for the status quo (Joint Economic Committee, 1968a, 8).

ity for housing and income distribution. Although it could not do much about the latter except to reduce reserve requirements for small banks, it moderated its actions to prevent sharp reductions in homebuilding. Adding homebuilding to a list of objectives that included sustained growth, full employment, low inflation, and international balance almost assured failure to reach most or all of the objectives.

When Arthur Burns replaced Martin, President Nixon recognized the independence of the Federal Reserve and then added: "I respect his independence. However, I hope that independently he will conclude that my views are the ones he should follow" (Wells, 1994, 41).

This was a forecast of the pressure the president and his advisers kept up. Burns, like Marriner Eccles before him, wanted to be a key presidential adviser while he was chairman. Possibly to satisfy the president's pressures for lower unemployment or because he shared the president's priority, Burns maintained relatively high money growth and in 1970–71 frequently and forcefully argued for a wage-price board to slow inflation by exhortation. More likely, as he claimed repeatedly at the time, monetary policy could not be used to reduce inflation. In his Per Jacobsson lecture (Burns, 1987), he showed that he recognized that the inflation was the result of overly expansive monetary policy, but there was little support in the administration, Congress, or the general public for the consequences of the policy that would be required.

> Viewed in the abstract, the Federal Reserve System had the power to abort the inflation at its incipient stage fifteen years ago [1964] or at any later point, and it has the power to end it today [1979]. At any time within that period, it could have restricted the money supply and created sufficient strains in financial and industrial markets to terminate inflation with little delay. It did not do so because the Federal Reserve was itself caught up in the *philosophical and political* currents that were transforming American life and culture. (Burns, 1987, 692; emphasis added)

Burns did not appeal to mistakes, bad luck, or misinformation. He appealed to philosophical and political beliefs.[266] Unlike Martin, who had more limited understanding of what had to be done, Burns knew "in the abstract" what was required. He was unwilling, or believed the Federal Reserve would be unable, to carry through an anti-inflation program that imposed heavy costs on employment, housing, and output.

266. Burns (1987, 693) recognized "errors of economic or financial judgment," called them significant, and cited the consensus view in the 1960s and early 1970s that "an unemployment rate of 4 percent corresponded to a practical condition of full employment" (ibid.).

Burns resented White House interference and pressure, but he did not often resist it. He took over a Board all of whose members had been appointed by Presidents Kennedy and Johnson. To varying degrees, a majority preferred to continue inflation rather than increase unemployment. If inflation could be reduced at an unemployment rate of 4.25 or 4.50 percent, they would accept it. But they did not want any higher unemployment rate. There was a minority that wanted more restrictive policy and more action against inflation. The few consistent anti-inflationists such as Hayes, Brimmer, and Francis were exceptions. They gained support when inflation rose but only until unemployment rose above the level the majority would accept. Brimmer (2002, 23) explained at the time that if fiscal policy was the way it was, you would have to tighten monetary policy to the point of inducing a recession. He added that in 1968 the Federal Reserve "didn't promise a tradeoff [of easier monetary policy] . . . if you get a tax bill but we came pretty close to it" (ibid., 23).

Many other reasons have been used to explain the persistence of inflation: the use of money market targets, failure to distinguish between real and nominal interest rates, and neglect of monetary aggregates (Mayer, 1999; Bordo and Schwartz, 1999; McCallum, 1999; Hetzel, 2003). Nelson (2003b) summarizes this literature and documents the importance of concentrating on cost-push and neglecting monetary policy—the monetary policy neglect hypothesis—both in Britain and the United States.

Orphanides (2003b) casts substantial doubt on claims that the FOMC did not raise nominal rates enough to compensate for inflation. Using the data available at the time, with the real-time smaller output gap, Orphanides showed that nominal rates rose at least one percent for every one percent increase in anticipated inflation. The appearance to the contrary depends on data that became available later, after revisions.

Several of these explanations correctly describe events and interpretations. Federal Reserve officials rarely distinguished real and nominal interest rates when discussing interest rates even if they responded as Orphanides's estimates suggest. Like many others, they overestimated the effect of the tax surcharge and underestimated subsequent inflation. Chart 4.14 shows that the survey of professional forecasts substantially underestimated inflation also.

Market participants may have relied on these or similar forecasts. We cannot know whether the increase in real rates was partly the result of underestimating future inflation, but that seems a very plausible conjecture. Chart 4.15 shows that the real long-term interest rate rose just as the smoothed real growth rate fell. Subsequently, a decline in real rates in 1970 contributed to the very gradual recovery from the 1969–70 recession.

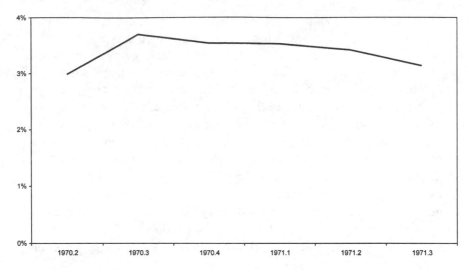

Chart 4.14. Mean error in four-quarter professional growth forecasts, implicit price deflator, 1970:2–1971:3.

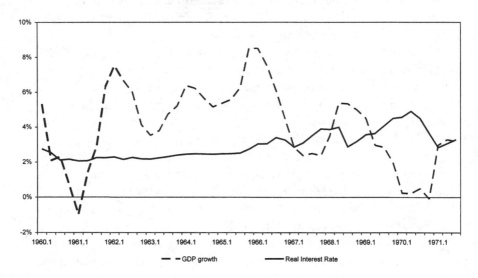

Chart 4.15. Four-quarter moving average real GDP growth versus ex ante real interest rate, 1960:1–1971:3.

The 1970–71 FOMC minutes make clear that slow growth and persistent unemployment were the main factors Burns cited to urge the FOMC to increase money growth.

Another factor slowing real growth has received less attention. The risk premium (Chart 4.16), measured by the spread between high-grade and lower-grade bonds, rose after the middle 1960s. The higher real interest

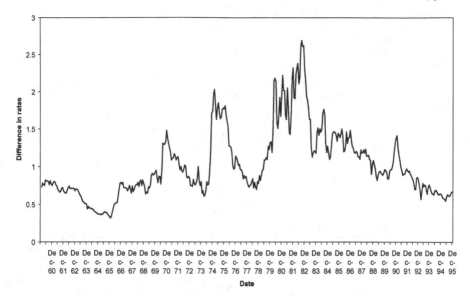

Chart 4.16. Spread, BAA minus AAA bonds, 1960–95.

rate for some more risky borrowers in this period incorporated a larger risk premium. The premium continued to increase to a local peak during the recession and declined, as expected, following the recession, but it did not return to the lower levels reached in 1963–65. Slower real growth meant that higher nominal growth occurred as inflation.

Analytic errors contributed to inflationary policy. Bad analysis and flawed theoretical understanding can lead to major policy mistakes, as in the Great Depression. The Federal Reserve policymakers made no effort to achieve analytic clarity on such basic issues as the causes of inflation. Several of its members doubted that it was worth the effort. They did not respond to Darryl Francis's efforts to explain that (1) in the long run, inflation was caused by money growth in excess of real growth, and (2) Federal Reserve policy produced excess money growth because it did not permit interest rates to increase enough. Similarly, they did not respond positively to Sherman Maisel's efforts to adopt a consistent policy framework.

Inaccurate forecasts added to the control problem. Chart 4.17 suggests that the Board's forecasts remained close to forecasts by the Society of Professional Forecasters. Both forecasts rarely overestimated inflation, but the underestimates are large and later highly persistent. Orphanides (2003a, 2003c) emphasized this error. The members of FOMC were aware that errors were made, and they attempted to correct or reduce the errors and the rate of inflation by giving more attention to money growth. But until

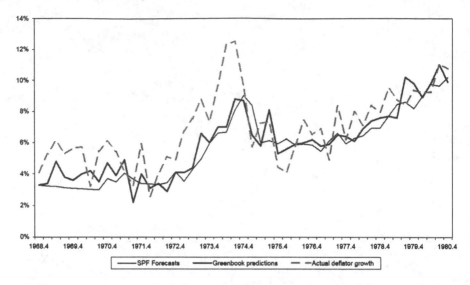

Chart 4.17. SPF vs. green book forecasts of GNP/GDP implicit price deflator annualized quarterly growth, compared with actual deflator growth, 1968:4–1980:4.

1979 or 1980 they remained as a group reluctant to let unemployment rise enough to reduce inflation permanently.

Inaccurate forecasts, mistaken beliefs, lack of a coherent framework, and the absence of agreement on an analytical framework all played a role. But criticism of these errors were made frequently and usually without effect. Missing from most explanations by economists is the political dimension. By law the Federal Reserve was an independent agency. In practice, it responded to political pressures to coordinate policy by financing deficits and giving primacy to reducing the unemployment rate and the impact of restrictive policy on home building.

Three morals stand out: you cannot end inflation (1) if you don't agree on how to do it; (2) if you and the public think it is less costly to let it continue; and (3) if you are overly influenced by politics. The Federal Reserve was better able to control inflation when the president was named Eisenhower or Reagan than when he was named Johnson, Nixon, or Carter. Book 2 of this volume contrasts the 1970s and the 1980s. The Federal Reserve sacrificed its independence in the 1970s by acting on the mistaken belief that it could avoid recessions by increasing inflation. When it reasserted its independence in 1979, many of its problems continued. It still lacked a coherent framework; it did not develop a common approach to analyzing the economy; it did not separate temporary from persistent changes. The most important change was a willingness to accept increased unemployment and to persist in a policy of reducing inflation. The economy suffered a deep recession, but inflation fell to low levels, and markets gradually became convinced that the Federal Reserve would persist in its disinflation policy.

Chapters 5 through 10, in book 2 of this volume, trace the mistaken and unsuccessful policies of the 1970s that ended in the Volcker disinflation.

APPENDIX TO CHAPTER 4

Chart 4A.1 shows the monetary base, its principal sources and the interrelation of the sources based on a vector autoregression (VAR) with two lags and eleven seasonal dummy variables. The VAR has four variables entered in the following order: discounts, gold, base, and government securities held by the reserve banks. Data are monthly from January 1961 to September 1971, the period discussed in chapters 3 through 5.

The chart offers a statistical analysis of the policy actions discussed in the text. It replicates for the 1960s the statistical analysis for the 1950s

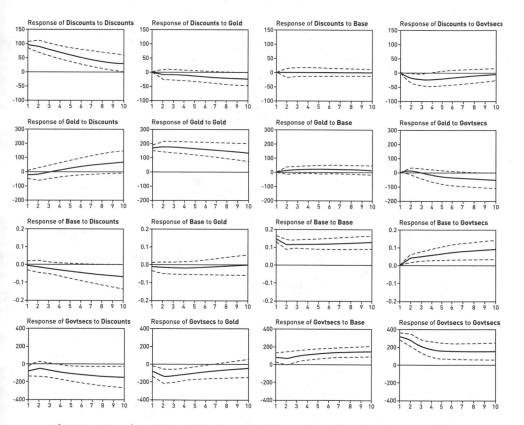

Chart 4.1A. Based on VAR with two lags and eleven seasonal dummies, January 1961:1–September 1971:9.

and 1920s in the appendix to chapter 2 of this volume and chapter 4 of volume 1.

Many of the statistical findings reflect a common source. The FOMC or the manager controlled free reserves or short-term interest rates. Any disturbance that changed interest rates induced offsetting actions. The gold outflows raised interest rates, inducing member bank discounts and open market purchases. Similarly, as discounts increased, the manager purchased fewer government securities.

Unlike the 1920s, when gold flow and discounts dominated changes in the base, the base responded mainly to open market purchases in the 1960s as in the 1950s. Gold movements had no significant effects on the base in this decade, but the components of the base—discounts and government securities—increased modestly as the gold stock fell. This is a change from the 1950s.